SLAVERY AND ANTI-SLAVERY;

A HISTORY OF THE

GREAT STRUGGLE IN BOTH HEMISPHERES;

WITH A VIEW OF

THE SLAVERY QUESTION

IN THE

UNITED STATES.

BY

WILLIAM GOODELL

NEGRO UNIVERSITIES PRESS
NEW YORK

Originally published in 1852 by William Harned

Reprinted in 1968
by Negro Universities Press
A DIVISION OF GREENWOOD PUBLISHING CORP.
New York

Library of Congress Catalogue Card Number: 68-55889

Printed in the United States of America

CONTENTS.

CHAPTER I.
PAGE.

Magnitude and necessity of the struggle............................ 1

CHAPTER II.

Origin of the modern Slave Trade and Slavery...................... 4

CHAPTER III.

Slavery and the Slave Trade in the British Colories in North America,
now the United States.. 10

CHAPTER IV.

Early testimonies against Slavery and the Slave Trade............. 27

CHAPTER V.

Action of religious bodies against the Slave Trade and Slavery, commencing before the American Revolution, and the results.......... 32

CHAPTER VI.

Of Slavery and its abolition in England.......................... 44

CHAPTER VII.

Of efforts for abolishing the African Slave Trade................ 53

CHAPTER VIII.

Period of the American Revolution, and the establishment of an independent Government.. 69

CHAPTER IX.

Era of forming the Federal Constitution.......................... 81

CHAPTER X.

Of direct anti-Slavery efforts, including ecclesiastical action, from the period of the Revolution to the close of the last century ; and the abolition of Slavery in the Northern States_____ 91

CHAPTER XI.

Decline of the spirit of Liberty, and growth of Slavery, since the Revolution ; their causes and early manifestations_____ 118

CHAPTER XII.

Position of the American Churches respecting Slavery, during the first half of the Nineteenth Century.—I. Methodist Episcopal Church. 143

CHAPTER XIII.

Position of the American Churches, &c. (continued).—II. The Presbyterian Church_____ 151

CHAPTER XIV.

Position of the American Churches, &c. (continued).—III. Congregationalists_____ 163

CHAPTER XV.

Position of the American Churches, &c. (continued).—IV. Baptists. 183

CHAPTER XVI.

Position of the American Churches, &c. (continued).—V. The Protestant Episcopal Church_____ 191

CHAPTER XVII.

Position of the American Churches, &c. (continued).—VI. Other Sects—General view _____ 195

CHAPTER XVIII.

Position of the American Churches, &c. (continued).—VII. Voluntary Associations connected with several Sects—Conclusion _____ 202

CHAPTER XIX.

Action of the Federal Government, to the close of the first Presidential Administration_____ 220

CHAPTER XX.

Subsequent action of the Federal Government—Colored people—Slave territory—New Slave States—Federal District_____ 237

CHAPTER XXI.

Further action of the Federal Government—American Slave Trade— African Slave Trade _____ 247

CHAPTER XXII.

Further action of the Federal Government—Continued subserviency
of the national diplomacy to the demands of the Slaveholders 263

CHAPTER XXIII.

Further action of the Federal Government—Hayti—Florida—Seminole War 268

CHAPTER XXIV.

Further action of the Federal Government—Acquisition of Texas... 272

CHAPTER XXV.

Conspiracy for the conquest of Mexico, and the disrupture of the
Federal Union in 1806—Controlling power of the Conspirators over
the Federal Judiciary 280

CHAPTER XXVI.

Further action of the Federal Government—The war with Mexico—
Acquisition of California, New Mexico, and Utah 287

CHAPTER XXVII.

Further action of the Federal Government—Result of the Conquest
of California—Its admission as a Free State—" The Compromise." 306

CHAPTER XXVIII.

Further action of the Federal Government—General policy, and
political economy, controlled by Slavery....................... 319

CHAPTER XXIX.

Colonization Society.. 341

CHAPTER XXX.

Abolition of Slavery in the British Colonies 353

CHAPTER XXXI.

Distinctive features of American Slavery 377

CHAPTER XXXII.

The present Anti-Slavery Agitation in America—Its causes, origin, and
character 382

CHAPTER XXXIII.

Opposition to Abolitionists—Its elements—Its nature and methods ... 400

CHAPTER XXXIV.

Attempts to silence the discussion by authority—State Legislatures—
Federal Executive—U. S. Mails—"Gag" Rules in Congress—
Right of petition 408

CHAPTER XXXV. PAGE.

Opposition from leading Clergy and Ecclesiastical bodies............ 425

CHAPTER XXXVI.

Persecutions of Abolitionists....................................... 434

CHAPTER XXXVII.

Of the elements and occasions of division among Abolitionists....... 447

CHAPTER XXXVIII.

Divisions in 1839–40... 457

CHAPTER XXXIX.

Organized political action—Liberty party—Liberty League—Free Soil
party 468

CHAPTER XL.

Anti-Slavery Church agitation—New Anti-Slavery Churches and Missionary bodies.. 487

CHAPTER XLI.

The Anti-Slavery Societies—Their relation to political and Church
action.. 509

CHAPTER XLII.

The American Anti-Slavery Society—Its further course on political
action.. 517

CHAPTER XLIII.

Second revolution in the position and policy of the American Anti-
Slavery Society in 1844 526

CHAPTER XLIV.

Further difficulties in the American Anti-Slavery Society 529

CHAPTER XLV.

Political course of the American Anti-Slavery Society, since its revolution of 1844.. 532

CHAPTER XLVI.

Course of Mr. Garrison and the American Anti-Slavery Society and
its members, since the division of 1840, in respect to Anti-Slavery
Church action.. 541

CHAPTER XLVII.

General estimate of the American Anti-Slavery Society and its labors,
since 1840.. 555

CHAPTER XLVIII.   PAGE.

Review of these divisions and their results 559

CHAPTER XLIX.

Different views of the Constitution and of the legality of Slavery.... 563

CHAPTER L.

The Slavery question in America—and the Crisis—What shall be done ? 583

OBJECT AND PLAN OF THIS BOOK.

THE *chief* design of this publication is to furnish, in *one volume*, an abstract, for convenient reference, of a great mass of *historical information* concerning slavery and the struggle against it (in this country and Great Britain), *that is now to be found only by looking over several volumes, numerous pamphlets, and the newspapers and scattered documents of the last twenty years.* This abstract, at the same time, was intended to have a bearing on the now-pending slave question in the United States, and to be so selected and arranged, as to facilitate a presentation of that question towards the close of the volume. It was designed to be as documentary in its *character* as the nature of an abstract would permit. Hence, it consists much in extracts, quotations, and abbreviated paragraphs, preserving as much as possible the significant portions, without giving the documents entire, which would have required volumes.

The writer was aware that the attempt to cover so much ground, in one volume, was a hazardous one. It could not be a *small* volume; and most readers, as well as some critics, will instantly pronounce a work "*too diffuse*" that exceeds three or four hundred pages, without stopping to consider whether or no it presents the substance of *several* such volumes on distinct points of history. They would find no fault with one book of that size that should only tell the story of the abolition of the African slave trade, nor with another that should only relate the measures that led to the abolition of slavery in the British West Indies, and the results of those labors; nor with another that should contain the story of Texas and the Mexican war. But if a writer should present the substance of all *three* of these histories, and *five or six more* in addition, of equal magnitude and importance, in a volume of six hundred pages, they would think him unpardonably *diffuse;* and the farther this condensing process was carried, *in one volume,* the more would he fall under censure for diffuseness. The

difficulty would not end here.   The same readers, or others, on referring to
the parts of the history that most interested them, would fail of obtaining
all the minute information they expected, or would wonder at the omission
of many things that they considered important.   Whether, on the whole,
the work will be found *too much* or *too little* condensed, is uncertain.   If
the latter, we may hereafter furnish a cheaper abridgment of it : if the
former, the present edition may hereafter take the name of ah abridgment
to the more copious work that may be written, and for which there are
ample materials at hand.

The writer has not *wholly* excluded from this volume all notice of the
principles that underlie history, nor of the workings of moral cause and
effect.   Nor has he suppressed his own sentiments, through fear of giving
offense.   He hopes he has not been uncandid or discourteous to others.

No *reasonable* pains have been spared to secure accuracy in dates and
facts ; and yet it is quite impossible to be certain of freedom from errors.
In some cases, the best authorities disagree.   Apparent or real discrepancies and mistakes are incident to all histories.   Biblical critics are not
always agreed in respect to the true solution of *apparent* discrepancies in
the inspired writers of history.   In preparing this book, several instances
have occurred in which good authorities have *seemed* to make irreconcilable
statements, but which have, nevertheless, with much labor, been reconciled.
Few of the books or pamphlets used by us have been free from real or
apparent mistakes that have perplexed us.   We hope we shall not be
accounted careless of our facts, if *some* of them should be found inaccurate,
or should be, by somebody, considered so.   We trust the book is as free
from mistakes as most other works of the kind.   We are certain of having
laboriously collected and carefully examined the statements presented, but,
like others who compile histories, we cannot be held responsible for the mistakes of the best authorities extant.

SLAVERY AND FREEDOM.

CHAPTER I.

MAGNITUDE AND NECESSITY OF THE STRUGGLE.

A World's Question—The Problem of the Present Age.

THE slave question in America is only one phase of the more comprehensive question of human freedom that now begins to agitate the civilized world, and that presents the grand problem of the present age.

Such a question must be met, must be discussed, must be decided, and decided correctly, before the nations of the earth can be enfranchised, and before this anomalous republic can either secure her own liberties, or find permanent repose.

In a nation whose declaration of self-evident and inalienable human rights has been hailed as the watchword for an universal struggle against despotic governments;—a nation whose support of human chattelhood has armed the world's despots with their most plausible pleas against republican institutions, it is in vain to expect that the discussion of such incongruities can be smothered, or the adjustment of them much longer postponed. In *any* age of the world, such expectations would be disappointed—in the *present* age, the indulgence of them can be little short of insanity—must be consummate folly. The question whether such a nation, at such a period of the world's progress, shall continue to tolerate human chattelhood, becomes, of necessity, a world's question. Universal human nature is knocking vehemently at our doors, and cannot be silenced. As well might we attempt to hush the thun-

1

ders of our own Niagara, or annul the laws by which the elements are governed.

Is this the language of enthusiasm? Ask counsel of existing facts. When a few voices were raised on this subject not many years since, the whole community, with few exceptions, north and south, demanded that the agitation should cease. But *has* it ceased? Or *can* it be made to cease? Most forward and even clamorous in the discussion, are those who, even now, have scarcely ceased to proscribe discussion! Our halls of legislation, that were to have been sealed against the discussion, nevertheless ring with it, to the exclusion of the most favorite topics! And those who were determined that the public mails should not transmit the agitating debate, are now gorging those mails to the full with their own eager debates! Not an important public measure can be proposed that is not found to involve, in some way, the much dreaded but ever present question. Can we not see the hand of an all-controlling Providence in all this? Can we not hear in it the voice of Nature and of Nature's God, demanding and ordaining a discussion of the slave question?

The history of Christian civilization is marked with successive eras of advancement, each one of which is distinguished by some particular phase or feature of human progress, and commonly involves the agitation of some great practical problem, the solution of which occupies the minds of thinking men until it is definitely settled. This is seldom effected without long and earnest discussions, sometimes protracted during one or two entire generations, and not completed until more enlarged views have displaced the prejudices and corrected the errors that preceded them. The responsibilities, as well as the dangers and the privileges of living in such an age of the world—stormy, perhaps, yet progressive—are not commonly appreciated as they should be. Not to have understood, correctly, the wants, and especially the grand problem of such an age, of the age one lives in, not to have taken the position, and to have exerted the influence demanded by the crisis, were equivalent to having wasted, or worse than wasted, one's probationary existence, so far as its bearing on general human progress is concerned; and this, too, at a time when one life is to be reckoned of more weight and significance than, perhaps, many lives, dreamed away in any of those dead calms in this world's history, in which little or nothing is done or devised for the elevation of the species.

Such an age of agitation and of corresponding responsibility is the present. The grand problem of the age is that of a more extended and better defined freedom, especially for the very lowest and most degraded portion of the species. Ours is an advanced period in the struggle for human freedom. It is not to the contest of the barons against an unlimited autocrat that we are summoned—nor to the struggle of the middle classes against the barons; nor to the question of taxation without representation; nor to the question of religious liberty, for those who are regarded as human beings. The demands of liberty strike deeper, now, and reach the ground tier of humanity, hid under the rubbish of centuries of degradation—classes who have scarcely been thought of, as human, and to whom no Magna Charta of Runny Meade, no organization of a House of Commons, no Declaration of Independence, have brought even a tithe or a foretaste of their promised blessings. The houseless, the landless, the homeless—the operatives of Manchester and Birmingham, the tenantry of Ireland, the Russian serfs,— above all, *the North American Slaves*—what have Christian civilization and democratic liberty and equality in reserve for these? And what are the responsibilities of Christians, of philanthropists, of statesmen, and of republican citizens, in respect to them? These questions to be properly decided, must be studied, must be understood.

We single out, for present inquiry, the North American slave. Who is he? What is his condition? How came he there? Who is responsible for his continuance in his present condition? What has been done, and what remains to be done in respect to him?

CHAPTER II.

ORIGIN OF THE MODERN SLAVE TRADE AND SLAVERY.

The Portuguese—The Spaniards—Charles V.—Ferdinand V.—The Hollanders, the Danes, the French, the English—Queen Elizabeth, John Hawkins, Louis XIII. of France—Act of George II.—Prohibition of Violence—Barbarity of the Traffic—Statistics—Imports into Jamaica.

"In the year 1442, while the Portuguese, under the encouragement of their celebrated Prince Henry, were exploring the coast of Africa, Anthony Gonzalez, who, two years before, had seized some Moors, near Cape Badajor, was, by that prince, ordered to carry his prisoners back to Africa. He landed them at Rio del Oro, and received from the Moors in exchange, ten blacks and a quantity of gold dust, with which he returned to Lisbon."—*Edwards' History of the West Indies, Vol. II., p.* 37.

"This new kind of commerce, appearing to be a profitable speculation, others, of the same nation, soon embarked in it."—*Godwin's Lectures on Slavery, p.* 184. (*American Edition.*)

THE Spaniards, on taking possession of the West India islands, compelled the native Charibs (or Caribs,) to work the mines of Hispaniola. In these and other exhausting labors, that feeble race became well nigh extinct,* and their place was supplied by importations of a hardier race from Africa. The infamy of having first projected this expedient has commonly rested on *Las Casas*, a priest much hated among the colonists for his uncompromising opposition to the ill treatment of the Charibs, whom he is represented as seeking to

---

* "Down to the dust the Charib people passed,
     Like autumn foliage withering in the blast;
     A whole race sunk beneath the oppressor's rod,
     And left a blank among the works of God."

                     Montgomery's West Indies.

relieve at the expense of the Africans.* With more probability, the crime has been charged on *Chievres* and the *Flemish nobility*, who obtained a monopoly of the traffic from Charles V., and sold it for 25,000 ducats to some Genoese merchants, who first commenced, in a regular form, the commerce in slaves that, with little intermission, has been continued ever since.

"As early as 1503," according to Clarkson, "a few slaves were sent by the Portuguese to the Spanish colonies."

In 1511, Ferdinand V. of Spain, is said to have permitted an importation of Negroes into the colonies. But while Cardinal Ximenes held the reins of government, and until the accession of Charles V. of Spain, he steadily refused to allow such a detestable commerce. Vide Godwin, p. 184.

It was in 1517 that Charles V., (who was sovereign of Germany, and of the Netherlands,) granted the exclusive patent before mentioned, to one or more of the Flemish nobility, to import four thousand Africans annually, for the supply of Hispaniola, Cuba, Jamaica, and Porto Rico.

"This great prince was not, in all probability, aware of the dreadful evils attending this horrible traffic, nor of the crying injustice of permitting it; for in 1542, when he made a code of laws for his Indian subjects, he liberated all the Negroes, and by a word put an end to their slavery. When, however, he resigned his crown and retired into a monastery, and his minister of mercy, Pedro de la Gasca, returned to Spain, the imperious tyrants of these new dominions returned to their former practices, and fastened the yoke on the suffering and unresisting Negroes."—*Godwin, p.* 185. See also *Clarkson's History, pp.* 28, 29.

The slave trade was prosecuted by the Portuguese, the

---

* Robertson, in his *History of America*, takes up and somewhat exaggerates this statement, on the authority of *Herrera*, an enemy of Las Casas, whose charge was first published 35 years after the philanthropist's decease. The previous writers make no mention of Las Casas in such a connection, though avowedly his enemies. The writings of Las Casas abound in denunciations against slavery; and from the language of Herrera himself, it would not conclusively appear that Las Casas designed to have the Africans imported by compulsion, or held as *slaves.—Vide* the *Abbe Gregoire's Defence of Las Casas*, approved by James Montgomery in a note to his poem, "*The West Indies.*" See also *Stuart's Memoir of Sharp, page 29.;* and preface to *Clarkson's Essay on the Slavery and Commerce of the Human Species.*

Spaniards, the Hollanders, the Danes, the French, the British, the Anglo-Americans, including the colonists of New England.

BEGINNING OF THE SLAVE TRADE BY THE ENGLISH.

" The first importation of Slaves from Africa by Englishmen was in the reign of Elizabeth, in the year 1562. This great princess seems, on the very commencement of the trade, to have questioned its lawfulness. She seems to have entertained a religious scruple concerning it, and, indeed, to have revolted at the very thought of it. She seems to have been aware of the evils to which its continuance might lead, or that, if it were sanctioned, the most unjustifiable means might be made use of, to procure the persons of the natives of Africa. And in what light she would have viewed any acts of this kind, had they taken place, we may conjecture from this fact; that when Captain (afterwards Sir John) Hawkins returned from his first voyage to Africa and Hispaniola, whither he had carried slaves, she sent for him, and, as we learn from Hill's Naval History, expressed her concern lest any of the Africans should be carried off without their free consent, declaring that ' it would be detestable, and call down Heaven's vengeance upon the undertakers.' Captain Hawkins promised to comply with the injunctions of Elizabeth in this respect. But he did not keep his word, for when he went to Africa again, he seized many of the inhabitants, and carried them off as slaves, which occasioned Hill, in the account he gives of his second voyage, to use these remarkable words: ' Here began the horrid practice of forcing the Africans into slavery, an injustice and barbarity which, so sure as there is vengeance in heaven for the worst of crimes, will sometime be the destruction of all who encourage it.' That the trade should have been suffered to continue under such a princess, and after such solemn expressions as those which she has been described to have uttered, can only be attributed to the pains taken by those concerned to keep her ignorant of the truth."—*Clarkson*, p. 30.

It may be proper to notice the view taken of this beginning of the slave trade and slavery in the British dominions by a writer decidedly averse to the abolition of the slave trade:

"In regard to Hawkins, himself, he was, I admit, *a murderer and a robber*. His avowed purpose, in sailing to Guinea, was to take, by stratagem or force, and carry away the unsuspecting natives, in the view of selling them as slaves to the people of Hispaniola. In this pursuit, his object was present profit, and his employment and pastime devastation and murder."—*Edwards' History of the West Indies*, Vol. II., pp. 43–4.

This authentic account of the origin of British Colonial slavery is worthy of profound study, and, in connection with other facts that may be presented, suggests thoughts that may have a decisive bearing upon the now pending slave question in America, in more aspects than one.

It is common to cast all the odium of slavery upon our fathers, and upon the governments that first permitted the slave trade. Could the dead rise up and plead their own cause, they might perhaps retort that they had no idea of lending their sanction to the system of American slavery, as *now* practiced. Queen Elizabeth permitted the Africans to be carried into the colonies with their own consent, but they were taken and are held by force. Louis XIII. of France was very uneasy, when about to sanction the importation of Africans into his colonies, until assured that they were to be educated in the Christian religion.* What would he say to the laws that forbid their Christian education? And what would he think of the statement that the colored people of America "must be colonized back to Africa," (a country they never saw), before they can be christianized?

If one monarch who authorized the importation of Africans into his American Colonies directed the liberation of the victims when he learned by what means and for what purposes they were imported—if another consented to the importation only on condition that they should be educated in the Christian religion—and if another only permitted their importation with their own free consent, (involving, by fair implication, the condition of their voluntary and compensated labor,) the question may arise whether the importation *originally* authorized was indeed that African *slave* trade that actually took place, and which history describes. And this may suggest the question how far the usages of slavery, as they now exist, can be said to have been authorized or legalized by the permission of such importations as were contemplated by those monarchs. Mr. Clarkson, who seems to have devoted much attention to the details of this history, considers them of the

---

* Vide Clarkson.

utmost importance to a right understanding of the question respecting the legality of the slave trade as it existed while he was laboring for its suppression.   He demands whether " the African slave trade ever would have been permitted to exist, but for the ignorance of those in authority concerning it."   And he affirms that the " trade began in piracy, and was continued upon the principles of force."   (Pg. 31.)

The *connivance*, rather than the "*ignorance* of those in authority," appears to have sheltered this execrable traffic, after the times of Elizabeth.   Even then it was rather tolerated than directly authorized.   It would be difficult, perhaps, to find any act of the British Parliament by which the *slave* trade was explicitly legalized.   The enactments seem to insinuate, or faintly imply, that the negroes imported are property, yet they studiously avoid to acknowledge them distinctly, or even by necessary implication, as such.   In the act of 10 William III., chap. 26, entitled an " Act to settle the trade to Africa," the negroes are not called *slaves*.   In the act of 23 George II., chap. 31 (1749–50), entitled " An Act for extending and improving the trade to Africa," it was provided (sect. 29) that "no commander or master of any ship trading to Africa shall by *fraud, force, or violence*, or by any other indirect practice whatsoever, take on board, or carry away from the coast of Africa, any negro or native of the said country, or commit, or suffer to be committed, any violence on the natives, to the prejudice of said trade."*   The 28th section of the same act did indeed recognize the holding of "slaves" at the station of the Trading Company in Africa, yet it gave no authority to transport *slaves* to America or elsewhere. Undoubtedly the *secret design* was to stimulate the slave trade. But a sense of shame, and a consciousness of wrong-doing, prevented the Parliament from employing the terms which, upon a strict legal construction, could give to *that* feature of the African trade the shelter of valid law.   [Vide Spooner, pp. 29–35.]

---

* Mr. Pitt's view of this statute, and of the legality of the slave trade, will be presented in the proper place.

Thus stealthily and almost imperceptibly was the idea of legalized human chattelhood introduced. Thus ambiguous and tortuous were the enactments under cover of which the slave traffic was prosecuted. A graphic and truthful description of that traffic we present in the language of Hon. Horace Mann, of Massachusetts.*

" One wants the plain, sinewy, Saxon tongue, to tell of deeds that should have shamed devils. Great Britain was the mother. Her American Colonies were the daughter. The mother lusted for gold. To get it, she made partnership with robbery and death. Shackles, chains, and weapons for human butchery, were her outfit in trade. She made Africa her hunting ground. She made its people her prey, and the unwilling colonies her market-place. She broke into the Ethiop's home, as a wolf into a sheep-fold at midnight. She set the continent aflame, that she might seize the affrighted inhabitants as they ran shrieking from their blazing hamlets. The aged and the infant she left to the vultures, but the strong men and the strong women she drove, scourged and bleeding, to the shore. Packed and stowed like merchandise between unventilated decks, so close that the tempest without could not ruffle the pestilential air within, the voyage was begun. Once a day the hatches were opened, to receive food and disgorge the dead. Thousands and thousands of corpses which she plunged into the ocean from the decks of her slave ships, she counted only as the tare of her commerce. The blue monsters of the deep became familiar with her pathway ; and, not more remorseless than she, they shared her plunder. At length the accursed vessel reached the foreign shore. And there, the monsters of the land, fiercer and feller than any that roam the watery plains, rewarded the robber by purchasing his spoils. For more than a century did the madness of this traffic rage.† During all those years the clock of eternity never counted out a minute that did not witness the cruel death by treachery or violence of some father or mother of Africa."

" Mr. Edwards says that from 1700 to 1786, the number imported into Jamaica was 610,000. ' I say this,' he observes, ' on sufficient evidence, having in my possession lists of all the entries.' ' The total import into all the British Colonies from 1680 to 1786 may be put down at 2,130,000.' In 1771, which he considers the most flourishing period of the trade, there sailed from England to the coast of Africa, one hundred and ninety-two ships, provided for the importation of 47,146 negroes. ' And now,' he observes, (1793) ' the whole number annually exported from Africa by all the European powers, is 74,000, of which 38,000 are imported by the British."—*Godwin, page* 187.

---

* Speech in the House of Representatives of the U. S., June 30, 1848.

† It has not ceased. It rages with violence still, as will be shown in another chapter.

CHAPTER III.

SLAVERY AND THE SLAVE TRADE IN THE BRITISH COLONIES IN NORTH AMERICA, NOW THE UNITED STATES.

Slavers from New England—Slavery in Massachusetts, Connecticut, Rhode Island, Maryland, Virginia, and the Carolinas—Condition of the Slaves—Testimony of Wesley and Whitefield—Inquiry into the legal foundation of Colonial Slavery—Complaints of the Colonies against the King of Great Britain, for favoring the traffic—Paradoxes—Absence of English Statutes legalizing Slavery—Common Law—Lord Mansfield—Colonial Charters—Slavery introduced in absence of Colonial enactments—Date and circumstances of introduction of Slavery into Virginia, South Carolina, and Georgia—Prohibition of Slavery in Georgia, (Gen. Ogelthorpe)—Dates of early enactments concerning Slavery in Virginia, N. Carolina, S. Carolina, Georgia, and Maryland—Loose and vague character of these enactments.

SOON after the settlement of the British North American Colonies, Africans were imported into them, and sold and held as slaves. Of the extent of these importations we have met with no authenticated statistics. The whole number of slaves in these states, by the first census under the present Constitution, 1790, was 697,697.

The colonies now known as the Southern or slave states, on the Atlantic coast, received the principal share of these importations. The middle and eastern colonies received comparatively few, and these chiefly for domestic servants in the cities, and in the families of professional gentlemen in the interior. As the soil was not adapted to slave culture, and was owned in small farms by a hardy race of agriculturists, inured to habits of labor, the process of cultivation by slaves never obtained, particularly in New England, except to a very limited extent. In New York, first settled by the Dutch, in New Jersey, and perhaps in some portions of Pennsylvania, the labor of slaves was introduced to a greater extent than further east. But in the *importation* of slaves for the southern colonies, the merchants of the New England seaports competed with those of New York and the South. They appear, indeed, to have outstripped them, and to have almost monopolized, at one time, the immense profits of that lucrative but detestable trade. Boston, Salem, and Newburyport, in Massachusetts, and Newport and Bristol in Rhode Island, amassed, in the persons of a few of their citizens, vast sums of this rapidly acquired and ill gotten wealth, which, in many instances, quite as rapidly and very remarkably, took to itself wings and flew away. In some cases, however, it remained, and formed the basis of the capital of some prominent mercantile houses, almost or quite down to the present time. Citizens, honored with high posts of office in the State and Federal Governments, have owed their rank in society, and their political elevation, to the wealth thus acquired, sometimes thus acquired by themselves, since the colonies became states, and while the traffic was tolerated as it was, till the year 1808. Among these was a late Senator in Congress, from Rhode Island, James D'Wolf, who, at the time, was reputed to be the owner of a large slave plantation in Cuba. Such incidents may convey some idea of the influence of the traffic in New England, even to the present day. The former seats of the traffic are still the centers of influences hostile to the agitation of the slave question.

The servitude of domestic slaves, in families, is known to be less intolerable than that of slaves on plantations. From this consideration, and from the limited extent of slavery in the northern and eastern colonies, it may be inferred that the slavery of that region was of a comparatively mild type. And yet we find sufficient evidence of its affinity, in many respects, with the present American slave system. Not even in Connecticut was there any recognition of the legality and validity of a slave's marriage.* A master's inadvertent con-

---

* According to Judge Reeve, however, as quoted by Stroud, the murder of a slave was held in Connecticut to be the same as the murder of a freeman. The

sent to the marriage of his female slave to a free colored
man, was held to be equivalent to her manumission, because

---

master could be sued by the slave for immoderate chastisement; the slave could
hold property, in the character of a devisee or legatee, and the master could not
take away such property, or might be sued for it on behalf of the slave by his next
friend.—*Reeve's Law of Baron and Femme*, &c., 340–1 ; Stroud, p. 24.

In Massachusetts, too, "if the master was guilty of a cruel or unreasonable casti-
gation of the slave, he was liable to be punished *for a breach of the peace*, and, I
believe, the slave was allowed to demand sureties of the peace against a violent and
barbarous master."—*Opinion of Chief Justice Parsons, case of Winchendon* vs.
Hatfield, Mass. Rep., 127–8, *cited by Stroud*, p. 23.

In Massachusetts colony, in 1641, the following law was enacted : " It is ordered
by this court and the authority thereof, that there shall never be any bond slavery,
villeinage, or captivity among us, unless it be lawful captives taken in *just war*,
(such) as willingly sell themselves or are sold to us, and such shall have the *liberties*
and Christian usage which the law of God established in Israel concerning such
persons doth morally require."—*See General Laws and Liberties of Massachusetts
Bay, chap.* 12, *sect.* 2 ; *Stroud, p.* 23.

Whether this act *prohibited*, or whether it *authorized* such slavery as afterwards
actually existed in the colony of Massachusetts, might not be very difficult to determine. It certainly prohibited such slavery as now exists at the South.

There is little doubt that slavery was introduced into Boston, by one Maverick,
previous to its settlement by George Winthrop and others, in 1630. There is no
evidence that Maverick was a Puritan. The Boston colonists, generally, were not
Puritans, and ought never to have been confounded with them by historians. The
Puritans, with all their defects and errors on this and other subjects, " made a wide
distinction between those who were stolen and seized by the violence of the slavers,
and those who" (as they supposed) "had been made captives in a lawful war, or
were reduced to servitude for their crimes by a judicial sentence."

This sentiment became current in the New England colonies. "An express law
was made, prohibiting the buying and selling of the former, while the latter were to
have the same privileges as were allowed by the laws of Moses." "In November,
1646, the General Court of Massachusetts passed a law against man-stealing, making
it a capital crime. They also ordered that two Africans, forcibly brought into the
colony, should be sent home at the public expense.—[*Felt's Annals of Salem.*]
The other colonies soon passed a law similar to that of Massachusetts. The Connecticut Code, prepared in 1650, has the following section : ' If any man stealeth a
man or mankinde, he shall be put to death.' The New Haven Code, printed in
London in 1656, contains a similar article : ' If any person steale a man, or mankind,
that person shall surely be put to death.' The Plymouth laws probably made man-
stealing a capital offence."—[*See First Annual Report of the New Hampshire Anti-
Slavery Society, penned by the late John Farmer, Esq., and published in the " Monthly
Emancipator," for August*, 1835.]

In all this we see the stealthy and deceptive introduction of chattel slavery. The
early laws did not authorize, but prohibited such slavery as was actually introduced !
The sin, the shame, and the curse would have been excluded, had it been clearly
understood that slavery is *malum in se*.

The action of the colony of RHODE ISLAND and PROVIDENCE Plantations, eleven
years later than that in Massachusetts, was more direct and explicit. The following

a slave could not be married, and because a husband could claim the assistance of his wife.

A still more discreditable illustration was previously furnished by a rural pastor in the same colony, the owner of a male and female slave. Having admitted them both to the communion of his church (Congregational) as members, and having himself officially pronounced them husband and wife, he afterwards separated them forever by the sale of the wife to a distant purchaser, in despite of the entreaties of both wife and husband. And no court of law, no church, no ecclesiastical body interposed, or even censured.

In Massachusetts, another Congregational pastor, of high reputation, is said to have reared up a female slave in his family in a state of almost absolute heathenism, and never attempted to teach her the alphabet.

When it is remembered that a large portion of the ministers of religion in New England were among the slave

---

document is said to be the first act of any government designed to prevent enslaving the negroes. It is copied from the records of the colony :

" At a general court held at Warwick, the 13th of May, 1652.

" Whereas, there is a common course practised among Englishmen, to buy negroes to that end they may have them for service or slaves forever; for the preventing of such practices among us, let it be ordered, That no black mankind or white being shall be forced, by covenant, bond, or otherwise, to serve any man or his assignees longer than ten years, or until they come to be twenty-four years of age, if they be taken in under fourteen, from the time of their coming within the liberties of this colony; at the end or term of ten years to set them free, as the manner is with the English servants. And that man that will not let them go free or shall sell them away elsewhere, to that end they may be enslaved to others for a longer time, he or they shall forfeit to the colony forty pounds."

To the credit of the members that enacted this law, we subjoin their names from the record :

" The general officers were, John Smith, president; Thomas Olney, general assistant, from Providence; Samuel Gorton, from Warwick; John Green, general recorder; Randal Holden, treasurer; Hugh Bewett, general sergeant.

" The commissioners were from Providence—Robert Williams, Gregory Dexter, Richard Waterman, Thomas Harris, William Wickenden, and Hugh Bewett; from Warwick—Samuel Gorton, John Wickes, John Smith, Randal Holden, John Green, jr., and Ezekiel Holliman."

The prevalence of slavery and the briskness of the slave trade in Rhode Island, long after the enactment of this law (which does not appear to have ever been repealed), furnishes another illustration of the fact that slavery grew up in the colonies in violation of law.

holding class of the community during the colonial state of the country, and many of them still later, that this was within fifty or sixty years of the beginning of the anti-slavery agitation in 1832, and that many of the present ministers of New England are the sons and most of them the successors, of slave holding ministers, it cannot reasonably be doubted that that untoward circumstance has had a bearing upon the position of the present generation of ministers in New England, in respect to the agitation of the subject, and especially in respect to the doctrine of the inherent sinfulness of slave holding. A similar remark might be made, with perhaps greater force, in respect to New Jersey, and, to a greater or less extent, in respect to a great part of the middle states. The beginning of the present agitation, in fact, *found* slavery existing, to a considerable extent, in New Jersey, and the influence of that fact has been seen and felt, wherever the slave question has been discussed, in this country.*

Slavery in the now Atlantic slave states received, substantially, its present complexion during the colonial period. The most important enactments on the subject bear date previous to the Declaration of Independence.

John Wesley, who visited this country during this period, characterizes " American slavery " as " the vilest that ever saw the sun."

George Whitefield, who travelled and preached extensively in the colonies, has drawn a vivid picture of the treatment of slaves at that period. This testimony, it should be remembered, is that of a devout man, whose type of piety is not exposed to the suspicion of tending to magnify, unduly, (as some are supposed to do) the *physical* privations and sufferings of slaves. Nor was he misled into any exaggeration by having imbibed the sentiment of the inherent and necessary criminality of slaveholding. Such a testimony is too important

---

* The Biblical defences of slaveholding, sent forth from the seat of the Theological Seminary at Princeton, took the lead of any thing of that description originating farther South.

to be omitted in this place. In a " Letter to the inhabitants of Maryland, Virginia, North and South Carolina," in 1739, he writes as follows:

" As I lately passed through your provinces on my way hither, I was sensibly touched with a fellow-feeling for the miseries of the poor negroes. Whether it be lawful for Christians to buy slaves, and thereby encourage the nations from whom they are bought to be at perpetual war with each other, I shall not take upon me to determine. Sure I am it is sinful, when they have bought them, to *use them as bad as though they were brutes, nay worse*; and whatever particular exceptions there may be (as I would charitably hope there are some), I fear the generality of you, who own negroes, are liable to such a charge ; for your slaves, I believe, work as hard, if not harder, than the horses whereon you ride. *These,* after they have done their work, are fed, and taken proper care of; but many negroes, when wearied with labor in your plantations, have been obliged to grind their corn, after their return home. Your *dogs* are caressed and fondled at your table, but your *slaves,* who are frequently styled dogs or beasts, have not an equal privilege. They are scarce permitted to pick up the crumbs which fall from their master's table. Not to mention what numbers have been given up to the inhuman usage of task-masters, who, by their unrelenting scourges, have plowed their backs, and made long furrows, and, at length, brought them even unto death. When passing along, I have viewed your plantations cleared and cultivated, many spacious houses built, and the owners of them faring sumptuously every day, my blood has frequently almost run cold within me, to consider how many of your slaves had neither convenient food to eat, nor proper raiment to put on, notwithstanding most of the comforts you enjoy were solely owing to their indefatigable labors."

In tracing the origin, progress, and history of American slavery, now claiming the high sanction and sacred guaranties of our Constitution and laws, and wielding both state and national governments for its support, it is important to note down with distinctness and precision all those facts of the history that may serve to throw any light upon the rise and growth of those high claims, and the methods that have been employed to swell them into their present magnitude, to give them their present hold upon the public mind, and upon the politics, the legislation, and the jurisprudence of the country.

Equally interesting will it be to trace, if we can, the process by which the murderous and piratical depredations of John

Hawkins, upon the unoffending inhabitants of Africa, scarcely three centuries ago, have been made to give not only legal validity, but biblical authority and sanction to the imbruting of three millions of native-born Americans, of all hues, the descendants of all the nations of Europe, as well as of the African tribes.

We pause, therefore, to inquire *on what authority*, divine or human, the North American colonies of Great Britain were inundated with a population of slaves? Was it the precedent of Gonzalez, the alleged recommendation of Las Casas, the importunate rapacity of Chievres, the permission of Ferdinand, the patent of Charles V., that gave legality to these proceedings? Was it the guarded and hesitant assent of Queen Elizabeth? Was it the treachery and perjury of Hawkins? Was it the ambiguity of the Act of Parliament "for extending and improving the trade to Africa," but forbidding "any violence to the natives," and imposing a petty fine upon any commander who, "by fraud, force, or violence, or any other indirect practice whatsoever," should "take on board or carry away from the coast of Africa, any Negro, or native of said country?"

And what was done by the colonial authorities to authorize the traffic?

"The New England colonies, New Jersey, Pennsylvania, Virginia, presented to the throne the most humble and suppliant petitions, praying for the abolition of the trade. *The colonial legislatures passed laws against it.* But their petitions were spurned from the throne. Their laws were vetoed by their Governors."—*Hon. Horace Mann.* Speech in Congress, June 30, 1848.

In the original draft of the Declaration of Independence, by Mr. Jefferson, this charge against the King of Great Britain is thus stated :

"He has waged cruel war against human nature itself, violating its most sacred rights of life and liberty, in the persons of a distant people who never offended him, captivating and carrying them into slavery in another hemisphere, or to incur miserable death in their transportation thither. This piratical warfare, the opprobrium of infidel powers, is the warfare of the Christian king of Great Britain. Determined to keep a market where men should be bought and sold, he has at length prostituted his negative for suppressing any legislative attempt to prohibit and restrain this execrable commerce."

This paragraph was objected to by the delegation from Georgia, and it was accordingly expunged from the document.

A bundle of incongruities here present themselves, attesting the monstrous and anomalous character of the usages in question. The British Government, that had never dared, in the face of British Common Law, to attempt legalizing, directly and unequivocally, the slave traffic, interposed, it would seem, to prevent the colonies from suppressing it. The colonies that, (as will be shown,) had transcended and even outraged their constitutional charters by their iniquitous slave code, are found petitioning and attempting to legislate against the slave *trade!* Slave-holding republicans stigmatizing a monarch as a tyrant beçause he had permitted them to be supplied with the subjects of their own tyranny! A revolutionary Congress compelled or consenting to strike out the most weighty item in the list of offences that characterized their repudiated king as a tyrant!

Whatever solution may be made of such paradoxes, or whatever may be inferred from them, they furnish a slippery and intricate labyrinth for slave-holders in search of their sacred and vested rights, the legal sanctions and the constitutional guaranties of their peculiar immunities, the very foundations of which were laid in piracy and crime.

Thus much in respect to the colonial slave *trade*, the foundation of colonial *slavery*. We inquire next respecting such facts of history, whatever they may be, as shall afford information concerning the authority, either divine or human, by which the colonists held slaves, and the colonial legislatures, (that attempted the suppression of the slave trade as criminal,) enacted their *slave laws*.

We are entering, here, upon no process of argument. We are only recording indisputable facts, without which our historical sketches would be unfaithful and incomplete. We know of nothing so sacred in the claims of slavery as could warrant the suppression of important historical facts.

One of those facts is, that there were no English statute laws, prior to the American Revolution, authorizing the holding of slaves, either in England or in the American colonies. None such, at least that we know of, have ever been alleged to exist.

Another fact is, that the common law of England was incompatible with slavery, and neither recognized nor permitted its existence.

Another fact is, that in the year 1772, the Court of King's Bench, Lord Mansfield presiding, affirmed, in respect to England, the legal facts above stated, and decided that there neither then was, nor ever had been, any legal slavery in England.

Another fact is, that the colonial charters, authorizing the colonial Legislatures to enact laws, gave no license to slavery, and contained the general proviso, that the laws of the colonies should "not be repugnant or contrary, but as nearly as circumstances would allow, conformable to the laws, statutes, and rights of our kingdom of England."*

Another fact is, that when slavery was first introduced into the Anglo-American colonies, and for some time afterwards, there were no colonial enactments that authorized the holding of slaves, or defined the relation and condition of slavery. The practice of slave-holding grew up and was tolerated without law, till at length it acquired power to control legislation and wield it in favor of slavery.

Another fact is, that when enactments were passed upon the subject, they *assumed* the existence of slavery, without so defining who were or might be slaves, as to enable any slave-master at the present day to prove that his slaves are held in virtue of any of the colonial enactments.

Another fact is, that the authority of the colonial " charters,

---

* The charters of Virginia, Maryland, the Carolinas, and Georgia, as well as of Pennsylvania and the New England colonies, were essentially alike in this particular. —*Spooner, p.* 24.

during their continuance, and the general authority of the common law, prior to the Revolution, have been recognized by the Supreme Court of the United States."*

These important historical facts should be borne in mind, pondered, and used, when there is occasion for them, by all who wish to oppose slavery, or to understand the relation of slave-holding to the laws and institutions of the country.

The landing of the founders of New England, at Plymouth, was in 1620. The first settlement in Virginia, at Jamestown, was in 1607. The charter to Lord Baltimore, of Maryland, was granted in 1632. The charter to William Penn, of Pennsylvania, in 1681. North Carolina began to be settled about 1650. South Carolina, about 1670, and Georgia in 1733.

Virginia was the first of the colonies that introduced slavery. Such an event was a natural consequence of the character and position of the first inhabitants.

" Of the one hundred and five persons on the list of emigrants destined to remain, there were no men with families,—there were but twelve laborers, and very few mechanics. The rest were composed of gentlemen of fortune, and of persons of no occupation,—mostly of idle and dissolute habits—who had been tempted to join the expedition through curiosity or the hope of gain ; a company but poorly calculated to plant an agricultural State in a wilderness."—*Willson's Am. Hist. p.* 162.

New emigrants arrived in 1609, " most of whom were profligate and disorderly persons, who had been sent off to escape a worse destiny at home."—*Ib. p.* 166.

" In the month of August, 1620, a Dutch man-of-war entered James River and landed twenty negroes for sale. This was the commencement of negro slavery in the colonies."—*Ib. p.* 169.

At this time " there were very few women in the colony"—" Ninety women of reputable character" were soon after sent over, and the colonists purchased them for wives, "the price of a wife rising from one hundred and twenty to one hundred and fifty pounds of tobacco."—*Ib. p.* 170.

Though these were not held as slaves, yet the state of society indicated by these historical incidents, illustrate the moral and social position of the colonists, at the time they com-

---

* 9 *Cranch's U. S. Reports,* 332-3, as quoted in " *The Unconstitutionality of Slavery, by Lysander Spooner,*" pp. 25-6.

menced the practice of slave-holding. And, so far as *law* was concerned, there was no more legal authority or sanction, at that time, in Virginia, for the holding of negroes in slavery, than there was for making slaves of the white women they purchased. And the incident of purchasing wives shows that the mere act of *purchasing* human beings (of which mention is made in the Scriptures,) does not, of necessity, involve the ideas of *chattelhood,* or of *forced servitude:* no, not even in Virginia !*

About the year 1671, Sir John Yeamans was appointed governor of South Carolina. " From Barbadoes he brought a number of African slaves, and South Carolina was, from the first, essentially, a planting State, with slave labor."—*Willson's Am. Hist. p.* 256.

The first settlement of Georgia was commenced under auspices decidedly hostile to slavery. Gen. James Oglethorpe, a member of the British Parliament, "conceived the idea of opening for the poor of his own country, and for the persecuted protestants of all nations, an asylum in America." Having obtained a grant from the king, he landed at Savannah with 120 emigrants, and commenced his settlement in 1733. The Trustees strictly prohibited slavery, and "de-

---

* Another fact, illustrative of the social and moral influences under which slavery grew up and entrenched itself in Virginia, deserves notice.

The following were the views of Sir William Berkeley, a royal Governor of Virginia, on the subject of popular education. In a letter descriptive of the state of that province, some years after the Restoration, he says :

"I thank God there are no free schools nor printing, and I hope we shall not have, these hundred years ; for learning has brought heresy and disobedience and sects into the world, and printing divulges them, and commits libels against the government. God keep us from both !"

This must have been since the year 1660, the era of the "Restoration" of Charles II., or nearly half a century after the lawless introduction of slavery into the colony. And it is among the archives of this dark period of Virginian brutality, sensualism, ignorance, lawlessness, despotism, servility, and semi-barbarism—in a community without wives, or with wives purchased like negroes with tobacco, without printing presses or free schools for *more* than half a century, and no prospect of them in future—*here* it is that our learned civilians and erudite theologians, in gowns and spectacles, are reverently searching for the credentials of the "peculiar institution," with its sacred *legal rights* and *Bible guaranties !* Worthy successors of Sir William Berkeley ! Accomplished expounders of *his* law, and of *his* gospel !—" *God keep us from both !*"

clared it to be not *only immoral, but contrary to the laws of England.*"—*Willson's Am. Hist., p.* 262.

Unhappily—" Most of those who first came over were unaccustomed to habits of labor." (*Ib.* 262.) " The Colony did not prosper," and some of the colonists began to " complain that they were prohibited the use of slave-labor.

" *The regulations of the trustees began to be evaded, and the laws against slavery were not rigidly enforced.* At first, slaves from South Carolina were *hired* for short periods; then, for a hundred years, or during life, and a sum equal to the value of the negro paid in advance ; and finally, slavers for Africa sailed directly from Savannah ; and Georgia, like Carolina, became a planting State, with slave-labor."—*Willson's Am. Hist. p.* 265.

" In 1752, the trustees of Georgia, wearied with complaints against the system of government which they had established, and finding that the Colony languished under their care, resigned their charter to the king," &c.—*Ib. p.* 266.

The historical evidence is here complete, that slavery and the slave trade were introduced into Georgia, not only without the sanction of either British or Colonial law, but in manifest and flagrant violation of both.

Gen. Oglethorpe, defeated in his laudable efforts, returned to England, in 1743. He afterwards became the friend and co-adjutor of Granville Sharp, and wrote against slavery, and the impressment of seamen. Under date of Cranham Hall, 13th October, 1776, he wrote to Mr. Sharp the following particulars respecting his former connection with the colony of Georgia:

" My friends and I settled the Colony of Georgia, and by charter were established trustees, to make laws, &c. *We determined not to suffer slavery there.* But the slave merchants and their adherents occasioned us not only much trouble, but at last got the then government to favor them. We would not suffer slavery, (which is against the Gospel, as well as the fundamental law of England) to be authorized under our authority ; we refused, as trustees, to make a law permitting such a horrid crime. The government, finding the trustees resolved firmly not to concur with what they believed unjust, took away the charter by which no law could be passed without our consent."—*Stuart's Memoir of Sharp, p.* 25.

The particulars which follow demand careful attention.

In Virginia, " slavery was introduced in 1620, but no act

was passed even purporting to tell who might be slaves, until 1670 "—and this act was afterwards found so defective in the description, as to need a new act for the purpose in 1748, one hundred and twenty-eight years after slavery had been introduced.—*Spooner's* " *Unconstitutionality of Slavery, pp.* 38–9.

" In North Carolina, no general law at all was passed, prior to the revolution, declaring who might be slaves." (*See Iredell's Statutes, revised by Martin*).—*Spooner p.* 40.

" In South Carolina the only statutes, prior to the revolution, that attempted to designate the slaves, was passed in 1740—after slavery had a long time" (sixty-nine years) " existed. And even this statute, in reality defined nothing, for the whole purport of it was to declare that all negroes, Indians, mulattoes, and mestizoes, *except those who were then free*, should be slaves."—*Spooner, p.* 40.

But no *previous* law had told who *were* then legally *slaves*, nor who were legally *free !*

" The same law, in nearly the same words, was passed in Georgia, in 1770," more than a quarter of a century after the introduction of slavery, and after the commencement and brisk prosecution of the African slave trade."—*Vide Spooner, pp.* 40, 41—*Willson's History, &c.*

The " earliest law " of Maryland, noticed by Judge Stroud, defining who might be held as slaves, was enacted in 1663, thirty-one years after the settlement of the colony. The language of the statute assumes the previous fact of slaveholding, and alludes also to a still more remarkable fact.

" Divers free-born *English* women, forgetful of their free condition, and to the disgrace of our nation, do intermarry with negro slaves; by which, also, divers suits may arise, touching the issue of such women, and great damage doth befall the master of such negroes," &c.

To deter from such matches, the statute enacts as follows:

" Whatsoever free-born woman shall intermarry with any slave, shall serve the master of such slave during the life of her husband, and that all the issue of such free born women, so married, shall be slaves, as their *fathers* were."—*Stroud's Sketch of the Slave Laws, p.* 10.

This last provision was a departure from the prevalent maxim of the slave code, that the child follows the condition of the *mother*. The temporary end of the statute of 1663 having been answered, it was repealed in 1681, with a clause saving the rights under the act of 1663, so that the masters might continue to hold in slavery the descendants, if any, of the "free born English women" who might have married slaves, during the operation of the act of 1663, which was repealed "to prevent persons from purchasing white women as servants, and marrying them to their slaves, for the purpose of making slaves of them and their offspring."

Yet "the doctrine of 'partus sequitur' obtained in the province" (*i. e.* the children of slaves followed the condition of the father) "till the year 1699 or 1700, when a general revision of the laws took place, and the acts in which this doctrine was recognized were, with many others, repealed. An interval of about *fifteen years* appears to have elapsed, *without any written law* on this subject; but in 1715 (chap. 44, sec. 22) the following one was passed : "All negroes and slaves already imported, or hereafter to be imported into this province, and all children now born or hereafter to be born of such negroes and slaves, shall be slaves during their natural lives.' Thus, (continues Stroud) was the maxim of the civil law, ' partus sequitur *ventrem*' introduced, and the condition of the *mother*, from that day to the present time, has continued to determine the fate of the child."—*Stroud's Sketch*, pp. 10, 11.

Had the opposite maxim prevailed—had the child followed the condition of the *father*, there would have been comparatively few slaves in Maryland, or in any of the southern states, at the present time.

The *dates* of colonial enactments on the subject of slavery are important historical items, as already hinted, because they are necessary in order to establish the fact of legalized colonial slavery, and to fix the period of its commencement, in a given colony, (if any such legislation under the Colonial Charters already alluded to, can be supposed to have been valid.) And we have already noticed that the practice of slaveholding obtained in the principal slave colonies, for long periods, and, in one instance, up to the period of the American Revolution, without any action of the colonial authorities, *attempting* to tell *who* were slaves ; viz. in Virginia, 50 years; in South Carolina, 69 years ; in Georgia, more than 25 years;

in Maryland, (from its first settlement), 31 years; and in North Carolina there was no colonial definition at all!

But the dates and the various *provisions* of the several colonial enactments, admitting them to have been constitutionally valid, become important historical facts in another point of view, not only as bearing upon the inquiry, *Who* were, legally, slaves, but also on the question, *What was the slavery* under which they were thus legally held, and *When* was it, that *that* slavery, as thus legislatively defined, became legalized?

For, if it were clearly ascertained and established, that "SLAVERY," in general terms, had been legalized by valid and constitutional enactments of the colonial legislatures, in the first commencement of their authority, the question would still remain whether the slavery thus legalized was identical with the slavery defined many years afterwards, or whether it was altogether *another thing*, though known by the same name. The South Carolina enactment of 1740, and the Georgia enactment of 1770, would tell us, distinctly enough, what was the slavery of those colonies at those periods: but they could not tell us whether the slavery legalized in those colonies (if, indeed, there were any) sixty-nine, and twenty-five years previous, was precisely the *same thing*. It *might* have been only the bond-service of Massachusetts, in 1641, defined by "the law of God established in Israel," and which, if followed out, would have secured "a jubilee throughout the land, to all the inhabitants thereof," long ago. In Georgia, as we have seen, the first slavery was the *hiring* of slaves for short periods, then for one hundred years—then buying, then importing them, and thus the whole system was changed.

When we are told of the inherited, imprescriptible, time-sanctioned, and guarantied rights of the present American slaveholder, it becomes a matter of the deepest interest to learn, if we may, the origin, the date, the tenure, and the *description* of those rights, as originally defined. Between the right to import Africans into the colonies, with "their own free consent" in the times of Queen Elizabeth or James I., and the right to hold the descendants of those Africans, and of all the nations of Europe, as chattels personal, in the present American States, there seems a perceptible chasm, and before the latter can be inferred from the former, some attention must needs be paid to the various arches of the bridge by which this chasm is conceived to have been spanned. A few missing links and bolts might endanger the safety of the transition. Into the requisite examination we cannot now enter. We only indicate the field of inquiry, and note down a few obvious facts.

In consulting Stroud's Sketch of the Slave Laws, one is struck with the fact that most, if not all of the colonial enactments cited, bear date many years after the practice of slaveholding is known to have been introduced, and after the slaves must have become numerous. From this fact, and from the implications or statements in the preambles to those acts, it appears evident that the *usages* of slavery grew up first, and that the colonial legislation came in, to sanction and shelter them, afterwards, indicating the fact of a *previously* existing slavery *without* statute, and consequently ILLEGAL, since no one maintains that it could have originated in natural right, or in the principles of common law.

Thus, in Virginia, where slavery, in *fact*, commenced in 1620, the first slave *law* cited by Stroud or by Spooner, is that of 1670, and most of the acts defining slavery are, perhaps, since 1700.—Of the slave laws of Maryland, (which was settled in 1632,) the first cited is that of 1663, and the remainder are from 1715 to 1751.—Of those of South Carolina, where slavery commenced in 1671, the first cited bears date 1695,—the remainder from 1711 to 1740, at which latter date the "peculiar institution" evidently received, (so far as the *statute* is concerned,) its full proportions and shape.—Of those of North Carolina, settled about 1650, the first cited is that of 1729, and the remainder bear date from 1741 to 1743, about which time the definition of slavery appears to have been settled, upon very nearly its present basis, in *that* Colony.— Of those of Georgia, where slavery commenced prior to 1743, the first and *only* distinct reference is to the law of 1770, by which, very manifestly, the cardinal features of the slave law, in *that* Colony, were determined.—*These eras* in colonial slave legislation are too distinctly marked to be mistaken or forgotten by the student of American slave law; though, doubtless, there must have been some earlier acts, not noticed by Judge Stroud, and some of his references are to Digests and Manuals, in which the dates of legislation are not given.

Slave legislation, since the American Revolution, has made some important strides. Virginian slavery reposes on her revised code of 1819, and *is* what *that makes* it, without dreaming of any hazard to the venerable antiquity of her claims.

CHAPTER IV.

EARLY TESTIMONIES AGAINST SLAVERY AND THE SLAVE TRADE.

THE Dominicans in Spanish America, as related by Clarkson, " considered slavery as utterly repugnant to the principles of the gospel, and recommended the abolition of it." Being opposed by the Franciscans, " a controversy on the subject between them was carried to Pope Leo X. for his decision."

Pope Leo X. declared that " not only the Christian religion, but that nature herself cried out against slavery."

Charles V. (as before stated) bore testimony against slavery, by abolishing it in his dominions, in the year 1542.

Between A. D. 1670 and 1680, Godwyn, a clergyman of the Established Church, and Richard Baxter, the celebrated Non-conformist, bore strong testimony against these oppressions, the former, describing, with nervous eloquence, the brutality of slavery, as he had witnessed it in Barbadoes ;— the latter protesting against the traffic, and denouncing those engaged in it as pirates and robbers. These writers were followed by Southern, Hutcheson, Foster, Atkins, Wallis, and others. [Vide Clarkson.]

Bishop Warburton, in 1676, preached a sermon, denouncing, in strong language, those who "talk, as of herds of cattle, of property in rational creatures !"

Dr. Porteus, Bishop of London, said that the slave trade was contrary to the religion we professed. He vindicated the Bible against the assertion that it sanctioned slavery—" Nay," (said he) " it classed men-stealers or slave traders among the murderers of fathers and mothers, and the most profane criminals on earth."

John Wesley, the founder of Methodism, who had witnessed the workings of slavery in our North American colonies and in the West Indies, declared " American slavery" to be " the vilest that ever saw the sun," and constituting " the sum of all villanies." Slave dealers, he denominated " man stealers ; the worst of thieves, in comparison of whom high-way robbers and house-breakers are comparatively innocent." He adds: "And men buyers are exactly on a level with men stealers."

Jonathan Edwards, the younger, said: "To hold a man in a state of slavery, is to be, every day, guilty of robbing him of his liberty, or of man stealing."

Bishop Horsley said: "Slavery is injustice, which no consideration of policy can extenuate."

Dr. Samuel Johnson said: "No man is by nature the property of another. The rights of nature must be some way forfeited before they can justly be taken away."

Edmund Burke said: "Slavery is a state so improper, so degrading, and so ruinous to the feelings and capacities of human nature, that it ought not to be suffered to exist."

Archdeacon Paley said: "Slavery is a dominion and system of laws, the most merciless and tyrannical that were ever tolerated upon the face of the earth."

Montesquieu ironically said: "If we allow negroes to be men, it will begin to be believed that we, ourselves, are not Christians!"

Blackstone, the jurist, sums up an elaborate scrutiny of the subject thus: "If neither captivity nor contract can, by the plain law of nature and reason, reduce the parent to a state of slavery, much less can they reduce the offspring."

William Pitt declared it to be "injustice to permit slavery to remain for a single hour."

Charles James Fox said: "With regard to a regulation of slavery, my detestation of its existence induces me to know no such thing as a regulation of robbery, and a restriction of murder." "Personal freedom is a right of which he who deprives a fellow-creature is criminal in so depriving him, and he who withholds is no less criminal in withholding."

Bishop Butler said: "Despicable as they" (the negroes) "may appear in our eyes, they are the creatures of God, and of the race of mankind, for whom Christ died, and it is inexcusable to keep them in ignorance of the end for which they were made, and of the means whereby they may become partakers of the general redemption."

Hannah More said: "Slavery is vindicated in print (1788), and defended in the House of Peers! Poor human reason! When wilt thou come to years of discretion?"

Dr. Samuel Hopkins said: "Slavery is, in every instance, wrong, unrighteous, oppressive, a very great and crying sin, there being nothing of the kind equal to it on the face of the earth."

The learned Grotius said: "Those are men stealers who abduct, keep, sell or buy slaves or free men. To steal a man is the highest kind of theft."

Dr. Benjamin Rush said: " Domestic slavery is repugnant to the principles of Christianity." " It is rebellion against the authority of a common Father."

Dr. Primatt said: " It has pleased God to cover some men with white skins and others with black ; but as there is neither merit nor demerit in complexion, the white man, notwithstanding the barbarity of custom and prejudice, can have no right, by virtue of his color, to enslave and tyrannize over the black man."

Dr. William Robertson said: " No inequality, no superiority in power, no pretext of consent, can justify this ignominious depression of human nature."

The Abbe Gregoire said: " The corruption of our times carries towards posterity all the elements of slavery and crime." " There is not a vice, not a species of wickedness, of which Europe is not guilty towards negroes, of which she has not shown them the example."

The Abbe Raynal said: " He who supports slavery is the enemy of the human race. He divides it into two societies of legal assassins, the oppressors and the oppressed." " I shall not be afraid to cite to the tribunal of reason and justice those governments which tolerate this cruelty, or which even are not ashamed to make it the basis of their power."

Dr. Price, of London, said: " If you have a right to make another man a slave, he has a right to make you a slave."

Joseph Addison said: " What color of excuse can there be for the contempt with which we treat this part of our species" (the negroes), " that we should not put them upon the common footing of humanity ?"—*Vide Spectator.*

Dr. Adam Clarke, the learned commentator, said: " How can any nation pretend to fast, or worship God, or dare profess to believe in the existence of such a being, while they carry on what is called the slave trade, and traffic in the souls, blood, and bodies of men? O ye most flagitious of knaves, and worst of hypocrites! Cast off at once the mask of religion, and deepen not your endless perdition by professing the faith of our Lord Jesus Christ, while you continue in this traffic."—*Comment. on Isa.*, 58 : 6.

Macknight, the commentator, in exposition of 1 Tim. 1 : 10, said: " Men stealers are inserted among the daring criminals against whom the law of God directed its awful curses. These were persons who kidnapped men to sell them for slaves ; and this practice seems inseparable from the other iniquities and oppressions of slavery ; nor can a slave dealer easily keep free from this criminality, if indeed the receiver is as bad as the thief."

Thomas Scott, the commentator, copied the preceding from Macknight, and in his practical observations on Rev. 18 : 13—" Souls of men"—said: " To number the persons of men with beasts, sheep, and horses, as the stock of a farm, or with bales of goods, as the cargo of a ship, is, no doubt, a most detestable and anti-Christian practice."

Abraham Booth (the Baptist theological writer) said : " I have not a stronger conviction of scarcely anything, than that *slave holding* (except when the slave has forfeited his liberty by crimes against society) *is wicked* and *inconsistent with Christian character*." " To me it is evident, that whoever would purchase an innocent black man to make him a slave, would with equal readiness purchase a white one for the same purpose, could he do it with equal impunity, and no more disgrace."

Mr. Booth preached a sermon (1792) entitled " Commerce in the Human Species, and the *enslaving* of innocent persons, inimical to the laws of Moses, and the Gospel of Christ." The text was from Exodus 21 : 16. " He that stealeth a man, and selleth him, or if he be found in his hands, he shall surely be put to death."

James Beattie said : " Slavery is inconsistent with the dearest and most essential rights of man's nature ; it is detrimental to virtue and industry ; it hardens the heart to those tender sympathies which form the most lovely part of human character ; it involves the innocent in hopeless misery, in order to procure wealth and pleasure for the authors of that misery ; it seeks to degrade into brutes, beings whom the Lord of Heaven and Earth endowed with rational souls, and created for immortality ; in short, it is utterly repugnant to every principle of reason, religion, humanity, and conscience. It is impossible for a considerate and unprejudiced mind, to think of slavery without horror."

George Fox, when in Barbadoes, in 1671, addressed himself thus, to those who attended his religious meetings : " Consider with yourselves, if you were in the same condition as the poor Africans are, who came strangers to you, and were sold to you as slaves ; I say, if this should be the condition of you or yours, you would think it a hard measure ; yea, and very great bondage and cruelty."

John Locke said : " Slavery is so vile, so miserable an estate of man, and so directly opposite to the generous temper and courage of our nation, that it is hard to be conceived that an Englishman, much less a gentleman, should plead for it."—*Essay on Government.*

Thomas Jefferson said : " The whole commerce between master and slave, is a perpetual exercise of the most boisterous passions ; the most unremitting despotisms, on the one part, and degrading submissions on the other." " I tremble for my country, when I reflect, that God is just ; that his justice cannot sleep forever."—*Notes on Virginia.*

John Jay said : " Till America comes into this measure" (abolition) " her prayers to Heaven will be impious. This is a strong expression, but it is just." " I believe that God governs the world, and I believe it to be a maxim in His, as in our courts, that those who ask for equity ought to do it." —*Letter from Spain,* 1780.

Dr. Benjamin Franklin said : " Slavery is an atrocious debasement of human nature."

James Oglethorpe, the founder of Georgia, said: "This cruel custom of a private man's being supported in exercising more power over the man whom he affirms to have bought as his slave, than the magistrate has over the master, is a solecism in politics."—*Stuart's Memoir of Sharp, p.* 25.

Rousseau said: "The terms *slavery* and *right*, contradict and exclude each other."

Buffon said: "It is apparent that the unfortunate negroes are endowed with excellent hearts, and possess the seeds of every human virtue. I cannot write their history without lamenting their miserable condition." "Humanity revolts at those odious oppressions that result from avarice."

Brissot said: "Slavery, in all its forms, in all its degrees, is a violation of divine law, and a degradation of human nature."

Sir William Jones said: "I pass with haste, by the coast of Africa, whence my mind turns with indignation at the abominable traffic in the human species, from which a part of our countrymen dare to derive their inauspicious wealth."

Our limits forbid us to extend this list of witnesses, into which we have introduced but few of the names most prominently connected, in England and America, with specific enterprises for abolishing the slave trade and slavery. Nor have we quoted the more modern writers on the subject, nor many of the American statesmen during and since the Revolution, (some of them slave-holders,) whose testimony would have been appropriate. In another connection we may refer to some of them. Nor have we cited the long catalogue of eminent poets, all of whom, with scarcely an exception, have deplored and condemned slavery. And yet, our chapter of testimonies is sufficient to show that the moral sense, the reason, the sympathy, the humanity, the philosophy, and the professed RELIGION of the civilized world, are against slavery, which is, of course, destined to fall.

CHAPTER V.

ACTION OF RELIGIOUS BODIES AGAINST THE SLAVE TRADE
AND SLAVERY, COMMENCING BEFORE THE AMERICAN REVO-
LUTION, AND ITS RESULTS.

George Fox in Barbadoes—William Edmundson, A.D. 1675—*Friends in England*,
A.D. 1727—1761—1763—1772—*Friends in America*—Yearly Meeting in Philadelphia, A.D. 1696—Gov. Penn, 1700—Quarterly Meetings of Chester, Haddonfield,
&c. Yearly Meeting, 1754—1774—1776—Friends in New England—Rhode Island
Quarterly Meeting, A.D. 1716—1727—1770—Yearly Meeting of New York,
1759—Purchase Quarterly Meeting, 1767. Yearly Meeting, 1771—1781—Yearly
Meeting of Virginia, A.D. 1757—1766—1767—1768—1773—1787—Compensation
provided for Emancipated Slaves—Stirring Agitations among Friends during
this Reformation—William Burling, Ralph Sandiford, Benjamin Lay, John Woolman, Anthony Benezet—Congregationalists in America—Dr. Samuel Hopkins—
Church at Newport, 1769.

FROM the records of early anti-slavery *testimony*, we turn to
those of early anti-slavery *action*. As those testimonies were
evidently founded, for the most part, in the principles of the
Christian religion, and were urged on religious considerations,
it was natural that the early efforts against slavery and the
slave trade should partake of the same character, and be propounded in religious bodies.

FRIENDS IN ENGLAND.

George Fox, as already mentioned, remonstrated with the
"Friends" in Barbadoes, concerning their treatment of the
negroes. This was in 1671. He exhorted them to give their
slaves religious instruction, and "bring them to know the
Lord Christ." In his journal he says:

" I desired, also, that they would cause their overseers to deal mildly and
gently with their negroes, and not use cruelty towards them, as the manner

of some had been; and that, after certain years of servitude, they should make them free."*

In a public discourse, he said:

" Let me tell you, it will doubtless be very acceptable to the Lord, if so be that masters of families here, would deal so with their servants, and negroes, and blacks, whom they have bought with their money, as to let them go free, after they have served faithfully a considerable number of years, be it thirty, more or less, and when they go, and are made free, let them not go away empty handed."†

William Edmundson, a fellow-laborer with Fox, bore a similar testimony. He complained of the herding of the slaves together like brute beasts, without any religious instruction, or a sufficiency of suitable sustenance.—*Clarkson*, p. 5.

Both Fox and Edmundson were charged with exciting the slaves to revolt, and the latter was arraigned before the governor, in 1675, on that false allegation.—" *Brief Statement*," p. 6.

Thus early began the false charge of bloody designs, and no peacefulness of principles, no mildness of manner and language, and no moderation of measures—though even faulty in that direction, have ever exempted the earnest friends of emancipation from these charges.

" I do not find any individual of this Society (i. e. in England) moving in this cause, for some time after the death of George Fox and William Edmundson. The first circumstance of moment which I discover, is a resolution of the whole society, on the subject, at their yearly meeting, held in London, in the year 1727. The resolution was in the following words" :---

" It is the sense of this meeting, that the importing of negroes from their native country and relations, by Friends, is not a commendable or allowed practice, and is therefore censured by this meeting."---*Clarkson's History*, p. 51.

From this record it is evident that Friends, in England, at this time, were, to a greater or less extent, implicated in the African slave trade. And it is equally clear from what follows, that this very cautious and gentle admonition had not

---

* *Clarkson's History*, p. 50.

† *Brief Statement*, &c., by the Philadelphia Yearly Meeting, 1843, page 6.

fully sufficed, in thirty-one years, to purge the Society from the guilt of that traffic. In 1758, the following resolution was adopted:

"We fervently warn all in profession with us, that they carefully avoid being in any way concerned in reaping the unrighteous profits arising from the iniquitous practice of dealing in negro or other slaves, whereby, in the original purchase, one man selleth another, as he doeth the beasts that perish, without any better pretension to property in him, than that of superior force, in direct violation of the Gospel rule, which teacheth all to do as they would be done by, and to do good to all. We, therefore, can do no less than, with the greatest earnestness, impress it upon Friends, everywhere, that they endeavor to keep their hands clear of the unrighteous gain of oppression."

Three years afterwards, 1761, the Society took a further step, as appears by the following:

" This meeting, having reason to apprehend that diverse, under our name, are concerned in the unchristian traffic in negroes, doth recommend it earnestly to the care of Friends, everywhere, to discourage, as much as in them lies, a practice so repugnant to our christian profession ; and to deal with all such as shall persevere in a conduct so reproachful to christianity ; *and disown them*, if they do not *desist therefrom.*"

In 1763, this action was repeated, and the cords drawn still tighter, in the following:

"We renew our exhortation that Friends, everywhere, be especially careful to keep their hands clear of giving encouragement, in any shape, to the slave-trade, being evidently destructive of the natural rights of mankind, who are all ransomed by one Savior, and visited by one divine light, in order to salvation, a traffic calculated to enrich and aggrandize some, upon the misery of others ; in its nature, abhorrent to every just and tender sentiment, and contrary to the whole tenor of the Gospel."

" By the minute which was made on this occasion, I apprehend that no one belonging to the Society, could furnish even materials for such voyages." —*Clarkson*, p. 52.

It is to be noticed that all this action was directed against the slave *trade*, or the importing of negroes. Nothing is said directly of slave *holding*, though slaves were then held in England, whether by Quakers we cannot tell, though Quakers in America held slaves at that time.

In 1772, the Society in England approved the "salutary

endeavors" of Friends in America, to discourage the holding of slaves.

FRIENDS IN AMERICA.

The movement among Friends in America began earlier:

" The Quakers in America, it must be owned, did most of them, originally, as other settlers there, with respect to the purchase of slaves."---*Clarkson*, p. 57.

They, however, treated them with peculiar lenity, yet individuals among them soon became uneasy about holding slaves at all.

In the year 1696 the yearly meeting of Philadelphia advised its members to " be careful not to encourage the bringing in of any more negroes, and that those who have negroes be careful of them, bring them to meetings, have meetings with them in their families, and restrain them from loose and lewd living, as much as in them lies, and from rambling abroad, on First days, or other times."*---" *Brief Statement*," &c., p. 8.

The quarterly meetings of Chester, Haddonfield, Philadelphia, Bucks, Burlington, and Salem, subordinate to the yearly meeting, took measures from time to time, on the subject. The quarterly meeting of Chester extended into Virginia.— " *Brief Statement*," &c.

In the yearly meeting, the subject was kept alive by renewed testimonies from time to time, and advance steps were taken, until, in 1754, the meeting recommended to "advise and deal with such as engage" in the traffic. They also expressed a desire to guard against " promoting the bondage of such an unhappy people." They "observe that their number is, of late, increased among us." They intimate the injustice of living upon their unrequited labor, and beseech those who have received slaves as an inheritance that they so train them

---

* William Penn, while Governor, in 1700, laid before the meeting his concern on the same subject, recommending religious meetings with the slaves. " His attempts to improve their condition by legal enactments were defeated in the House of Assembly."—*Ib.*, p. 9. A law imposing a duty of twenty pounds upon every slave imported, was a few years afterwards enacted, but disannulled by the British Crown.—*Ib.*, p. 11.

as to prepare them for freedom, if they should hereafter set them at liberty.—*Clarkson's History*, pp. 58, 59.*

In 1774 another advance step was taken.

" By a resolution of that year, all members concerned in importing, selling, purchasing, giving, or transferring negroes or other slaves, or otherwise acting in such a manner as to continue them in slavery beyond the term limited by law or custom (*i. e.*, for white persons), were directed to be excluded from membership, or disowned."—*Clarkson's History*, p. 60.

" In the year 1776, the same yearly meeting carried the matter still farther. It was then enacted, That the owners of slaves, who refused to execute proper instruments for giving them their freedom, were to be disowned likewise."—*Ib.*

As the result of this action, it appears that the practice of slaveholding was generally discontinued within the bounds of the Philadelphia Yearly Meeting, not many years afterwards. The subordinate meetings took early measures for carrying out the views of the Yearly Meeting. The Philadelphia Monthly Meeting reported, in 1781, that "there was but one case," under care, and, in 1783, that "there were no slaves owned by its members."

" As the minute of 1781 is the last on record " (of the Yearly Meeting) " on this subject, which speaks of slaves being still owned by our members, it is probable that before the succeeding Yearly Meeting, they had all been freed."—*Brief Statement*, p. 35.

These measures were followed by efforts for the religious instruction of the emancipated negroes; and in some instances they were compensated for their past services.

---

* From the more full quotation of this document, in the *Brief Statement* of 1843, we learn that it also held the more stern language that follows :

" And we entreat all to examine, whether the purchasing of a negro, either born here or imported, doth not contribute to a further importation, and consequently to the upholding all the evils above mentioned, and promoting *man stealing*—the only theft which, by the Mosaic law, was punished with death : ' He that stealeth a man, and selleth him, *or if he be found in his hand*, he shall surely be put to death.'— Ex. 21 : 16."—*Brief Statement*, see p. 18.

So that the ecclesiastical testimony of the " Friends"—invidiously commended by some for its mildness, did not reach its object, till it had identified slaveholding with man stealing. This testimony is recorded as being "supposed to have been from the pen of Anthony Benezet."

The course of action by the New England Yearly Meeting, and its subordinate meetings, was very similar, and but little later in dates.   The earliest action on record is a query by the Monthly Meeting of Dartmouth to the Rhode Island Quarterly Meeting, in 1716, asking " whether it be agreeable to Truth, for Friends to purchase slaves, and keep them for a term of life?"   The question was referred back to the different monthly meetings composing that quarterly meeting.   The answers of several meetings were in the negative.   The matter came up again before the Rhode Island Quarterly Meeting, in 1717, but no decisive minute was made on the subject.—In 1727, the Yearly Meeting made a short minute censuring the practice " of importing negroes from their native country and relations."   In 1760, the discipline was revised, and the language of the "printed epistle of the London Yearly Meeting of 1758, against dealing in negroes and other slaves," was incorporated into the discipline.   In the same year the following inquiry was adopted:

" Are Friends clear of importing negroes, or buying them when imported ; and do they use those well, where they are possessed by inheritance or otherwise, endeavoring to train them up in the principles of religion ?"

In 1769, the Rhode Island Quarterly Meeting proposed to the Yearly Meeting such an amendment of this query as should not imply that the holding of slaves was allowed. The Yearly Meeting deferred action until 1770, when the query was so amended as to include the following:

" And are all set at liberty that are of age, capacity and ability, suitable for freedom ?"

This action was carried forward until, in 1782, the Yearly Meeting says—

" We know not but all the members of this meeting are clear of that iniquitous practice of holding or dealing with mankind as slaves."—*Brief Statement*, &c., pp. 44 to 47.

It was not, however, until 1787, that the Yearly Meeting could report a satisfactory settlement for the past services of those who had been held in slavery.   (*Ib.*)

The Yearly Meeting of New York, previous to 1759, had manifested its disapprobation of the slave trade.—The Purchase Quarterly Meeting, in 1767, suggested the inquiry, "whether it is consistent with a Christian spirit to keep those in slavery we have already in possession, by purchase, gift, or any other way?"

In 1771, the Yearly Meeting concluded " that those Friends who have negroes shall not sell them for slaves, excepting in cases of executors," &c., who are, in that case, to advise with their respective monthly meetings.—Measures were taken, the same year, to encourage manumissions.

In 1776, the Yearly Meeting took still higher ground, refusing to accept or employ the services in the church, or "receive the collections," of those who "continue these poor people in bondage."

In 1784, a solitary case of slaveholding was reported—and in 1787 there were none at all.

In 1781, the Yearly Meeting advised each monthly meeting to appoint suitable persons to inspect the cases of the recent emancipations, and afford such assistance and advice, both in respect to the temporal and spiritual good of the emancipated, as might be in their power, and "endeavor to find what, in justice, may be due them." At the succeeding Yearly Meeting, it was recommended that committees be appointed by the monthly meetings to "hand out to the said negroes" "the sum or sums which may appear to be due them."——"So faithfully and earnestly did Friends carry out these views of the Yearly Meeting, that in the year 1784 there appear to have been but three unsettled cases remaining.—" *Brief Statement*," &c., pp. 47 to 51.

The Yearly Meeting of Virginia introduced a query " designed to forbid the trafficking in slaves," in 1757. In 1764, the Meeting advised additional attention to the religious instruction and clothing of slaves. In 1766, it was proposed to forbid its members to purchase any more negroes, and the subject was referred back to the quarterly meetings. In 1767, the Yearly Meeting could not unanimously conclude upon issuing any injunctions either with regard to purchasing or setting them free, but earnestly desired each member to be careful and not encumber himself or posterity with any further purchases.—In 1768, this advice was made a rule of discipline.—In 1773, the Yearly Meeting earnestly recommended manumissions, and quoted the words of the prophet— " The people of the land have used oppression and exercised *robbery*," &c. The measure was followed up till 1787, when it appeared that there were still some members who held slaves. It is stated that, after this, " the Yearly Meeting of Virginia gradually cleared itself of this grievous burthen:" but the precise date of its final extinction is not given.— "*Brief Statement,*" &c., pp. 51 to 56.

A very interesting feature of this reformation among the Friends, was the compensation provided for the emancipated slaves, in striking contrast with the absurd claim, sometimes set up, for compensation to the master. Another circumstance worthy of note is the uniformity and celerity with which the reformation was effected, so soon as the ecclesiastical bodies adventured to characterize slaveholding, in the strong but truthful language of Scripture, as robbery and man-stealing; giving proof of the earnestness and sincerity of their testimony, by taking measures for withdrawing religious fellowship from slaveholders. It is stated that some were actually " *disowned,*" for non-compliance.—" *Brief Statement,*" &c., p. 46.

Nor was this great change effected in the Society of Friends without stirring agitations, exciting appeals, and long-continued and earnest debates and discussions. The cautiously guarded and modified records of the ecclesiastical bodies, especially the more early testimonies, expressing, perhaps, in the language of compromise, the hesitant and even reluctant assent of the predominating and conservative portion of the body, must not be taken as specimens of the tone and manner of the agitators by whom the subject was continually pressed upon the attention of the Society, until final action was reached. A long succession of these untiring and zealous laborers were engaged in this great work.

William Burling, of Long Island, was, perhaps, the first of these. He began his testimony early in life, and seldom if ever permitted a Yearly Meeting to assemble and separate without hearing his earnest remonstrance against their toleration of slavery.

Ralph Sandiford, of Philadelphia, was another earnest agitator. He published his "Mystery of Iniquity, in a brief examination of the practice of the times," in the year 1729. The language is described as bold, stirring, energetic, and uncompromising. The very title-page is a sufficient indication of the fact.

Benjamin Lay published his Treatise on Slave-keeping in 1737. It was printed by Benjamin Franklin. The title of this book* shows that he opposed not merely the slave trade and slave buying, (which was all that the Yearly Meeting was prepared to do, six years afterwards,) but likewise the practice of slaveholding, and denounced it as a high crime. He is described by Clarkson as "a man of strong understanding, and of great integrity, but of warm and irritable feelings, and more particularly so when he was called forth on any occasion in which the oppressed Africans were concerned."†

---

* "All Slave-keepers, that keep the innocent in bondage, *apostates.*"

† Some specimens of his manner of agitating "the delicate question" may be interesting.

"Calling on a Friend in the city (Philadelphia), he was asked to sit down to breakfast. He first inquired, 'Dost thou keep slaves in thy house?' On being answered in the affirmative, he said, 'Then I will not partake with thee of the fruits of thy unrighteousness.'—After an ineffectual attempt to convince a farmer and his wife in Chester county of the iniquity of keeping slaves, he seized their only child, a little girl of three years of age, under pretence of carrying her away, and when the cries of the child and his singular expedient alarmed them, he said, 'You see and feel, now, a little of the distress which you occasion by the inhuman practice of slave-keeping."—*First Annual Report, N. Hampshire A. S. Society, by John Farmer, Esq.—Emancipator for August,* 1835.

At Friends' Monthly Meetings, if a slaveholder rose to speak, Benjamin Lay would rise and exclaim—"There's another negro master!"

On one occasion he seated himself in a Friends' Meeting among slaveholders, with a bladder of bullock's blood secreted under his mantle, and at length broke the quiet

For forty-one years, and until his death, in 1759, he bore an uncompromising and zealous testimony against the sin of slavery.

John Woolman travelled through the provinces as a preacher and anti-slavery agitator, from 1746 to 1767. He travelled much of the time on foot, conversing with the people, and discoursing to public assemblies.

Anthony Benezet published a work against slavery in 1762, and another in 1767. He wrote also in the public journals, in the almanacs, and labored in every practicable and suitable manner to convince the people of the unlawfulness of slavery.

"Let all the evangelical denominations but follow the simple example of the Quakers in this country, and slavery would soon come to an end."— *Albert Barnes.*

If to this statement were added the condition that the members of all these religious denominations, including the Quakers, would support the cause of righteousness in their political as well as ecclesiastical relations, the result could not be a matter of doubtful speculation.

CONGREGATIONALISTS IN NEW ENGLAND.

The brightest as well as the earliest exhibition of Christian church discipline against *slavery*, however, was in the instance, not of an extended ecclesiastical organization or sect, but of an Independent or Congregational Church in New England. When Dr. Samuel Hopkins, the celebrated theologian, removed to Newport, Rhode Island, in 1769, he found himself pastor of a church involved deeply in slaveholding and the African slave trade. He was not long in applying to those

---

stillness of the worship by deliberately rising in full view of the whole audience, piercing the bladder, spilling the blood on the floor and seats, thus sprinkling some of it on the raiment of those near him, and exclaiming with all the solemn authority of an ancient prophet—"Thus shall the Lord spill the blood of those that traffic in the blood of their fellow-men!"—Some shrieked—some fainted, and the meeting broke up in confusion.

"Modern" abolitionists have been censured as too denunciatory and violent. Not unfrequently they have been advised to take the good old Quaker abolitionists as models of mildness ! Do the advisers understand what they are saying ?

practices the stern and unbending ethics derived from his *then* somewhat peculiar and most uncompromising theology, according to which, slaveholding could be nothing less than *malum in se*, in every instance sinful, without any valid excuse, or apology : a sin, like all other sin, to be cured or purged in no way but by its present and unconditional abandonment, at whatever cost, the case admitting of no prudential stipulations, and no delay. Admitting into his theory no such idea as that of a gradual regeneration or repentance, he could, of course, listen to no proposition for a gradual abandonment of slaveholding. His measures, therefore, were prompt, his purpose inflexible, his object determinate. It was not to the abuses of the system, nor to particular cases of cruelty that he directed attention, further than to ascertain and exhibit the *principle* that lay at the bottom of the mischief. His remedy was radical, applying to the root, not to the branches. In the slave *trade*, with all its abominations and horrors, he saw only a particular manifestation or phase of *slavery*. With no extended ecclesiastical body to consult, to assist, or to impede him, he addressed his appeals and arguments directly to the consciences and the intellects of his congregation,—the party immediately concerned, and on *them*, in view of the coming Judgment, he cast the tremendous responsibility of direct and unambiguous *action* :

The church was soon induced, as a Congregational body, to take the following action :

"Resolved, that the slave trade and the slavery of the Africans, as it has existed among us, is a gross violation of the righteousness and benevolence which are so much inculcated in the gospel, *and therefore we will not tolerate it in this Church.*"

The doctrines of modern abolitionists, of the inherent sinfulness of slaveholding, and of the duty of immediate and unconditional emancipation, were distinctly enunciated and consistently reduced to practice in this action of the Congregational church in Newport. This was long before the commencement of any systematic efforts for abolishing the African slave trade, before the decision of the Somerset case, and before any body of " Friends " had taken a similar position in respect to slavery, or had discontinued the practice. Had all the Congregational ministers and churches in this country taken the stand of Samuel Hopkins, and the church at Newport, from that time to the present, there is no reason to think that the condition and prospects of the nation would have been, at this time, what they now are. How many, or which of the Congregational churches in New England, at that period, came up to the standard of the church at Newport, we are unable to say. It is understood that there were several.* And it is certain that the sentiment was very generally received, for a time, and that the result was the termination of slavery in New England. Of this, and of the concurrent action of the Methodist Conference, and Presbyterian General Assembly, we shall treat, in connection with the records of a later period. We must first dispose of some points in the earlier history.

---

* In a note to the second edition of *Dr. Hopkins' Dialogue on Slavery*, re-published in 1785, it is said : "Since the first edition of this *Dialogue*, *a number of churches in New England* have purged themselves of this iniquity, and determined not to tolerate the holding of Africans in slavery."

CHAPTER VI.

OF SLAVERY, AND ITS ABOLITION IN ENGLAND.

Judicial Action—Granville Sharp—Early Introduction of Slavery into England; its supposed legality (1700)—Opinion of York and Talbot, in favor of its legality (1729)—Effects of this Opinion—Slave Traffic in England—Case of Jonathan Strong—Efforts of Sharp—His Investigation of British Law—Declares Slavery to be illegal—Publishes his argument—*Treats* Slavery as illegal, though the Courts and Public Sentiment were against him—Case of Thomas Lewis—Decision of Lord Chief Justice Mansfield, sustaining the legality of Slavery—Sharp enters his Protest—Blackstone alters his *Commentaries* to defeat Sharp, and favor the Slaveholders—Case of James Somerset—The Argument—A Decision found against Slavery in the times of Queen Elizabeth—Lord Mansfield hesitates—An interval before the decision—*Sharp anticipates the result, and memorializes Lord North against Slavery in the Colonies*—State of Public Sentiment against Slavery—Final decision of Lord Mansfield (1772), releasing Somerset, and declaring Slavery illegal in England—Second Memorial of Sharp to Lord North, admonishing him of the duty of suppressing Slavery in the Colonies, agreeably to the decision of Lord Mansfield.

As church action against slavery naturally follows and grows out of religious teachings and testimonies against the sin of slavery, so judicial and legislative action against the practice, naturally follows and grows out of both the preceding. The laws of a country are an index, to a great extent, of the prevalent religion of a country, and it is difficult, if not impossible, to maintain, for any length of time, a code of laws that essentially conflict with the religion of the people.

From the records of early religious testimony and action against slavery, we come to those of judicial action.

The first laborer in this department of benevolent enterprise, in England, says Clarkson, was Granville Sharp, "distinguished from those who preceded him in this particular, that whereas they were only writers, he was both a writer and an *actor* in the cause." His first effort in 1767, for the release of an individual slave, was followed, not long afterwards, by systematic endeavors to overthrow slavery itself in the British dominions, and particularly in England.

The introduction of slavery into England, appears to have been upon the same foundation, (in respect to its legality,) as its introduction into the North American colonies. That is, it was done without the authority of any direct statute; and it was done in the presence and in palpable violation of English Common Law. If it could plead any legal warranty, it was that of the royal permission to transport *Africans* "with their own free consent," into the colonies, and the Act of Parliament "for extending and improving the trade to Africa," which prohibited "any violence to the natives."

How early slaves were introduced into England, we cannot exactly determine. "Before the year 1700," says Clarkson, "planters, merchants, and others, resident in the West Indies, but coming to England, were accustomed to bring with them certain slaves, to act as servants with them during their stay." They frequently absconded, and were sometimes seized and sent back by force. A sentiment had come down from former ages that Christians could not enslave Christians, and that as soon as an Englishman's slave was baptized, he became free. In consequence of this sentiment, it became common for pious clergymen to baptize all the slaves they could, providing "god-fathers" for them, according to the usages of the Church of England. These god-fathers were in the habit of vindicating their high claim to the title, by espousing the cause of their god-children, and demanding their freedom. For a time, this held the slave-masters in check, as they were "afraid to carry off their slaves by force, and equally afraid to bring any of the cases before a public court."

"In this dilemma, they applied, in 1729, to York and Talbot, the Attorney and Solicitor-General, for the time being, and obtained from them, the following strange opinion :—' We are of opinion that a slave, by coming from the West Indies into Great Britain or Ireland, either with or without his master, does not become free, and that his master's right and property in him is not thereby determined or varied, and that baptism doth not bestow freedom upon him, or make any alteration in his temporal condition, in these kingdoms. We are also of opinion that the master may legally compel him to return again, to the plantations.' "

" This cruel and illegal opinion was delivered in 1729. The planters, merchants, and others, gave it, of course, all the publicity in their power; and the consequences were as might easily have been apprehended. In a little time, slaves absconding, were advertised in the London papers, as runaways, and rewards offered for the apprehension of them; in the same brutal manner as we find them advertised in the land of slavery. They were advertised, also, in the same papers, to be *sold at auction*, sometimes by themselves, and at others, with horses, chaises, and harness. They were seized also by their masters, or by persons employed by them, in the very streets, and dragged from thence to the ships; and so unprotected, now, were these poor slaves, that persons, no wise concerned with them, began to institute a trade in their persons, making agreements with captains of ships, going to the West Indies, to put them on board at a certain price." This "shows, as all history does, that where there is a market for the persons of human beings, all kind of enormities will be practiced to obtain them."— *Clarkson's History*, &c., pp. 38–9.

For forty-three years did this "illegal opinion" of York and Talbot prevail in Great Britain instead of law; nay, in opposition to the fundamental law of the realm. Such was the state of things when, in 1767, as before mentioned, Granville Sharp undertook the liberation of Jonathan Strong, claimed as a slave by David Lisle, a lawyer and slave-master of Barbadoes, then residing in London.

" But the lawyers whom Sharp consulted, declared the laws were against him. Sir James Eyre, Recorder of the city, whom he retained as his counsel, adduced to him York and Talbot's opinion, and informed him that Lord Chief Justice Mansfield agreed with those gentlemen."—*Stuart's Memoir of Sharp*, p. 8.

" Mischief framed by law, yet *against* law, thus took deep root in Britain." " At this time slavery had disgraced the British Colonies in America and in the West Indies, for two hundred years. The righteous law of the empire had been evaded or perverted, and *opinion* and *precedent* had been substituted for *law*."—*Ibid*, pp. 6–7.

This, Granville Sharp understood, though he stood alone. He had not been educated a lawyer. But he understood, better than York and Talbot, (as the event proved,) and better than Mansfield and Blackstone, the sacred and the change-less nature of LAW. A legal triumph was in reserve for him, the most sublime and august of any on the records of modern jurisprudence.

But it was not won in the controversy concerning Jonathan Strong. Some informality in the proceedings led to his discharge by the Mayor. He was, however, instantly seized again by Captain Laird, (about to sail for the West Indies,) on behalf of John Kerr, to whom Lisle had sold him. This seizure was made in the presence of the mayor and others, before whom also, Granville Sharp, with consummate general-ship and promptitude, stepped up to Captain Laird, and, tapping him on the shoulder, exclaimed: "I charge you, in the name of the king, with an assault upon the person of Jonathan Strong, and all these are my witnesses!" Laird was intimidated, let go his grasp, and Sharp conveyed away the ransomed captive in triumph. This led to a suit against Sharp, the trial of which was deferred by the plaintiffs for two years, and then withdrawn by them under charge of treble costs for the delay.

During these two years, Mr. Sharp applied himself, diligently, to a further study of the law, by which his former position was fortified, and he was prepared for any future litigation on the subject. In the course of this investigation, he applied to the great Doctor (afterwards Judge) Blackstone, for his opinion. "He was not, however, satisfied with it," says Clarkson, "when he received it, nor could he obtain any satisfactory answer from several other lawyers, to whom he afterwards applied." Thrown, therefore, upon his own industry and resources, he worked out the problem alone.

"The result of his research, was a tract, ' *On the injustice and dangerous tendency of tolerating slavery, or even of admitting the least claim to private property, in the persons of men, in England.*"—*Stuart's Memoir*, p. 8.

"In this work"* (says Clarkson) "he refuted, in the clearest manner, the opinion of York and Talbot. He produced against it the opinion of

---

* Mr. Clarkson gives, as the title of the book, "A Representation of the Injustice and Dangerous Tendency of Tolerating Slavery in England."

Lord Chief Justice Holt, who, many years before, had determined that every slave coming into England became free. He attacked and refuted it, again, by a learned and laborious inquiry into all the principles of villeinage. He refuted it, again, by showing it to be an axiom in the British Constitution, ' That every man in England, was free to sue for, and defend his rights, and that force cannot be used without a legal process,' leaving it with the judges to determine whether an African was a man. He attacked also, the principle of Judge Blackstone, and showed where his error lay. This valuable book, containing these and all other kinds of arguments, on the subject, he distributed, but particularly among the lawyers, giving them an opportunity of refuting or acknowledging the doctrines it contained."— *Clarkson's History*, p. 42.

Several cases were afterwards tried, in which the slaves were set at liberty; but "none of the cases had yet been pleaded upon the broad ground, 'Whether an African slave coming into England, became free.' This great question had been studiously avoided. It was still, therefore, left in doubt." Mr. Sharp continually *acted* on the ground that there was no legal slavery in England, though the judges had not so decided. The suspense at length became painful to both parties, and there was a general anxiety to have the controversy decided.—*Clarkson*, p. 42, *Stuart*, p. 10.

In the meantime, some of the cases were so decided as to afford great encouragement to the slave party. An African. named Thomas Lewis, had escaped from his master, Mr. Stapylton, in London. He was recaptured, and put on board a vessel for the West Indies. The vessel had reached the Downs, and was already under way, when a *habeas corpus* was carried on board, and the man released, and sent on shore. A bill was found against Stapylton and his two assistants, and the case was tried before the Court of King's Bench, Lord Chief Justice Mansfield presiding, the 20th of February, 1771. The jury returned a verdict of guilty : "but so fraught was Mansfield's mind, still, with the false views of the day, that he refused to proceed to judgment, and the criminals escaped." —" Against this proceeding of the Judge, as *an open contempt of the laws of England*, Granville Sharp prepared a strong protest."—*Stuart's Memoir*, p. 10.

Another incident, and a very remarkable one, illustrates the methods resorted to, by gentlemen of the highest standing in the legal profession, at that time, in England, to sustain the slave interest, at the expense of those great fundamental maxims of Common Law, of which they were themselves the recognized expounders, and which they could enunciate, distinctly enough, except when overawed by " the mighty wealth and influence of the West India faction," before whom, king and nobles, courts of justice, parliaments and doctors of the law, bowed down in abject submission.

" In the beginnings of his researches, Granville Sharp had found and *noted* the following passage in Blackstone's Commentaries, Book I., page 123, Edition 1st—' And this spirit of liberty is so deeply implanted in our Constitution, and rooted in our very soil, that a slave or a negro, the moment he lands in England, falls under the protection of the laws, and, with regard to all national rights, becomes *eo instanti*, a freeman.'

" This passage being quoted in one of the trials, was triumphantly repelled by the opposite counsel, who produced the volume from which the quotation was made, and instead of the words as noted by Granville Sharp, read as follows : ' A negro, the moment he lands in England, falls under the protection of the laws, and so far becomes a free man, though the master's right to his service may possibly remain.'

" Upon further investigation, it was found that, *in the course of the trials, Dr. Blackstone himself had made this alteration in the subsequent editions.*"
—*Stuart's Memoir of Sharp*, p. 19.

Such was the condition of things, when, at length, a case came before the courts that presented a fair opportunity to test the great question of legal slavery in England. This opportunity was improved, and the issue was joined.

James Somerset " had been brought to England in November, 1769, by his master, Charles Stewart, from Virginia, and in process of time had left him. Stewart had him suddenly seized, and carried on board the Ann and Mary, Captain Knowles, in order to be taken to Jamaica, and there sold for a slave."

" On February 7, 1772, the cause was tried in the King's Bench, before Lord Chief Justice Mansfield, aided by Justices Ashton, Welles and Ashhurst. The question at issue was—' Is every man in England entitled to the liberty of his person, unless forfeited by the laws of England?' This was affirmed by the advocates of Somerset; and Mr. Sergeant Davy, who opened his cause, broadly declared, ' that no man at this day *is*, or *can* be, a slave in England.' "—*Stuart's Memoir*, p. 11.

In the course of the argument a precedent was adduced in favor of freedom. "This was the case of Cartwright, who brought a slave from Russia, and would scourge him. For this he was questioned, and it was resolved, *that England was too pure an air for slaves to breathe in.*"—See *Rushworth's Collections*, p. 468. This was in the 11th of Queen Elizabeth.—*Ib.*

Lord Mansfield was evidently beginning to waver.

" In order that time might be given for ascertaining the law fully on this head, the case was argued at three different sittings. First in January, secondly in February, and thirdly in May, 1772. And that no decision otherwise than what the law warranted, might be given, the opinion of the judges were taken on the pleadings."—*Clarkson's Hist.* p. 43.

" Granville Sharp availed himself, with his usual zeal, of this interval, and, among the other measures by which he sought to obtain an equitable decision, he addressed a Letter to Lord North, dated Feb. 18th, 1772."—*Stuart's Memoir*, p. 12.

In this Letter Mr. Sharp anticipates a decision of the courts against slavery, and says—"We must judge by *law*, not by *precedent.*"—He further intimates the illegality of slavery in the American Colonies, in the following paragraph :

" I might indeed allege that many of the plantation laws (like every other act that contains anything which is *malum in se*, evil in its own nature,) *are already null and void in themselves ;* because they want every necessary foundation to render them valid, being absolutely contradictory to the laws of reason and equity, as well as the laws of God."—*Ib.* p. 13.

By this time the eyes of the British public, from the members of the administration down to the mass of the intelligent inhabitants, were fixed upon Lord Mansfield and the Court of King's Bench, awaiting, with deep interest and anxious suspense, their decision. It was a healthful scrutiny, not unfelt by the Lord Chief Justice and his associates. New and enlarged views of the nature and character of LAW had been impressed upon the nation and upon the national judiciary, by the tireless labors and profound investigations of Granville Sharp. And yet it required a desperate struggle to break away from the meshes of precedent and opinion, and restore the ascendancy of impartial and equitable law.

" Lord Mansfield delayed judgment, and twice threw out the suggestion ' that the master might put an end to the present litigation, by manumitting the slave.' But the base suggestion was, providentially, not attended to. The judgment was demanded ; and the judgment was given on Monday, 22d of June, 1772. After much lawyer-like circumlocution, Lord Mansfield decided as follows :

" Immemorial usage preserves the memory of *positive law*, long after all traces of the occasion, reason, authority, and time of its introduction are lost, and in a case so odious as the condition of *slaves*, must be taken *strictly :* (tracing the subject to *natural principles, the claim of slavery can never be supported.*) The power claimed by this return *never was in use here.* We cannot say the cause set forth in this return is allowed or approved of by the laws of this kingdom, and therefore the man must be discharged."—*Stuart's Memoir*, p. 17. " Mr. Sharp felt it his duty, immediately after this trial, to write" (again) " to Lord North, then principal minister of State, warning him, in the most earnest manner, to abolish, *immediately*, both the slave *trade* and the *slavery* of the human species, IN ALL THE BRITISH DOMINIONS, *as utterly irreconcilable with the principles of the* BRITISH CONSTITUTION, and the established religion of the land."— *Clarkson's Hist.*, p. 44.

The measure here insisted on by Granville Sharp, was evidently required by the decision of the Somerset case, and had it been carried into effect, at that time, there would have been no slavery now in the United States.

Mr. Clarkson awards much credit to the counsel employed on this trial, Davy, Glynn, Hargrave, Mansfield, and Alleyne, but chiefly to Granville Sharp, " who became the first great actor in it, who devoted his time, his talents, and his substance to this Christian undertaking, and by whose laborious researches the very pleaders themselves were instructed and benefited."—p. 44.

" It ought to be remembered that, while Granville Sharp thus boldly remonstrated with the government of his country, he filled a government situation, and was dependent for his present subsistence, and his future prospects in life, upon the ministry of the day."—*Stuart's Memoir*, p. 15.

Thus was the guilty fiction of legal slavery in England exploded, after having been acted upon as though it were a

truth for at least three-fourths of a century, and confirmed
by the highest official authority for forty-three years. Of the
magnitude, the importance, and the legal consequences of this
judicial decision, which forever settled the slave question in
England, without legislative action or executive interference,
we propose not to speak here. In another connection it may
be adverted to again. Very possibly its study may assist in
the detection and correction of similar mistakes in the judicial
action of other countries, besides England. If York and
Talbot, and Blackstone and Mansfield were mistaken, other
learned judges may be. If, under the British monarchy, a
private individual may peacefully revolutionize the jurisprudence of his country, it cannot be out of place, nor arrogant
for the friends of liberty in republican America to study, to
understand, to insist upon the principles of constitutional and
common law, in their bearing upon the same great practical
question, in their own country, as Granville Sharp did in his.

CHAPTER VII.

OF EFFORTS FOR ABOLISHING THE AFRICAN SLAVE TRADE.

Relaxation of effort—American Revolution—Sharp espouses the cause of the Colonies—Thomas Clarkson's early life—Granville Sharp—Slave ship "Zong" (1781) —Trial of this case (1783)—Slave-traders sustained—Sharp's Report of the Trial —Committee instituted to act against the Slave Trade (1787)—Unfortunate Compromise—Policy of opposing the Slave *Trade*, but not *Slavery*—Solemn Protest of Granville Sharp—William Wilberforce—Public Agitation—Abstinence from Slave Products—Wilberforce denounced in the House of Lords—Influence of John Wesley—of the Quakers—the Baptists—Inquiry in King's Privy Council, 1788; also in House of Commons, introduced by Wm. Pitt—Dates of various movements in Parliament till 1806—Slave Trade abolished in Parliament in 1807— *Review of this struggle*—*Slavery* declared illegal in 1772, yet the Slave *Trade* tolerated till 1807—The turning point—The legality of the Slave Trade—Pitt proved it *illegal*—*Abolition of the Slave Trade abortive*—Premature and misplaced gratulation and triumph. Mr. Clarkson's late retraction of his grand error (1845). Testimony to the impossibility of suppressing the traffic while Slavery continued (1845)—Continued profitableness of the Slave Trade—Increased horrors of the Middle Passage—Slave Trade actually increased instead of being suppressed.

THE speedy and glorious success of the efforts of Granville Sharp and a few others for uprooting slavery from the soil of Great Britain, should have encouraged Christian philanthropists, in both hemispheres, one would think, to co-operate in similar efforts to uproot slavery throughout the colonial possessions of Great Britain, over which the same great principles of the British Constitution, and of English Common Law, were recognized as holding paramount authority. It is not improbable that the growing difficulties between the North American colonies and the mother country, ripening into a civil war, soon after the decision of the Somerset case, may have interrupted the correspondence just beginning to be opened between the friends of liberty in the two countries. The British West India Islands, however, might have presented a field of operation for the abolitionists in England, though there may have been none in the islands to co-operate with them.

From some cause, no such efforts were made. Granville Sharp, in 1774, published a tract in favor of the rights of the American colonies, of which he presented two hundred and fifty copies to Dr. Franklin, who dispatched them to America. " It was immediately and extensively republished in the colonies." The next year, 1775, on hearing of the commencement of hostilities, near Boston, he retired from the post he had held under the British administration, which was his only means of subsistence.—*Stuart's Memoir of Sharp*, pp. 21, 22.

The entire period of the American Revolutionary War, terminating in 1783, appears to have been marked by an almost total suspension of active labors on the part of the friends of the negroes in England. And when, not long after, their labors were renewed, they took the form of opposition to the African slave *trade*, the horrible cruelties of which, at that time, having been, in some cases, exposed, excited the sympathies and the indignation of many who had never reflected profoundly upon the iniquity involved in the slave system itself.

Thomas Clarkson, the chief actor, for a long time, in this enterprise, then a young man, a student at Cambridge, had obtained a college prize for an Essay on the Slave Trade, which was printed in 1785, and attracted some attention. He frankly confessed afterwards, that his only motive, in the first place, was " that of other young men in the University, the wish of being distinguished, or of obtaining literary honor." But the facts he had collected, made so deep an impression upon him, that he soon " interested himself in it, from a motive of duty," and afterwards relinquished his prospects of promotion in the profession of a clergyman in the established church, for which he was preparing, in order to devote himself to the enterprise of abolishing the African slave trade.— *Clarkson's History*, pp. 79–86.

The attention of Granville Sharp, some time previous, had been intensely directed to the slave trade, by a most thrilling illustration of its atrocity. The slave ship Zong, Captain Collingwood, from Africa, freighted with slaves for Jamaica, in 1781, was visited with a dreadful mortality among the slaves. Under a false pretence of scarcity of water, the captain ordered a large number of the sick slaves thrown overboard, that the loss might fall on the insurers, (as merchandize thrown overboard for the safety of the vessel,) instead of falling on the owners, if they died from sickness. The question growing out of this transaction, and before the court, in 1783, was *not* concerning the *murder* of these men, but simply whether the owners or the insurers should lose the pecuniary amount of their value! The Solicitor-General, J. Lee, said:

" This is a case of goods and chattels. It is really so ; it is a case of throwing over goods, for, to this purpose, and for the purpose of insurance, they are goods and property ; whether right or wrong, we have nothing to do with it."

Lord Mansfield said:

" The matter left to the jury is—Was it from necessity ? for they (the court) had no doubt (though it shocks one very much) that the case of *slaves* is the same as if *horses* had been thrown overboard. It is a very shocking case."

The verdict of the jury, on the first trial, was for the captain and owners. A new trial was granted, and the insurers gained their cause. *But no criminal prosecution could be had against the murderers!* Any *such* accusation, legal gentlemen agreed, " would argue nothing less than madness !"—*Clarkson's History*, p. 45. *Stuart's Memoirs*, pp. 29–31.

Granville Sharp " was present at this trial, and procured the attendance of a short-hand writer, to take down the facts," " which he communicated to the public afterwards. He communicated them also, with a copy of the trial, to the Lords of the Admiralty, as guardians of justice on the high seas, and to the Duke of Portland, as Minister of State. No notice, however, was taken, by any of these, of the information which had thus been sent to them."—*Clarkson*, p. 46.

In his address to the Duke of Portland, Mr. Sharp warned him of "the absolute necessity to abolish the slave trade, and *West Indian slavery.*"—*Stuart,* p. 31.

It is easy to conceive that while the public sympathy was so strongly acted upon by such astounding developments concerning the slave *trade,* an effort for its abolition would be more likely to win at once a cheap general favor, than an effort for the abolition of slavery. But benevolent enterprises, founded on mere sympathy, are not likely to be as wisely directed, as consistently supported, or as really and permanently successful as those that are likewise seen to be deeply imbedded and fortified in the fundamental principles of moral right. The history of the nominal abolition of the African slave trade is deeply interesting, as affording a striking exemplification of one class of these experiments.

The committee instituted in June 1787, for "effecting the abolition of the slave trade," was composed of twelve members, nine of whom were Quakers. Of the three others, one was Thomas Clarkson, and one was Granville Sharp, the latter of whom was appointed chairman. An earnest discussion took place in the committee, on the question whether they should direct their efforts against the slave trade alone, or against the slave trade and slavery. All the members, except Granville Sharp, were in favor of acting only against the slave *trade.*

The arguments in favor of this course are stated in his history, at some length, by Mr. Clarkson. Two distinct evils, the slave trade and slavery, presented themselves, he says, to their attention, and both needing removal. "It soon appeared to the committee that to aim at the removal of both, would be to aim at too much, and that by doing this, we might lose all." "The question then was, which of the two would they take as their object." "By aiming at the slave trade, they were laying the axe at the very root." Pp. 27, 28.

This view is the more remarkable as being found in the same volume in which the same writer had said: "All history shows, from the time of Joseph, that where there is a *market* for the persons of human beings, all kinds of enormities will be practiced to obtain them." P. 39.

It is still more mortifying to find Mr. Clarkson, at different points in the succeeding history, in the attitude of disclaiming on behalf of the committee, any intention of promoting emancipation. Thus, in his intercourse with Mirabeau, and the French National Assembly:

" Emancipation is now stated to be the object of the friends of the negroes. *This charge I repelled*, by addressing myself to Monsieur Beauvet. I explained to him the views of the different societies which had taken up the cause of the Africans, and *I desired him to show my letters to the planters*."—p. 241.

Though it was held by the committee, including Mr. Clarkson, that " in aiming at the slave trade they were striking at the root," yet, in his " Summary View of the Slave Trade, and of the probable consequences of its abolition," Mr. Clarkson apparently labors to reconcile the abolition of the slave *trade* with the continuance and increase of slave-*holding*, a view which seems designed to conciliate the planters.

" If the slaves were kindly treated in our colonies, *they would increase.* The abolition of the slave trade would necessarily secure such a treatment, and would produce many other advantages," &c.—p. 96.

The same view was afterwards taken by Mr. Wilberforce and Mr. Pitt, in their speeches in Parliament. Little did they imagine that the slave *trade*, though *legally* abolished, would survive and flourish after the actual abolition of *slavery* in the British colonies, because slavery would exist elsewhere.

Even at the time of writing his History of the enterprise, Mr. Clarkson seems to have entertained a high opinion of the sagacity of the committee in making this decision.

" Thus, at the very outset," says he, " they took a ground which was forever tenable. Thus they were enabled to answer the *objection* which was afterwards so constantly and so industriously circulating against them, *that they were going to emancipate the slaves.* And I have no doubt that this was a wise decision, contributing greatly to their success, for I am persuaded that if they had adopted the other object, they would not, for years, if ever, have succeeded in their attempt."—*Clarkson's History*, p. 98.

What kind of "success" was realized, after twenty years of labor, and forty more of triumph and gratulation, will be seen in the sequel.

Granville Sharp stood alone in the committee, in opposing their decision in this matter.

" He solemnly and vehemently remonstrated with the Committee against the resolution which they had adopted.   He declared that, ' as *slavery* w?, as much a crime against God as the *slave trade*, it became the committee to exert themselves equally against the continuance of both, and he did not hesitate to pronounce all present *guilty before God*, for shutting those who were then slaves out of the pale of their approaching labors.' He delivered this protest with a loud voice, a powerful emphasis, and both hands lifted up towards heaven, as was usual with him when much moved.   The Committee acknowledged the criminality of *both* to be the *same*, but they adhered to their resolution, fearing that if they attacked, at once, both slavery and the slave trade, they would succeed against neither."—*Stuart's Memoir of Sharp*, p. 56.

Having delivered this testimony, and conceiving, as he seems to have done, that the responsibility rested on him no longer, he consented to act with the committee, though with such singular modesty, (notwithstanding his Christian boldness) that " he would never assume the chair "—" while he sustained the responsibility and discharged the duty of the office."*

" I have attended above seven hundred Committees and Sub-Committees with him," says Clarkson, "yet, though sometimes but few were present, he always seated himself at the end of the room ; choosing rather to serve the glorious cause, in humility, through conscience, than in the character of a distinguished individual."

Among the early patrons of the enterprise of abolishing the slave trade, was William Wilberforce, member of Parliament, with whom Mr. Clarkson, Mr. Sharp, and several others, had been in the habit of holding consultations before the organization of the Committee, and preliminary to that measure.

Mr. Clarkson, at the request of the Committee, visited

---

* Vide *Stuart's Memoir*, p. 56.

several different commercial cities in the kingdom, to obtain further information, before commencing the agitation of the subject in Parliament. He likewise visited France, to secure the co-operation of the French National Assembly; but this mission was a failure. Correspondence was likewise held with friends of the cause in America, and their co-operation secured, to effect the abolition of the slave trade by our Government. The public mind was operated upon in various ways. A sentiment averse to the use of slave-grown products was cherished in the literature of the country. At one period, the school books, both of England and of the United States, abounded in expressions of this sentiment.

"Three hundred thousand persons, at this period, refrained from sugar altogether, perceiving that by using it they were directly supporting the slave system they abhorred. Three hundred and ten petitions were presented from England, one hundred and eighty-seven from Scotland, and twenty from Wales."—*Stuart's Memoir*, p. 51-2.

Could this *sentiment* against the use of slave products have arisen to the dignity of a *moral principle*, in the minds of these philanthropists, and had it been guided by a sufficient degree of reflection and intelligence, it might have suggested the necessity of an enterprise against SLAVERY—which furnishes slave *products*—as well as against the slave *trade*.

As it was, the country was extensively agitated, and a violent opposition was roused, which was continued for twenty years, led on by some of the principal men of the nation, and sustained by the entire West India interest. In the cities the opposition was violent. At Liverpool, attempts were made to throw Mr. Clarkson into the dock. In the House of Lords, the abolitionists were stigmatized by the Duke of Clarence, afterwards King William IV., "as fanatics and hypocrites, among whom he included Mr. Wilberforce, by name."* Many years afterwards, he had the honor of giving the royal assent to a bill for abolishing, *not* the African slave *trade*, but *slavery itself*, in the West Indies!—A more protracted or a more vio-

---

* *Clarkson's History*, p. 323.

lent contest could hardly have been witnessed, had the effort
been made against slavery itself. While the ranks of the
opposition could have done nothing more, the friends of the
negroes would have been doubly armed with the whole pano-
ply of divine truth, and would have been spared those pitiful
and indefensible disclaimers that so much crippled and embarrassed them, and their successors, at a later day.

We must not forget to notice the important fact, that during
the whole of this contest against the slave trade, as in the
previous one of Granville Sharp against slavery in England,
the conscience and the humanity of the country were neither
counteracted nor unsustained by the religion of the country.
Churches and Ministers, so far from opposing human progress
and liberty, very extensively regarded it their proper business
to urge them onward. The Society of Friends, having previously purged their own community, were ready to cast their
influence on the right side.

But the Friends were not alone. The eloquent and celebrated letter of John Wesley, on his death-bed, (1791) to
William Wilberforce, is to be regarded not merely as an expression of his own personal feelings in respect to the pending
contest, but as a specimen of the religious sentiment in the
midst of which he was moving, and which it was the business
of his life to commend and communicate to others, as belonging to the sanctification which fits men for heaven. In this
letter the opponents of abolition are alluded to as the confed-
erates of "devils," and American slavery is denominated
"the vilest that ever saw the sun." This was Methodism,
when Methodism was vitalized by the Spirit of God, and
clothed with Divine power.

But Baptists in England were not behind Methodists, at
this period, nor have they since been. It was during the progress of this same contest, and very nearly at the same date,
that " one of the ablest writers and soundest divines who have
ever adorned the Baptist denomination, good old Abraham
Booth," by his preaching and in his correspondence (1792) with
brethren in America, bore a similar testimony. He, too,

along with Grotius, and Wesley, and Edwards, and Porteus, and Macknight, and Scott, and the American Presbyterian Church, (previous to 1818), understood that modern slave-holding falls under the condemnation of "man-stealing," as prohibited by Moses, in Exodus 21 : 16, and condemned by Paul in 1 Tim. 1 : 10. The sermon of Eld. James Dove was still earlier, (1789,) and had direct and special reference to the same great struggle, in which no good men were neutral.

Not only Baptist ministers but Baptist Churches and Baptist Associations in England, came up to the work, in good earnest. The idea that the enterprise was too secular or too political for the co-operation of churches and ecclesiastical bodies, seems not to have embarrassed them.*

The King directed a privy council to consider the state of

---

* "The Elders and Messengers of the several Baptist Churches meeting at Falmouth, Chasewater, Plymouth Dock, Plymouth," and (twelve other Churches) "having received letters also from Portsmouth, Sarum" (and twenty other churches —making 38 Churches in all), "being met in association at Plymouth, May 25–6, 1790, a letter received last year from Granville Sharp, Esq., was read, and a *third* benefaction of five guineas was voted to the treasurer of the truly noble Committee for the Abolition of the Slave Trade, as a further testimony of our high approbation of their zealous efforts to remove so great an evil."

"*Northampton and other Churches in Association.*
"*Oakham, June* 14–15, 1791.

"It was unanimously voted that five guineas be sent up to the treasurer of the Society for Procuring the Abolition of the Slave Trade," &c. A part of the statement speaks of "the iniquitous, disgraceful practices of slave-dealing and *slaveholders.*"

"*Baptist Association, Wooten-under-edge,*
"*June* 14–15, 1791.

"Voted, particularly, a *fourth* benefaction of five guineas to the Committee for Abolishing the Slave Trade."

Similar minutes are on record of the Northamptonshire Association.

York and Lancashire Association.—"The ministers, met in association at Salendine, June 15–16, 1791, send Christian salutations to the several Churches with which they are connected" (here follow their names, eighteen in number), &c.

Then follows *a letter* from the ministers to these Churches, urging upon them renewed and continued effort in the cause of abolition, adding : "Ye friends of humanity, heaven will reward and approve your conduct."

[See "*Facts for Baptist Churches,*" by A. T. Foss and E. Mathews. Utica : Published by the American Baptist Free Mission Society," 1850—a book of 408 pages, and containing a mass of documentary information, chiefly concerning Baptists in America.]

the African Slave Trade, in February, 1788.   In May of the
same year, the same subject of inquiry was introduced into
the House of Commons, by Mr. Pitt, during the sickness of
Mr. Wilberforce.   The investigation was urged by Pitt, Wilberforce, Fox, and Burke, but delayed by opposition, until, in April, 1791, Mr. Wilberforce moved for leave to bring
in a bill to prevent the further importation of slaves into the
colonies.   After a long debate, the motion was lost.   He renewed his motion in 1792, when an amendment in favor of
gradual abolition prevailed in the Commons, but was not acted
upon in the House of Lords.

"In 1793, Mr. Wilberforce renewed and lost his motion.   In 1794, he
renewed and carried it in the House of Commons, but the House of Lords
rejected it.   In 1795-6, the effort was renewed and negatived.   In 1797,
an address was carried to the king.   In 1798-9, Mr. Wilberforce renewed
his motion, and was defeated, but Dr. Horsley, Bishop of Rochester, in the
House of Lords, nobly and effectually vindicated Scripture from the blasphemous imputation of tolerating *slavery*."—*Stuart's Memoir*, p. 54.

So the *argument* must needs be made against *slavery*, though
the proposition was only to abolish the *traffic* from Africa!
And the Bible argument, from the lips of religious teachers,
must needs precede legislative action.

From 1799 till 1804, the agitation in Parliament was suspended; but, in the mean time, public sentiment appears to
have undergone a favorable change, and in Parliament the
cause was strengthened by the accession of the new representation from Ireland.

"In 1804, the bill passed the Commons, but its discussion
was deferred in the House of Lords.

"In 1805, Wilberforce renewed his motion, but lost it.   Mr.
Pitt, who had thus far fostered the bill, soon after died.

In 1806, a bill was introduced by Sir Arthur Piggott, to
give effect to a previous proclamation of the King, restricting
and crippling, in some particulars, the slave trade.   This bill
passed both houses, whereupon Mr. Fox moved "That the
House, considering the slave trade to be contrary to the principles of justice, humanity and policy, will, with all practica-

ble expedition, take effectual measures for its abolition."—
"This was carried by a majority of 114 to 15 in the Commons,
and 41 to 20 in the Lords. Mr. Fox died before the next
session."

"In 1807, Lord Granville brought into the House of Lords
a Bill for the Abolition of the Slave Trade." After mature
discussion, during which, counsel was heard against it, four
days, the Bill was passed in the House of Lords, 100 to 36,
and the House of Commons, 283 to 16. It received, almost
immediately, the Royal assent. This was March 16th, 1807.
The bill provided that no vessel should clear out from any
British port for slaves after the 1st of May, 1807, nor land
any in the colonies after the 1st of March, 1808.—*Stuart's
Memoir*, p. 54. *Clarkson's Hist. passim.*

Similar action was going on in the Governments of other
nations, or soon followed. In the United States, a Statute of
Congress, enacted in 1807, prohibited the importation of
slaves, after January 1, 1808. In 1818, Congress declared
the traffic to be piracy. In 1819, the President was authorized to provide for the removal of imported slaves beyond
the limits of the United States.

REVIEW OF THIS STRUGGLE.

This memorable and protracted struggle is instructive, in
many respects. Among other things, it shows how blindly
public men may follow mere technicalities and precedents,
and how difficult it is to overcome the *prejudices* associated
with these, in the effort to restore the reign of impartial *law*.
A similar struggle had resulted in the decision of Lord
Mansfield in the Somerset case, in 1772. The illegality of
slave *holding* was then fully established, under the fundamental principles of the British Constitution and Common
Law, which were not then first brought into existence, but
had been the same, from the beginning of the slave *trade*.
The decision had labeled "ILLEGALITY" upon the whole
procedure, from beginning to end, upon the slave trade as

well as slavery, upon the *past* slave trade and slavery as well as present, so far as the *principle* involved was concerned. To have admitted that there *had* been, or then *was*, any legality in the slave *trade*, under that same British Constitution and Common Law, would have been, in effect, to have impugned the decision of Lord Mansfield in the Somerset case, and to have set it aside as erroneous. No one thought of attempting this. And yet, strange to tell, the then *present* legality of the slave *trade* appears to have been taken for granted, on all hands, at the commencement of this long struggle for its Parliamentary suppression.

It is curious to observe, that while in America, at the present time, slave *holding* is held to be legal and not disreputable, and yet the slave *trade* is branded as piracy ; the corresponding prejudice in England took an *opposite* direction; insomuch that slave *holding* was considered a high crime, while around the slave *trade* was supposed to cluster all the sacred sanctions and guaranties of obligatory and *valid law !*

It was not until this falsehood was ferrited out of its hiding places, dragged into daylight, and dissected by Mr. Pitt, that the power of the slave trade, in the Parliament, was broken, and the charm of its invincibility, as an interest fostered by the Government, was dissolved.

To every thing that could be urged by the eloquence of Wilberforce, against the wickedness, the injustice, the inhumanity, the cruelty, the impolicy, and the blighting effects of the slave trade, the ready answer of the interested opposition was, the *legality* of the traffic, the sacred and inviolable guaranties, the legal inheritance, the patrimonial rights of the parties concerned, and especially of the West India planters, who were supposed to need further supplies of slaves.

In answer to Mr. Dundas, who, for the fortieth time, perhaps, had been parrying off Parliamentary proceedings, by urging pleas of this sort, Mr. Pitt, upon whose vision new light on the subject appears to have suddenly gleamed, rose up, astonished the House, and overwhelmed his antagonist by a bold *denial* of the *legality* of the *slave trade*, under any supposed laws of the realm! He proceeded to dash in shivers the flimsy pretext, in a manner that precluded all attempts at reply.

" *Any* contract," he said, " for the promotion of this trade *must*, in his opinion, have been VOID FROM THE BEGINNING, for if it was an outrage upon justice, and only another name for fraud, robbery, and murder, what pledge could devolve on the legislature to incur the obligation of becoming principals in the commission of such enormities, by sanctioning their continuance ?

" But he would appeal to the acts themselves. That of 23 George II., c. 31, was *the one upon which the greatest stress was laid.* How would the House be surprised to hear that these very outrages committed in the prosecution of this trade had been *forbidden* by that act! ' No master of a ship trading to Africa,' says the act, ' shall, by fraud, force, or violence, or by any indirect practice whatever, take on board or carry away from that coast any Negro, or native of that country, or commit any violence upon the natives, to the prejudice of said trade ; and every person so offending shall, for every such offence, forfeit one hundred pounds.' But the whole trade had been demonstrated to be a system of fraud and violence, *and therefore the contract was daily violated* under which *the Parliament allowed it to continue.*"—*Clarkson's History*, p. 314.

Thus was the notion of the legality of the slave *trade* exploded, (as that of the legality of *slavery* had previously been) and the mind of the British nation forever emancipated from that ensnaring and enslaving delusion. Thenceforward the real question was, how that lawless traffic could be suppressed and terminated.

ABOLITION OF THE SLAVE TRADE ABORTIVE.

One of the most instructive though mortifying lessons to be deduced from this history, as expounded in the light of its results, is the utter futility of all attempts to suppress the slave *trade*, without breaking up the market, by the abolition of *slavery itself*. So slow have philanthropists been to learn this plain lesson, that, during one entire human generation, the glorious abolition of the African slave trade was celebrated by public demonstrations, by orators, by poets, by historians, in almost universal inattention to the fact, that the slave trade, though prohibited by *law*, was increasing, both in extent and in cruelty, amid all this misplaced gratulation and triumph.

Disregarding chronological order, for a few moments, we must leap over a chasm of thirty-five years, to witness the historical confirmation of Granville Sharp's solemn protest against the deplorable error of the Committee.

Mr. Clarkson lived to see and to retract the error. As President of the Anti-Slavery Society, in 1845, he addressed a letter to Lord Aberdeen, on the mode of suppressing the traffic, in which he solemnly affirmed, " that by the total abolition of slavery only, can the slave trade be annihilated." This view was "sustained by the high authority of Lord John Russell, who, when Colonial Minister, addressed a communication to the Lords Commissioners of Her Majesty's Treasury, in which he says,—'To repress the Foreign Slave Trade by a marine guard would scarcely be possible.'" This view was afterwards amply sustained by evidence before a Select Committee of Parliament, and embodied in two Reports presented to the House of Commons, showing not only the increase and the horrors of the Slave Traffic, but the utter inefficiency of an armed force for its suppression. A number of Commanders in the Royal Navy, employed in that service, gave explicit testimony to that import, and that the horrors of the middle passage and the miseries of the slaves are greatly aggravated by the efforts to suppress the traffic. The reason, as stated by the witnesses, is obvious. The trade, after deducting losses by deaths on the passage, yields a profit of about 200 per cent. on the investment! The amount of re-captures, though very great, and indicating the vast extent and briskness of the traffic, is only from four to ten per cent. of the estimated amount of shipments, and consequently interposes no serious check to the business. Yet the danger of capture induces the use of smaller vessels, in order to escape more easily the cruisers, and the consequent crowding of the slaves into a much smaller space.

The picture of the middle passage, in former times, as drawn by Mr. Mann, (already quoted,) falls short of the reality, as existing at *present*. It was testified that " in Brazil the number of slaves imported are now beyond what they were before Great Britain first used her efforts to put down the trade." Between 60,000 and 65,000 were computed to have been landed alive in Brazil, in the year 1847, after a loss of 35,000 by deaths, on the passage. In short, " the horrors of the slave trade appear to increase, just in proportion to the rigor used for its suppression." The French and American squadrons have, however, done little or nothing for the suppression. And, under cover of the American flag, which, by treaty, the British cruisers are prohibited from molesting, the slavers, of whatever nation frequently defeat the object of the British cruisers. The whole number of slaves computed to have been exported from Africa, westward, in 1788, was 100,000. The annual export from 1798 to 1805 was computed at 85,000. For the year 1847, it was computed at 88,000. This shows that the decrease of the slave trade since the first organized agitation on the subject has not kept equal pace with the extent to which slavery itself has been abolished, diminishing the field resorted to as a market. In other words, if slavery now existed, as it recently did, in the British West Indies, in Mexico, and all the South American countries, we should witness a greater amount of slave exportations from Africa than in 1788. This is confirmed by the fact that in 1825, such was actually the case, the exportations for that year having been computed at 125,000, and from some causes, the average of exportations from 1835 to 1840, inclusive, were computed at 135,000.* Towards the close of this period, Thomas Fowell Buxton, Esq., Member of Parliament, wrote an account of the African slave trade, in which he says :

" It has been proved, by documents which cannot be controverted, that for every village fired, and every drove of human beings marched, in former times, there are now double. For every cargo then at sea, two cargoes,

---

* See Annual Reports of the British and Foreign Anti-Slavery Society, for 1847 and 1848 ; also, the (British) Anti-Slavery Reporter, for August 1, 1848, containing an abstract of the evidence before the Select Committee of Parliament.

or twice the number in one cargo, wedged together, in a mass of living corruption, are now borne on the wave of the Atlantic."—*Buxton's Slave
Trade*, p. 159.

But the efforts of philanthropists for the abolition of the
African slave trade were not wholly in vain. They demonstrated the necessity of abolishing slavery itself. They branded
with the infamy of piracy the *African* slave trade, and, by
unavoidable implication, the same traffic everywhere else,
thus striking at the very idea of human chattelhood throughout
the world. If the process of teaching these truths has been a
slow one, it has nevertheless been effective.

CHAPTER VIII.

PERIOD OF THE AMERICAN REVOLUTION, AND THE ESTABLISH-
MENT OF AN INDEPENDENT GOVERNMENT.

Natural Tendencies of the Revolutionary Struggle—Its principle educed from previous Anti-Slavery Discussion—Originated in the States least influenced by
Slavery—First Congress (1774)—Action in favor of "*the abolition of Domestic
Slavery*"—Resolutions against the Slave Trade—Previous action in Provincial and
Local Conventions—In North Carolina and Virginia—"Articles of Association"
against Slave Trade—Concurrent Action in Georgia, Maryland, Virginia, and Con-
necticut—Anti-Slavery Literature of 1776—Implied illegality of Slavery—Decla-
ration of Independence—The unanimous act of the Thirteen *United States*—
"The Union" formed then, and not by the Federal Constitution of 1789—John Q.
Adams—This Declaration equivalent to a Constitution of Government—State
Constitutions—Articles of Confederation (1778) make no compromise with Slavery
—Sentiments published by order of Congress (1779)—Jefferson's Notes on Virginia—Peace of 1783—Address of Congress to the States—Sentiments of promi-
nent Statesmen—Legislation in Virginia.

THE state of the slave question in America, from about the
time of the commencement of the Revolution in 1774, till the
adoption of the Federal Constitution in 1789, requires to be
correctly understood, in order to any trustworthy estimate of
the bearing of our political institutions upon the present
existence of slavery.

It was by no accidental coincidence that the period of the
Revolution was the period of a more general and deep seated
opposition to slavery than had been before visible, or than
has been witnessed since. The religious sentiment against
slavery, as a violation of heaven established rights, a sentiment that had been rising for some time previous, and that
was now beginning to reach the point of disfellowship with
slave-holders, was a sentiment that naturally assimilated itself.

with the rising opposition to the British Government for its invasions of the same sacred rights; and that as naturally sought the same remedy; to wit, the separation of freedom from the embraces of despotic power. A spirit of liberty, humanity, and justice, in the church, may be regarded as the best foundation for the establishment of liberty, humanity, and justice in the State,* and a proper regard for the rights of others will ever be found essential to a healthful jealousy and timely vindication of our own.

It is equally evident that the rising opposition of the community in general to the despotic assumptions of the British Government, so far as it had anything in it like a manly regard to free principles for its basis, compelled that community to look at the more grievous wrongs of the slaves, and created an earnest sympathy in their favor. A decent regard to self-consistency, in that unsophisticated and earnest age, could scarcely fail to produce some such effects. The only just ground for regret or astonishment is that the spirit of freedom then seeming to be in the ascendant, did not secure and maintain a more complete and permanent triumph.

It is instructive to notice how the spirit of republican liberty and independence, in the different colonies, was found most predominant and most efficient, precisely where there were

---

* It may be doubted by some whether the religious sentiment and the testimony and action of religious bodies against slavery in this country, had been sufficiently extensive to make any very deep impression either upon the public conscience, in general, or upon the minds of our prominent statesmen. But the power of such influences is greater than is commonly understood. True statesmen, and even shrewd politicians, always keep themselves informed in respect to the religious tendencies of a country. Especially was this true in the last century. There can be no doubt that such men as Jefferson and Madison were familiarly acquainted with all that theologians in this country and Europe had written concerning slavery.

The letter of Patrick Henry to Robert Pleasants (afterwards President of the Virginia Abolition Society), written Jan. 18, 1773, sufficiently shows that his mind had been deeply affected with the movements among the " Friends."

" Believe me," says he, " I shall honor the Quakers for their noble efforts to abolish slavery. It is a debt that we owe to the purity of our religion to show that it is at variance with that law that warrants slavery. I exhort you to persevere in so worthy a resolution." " I believe a time will come when an opportunity will be offered to *abolish* this lamentable evil."

fewest slaves, and where the spirit of opposition to slavery was likewise most efficient and most predominant; while the regions most deeply involved in the sin of slaveholding and least accessible to the principles of emancipation, were precisely the same regions in which the apologists and partizans of British usurpation were most numerous and influential— the regions in which the spirit of opposition to that usurpation was, to the smallest extent, and with the greatest difficulty roused. The South was overrun with tories, while New England was united in favor of independence, almost to a man. Particular localities at the North, might be mentioned, where the prevalence of slaveholding and slave trading was connected with a corresponding sympathy with despotic government.

It may be added, that the names most prominent in the Revolutionary struggle were also among the names most prominent in opposition to slavery, and it is not known that a single advocate of the abolition of slavery was otherwise than a firm asserter of the rights of the Colonies.

That the subsequent decline of the spirit of general liberty, and the corresponding decline of opposition to slavery, have steadily gone hand in hand, until the propagandists of interminable slavery have derided the self-evident truths of the Declaration of Independence, and the people of the free States have listened with comparative apathy, are equally undeniable facts.

A full and correct history of the American Revolution, and of the incipient and successive steps taken to unite the Colonies under a new government, cannot fail to identify the movement with opposition to slavery, and the purpose and anticipation of its overthrow. A few documentary facts, in illustration, must suffice here.

The first general Congress of the Colonies assembled in Philadelphia, in September, 1774. Preparatory to that measure, the Convention of Virginia assembled in August of that year, to appoint delegates to the general Congress. An exposition of the rights of British America, by Mr. Jefferson, was laid before this Convention, of which the following is an extract:

"THE ABOLITION OF DOMESTIC SLAVERY is the greatest object of desire in these Colonies, where it was unhappily introduced in their infant state. But previous to the enfranchisement of the slaves, it is necessary to exclude further importations from Africa. Yet our repeated attempts to effect this by prohibitions, and by imposing duties which might amount to prohibition, have been hitherto defeated by his Majesty's negative ; thus preferring the immediate advantage of a few African corsairs to the lasting interests of the American States, and the rights of human nature, deeply wounded by this infamous practice."—*Am. Archives*, 4th series, Vol. I., p. 696.

The Virginia Convention, before separating, adopted the following resolution :

"*Resolved*, We will neither ourselves import nor purchase any slave or slaves imported by any other person after the first day of November next, either from AFRICA, the WEST INDIES, or ANY OTHER PLACE."—*Ib.* p. 687.

Similar resolutions, had been adopted by primary meetings of the people in county meetings throughout Virginia, during the month of July preceding the State Convention. At the meeting in Fairfax county, WASHINGTON was chairman.

North Carolina also held her Provincial Convention in August, of the same year. Nearly every county in the State was represented. There were sixty-nine delegates. The following resolution was adopted :

"*Resolved*, That we will not import any slave or slaves, or purchase any slave or slaves imported or brought into the Province by others, from any part of the world, after the first day of November next."—*Ib.*, p. 735.

Similar resolutions had been previously adopted in primary meetings of the citizens in other Southern provinces, now States.

It was after such demonstrations that the first General Congress assembled. Their first and main work was the formation of the " ASSOCIATION " which formed *a bond of Union between the Colonies*. This was nearly two years before the Declaration of Independence, so that " *the Union* " of the future States was effected before their *Independence*, a fact subversive of the common theory of the Constitution, which supposes independent States *first*, and a compromise of the slave question, in order to the effecting of a Union, *afterwards*. The following extracts from the articles of Association will show the principles and the terms, so far as the slave question is concerned, upon which this first union was effected :

"We do, for ourselves and the inhabitants of the several Colonies whom we represent, firmly agree and associate under the sacred ties of virtue, honor, and love of our country, as follows :

*   *   *   *   *   *   *

2. "THAT WE WILL NEITHER IMPORT NOR PURCHASE ANY SLAVE imported after the first day of December next ; after which time we will wholly discontinue the SLAVE TRADE, and will neither be concerned in it ourselves, nor will we hire our vessels, nor sell our commodities or manufactures, to those who are concerned in it."

*   *   *   *   *   *   *

11. "That a committee be chosen in every county, city, and town, by those who are qualified to vote for Representatives in the Legislature, whose business it shall be attentively to observe the conduct of all persons touching this Association ; and when it shall be made to appear, to the satisfaction of a majority of any such committee, that any person within the limits of their appointment has violated this Association, that such majority do forthwith cause the truth of the case to be published in the gazette, to the end that all such FOES to the rights of British America may be publicly known, and universally contemned as the ENEMIES OF AMERICAN LIBERTY ; and thenceforth we respectively will break off all dealings with him or her."

*   *   *   *   *   *   *

14 "And we do further agree and resolve that we will have no trade, commerce, dealings, or intercourse whatever, with any colony or province in North America, which shall not accede to, or which shall hereafter violate this Association, but will hold them as UNWORTHY OF THE RIGHTS OF FREEMEN, and as inimical to the liberties of this country."

*   *   *   *   *   *   *

"The foregoing Association, being determined upon by the Congress, was ordered to be subscribed by the several members thereof ; and thereupon, we have hereunto set our respective names accordingly.

In Congress, Philadelphia, October 20, 1774.

PEYTON RANDOLPH,
President.

NEW HAMPSHIRE—John Sullivan, Nathaniel Folsom.

MASSACHUSETTS BAY—Thomas Cushing, Samuel Adams, John Adams, Robert Treat Paine.

RHODE ISLAND—Stephen Hopkins, Samuel Ward.

CONNECTICUT—Eliphalet Dyer, Roger Sherman, Silas Deane.

NEW YORK—Isaac Low, John Alsop, John Jay, James Duane, Philip Livingston, William Floyd, Henry Wisner, Simon Boerum.

NEW JERSEY—James Kinsey, William Livingston, Stephen Crane, Richard Smith, John De Hart.

PENNSYLVANIA—Joseph Galloway, John Dickinson, Charles Humphreys, Thomas Mifflin, Edward Biddle, John Morton, George Ross.

THE LOWER COUNTIES, NEWCASTLE, &c.—Cæsar Rodney, Thomas McKean, George Read.

MARYLAND—Matthew Tilghman, Thomas Johnson, jr., William Paca, Samuel Chase.

VIRGINIA—Richard Henry Lee, George Washington, Patrick Henry, jr., Richard Bland, Benjamin Harrison, Edmund Pendleton.

NORTH CAROLINA—William Hooper, Joseph Hewes, Richard Caswell.

SOUTH CAROLINA—Henry Middleton, Thomas Lynch, Christopher Gadsden, John Rutledge, Edward Rutledge.—*American Archives*, 4th Series, p. 915.

Such was the action of the first American Congress. These were items in the " Articles of Association." How they were received in the Colonies will appear from the following :

" We, therefore, the Representatives of the extensive District of Darien, in the colony of Georgia, having now assembled in Congress, by authority and free choice of the inhabitants of said District, now freed from their fetters, do resolve :

" 5. To show the world that we are not influenced by any contracted or interested motives, but a general philanthropy for ALL MANKIND, of whatever climate, language, or complexion, we hereby declare our disapprobation and abhorrence of the unnatural practice of slavery in America, (however the uncultivated state of our country, or other specious arguments may plead for it,) a practice founded in injustice and cruelty, and highly dangerous to our liberties, (as well as lives,) debasing part of our fellow-creatures below men, and corrupting the virtue and morals of the rest, and is laying the basis of that liberty we contend for, (and which we pray the Almighty to continue to the latest posterity,) upon a very wrong foundation. We, therefore, Resolve, at all times to use our utmost endeavors for the manumission of our slaves in this colony, upon the most safe and equitable footing for the master and themselves."—JAN. 12th, 1775.—*Ibid.*, p. 1136.

The following action was taken by the Convention of Maryland, held in November, 1774, and re-adopted by a Convention more fully attended, in December :

" *Resolved*, That every member of this meeting will, and every person in the province should, strictly and inviolably observe and carry into execution the Association agreed on by the Continental Congress."

The declaration adopted by a general meeting of the freeholders in James City county, in Virginia, in November, 1774, is in these words:

" The Association entered into by Congress being publicly read, the freeholders and other inhabitants of the county, that they might testify to the world their concurrence and hearty approbation of the measures adopted by that respectable body, very cordially acceded thereto, and did bind and oblige themselves, by the sacred ties of virtue, honor, and love to their country, strictly and inviolably to observe and keep the same in every particular."

The proceedings of a town meeting at Danbury, Connecticut, Dec. 12th, 1774, contained the following:

" It is with singular pleasure we notice the second article of the Association, in which it is agreed to import no more negro slaves, as we cannot but think it a palpable absurdity so loudly to complain of attempts to enslave *us* while we are actually enslaving *others*."—*Am. Archives*, 4th series, Vol. I., p. 1038.

These are but " specimens of the formal and solemn declarations of public bodies." "The Articles of Association were adopted by Colonial Conventions, County Meetings, and lesser assemblages throughout the country, and became the law of America—the fundamental Constitution, so to speak, of the first American Union." " The Union thus constituted was, to be sure, imperfect, partial, incomplete, but it was still a Union, a union of the Colonies and of the people for the great objects set forth in the articles. And let it be remembered, also, that prominent in the list of measures agreed on in these articles, was the discontinuance of the slave trade, with a view to the ultimate extinction of slavery itself."*

That this "sentiment pervaded the masses of the people," and that they understood themselves *as laying the constitutional foundations of a permanent union and general government* by these measures, may be seen by the following extracts from an eloquent paper, entitled "Observations addressed to the people of America," printed at Philadelphia, in Nov., 1774:

---

* Speech of Hon. S. P. Chase, of Ohio, U. S. Senate, March 26, 1850. To this speech, and to that of Hon. Lewis D. Campbell, of Ohio, in the House of Representatives of the U. S., Feb. 19, 1850, we are indebted for the quotations made from the American Archives.

" The least deviation from the resolves of Congress will be treason ; such treason as few villains have ever had an opportunity of committing. It will be treason against the present inhabitants of the colonies—against the millions of unborn generations who are to exist hereafter in America— against the only liberty and happiness which remain to mankind—against the last hopes of the wretched in every corner of the world ; in a word, it will be treason against God. *   *   *   WE ARE NOW LAYING THE FOUN- DATIONS OF AN AMERICAN CONSTITUTION. Let us, therefore, hold up everything we do to the eye of posterity. They will most probably mea- sure their liberties and happiness by the most careless of our footsteps. Let no unhallowed hand touch the precious seed of liberty. Let us form the glorious tree in such a manner, and impregnate it with such principles of life, that it shall last forever. *   *   *   *I almost wish to live to hear the triumphs of the jubilee in the year* 1874 ; to see the models, pictures, fragments of writings, that shall be displayed to revive the memory of the proceedings of the Congress of 1774. If any adventitious circumstance shall give precedency on that day, it shall be to inherit the blood, or even to possess the name, of a member of that glorious assembly."—*Amer. Arch.*, 4 ser., vol. i, p. 976.

The spirit of 1774 was not extinct or languishing in 1776, a year memorable not only for the Declaration of American Independence, but for the previous enunciation of the same self-evident truths, applied to the sin of slavery, in a more elaborate and thorough elucidation of the whole subject than had before appeared.* The argument of Dr. Hopkins against slavery is introduced by a notice of the action of Congress against the slave trade, and the statement that the traffic " has now but few advocates, and is generally exploded and con- demned." The treatise contains the remarkable statement that " the slavery that now takes place," (in distinction from that of ancient times,) is " *without the express sanction of civil government.*"† This idea will now appear strange to most per-

---

* " A Dialogue concerning the Slavery of the Africans, showing it to be the duty and interest of the American States to emancipate all their African Slaves. Dedi- cated to the Honorable the Continental Congress." By Samuel Hopkins, D.D., of Newport, R. I.

† The same idea seems involved in another portion of the treatise. " The *several legislatures* in these colonies," says the writer, " the *magistrates* and the body of the people, have doubtless been greatly guilty in approving and encour- aging, *or at least conniving at*, this practice" (*i. e.*, slaveholding).

This is certainly remarkable language, especially from so accurate and discrimin-

sons. But the careful and reflecting reader of the history we have given in the preceding chapters, will have been led to inquire *when* and *how* the "express sanction," of "civil government" had been given to slavery in any form that could entitle it to the reputation of being legalized. The decision of Lord Mansfield in the Somerset case, four years previous, may have been in the mind of Hopkins, and he is known to have been in correspondence with Granville Sharp, with whose views the reader is acquainted. What seems most remarkable is, that a treatise containing such a statement should not only have been extensively circulated without being questioned, but republished, and still more extensively circulated, nine years afterwards, by anti-slavery societies under the auspices of such statesmen as Franklin and Jay. If it be conceded that American slavery was "without the express sanction of civil government," that it was not, in a strict and proper sense, legalized, at the time when Hopkins wrote his treatise, a few months before the Declaration of Independence, it would be a curious question how it could have become legalized since. Assuredly, the far-famed Declaration of inalienable human rights cannot have given it any new validity!

" We hold these truths to be self-evident, that all men are created equal; that they are endowed by their Creator with certain inalienable rights, among which are life, liberty, and the pursuit of happiness." " To secure these rights, *governments* are instituted among men." " We, *therefore*, the representatives of the United States of America," &c. &c.

We enter into no argument here concerning the legal effect of that immortal Declaration, upon the tenure of slave property. But it is important to note down distinctly the historical facts. It was the "unanimous Declaration of the thirteen United (not disunited) States of America." The " Union " had already been formed, and has never since been dissolved.

---

ative a writer as Hopkins, if slavery were universally and unhesitatingly held to be *legal*. Legislatures and magistrates are not commonly spoken of as "*conniving*" (closing their eyes upon) practices which are admitted to be legal! Such language describes their culpable neglect to suppress and punish practices that are unlawful.

On this point, there can be no mistake.* It was not only a Declaration of the States by their delegates, but was separately ratified by all the States, afterwards, and has never been repudiated or repealed since. In connection with the previous Articles of Association, it was the only constitution of the United States, until the adoption of the " Articles of Confederation" in 1778; and with these, thenceforward, until the adoption of the present Federal Constitution, in 1789. It had power to legalize Acts of Congress and Treaties, as also to absolve citizens from their allegiance to the king of Great Britain.† Its repeal would have been an abandonment of Independence, and a return to the condition of colonies.

Besides this, the original thirteen States, except Connecticut and Rhode Island, formed Constitutions bearing date, variously, from 1776 to 1783. " They generally recognized, in some form or other, the natural rights of men, as one of the fundamental principles of the government. Several of them asserted these rights in the most emphatic and authoritative manner." So that the fundamental principles and self-evident truths of the Declaration of 1776 became the constitutional law of the several States. *Vide Spooner*, p. 46.

The Articles of Confederation, formed in 1778, contained no recognition of slavery, nor of distinctions of color. It was never pretended that, under these articles, the slaveholder whose slaves had escaped to another State, had any legal power to force him back.

In 1779 the Continental Congress ordered a pamphlet to be published, entitled, " Observations on the American Revolution," of which the following is an extract:

" The great principle (of government) is and ever will remain in force,

---

* The reader is referred to the unanswered and unanswerable argument of John Quincy Adams on this point, in his address at Newburyport, 4th of July, 1837.

† John Hancock, President of Congress, in a letter to the Convention of New Jersey, then in session, and inclosing a copy of the Declaration of Independence, speaks of it as being " the *ground and foundation* of a future *government*." If the " ground and foundation" be removed, what becomes of the superstructure? But if this " ground and foundation" remains, what becomes of the validity of slave laws?

that men are, by nature, free; as accountable to Him that made them, they must be so ; and so long as we have any idea of divine *justice,* we must associate that of *human freedom.* Whether men can part with their liberty is among the questions which have exercised the ablest writers ; but it is *conceded, on all hands, that the right to be free* CAN NEVER BE ALIENATED ; still less is it practicable for *one* generation to mortgage the privileges of *another."*

A more forcible denial of the possibility of legalizing slavery could not easily have been penned.

About this time, or not long after, Mr. Jefferson wrote his celebrated Notes on Virginia, in which his testimonies against slavery are so various and emphatic, that we hesitate what paragraph to select for quotation. The following serves to show what such men, at that time, expected and desired to see accomplished, and what was then, in Mr. Jefferson's opinion, the state of sentiment in the Southern States.

" I think a change is already perceptible since the origin of the present revolution. The spirit of the master is abating, that of the slave is rising from the dust, his condition mollifying, THE WAY, I HOPE, PREPARING, UNDER THE AUSPICES OF HEAVEN, FOR A TOTAL EMANCIPATION."

General Gates, the conqueror of Burgoyne, emancipated, in 1780, his numerous slaves.

From the beginning to the close of the war, one uniform language was held. Soon after the peace of 1783, Congress issued an address to the States, drawn up by Mr. Madison, a main object of which was to ask the provision of funds to discharge the public engagements. The plea is thus urged:

" Let it be remembered, finally, that it has ever been the pride and boast of America that the rights for which she contended were the rights of human nature. By the blessing of the Author of these rights on the means exerted for their defence, they have prevailed against all opposition, and form the basis of THIRTEEN INDEPENDENT STATES."

The expression of similar sentiments did not then cease, nor were they confined to public acts.

" Jefferson, Pendleton, Mason, Wythe, and Lee, while acting as a committee of the House of Delegates of Virginia, to revise the State Laws, prepared a plan for the gradual emancipation of the slaves, by law."

In addition to these, " Grayson, St. George Tucker, Madison, Blair, Page, Parker, Edmund Randolph, Iredell, Spaight, Ramsey, McHenry, Samuel

Chase, and nearly all the illustrious names south of the Potomac, proclaimed it before the sun, that the days of slavery were beginning to be numbered."—*Power of Congress over the "District of Columbia,"* by T. D. WELD.

But it is needless to multiply these references. So universal were these sentiments, that Mr. Leigh, in the Convention of Virginia, in 1832, took occasion to say :

"I thought, till very lately, that it was known to every body that, during the Revolution, and for many years after, the abolition of slavery was a favorite topic with many of our ablest statesmen, who entertained with respect all the schemes which wisdom or ingenuity could suggest for its accomplishment."

Mr. Faulkner, in the same Convention, alluded to the same fact, as did also Gov. Barbour, of Virginia, in the United States' Senate, in 1820.

These professions of the fathers of our republic were not totally unaccompanied with corresponding action.

The articles of Association, including the solemn pledge to discontinue the slave trade, appear to have been generally respected and observed. That there were unprincipled men who evaded or transgressed them, as there were other traitors to the cause of liberty, there can be no doubt. After the close of the war, this is known to have been the fact. But the States took early measures for its suppression.

"The first opportunity was taken, after the Declaration of Independence, to extinguish the detestable commerce so long forced upon the province (Virginia). In October, 1778, during the tumult and anxiety of the Revolution, the General Assembly passed a law, prohibiting, under heavy penalties, the further importation of slaves, and declaring that every slave imported thereafter, should be immediately set free." "The example of Virginia was followed, at different times, before the date of the Federal Constitution, by most of the other States."—*Walsh's* "*Appeal*"—*Vide* "*Friend of Man,*" June 21, 1837. Copied from "*Human Rights.*"

"We are not aware that any State allowed the importation of slaves at the time," when the Constitution was adopted. "The first State that renewed the traffic, so far as we know, was S. Carolina." in 1803.—"*Human Rights*"—"*F. of Man,*" as above.

Under what influences, and with what activity, the slave trade was resumed, from 1803 to 1808, will be shown in the proper place.

CHAPTER IX.

ERA OF FORMING THE FEDERAL CONSTITUTION.

Prevailing Sentiment—Washington—Luther Martyn—William Pinckney—North-Western Territory—Ordinance of 1787—Madison—" Understandings"—Wilson—Heath—Johnson—Randolph—Patrick Henry—Iredell—" The Federalist," by Jay, Madison, and Hamilton—Ratifications—Rhode Island—New York—Virginia—North Carolina—Amendment—" Due process of law."

FROM the close of the Revolutionary war in 1783, to the sitting of the Constitutional Convention, was a space of only four years. Thence, two more years bring us to the adoption of the Constitution, in 1789. What was the prevailing sentiment of that period?

In a letter to Robert Morris, dated Mount Vernon, April 12, 1786, George Washington said:

" I can only say that there is not a man living who wishes more sincerely than I do to see a plan adopted for the abolition of it, (slavery;) but there is only one proper and effectual mode in which it can be accomplished, and that is by legislative authority; and this, so far as my suffrage will go, shall never be wanting."—9 *Sparks's Washington*, 158.

In a letter to John F. Mercer, September 9, 1786, he reiterated this sentiment:

" I never mean, unless some particular circumstances should compel me to it, to possess another slave by purchase, it being among my first wishes to see some plan adopted, by which slavery in this country may be abolished by law."—*Ibid.*

And in a letter to Sir John Sinclair, he further said:

" There are in Pennsylvania laws for the gradual abolition of slavery, which neither Virginia nor Maryland have at present, but which nothing is more certain than they must have, and at a period *not remote.*"

By his last will and testament he made all his slaves free.

The testimonies of Franklin, Rush, and Jay, in strong opposition to slavery, have been cited in another connection.*

We have now traced the history of the " peculiar institution" down to the time when the Federal Constitution was about to be formed. *Exceedingly* " peculiar " indeed, are the vouchers for its authenticity and legality down to that point in our national history. What occurred while the Federal Constitution was in process of forming, is the next historical fact to be inquired after. What was *likely* to have occurred, and even, indeed, what *could* have occurred, may well nigh be read in the mere light of the historical facts already noticed. Those facts, at least, should not be left out of the account, in any attempts at a *historical* exposition of the Constitution, if, indeed, the advocates of the "institution" adventure into the field of history at all, in defence of their claims. The simple history, and not the argument, must occupy, at present, our attention, and yet it is in the light of the pending controversy that we should ponder the facts. It is that contest that gives them their value, and they should be collected, arranged and studied with a view to the points to be illustrated and determined by them.

Luther Martin, of Maryland, advocated the abolition of slavery, in the Federal Convention of 1787, and in his Report of the proceedings of that Convention to the Legislature of his own State.

William Pinckney, of Maryland, in the House of Delegates in that State, in 1789, urged, strongly, the abolition of slavery. We will give but a specimen of his language on that occasion.

" Sir—Iniquitous and most dishonorable to Maryland, is that dreary system of partial bondage which her laws have hitherto supported with a solicitude worthy of a better object, and her citizens by their practice, countenanced. Founded in a disgraceful traffic, to which the parent country lent its fostering aid, from motives of interest, but which even she would have disdained to encourage, had England been the destined mart of such inhuman merchandize, its continuance is as shameful as its origin."

---

* Chapter IV.

NORTH-WESTERN TERRITORY—ORDINANCE OF 1787.

While the Convention for drafting the Constitution of the United States was in session, in 1787, the Old Congress passed an ordinance abolishing slavery in the North-Western Territory, and precluding its future introduction there. The first Congress under the new Constitution ratified this ordinance, by a special act. It received the approval of Washington, who was then fresh from the discussions of the Convention for drafting the Federal Constitution. The measure originated with Jefferson, and its ratification in the new Congress received the vote of every member except Mr. Yates, of New York, *the entire Southern delegation voting for its adoption.* By this ordinance slavery was excluded from Ohio, Indiana, Illinois, Michigan, Wisconsin, and Iowa.

The series of articles is preceded by this preamble :

" And for extending the fundamental principles of civil and religious liberty, which form the basis whereon these republics, their laws and constitutions, are erected ; to fix and establish those principles as the basis of all laws, constitutions, and governments, which forever hereafter shall be formed in said Territory ; to provide also for the establishment of States, and permanent government therein, and for their admission to a share in the Federal Councils at as early a period as may be consistent with the general interest :—Be it ordained and established," &c. &c.

Then follow the articles. The sixth is as follows :

" There shall be neither slavery nor involuntary servitude, otherwise than in the punishment of crimes, whereof the party shall have been duly convicted ; provided, always, that any person escaping into the same, from whom labor or service may be lawfully claimed, in any one of the original States, such fugitive may be lawfully reclaimed, and conveyed to the person claiming his or her labor or service, as aforesaid."

" The Constitution," it is claimed, "guaranties slavery." And "the compromises of the Constitution" are very generally conceded, even among those who disrelish and controvert the claim. We enter not now into matters of mere opinion. But the continuity and fidelity of the *history* we have attempted, compel us to attend to the *facts*.

Whatever those facts are, they are such as are interlinked, indissolubly, with the historical facts of the last previous chapter, and the preceding ones. History must be understood, if at all, in its connections.

The Constitution is in the hands of the people. We need not copy here its provisions. No claimant of the Constitutional guaranties of slavery adventures to rest the claim on the mere *words* of that instrument. He well knows that neither the terms "slave" nor "slavery" are to be found there. He goes *out* of the instrument for its exposition, and reposes on supposed *facts*, in the shape of "*understandings*" then entertained. What were the "understandings" of that period? In the preceding chapter may be seen some of them. It is in place here to record more. We have seen what they were, up to the time of the framing and adopting of the Federal Constitution. What were they, then?

In the Convention that drafted the Constitution—

Mr. Madison declared, he "thought it wrong to admit in the Constitution the idea that there could be property in men."—3 *Mad. Pap.*, 1429.*

" On motion of Mr. Randolph, the word ' SERVITUDE' was struck out, and ' SERVICE' unanimously inserted—the former being thought to express the condition of SLAVES, and the latter the obligation of FREE PERSONS."—*Ib.* 3, p. 1569.

Such were the "understandings" of the Convention that drafted the Constitution. And with what "understanding" was it adopted by the people, in their State Conventions? Let us see.

James Wilson, of Pennsylvania, had been a leading member of the Convention, and in the Ratification Convention of his State, when speaking of the clause relating to the power of Congress over the slave trade after twenty years, he said :

" I consider this clause as laying the foundation for banishing slavery out of this country ; and though the period is more distant than I could wish it, it will produce the same kind, gradual change as was produced in Pennsyl-

---

* In other words, Mr. Madison would not consent that the Constitution should recognize even the *legality* of slavery ! This was a still more full, confident, and emphatic expression of the idea we have before quoted from Dr. Hopkins.

vania. * * * The new States which are to be formed will be under the control of Congress in this particular, and slavery will never be introduced among them."—*2 Elliot's Debates*, 452.

In another place, speaking of this clause, he said :

" It presents us with the pleasing prospect that the rights of mankind will be acknowledged and established throughout the Union. If there was no other feature in the Constitution but this one, it would diffuse a beauty over its whole countenance. Yet the labor of a few years, and Congress will have power to exterminate slavery from within our borders."—*Ib.* 2, p. 484.

In the Ratification Convention of Massachusetts, Gen. Heath said :

" The migration or importation, &c., is confined to the States now existing only ; new States cannot claim it. Congress by their ordinance for creating new States some time since, declared that the new States shall be republican, and that there shall be no slavery in them."—*Ib.* 2, p. 115.

Nor were these views and anticipations confined to the free States. In the Ratification Convention of Virginia, Mr. Johnson said :

" They tell us that they see a progressive danger of bringing about emancipation. The principle has begun since the Revolution. Let us do what we will, it will come round. Slavery has been the foundation of much of that impiety and dissipation which have been so much disseminated among our countrymen. If it were totally abolished, it would do much good."—*Ib.* 3, pp. 6—48.

Gov. Randolph rebuked those who expressed apprehensions that its influence might be exerted on the side of freedom, by saying :

" I hope that there are none here who, considering the subject in the calm light of philosophy, will advance an objection dishonorable to Virginia, that, at the moment they are securing the rights of their citizens, there is a spark of hope that those unfortunate men now held in BONDAGE may, by the operation of the General Government, be made FREE."—*Ib.* 3, p. 598.

Patrick Henry, in the same Convention, argued " *the power of Congress, under the United States' Constitution, to abolish slavery in the States*," and added :

" Another thing will contribute to bring this event about. Slavery is detested. We feel its effects. We deplore it with all the pity of humanity."—*Debates Va. Convention*, p. 463.

" In the debates of the North Carolina Convention, Mr. Iredell, afterwards a Judge of the United States Supreme Court, said—' When the entire abolition of slavery takes place, it will be an event which must be pleasing to every generous mind, and every friend of human nature.' "—" *Power of Congress*," &c., pp. 31–2.

Such are a few specimens of the expressed "understandings" with which the people adopted the Constitution.

Another class of historical facts, of the utmost importance to a right understanding of the slave question in America, relates to the expositions and arguments addressed to the people of the United States to persuade them to adopt the Federal Constitution. It is well known that the people were sensitively jealous of their rights at that period, and fearful of the encroachments of despotic power. A strong party, of which Mr. Jefferson (a prominent and zealous propagandist of abolitionism) was understood to be the nucleus, and afterwards became the successful presidential candidate, opposed the adoption of the Federal Constitution, as prepared by the Convention, on the ground of its alleged defects in not providing sufficient securities for *personal rights*, and a more ample and explicit enunciation of the self-evident truths of the Declaration of 1776. This opposition drew out the distinguished statesmen, Madison, Jay, and Hamilton, in a joint and elaborate defence of the Constitution as drafted, comprising a series of papers known as "The Federalist," and since collected into a large volume. These papers were extensively circulated before the action of the States, and were largely instrumental in securing their desired object.—No. 39 of "The Federalist," by James Madison, contains the following:

"*The first question* that offers itself is, whether the general form and aspect of the government be strictly *republican*. It is evident that no other form would be reconcilable with the genius of the people of America, and with *the fundamental principles of the Revolution*, or with that honorable determination which animates every votary of *freedom*, to *rest all* our political experiments on the capacity of MANKIND for SELF-GOVERNMENT. If the plan of the Convention, therefore, be found to depart from the republican character, its advocates must abandon it, as no longer defensible."

Mr. Madison proceeds, at some length, to discuss the question, "What are the distinctive characters of the republican form"? After distinctly repudiating the aristocracies and oligarchies of Holland, Venice, Poland, and England, as not being republican, though sometimes "dignified," very impro-

perly, "with the appellation," Mr. Madison proceeds further
to define a republican government as one whose officers are
appointed by THE PEOPLE, &c. "It is *essential* to such a government," says he, "that it be derived from the *great body of
society*, NOT from an inconsiderable portion, OR, a favored *class*
of it." And this is the same Mr. Madison, who, in the Convention for drafting the Constitution which he was now recommending, had insisted that the instrument must not recognize the legality of slavery.

The adoption of the Federal Constitution was thus successfully urged upon the people, by representing it as laying the
foundation of the Government upon "the principles of the
Revolution"—the principles of '76,—the principles promulgated so effectively by Mr. Jefferson, who had said—

"The true foundation of republican government is the EQUAL RIGHTS OF
EVERY CITIZEN, in his PERSON and PROPERTY, and in their MANAGEMENT,"
and who had explicitly designated the slaves as "citizens."*

In No. 84 of "The Federalist" several pages are devoted
to a consideration of what was evidently understood to be a
vital point, in the minds of the people, who were so soon to
decide on the adoption or rejection of the proposed Constitution.

"The *most considerable* of the remaining objections," says
the writer, "is, *that the plan of the Convention contains no bill
of rights*."

The writer speaks of "the *intemperate partizans* of a bill of
rights," and of their "*zeal* in this matter." This shows that
many of the people were sensitive on this point, and that the
friends of the proposed Constitution were afraid of its being
rejected in consequence.

And how did "The Federalist" successfully allay this
jealousy, and persuade the people to adopt the proposed Constitution?

---

* With what execration should the statesman be loaded, who, permitting *one half*
of the *citizens* thus to trample upon the rights of *the other*, transforms those into
despots, and these into enemies, destroys the morals of the one part, and the *amor
patriœ* of the other."—*Notes on Virginia*.

It was done, *first*, by citing a number of specific provisions in the Constitution, equivalent, (as was claimed) to so many corresponding items in a bill of rights; and, *second*, by citing the PREAMBLE to the Constitution, setting forth its objects "*to secure the blessings of liberty*," &c. to "the people of the United States." This Preamble, as being a part of the Constitution, and its very basis, to which all the rest was conformed, was represented as being not only a bill of rights in the general, but "a *better* recognition of popular rights" than could otherwise have been framed, and *less* liable to be set aside, under a "plausible pretence," by men "disposed to usurp power."*

The objectors had desired such a bill of rights as several of the States, particularly Massachusetts, had already adopted, and *under* which, *before that time*, the Courts of Massachusetts had decided slavery to be illegal. Yet "The Federalist" assured them that the Constitution was *more* than the equivalent of such bills of rights.

It was under the pressure of expositions and arguments like these, from leading members of the Convention, that the people were persuaded to ratify the Constitution that had been elaborated with closed doors. They ratified it with "the understanding," so frequently expressed by and among them, that the Constitution was in favor of freedom. We know of no record in which the ratification of that instrument was urged, either at the North or at the South, on the ground that it was the guaranty of any form of despotism—or on the ground that the conflicting interests of liberty and slavery had been compromised. The whole current of the political literature of that period forbids the idea that any such appeals could have been adventured.

But the people, though they ratified the Constitution, were

---

* The reader is doubtless familiar with the *modern* pleas, that the Preamble has no controlling power over the Constitution; that it does not furnish a criterion for Constitutional exposition; and that, in fact, it is no part of the Constitution! We may judge what would have been the fate of the proposed Constitution, if its friends had outstript its enemies in representing it thus!

not satisfied to do so without insisting upon important amendments. The Conventions of Virginia, North Carolina and Rhode Island, proposed a provision as follows :

" No FREEMAN ought to be taken, imprisoned, or disseized of his freehold, liberties, privileges, or franchises, or outlawed, or exiled, or in any manner despoiled or deprived of his life, liberty, or property, BUT BY THE LAW OF THE LAND."—*Elliot's Debates*, 658.

New York proposed a different provision :

" No PERSON ought to be taken, imprisoned, or disseized of his freehold, or be exiled, or deprived of his privileges, franchises, life, liberty, or property, but by due process of law."—1 *Ibid*, 328.

These various propositions came before Congress, and that body, at its first session, agreed upon several amendments to the Constitution, which were subsequently ratified by the States. That which related to personal liberty was expressed in these comprehensive words :

" No person * * * * shall be deprived of life, liberty, or property, without due process of law."—*Cons., Amend., Art.* 5.

It is to be noted, as an important historical fact, that this remarkable provision is *an amendment*, coming in after the original instrument had been ratified, thus over-riding and controlling, like all other amendments, whatever in the original instrument may have been supposed to be of a contrary bearing.

The ratification of Rhode Island was longest withheld, and was most remarkable in its mode of expression. It was, in fact, *conditional*. It specified a long list of declarations of rights, and then said :

" Under these impressions, and declaring that the rights aforesaid *cannot be abridged*, and that the explanations aforesaid are *consistent with* the said Constitution, and in confidence that the amendments hereafter mentioned will receive an early and mature deliberation, and conformably to the 5th article of said Constitution, speedily become parts thereof : We the said delegates," &c., &c., " do assent to and ratify the said Constitution."

Among these declarations of rights were some equivalent to those of the Declaration of Independence.

Among the proposed amendments, above mentioned, was the following :

" As a traffic tending to establish or *continue the slavery* of any part of the human species, is disgraceful to the cause of religion and humanity, that

Congress as soon as may be, promote and establish such laws as may effectually prevent the importation of slaves, of any description, into the United States."

From this it is seen, that the State whose citizens were most deeply engaged in the lucrative importation of slaves, the only State, perhaps, that was growing rich *by the continuance of the slave system*, consented to ratify the Federal Constitution only *on condition* that the traffic should be speedily prohibited. No other ratification of the Constitution was ever made by Rhode Island. She *never consented* to the twenty years' delay of that prohibition.

CHAPTER X.

OF DIRECT ANTI-SLAVERY EFFORTS, INCLUDING ECCLESIASTI-
CAL ACTION, FROM THE PERIOD OF THE REVOLUTION TO
THE CLOSE OF THE LAST CENTURY, AND THE ABOLITION
OF SLAVERY IN THE NORTHERN STATES.

Republication of Hopkins' Dialogue (1785)—Edwards' Sermon (1791)—Anti-Slavery
Meeting at Woodbridge, N. J. (1783)—Abolition Societies in Pennsylvania, New
York, Rhode Island, Connecticut, Maryland, Virginia, New Jersey, Delaware—
Names of distinguished abolitionists—Memorial to Leg. of New York, by Jay,
Hamilton, &c.—Petitions to Congress, by B. Franklin and others—Discussions in
Congress—William and Mary College (Va.)—Action of Methodist E. Conference—
Presb. General Assembly—Baptists—Action of the States—Virginia, Delaware,
Rhode Island, Vermont—Massachusetts—Pennsylvania—New Hampshire, Con-
necticut—New York—New Jersey—Census of remaining slaves.

SIGNIFICANT as are the facts recorded in the two preceding
chapters, they would fail of producing their full and proper
impression, unless connected with an account of other movements witnessed at the same time, and extending to a still
later period of our history. It was not in the National Councils alone, the resolutions and acts of Congress, the corresponding proceedings of State and County Conventions, the
action of State legislatures, and the declarations of prominent
statesmen, that the rising of sentiment against slavery was
apparent. Then, as at other times, under popular institutions, such manifestations were to be regarded as evidences of
a still broader and deeper current of public opinion, that was
producing them. Then, as now; here, as in Great Britain,
the public bodies and functionaries nearest to the people,
freshest from their bosom, most accessible to their inspection,

and most directly and vitally amenable to them ("Representatives" and "Commons," in distinction from "Lords" and "Senates"), were most deeply imbued with the principles of justice and freedom—a general fact of incalculable weight in the argument for thoroughly democratic institutions.

And back of this general public sentiment against slavery, were the moral influences that had been operating in that direction—the religious testimonies and the ecclesiastical action before mentioned. The power of the press, and of voluntary association, irrespective of sect, followed soon afterward.

The first edition of Hopkins' Dialogue was published at Norwich, Connecticut, early in 1776, as before stated. Its circulation was extensive, and is known to have produced a powerful impression upon the minds of reflecting men, including some in high stations. A second edition was issued in New York in 1785, "by vote of the society for promoting the manumission of slaves"—of which John Jay was President, and which had been formed January 25th of that same year.

Another publication, of great weight and influence, was the celebrated sermon of Dr. Jonathan Edwards, of New Haven, Conn., afterwards President of Union College, Schenectady, preached before the Connecticut Society for the Promotion of Freedom, &c., Sept. 15, 1791. It is a masterpiece of logical argument, and was extensively circulated by the manumission and abolition societies of that period, as it has been since by the more modern anti-slavery societies.

By these two publications, the argument against slavery was placed upon a deeper and broader theological and metaphysical basis, and was pushed to more startling and radical conclusions, than in any previous writings on the subject with which we are acquainted. And it may safely be said that no later writers have gone beyond them in affirming the inherent sinfulness and deep criminality of slaveholding, and the duty of immediate and unconditional emancipation. Particularly is this true of the sermon of Edwards. If others have insisted upon these points with more vehemence of declamation, or with a more brilliant display of rhetoric, there is no one who has more deliberately and triumphantly demonstrated those truths by a process of cool iron-linked argument, placing it forever beyond the power of man to unsettle them, without dethroning the moral sense, rejecting the inductions of reason, and abjuring the Christian religion. It is not known that any writer or public speaker of any note, has ever attempted to grapple with that sermon, attempting to criticize, or to confute it. And yet this forbearance cannot be because the language employed is more smooth and mild than that of other writings that have been criticized as denunciatory. The preacher distinctly charges upon the slaveholder the crime of man-stealing, and the repetition of the crime every day he continues to hold a slave in bondage. He charges him also with "theft or robbery"—nay, with "a *greater* crime than fornication, theft, or robbery." He predicts that, "if we may judge the future by the past, within fifty years from this time it will be as shameful for a man to hold a negro slave, as to be guilty of common robbery or theft." In an appendix, Dr. Edwards answers objections against immediate emancipation, just as modern abolitionists answer them now.

Such were the sentiments which the abolition societies of the last century, directed by the patriots of the American Revolution, the founders of the Union, the framers and the adopters of the Federal Constitution, were intent to circulate through the country. If some of them, as statesmen, did not fully carry out the idea of immediate emancipation taught in such writings, they circulated them among the people, nevertheless. These were the effective weapons of their warfare against slavery, so far as they succeeded at all. By these doctrines, mainly, the public conscience was reached, and the measures put in progress, which finally resulted in the abolition of slavery in some of the States. The doctrines are none the less true and trustworthy because the partial adoption of them produced but partial and tardy results. If the abolition of slavery in some of the States was so slow and gradual as to occupy a whole generation or more in the process, if in some others it still lingers, or has been indefinitely postponed, while the system has strengthened itself, and the slave power has assumed the control of the nation and stealthily reversed its policy, the fault does not lie in the teachings of Hopkins and Edwards, but in the mistaken prudence of those who thought it more wise and safe to follow but partially in practice what was admitted to be right and true in the abstract. To this single fallacy, the failure of the Revolutionary abolitionists, in their intended overthrow of American slavery, may be distinctly traced. "The ruse of gradualism," identical with deferred repentance for sin, produced its accustomed and legitimate fruits. It deceived them, as it deceives the greater portion of mankind.

We may honor their earnest endeavors, nevertheless, and rejoice in the success, however limited, with which their labors were crowned. It should be ours to emulate their love of freedom, and avoid their mistakes, the repetition of which would be less excusable in us.

An important and highly spirited anti-slavery meeting is said to have been held at Woodbridge, New Jersey, appropriately convened on the 4th of July, 1783, just seven years after the Declaration of inalienable rights that was now admitted to have been manfully and successfully sustained. Dr. Bloomfield, father of Governor Bloomfield of New Jersey, is said to have presided on that joyous occasion, which was celebrated by a public dinner, for which was provided a roasted ox—a circumstance that attests the general and cordial attendance of the citizens. Who could have predicted the era of pro-slavery mobs against abolition meetings then? Who would have looked for biblical defences of slaveholding, from the high places of Princeton? Who would have believed that churches and pulpits, generally, throughout the country, would ever be closed against the discussion of slavery, for fear of "disturbing the peace of our Zion?" Who would have believed that anti-slavery agitation would ever have been regarded with abhorrence, as adverse to "the perpetuity of our glorious Union?" What value could the patriots of that day have attached to any union that was not cemented on the basis of freedom, and designed for its guaranty?

ABOLITION SOCIETIES.

It may be difficult to enumerate all the manumission and abolition societies of this period, or to fix, accurately, the precise dates of their organization. The particulars that follow embody what we have at command.

Dr. Holmes, in his "American Annals," says that the Abolition Society of Pennsylvania was formed in 1774, and was enlarged in 1787. Hildreth, in his "History of the United States," says the Pennsylvania Society was the first. Edward Needles, in his "Historical Memoir of the Pennsylvania Society for the abolition of Slavery, the relief of free negroes unlawfully held in bondage, and for improving the African race," says the first associated action in Philadelphia was a meeting of a few individuals at the Sun tavern in Second-street, April 14, 1775,* when a society was formed "for the relief of free negroes unlawfully held in bondage." The society met four times in 1775, and adjourned to meet in 1776; but, on account of the war, no meeting occurred till February, 1784, after which its meetings were continued till March, 1787, when the Constitution was so revised as to include prominently "*the abolition of slavery,*" as in the above title. Of this Society, Dr. Benjamin Franklin was chosen President.

The New York "Society for promoting the Manumission of Slaves, and protecting such of them as have been or may be liberated," was formed January 25, 1785, as before mentioned. Of this society, John Jay was the first President. On being appointed Chief-Justice of the United States, he resigned, and was succeeded by Gen. Alexander Hamilton, who held the office a few months, until, on receiving an appointment in the Federal cabinet, he removed to Philadelphia, and soon after his place was filled by "Gen. Matthew Clarkson, *the United States Marshal for New York*, a very pious, good

---

* One year later than the statement of Dr. Holmes.

man, and belonging to a different species from the general race of slave-catching marshals."*

May 5, 1786, the committee of the New York Society reported that a similar society was about to be established at Providence, Rhode Island. In 1788 the Pennsylvania Society addressed their corresponding members in Rhode Island, about vessels fitting out there in defiance of the laws against the slave trade. In 1791 the Rhode Island Society is alluded to as having memorialized Congress, in conjunction with the abolition societies of Connecticut, New York, Pennsylvania, Baltimore, Virginia, and two societies on the eastern shore of Maryland.

The Maryland Abolition Society was formed in 1789. The Connecticut Abolition Society in 1790; the Virginia Abolition Society in 1791. The New Jersey Society "for promoting the Abolition of Slavery," in 1792.

The Maryland and Virginia Societies had auxiliaries in different parts of those States.

There was also a society in Delaware. In 1794, ten societies met in convention in Philadelphia, and continued to meet annually, for a number of years afterwards.

Of the Pennsylvania Abolition Society, Benjamin Franklin was chosen President, and Benjamin Rush Secretary, both signers of the Declaration of Independence, and the first-named just returned from the convention that drafted the Federal Constitution. Among the officers of the Maryland Society was Samuel Chase, one of the signers of the Declaration of Independence, afterwards Judge of the United States' Supreme Court, and Luther Martin, a member of the Constitutional Convention. Of the Connecticut Abolition Society, Dr. Ezra Stiles, President of Yale College, was the first President, and Simeon Baldwin was Secretary.

"Among other distinguished individuals who were efficient officers of these abolition societies, and delegates from their respective State societies, at the annual meetings of the American Convention for Promoting the

---

* MSS. by Hon. Wm. Jay.

Abolition of Slavery, were Hon. Uriah Tracy, United States Senator from Connecticut; Hon. Zephaniah Swift, Chief Justice of the same; Hon. Cæsar A. Rodney, Attorney-General of the United States; Hon. James A. Bayard, United States Senator from Delaware; Gov. Bloomfield, of New Jersey; Hon. Wm. Rawle, the late venerable head of the Philadelphia bar; Dr. Casper Wistar, of Philadelphia; Messrs. Foster and Tillinghast, of Rhode Island; Messrs. Ridgley, Buchanan, and Wilkinson, of Maryland; and Messrs. Pleasants, McLean, and Anthony, of Virginia."—*Power of Congress*, &c., pp. 30, 31.

These Abolition Societies and the officers and members of them were not idle. They agitated the subject, circulated publications, and petitioned legislative bodies.

In 1786, John Jay drafted and signed a memorial to the Legislature of New York against slavery, and petitioning for its abolition, declaring that the men held as slaves by the laws of New York, were free by the law of God. Among the other petitioners were James Duane, Mayor of the City of New York, Robert R. Livingston, afterwards Secretary of Foreign Affairs of the United States and Chancellor of the State of New York, Alexander Hamilton, and many other eminent citizens of the State.*

Nor were petitions addressed only to the legislatures of the States in which the petitioners resided. The doctrines of moral and political non-intervention with the delicate subject had not then been discovered. The dogma that Congress has nothing to do with slavery in the States does not appear to have obtained general currency at that period. These statements are believed to express *simple historical facts*, and applicable up to a point of time after the Federal Constitution had been drafted, discussed, and adopted, and the Federal Government under that Constitution organized and put in operation. A few particulars will suffice to justify these statements.

Both the Virginia and Maryland Abolition Societies, at an early day, sent up memorials to Congress. We have not at hand the precise dates, nor is this important. The dates of the organization of these societies, particularly that of Vir-

---

* MSS. by Hon. Wm. Jay.

ginia, make it evident that their petitions were addressed to the new Federal Government. The Connecticut Abolition Society sent up a petition in 1791. The Society of Friends and the Pennsylvania Abolition Society had done so, still earlier, and their petitions came before the first Congress under the new Constitution, and were debated February 12th, 1790.*

These petitions were addressed to Congress. What could the petitioners have supposed that Congress had to do with the subject? The Foreign Slave Trade, at that time, appears to have been interdicted by most of the States, in conformity with the original compact of 1774, and was not resumed, even by South Carolina, as has already been stated, until 1803. And among the "compromises of the Constitution," since claimed, a prominent one, and the best authenticated, is that which prevented *Congress* from interdicting the foreign traffic, until 1808. The cession of the District of Columbia was not accepted by Congress until July 16, 1790, some time after the presentation of the Pennsylvania petition. The seat of the Federal Government, then, and for some years afterwards, was at Philadelphia. By the ordinance of 1787, slavery had been prohibited in the North Western Territory, and no one anticipated the admission of any new slave states. What, then, was there for Congress to do, according to the doctrine of non-intervention now entertained? What was it that the petitioners asked? Against what did they petition? And where did it exist?

A copy of the Pennsylvania petition is before us, and portions of those from Connecticut and Virginia.

The Connecticut petitioners, (Pres. Stiles, Simeon Baldwin, &c.) say :

" From a sober conviction of the UNRIGHTEOUSNESS OF SLAVERY, your

---

* Mr. Weld's pamphlet and the *Liberty Bell* give the date 1789, but Washington was not inaugurated until April 30th of that year, and the "first Congress" commenced its first session, April 7th. Besides, the petition of the Pennsylvania Society, signed by Benjamin Franklin, as published in the *Liberty Bell*, bears date Feb. 3, 1790, and the Journal of Congress mentions its presentation, Feb. 12, 1790.

petitioners have long beheld with grief our fellow-men doomed to perpetual bondage in a country which boasts her freedom. Your petitioners are fully of opinion that calm reflection will at last convince the world that THE WHOLE SYSTEM OF AMERICAN SLAVERY is unjust in its nature, impolitic in its principles, and in its consequences ruinous to the industry and enterprise of the citizens of THESE STATES."

The " *Virginia* Society for the *Abolition of* SLAVERY," &c., in addressing the *Congress of the United States*, say :

" Your memorialists, fully aware that righteousness exalteth *a nation*, and that SLAVERY is not only an odious degradation, but an outrageous violation of one of the most essential rights of human nature, and utterly repugnant to the precepts of the Gospel, which breathes 'peace on earth and good will to men,' lament that a practice so inconsistent with true policy and the inalienable rights of men, should subsist in so enlightened an age, and among a people professing that all mankind are, by nature, equally entitled to freedom."

" The memorial of the Pennsylvania Society for promoting the *abolition of* SLAVERY," &c., addressed " to the Senate and House of Representatives of the *United States*," contains the following :

" Your memorialists, particularly engaged in attending to the distresses arising from SLAVERY, believe it to be their indispensable duty to present this subject to your notice. They have observed, with real satisfaction, that many important and salutary powers are vested in you, for 'promoting the welfare and *securing the blessings of* LIBERTY to the PEOPLE of the UNITED STATES ;'* and as they conceive that these blessings ought rightfully to be administered, WITHOUT DISTINCTION OF COLOR, to all descriptions of people, so they indulge themselves in the pleasing expectation that nothing which can be done for the relief of the unhappy objects of their care, will be either omitted or delayed.

" From a persuasion that equal liberty was originally the portion, and is still the birth-right of all men, and influenced by the strong ties of humanity and the principles of their institution, your memorialists conceive themselves bound to use all justifiable endeavors to LOOSEN THE BONDS OF SLAVERY, and promote a general enjoyment of the blessings of freedom. Under these impressions, they earnestly entreat your attention to the subject of *slavery* ; that you will be pleased to countenance the RESTORATION TO LIBERTY of

---

* This language is evidently taken from the Preamble to the Federal Constitution. " We, the people of the United States, in order to promote the general welfare, and secure the blessings of liberty," &c., &c.

those unhappy men, who, alone, *in this land of freedom*, are degraded into perpetual bondage, and who, amid the general joy of surrounding freemen, are groaning in servile subjection ; THAT YOU WILL DEVISE MEANS FOR RE-MOVING THIS INCONSISTENCY OF CHARACTER FROM THE AMERICAN PEOPLE ; that you will promote mercy and justice towards this distressed race ; and that you will step to the very verge of the power vested in you for discouraging every species of traffic in the persons of our fellow-men.

BENJAMIN FRANKLIN, PRESIDENT."*

PHILADELPHIA, Feb. 3, 1790.   [*Federal Gazette*, 1790.]

DISCUSSIONS IN CONGRESS.

How were these petitions understood in Congress ? How were they received and treated ? Were they understood to look in the direction of a general removal of slavery, as well as the slave trade ? Were the petitioners denounced as fanatics and madmen ? Was the application repelled as treason against the Constitution and the Union? On the other hand, were there any who expressed a readiness "to espouse their cause"? The reader of the following extracts from the discussions, will judge.

In the debate on the petition from Pennsylvania, Mr. Parker, of Virginia, said:

" I hope, Mr. Speaker, the petition of these *respectable people* will be attended to, with all the readiness the *importance* of its object demands ; and I cannot help expressing the pleasure I feel in finding *so considerable a part of the community* attending to matters of such a momentous concern to the future prosperity and happiness of the people of America. I think it my duty, *as a citizen of the Union*, TO ESPOUSE THEIR CAUSE."

Mr. Page, of Virginia (afterward Governor) " was in favor of the commitment. He hoped that the designs of the respectable memorialists would not be stopped at the threshold, in order to preclude a fair discussion of the prayer of the memorial. With respect to the alarm that was apprehended, he conjectured there was none ; but there might be just cause, if the memorial was NOT taken into consideration. He placed himself in the case of the slave, and said that, on hearing that Congress had refused to listen to the decent suggestions of a respectable part of the community, he should infer that the general Government, FROM WHICH WAS EXPECTED GREAT

---

* This was probably the last important public act of Franklin, who died the same year.

GOOD WOULD RESULT TO EVERY CLASS OF CITIZENS,* had shut their ears against the voice of humanity, and he should despair of any alleviation of the miseries he and his posterity had in prospect. If anything could induce him to rebel, it must be a stroke like this, impressing on his mind all the horrors of despair. But if he was told that application was made in his behalf, and that Congress were willing to hear what could be urged in favor of discouraging the practice of importing his fellow-wretches, he would trust in their justice and humanity, and wait the decision patiently."

Mr. Scott, of Pennsylvania : " I cannot, for my part, conceive how any person CAN BE SAID TO ACQUIRE PROPERTY IN ANOTHER ;† but—enough of those who reduce men to the state of transferable goods, or use them like beasts of burden, who deliver them up as the patrimony or property of another man.‡ Let us argue on principles countenanced by reason and becoming humanity. I do not know how far I might go if I was one of the Judges of the United States, and those people were to come before me, and claim their *emancipation;* but I am sure I would go as far as I could."§

Mr. Burke, of South Carolina, said : " He saw the disposition of the House, and he feared it would be referred to a committee, maugre all their opposition."

Mr. Smith, of South Carolina, said : " that on entering into this government, they (South Carolina and Georgia) apprehended that the other States, not knowing the necessity of the citizens of the Southern States, would, from motives of humanity and benevolence, be led to vote for a GENERAL EMANCIPATION ; and, had they not seen that the Constitution provided against the effect of such a disposition, I may be bold to say they never would have adopted it."

" In the debate, at the same session, May 13th, on the petition of the Society of Friends respecting the slave trade, Mr. Parker, of Virginia, said : ' He hoped Congress would do all that lay in their power *to restore to human nature its inherent privileges,* and, if possible, wipe out the stigma that America labored under. The inconsistency in our principles, with which we are justly charged, *should be done away*, that we may show, by our actions, the pure beneficence of the doctrine we held out to the world in our Declaration of Independence.' "

" Mr. Jackson, of Georgia, said : ' IT WAS THE FASHION OF THE DAY TO FAVOR THE LIBERTY OF THE SLAVES. * * * What is to be done for compensation ? Will Virginia set all her negroes free ? Will they give

---

* Here, again, we find the negro slaves expressly designated as *citizens.*

† Another blow at the idea of the legality of slavery.

‡ How does this harmonize with the Constitutional obligation of delivering up fugitive slaves ?

§ A pregnant hint of the speaker's impression of the duties of the Federal Courts.

up the money they have cost them, and to whom? When this practice
comes to be tried, then the sound of liberty will lose those charms which
make it grateful to the ravished ear.' "

" Mr. Madison, of Virginia: ' The dictates of humanity, the principles
of the people, the national safety and happiness, and prudent policy, require
it of us. The *Constitution* has particularly called our attention to it. * *
I conceive the Constitution in this particular was formed in order that the
Government, whilst it was restrained from laying a total prohibition, might
be able to give some testimony of the sense of America, with respect to
the African trade. * * * It is to be hoped, that by expressing a
national disapprobation of the trade, we may *destroy* it, and save our
country from reproaches, and our posterity from the imbecility ever attendant on a country filled with slaves. I do not wish to say anything harsh
to the hearing of gentlemen who entertain different sentiments from me, or
different sentiments from those I represent. But if there is any one point
in which it is clearly the POLICY OF THIS NATION, so far as we constitutionally can, to vary the practice obtaining under some of the State Governments, it is this. But it is certain that a majority of the States are
opposed to the practice."—*Cong. Reg.*, v. i., pp. 308–12; *Weld's Power of
Cong.*, &c., pp. 30–32.

There may be some difficulty in apprehending, clearly, the
import of some of the expressions used in this debate. This
may be owing to our making a broad distinction, now, which
seems scarcely to have been recognized at all, then, between
the slave trade and slavery. It seems to have been taken for
granted that the prohibition of the former would involve,
virtually, the extinction of the latter. Georgia had desired a
respite of twenty years, which, by the Constitution, had been
granted. Thus far the hands of Congress were tied. Thus,
at least, it was understood by the speakers. *This was the compromise claimed.* This exposition of the position of the speakers, if it be correct, enables us to understand the drift of their
arguments. What then do we find?

First, we have the presentation of petitions, some of them
said to be in respect to the slave *trade*, others of them (including that of Dr. Franklin) as evidently bearing upon "SLA-
VERY" itself, desiring for the slaves their "*restoration* to
liberty," and that Congress would "*devise means*," in some
way, for "removing this inconsistency from the *American*

character." The two descriptions of petitions appear to have had the same object, and to have been received and considered accordingly.

Next, we have two gentlemen from Virginia decidedly " espousing the cause " of the petitioners, followed up by a representative of Pennsylvania, on the same side.

Then, we have a specimen of the opposition, from South Carolina and Georgia; and finally, an effort, by Mr. Madison, to reconcile the difference between the parties, though strongly leaning to the side of the petitioners, and declaring that *he represented*, for his constituents, those sentiments.

The main object of the slave party, seems to have been to stave off present action. The House, and the Country, they saw and acknowledged, were disposed to be against them— disposed to *liberate* "*the slaves.*" They pleaded the constitutional compromise, that is, the postponement till 1808. Yet they raised the question of *compensation*, as much as to intimate that if the country was ready to meet their demands in this respect, they might waive their constitutional objections. And this was then the extent of South Carolinian and Georgian opposition! "*Humanity and benevolence,*" they admitted, was on the side of the petitioners, and of those who might " vote for a general emancipation." Not a word of the dangers of turning the slaves loose. Not a single threat of dissolving the Union. Not a lisp of the sacred guaranties of the Constitution, of the obligation to protect and extend slavery !

From the advocates of liberty, in the House, then, we hear no concessions of the compromises of the Constitution. Those, they left in the hands of their opponents, and in the hands of the illustrious pacificator between the two parties. And even his (Mr. Madison's) speech, would be accounted a radical abolition harangue, were it uttered in Congress now. It is instructive to ponder these contrasts. We need to be disabused of our vague impressions and educational prejudices, if we would understand the relation of slavery to our political institutions, as at first established.

Little incidents, often, more than imposing official documents, and public records, reveal public character, and assist us to understand the spirit and temper of a particular age or people. " In 1791, the university of William and Mary, in Virginia, conferred upon Granville Sharp, of England, the Degree of *Doctor of Laws*."* Who was Granville Sharp? And by what discoveries in the sublime science of jurisprudence had Granville Sharp, a clerk in the ordinance department of Great Britain, commended himself to a Virginian University, for so distinguishing an honor? The reader of the preceding chapters understands. Granville Sharp had discovered and announced the utter and absolute *illegality of slavery* under the ægis of the British Constitution, and under the jurisdiction of English Common Law. With this discovery he had enlightened the British mind, had reversed the legal decisions and opinions of York and Talbot—of Blackstone and Mansfield. Without a seat in the Court of King's Bench, nay, without the credentials that could entitle him, by the usages of Court, to stand up in its presence and plead a cause, Granville Sharp, by the simple force of his lofty intellect and indomitable and righteous purpose, had laid his hand on that Court of King's Bench, and compelled it to do (unwillingly enough) his bidding, in the decree that " slaves cannot breathe in England." More than this—Granville Sharp, perceiving that this decree was binding on the colonies of Britain, as well as on the mother country, had solemnly admonished the British prime minister of his high responsibilities in this respect, and with all the majesty of a holy prophet had charged him, on the peril of his soul, to lose no time in suppressing slavery in America. This was the high merit of Granville Sharp. For this, he wore, meekly, the clustering homage of the wise and good, of two hemispheres. The University of William and Mary, in Virginia, eagerly honored herself by honoring Granville Sharp. What a change has since taken place! Had Granville Sharp lived to visit the Univer-

---

* *Power of Congress*, &c., p. 86.

sity of William and Mary, in 1835, his temerity would probably have cost him his life. He would have subjected
himself to the liability of being ignominiously and uncere-
moniously hanged up, without judge or jury, or condemned
to death under the laws of the State.* Were the public sentiment of Virginia, and of the whole country, now, what they
were in 1791, those English philanthropists who are now denounced as impertinent intermeddlers, would be fair candidates for the highest honors of the University of William and
Mary, in Virginia.

Can it be credible that a change of sentiment like this can
have come over Virginia, and over the nation, without bringing along with it new maxims of state policy, new principles
of jurisprudence, new views of the relation of slavery to our
Constitution and laws?—and with these—of necessity—new
usages of Constitutional exposition,—new conceptions of the
relations described by it, and of the obligations and rights
growing out of those relations? May it be assumed, without
scrutiny, that the usages and expositions with which we, in
this age, have become familiarized, are trustworthy?

---

* No exaggeration in this. The very *writings* of Granville Sharp could not have
been safely circulated in Virginia in 1835, if indeed they can be at present. On
charge of having circulated anti-slavery writings, Dr. Reuben Crandall was arrested
and tried for his life, in the District of Columbia, and on prosecution of the late
Francis S. Key, Esq., one of the most popular citizens of the District. The "incendiary publications," for the publishing of which the late R. G. Williams, of New
York, was indicted, and demanded to be given up to the authorities of Alabama,
by the Executive of that State, included the writings of Granville Sharp, and
nothing beside them that could have been more offensive than they must have
been. Nothing more strongly condemnatory of slavery and of slaveholders could
have been found in the papers pillaged from the U.S. mail at Charleston, and burnt.
By the laws of Virginia, the publishing or circulating of publications having *a tendency* to excite slaves or free people of color to insurrection or resistance, is punished
with thirty-nine lashes ; *the second with death.*" Amos Dresser, though without the
forms of a legal trial, suffered a public whipping in Tennessee. Whatever may have
appeared on the antiquated statute books of Virginia, in 1791, the simple incident
we have recorded affords evidence of the change of public sentiment we have described—a change the more marked, in proportion as the sentiment of 1791 was in
opposition to her own statutes.

ECCLESIASTICAL BODIES—METHODISTS.

The position and language of ecclesiastical bodies at that era, furnish another significant feature of our history.

In the year 1780, the sentiments of the Methodist societies in this country were thus expressed in the minutes of the Conference for that year:

"The Conference acknowledges that slavery is contrary to the laws of God, man,* and nature, hurtful to society; contrary to the dictates of conscience and pure religion, and doing what we would not that others should do unto us, and they pass their disapprobation upon all our friends who keep slaves, and they advise their freedom."—*A. S. Manual, by Sunderland,* p. 58.

In 1785, the following language was held by the M. E. Church:

"We do hold in the deepest abhorrence the practice of slavery, and shall not cease to seek its destruction, by all wise and prudent means."

The following is extracted from Sunderland's Anti-Slavery Manual, published in 1837:

From Lee's History of the Methodists, p. 101, we learn that the M. E. Church was organized with a number of express rules on the subject which stipulated THAT SLAVERY SHOULD NOT BE CONTINUED IN THE CHURCH. One of them was as follows:

"Every member in our Society shall legally execute and record an instrument [for the purpose of setting every slave in his possession free] within the space of two years."

Another was as follows:

"Every person concerned who will not comply with these rules, shall have liberty quietly to withdraw from our Society within twelve months following the notice being given him as aforesaid:—otherwise, the assistant shall exclude him from the Society."

Another rule declared that

"Those who bought or sold slaves, or gave them away, unless on purpose to free them, should be expelled immediately."

---

* "Contrary to the laws of *man*." Here we find another admission of the illegality of slavery, corresponding with the doctrines of Granville Sharp, the decision of Lord Mansfield in the Somerset case, the expressions of Dr. Hopkins, the declaration of James Madison, and the speech in Congress of Mr. Scott, of Pennsylvania. Were all these ignorant enthusiasts? Or has slavery become legalized since?

" And forty years ago" (*i. e.* in 1797), the discipline of this church contained the following directions on the subject :

" The preachers and other members of our Society are requested to consider the subject of negro slavery, with deep attention, and that they *impart to the General Conference*, through the medium of the Yearly Conferences, or otherwise, any important thoughts on the subject, that the Conference may have FULL LIGHT, in order to take further steps towards eradicating this enormous evil from that part of the Church of God with which they are connected. The Annual Conferences are *directed* to draw up addresses for the gradual emancipation of the slaves, to the legislatures of those States in which no general laws have been passed for that purpose. These addresses shall *urge*, in the most respectful but pointed manner, the necessity of a law for the gradual emancipation of slaves. Proper committees shall be appointed by the Annual Conferences, out of the most respectable of our friends, for conducting the business ; and presiding elders, elders, deacons, and travelling preachers, *shall* procure as many proper signatures as possible to the addresses, and give all the assistance in their power, IN EVERY RESPECT, to aid the committees, and to forward the blessed undertaking. Let this be continued from year to year, till the desired end be accomplished."—*A. S. Manual*, pp. 58–9.

These directions were not a dead letter. Persons still living can remember the circulating of anti-slavery petitions, and the distributing of Wesley's Tract on Slavery, by the Methodist travelling preachers, as a part of their official business. So late as the year 1803, the Hymn Books of the M. E. Church, published by Ezekiel Cooper for the M. E. Book Concern, at Philadelphia, contained advertisements of the " Tract on Slavery." Here then was the entire Methodist Episcopal connection organized into a society for anti-slavery agitation, its Annual Conferences inviting *free discussion* and seeking for *more light*, its preachers and church officers circulating anti-slavery publications and petitions to legislative bodies. The contrast with later times we cannot stop here to present.

PRESBYTERIANS.

The General Assembly of the Presbyterian Church adopted, in 1794, a note to the one hundred and forty-second question in the larger Catechism, in the Confession of Faith, in the words following:

"1 Tim. 1 : 10. 'The law is made for MAN-STEALERS.' This crime, among the Jews, exposed the perpetrators of it to capital punishment, Exodus 21 : 16, and the apostle here classes them with sinners of the first rank. The word he uses, in its original import, comprehends all who are concerned in bringing any of the human race into slavery, or *retaining them in it. Hominum fures, qui servos, vel libros abducunt, retinent vendunt, vel emunt.* Stealers of men are those who bring off slaves or freemen, and KEEP, SELL, or BUY THEM. To steal a freeman, says Grotius, is the highest kind of theft. In other instances we only steal human property, but when we steal *or retain* men in slavery, we seize those who, in common with ourselves, are constituted by the original grant, lords of the earth. Gen. 1 : 28. *Vide Poli Synopsin in loc.*"

BAPTISTS.

"At a meeting of the General Committee of the Baptists of Virginia, in 1788, the following point came up.—*Semple's Hist. of Baptists in Virginia.*

"Whether a petition should be offered to the General Assembly, praying that the yoke of slavery may be made more tolerable. Referred to the next session."

"1789. At this session the propriety of hereditary slavery was also taken up, and after some time employed in the consideration of the subject, the following resolution was offered by Eld. John Leland, and adopted :

"*Resolved,* That slavery is a violent deprivation of the rights of nature, and inconsistent with republican government, and therefore (we) recommend it to our brethren to make use of every measure to extirpate this horrid evil from the land ; and pray Almighty God that our honorable legislature may have it in their power to proclaim the great jubilee, consistent with the principles of good policy."—"*Facts for Baptist Churches,*" p. 365.

Action in Vermont.—The minutes of the Shaftsbury Association, in 1792, contain an expression against the slave trade, and in favor of universal liberty.—*Ib.*

"According to Benedict (History of the Baptists, first edition), there was, in 1805, an Association of Baptists in Northern Kentucky, who separated themselves from slaveholding Baptists," &c. "Eld. David Barrow, once a Virginia slaveholder, became, after emancipating his slaves, one of their principal men. He wrote a pamphlet on slavery, entitled 'Involuntary, unmerited, perpetual, absolute, hereditary slavery, examined on the principles of nature, reason, justice, policy, and Scripture.'—Other prominent advocates of these principles were, Elders Dodge, Carman, Sutton, Holmes, Tarrant, Grigg, and Smith."—*Ib.* p. 366.

LEGISLATIVE AND JUDICIAL ACTION.

Legislative and judicial action against slavery in several of the States, was the natural result of the moral and religious influences described in this and the preceding chapters, and on the whole the effects may be considered commensurate with the causes operating for the production of them. If it be said that the gradual and prospective emancipation provided for by the legislatures of several States did not correspond with the doctrines of the inherent sinfulness of slavery and of the duty of immediate and unconditional abolition, insisted on by Hopkins and Edwards, and exemplified by some of the Congregational churches, it must be remembered that these testimonies were not fully received and adopted by some of the eminent statesmen at the head of the anti-slavery societies by whom these writings had been circulated. Ideas of supposed necessity, expediency, or convenience, were permitted to modify and control the direct and full application of principles admitted to be true and right in the abstract. Those testimonies, moreover, had been counteracted and neutralized by the gradual and tardy action, with few exceptions, of ecclesiastical bodies, including even the Society of Friends. It was hardly to be expected that the work of purification in the State would be more speedy and thorough than in the Church.

A paragraph from an Appendix, by Dr. Hopkins, to the second edition of his Dialogue on Slavery, printed at New York, under sanction of the Manumission Society, in 1785, embraces, in a few words, an account of the progress that had been made since the publication of the first edition, early in 1776.

" Since the publication of this Dialogue, many things have been done and steps taken towards a reformation of this evil. In the States of Massachusetts and New Hampshire the slavery of the blacks is wholly abolished. And it is one of the fundamental articles in the Constitution of the proposed State of Vermont, that no slavery shall be tolerated there. The States of Rhode Island, Connecticut, Pennsylvania, and the lower counties of the

Delaware, have provided for the gradual abolition of slavery, and have ordered that all the blacks who shall be hereafter born in these States, shall be free at a certain age, and that no more slaves shall be introduced among them. And the State of Virginia has repealed a law, which was formerly in force there, against the freeing of the blacks, and now allows the masters of slaves to free them when they please. Thus, ALL THE STATES BUT FIVE,* have manifested a disposition to promote the freedom of the Africans.† And numbers of slaves have been liberated by their masters, under a conviction of the unrighteousness of holding them in slavery. This is a great advance in the desired reformation, and has given ground to hope that slavery will be *wholly abolished* in all the United States of America."

To this it might have been added, that "in the Convention that formed the Constitution of Kentucky, in 1780, the effort to prohibit slavery was nearly successful." "But for the great influence of two large slaveholders—Messrs. Breckinridge and Nicholson"—the measure, it is believed, would have been carried.—" *Power of Congress,*" &c. p. 34.

Virginia, in 1786, enacted that every slave imported into the Commonwealth should be free.

It is to be lamented that Virginia should have since re-enacted her laws against emancipation, and in many ways sought to strengthen the slave system. In Delaware, too, there must have been some retrograde steps, though the number of slaves has greatly diminished since 1785.

In 1777, the people of Vermont met in Convention and proclaimed Vermont an independent State. The first article of their bill of rights excluded slavery. Though not admitted into the Confederacy (owing to some claims of New York) till 1789, Vermont has the honor of having first provided for the abolition of slavery. Seventeen slaves are indeed set

---

* The statement should have been *six,* viz. New York, Maryland, New Jersey, the two Carolinas, and Georgia. Vermont, a new State, having been reckoned, there were fourteen States then in the Union, instead of the original thirteen, in the mind of the writer.

† Virginia and Delaware, it seems, were *then* counted upon as being on the side of freedom, while New York and New Jersey were reckoned on the other side. Another fact to be adjusted to the current theory of constitutional guaranties, which would present to us New York and New Jersey refusing to come into the Union, unless Virginia and Delaware would enter into the "compact" to hunt fugitive slaves, &c.!

down to Vermont in the census of 1790. The revised Constitution of 1793 retains the prohibition of slavery.

" In Massachusetts, it was judicially declared, soon after the Revolution, that slavery was virtually abolished *by the Constitution*, and that the issue of a female slave, though born *prior* to the Constitution, was born free."— *Kent's Commentary*, p. 252.

" In Massachusetts, all the negroes in the Commonwealth were, *by their new Constitution*, liberated in a day, and none of the ill consequences objected, followed, either to the Commonwealth or to individuals."—*Appendix, by Dr. Edwards, to his Sermon against Slavery*, Sept. 15, 1791.

In giving the opinion of the Court in the case of the Commonwealth *versus* Thomas Aves, in 1833, Chief Justice Shaw said :—

" How, or by what act particularly, slavery was abolished in Massachusetts, whether by the adoption of the opinion in *Somerset's case*, as a declaration and modification of the *Common Law*, or by the *Declaration of Independence*, or by the [State] *Constitution of* 1780, it is not now very easy to determine, and it is a matter rather of curiosity than utility, *it being agreed on all hands* that, if not abolished before, it was so by the declaration of rights." * * * " Without pursuing this inquiry further, it is sufficient for the purpose of the case before us, that by the *Constitution* adopted in 1780, slavery was abolished in Massachusetts, *upon the ground* that it is contrary to natural right and the plain principles of justice. The terms of the first article of the Declaration of Rights are clear and explicit. ' All men are born free and equal, and have certain natural, essential, and inalienable rights, which are the right of enjoying and defending their lives and liberties, that of acquiring, possessing, and protecting property.'—It would be difficult to select words more precisely adapted to the abolition of slavery."—*Pickering's Reports*, pp. 209–10.

The suggestion of Chief Justice Shaw, that slavery *may have been* abolished in Massachusetts by the National Declaration of Independence, may be startling to some readers, but the similarity, not to say identity of that declaration with the article in the Massachusetts Constitution, and the coincidence of both with the well known powers of the Common Law, as applied and exemplified "in Somerset's case," may induce the inquiry whether or how either one of the three " acts " specified by Judge Shaw could have had power to abolish slavery, unless *either of the others* possessed likewise the *same* power?

The answer to this query seems suggested by the intimation of Judge Shaw, that "it is matter rather of curiosity than utility" to fix upon a selection of the implements or "acts" of freedom.*

The first Federal Census, 1790, contains no enumeration of slaves in Massachusetts.

In Pennsylvania a law was passed the first of March, 1780, declaring all persons born in the State after that day, to be free at the age of twenty-eight years. Penalty seventy-five pounds for carrying a slave beyond the limits of the State.†

The first section of this act, of the nature of a preamble, recapitulates the condition into which the colonies were expected to be reduced by the tyranny of Great Britain, the grateful sense due for so great a providential deliverance, and the corresponding obligation and privilege of extending the blessings of freedom to others. The second section brings directly into view the condition of the negro slaves, and the demands of justice on their behalf, and then proceeds to the enactment above described.

There were those, it would seem, who were not satisfied

---

* Since writing the above, the following item reaches us through a new work of Mr. Spooner—"A Defence for Fugitive Slaves." We deem it altogether too important to be omitted here:

"As early as 1770, and two years previous to the decision of Somerset's case, so famous in England, the right of a master to hold a slave had been denied by the Superior Court of Massachusetts, *and upon the same grounds, substantially, as those upon which Lord Mansfield discharged Somerset, when his case came before him.* The case here alluded to was James *vs.* Lechmere, brought by the plaintiff, a negro, against his master, to recover his freedom."—*Washburn's Judicial History of Massachusetts*, p. 202.

That slaves should have been held in Massachusetts *after* this decision, that a *new* judicial decision should have been needed after the Revolution, and that Chief Justice Shaw, in 1833, should have been at a loss to fix, with precision, the earliest date and the grounds of the previous decisions, are very remarkable circumstances, all tending to illustrate the facility with which the *practice* of slaveholding has been continued, *contrary to law*, and the inattention of learned jurists to the *facts* as well as the *law*, on the subject.

The case mentioned by Washburn confirms very strongly the impression that slavery was as illegal in the *Colonies*, before the Revolution, as it is known and admitted to have been in *England*.

† Genius of Temperance, Sept. 19, 1833, copied from *Emancipator*.

with this partial and tardy justice. " Petitions in favor of the oppressed Africans " were again presented to the Legislature in 1798, and a committee made a favorable report, March 8. They intimated that if the Bill of Rights, the Declaration of Independence, and the paternal character and overruling providence of a common Creator, were to be recognized, "the petitioners but speak the divine will, in requesting that this evil be *done away from the land*."*

Of the specific points of this petition, and of the legislative action had on it, we are not informed. The United States census for Pennsylvania, in 1790, exhibits 3,737 slaves, and in 1840, *sixty-four*.

It deserves notice that the efforts of that period had reference to the removal of slavery "from the land," and not merely from particular portions of it.

In New Hampshire, slavery was said to have been abolished, by constitutional declarations of rights, similar to those of Massachusetts, adopted in 1783, and taking effect in June, 1784. And yet, singularly enough, the census of 1790 shows 158 slaves in New Hampshire, and even that of 1840 gives *one !* By what tenure, and under what circumstances or pretexts slaves are held in New Hampshire, we are not informed. State Constitutions, it seems, as well as National Declarations, may be violated in practice, but the *legality* of such practices presents another question—the same that was agitated by Granville Sharp in Great Britain.

Rhode Island, the very seat of the African Slave Trade, was the seat also of early efforts in favor of freedom. The exact date, or the precise form of the earliest legislative movements are not before us, but a note of Dr. Hopkins to his Dialogue, in 1776, mentions a *proposed* act, prohibiting the importation of negroes into this colony, and asserting the rights of freedom of all those hereafter born or manumitted within the same." He gives the preamble to this proposed act in the following words :

---

* Statutes of Pennsylvania, *vide National Era*, Aug. 22, 1850.

"Whereas, the inhabitants of America are generally engaged in the preservation of their own rights and liberties, among which those of personal freedom must be considered as the greatest; and, as those who are desirous of enjoying all the advantages of liberty themselves should be willing to extend personal liberty to others, therefore, be it enacted," &c.

"Is it possible," exclaims Hopkins, "that any one should not feel the irresistible force of this reason?" In a note to the second edition, in 1785, he adds:

"Since the above was published, the General Assembly of that State have made a law, that all the blacks born in it after March, 1784, are made free. And the masters who have slaves under forty years old, are authorized to free them, without being bound to support them if afterwards they should be unable to support themselves."

The census of 1790 reports 952 slaves in Rhode Island, and in 1840, FIVE.

In Connecticut, a law providing for the gradual abolition of slavery was enacted in 1784. In 1790, the number of slaves in that State was 2,759; in 1840, there were only SEVENTEEN.

In New York, "in 1799, an act of gradual emancipation was passed, declaring all children born thereafter to be free, males when coming to the age of twenty-eight, and females at twenty-five. A fine of two hundred and fifty dollars was the penalty, and the freedom of the slave was the result of an attempt to sell him out of the State. Although masters were allowed to travel with their slaves, yet under severe fines they were obliged to return them; or, under oath, to make proof that unavoidable accident prevented the returning.

"In 1817 another act was passed, declaring all slaves to be free in 1827, and on July 4th of that year the act took effect, and every slave, nearly ten thousand, was manumitted *without compensation to their owners.*"*

And yet, from some cause, the census for 1840 reports four slaves in the State of New York. In 1790 there were 21,324, being nearly three-fourths as many as there were in Georgia

---

* H. W. Beecher, *New York Tribune*, June 1, 1850.

at that time, nearly twice as many as there were then in Kentucky, and more than six times as many as there were in Tennessee! The proportion, when the Federal Constitution was adopted a year or two previous, could not have greatly varied, throwing New York, at that time, and for several years afterwards, somewhat conspicuously, into the ranks of the Slave States. Even down to 1800 there were 20,343 slaves, the number having decreased but 881 in ten years.

New Jersey took measures, in 1804, for the prospective abolition of slavery, but the process must have been a tardy one. In 1790 the number of slaves was 11,423. In 1840, it was 674.

In 1820 an act was passed emancipating all slaves born after 1805 at the age of twenty-five years, and imposing a fine of one hundred dollars and imprisonment for transporting slaves beyond the limits of the State, except slaves of full age who freely consented to go, before a judge of one of the courts in private.—*Statutes of New Jersey, Congress Library. National Era, August* 22, 1850.

In April, 1846, a law was passed and approved, ostensibly abolishing slavery, and declaring that every person then held in slavery was *free*, subject, however, to certain restrictions, which retain the same persons under the control of their masters, *for an indefinite period, as apprentices.* They are to "serve *until discharged*," and the master is *permitted* "to discharge them by a writing executed in the presence of at least one witness, *provided* the apprentice be of sound mind, and capable of procuring a livelihood, and upon certificate of the overseers of the poor and two justices of the peace, to such capacity," &c., &c. Such is the definition of freedom, and of the abolition of slavery, in New Jersey!—*MSS. by Gov. Haines.*

The census of 1840 records 3 slaves in Ohio, 3 in Indiana, 331 in Illinois, 11 in Wisconsin, and 16 in Iowa. The only States, at that time, *without slaves*, were Massachusetts, Maine, Vermont, and Michigan. A short list of really *non*-slaveholding States!

In the States now commonly denominated non-slaveholding,

there were, in 1776, by computation, 46,099 slaves. In 1790 there were, by census, 40,370. In 1840, there were 1,129.

This decrease, though chiefly the effect of legislative and judical action, was not wholly so. By voluntary manumissions, the slave population must have been very essentially diminished. Particularly must this have been the case in Rhode Island, where the dimunition between 1776 and 1790, an interval of only fourteen years, was from 4,370 to 932, since the law of 1784 liberating only those who were born after that time, could have operated only to a very limited extent, in checking the increase of slave population. In Pennsylvania, too, where legislation had only liberated those born after 1780, we find the decrease of slaves between the years 1776 and 1790, to have been from 10,000 to 3,737. Church action, rather than legislative or judicial, is to be credited with these manumissions in Pennsylvania and Rhode Island.

It is somewhat remarkable that South Carolina, between 1776 and 1790, exhibits a decrease of slave population, from 110,000 to 107,094, while the slaves of New York, in the same time, increased from 15,000 to 21,324. But the number of slaves in S. Carolina had increased, in 1840, to 327,038.

The increase of slavery in the Southern States, presents a striking contrast to the decrease in the Northern and Eastern States. In 1776 the number of slaves in these is computed at 456,000. In 1790, by census, it was, 567,527. In 1840, it was 2,486,126, including the District of Columbia.

Thus, while in one part of the country, the slave population increased from less than half a million to nearly two and a half millions, in another part of the country it was diminished from above 46,000 to a little more than 1,100.

This diminution, whether in the form of voluntary manumissions, or in consequence of legislative or judicial action, may be traced, almost entirely, to the moral, religious and political influences, exhibited in this and the preceding chapters. But for these, the eastern, middle, and north-western

States—in despite of all that has been said of soil and climate —would probably have been overspread with the foul stain and the blighting curse of slaveholding. It was the prevailing moral sentiment of the North that led to the abolition of slavery there. This is manifest from the fact that the emancipated slaves and their children, are for the most part, still to be found at the North. They were not, in anticipation of emancipation acts, exported to other States, to any observable extent.

When, in 1827, ten thousand slaves were, in one day, set free, in the State of New York, they remained on the soil, and it is not known that a single slave had been sold into another State, in anticipation of that long expected event. Transportation has never been made, in these States, a condition of freedom; nor, until after the organization of the Colonization Society, was their removal sought as an advantage to the communities in which they resided.

CHAPTER XI.

DECLINE OF THE SPIRIT OF LIBERTY, AND GROWTH OF SLAVERY, SINCE THE REVOLUTION—THEIR CAUSES AND EARLY MANIFESTATIONS.

Importance of tracing disastrous social changes to their moral causes—Promises made in adversity forgotten in prosperity—View of Dr. Hopkins—A humiliating fact—Partial revival of the Slave Trade—Fallacy of expecting to abolish the traffic during the existence of Slavery—The strategy of postponement—General decline of Religion and Morals—Disbanding of the Army—Habits of idleness, and tendency to Piracy and Slave Trade—Relaxation of vigilance—Decline of public spirit—Vicissitudes of poverty and returning wealth—Concentration and control of capital—Anti-Democratic Conservatism, and semi-infidel French Democracy—The two rival parties—Misunderstood "horrors of St. Domingo"—Unforeseen profitableness of cotton-growing—Unequal apportionment of representation—Declining standard of morals in the Church—Rivalry of the Sects—Growing prejudice against color—Influence of the Colonization project—Fatal fostering of this prejudice—corroborated by estimate of Henry Clay.

THE study of history is like a journey, or an exploring tour, in the course of which, cheering prospects are sometimes unexpectedly succeeded by scenes less promising, but necessary to be traversed, or the proposed end is not reached. If we would faithfully explore a country, we must not confine our attention to the pleasant portions of it. If we would improve it, we must acquaint ourselves with the unseemly features and untoward influences to be removed or remedied. If fields once fertile are becoming sterile, we must learn under what modes of tillage they have become so. If the buildings just erected and yet unfinished, are beginning to crumble, we must inquire after the nature of the materials, and the process of the structure.

The marked decline of the spirit of liberty in this country for half a century after the Revolution, is a fact too palpable to escape notice. Between the historical details of the last three chapters, and those that must appear in the following, there will be found, we fear, a chasm too wide and abrupt to comport with the ordinary vicissitudes of credible history. To the reader, of another country, or a future age, we shall appear to have been writing fiction, and even the verity of the public documents cited, will scarcely escape suspicion. But "truth is stranger than fiction." The details to be presented will appear credible enough when we shall have become conversant with the moral causes at work beforehand, adapted to the production of them. To the reader who never stops to inquire after moral causes, or who reads on, without keeping them steadily in mind, the perusal of history can be of little value. It can supply him with no guide to the future, no element of congruity for the past. Such causes constitute, in reality, the most essential ingredient of true history. They are facts, at wholesale, fountains of facts, from whence all minor facts flow. We make no digression, then, in stating them. We cannot promise a complete enumeration of all these causes. We may not be able, always, to distinguish causes from effects, nor to designate the precise point, in the history, where the defection began, nor decide positively what portion of the body politic was first corrupted, or first became corrupting. But we can note down a few general facts.

1. We shall first venture to suggest, that the regard for human liberty, and the opposition to the slave trade and slavery, that were manifested during the revolutionary period, may have failed to prove permanent and abiding, because, in respect to great numbers of the people, including some prominent citizens, those sentiments were not as deep seated and as disinterested as they should have been, and therefore a change in the aspect of public affairs would naturally bring with it a change in the manifestation of such sentiments. To suppose otherwise would be to suppose an unprecedented purity of purpose, of which no other nation has yet furnished a parallel. This suggestion does not discredit the fact of an actual declension. It only indicates one of the causes of it. Without any

previous tendency to declension, other causes would have had little power.

It is easy to see, that, in many ways, the revolutionary period presented peculiar inducements to the abolition of the slave trade and slavery. To fight for their own liberties while enslaving others, was an incongruity too glaring to consist with national reputation, or with intelligent self-respect. Like all other men, in times of pressing danger and sore calamity, our fathers might make solemn promises of amendment, which would be liable to be forgotten and disregarded, on the return of security and peace. The fear of an insurrection of the slaves, or of their desertion to the enemy, in time of war, might present an argument in favor of their emancipation, that would influence many minds, until the danger had passed away. Such, indeed, was the fact. A note of Dr. Hopkins to his Dialogue, in 1776, will place this fact in a clear and impressive light.

" God is so ordering it, in his providence, that it seems absolutely necessary that something should speedily be done in respect to the slaves among us, in order to our safety, and to prevent their turning against us, in our present struggle, in order to get their liberty. Our oppressors have planned to gain the blacks, and induce them to take up arms against us, by promising them liberty on this condition ; and this plan they are prosecuting to the utmost of their power, by which means they have persuaded numbers to join them. And should we attempt to restrain them by force and severity, keeping a strict guard over them, and punishing those severely who shall be detected in attempting to join our opposers, this will be only making bad worse, and serve to render our inconsistency and cruelty more criminal, perspicuous, and shocking, and bring down the righteous vengeance of heaven on our heads. The only way pointed out to prevent this threatening evil, is to set the blacks at liberty ourselves, by some public act and laws, and then give them encouragement to labor, or take up arms in defence of the American cause, as they shall choose. This would, at once, be doing them some degree of justice, and defeating our enemies in the scheme they are prosecuting."

This wise and righteous counsel was not followed, but it is impossible to tell how extensively the slaves were kept quiet, by the public testimonies made in favor of their freedom, and by the hopes thus inspired.

In his Dialogue, Dr. Hopkins had insisted so strongly on the tokens of divine displeasure hanging over the nation, on account of this crying sin, that on the re-publication of the work, after the return of peace, he thought it necessary, in an Appendix, to notice the objection, that if slavery were so great a national sin, as had been represented, Divine Providence would not have favored the cause of America; and therefore, the representations that had been made of the danger of defeat, in consequence of this wickedness and inconsistency, had been unfounded and rash. One answer of Dr. Hopkins to this objection, was, that "since the publication of this dialogue, many things have been done and steps taken, towards a reformation of this evil"—proceeding to enumerate, (as we have before quoted,) the States that had either abolished slavery or taken measures in that direction. He adds, that if these hopeful beginnings, commenced in times of affliction, were not followed up and completed in prosperity, we may expect divine judgments, still. And here, he quotes as applicable to this country, in such a case, that remarkable passage in the prophecy of Jeremiah, Chapter 35, where it is recorded that the king and princes of Judah, in a time of siege and distress entered into a solemn "resolution and covenant to free all their slaves"—but "when their fears and distress were removed, they returned to their former practice," —for which God commissioned Jeremiah to tell them that since they had "refused liberty to their brethren, he would proclaim a liberty for them, even a most dreadful liberty to the sword, to the pestilence, and to the famine, and cause them to be removed into all the kingdoms of the earth," &c.

The contrast between Hopkins and some of his successors, in the same religious denomination in New England, who have recently applauded the efforts of our most recreant politicians to draw, still closer, the fetters of the enslaved, and to punish those who shelter the outcasts, is too palpable and glaring to escape observation: and the question forces itself upon our attention, notwithstanding their technical agreement in creeds and forms, whether teachers so opposite in their practical expositions, should be regarded as teaching, in reality, the same religion, and serving the same Master.

It is in the same connection, in that Appendix, that Dr. Hopkins notices the pecuniary troubles and distresses that still, at that time, (1785) embarrassed the country, and threatened its ruin, in evidence that the danger of divine judgments had not yet disappeared. And as a reason for fearing yet greater judgments, he proceeds to mention, what belongs to this portion of our history, as an important, but painfully humiliating fact. Though the General Congress and the Colonies or States had solemnly covenanted to discontinue the slave traffic, and had interdicted it, yet, by prominent and wealthy individuals, it was now beginning, on the return of peace, to be revived, and was not effectually suppressed by the authorities. We will state this in the words of that celebrated author.

"We are again going into the practice of that seven-fold abomination, the slave trade, against which, in the beginning of the war, we bore public testimony, and entered into a united and solemn resolution wholly to renounce it, and all connection with those who should persist in this evil practice. A number of vessels have been sent from some of the States in New England, and other States, to Africa, to procure slaves, and they are in such demand in the West Indies, and in some of the Southern States, and especially South Carolina, that several successful voyages have been made, thousands of slaves brought into these United States, and sold at extraordinary prices, by which others are tempted and encouraged to go into this trade, and there is a prospect that it will take place to as great a degree as it has heretofore, unless it should be suppressed by those in public authority, or by the people at large."

The precise extent to which this infamous traffic was resumed, cannot now be ascertained. But there is reason to think it was quite limited, until (as before stated) it was allowed by South Carolina, in 1803.

2. The experiment of putting a stop to the slave trade during the existence of slavery—and the policy of attempting to abolish either the one or the other, or both of them, by the mere force of moral suasion, without corresponding and adequate political action, was fully tried by the philanthropists and patriots of the revolutionary period, and with a result

that should prove a caution to all their successors who may be engaged in the cause of human freedom. To maintain penal laws against any other forms of crime, and permit this crime of crimes to go "unwhipt of justice," is a solecism in legislation, in jurisprudence, and in civil polity, without a parallel for inconsistency and folly. This capital error we put down as one of the leading causes or outstanding signs of the lamentable defection of this nation from the principles of civil government they had marked out for themselves, in their declaration of human rights, and their definition of the objects and characteristics of a legitimate and just civil government.

3. "The ruse of gradualism"—the strategy of delay—the contamination of temporary compromise, was another kindred error, (if it may be called another) and the same with which the friends of liberty have been frequently beset, and sometimes foiled, in their more recent as well as more early endeavors.

4. The general decline of pure religion and sound morality, after the close of the revolutionary struggle, another fact commonly noticed by the better portion of the community at that period, was almost certain to include in it a decline of the spirit of liberty, of a tender regard for human rights, and of sensibility to the flagrant iniquities of the slave trade and slavery.

Though the war of the Revolution contributed, in many respects, and with the better portion of society, to foster the spirit of freedom; yet, like other wars, it had its demoralizing tendencies, and the disbanding of the army was the occasion for the development of them. Not a few of the soldiers, and some of the officers, had contracted a distaste for the habits of sober and patient industry, in which they had, in earlier life, been educated; and, to a frightful extent, the spirit of lawlessness and licentiousness had been mistaken for the spirit of freedom. The spirit of gambling adventure, amid the pecuniary fluctuations of that period, and the depreciation of the continental paper currency, contributed its share to pro-

duce the recklessness, unscrupulousness, and hap-hazard adventure for which a considerable portion of that generation
were distinguished. The anti-slavery writings of a Hopkins
and an Edwards can hardly be supposed to have had much
effect upon this class of society, who had learned to cast off
their respect for moral and religious instructions and restraints
in general. The rapid inroads of intemperance, profanity,
and irreligion, were among the marked features of that period,
even in New England, as we learn from the testimonies of
such writers as Emmons. The class of the community just
alluded to, were ripe for any unlawful enterprise rather than
for patient, quiet rural labor. The slave trade, as well as
other forms of piracy, was not lacking for men of this class
to man its vessels, and even to take charge of them, as super-
cargoes and captains. And in how many ways the characteristics of such an age would tend to strengthen and perpetuate
slavery, we need not stop to describe.

5. A general decline of the spirit of liberty succeeded to
the exhausting struggles of the Revolution, almost by a law of
the human mind, if we may adventure to say so, a process in
human affairs very difficult to be counteracted, except by the
most resolute and disinterested exertions. The *one idea* of
national independence, which had come to stand as the syno-
nym of the idea of freedom, had so long held the mind of the
nation in an agony of attention and suspense, that when the
struggle was over, and the national independence acknowledged, it was taken for granted that the liberties of the nation
were secured. Even with the most philosophical and philanthropic, a vague, indefinite, and ill-conceived impression of
the " *spirit of the age* " as it is called, that was to carry everybody onward and upward to the dignity of freemen, without
the exhausting cares, anxieties, and solicitudes of those who
had almost worn themselves out in the long struggle, had
operated as a welcome furlough, or discharge from service.
When the army and the commander-in-chief were permitted
to retire from the public defence, why should not they ? The
human mind, so long and so intensely kept on the stretch,

sought repose, and, unhappily, in this case, before the giant despotism of the age had been vanquished. Even the strong-minded and the keen-sighted failed to perceive this! How much more the masses of the people, whose vigilance and combined efforts were then needed? Withdrawing their attention too much from public affairs, they expended their strength on their own personal and domestic concerns, that now needed unusual care, after a season of comparative neglect. A people impoverished by a seven years' war, were now to replenish their exhausted stores, and pay off their public and private debts, at a time when the proportion of producers had been diminished, first by the demands of the war, and next, by the flood of idlers, or worse than idlers, which had come with the return of peace. How easily would most men excuse themselves from anti-slavery agitation at such a period, to say nothing of an unwillingness to hazard, afresh, at the close of a civil war, the amicable relations that remained. In all this we see a cause, not an adequate excuse, for the general apathy that succeeded to the revolutionary struggle. The lesson for our instruction is, the importance of never relinquishing a contest for freedom, till it is thoroughly secured, or of never yielding a moral controversy till it is settled on the right basis.

6. When the private and the public purse were replenished, when prosperity had succeeded to poverty, when wealth, at the opening of the present century, rolled in upon the nation, the former habits of disinterested or even of patriotic devotion to public affairs and the interests of human freedom did not return. The pursuit of wealth had begotten the inordinate love of it. Inattention to the demands of liberty and justice had resulted in the disregard of them. Inequality of possession, continually increasing and in striking contrast to earlier times, had undermined the spirit of equality, and introduced aristocratic tastes. Humanity and human rights were less valued than wealth. The concentration of capital created a new element of political power, and diverted it from its former channels. The possession of wealth, or of talents prostituted

to the support of its claims, instead of a disinterested advocacy of human liberty and equal justice, supplied passports to seats in the State and National Councils, to places of authority and power. Here was another cause, and another step in the downward tendencies of the nation; the beginning of that powerful aristocracy of wealth that afterwards openly opposed the discussion of the slave question.

7. Earlier than this, and somewhat if not altogether distinct from it in the first place, though afterwards learning to combine with it, and becoming at length wholly absorbed in it, and obliterated by it, was a more elevated aristocracy, (not using the word in its most odious sense,) beginning to exhibit itself, almost immediately after the close of the revolutionary struggle. In the effort to establish a national Constitution, to organize a new general government, and to mark out a course of national policy, this element became distinctly visible. It might be described as the aristocracy of intellect, combined, to a great extent, (though with some marked exceptions,) with high moral worth, which, in the absence of numbers, gave it, for a time, great weight and power. It was not so much, if at all, an aristocracy of misanthropy or of gross selfishness, as of conscious superiority of intelligence and character, and a distrust in the capacities of the mass of the people for self-government. With a goodly share of the friends of humanity and justice in its ranks, (the friends of the enslaved,) seeking earnestly their future or ultimate freedom, it nevertheless failed to yield its full assent to those self-evident truths of the Declaration of Independence which must lie at the basis of any consistent and thorough agitation for the present removal of slavery. If the masses of the people could not safely be intrusted with the experiment of self-government, as this class of statesmen seem to have supposed, it would have been the consummation of folly and madness to have set the slaves all loose, at once, without any previous preparation for freedom. Even the professedly democratic portion of our public men were, by no means, prepared to apply their principles to the case of the unlettered and uncultivated negro

population, though they were willing to hazard the experiment with the more favored and better educated whites. Was it to be expected, then, of those who trembled at the experiment of republican institutions even for the educated yeomanry of New England, without the protecting shadow of a royal throne, or its equivalent in some form—those who sought to restrict as much as possible the right of suffrage, making property the evidence of qualification; those who sought for balances and checks against the people, and the placing of the highest officers of government at the greatest practicable distance from their control—was it to be expected, we demand, of such a school of statesmen, that they should signalize themselves by demanding the immediate and unconditional emancipation of the enslaved? Most assuredly it was not. And no such anomaly was witnessed. Admit that they embodied a majority of the most intelligent, respectable, philanthropic, and religious portion of the community, as has been plausibly, and perhaps justly, claimed for them—admit that among their prominent men were some of the most prominent and worthy patrons of manumission, and even of abolition societies—admit that they favored the circulation of the more radical and truly democratic anti-slavery doctrines of Hopkins and Edwards*—it nevertheless remains true that no prominent statesman of this class, (nor even of their more democratic opponents,) proposed an immediate and unconditional abolition of slavery. The democratic theory of human rights and corresponding capabilities, was not then sufficiently understood, to warrant such a movement. We mention this as an indisputable and important historical fact—not for any purposes of invidious reproach. If the best friends of the enslaved among our purest and most prominent statesmen were not ready to demand for them immediate justice, then their continued enslavement was a matter of course, until the rise

---

* We cannot say that Hopkins and Edwards were not both identified, in their political influence, as most of their clerical associates were, with the school of politics we have described. It would be remarkable if they were not. But their writings on slavery are among the most radically democratic of their times.

and ascendency of the slave power riveted their chains. The fact and philosophy of gradualism, and consequent postponement, has, in part, its historical elucidation just here.

Fidelity to historical truth compels us to add, that the class of statesmen just described exerted a powerful influence in moulding the Federal Constitution; that they distinguished themselves and obtained their political name, as Federalists, by advocating its adoption; that the administration of the Federal Government, on its first organization, came into their hands; that they administered it for the first twelve years, during which time the national policy was gradually but substantially settled upon the basis upon which it has been administered ever since,* so far as the slave question is concerned, only that the exorbitant demands of the slave power have been constantly "growing with its growth, and strengthening with its strength."

Impartiality requires us to notice these facts concerning the Federal party while in power, as the Democratic party so called, is justly obnoxious to the charge of violating, even more conspicuously and outrageously, the free principles of which they boast, during their much longer administration of the government in after years.

The want of a thorough, consistent, and Christian democracy, therefore, is distinctly visible in the origin and continuation of the pro-slavery policy of the national government, and to this fact, as to a comprehensive cause, the present ascendency of the slave power may be traced. Had the "Federalists" been more democratic in their theory of civil government—had the "Democrats" (or "Republicans," as they were then called) reduced their own theory to practice,†

---

* Facts, in evidence of this, will be adduced in the proper connection of the history.

† Having never belonged to either of those parties, nor voted more than twice or thrice before the formation of the Liberty party in 1840, (though an attentive witness of party struggles since 1804,) the writer hoped to have presented a picture which would have been admitted by all the intelligent friends of liberty to be a just and impartial one. But on submitting his manuscript to the inspection of judicious friends, he finds his mistake. He now makes up his mind that some good men of

the system of American slavery would have been abolished at an early period of our history.

8. In close connection with the preceding facts, it should be noticed that the excesses of the first French Revolution, commencing soon after our Federal Government went into operation, must have contributed largely, as we know it did, to bring democratic principles into disrepute, to increase and fortify the jealousies and fears of conservatists, and confirm the impression of insecurity to life, to property, and to civil order, if large masses of men should at once be released from absolute control. If millions of educated and polished Frenchmen could not be transferred at once from a state of mere political servility to a state of civil and political freedom, without becoming fired with the frenzy of demons, abjuring all the restraints of religion, subverting the state, proscribing the church, engulfing society and property in the wildest chaos of disorder; drenching the land with blood, and exterminating each other by the rapid succession and violent proscription of rival factions, how could it be thought safe or prudent to release suddenly from a state of still deeper degradation a more ignorant population of slaves? Thus it must have been that men reasoned, especially that portion of them whose previous jealousy of popular ascendency had been so unequivocally manifested, who looked upon these trans-atlantic developments with unmingled horror, and pointed to them as evidences in confirmation of their predictions. Even the most sanguine and democratic among our American statesmen, and those who had most joyfully hailed the dawn of liberty in France, were compelled, though reluctantly, at length to join in the general condemnation of such excesses, and to feel if they could not re-echo the appeals now so eloquently made

opposite parties will think him unjust to *their* party. No course seems to remain for him but the expression of his own convictions. He has no desire nor temptation to follow the bad custom of abusing the obsolete Federal party, the representative of a former age. A more honest and patriotic party never administered the government. We have only attributed to it a defective theory, consistently followed—a less reprehensible error than that of its opponent, the holding of a better theory in abeyance, for the sake of pro-slavery support and the spoils of office.

concerning the dangers of *such* freedom. If a conclusion adverse to the sudden emancipation of the slaves was not logically deduced and propounded in the form of a syllogism, the *impression* must have been effectually made. The horrors of the French Revolution, like the perverted story of " the horrors of St. Domingo,"* some time afterwards, have ever since been on the lips of the conservators of slavery. So late as the beginning of the present anti-slavery agitation, in 1833, the " reign of terror " in France, and " the horrors of St. Domingo," were successfully adverted to by opposers ; and the doctrines of immediate and unconditional emancipation, as taught by Edwards, were systematically confounded with the " Jacobinism of the first French Revolution "—a misrepresentation less excusable now, than during the dimness and confusion near the close of the last century.

9. This untoward influence of the French Revolution was increased by the undeniable fact, that a leaven of the French infidelity, and the maxims of disorganization, had insinuated themselves into the ranks of the democratic party in this country, and appeared to find favor with some of the popular leaders of that school, some of whom had advocated slave emancipation. The cry of the French atheists—" No monarch in heaven, no monarch on earth," if not re-echoed in this

---

* The story of St. Domingo, correctly told, gives no countenance to the idea of the dangers of emancipation. The first act in the tragedy of horror, was before emancipation had been proposed. The abolition of slavery, some time after, took place quietly, and was followed by years of good order and prosperity. It was the perfidious attempt of Napoleon, after all this, to subjugate the island, and re-enslave the colored inhabitants, that opened the second scene of the tragedy, which was indeed enacted in blood, and drove the surviving whites from the island. The danger of *slavery*, not of *freedom*, is the only legitimate inference from this history.

The horrors of the French Revolution, too, in like manner, are to be charged mainly upon the corruption in the Church and the despotism in the State, that seduced the French philosophers into atheism, and drove the populace to desperation. And then it was but a counterfeit of *true* democracy that was introduced, and holding no nearer affinity to it than the corrupted Christianity of France had held to the Christianity of Christ. In fact, the anarchy that was misnamed *liberty*, was only a reproduction of the old despotisms in another form, trampling all the inalienable rights of humanity under foot, and resulting in a settled military despotism in the end.

country, was listened to by many without marked disfavor. The violent overthrow of a corrupt and oppressive Church in France, had involved along with it the open repudiation of Christianity and the Bible, and had suggested the idea of the overthrow of all churches. Thomas Paine, a leading democratic writer of this country during the Revolution, and the intimate friend of Thomas Jefferson, came home from a sojourn in France, deeply imbued with these sentiments, and found kindred spirits here, where his infidel writings had preceded him.

In the ranks of this school might be numbered not a few of that class of American revolutionists, before noticed, whose influence and example, like Paine's,* were not on the side of morality and social order, and who could not have contributed, had they been thus disposed (as very many of them were not) to any healthful or hopeful enterprise for slave emancipation. Had any thing been desired or attempted† in that direction, by the party absorbing this class of influences, and coming into power with Mr. Jefferson, in 1801, it is not improbable that the cry against them, of "infidelity, anarchy, and bloodshed" would have been, if possible, redoubled. That the opposite

---

* Paine was an advocate of the abolition of slavery, and as clerk of the Pennsylvania House of Assembly, affixed his signature to the act of prospective emancipation in that State. The infidel principles and lax morals of Paine occasioned much prejudice against his doctrine of the "rights of man."

† There is no evidence that the Democratic or Republican party, at any period, was inclined to abolish slavery. Among all the loud and bitter complaints raised by them against the alleged despotic tendencies of the Federal party, its support of slavery was never mentioned. And among all the democratic measures proposed by Mr. Jefferson while in office, the abolition of slavery was not one. His own eloquent writings against slavery could not persuade him to emancipate (as Washington had done) his own slaves. The early identification of a majority of leading slaveholders with the Democratic party, and the steady control of that party by them, ever since, has always been a great puzzle and a great stumbling-block in the way of Democratic progress.

The historical solution seems to be, that Northern talent and Northern capital (the natural rivals of Southern talent and capital) had committed themselves against the democratic theory. The only way to "get up an issue" was to espouse the theory, but blink the particular application to slavery, with the double advantage of neutralizing and disarming the hostile principle. And if democratic measures favored *labor*, the slaveholder adroitly stood in the place of the Southern laborer, and might count on the co-operation of the Northern laborer.

party, while in power, under Washington and Adams, and
amid the opposition they encountered, and the jealousies, the
panic, and the confusion of that singular crisis, should have
attempted anything so radically democratic and unprecedented
as the sudden emancipation of all the slaves, most assuredly
was not to have been expected. We say nothing in excuse
of the derelictions of either of these parties, nor in peculiar or
exclusive reproach of either of them, but we think it important to present a true and impartial account of the facts of
that period, that the causes of our present unhappy position
may be understood, and avoided in future. A Christianity
crippled by an alliance with even the most pure and elevated
description of aristocracy, is incompetent to the task of securing human freedom. A democracy, or a philanthropy, however ardent and radical, that is not based upon the Christianity
of the Bible, is equally impotent, for the same sublime mission.*

10. Among the influences tending strongly to bribe the public sentiment, and change the political tendencies of the country, especially at the South, on the slave question, have been
justly reckoned the increased and unforeseen profitableness of
slave labor, in consequence of the invention of the cotton-gin,
by Mr. Whitney. Of the reasons which had operated to produce the conviction, during the revolutionary period, that
slavery was a waning system that must soon be abandoned,
the unprofitableness of slave labor was doubtless, in many
minds, a leading one. This economical view of the subject
must have become the more prominent as the moral influences
and the generous enthusiasm of the revolutionary period gave
place to plans of individual thrift and accumulation. Then it
was that the blighting influences of slavery must have begun
to be felt; but a wonderful change was at hand, the almost
magical result of a labor-saving machine, in the hands, not of

---

* It belongs to a later period of the history of the parties to remark, that the
rival aristocracies of the *North* and *South*, throwing the Federal party and its successors into the embraces of the one, and the Democratic into the hands of the
other, have effectually prevented the abolition of slavery.

the laborer himself, but of the capitalist who controlled him, and appropriated the avails of his labor. And thus, at the very moment when the more worthy and noble considerations in favor of liberty had almost ceased to occupy the slaveholder's attention, the most powerful temptations were presented to his cupidity and avarice. Under this temptation, he fell. And the policy of the national government was, in consequence, changed. On this point, we present the testimony of two statesmen holding opposite views, in general, of the slave question.

"What, then, have been the causes which have created so new a feeling in favor of slavery in the South—which have changed the whole nomenclature of the South on the subject—and from being thought of and described in the terms I have mentioned and will not repeat, it has now become an institution, a cherished institution there; no evil, no scourge, but a great religious, social, and moral blessing, as I think I have heard it latterly described? I suppose this, sir, is owing to the sudden uprising and rapid growth of the cotton plantations of the South. * * * * * * The tables will show that the exports of cotton for the years 1790 and 1791 were hardly more than forty or fifty thousand dollars a year. It has gone on increasing rapidly until it may now be, perhaps, in a season of great product and high prices, a hundred millions of dollars. Then there was more of wax, more of indigo, more of rice, more of almost everything exported from the South than of cotton. I think I have heard it said, when Mr. Jay negotiated the treaty of 1794 with England, he did not know that cotton was exported at all from the United States; and I have heard it said that, after the treaty which gave to the United States the right to carry their own commodities to England in their own ships, the custom-house in London refused to admit cotton, upon an allegation that it could not be an American production, there being, as they supposed, no cotton raised in America. They would hardly think so now."—*Speech of D. Webster,* U. S. Senate, March 7, 1850.

"Unhappily, the original policy of the Government and the original principles of the Government in respect to slavery, did not permanently control its action. A change occurred—almost imperceptible at first, but becoming more and more marked and decided, until nearly total. The Honorable Senator from Massachusetts, in the course of his late speech, noticed this change, and ascribed it to the rapid increase in the production of cotton. Doutless, sir, this was a leading cause. The production of cotton, in consequence of the invention of the cotton-gin, increased from 487,600 pounds in 1793, to 6,276,300 pounds in 1796, and continued to increase very rapidly afterwards.   Of course the market value of slaves advanced, and masters were less inclined to emancipation."—*Speech of S. P. Chase*, U. S. Senate, March 26, 1850.

When the cotton manufacture of the North came to engross so great an amount of northern capital, a bond of affinity between northern and southern capitalists was created, which at length, has almost indissolubly interwoven the Eastern States in the web of the slave power.   If anything is to be done to disentangle or cut the threads, it must be done soon.

11. There is yet another cause to be mentioned, that operates, perhaps, still more strongly to attach the slaveholders to their present system, and bind the North to their car.   Except to the growers of cotton and those who raise human herds, further north, to sell to them, the slave system, even now, is not a pecuniary benefit to the slaveholder.   Though many individuals are enriching themselves by the system, the southern country, on the whole, is becoming impoverished by it.   But there is, at the South, a still more potent passion than the love of wealth.   It is the lust of political power, and slavery has always been an element of political power to the slaveholders in the Southern States.   Though frequently, if not commonly, a minority, in the different States, (counting slaves, free colored persons, and non-slaveholding whites,) the slaveholders have always held the political power of the slave States in their own hands, and may calculate upon doing this while the slave system continues.   Since the adoption of the Federal Constitution, in 1789, slavery has also become an all-controlling element of political power in this nation, in the hands of an oligarchy of slaveholders.   This element, at first, was scarcely perceived.   It originated in that provision of the Constitution which gives to the South a representation for their slaves, in the apportionment of representatives, and in the election of President and Vice President of the United States.   A perception of this advantage has taught the slaveholders to regard the slave system as the grand instrument of their political ascendency in the nation.   It has taught political aspirants at the North to become sycophantic and servile.

These joint influences, like the upper and nether mill-stone, are rapidly grinding to powder the last hopes of American freedom, unless the remedy be promptly applied by the resolute withdrawal of votes from slaveholders and their sycophants. The federal patronage, and the national policy, in the hands of slavery, have been found too powerful for the remaining energies of freedom. These advantages remaining with the slave power, the nation becomes enslaved.

12. Of all the causes or indications, in that period, of a decline of the spirit of liberty, and of a corresponding resuscitation of the once waning system of slavery, there was none more comprehensive, more significant, or more influential than the changed spirit and position of the *Church*.

Not one of the causes or indications already enumerated, has failed to affect, most injuriously, the character and the influence of the Church, and when the weight of the Church itself came to be thrown into the scale of slavery, each one of the causes or indications connected with the transition could not fail to receive fresh accessions of strength; and, by being combined in the bosom of the Church, consolidating and intrenching themselves there, with a compactness and solidity unknown before, they have rendered themselves almost impregnable, ever since.

In speaking of this transition of the Church, we do not forget that the Church had not, at any period, divorced herself wholly from slavery, nor even, as a whole, taken the ground of immediate and uncompromising action on the subject. The doctrine of "*gradual*" repentance, resulting, in part, from the defective theologies then commonly in vogue, and which rejected the idea of sudden moral transformations, was the fatal error of the Church, and from her it had been imbibed by the best statesmen of the age, nurtured and taught in her bosom.

But we speak of the transition of the Church as we do of the corresponding transition of the State. We give both bodies the credit of no small degree of earnestness and honesty, in their opposition to slavery during the revolutionary period, though they failed of applying promptly the appropriate remedy, in its proper form. The transition of which we speak was from this state of honest opposition to slavery and incipient though dilatory action against it, to a state of comparative apathy, first; of a quiescence, next; and finally, of apology, of biblical defence, and of opposition to all earnest endeavors to diffuse information on the subject, and to array a public sentiment against slavery.

When the external pressures, and the special dangers incident to the slave system, during the war, were removed from the *community* by the return of peace, they were removed also from the *Church*. The Church, too, as well as the world, forgot her solemn resolutions, in the hour of distress, to put away this iniquity from her bosom. When philanthropists contented themselves with mere moral suasion, without demanding distinct and effective legislation on the subject, they acted upon maxims they had imbibed in the Church; a Church that neglected to preach the religious duty of political justice in "delivering the spoiled out of the hands of the oppressor," and "executing judgment between a man and his neighbor." When projects of gradualism deceived the friends of the oppressed, it was because the Church had taught the doctrines of gradualism rather than those of immediate and unconditional compliance with all the divine precepts. When the moral reformers of those times consented to moral compromises, they were kept in countenance by the corresponding policy of the Church, from which they had received, directly or indirectly, their moral education, and of which the greater part of them were members. The general decline of pure religion and sound morality after the Revolution, is known to have affected, very seriously, the Church, and it was the testimony and the complaint of her most vigilant watchmen, that her standard of morality, and the efficacy of her discipline could not be restored to their former state. How evidently and how disastrously must such a fact have affected the position of the Church on the slave question! And how notoriously have these manifestations been increasing ever since!

Even revivals of religion have done little towards restoring the ancient standard of morals. The moral duties have been less insisted on from the pulpit, and the religion revived and propagated in times of religious awakening, has been common-ly of a corresponding type, till the idea that ministers and churches must not meddle with political sins, has grown up into theories concerning "organic sins," that would have astonished our fathers.

The general decline of the spirit of liberty that was witnessed in the community, was witnessed also in the Church, and the same moral lethargy and stupor came over them both. The influx of wealth, the erection of castes and aristocracies in society, that displaced simplicity and equality in the State, produced similar effects in the Church. Especially was it true that the more elevated aristocracy of intelligence, of character, and of spiritual pride, that led prominent statesmen to distrust their fellow-citizens in the exercise of their God-given rights, found its home and its sanctuary in the high places of the Church and the ministry, by whom the policy of those statesmen was most earnestly and effectively sustained. By these, in an especial manner, were the horrors of the French Revolution so exhibited as to teach the danger of according to human beings, as such, the exercise of essential human rights. However honest may have been the error, and however plausibly maintained, it was none the less to be deplored. The unexpected profitableness of slave labor in the production of cotton was a temptation to the Church, as well as to the rest of the community, and with the rest of the community the Southern Church fell into the snare. And the profitableness of the cotton manufacture at the North, and the consequent sympathy of the manufacturer with the planter, has influenced the Northern Church, not ex-cepting the Society of Friends, as really (if not as universally) as it has the rest of the community. The same may be said of the temptations of ambition, connected with this anomalous element of political power, and among our most supple and obsequious politicians, are honored and even devout members of the Church.

So that all the elements and causes of declension, in respect to the treatment of slavery, that have appeared and operated in the body politic, have appeared and operated likewise in the Church. *There* they have become concentrated, *there* they have been strengthened, *there*, above all, they have been baptized "into the name of the Father, and of the Son, and of the Holy Ghost"—have been seated at the communion table, have been elevated into the pulpit, have been installed trustees and professors of Colleges and Theological Seminaries; have been made managers and life members of Bible, Tract, and Missionary Societies, have shaped the course of ecclesiastical bodies, and revised and controlled the discipline of the Church.

Besides all this, the Church has seemed to embody elements of deterioration peculiarly her own. Her divisions into rival sects and theological schools have ensnared her; she has compromised her christian principles, has neutralized, or withdrawn her testimony, and has faltered in her administration of discipline, to gain strength and numbers wherewith to carry on schismatic and polemic wars within her own bosom! When the Methodist testimonies against slavery were found to stand in the way of the comparative growth and prospective ascendency of the Methodist sect, then the severity of Methodist discipline against slavery must be relaxed (so we have been told by the apologists of that policy) to propitiate the favor of slaveholders. In the same way, and for the same object, the testimonies of the Presbyterian sect against slavery must be rendered a dead letter, and the most pointed of them at length, expunged. The unity and extension of the sect, and the harmony of its ecclesiastical action throughout the country, must not be disturbed by any agitation of the exciting question. The cry of "peace, peace," must drown the voice of remonstrance against the crying sin of the Church. And thus the Church becomes a privileged body, the members of which appear to claim peculiar exemption from reproof for their sins.

13. There is still another and a most potent element and evidence of deterioration, on this subject, that we know not how to treat of, as its magnitude and its meanness demand. Whenever we attempt to speak or write upon it, we feel our cheeks burning with indignation and shame. We know not how or in what terms to describe it, to what origin to trace it, or by what considerations to attempt to dislodge it from the minds of sane men. From its flat contradiction of the Bible, we should characterize it as decidedly of infidel parentage, yet we find it nestling in the bosom of the Church. From its unaccountableness, we should describe it by the names of hypocrisy and pretence, did not its malignity prove its sincerity and reality. Were it less murderous and less blasphemous, we might laugh at it; were it less ludicrous, we might reason against it; were it less mean, we could enter the lists against it, as an object of honorable warfare. We should attribute it to sheer vulgarity and ignorance (where we find it signally at home) but that we meet with it also in circles claiming refinement and learning. We allude to the infatuation that virtually predicates humanity upon the hue of the skin, that disbelieves that "God had made of one blood all nations of men," that arrogates to less than one-sixth part of the human race the exclusive monopoly of our common humanity, that thus falsifies the self-evident truths of our Declaration of Independence, and sets up, in the temples of Jehovah, the monuments of heathen caste.

Existing in and controlling both the community and the Church, this prejudice should have been noticed earlier in our enumeration of evil influences, but it seems not to have attained its gigantic growth till the united energies of a lapsed Church and State had first provided for it, new methods of culture. We do not say that the Colonization Society organized in 1816, created this prejudice, for without such a prejudice the idea of colonizing a portion of our citizens on the ground of their color could not have been conceived.

But we do say that the existence and operations of that Society, have more than quadrupled the strength and the extent of that prejudice, in a few brief years. It is a prejudice stronger at the North than at the South, because the two colors do not come so constantly in contact. Yet, at the North, it had scarcely made its appearance in common schools and worshiping assemblies, at the beginning of the present century, as many can testify.

The Maryland laws, before quoted, forbidding white women to marry negroes, simply for the reason stated, that the latter were *slaves*, afford sufficient proof of the modern date of this prejudice, and of its origin in the slave system.

In countries not familiarized with a population of colored slaves, (as in Russia and Poland, where the serfs are all whites,) the prejudice against colored people is unknown, and its existence among us is there discredited, or considered an inexplicable phenomenon. In France, in England, in Germany, and throughout all Europe, though the *Jews* are a degraded caste, the educated *negro* has free access, and on terms of unquestioned equality, to the very highest circles of society. It is reserved to a nation pluming itself upon being the world's teacher of the doctrine of human equality, to deny the common courtesies of life, along with the essential rights of humanity, to a large part of the human species, (to the very race first proficient in literature and civilization,) on account of their color! Thus do we invite and merit a world's scorn!

Were it not for this stupid prejudice against color, the sceptre of the slaveholding oligarchy would drop powerless at once, and the nation would be disenthralled. Sustained by this debasing prejudice, its supremacy must remain unbroken, and the nation must be enslaved. *Slavery knows no color.*— "In the progress of time, some one hundred and fifty or two hundred years hence, but few vestiges of the black race will remain *among our posterity*." So says Henry Clay,* and the

---

* Speech of Henry Clay, in the U. S. Senate, in 1839. In this speech Mr. Clay urged arguments against "emancipation, immediate or gradual." "The first impediment, is the absolute want of power in the Federal Government to effect the

constant and rapid blending of colors at the South justifies the estimate. But the bleaching process removes not the taint of slavery. The child of the slave mother follows her condition. Persons of the whitest complexion are already held as

---

purpose." " The next obstacle in the way of abolition arises out of the fact of the presence, in the Slave States, of three millions of slaves. No practical scheme for their removal or separation from us, has yet been devised or proposed." [The Colonization scheme, then, is *not* "practical."] " The third impediment to immediate abolition, is to be found in the immense amount of capital which is invested in slave property." " The total value of slave property then, by estimate, in the United States, is twelve hundred millions of dollars. And now it is rashly proposed, by a single fiat of legislation, to annihilate this immense amount of property ! To annihilate it without indemnity, and without compensation to the owners." " I know there is a visionary dogma which holds that negro slaves cannot be the subject of property : I shall not dwell long on the speculative abstraction. That *is* property which the law declares *to be* property. Two hundred years of legislation have sanctified and sanctioned negro slaves as property." " It is frequently asked, What is to become of the African race among us ? Are they forever to remain in bondage ?" * * * " Taking the aggregate of the two races, the European is constantly, though slowly, *gaining on the African portion*. In the progress of time, some one hundred and fifty or two hundred years hence, but few vestiges of the black race will remain among our posterity."

The speech will repay close study. In no part of it does Mr. Clay intimate a future abolition of slavery. The " impediments" he urges will not diminish. The limited powers of the Federal Government—the sanction of centuries of legislation —the impossibility of separation or removal—the appalling amount of property invested—all these, except the first item, must increase. Neither does Mr. Clay predict the future *extinction* of SLAVERY, but only the disappearance of the "*black race* from *among* OUR *posterity !*" The language is exceedingly guarded, and commendably accurate. Mr. Clay knows that the slave population, like the free, are increasing in a geometrical ratio. And that, if it be true that the free (or as he has it, the European portion) are gaining a little more rapidly, this does not alter the fact of the rapid increase of slaves, *whatever their color may be*. Indisputably it is the process of amalgamation, and *nothing else*, that lays the foundation for the estimate that one hundred and fifty or two hundred years will " leave but few vestiges of the black race AMONG our posterity !" Neither the " slaves" nor the " blacks" are diminishing by depopulation, like the Indians and the Sandwich Islanders. The reverse is the known fact. Mr. Clay's remedy for the " bondage of the *African* race" is manifestly a future enslavement of a vastly greater number of " *our posterity*," " AMONG" whom will remain " but few vestiges of the black race in one hundred and fifty or two hundred years."

Gov. McDuffie, of South Carolina, had declared a laboring community, " bleached or unbleached," " a dangerous element in the body politic." He had anticipated their enslavement, in the Northern States, in " less than a quarter of a century." To Mr. Clay it was reserved to intimate a respite of one hundred and fifty or two hundred years, showing how it must then be inevitably introduced, by causes already in operation, and fortified by formidable " obstacles" and " impediments" in

slaves—fugitives are thus described in advertisements, hunted, captured at the North, and taken back again. And it is known that, in some cases, white persons have been kidnapped who had no African blood in their veins.

To this point, then, at length, our declension has reached. We hesitate to give up the insane prejudice that supports slavery, though told never so plainly, and from the best authority, that the consequence must be the loss of our own liberties—the enslavement of our own children! Nay, while we hear it proclaimed from the loftiest battlements of slavedom, that "the noblest blood of Virginia," the noblest blood of our revolutionary sires, runs in the veins of slaves.*

---

the way of their removal. Those "obstacles" and "impediments" present the problem for the laboring people of the free States. Unless overcome, the prophecy of Mr. Clay must become history. There is no possible or conceivable alternative. Let the people banish *prejudice against color*, and all Mr. Clay's "impediments" and "obstacles" would vanish in twenty-four hours.

* It has been credibly reported, over the signatures of respectable citizens, that a reputed daughter of Thomas Jefferson has been seen exposed for sale at auction in New Orleans, as a slave. The known usages of slavery in America are such as to render the statement a highly probable one. It is also said that a grand-daughter of Mr. Jefferson is among the colonists of Liberia. The statement, along with the following, is from a communication in " Frederick Douglass' paper" for March 25, 1852 : " I have heard from an eye witness, that on more than one occasion, when the sage of Monticello left that retreat for the Presidential abode at Washington, there would be on the top of the same coach a yellow boy 'running away.' And when told that one of his slaves was going off without leave, Jefferson said, ' Well, let him go, his right is as good as his father's !' And, somehow, *that* boy would get a doceur before the ' parting of the ways.' "

CHAPTER XII.

POSITION OF THE AMERICAN CHURCHES RESPECTING SLAVERY
DURING THE FIRST HALF OF THE NINETEENTH CENTURY.

I.—METHODIST EPISCOPAL CHURCH.

General Conference of 1801—do. of 1836—Contrast with 1797—Leading Ministers—
Prof. E. D. Sims—Dr. S. Olin—Pres. Thornton—Bishop Soule—Dr. Bond—Pres.
Fiske—Bishop Hedding—Refusal to put to vote Anti-Slavery Resolutions in Con-
ference—Georgia Annual Conference—S. Carolina Conference—" Book Concern "
—General Conference for 1840—Division concerning slaveholding Bishops—
Grounds of the division—Slaveholding statistics of M. E. Church, *North*.

In speaking of the position of the churches, we shall have
reference to the general fact—the principal religious denominations—the leading influences—not forgetting that there are
honorable exceptions to the picture we shall be compelled to
present.

The former anti-slavery testimonies of the Society of
Friends, and also of the Presbyterian and Methodist, and
some of the Baptist churches, until near the close of the last
century, we have presented already.* Of other denominations, as such, at that period, we had nothing of an authentic
character to record. We are assured that there were earnest
opposers of slavery among Episcopalians, and other religious
communions.

Of the course of the principal denominations since that time,
and their position at present, we propose now to treat; in doing
which, such facts will be brought forward as will enable the
reader to form his own judgment in the premises.

---

* See Chapters IV. and IX.

METHODIST EPISCOPAL CHURCH.

In reverting to the action of the Methodist Conferences, towards the close of the last century (Chap. IX.), the reader would almost be warranted to take it for granted that slaveholding, in that religious denomination, must have speedily come to an end. There can be no doubt that such was the intention of the Conferences, and that such was the general expectation at the time. Such, however, was not the fact. The fatal error seems to have consisted in an unwarrantable lenity towards delinquent members, in not promptly enforcing the discipline, and this under the delusive expectation that they would, in a short time, be prepared to take the step, voluntarily, themselves, without being authoritatively coerced. Never, perhaps, was there a more striking illustration of the danger of such delays. The church that, with a full and clear perception of the iniquity of a practice existing among its members, has not fidelity and energy to expel it at once, has no reason to flatter itself that it ever will. If the Friends were more successful, notwithstanding their tardy process, the reason may perhaps be found in the fact, that they did not so directly sin against their own conscientious convictions, in withholding church discipline. They were first led to condemn what appeared to be the *abuses* of slavery, then the slave *trade*, and at last, slaveholding *itself*. And so far as their convictions went, they put them in practice. But Methodism, which had its rise amid the testimonies and the conviction that " SLAVERY *is the sum of all villanies*," could not sit down with that iniquity in her skirts without being overcome by it.

1n 1801, the General Conference said—

" We are more than ever convinced of the great evil of African Slavery, which still exists in these United States."

And there the testimony still stands. "More than ever convinced of the great evil," and "more than ever" wedded to it and embedded in it. Such testimonies, though sometimes apparently relied upon, to disprove the pro-slavery character of the Church, contain the strongest proof of the inexcusableness of its position. The Church knows the evil, but nevertheless hugs it to her bosom.

Yet there should be noticed here, perhaps, a studied dilution of the testimony previously given. In 1780, slavery was admitted to be " contrary to the laws of God, man, and nature, and hurtful to Society, contrary to the dictates of conscience and true religion, and doing what we would not that others should do unto us." This clearly describes it as a *sin*. But in 1801 it is only designated, in vague terms, as *an evil ;* whether physical or moral, is not expressed. To those who would understand the course and the position of our ecclesiastical bodies, these nice distinctions should be noticed with care. " Fraud lurketh in generalities," said Lord Coke.

" Rev. Robert Emory, in his history of ' The Discipline,' informs us that he finds the following :—

" In 1789, ' The buying and selling the bodies and souls of men, women, or children, with intention to enslave them.'

" In 1792, it reads ' The buying or selling of men, women, or children, with an intention to enslave them.'

" In 1808, it reads ' The buying *and* selling of men, women, *and* children,' &c.

" For this alteration no authority is found in the Journal of the General Conference."—" *The Grounds of Secession, from the M. E. Church*"—*By O. Scott*, p. 45.

" And the following, from a letter published in the Pittsburg Christian Advocate, by Rev. Mr. Drummond, is not less important :

" If we take the action of the General Conference as a true index of antislavery feeling and zeal in the Church, I think it apparent that these have been considerably diminished, since 1800."—*Ib*. pp. 45–46.

" In 1804, the paragraphs about considering the subject, and petitions to the legislatures (viz : No. 4, of 1796, and No. 6, of 1800) were stricken out."

1808—Paragraph 2 and 3 of 1796 were struck out, and the following substituted :

" 3. The General Conference authorizes each Annual Conference to form their own regulations, relative to buying and selling slaves."—*Ib*. p. 47.

The General Conference of the Methodist Episcopal Church, held at Cincinnati, in 1836, declared that they " wholly disclaim any right, wish, or intention, to interfere with the civil and political relation of master and slave, as it exists in the slave-holding States of this Union." This was adopted by a vote of 120 to 14.

The action of the Conference, at the same time *against abolitionists*, will be noticed in another chapter. What we have to do with, *now*, is the changed attitude of the Methodist Episcopal Church, respecting *slavery*. We quote their proceedings still farther on this point. In their Pastoral Address, dissuading their members from agitating the subject, they say—

" The question of slavery in the United States, by the constitutional compact which binds us together, as a nation, is left to be regulated by the several State Legislatures themselves; and thereby is put beyond the control of the general government, *as well as of all ecclesiastical bodies ;* it being manifest that in the slaveholding states themselves the entire responsibility of its existence or non-existence rests with those State Legislatures."

What "Constitutional Compact" had there been made since 1797, when the General Conference, as before shown,[*] had *required* its preachers to memorialize the legislatures ? And if, as stated in 1836, the sole responsibility rested on the State Legislatures, why not continue to memorialize them still? There must have been Methodists in those legislatures, and probably few or no members of those bodies held seats there without the aid of Methodist votes? Aside from this, how could any state or national arrangements relieve *the Church* from the responsibility of carrying out its own *Church discipline?* The *truth* was expressed in the Resolution just now quoted. The Conference had " *no wish*" " to interfere in the civil and political relation of master and slave." Too many of them were slavemasters themselves.

Another important thing to be noticed here, is, the new views of the M. E. Conference, since 1797 or 1801 and 1836, on the subject of the bearings of the Federal Constitution on the question. It indicates a corresponding change in the community in general. New expositions and applications of

---

* Chap. IX.

constitutional law must have grown up, or we should not witness such a change of language.

Leading non-slaveholding ministers of the M. E. Church, were now forward to take similar ground, and even to vindicate the rightfulness of slaveholding.

" Having established the point, that the first African slaves were legally brought into bondage, the right to detain their children in bondage, follows as an indispensable consequence. Thus we see that the slavery which exists in America, was founded in right."—*Professor E. D. Simms of Virginia Conference.*

" Not only is holding slaves, on the conditions and under the restrictions of the discipline, no disqualification for the ministerial office ; but I will go a little further, and say, that slaveholding is not constitutionally a forfeiture of a man's right, if he may be said to have one, to the office of a bishop."—*Dr. S. Olin, Pres. of the Wesleyan University, Middletown, (Ct.)*

" That God not only permitted it, but absolutely provided for its perpetuity. The act of holding a slave then, under all circumstances, God being judge, is not sin."—*Pres. S. C. Thornton, Centenary College, Miss. Conference.*

" I have never yet advised the liberation of a slave, and think I never shall."—*Bishop Soule at the Pittsburg Conference,* Washington, Pa., July, 1839.

" The buying of a slave may be an act of great humanity under certain circumstances, as well as the holding of those already in possession. And, moreover, we should be as much opposed to the introduction of a rule of discipline, to expel from our communion all who bought a slave, whatever the motives might be, as we are to a rule to expel all slaveholders under all circumstances."—*Dr. Bond of N. Y., to R. Boyd,* 1840.

The late Wilbur Fisk, D. D., President of the Wesleyan University, Middletown, Conn., said :

" The relation of master and slave may, and does, in many cases, exist under such circumstances as free the master from the just charge and guilt of immorality."

" The general rule of Christianity not only permits, but in supposable cases enjoins, a continuance of the master's authority."

" The New Testament enjoins obedience upon the slave, as an obligation DUE to a present *rightful* authority."

" Rev. Elijah Hedding, D. D., one of the six Methodist Bishops," and also a northern man, said :

" The right to hold a slave is founded on this rule : ' Therefore, all things whatsoever ye would that men should do to you, do ye even so to them ; for this is the law and the prophets.' "—*Ch. Adv. and Jour.*, Oct. 20, 1837.

Bishop Hedding, presiding at the New England Conference, in 1838, refused to put resolutions, condemning the buying and selling of slaves, and at the same time refused to put a motion declaring slavery to be a moral evil.

" In the year 1837, the Baltimore Conference passed the following resolution :

" That in all cases of administration under the General Rule in reference to buying and selling men, women, and children, &c., it be, and hereby is recommended to all committees, as the sense of this Conference, that the said rule be taken, construed, and understood so as NOT to make the guilt or innocence of the accused to depend upon the SIMPLE FACT OF PURCHASE OR SALE, but upon the attendant circumstances of cruelty, injustice, or inhumanity on the one hand, or those of kind purposes or good intentions on the other, under which the actions shall have been perpetrated ; and further it is recommended, that, in all such cases, the charge be brought for immorality, and the circumstances be adduced as specifications under that charge.' " *The Grounds of Secession,* &c., pp. 53–4.

" The General Conference of 1840 approved of the journals of the Baltimore Conference, with this resolution in them—approved of them, this resolution and all ; consequently, approved of it, and made it their own."—*Ib.*

For a full account the reader is referred to the work just quoted, and also to Lucius C. Matlack's " History of American Slavery and Methodism," from 1780 to 1849, an elaborate and documentary work of nearly 400 pages.

The Georgia Annual Conference unanimously resolved, " that slavery, as it exists in the United States, is not a moral evil."

The South Carolina Conference unanimously adopted the following : " Whereas, we hold that the subject of slavery in these United States is not one proper for the action of the Church, but is exclusively appropriate to the civil authorities, therefore, resolved, that this Conference will not meddle with it, farther than to express the regret that it has ever been introduced, in any form, into any of the judicatures of the Church."

" Rev. W. Capers, D.D.," who offered this resolution, explained it as " implying that slavery is not a moral evil. He understood it as equivalent to such a declaration. His purpose was that of not only reproving some wrong doings at the North, but with respect also to the General Conference," &c. " If slavery were a moral evil—that is, sin—the Church would be bound to take cognizance of it."—[January, 1839.]

" The Book Concern, in New York, up to the division which followed the General Conference of 1844, published books for the whole connection, North and South ; hence, in the republication of English works which have contained allusions to slavery, various expedients were resorted to, to render them acceptable to slaveholders. Sometimes the anti-slavery matter is said to have been expunged, and in other cases it has been attempted to explain it away by notes appended by the American Book-room editor."— *True Wesleyan*, Jan. 24, 1852.

The Editor of the True Wesleyan, proceeds to specify an instance of the latter. In re-publishing Watson's Theological Institutes, in which were found some pointed remarks against slaveholders, a note is appended, evidently designed to make the impression that it is not applicable to *American* slavery.

The General Conference for 1840 adopted the following:

" Resolved, that it is inexpedient and unjustifiable for any preacher to permit colored persons to give testimony against white persons, in any State where they are denied that privilege by law."

A motion was made to re-consider this Resolution, and several attempts were made at compromise, but after a long discussion, the resolution was permitted to stand. Thus was the ecclesiastical polity of the Church conformed to the slave code.

Some time after the "Wesleyan" secession from the M. E. Church on account of slavery, a division took place in the Methodist Episcopal Church, growing out of the refusal of the Church to consent to having slaveholding bishops. Of this division we present the following account ... the True Wesleyan (a paper of the Wesleyan Secession,) then edited by by Rev. Luther Lee, as copied into the Annual Report of the Am. and For. A. S. Society, for 1850 :

" The action of the General Conference which led to the separation, was not against slavery or slaveholding by the membership or ministers, but simply against slaveholding by the Episcopacy, and that not upon principle, but wholly upon the ground of expediency. This division was brought about by the Southern and not by the Northern members, who did what they could to prevent it, and now condemn the act as unjustifiable ; but it did not throw all the slave States into the South 1 General Conference. Official documents show that there are, at the present time, in the Northern

General Conference, eight annual Conferences, a part or the whole of whose territory is in the slaveholding States. There are many slaveholding preachers in the M. E. Church, and it ordains slaveholders to the ministry. It is computed that there are in the M. E. Church, North, not less than four thousand slaveholders, and twenty-seven thousand slaves."*

It would be difficult to reconcile with these facts the strong anti-slavery resolutions of the General Conference of the Methodist Episcopal Church North, in 1849 and in 1850, denouncing slavery in severe terms, repudiating "the low standard of morality that sanctions the settlement of any difficulties by a compromise of moral principles," and concluding the whole by the following:

"Resolved, that Christians cannot consistently give their influence to elevate men to places of honor and trust who are known to be supporters of any great social and moral evil.

"Resolved, that the glory of God and the good of mankind require the exclusion of slaveholders from the Christian Church."—*Annual Report American and Foreign Anti-Slavery Society*, 1850.

This progress, (if it *be* progress) as well as the inconsistencies connected with it, may perhaps be accounted for, by the movements among Northern Methodist Abolitionists, resulting in a secession, and in the organization of a new ecclesiastical connection, called the Wesleyan Church. These movements *made it necessary* to oppose the election of a slaveholding bishop, and to adopt strong resolutions against slavery.

---

* The following statement apparently varies from the preceding, in respect to the number of slaveholding Conferences:

"The Methodist Church *North* has about one-fifth part as many slaveholding societies as the entire Church South. It reports in the slave States *three* annual conferences, 857 preachers, and 86,627 members, all in actual and full fellowship with slaveholding."—*Pres. Blanchard, as reported by Cleveland True Democrat*, Sep. 26, 1851.

The solution, as furnished us by Mr. Lee, is, that *five* of the Conferences, viz., the Pittsburg, the Ohio, the Indiana, the Illinois, and the Philadelphia, though bearing Northern names, include portions of slave territory; while the Western Virginia, the Missouri, and the Baltimore, are slaveholding, of course: *eight in all.*

CHAPTER XIII.

POSITION OF THE AMERICAN CHURCHES, ETC. CONTINUED.

II.—THE PRESBYTERIAN CHURCH.

General Assembly, 1815—1816—1818—Erasure of anti-slavery testimony of 1794—Synod of Kentucky, 1834—Anti-slavery testimony and pro-slavery practice—General Assembly, 1835—"Doctors of Divinity" engaged in the traffic—1836—Pro-slavery pamphlet from Princeton—Discussion—Indefinite postponement—General Assembly of 1837—Anti-slavery memorials laid on the table—Excision of four Northern Synods—Division of General Assembly in 1838—And the reason—"OLD-SCHOOL." Assembly declined discussing Slavery—In 1843, laid Anti-slavery memorials on the table without reading—In 1845, declared that "to treat slavery as necessarily a sin, would be to dissolve itself"—In 1847, re-affirmed its former testimonies—In 1850, declared the "interference" of the General Association of Massachusetts on the subject "offensive"—NEW-SCHOOL GENERAL ASSEMBLY, 1838, Anti-slavery memorials withdrawn—In 1839, "referred the whole subject to the Presbyteries"—In 1840, "indefinitely postponed"—"Vesuvius capped for three years"—In 1843, censured Presbyteries that had excluded slaveholders—In 1846, declared Slavery unrighteous, but could not exclude slaveholders—In 1849, was ignorant of any blame resting on its slaveholding members—In 1850, refused to call slaveholding "an offence under the discipline"—"Deplored the workings of the whole system"—Again "referred it to the Presbyteries"—And invited the "Old-School" Assembly to commune with them.

Notwithstanding the testimony of the Presbyterian Church, in 1794, that it is "man-stealing" to "keep, sell, or buy slaves," or "retain men in slavery," yet the Church contented itself with recording its doctrine without reducing it to practice. No discipline was enforced, and the custom of slaveholding, among its members and even among the officers of the Church, became general, in the slave states.

In 1815, the General Assembly declared their "approbation of the principles of civil liberty," and their "deep concern at any vestiges of slavery which may remain in our country." This is theory. In practice, they urge the lower judicatures to prepare the young slaves "for the exercise of liberty when God, in his providence, shall open a door for emancipation."

" This recommendation is an implied permission to their slaveholding members to dismiss all thoughts of emancipation at present, waiting for some colonization opening, or some undefined providence of God."—*Statement of Pres. Blanchard and others, in letter to Chr. A. S. Convention in Cincinnati.*

In 1816, the General Assembly, while it called slavery a " mournful evil," directed an erasure of the note (of 1794) to the eighth commandment.

" In 1818, it adopted an ' expression of views' in which slavery is called a ' gross violation of the most precious and sacred rights of human nature, utterly inconsistent with the law of God, which requires us to love our neighbor as ourselves, and totally irreconcilable with the spirit and principles of the gospel of Christ, which enjoin that ' all things whatsoever ye would that men should do to you, do ye also to them.' But, instead of requiring the instant abandonment of this ' gross violation of rights,' &c., the Assembly exhorts the violators to ' continue and increase their exertions to effect a total abolition of slavery, with no greater delay than a regard to the public welfare demands,' and recommends, that if ' a Christian professor shall sell a slave, who is also in communion with our Church,' without the consent of the slave, the seller should ' be suspended till he should repent and make reparation.' "*

The effect of this temporizing and procrastinating policy was precisely such as might have been anticipated. The " mournful evil" only struck its roots deeper under such pruning.

In 1834, the Synod of Kentucky adopted a report on slavery, in which they draw a thrilling picture of the cruelties and horrors of the internal slave trade, in which families are forcibly separated from each other. They say :

" These acts are daily occurring in the midst of us." " There is not a village or road that does not behold the sad procession of manacled outcasts, whose chains and mournful countenances tell that they are exiled by force from all that their hearts hold dear. Our church, years ago, raised its voice of solemn warning against this flagrant violation of every principle of mercy, justice, and humanity. Yet we blush to announce to you, that this warning has been often disregarded, even by those who hold to our communion. Cases have occurred in our own denomination where professors of the reli-

---

* Vide *Amer. Churches*, &c., by J. G. Birney, to whose statement we have added a further extract from the *Expression of Views*, as republished by the General Assembly in 1846. (*Ch. In.*, April, 1846.)

gion of mercy HAVE TORN THE MOTHER FROM THE CHILDREN, AND SENT HER INTO A MERCILESS AND RETURNLESS EXILE. Yet acts of discipline have rarely [*never!**] followed such conduct."

But, who would have believed it?—the Synod of Kentucky *were* not, and *are* not, in favor of *present* emancipation on the soil. With a knowledge of the "incontestible fact" (as Henry Clay calls it), that the internal slave trade is inseparable from slavery, and equally aware, as they must be, that no removal of the slaves could be effected in a century, the Synod of Kentucky, and its leading members, who tell us this sad story, are unwilling to listen to any proposal for emancipation, without the colonization of the slaves. And the one only Presbyterian minister within their bounds who advocated immediate and unconditional emancipation on the soil, was given to understand by his Presbytery, that he could not consistently remain with them.† The Synod has fresh cause to "blush"—but it will need something besides blushes to purge out the plague spot. To "*confess*" avails little, unless they "*forsake*."

In 1835, Mr. Stewart, of Illinois, a ruling elder, in advocating sundry anti-slavery memorials, urged the General Assembly to take action on the subject. He said:

"In this church, a man may take a free-born child, force it away from its parents, to whom God gave it in charge, saying, ' Bring it up for me,' and sell it as a beast, or hold it in perpetual bondage, and not only escape corporal punishment, but really be esteemed an excellent Christian. Nay, even ministers of the Gospel, and Doctors of Divinity, may engage in this unholy traffic, and yet sustain their high and holy calling."—" Elders, ministers, and Doctors of Divinity, are, with both hands, engaged in the practice."

The facts were not disputed; yet nothing was done to censure the act or the actors, further than to appoint a committee, a majority of whom were known to be opposed to the prayer of the memorialists (of which the late Dr. Samuel Miller,

---

* J. G. Birney, long resident in Kentucky, says " *never*."
† J. G. Fee.—The intimation was heeded.

Professor at Princeton, was chairman), to report at the next session.

In 1836, this report was presented at Pittsburg. In a preamble, it is said that "the subject of slavery is inseparably connected with the laws of many of the States of this Union, with which it is *by no means proper for an ecclesiastical body to interfere*,* and that "any action on the part of this Assembly, &c., would tend to distract and divide our churches," &c. Resolutions were therefore recommended declaring it "*inexpedient* for the Assembly to take any further order in relation to this subject;" also affirming that the note on the eighth commandment, in 1794, was "introduced irregularly—never had the sanction of the church, and therefore never possessed any authority," &c.

A minority of the committee, Messrs. Dickey and Beman, presented a report, declaring "the buying, selling, or holding a human being as property" "a heinous sin," that "ought to subject the doer of it to the censures of the church," &c., &c.; whereupon forty-eight slaveholding delegates met apart, and resolved that if any such action was taken by the Assembly they would not submit to the decision. They also, at an adjourned meeting, prepared a substitute for Dr. Miller's resolution, declaring that "the General Assembly have no authority to assume or exercise jurisdiction in regard to the existence of slavery."

The subject was finally disposed of by a long preamble and a brief resolution, that "this whole subject be indefinitely postponed."

In the meantime, while the Assembly were in session, a pamphlet, being a reprint of an article in the *Princeton Repertory*, was issued from the Pittsburg press, labelled, "for gratuitous circulation" among the members of the Assembly. It is said to have been written by Prof. Hodge, of Princeton,

---

* Yet the funds of the Presbyterian Church, at this moment, to the amount of more than $94,000, were invested in the South-Western banks, in prospect of gaining more than 6 per cent. interest, on account of the unprecedented briskness of the domestic slave trade. For the sequel see a succeeding Chapter.

and is regarded at the South as the strongest Bible argument for slavery. It contained the following:

> "At the time of the advent of Jesus Christ, slavery in its worst forms prevailed over the world. The Savior found it around him in Judea, the apostles met with it in Asia, Greece, and Italy. How did they treat it? Not by the denunciation of SLAVEHOLDING as necessarily SINFUL. The assumption that slaveholding is, in itself, a crime, is not only an error, but it is an error fraught with evil consequences."

In 1837, many anti-slavery memorials were presented to the Assembly. They were referred to a committee, of which Dr. Witherspoon, a slaveholder, of South Carolina, was chairman, and which reported, near the time for adjournment, that the memorials be "returned to the house," and the chairman moved to lay the whole subject on the table. This was done by a vote of 97 to 28.

At this same session the General Assembly excinded four northern Synods, called New School, containing a Presbyterian population of about sixty thousand persons. This was done ostensibly on account of theological differences, but it is remarkable that it cut off a very large proportion of the active opponents of slavery in the communion of the Presbyterian Church. Dr. G. A. Baxter, President of the Union Theological Seminary, Prince Edward Co., Va., changed sides suddenly from New School to Old, about the same time, and justified the change by avowing that "one motive" was the firm position of the Old School against abolition. And since the separation, in 1838, some anti-abolition clergyman, once known as New School, within the bounds of the excinded Synods, in the State of New York, have transferred their relations to the Old School.

OLD SCHOOL GENERAL ASSEMBLY.

"In 1838, the two Schools separated,* leaving three slaveholding Presby-

---

* The separation in 1838 is understood to have been for the same cause as the excision of 1837.

According to a correspondent of the *New York Observer*, Dr. Gardiner Spring, of New York, at a Colonization Meeting in Washington City, in 1839, held the following language:

teries represented in the New, and between thirty and forty in the Old."—
" Since that time the Old School has abode firmly on the Princeton ground."

In 1838, the O. S. General Assembly resolved that "it is of the greatest consequence to the best interests of our church, that the subject of slavery shall not be discussed in the ensuing General Assembly," &c.

In 1843, they laid anti-slavery memorials on the table without reading.

In 1845, after an hour's discussion, at Cincinnati, they adopted a report that they could not treat slavery as necessarily a sin, " without charging the apostles of Christ with conniving at such sin." " For the Assembly to make slaveholding a bar to communion would be to dissolve itself."— *Vide statements of Pres. Blanchard and Cincinnati Herald* of May 28, 1845 ; *Chr. Inv.*, June, 1847.

In 1847, the General Assembly reaffirmed all its former testimonies on slavery, contradictory as they were.

In 1850, in reply to a resolution of the General Association of Massachusetts communicated to the General Assembly, and very courteously expressing their conviction that the cause of religion required the removal of slavery from the churches, the General Assembly adopted the following:

Resolved, " That our delegates to the next General Association of Massachusetts be directed to inform that venerable body that this General Assembly must consider itself the best judge of the action which it is necessary for it to take as to all subjects within its jurisdiction, and that any interference on the part of that General Association with its action upon any subject upon which this General Assembly has taken action, is offensive, and must lead to an interruption of the correspondence which subsists between that Association and the General Assembly."—*Oberlin Evan.*, June 19, 1850.

From the Old School we now turn to the New.

" He stated that the unhappy divisions in the Presbyterian Church had grown out of this opposition" (*i. e.* to " the proceedings and designs of the Abolition Society"), " and, painful as it was, they were obliged to rend the church to avoid being engulfed in the sentiments, feelings, and schemes of abolitionists."

At other times, the ground of division had been stated to be the heresy of " New School" theology, and tendencies towards Congregational Church government in the New School portion of the Presbyterian Church.

NEW-SCHOOL GENERAL ASSEMBLY.

" In 1838, the New-School General Assembly appointed a committee on anti-slavery memorials, which reported ' that the applicants, for reasons satisfactory to themselves, have withdrawn their papers.' The committee was discharged."—*Birney's American Churches*, &c., p. 33.

The excuse was, that business connected with the division of the two assemblies made it difficult to attend to another subject.

" In 1839, it referred the whole subject to the Presbyteries, to do what they might deem advisable."

In 1840, a large number of memorials and petitions against slavery were sent in, and referred to the usual committee. The committee reported a resolution—referring to what had been done last year*—declaring it inexpedient for the Assembly to do anything further on the subject. Several attempts were made by the abolition members of the Assembly to obtain a decided expression of its views, but they proved ineffectual, and the whole subject was indefinitely postponed."—*Ib.*

This measure was adopted on motion of " Rev. Samuel H. Cox, D.D., of the city of Brooklyn (N. Y.) On the motion being carried, he exultingly said : " Our Vesuvius is safely capped for three years"—the Assembly not meeting again till 1843.—*Ib.*

" In 1843, the General Assembly censured the action of those anti-slavery Presbyteries which had excluded slaveholding from their pulpits and communion tables, and requested them to rescind their acts; thus condemning them for obeying their own advice, or excluding slaveholding from fellowship."—*Letter of Pres. Blanchard*, &c.

In 1846, the General Assembly adopted a paper drawn up by Dr. Duffield, declaring the unrighteous and oppressive character of slavery, lamenting its continued existence in the churches, exhorting to the use of all means in their power to put it away from them, since no mere mitigation of its severity "would be regarded as a testimony against the system, or as, in the least degree, changing its essential character."

After all this, the Assembly, nevertheless, at the same time,

---

* The language employed, either in 1839 or '40, we believe, was this: "Solemnly referring the whole subject to the lower judicatories, to take such action as in their judgment is most judicious and adapted to remove *the evil* "—refusing the request of Rev. Geo. Beecher to insert the word *moral* before *evil ;* that is, they refused to call slavery a *moral evil.*—*Vide Letter of Pres. Blanchard and others.*

proceeded to say that it "cannot determine the degree of moral turpitude involved"—"cannot pronounce a judgment of general and promiscuous condemnation,"—it recognizes "embarrassments and obstacles in the way of emancipation"—it cannot "exclude slaveholders from the table of the Lord"—it would rather "sympathize with and succor them in their embarrassments"—it condemns all divisive and schismatic measures *tending to destroy the unity, and disturb the peace of our Church*." The "Assembly possesses no legislative or judicial authority;" it must, therefore, "*leave it with the Sessions, Presbyteries, and Synods*," &c., &c.!—*Vide Chr. Inv., June,* 1847.

The confusion, incongruity, and self-contradiction of this action, can hardly escape notice, even when our attention is confined to the doings of this one session. Slavery is characterized as unrighteous and oppressive; but this unrighteousness and oppression must not be promiscuously condemned, nor excluded from the table of the Lord, lest it should destroy the unity and disturb the peace of the Church.

Still more confused, incongruous, and self-contradictory does the action of the General Assembly appear, when the doings of one session, in one year, are compared with those of another. In 1839, the whole subject was referred to the Presbyteries; in 1843, the Presbyteries were censured for acting, and requested to rescind their acts; but in 1846 the subject was again referred to the Presbyteries. In 1846, as in 1839, the Assembly possessed no legislative or judicial authority; but in 1843 its powers appear to have been ample. The true solution seems to be that the Assembly has no power *against* slavery, but claims and exercises power in *its favor*. It could not censure slavery, but it could censure Presbyteries by whom slavery is censured. It could go further than this, and restore to his former standing, a minister (Dr. Graham) who, in 1845, had been suspended by his Presbytery (acting on recommendation of the Assembly,) for defending slavery by the Bible.* This was done in 1846, or afterwards.

---

* He maintained that Jesus Christ "has authorized slaveholding, in the charters of the Church, and in all the laws he ever made, for its regulation."

The General Assembly of 1846 also invited the Old School General Assembly, then sitting in the same city, to unite with them in a celebration of the Lord's Supper, but the invitation was declined, and the Old School Assembly bears the blame of the "schism."

Thus does the Presbyterian New School, like the Methodist Episcopal Church North, by a fair implication, profess that slavery is not to be regarded as a sufficient cause of division, or a bar against Christian communion. This will further appear as we proceed.

In 1849, the General Assembly, in strange forgetfulness, one would think, of the facts conceded or implied in its testimony of 1846, declared:

"That there has been no information before this Assembly to prove that the members of our Church, in the slave States, are not doing all they can (situated as they are, in the providence of God) to bring about the possession and enjoyment of liberty by the enslaved."—*Copied from Letter of Pres. Blanchard*, &c.

The slaveholders could, at any time, if they pleased, give their slaves a "pass" into the Free States, which, in most cases, would not only be eagerly accepted, but carried into operation with little or no expense or trouble to the masters, to say nothing of the practicability, in Kentucky, &c., of making them legally free on the soil.

In 1850, the General Assembly, (no longer triennial,*) came together again, and after a long discussion, during which a number of propositions for acting against slavery were rejected, settled down upon a declaration very closely resembling that of 1846, so far as direct action by the General Assembly is concerned.

Among the propositions rejected, one, presented by "Rev.

---

* In 1849, overtures were sent down to the Presbyteries in favor of making the General Assemblies annual again, instead of triennial, and in 1850, on their coming together, the answers being favorable, the constitution was changed back again, making the meetings henceforth annual. The policy of having triennial conventions had answered its purpose, there being now no fires in the "Vesuvius" to threaten an explosion.

H. Curtiss of Indiana," was, "That the enslaving of men, or the holding of them as property, is an offence, as defined in our Book of Discipline, Chap. I., Sec. 3, and that as such, it calls for inquiry, correction, and removal, in the manner prescribed by our rules, and should be treated with a due regard to all the aggravating or mitigating circumstances of each particular case "—also, " that this General Assembly, in the exercise of its power of bearing testimony against immorality in practice, and "of attempting reformation of manners, and the promotion of charity, truth, and holiness, through all the churches under their care,' do most earnestly recommend to the proper judicatories to take measures in accordance with the foregoing principles."

This would seem sufficiently mild and guarded, if the Assembly had been willing to meet directly, the sin, in any way of effective reproof.

Equally so was another proposition presented by P. F. Smith, an Elder, from Pennsylvania, affirming that slaveholding was "*prima facia* an offence within the meaning of our Book of Discipline," and throwing upon the slaveholder " the burden of showing such circumstances," as "will take away from him the guilt of the offence."

The *rejection* of these propositions will assist the reader to a better understanding of the propositions *adopted* by the Assembly, the most pointed of which was the following :

That slavery " is fraught with many and great *evils*." That they " deplore the workings* of the whole system of slavery," and that " the holding of our fellow-men in the condition of slavery, *except* in those cases where it is unavoidable by the laws of the *State*, the obligations of *guardianship*, or the *demands of humanity*, is an offence in the proper import of that term, as used in the Book of Discipline, Chap. I., Sec. 3, and should be regarded and treated in the same manner as other offences." Also *referring* the subject to the " Sessions and Presbyteries, &c."

---

* In 1846, the General Assembly had called slavery "unrighteous." Having failed to purge away this "unrighteousness," it must, in 1850, be spoken of in milder terms. It is only an "evil," the "workings" of which are "deplorable." Among its "deplorable workings" should be reckoned its power to neutralize and alter the moral creed of the church.

The *exceptions* above specified will be found to embrace the very excuses in view of which all slaveholders continue the practice, except those who justify slavery "in the abstract," and consider it a blessing instead of an evil.

Even this action, however, was strenuously opposed.

"The vote stood 84 to 16, under a written protest of the minority who were for no action, in the present state of the country. Two were excused from voting."—*N. Y. Observer*, June 15, 1850.

The adoption of even this evasive testimony is to be construed in the light of the following action, by the same body, at the same session, by which, after this idle show of threatening *some sorts* of slaveholders with Church discipline, the New School General Assembly eagerly throws its arms of embrace around *all* sorts of slaveholders in the Old School Assembly, including slavery propagandists, extensionists, slave sellers, and all. A statement was *unanimously* adopted, of which the following is the substance :

This Assembly cherished the idea of re-union, (with the Old School Assembly,) until 1841, when it was reluctantly relinquished. "Again, in 1846 they expressed the desire for union with our brethren, and, pained by the unusual exhibition of two such bodies, at apparent strife with each other, they proposed to the other Assembly, a mutual recognition of each other, by communing together at the table of our Master." " These propositions and overtures were all made in good faith." " We do not pretend to question the motives of our brethren in rejecting them."

Declining, under these circumstances, to make any new overtures, the Report and the Assembly, say :

" We should be untrue to ourselves, before God and the world, did we not frankly avow our readiness to meet in a spirit of fraternal kindness and christian love, any overtures which may be made to us by the other body."
—See *N. Y. Observer*, June 15, 1850.

Thus, then, " before God and the world," the New School General Assembly of 1850 "unanimously" declared itself ready to commune with the Old School, at a time when the great body of Old School Presbyterians at the South were zealous for the extension of slavery, claimed of the Federal Government its extension as an act of justice, and defended it as a Bible institution.—*See letter of a Southern Clergyman in New York Observer, same date as the above.*

The discriminating reader will now judge for himself respecting the moral difference between the Old School and the New, in their relations to slavery. The one has more slaveholders under its jurisdiction than the other, but both tolerate the practice.* The one does this to retain many members; the other to retain a few. The one does it believing slavery to be a Bible institution; the other, believing it to be "unrighteous" and "oppressive." The one makes no pretence of any intention to discipline any sort of slaveholders; the other holds the rod over a class of them that it "has no information" of being found within its enclosures, but yearns to go out of its boundaries to clasp them to its bosom.

In 1851, the General Assembly met at Utica, New York. It declined to take action against slavery, and won the commendation of President Fillmore, who expressed to some members of the Assembly his high gratification with the proceedings.

---

* The following statement is from a lecture by Pres. Blanchard, as reported in the *Cleveland True Democrat* of Sept. 26, 1851 :

"The Old School branch has now *fifty* slaveholding Presbyteries; more than one-third of its whole number.

"The New School Assembly, at its first separate meeting, in 1838, was followed by but three slaveholding commissioners, and there was fervent prayer and strong hope that this might become an anti-slavery body. But once separated from the Old School, and seized by the natural desire for denominational success, its has steadily increased its slaveholding wing till it has now *twenty* slaveholding Presbyteries, between one and two hundred ministers, *and from fifteen to twenty thousand members, in the slave States, all walking in Christian fellowship with slaveholders.*

CHAPTER XIV.

POSITION OF THE AMERICAN CHURCHES, ETC. CONTINUED.

III.—CONGREGATIONALISTS.

Connection with Presbyterians and the South—Pro-slavery Sermons—Prof. Stuart—
Andover Theo. Seminary—General Association of Connecticut, 1834, 1836, 1840,
1845—Rejected Resolutions compared with Resolutions Adopted—General Asso.
of Massachusetts, 1834, 1837, 1849—Convention of Cong. Ministers, 1848—Gen.
Conf. of Maine—Cong. Periodicals, N. E. Spectator, Vermont Chronicle.

CONGREGATIONALISTS, like Baptists, are subject to the control of no ecclesiastical body, holding jurisdiction over the
whole country. Unlike Baptists, Presbyterians, and Methodists, they number no churches, or none sufficient to deserve
notice, in the present slaveholding States. They claim to be,
emphatically, the descendants and successors of the Puritans,
and of that particular branch of them whose democratic polity
gave origin to the free institutions—so far as they *are* free—
of republican America. Congregationalists have had, moreover, the chief influence in moulding the religious and moral
sentiment of New England; they have their central home and
seat in the birth-place of Hopkins and Edwards, the scene of
their agitating anti-slavery labors, in the atmosphere of a theological literature enriched by those luminaries, and still cherished in the churches as a badge of honorable distinction.
Theoretically, they are, for the most part, or claim to be, of
the same creed or phase of religious faith, the very technicalities of which are identified with the most uncompromising of
all schemes of ethics, allowing no palliatives of transgression,
no exceptions to the demand of immediate and unconditional

abandonment of all sin. Assuredly, then, Congregationalists can have no valid excuse, if they are not foremost in their opposition to slavery. Of those to whom much is given shall much be required.

But Congregationalists, through their Associations of Ministers, have held regular correspondence and close affinity with Presbyterians; have received delegates from the General Assembly, and sent delegates to them. Congregational ministers removing out of New England, have readily become Presbyterian. And Presbyterian ministers have been received as pastors of Congregational churches. Congregationalism in Connecticut has been so modified as to be claimed by Presbyterian writers as being virtually Presbyterian. In the Middle and Northwestern States, a "plan of accommodation," so called, has brought churches claiming to be Congregational into connection with the Presbyteries. In all these ways, as well as by missionary co-operation, by plans and processes of ministerial education, as well as by similarity of creed, and identity of rituals and forms of public worship, the cord of sympathy and the bond of unity between Congregationalists and Presbyterians have been strengthened. Congregational ministers, educated in New England, transferred to the Presbyterian church, and located, by the enterprising spirit of New England emigration, *in the slaveholding States,* have often become slaveholders themselves, and defenders or apologists of the slave system, and commonly without forfeiting their religious character or ecclesiastical standing with their friends and relatives in New England.* The same spirit of emigra-

---

* The following statement, made by "Rev. A. H. H. Boyd, of Virginia," in the New School General Assembly of the Presbyterian Church, in 1850, has a bearing quite as appropriate and significant upon northern Congregationalists, as upon northern Presbyterians:

"In the Southern country *we depend* upon the north for ministers, in a great measure. *Few* of our Southern young men are educated for ministers. In some parts it is necessary that some born South should endorse a minister, before commencing his labor, because *some* have endeavored to loosen the relation of master and slave."—*N. Y. Observer,* June 15, 1850.

A similar remark would apply to schoolmasters, only that there is, perhaps, less

tion, and especially the habit of temporary sojourn, or residence, as school teachers, or as commercial adventurers, in the slaveholding States, has drawn large numbers of Congregational laymen into close sympathy with Presbyterian slave holders at the South, with whom they have worshipped. Becoming comparatively wealthy, and returning home to the North, to settle for life, not a few of them, though preferring for their own comfort a residence in a free State, have lost their abhorrence of the *sin* of slavery, and have exerted a wide and strong influence in favor of a religious fraternity with slaveholders. Intermarriages between slaveholding and non-slaveholding families, commercial intercourse, and political co-operation, are thrown into the same scale.

Congregationalists in New England, as well as other members of churches, and perhaps to a greater extent than in most other sects at the North, as being most numerous and enterprising, have been subjected to influences of this character. Besides all this, Congregational ministers in New England, along with other gentlemen of the learned professions, (who were then chiefly members of congregational churches,) constituted a large portion of the few who were slaveholders, during the existence of slavery in the Northern and Eastern States, there being few, then, in New England, of other religious sects, thus making that denomination responsible for a very great portion of all the slaveholding that ever existed in New England. And there is no reason to think that all of these slaveholding Congregationalists, whether laymen or ministers, ever welcomed heartily and fully the radical views of Hopkins and Edwards on this subject, or ceased to become slaveholders until slaveholding became impracticable under the State laws.

It would be idle to suppose that facts like these would be without their significance and bearing in that general decline

---

jealousy of them. Schoolmasters and ministers for the South have been reckoned among the staple exports of New England, and they are commonly adapted to the market. Can the Congregational churches of New England, which supply a large share of these teachers of religion and literature, be uninfluenced by such facts?

of the spirit of liberty already noticed, or that they could fail to affect the position of the Congregational ministers and churches of New England, on the opening of the present anti-slavery contest.

The distribution of the Princeton pamphlet among the members of the Presbyterian General Assembly, at Pittsburg, in 1836, before mentioned, was the beginning of a series of similar demonstrations among clergymen at the North, not excepting Congregational ministers in New England, from whom at least three printed sermons in biblical defence or palliation of slavery appeared not long afterwards. They were echoes of the Princeton doctrine, not marked with any unusual force of reasoning; and, not coming from sources particularly suited to arrest attention, they produced no very deep, general, or permanent impression. The most remarkable thing in respect to them was, that they procured for their authors no such ecclesiastical disclaimers, in the proceedings of their respective associations and consociations, as those with which the doctrines or measures of abolitionists in the same ecclesiastical connections were so bountifully visited about the same time. If not fully approved, they were not accounted so heretical as to deserve the notice that would have been given to any departure from their recognized theological standards. The same doctrine from Dr. Graham, some years afterwards, was branded as a heresy by the Presbyterian Synod of Cincinnati. But in 1836 it does not appear to have been regarded as "heresy," by the Congregational bodies in New England, whatever may be supposed to have been the prevalent sentiment among them.

Nor can it be said that any remarkable improvement was perceptible in 1837. In that year an occasion presented itself for remonstrating against the heresy of biblical human chattelhood, had it been accounted a heresy, as promulgated from a quarter that could not be accounted too obscure to require notice.

MOSES STUART, Professor in the Theological Seminary at Andover, Mass., stood then, and for many years afterwards, at the very head of the department of sacred literature among the Congregationalists in New England. *To him*, more than to any other man living at that time, and while he held his professorship, were biblical students of the Congregational order encouraged to look up for solid instruction in the science of expounding the Scriptures. What *he* might say concerning the teachings of the Bible on the subject of slavery would be likely to exert, at least, as powerful an influence among Congregationalists as the expressed opinions of any other man.

The late Dr. Fisk, then President of the Wesleyan University, at Middletown, Conn., whose views of slavery the reader has seen in our account of the position of the Methodist Episcopal Church, addressed a letter to Prof. Stuart, designed to draw out, for publication, his views of the slave question. The following is an extract from Prof. Stuart's answer:

" 1. The precepts of the New Testament respecting the demeanor of slaves and of their masters, beyond all question recognize the existence of slavery. The masters are, in part, ' believing masters,' so that a precept to them, how they are to behave, as *masters*, recognizes that the relation may exist, *salva fide, et salva ecclesia.** Otherwise, Paul had nothing to do but to cut the bond asunder at once. He could not lawfully and properly temporize with a *malum in se.*†

" If any one doubts, let him take the case of Paul's sending Onesimus back to Philemon, with an apology for his running away, and sending him back to be a servant for life. The relation did exist, may exist. The *abuse* of it is the essential and fundamental wrong. Not that the theory of slavery is, in itself, right. No. ' Love thy neighbor as thyself'—' Do unto others that which ye would that others should do unto you,' decide against this. But the relation once constituted and continued, is not such a *malum in se* as calls for immediate and violent disrupture, at all hazards. So Paul did not counsel.

" 2. 1 Tim. 6 : 2, expresses the sentiment that slaves who are Christians, and have Christian masters, are not, on that account, and because, *as Christians they are brethren*, to forego the reverence due to them as masters. That is, the relation of master and slave is not, as a matter of course, abrogated between all Christians. Nay, servants should, in such a case,

---

* i. e. " *Without violating the Christian faith, or the Church.*"
† i. e. *That which is, in itself, sin.*

a fortiori, do their duty cheerfully. This sentiment lies on the very face of the case. What the master's duty in such a case, in respect to *liberation*, is another question, and one which the apostle does not here treat of."

Learned men are not always wise. Beneficial as the science of biblical exigesis may be, when needed, and when directed by Christian simplicity and manly common sense, it can never be otherwise than powerless, except for mischief, when wielded either without or against them, or when used to mystify and perplex what is already plain. Aside from such glosses as those just now quoted, and in the absence of the iniquitous practices that gave rise to them, no simple-minded reader of the New Testament would ever have detected in the passages commented upon, the slightest sanction of such usages as those that go to define modern slaveholding. The art, most assuredly, is not a desirable one, that could thus torture and invert the plain import of Paul's Letter to Philemon. In this instance, the beautiful and affectionate dissuasive of "Paul the aged" against the too rigid exaction of an honest debt, voluntarily assumed, is transmuted into an apostolic warranty and example for the rendition of fugitive slaves. This result could not be reached without a palpable and direct falsification of the text; which says, "Receive him"—"*Not* now as a servant, but above a servant, a brother beloved," "both in the flesh, and in the Lord :"—a brother, in the secular as well as the religious acceptation of the term. Instead of this, the apostle is represented as "sending him back to be a servant for life." Onesimus was not a slave, for a slave can make no contract and incur no debt. Yet Paul entreated (what he says he might have enjoined by authority), that the obligation should be cancelled. But whatever we consider to be the relation between the parties, the entire drift of the epistle was evidently to induce a change, and not a continuance, of the relation.

In his exposition of 1 Tim. 6 : 2, the learned writer coolly took for granted the very gist of the controversy, by assuming that the word rendered "master" is equivalent to "slaveholder," and that there could have been no "servants" but

" slaves." It had often been shown that this was not the fact, but the Professor takes no notice of this, and makes no attempt to prove or show the contrary.

It would be difficult to reconcile Prof. Stuart with himself, or with the plain dictates of the Christian religion and of common sense, which the learned and the unlearned can equally understand. The following propositions and results will be found involved in his statements:

" The theory of slavery is not, in itself, right;" but the practice of slavery is not, in itself, wrong.

The law of love and the golden rule decide the question of slavery *one* way, but Paul's advice to servants and masters, and his sending back Onesimus, decide it *the other* way.

The relation may exist without violating Christianity or the Church, but the relation is founded in a theory that is not, in itself, right; in other words, Christianity and the Church are not violated by the opposite of moral right.

The "*abuse*" of the relation "is the fundamental and essential *wrong*," but the relation itself cannot claim its origin in moral *right*.

The relation, though not founded in moral *right*, when "*once constituted*" is not a moral *wrong*.

Paul "could not temporize with" what was wrong in itself; but he would not "cut asunder at once" the bond of a relation that was the opposite of moral right.

And while the Professor decides promptly that Paul would not do this, he confesses he cannot tell what Paul would say of "*the duty of the master in respect to liberation*," because *that* question was "one of which the apostle does not here treat of."

" The duty of the master in respect to liberation" was the very question that then agitated the country. It was because abolitionists insisted upon this "duty," that they were opposed and censured, and the pen of Prof. Stuart was invoked to counteract their influence. To this end he controverted their doctrine, that slaveholding is sinful. If not sinful, who could urge upon them the "duty" of giving up the practice? But, after all, it is conceded that Paul was not treating of the duty of liberation, and Prof. Stuart does not know what he would have said on that subject.

Then Paul was not treating of the lawfulness or unlawfulness of slaveholding:—he was not treating on the question whether "the relation of master and slave" was "abrogated among Christians." If Prof. Stuart was aware of all this, why did he labor to make the contrary impression?

Does any one now inquire whether, or to what extent, the Congregationalists of the North and of New England were responsible for these opinions of Prof. Stuart? We will answer by propounding another inquiry.

Suppose Prof. Stuart, instead of writing what we have here quoted concerning slavery, had written a biblical defence of Universalism, or of some other doctrine that orthodox Congregationalists had considered "heresy." Then suppose the intercourse, the bearing, and the relations of the Congregational sect towards Prof. Stuart had continued to be what every one knows they were, at the time of his writing on slavery, and for fifteen years afterwards—we ask, whether orthodox Congregationalists in England, and whether public sentiment, the world over, would not inevitably have held New England Congregationalists, as a body, responsible for his doctrines?

When Dr. Graham, in the Presbyterian Church, wrote a biblical defence of slaveholding, his Synod suspended him from the ministry. Why? Because they knew that they should otherwise be held responsible for his heresy; which was substantially the same with that of Prof. Stuart,* who, had he been a member of the Synod of Cincinnati, would probably have been suspended, likewise.

It may be said that Congregationalists hold no such ecclesiastical powers. But they hold and freely exercise (no

---

* It may be said that Prof. Stuart's defence of slavery was less self-consistent than Dr. Graham's, containing concessions that overturned his whole argument. This only shows that he was not unaware that the principles of Christianity were hostile to slavery, while he was laboring to construe particular texts in its favor.

"General Assembly" forbidding them) the power of withdrawing religious co-operation and communion. Had Prof. Stuart avowed himself a Universalist, it would have been promptly done. And the same result would have been witnessed had a defence of slavery been thought as heretical as Universalism.

Suppose, again, that Prof. Stuart had written concerning adultery, or concubinage (one feature of slavery), or concerning robbery, or horse-stealing, or any other known and proscribed crime, as he wrote concerning slaveholding. Would or would not an impartial public sentiment abroad, or in coming ages, hold the sect responsible that continued to hold fraternity with him, to confide in him as a religious teacher, an accomplished educator of religious teachers?

No personal dislike of Prof. Stuart has occasioned these remarks. He had his attractive traits of character. He was the admired representative of a class—a very large class—of Congregational ministers, his associates and pupils. His memory is still venerated; he is proudly pointed to, by his sect, as "the father of the science of biblical criticism in America;" and the clergy of other sects recognize the validity of the claim. All this tends directly and almost irresistibly to confirm, in the community, the belief that slaveholding is not inconsistent with the Bible. If "the father of biblical criticism" says so, who shall contradict it? One in ten of those who receive his testimony, may infer the innocency of slaveholding; while nine in ten will infer the moral deficiency of the Bible, and this will swell the tide of horror and amazement at "infidel abolitionism." Impartial history, if it attempts to look below the surface of things, and trace effects to their causes, must give marked prominence to influences like these. The real position of the sects could not otherwise be understood.

It is not known that the Trustees, Faculty, and friends of the Theological Seminary at Andover, were ever distressed with the apprehension that Prof. Stuart's heresy on the slave question would diminish the patronage, or injure the reputation of their institution, in which he held so conspicuous a post. But no one will doubt that those fears would have risen to a high pitch, had he dissented from the policy of the Colonization Society, or avowed himself an advocate of immediate and unconditional emancipation. The views of Prof. Stuart were extensively circulated among the Congregational churches and ministry of New England. Had there been any general or earnest dissent from them, or if his intimate associates had been grieved at his course, the religious journals of the denomination would have contained evidence of the fact. Slight shades of difference in metaphysical speculation, among professors of theology, have given rise to rival claims among the Theological Seminaries of New England, but the position of the learned Professor at Andover concerning slavery has occasioned no manifestations of that character. Dissent was indeed strongly expressed; but it was the dissent of an inconsiderable though increasing minority, not of the main body.

It may be in place to add here, that soon after the passage, by Congress, of the Fugitive Slave Bill, in 1850, Prof. Stuart (who had previously resigned his Professorship at Andover), appeared as the public defender and eulogist of Hon. Daniel Webster, for the part he took in procuring and vindicating that iniquitous measure. In company with Dr. Leonard Woods, late Professor at Andover, Prof. Ralph Emerson, of the same institution, and other Congregational ministers,* he gave his signature to a paper drawn up for the purpose. And afterwards he vindicated his position in a pamphlet, at some length.

This new demonstration in favor of slavery, we are happy to add, appears to have been less favorably received among Congregationalists, than the former one. It is understood that most of the Professors at Andover declined signing the paper above-mentioned (though they entered no public protest

---

* Among the names appended to this paper were those of Dr. Dana of Newburyport, Rev. W. W. Rogers of Boston, Pres; Sparks of Harvard College (Unitarian), &c., &c.

or disclaimer against it), and the pamphlet has probably exerted an influence in the direction opposite to its design.*

GENERAL ASSOCIATION OF CONNECTICUT.

The General Association of Congregational Ministers in Connecticut have repeatedly defined their position in respect to slavery. The resolutions adopted at different times are as follows:

At Vernon, in 1834. *Resolved,* That to buy and sell human beings, or to hold and treat them as merchandise, or to treat servants, free or bond, in any manner inconsistent with the fact that they are intelligent and voluntary beings, made in the image of God, is a violation of the principles of the word of God, and should be treated by all the churches of our Lord Jesus Christ as an immorality, inconsistent with a profession of the Christian religion.

Resolved, that this Association regards the laws and usages in respect to slavery, which exist in many of the States of this Union, as inconsistent with the character and responsibilities of a free and Christian people, and holds it to be the duty of every Christian, and especially of every Minister of the Gospel, to use all prudent and lawful efforts for the peaceful abolition of slavery.

"At Norfolk, in 1836. *Resolved,* that in the judgment of this Association, the buying and selling of human beings, and the holding them for selfish ends, by the ministers and members of our Churches removing to the South, is a great sin, and utterly inconsistent with their Christian profession.

At New Haven, in 1840. *Resolved,* that American slavery, is, in the opinion of this body, inconsistent with the principles of the Gospel, and its immediate abolition by those who have the legal power, is a duty in the discharge of which the blessing of heaven may be expected.

Resolved, that we recommend to the churches under our care, a prayerful consideration of this important subject, and the exertion of their appropriate influence for the emancipation of all the enslaved throughout this land and throughout the world.

---

* And yet it remains true that the Fugitive Slave Bill of 1850 has its earnest advocates among Congregationalists, as it certainly has among the leading ministers and editors of the Presbyterian and other denominations, by whom a strenuous effort has been made to cast odium and reproach upon those who maintain, in reference to this enactment, that the laws of God are paramount to the unrighteous edicts of man, and annul them. Under such circumstances, it would seem the duty of all who fear God, to bear solemn testimony against such impiety.

In 1845. *Resolved,* that we again adopt these resolutions, as the expression of our present views, and direct our scribe to transmit a copy of them to the stated clerks of each of the bodies, styled " The General Assembly."

To the reader uninitiated in the nice distinctions elaborated by the New England Congregational Clergy, in their discussions on this subject, these Resolutions, standing by themselves, would appear to be tolerably distinct testimonies against the practice of slaveholding. To understand them correctly, they must be construed in the light of what the same bodies *refused* to say, on the same subject, and also in the light of the discussions had, at the time of adopting them.

We will, therefore, put them by the side of the resolutions " offered by Rev. Mr. Perkins of Meriden, in 1845," but not adopted :

" Whereas, this Association has frequently delivered its opinions in relation to slaveholding—and whereas, recent events, such as the imprisonment of Christian men, on the charge of aiding slaves to escape, and the late action of the General Assembly of the Presbyterian Church, seems to require the reiteration of our views, therefore resolved :

" 1st. That we consider slaveholding as an outrage on human rights, and at variance with the spirit of Christianity.

" 2d. That no man is bound in conscience to obey slave law.

" 3d. That while it may be matter of judgment and expediency what measures should be taken, and what risks incurred in aiding the colored man to escape from bondage, as once the like considerations should have been weighed in deciding how far we should have gone in aiding a white slave to escape from Algiers ; yet the right to give such aid, we hold to be undeniable.

" 4th. That we recommend, to our churches, to give a place to the slave in their prayers and benevolent efforts, together with the usual religious objects of the day.

" 5th. That our delegate to the General Assembly of the Presbyterian Church, carry from us to that body, a letter on its connection with slavery."

After a long debate, *these* Resolutions were set aside, and the action taken which has already been recorded. On a comparison it will be seen that the Association declined saying that "no man is bound in conscience to obey slave law"— declined expressing sympathy for " Christian men," imprisoned on charge of aiding fugitive slaves—declined affirming the *right* of assisting such fugitives—declined recommending to the Churches to place anti-slavery efforts with other benevolent and religious objects—declined addressing to the General Assembly of the Presbyterian Church, a letter on *its connection* with slavery.

On a further examination of the Resolutions at different times adopted by the General Association, and re-affirmed in 1845, some further differences between the sentiments express-ed, and the rejected resolutions of Mr. Perkins, will be manifest.

The General Association, even in 1834, had learned, it seems, to condemn "*slavery*," rather than "*slaveholding*." The distinction was not then understood by the public as it has since been insisted on, and the preamble of Mr. Perkins, stat-ing that the General Association had "frequently delivered its opinions in relation to *slaveholding*," seems to have been considered too inaccurate a statement (as doubtless it was) to be endorsed. The Association had not condemned the *act*, but only the *abstraction*.

The resolutions of 1834 expended their strength upon "laws and usages," rather than upon persons doing a wrong act un-der shelter of them. They would be understood at the South as bearing against the slave *trade*, rather than against slave *holding*. They suggested, likewise the implication of a senti-ment since insisted on, that slaves *may* be held *without* being "treated as merchandise," and that the distinction between "bond *and* free" is, by no means, the significant point in that matter.

The resolution of 1836, plainly condemns buying, selling, and holding human beings as slaves, only when it is done for *selfish ends;* thus teaching, by implication, the doctrine now openly insisted on, that all this may be innocently and even laudably done, for *benevolent* ends—which is all the license the slaveholder asks. He thinks he only holds slaves for their own good.

The resolution of 1840 retains the same distinction between *slavery* and slave-*holding;* that is, slavery in the *abstract*, and slavery in *practice;* the former being almost universally condemned : the latter, very extensively defended or palliated.

The debates on the proposed Resolutions of Mr. Perkins illustrate the meaning of the Resolutions adopted.

Rev. Mr. Andrews vindicated the course of the General Assembly. Slavery (he said) existed in the time of Christ and his apostles. *They* did not condemn it. He would vote for no resolution that did not distinctly avow that slaveholding was not sin.

Rev. E. Hall, of Norwalk, said that if he supposed there was the least danger that these resolutions would pass, he would make a strenuous speech. He abhorred slavery totally, and from the bottom of his heart, but these resolutions were rank Garrisonism and Dorrism. He could not think more than one or two persons would vote for them.

Dr. Bennett Tyler (of the Theological Seminary at East Windsor) said that " Christ and his apostles did not condemn slaveholders, nor command them to emancipate their slaves."

" Rev. Mr. Ely" repeated the old story of Paul's returning a fugitive slave to his master. He would seek the conversion of the slaves first, and then seek their liberty in the Lord's way and in the Lord's time.

The *New York Observer*, in its account of this matter, declares that the resolutions introduced by Mr. Perkins were the most ultra and untenable ever heard of in any ecclesiastical body.

A severer satire upon " ecclesiastical bodies " it would be difficult to indite. If the Resolutions of Mr. Perkins were too ultra, there was an opportunity presented to the General Association, had they been disposed, to have adopted others of a sufficiently accommodating character.

Rev. S. W. S. Dutton was convinced that the resolutions of Mr. Perkins would not pass. If they were disposed of, he would offer the following :

" 1. *Resolved*, That the buying and selling of human beings for gain ; the forced separation of husbands and wives, parents and children ; the permission, by masters, to servants under their control, to live in a temporary concubinage, liable to be ended at any time by the caprice of either party, or by the caprice of others ; the withholding the Bible and the ability to read the Bible, by masters, from servants under their control and care ; and in general, the treatment of servants by masters in any manner inconsistent with their nature as immortal beings, for whom Christ gave himself to die, are crimes utterly inconsistent with a standing and a name in the Church of Christ.

" 2. *Resolved*, That all those laws, whether of individual States or of the United States, which, instead of prohibiting and punishing these crimes, require, or encourage, or allow them, are a foul disgrace to a people who glory in the possession of freedom as God's inalienable gift to man, and are deeply to be deplored by all friends of their country, as fitted to call down upon it the direst judgments of heaven.

"3. *Whereas*, There is a common fame, the cry of which has gone abroad to the ends of the earth, that these crimes are perpetrated by ministers and members in both branches of the Presbyterian Church in this country ; therefore,

"*Resolved*, That our delegates be directed to present a copy of these resolutions to each branch of the Presbyterian Church, with our fraternal request, that the truth of this common fame be publicly denied, or, if that be inconsistent with facts, that proper and effectual measures be taken to bring the offenders to repentance."

These Resolutions are similar in spirit to those presented to the American Board at Brooklyn, the same year, by Dr. Leonard Bacon of New Haven, and unsuccessfully advocated by him, on that occasion. He also advocated the above resolutions of Mr. Dutton, before the General Association of Connecticut.

What objection could there have been against them ? They were specially designed to waive the mooted questions of the sinfulness both of slavery and slaveholding, and fix upon what are claimed to be the *abuses* of the system. He urged upon the Board, and upon the General Assembly, the importance of condemning, distinctly, *these practices*.

Why could it not be done ? Why, but because, instead of an indefinite and vague *abstraction* there was an inconvenient and well understood specification of prevalent *practices ;* of practices which would criminate the great body of religious slaveholders at the South ? Because, moreover, the third Resolution would be understood at the South as evidence that the General Association of Connecticut were *in earnest* for the removal of *these practices*.

It will be seen, on inspection, that the action of the General Association of Connecticut does not conflict with the positions of Professor Stuart, or, at least, only as Professor Stuart's positions conflict with each other. Self-consistency is not to be expected, where the effort is to avoid the condemnation of that which common sense and common decency will not consent to defend.

GENERAL ASSOCIATION OF MASSACHUSETTS.

This body of Congregational Ministers have been led to record a somewhat different testimony, and one which it might be difficult to reconcile with their patronage of Professor Stuart, and of the American Board.

In 1834 the General Association adopted the following Resolutions:

" 1. *Resolved,* That the slavery existing in this country, by which more than two millions of our countrymen are deprived of their inalienable rights, and held and treated as mere merchandise, is a violation of the law of God and the fundamental principles of our national government.

" 2. That this Association regards those usages and laws in the slave-holding States which withhold the Bible as a book to be read from the slave population, as inconsistent with the spirit of Christianity.

" 3. That we deeply sympathize with our enslaved brethren, and commend their cause to the prayers of the Christian Church.

" 4. That the efforts recently made in some of the slaveholding States for imparting religious instructions to the slaves, are regarded by us with lively hope and earnest prayers for their universal extension.

" 5. That the principles and objects of the American Anti-Slavery Society, so far as they do not come in collision with the American Colonization Society, meet with our approbation."

A sixth resolution recommended the *Colonization* Society to the continued *support* of the churches, by collections on the Fourth of July, &c. How far the first three resolutions were congruous with the remaining ones, and how well they comported with the subsequent activities of those who voted for them, we do not now stop to inquire. But it is proper to remark that these resolutions were adopted in the presence of the agents of the two societies, (the Anti-slavery and the Colonization,) who were pressing their rival claims, and at a time when the opposition of leading Colonizationists to the Anti-slavery movement had diminished the receipts of the Colonization Society.

In 1837, the General Association adopted the following :

" *Whereas*, Slavery, as it exists in our country, is a great moral and social evil ; and whereas, no man should feel indifferent respecting that which the God of heaven disapproves, therefore,

" 1. *Resolved*, That the assumed right of holding our fellow-men in bondage, working them without wages, and buying and selling them as property, is obviously contrary to the principles of natural justice and the spirit of the gospel, offensive to God, and ought to cease with the least possible delay.

" 2. *Resolved*, That we approve of free and candid discussion on the subject of slavery, and also of all other proper methods of diffusing light and promoting correct moral sentiment, which may have an influence to do away the evil."—*Eman.*, Aug. 10, 1837.

How well these resolutions, especially the second, correspond with the action of the General Association at the same session, and the year previous, in respect to the labors of anti-slavery lecturers among their churches, the reader will judge when he shall have seen the record, in another chapter, of the opposition raised against abolitionists. For the present, we let it stand disconnected with those matters, and by the side of other Congregational testimonies concerning slavery.

In 1849, the General Association adopted the following :

" *Resolved*, That, in maintaining correspondence and connection with the two General Assemblies of the Presbyterian Church, we look with deep solicitude upon the position of those bodies with respect to the sin of slavery ; that our own strong sympathies are with those brethren in these Assemblies who are laboring in an earnest and Christian spirit to put an end to this evil ; and that we desire our delegates to those Assemblies, in a decided but courteous manner, to express our deep conviction, that the right of the enslaved, the cause of true religion, and the honor of the Great Head of the Church, require those ecclesiastical bodies to use all their legitimate power and influence for the speedy removal of slavery from the churches under their supervision."

The fact of a religious connection and fraternal intercourse between the Congregationalists of Massachusetts and the slaveholding Presbyterians of the South, is here distinctly recognized, an item of some importance, as we sometimes hear it confidently denied. The manner in which the Old School General Assembly, as already mentioned, repulsed this remonstrance, affords some evidence that they regarded it as having been uttered in earnest. It affords, at the same time, an occasion and an opportunity for the General Association of Massachusetts to show, by their future course and position, whether they are prepared to carry out the principles involved in this testimony. The alternative is now fairly presented to them, of forbearing a repetition of that testimony, or of ceasing to " maintain correspondence and connection " with the Old School Presbyterian Church.

THE CONVENTION OF CONGREGATIONAL MINISTERS of Massachusetts, in 1848, appointed a committee to prepare a report on slavery. The committee made an elaborate report in 1849. The Convention approving of " the general principles and results of the same," authorized its publication.* The annual report of the Am. & For. A. S. Society says, that it contains some things which they (the anti-slavery committee) cannot approve, but that, on the whole, it bears " a faithful testimony against the wrongfulness of slavery." From some extracts it appears that this document denies that " slavery, as it exists in the United States, and as it has been legalized," is sanctioned by the Bible. It affirms that the Mosaic institutions are " utterly repugnant, and destructive to, all slaveholding and slavery ;" and finally, that " it well becomes the Convention of Congregational Ministers of this ancient Commonwealth solemnly to declare to the world their deep conviction of the injustice and inhumanity of the system of slavery, and of its absolute repugnance to all the principles of the word of God."

GENERAL CONFERENCE OF MAINE.

This body is composed of Congregational ministers and lay delegates. In 1836, the Conference

" *Resolved*, That slaveholding, as it exists in a portion of these United States, is a great sin against God and man, for which the nation ought to

---

* Published by T. R. Marvin, Boston : 92 pages. This Convention consists of both " Orthodox " and Unitarian Congregational ministers, associated for some special objects.

humble itself, and for the speedy and entire removal of which, every Christian ought to pray, and use all suitable means within his reach."—*Eman.*

The Congregational ministers and churches of Maine, as a body, have appeared to be more earnest in their condemnation of slavery, than those of Massachusetts and Connecticut.

In 1846, the General Conference adopted a paper expressing their "surprise and grief" at the then recent action of the General Assembly of the Presbyterian Church, which, say they, "appears to be directly at variance with the former report made by the General Assembly in 1818, and to be intended as a justification of the system of slavery now existing in the Southern States."—*Chr. Inv.*, Feb. 1846.

CONGREGATIONAL PUBLICATIONS.

The Christian Spectator, the organ of the New Haven or New School Theology of New England, was earlier in its defence of slavery than the Old School Doctors at Princeton, or the Professor at Andover.

"The Bible contains no explicit prohibition of slavery. It recognizes, both in the Old and New Testaments, such a constitution of society, and it lends its authority to enforce the mutual obligations resulting from that constitution. Its language is, ' Slaves, obey your masters, and, masters, give unto your slaves that which is just and equal, knowing that ye also have a master in heaven.' There is neither chapter nor verse of holy writ which lends any countenance to the fulminating spirit of universal emancipation, of which some specimens may be seen in some of the newspapers."—*New Haven Chr. Spectator*, Sept., 1832, Vol. II., No. 5, p. 473 ; *Gen. Temp.*, April 17, 1833.

"Domestic slavery, in the light of the Scriptures, and in the light of common sense, is justifiable to the same extent, and on exactly the same principles with despotism on a larger scale. The right and the wrong of both is, materially, perhaps we should say precisely, the same." * * * "What is the duty of the Emperor of Russia towards his fifty millions of slaves? Is it his crime that they are his slaves?" &c., &c.—*Ib.*

The innocency of "despotism" in general is strange doctrine in America, and among the sons of the Puritans, admitting, for the sake of the argument, that chattel slavery is no worse—which is not true.

On the vitally important subject of *oral instruction* for slaves, as a substitute for the reading of the scriptures, the Congregational press, in New England, to some extent, took substantially, the ground of the following extracts, The Portland Christian Mirror, if we mistake not, contained some suggestions in that direction.

The Editor of the Vermont Chronicle, (Rev. Joseph Tracy,) afterwards Editor of the Boston Recorder, and more recently assistant Editor of the N. Y. Observer, wrote of the slaves as follows :

" They have a right to such religious and other instruction as they are capable of receiving. When they have profited by that, they will be capable of receiving more, and so on, till they become capable of performing the duties of freemen and THEN they will have a right to be FREE. *That they have a right to be taught to read, immediately, we do not say,* but their right to be taught that which it will be immensely difficult, all but impossible, to teach them without reading, is as evident as the sun at noon-day."—*Vermont Chronicle, vide Emancipator,* March 11, 1834.

" The art of reading, we know, wonderfully increases the facility with which we may fit ourselves for the performance of duty, but it is possible to become safe citizens without it. We, therefore, PASS NO SENTENCE, either OF CONDEMNATION OR APPROVAL, ON THOSE WHO WITHHOLD THIS ART FROM THEIR SLAVES. We only say *they must be educated.* You must educate them. *Take your own way to do it.* If you find it SAFE to put books into their hands, it will diminish your labor immensely. If not, you must do it, nevertheless. The labor of educating them without books will be immense, but, books or no books, it must be done, and if books are UNSAFE instruments, you must work the harder."—*Sermon of Rev. Joseph Tracy,* before the Vermont Col. Soc.

" *Capable* of receiving!" How long before they will be " *capable*" of learning to read ? What right have one class of men to sit in judgment, and decide upon the *capabilities* of *another* class to receive and study the scriptures ? If we may " pass no sentence of condemnation" on this assumption in America, then we must cease our condemnation of it in Spain and Italy.

CHAPTER XV.

POSITION OF THE AMERICAN CHURCHES, ETC. CONTINUED.

IV.—BAPTISTS.

Charleston (S. C.) Association—Savannah River (Geo.) ditto—Goslein (Va.) ditto—Rev. Dr. Furman—Sale of his negroes—Dr. Bolles—"Pleasing union" among Am. Baptists—"Southern brethren, generally Slaveholders"—North Carolina Association—Baptist Triennial Convention—Board of Foreign Missions—Acting Board at Boston—Baptist Home Mission Society—Am. and For. Bible Society—Am. Bap. Publication Society.

UNLIKE Presbyterians and Methodists, the Baptists are subject to no great ecclesiastical body, holding supervision over all the Churches and members of the denomination, Northern and Southern. The non-slaveholding portion, therefore, of the Baptist sect, at the North, can plead no organic difficulties, of an ecclesiastical character, in the way of their entire separation from the sin of slaveholding, and their untrammeled religious testimony against it. If they receive the sin into their pulpits, and seat it at their communion tables, it is not because the canons of their church require them to submit to such arrangements, nor because any Bishops, Conferences, or General Assemblies, have imposed the burthen upon them. The bond of affinity and sympathy between Baptist slaveholders and Baptist Anti-Slavery men, if it exists at all, exists voluntarily, and not by compulsion—exists as a veritable reality and not as a mere matter of appearance and form.

That Southern Baptists, like Southern Methodists, Presbyterians, and Episcopalians, are commonly slaveholders (except those of them who are *slaves,*) we need not spend time to prove, as it will not be denied. A few facts will show the general position of Southern Baptists, on the subject.

In 1835, the Charleston Baptist Association addressed a memorial to the Legislature of South Carolina, in defence of slavery. They say:

"The said Association does not consider that the holy scriptures have made the fact of slavery a question of morals at all. The Divine Author of our holy religion, in particular, found slavery a part of the existing institutions of society, with which, if not sinful, it was not his design TO INTERMEDDLE, but to leave them entirely to the control of men. *Adopting it, therefore, as one of the allowed relations of Society*, he made it the province of his religion only to prescribe *the reciprocal duties of the relation.* The question it is believed is purely one of political economy, &c."

As it is here assumed that Christ and Christianity do not "intermeddle" with questions of mere "political economy," and as slavery is affirmed to be purely such a question, and not a question of morals, it might be inquired *why* an *ecclesiastical body* should depart from what it alleged to be Christ's example, by "intermeddling" with this purely political subject? The "Association" proceeded to affirm their right to hold slaves, and to say:

"Neither society nor individuals, have any more authority to demand a relinquishment without an equivalent, in the one case than in the other," (that is, their right to) "*the money and lands inherited from ancestors or derived from industry.*"

The Association then claims for the State of S. Carolina, the exclusive right "to regulate the existence and continuance of slavery within her territorial limits," and they add:

"We WOULD RESIST, TO THE UTMOST, every invasion of THIS RIGHT, come from what quarter and under whatever pretense it may."

The object, then, of this ecclesiastical memorial to the State Legislature, was to affirm the inherent right of slaveholding, on the same basis of the rights of property in "money and lands," to invoke or encourage a continued legislative protection of this supposed right, and to pledge *The Charles-*

ton Baptist Association, to the support of this legislative action, even to the point of *resistance to the utmost.*

Sad business for the professed disciples of him who came to proclaim the jubilee of deliverance to the captives !

How Baptist slaveholders understand the tenure of their assumed rights of property in man, and at what expense they expect those rights to be maintained by their State Legislatures, may be learned from the following :

In 1835 the following *query,* relating to slaves, was presented to the Savannah River Baptist Association of ministers :

"Whether, in case of involuntary separation of such a character as to preclude all future intercourse, the parties may be allowed to marry again ?"

ANSWER.

"That such separation among persons situated as our slaves are, is civilly a separation by death, and they believe that, in the sight of God, it would be so viewed. To forbid second marriages in such cases, would be to expose the parties not only to greater hardships and stronger temptations, but to *church censure* for acting *in obedience to their masters,* who cannot be expected to acquiesce in a regulation at variance with justice to the slaves, and to the spirit of that command which regulates marriage between Christians. *The slaves are not free agents,* and a dissolution by death is not more entirely without their consent and beyond their control than by such separation."

Incidentally here, the fact leaks out that slave cohabitation is enforced by the authority of the masters, for the increase of their human chattels, and that this is done in utter contempt of the divine institution of marriage. And a body of devout ecclesiastics gravely decide that inasmuch as this process, in connection with the frequent and forced separation from each other of wives and husbands belonging to Baptist churches, is inseparable from the slave system, the divine institution of marriage, as expounded by Christ, must be modified in conformity with the slave code, in order that those whom God hath joined together, may, by man, be put asunder, so that Baptist wives may have two husbands and Baptist husbands may have two wives, without being subjected to *"church censure."*

The "censure" of *such* churches, verily, must be of vast

benefit in rebuking the sin of adultery! If any testimony were wanted, to establish the fact that slavery is incompatible with marriage, the Savannah River Baptist Association have furnished it to our hands.

In the same year, 1835, the ministers and messengers of the Goslein Baptist Association, assembled at Free Union, Virginia, adopted resolutions, affirming their right to slave property.

In 1833, Rev. Dr. Furman addressed to the Governor of South Carolina an exposition of the *views of Baptists*, in which he said :

"The right of holding slaves is clearly established in the Holy Scriptures, both by precept and example."

"Dr. Furman died not long afterward. His legal representatives thus advertised his property for sale :

"' NOTICE.

"' On the first day of February next will be put up at public auction, before the Court-house, the following property, belonging to the estate of the late Rev. Dr. Furman, viz. :

"' A plantation or tract of land on and in Wateree Swamp ; a tract of the first quality of fine land on the waters of Black River ; a lot of land in the town of Camden ; a library of a miscellaneous character, CHIEFLY THEOLOGICAL;

27 NEGROES,

some of them very prime ; two mules, one horse, and an old wagon.' "

This is Baptist religion at the South. And what is it at the North?

"The late Rev. Lucius Bolles, D.D., of Massachusetts, Cor. Sec. Amer. Bap. Board for Foreign Missions, in 1834, said :

"' There is a pleasing degree of union among the multiplying thousands of Baptists throughout the land.' * * * * * 'Our Southern brethren are generally, both ministers and people, slaveholders.' "—*American Churches*, &c.

The great majority of northern Baptists endorse this statement and certify the essential identity of their religion with that of Southern Baptists, by *joining with* them in sending THEIR religion . . . *to the heathen.*

The North Carolina Baptist Convention, in 1838 or 1839,

adopted a report of a Committee on the religious instruction of people of color. After urging, in a series of Resolutions, the duty of instructing slaves, they close with the following:

" Resolved, That by religious instruction be understood, VERBAL communications on religious subjects."—Vide *Cincinnati Cross and Baptist Journal*, as quoted in *A. S. Lecturer*, No. 3.

Thus careful were they to be understood as not intending to recommend giving slaves the Bible and permitting them to read.

THE BAPTIST TRIENNIAL CONVENTION.

This body was organized in 1814.

" Under its constitution, slaveholders and non-slaveholders united on terms of social and moral equality. This was its fatal error. It caused the Convention, from its birth to its dissolution, to sanction as Christian a slaveholding religion." "The first President was Richard Furman, a slaveholder of South Carolina. He filled the office till 1820, when another slaveholder, Robert B. Semple, of Virginia, succeeded him, and was President till 1832, when Spencer H. Cone,* of New York (City) was elected, who held the office till 1841, when another slaveholder, William B. Johnson, of South Carolina, was elected, at the close of whose term of office, 1844, Francis Wayland became President. Thus, for twenty-one of the thirty years of this organization, slaveholders were its Presidents."—*Facts for Bap. Churches*, pp. 14, 15.

Connected with the Triennial Convention was a General Board of Baptist Foreign Missions; and subordinate to this was an " Acting Board," located in Boston.

So late as 1844, near the time of the dissolution of that body, it came to light that there was a slaveholding missionary in its employ, a Mr. Bushyhead, who was laboring among the Cherokees. He lived in a fine dwelling, had a plantation, and several slaves.—*Ib.* p. 102.

It also appeared, not long after, that there were several southern missionaries employed by the Board, and that, among these, Mr. Davenport and his wife, at Siam, were slaveholders.

---

* In 1823 or 1824, Mr. Cone was pastor of a slaveholding Baptist Church in Alexandria (D. C.)

This was stated, on authority of the "Christian Index," (a Southern Baptist paper) by the New York Baptist Register, of Utica, N. Y., April 6, 1845.—*Ib.* p. 113–17.

It was also stated, on good authority, that several others among the foreign missionaries were slaveholders.—*Ib.* p. 122–3.

"THE AMERICAN BAPTIST HOME MISSION SOCIETY

was organized in the City of New York, April 27, 1832." "Missionary Societies" (northern and southern) "by paying into its treasury their surplus funds, become auxiliary." Its constitution makes no distinction between slaveholders and non-slaveholders. "The Society has elected slaveholding officers, sent out slaveholding missionaries, and planted slaveholding churches, and all this in perfect keeping with its Constitution. Slaveholders are, to-day, (1850) on its list of life members, and its treasury is open to the price of men and women and little children." "As the Missionary of this Society, (Mr. Tryon,) entered Texas, he drove his slaves before him."—*Ib.* p. 63–65.

It was publicly stated, at a meeting in Philadelphia, by Eld. Duncan Dunbar, that *twenty-six slaveholders* had been employed by the Board.—*Ib.* p. 65.

The subject of employing slaveholding Missionaries came up for consideration, at its twelfth annual meeting, at Philadelphia, in 1844, but, after discussion, no action was taken against it. Instead of this, a Resolution (drawn up by Eld. R. Fuller, a slaveholder of South Carolina, and a Biblical defender of slavery,) was adopted, assuming neutral ground, and disclaiming fellowship, as a Society, either with slavery or anti-slavery. At this meeting, Eld. B. M. Hill, Corresponding Secretary of the Society, stated that the Southern States paid more into the treasury than the Northern States, and therefore more southern missionaries were appointed than northern ones.—*Ib.* p. 88–90.

At the meeting of the Society at Providence, R. I., April, 1845, some further discussion was had, and some incipient measures for a division between the North and the South were considered, and a committee appointed to mature a plan. Assurances were given that, in the meantime, no more slave-holding missionaries should be appointed. But the promise was violated. "Two slaveholding missionaries had been appointed in February, and one of them was appointed again the next year, after the fact of his slaveholding had been published in the Minutes of the Baptist Convention of North Carolina, as a proof that the Home Missionary Society was willing to employ slaveholders, and as an evidence that no rule had been adopted at Providence prohibiting the appointment of slaveholders."—*Ib.* 149–162.

THE AMERICAN AND FOREIGN BIBLE SOCIETY,

(Baptist) was organized in 1837, the year of the martyrdom of Lovejoy, and after the murderous spirit of slaveholding ministers and church members against northern abolitionists had been fully revealed. It was a fraternal union between the leading ministers and the great majority of the lay brotherhood of Baptists, at the North and at the South. It had, in 1841, fifty-eight auxiliary societies in the slaveholding states. It has never been without slaveholding officers.—*Ib.* p. 58–9.

The (Baptist) "Christian Index," Georgia, of November 16, 1848, contained an appeal in behalf of this Bible Society, and also an advertisement, in which "a plantation with some twenty negroes, stock of every kind," &c., were offered for sale.—*Ib.* p. 323–4.

At a meeting of this Society, it was "Resolved to furnish every family in the United States with a Bible."

Eld. Abel Brown immediately rose and inquired, mildly, whether the resolution embraced slaves? Scarcely had the words escaped his lips, when the house resounded with the cry of "Order! order! order!" and the President, Eld. Spencer H. Cone, with emphatic voice and gesture, called out to him,—"Sit down, Sir! you are out of order."—*Ib.* 327.

The Society has never published its intention of giving the Bible to the poor heathen in the slave states, though it is be-

lieved that money has been repeatedly offered to the Society
for the object, and that they have, invariably, refused to receive it.—*Ib.* 327–8.

And yet, in a communication to the committee of the (English) General Baptist Missionary Society, the Board of the
American and Foreign Bible Society, Nov. 3, 1847, over the
signature of Eld. Spencer H. Cone, said, of the Society,—

"They have never withheld the Bible from the slave." And they further say they have reason to believe that "the colored race, bond and free,"
receive a fair proportion of their books!

Of the credibility of these statements, the *American* reader
can judge.—*Ib.* 325–334.

The Board further says: "We have never designed, nor
are we conscious that we have done aught to abet the system
or practice of slavery." Yet the Society (1849) receives slaveholders to membership, has 59 auxiliaries, 506 life members,
99 life directors, and 9 Vice Presidents, in the slave states.—
Ib. p. 333–4.

"THE AMERICAN BAPTIST PUBLICATION SOCIETY,"

is also "a bond of union between the North and the South,"
publishing nothing againt slavery.—*Ib.* p. 340–44.

A further account of the position of Baptist organizations
in respect to slavery, will appear in another chapter, as connected with the movements of abolitionists, and Baptist "Free
Missions."

CHAPTER XVI.

POSITION OF THE AMERICAN CHURCHES, ETC., CONTINUED.

V. THE PROTESTANT EPISCOPAL CHURCH.

Testimony of John Jay, Esq.—Sermon of Mr. Freeman—Bishop Ives—Protestant Episcopal Society of South Carolina—Bishop Bowen—"The Churchman"—Prohibition of reading—General Theological Seminary—Treatment of a Colored student, Alexander Crummel—Position of Rev. Drs. Milnor, Taylor, Smith, and Hawks—Dissent of Bishop Doane—Exclusion of Colored Ministers from Ecclesiastical Councils—Episcopal Convention at Philadelphia—St. Thomas' Church.

THE prevailing temper of the Protestant Episcopal Church is thus testified of, by John Jay, Esq., of the City of New York — himself an Episcopalian—in a pamphlet entitled, "Thoughts on the Duty of the Episcopal Church, in relation to Slavery."

"Alas! for the expectation that she would conform to the spirit of her ancient mother! She has not merely remained a mute and careless spectator of this great conflict of truth and justice with hypocrisy and cruelty, but her very priests and deacons may be seen ministering at the altar of slavery, offering their talents and influence at its unholy shrine, and openly repeating the awful blasphemy, that the precepts of our Saviour sanction the system of American slavery. Her Northern (free State) clergy, with rare exceptions, whatever they may feel on the subject, rebuke it neither in public nor in private, and her periodicals, far from advancing the progress of abolition, at times oppose our societies, impliedly defending slavery, as not incompatible with Christianity, and occasionally withholding information useful to the cause of freedom."—*Birney's American Churches*, &c., pp. 39, 40.

"In 1836, a Clergyman of North Carolina, of the name of Freeman, preached, in presence of his bishop (Rev. Levi S. Ives, D.D., a native of a free State), two sermons on the rights and duties of slaveholders. In these he essayed to justify, from the Bible, the slavery of both white men and negroes, and insisted that, ' without a new revelation from heaven, no man was authorized to pronounce slavery *wrong*.' The two sermons were printed in a pamphlet, prefaced with a letter to Mr. Freeman from the Bishop of North Carolina, declaring that he had ' listened with most unfeigned pleasure' to his discourses, and advised their publication, as being ' urgently called for at the present time.'

" The Protestant Episcopal Society for the Advancement of Christianity in South Carolina thought it expedient, and, in all likelihood, with Bishop Bowen's approbation, to republish Mr. Freeman's pamphlet as a *religious tract* !"—*Ib.*, p. 41.

The Churchman, edited by a Doctor of Divinity, and previously an instructor in a theological seminary, held the following language, in respect to the legal prohibition of teaching the colored population to read:

" All the knowledge which is necessary to salvation—all the knowledge of our duty towards God, and our duty to our neighbor, may be communicated by oral instruction, and therefore a law of the land interdicting other means of instruction, does not trench upon the law of God."—*Ib.*

This argument would justify the Romish Church in withholding the Bible from the laity. And by the same kind of logic it might be argued, with much greater force, that, since "the holy scriptures are able to make men wise unto salvation," therefore, in a community that can read and that has Bibles, " a law of the land interdicting *other* means of instruction" (oral instruction by preaching) "does not trench upon the law of God." If the civil or ecclesiastical authorities may interdict some means of religious instruction they may interdict others. If they may interdict the Bible, they may, doubtless, interdict the " Book of Common Prayer" and *all* the forms of instruction, including the rituals of the Episcopal or any other church. To such results do those drive their arguments who would defend the usages of slavery. The employment of such arguments certifies what those usages are, and that the slave code is not a dead letter. The quarter they come from indicates the relative position, in respect to them, of the Church and the State. If the prevailing *religion* of the country did not sanction them, they could not be protected by the State laws ; nay, such enactments would not have been made. No civil government, however despotic, can "interdict" the standard books of the prevailing and predominant religion, and survive the process. Whenever the prevailing religion of the country shall be the religion of *the Bible*, in which is contained the divine injunction, "*Search the Scriptures*," the laws and the usages "*interdicting*" the same Scriptures will, of course, become obsolete, and the slave system, which can be supported only by such interdiction, will fall.

Alexander Crummel, a colored young gentleman of the city of New York, made application to "become a candidate for holy orders." He received from his bishop the usual circular in such cases, in which he was encouraged to "belong to the General Theological Seminary," located at New York. In the statutes of the Seminary it is expressly said, "*Every* person producing to the *Faculty* satisfactory evidence of his *having been* admitted a candidate for holy orders," &c., "shall be received as a student of the Seminary." He was, however, referred to the Board of Trustees. A committee was appointed to consider and report, consisting of Bishop Doane, Rev. Drs. Milnor, Taylor, and Smith, and Messrs. D. B. Ogden, Newton, and Johnson. The next day (June 26, 1839), Bishop Doane, on request, was excused from further service on this committee, and Bishop Onderdonk, of Pennsylvania, appointed to fill the vacancy. This committee reported, June 27th, that "having *deliberately* considered the said petition, they are of opinion that it *ought not to be granted*," and they recommended a resolution accordingly, which, on motion of Rev. Dr. Hawks, was adopted. Mr. Huntington moved that the subject be referred to the *Faculty*, which was lost. Bishop Doane, June 28th, asked leave to state to the Board his reasons for dissent, with a view to the entering of the same on the minutes. *Leave was not granted*. During these proceedings Mr. Crummel was advised by the Bishop of New York to withdraw his petition, and was assured that the Faculty were willing to impart to him private instruction. In the minutes of the proceedings there was a careful avoidance of all allusion to the *cause* of excluding Mr. Crummel, leaving it to be inferred that it was for some cause besides his *color*, which was not the fact. Mr. Crummel afterwards became a member of the Theological department of Yale College, but not being treated there as white students are, he was compelled to complete his education in Europe! He is *now* an ordained clergyman of the American Protestant Episcopal Church.

Regularly ordained ministers and rectors of parishes have been excluded from seats in the ecclesiastical councils of their church, solely on account of their color. "The rector of a colored church in Philadelphia is excluded by an express canon of the Diocesan Convention."—*Vide J. G. Birney's Am. Churches*, pp. 39–41.

Quite recently, the Episcopal Convention of Pennsylvania, sitting in Philadelphia, after discussion, decided against the admission of colored delegates.

We learn from the *Saturday Evening Post*, that at the late Episcopal Convention, a final decision was made upon the question of admitting representatives from the African Church of St. Thomas.

The majority of the committee appointed to consider the subject, reported adversely to the admission, arguing that the color, and physical and social condition and education of the blacks, render them unfit to participate in legislative bodies. The Rev. Mr. Montgomery submitted a minority report, which stated that, in the month of September, 1794, Bishop White laid before the Convention the Constitution of St. Thomas's Church, and it was then resolved, that as soon as they should sign the Act of Association, they should be entitled to all the privileges of the Diocese. It also urged that the exclusion of delegates on account of their color, was contrary to the spirit of Christianity, and the practice of the church in apostolic times.

After a short discussion, the vote was taken upon adopting the report of the *majority*, which was decided as follows: Clerical, ayes 44, nays 42. Lay votes, by churches, ayes 50, nays 17. So it was resolved that the delegates from St. Thomas' Church should not be admitted to seats in the Convention!!—*Liberator*, June 28, 1850.

The large number of nays, in the *clerical* vote, deserves notice, as an encouraging indication, and as contrasting strongly and remarkably with the vote of the *laity*.

CHAPTER XVII.

POSITION OF THE AMERICAN CHURCHES, ETC. (CONTINUED.)

VI.—OTHER SECTS—GENERAL VIEW.

Protestant Methodist Church—Dutch Reformed—Roman Catholics—Unitarians, Universalists and Restorationists—Free Will Baptists—Cumberland Presbyterians—Orthodox and Hicksite Friends—Scotch Covenanters—*General View.* Testimony of Rev. James Smylie, of Mississippi—S. W. Chr. Adv. & Journal—Presb. Synod, Kentucky—Rev. C. C. Jones, of Georgia.

WE have now spoken of the principal religious denominations in America. The reader has already noticed our cheerful recognition of the fact that in *all* of them there are earnest friends of the slaves. Of some of the smaller sects, it cannot be said that their position essentially differs from the preceding, though smaller and younger sects are commonly more free than larger ones.

THE PROTESTANT METHODIST CHURCH (which rejects Episcopacy) has a Southern as well as a Northern membership, and allows slaveholding. After some agitation in their General Conference, and some signs of a Northern secession in Western New York, a General Conference at Cincinnati declined any anti-slavery action, the Northern Conferences did not secede, and there has been little or no agitation since.

THE DUTCH REFORMED CHURCH is not known to differ in respect to slavery from northern Congregationalists and Presbyterians with which sects it co-operates in the enterprise of Foreign Missions.

There are some advocates of emancipation among the ROMAN CATHOLICS, but it is not known that the number is large, or that the question of slavery, or of the treatment of the colored people, has been agitated in that communion. The Catholics in the Slave States are as generally slaveholders as others.

UNITARIANS, UNIVERSALISTS, and RESTORATIONISTS, whose church polity is generally Congregational, were not included in our account of the Congregational sect. We cannot say that they differ widely from other sects at the North, though they have little or no direct ecclesiastical connections or branches at the South. They are divided on the abolition question, as other sects are.

A large, though select number of UNITARIAN MINISTERS, signed, some time since, an extended document against slavery, but not taking, it is believed, higher ground than the "orthodox" General Association of Massachusetts and General Conference of Maine had taken several years before. Whether the document is better honored by them, in practice, as a general fact, we cannot tell. Nor can we conjecture how anti-slavery resolutions would be disposed of in their regularly constituted Associations, if it were their habit to bear testimonies in that way. We have heard of no thorough anti-slavery churches of that sect, or of the withdrawal of ministers and laymen for re-organization, on account of the slave question, though there are earnest and active abolitionists among them, and of the radical type not approved by the late Dr. Channing.

The statements made in the last sentence may, perhaps, apply to Universalists and Restorationists. A large, if not a general ASSOCIATION OF UNIVERSALISTS, some time since, adopted a general testimony against slavery.

Of all these, *as sects*, we must however say, that the weight of their influence, especially at the ballot-box, as in the case of the larger sects, is not against slavery, but in its support.

And we cannot here, and in this particular, make an exception in favor of some other sects, as the "ORTHODOX" and the "HICKSITE" FRIENDS, and the FREE-WILL BAPTISTS, who claim the merit of being opposed to slavery, and whose printed "testimonies" to that effect have not been wanting.* To say nothing now of their general treatment of active abolitionists belonging to their own sect (a topic of which we are not directly speaking in this chapter), the general influence of even *these* sects, or of a majority of their members, especially at the ballot-box, has been, and still is, on the side of the slave power, in voting for slaveholders and their supporters.

The majority of "FRIENDS," of both classes, have not only voted for slaveholding candidates for the Presidency, but, in the case of the late General Taylor, for a candidate whose sudden and surprising popularity (first at the South, and then at the North) was owing wholly to the terrible success (sometimes by the aid of bloodhounds) with which he prosecuted aggressive pro-slavery wars, in further contempt of the professed principles of *Friends*.

If such be the position of what have been called the anti-slavery sects, by way of distinction, what must be the position of the others? Who can marvel that, in the case just adverted to, the preponderating influence of Presbyterian and Congregational ministers should have been cast into the same scale with the Friends? And what can be said in excuse of such a course, when an united rally at the polls, by professed Christians of all sects, even in the free States alone, in opposition to the slave power, would so manifestly and so speedily terminate its iron and bloody sway?

In due justice to FREE-WILL BAPTISTS, it should be further said, that their periodical publications and ecclesiastical bodies have generally, if not uniformly, taken anti-slavery ground, from the beginning of the agitation on the subject. And at an early day they separated themselves (the Northern and principal portion of them) from a considerable body of Southern Free-Will Baptists, who refused to relinquish slavehold-

---

* It is possible for a sect or religious body, in its public or corporate character, and by its official and formal declarations and proceedings, to maintain a strong testimony against slavery, and even (as in the case of the Free-Will Baptists and Friends) to withdraw religious fellowship from slaveholders; while the great body of its members and officers, *for political ends*, sustain slavery at the polls.

ing. Their testimony, on the whole, is perhaps not behind that of the " Friends."

THE SCOTCH COVENANTERS, or Associate Reformed Presbyterian Church, is anti-slavery, and having scruples (on other grounds) that deter them from voting at all under our government, they are free from pro-slavery voting.

THE CUMBERLAND PRESBYTERIANS have sometimes been described as anti-slavery, but their " General Assembly refuse to legislate on the subject of slavery, on the plea that, as spiritual bodies, they have no cognizance of civil matters."—*An. Report Am. & For. A. S. Soc.*, 1852, p. 19.

"THE DISCIPLES"—sometimes called Campbellites (from their founder, Alexander Campbell)—are numerous at the West and South. They are slaveholders and slaves. Pres. Shannon, of Bacon College, a prominent member of the sect, says :

" Thus did Jehovah stereotype his approbation of domestic slavery, by incorporating it into the Jewish religion, the only religion on earth that had the divine sanction."

Alexander Campbell himself, in his "*Millennial Harbinger*," says :

" There is not one verse in the Bible inhibiting it, but many regulating it. It is not, then, we conclude, immoral."—*Pillsbury's* " *Church as it is*," pp. 52–3.

Of the anti-slavery churches, sects, ecclesiastical bodies, and missionary organizations that have grown out of the abolition movement, and which are controlled by abolitionists, we shall give some account in another connection.

GENERAL VIEW.

The record we have presented looks in the direction of a general estimate of the religious influences of the country on the slave question. And it indicates the position of the professed Christianity of the North, as represented by the different sects. If there be any further inquiry needed respecting the system that is thus sustained, or whether, in the hands of professing Christians of the different sects at the South, it be the thing that its opposers represent it to be, a few testimonies may satisfy the inquirer.

" The Rev. James Smylie, A.M., of the Amite Presbytery, Mississippi, in a pamphlet published by him" (about fifteen years ago), " in favor of American slavery, says :

" If slavery be a sin, and advertising and apprehending slaves, with a view to restore them to their masters, is a direct violation of the divine law, and if THE BUYING, SELLING, AND HOLDING a slave FOR THE SAKE OF GAIN, is a heinous sin and scandal, then verily, *three-fourths of all the Episcopalians, Methodists, Baptists, and Presbyterians*, in eleven States of the Union, are of the devil. They hold, if they do not buy and sell slaves, and, (with few exceptions,) they hesitate not to apprehend and restore runaway slaves, when in their power."

The Editor of South West Christian Advocate and Journal, a periodical of the Methodist Episcopal Church, corroborates this general statement, so far as that Church is concerned, as follows :

" If, however, the holding of men, women, and children, in bondage, UNDER THE ORDINARY CIRCUMSTANCES *that connect themselves with slavery in the* SOUTHERN STATES, constitutes us a pro-slavery Church, then we are a pro-slavery Church in this restricted or privately understood interpretation, for we do not regard slaveholding as sinful, AS IT EXISTS IN THE SOUTHERN STATES, provided the master feeds, instructs, and governs his slaves, according to the directions laid down in God's word."

By the testimony of the Presbyterian Synod of Kentucky, of Rev. C. C. Jones of Georgia, and also of the Synod of S. Carolina and Georgia, the fact is established that slaveholding church members in general do not give their slaves any more religious instruction than other slaveholders do, which, in most cases is none at all, so that the slaves—to use their own language—are in the condition of heathenism.

Putting these things together, we have a complete and full refutation of the pretence that Christian slaveholders hold slaves *for their own good*, that they make a wide distinction between slavetrading and slaveholding, and that they treat their slaves better than they are generally treated by others.

Any amount of testimony might be added, to the same point. We only advert to the topic, in this place, to exhibit, as clearly as we can, in one view, the relation of our religious sects, in America in general, to the condition and treatment of the slaves, and to slaveholding.

PREJUDICE AGAINST COLOR.

That prejudice against the colored people, which constitutes one of the main pillars of slavery, is fostered in most of the Churches, including some that—in other respects—bear testimony against the system. Their support of the Colonization Society (as will be shown in its place,) is a sufficient indication of the fact. Another evidence is the erection of the negro pew, and, in some Churches, the custom of administering the Lord's Supper to colored persons, by themselves, after the distribution to the whites. In Theological Seminaries, as well as in Colleges, the same spirit of caste is commonly witnessed. In some cases, it invades the sanctuary of the dead, and forbids the interment of colored persons in burial places designed for the whites.

A Protestant Episcopal Church at Rye, Westchester Co., (N. Y.,) accepted a deed of gift of ground for a cemetery, a condition of which deed was, that no colored person should be buried within the enclosures. The condition is carefully fulfilled. In selling burial lots to individuals, the officials of the Church having charge of that business, insert the same conditions in the conveyance. This fact is stated on authority of Hon. William Jay, a member of the Protestant Episcopal Church, and residing in the same county.

A Presbyterian Church in Philadelphia advertised burial lots for sale, with the particular recommendation of them, that no colored persons, or executed criminals, were buried in the cemetery.

A Congregational Church in New Haven, Con., parcelled off, in its cemetery, a side lot, for the burial of colored persons, after the manner of the negro pew. But it became necessary to enlarge the cemetery, and bury whites on the other side of the colored people, so that they now occupy the center! An omen, perhaps, of the future position of that despised race, in America.

To the credit of Roman Catholics, it must be said, that they maintain no arrangements of caste founded in color, in their Churches.

CHAPTER XVIII.

POSITION OF THE AMERICAN CHURCHES, ETC. CONTINUED.

VII.—VOLUNTARY SOCIETIES CONNECTED WITH SEVERAL SECTS. CONCLUDING REMARKS.

AMERICAN BOARD—Employment of Slaves by Missionaries—A Missionary a slave-owner—Slaveholding tolerated in Mission Churches—Board, at Rochester, decline interfering (1844)—At Brooklyn, 1845, decide against excluding *pious* Slaveholders from Church ordinances—In 1846, at New Haven, decline further action—In 1847, at Buffalo, promise inquiry—Mission and Letter of Mr. Treat—Reply of Choctaw Missionaries—Vindicate their right to have slaves—Rejected resolutions of Dr. Bacon, at Brooklyn (1845)—Doctrine of " organic sins."—AMERICAN HOME MISSIONARY SOCIETY—No rule to exclude Slaveholders from Mission Churches—Has greatly increased the list of its slaveholding Churches since 1842—*Other agencies.* —AMERICAN BIBLE SOCIETY—No Bibles for Slaves—Offer of funds for that object rejected—Auxiliary Society at New Orleans disclaimed the intent to supply colored people—Auxiliary Society, Orleans County, N. Y., refused a donation of Bibles to fugitives—Modified but doubtful position of the Parent Society in 1849. —AMERICAN TRACT SOCIETY—Publishes nothing against Slavery—Mutilation of books.—AMERICAN SUNDAY SCHOOL UNION—Rejects books that disapprove slavery—Closing remarks.

MISSIONS—AMERICAN BOARD.

THE following statements are from a paper, adopted by the Illinois Central Association, and prepared by a committee, consisting of Pres. Blanchard, Rev. D. Gore, and G. Dewy, at Lafayette, October 9th, 1849* :

" The action which the Board has taken from year to year, on the subject of slavery, is as follows, viz:

" 1. Some thirteen years since, the Prudential Committee, in correspondence on the subject, declared against the missionaries hiring slaves, except in cases of emergency.

---

* *National Era*, Nov. 8, 1849.

"2. In 1841, eight years ago, at Philadelphia, the subject came before the Board on petition of certain ministers of New Hampshire, who represent themselves as supporters of the Board, not Abolitionists, yet opposed to slavery ; and they ask the Board to declare itself distinctly on that subject, as they had done on the subject of other public vices which obstructed the missionary work. To this New Hampshire petition, the Board, by their committee's report, adopted, reply that :

"'The Board can sustain no relation to slavery which implies approbation of the system, and, as a Board, can have no connection or sympathy with it.'

"At that time, however, slaves were employed in the service of the mission-schools, the owners being paid for their service, and slaveholders were without objection received to the mission churches ; both which practices have continued ever since, and still continue. One of their missionaries, too, was at that time a slave owner—the Rev. Mr. Wilson, of Africa.

"In 1842, at Norwich, Connecticut, several 'memorials and other papers on the subject of slavery' were read by Mr. Greene, and referred. The Board, in their answer, say, 'They cannot but hope that he (Mr. Wilson) will ere long be able, with such counsel and aid as the Prudential Committee may give, to accomplish the object (the liberation of his slaves) in a manner satisfactory to himself, and kind and beneficent to them (i. e., his slaves).'

"In 1843, at Rochester, New York, one memorial on slavery was read by Mr. Greene, and the Board refer, for answer, to their former action on the subject.

"In 1844, at a very large meeting of the Board at Worcester, Massachusetts, memorials on the subject of slavery were committed to Drs. Woods and Tyler, Chancellor Walworth, Chief Justice Williams, Drs. Stowe, Sandford, Pomroy, Tappan, McLane, and Secretary Greene.

"The memorials this year set forth that slavery is '*actually tolerated*' in the Mission Churches among the Choctaws, 'by the admission of slaveholders as members,' to the hindering of the missionary work, and diminishing the funds of the Board. In their answer, which was adopted by the Board, the committee reiterate the words of the Philadelphia report, three years before, 'That the Board can sustain no relation to slavery which implies approbation of the system,' &c. But they add, as explaining that clause, ' plainly intimating that we consider it an obvious evil, the removal of which does not fall within the province of the Board.'

"They ask further time to obtain information as to slavery in the Choctaw mission churches, but observe, meantime, that missionaries there, so far as facts appear, have been guilty of 'no violation or *neglect* of duty.'

"In 1845, the Board met at Brooklyn, New York, and much discussion was elicited by a long report from the above committee, which report, with proposed amendments, was re-committed, reported again, and finally unanimously adopted. This celebrated Brooklyn report declares, among other things, that in the Cherokee and Choctaw missions, 'both masters and slaves were received into the churches on the same principles.'

" ' That Baptism and the Lord's Supper cannot be scripturally and rightfully denied to those who give credible evidence of piety ;' and that,

" ' The missionaries, in connection with the churches which they have gathered, are the sole judges of the sufficiency of this evidence.'

" The committee further report, that at that time there were in the Choctaw churches 20 slaveholders and 131 slaves. In the Cherokee churches, 15 slaveholders and 21 slaves. Total, 35 slaveholders and 152 slaves, in a total membership of 843. And this Brooklyn report further explicitly recognizes the doctrine that both ' master and slave may be gathered into the fold of Christ,' and intimates that this is the way to prepare the master to consent to emancipation.

" In 1846, at New Haven, Connecticut, papers on the subject of slavery were laid before the Board, from the General Congregational Association of Illinois, New Haven East Association, and other bodies. They were referred to a committee, consisting of Chancellor Walworth, Drs. Parker, Stowe, and others, and they reported :

" ' That they consider the further agitation of the subject here as calculated injuriously to affect the great cause of missions in which the Board is engaged.'

" Up to this time, the doctrines on which the Board stands respecting slavery are :

" 1. That slavery, though an admitted evil, is one which the Board is not responsible for removing ; and

" 2. That masters and slaves are to be received into fellowship in the churches, giving evidence of piety ; and

" 3. That the missionaries and churches among the Choctaws are the only judges of the credibility of that evidence.

" In 1847, the Board met at Buffalo, New York, when an honorary member of the Board moved that a committee be appointed to inquire whether any further action was required in reference to slavery among the Choctaws and Cherokees. The Secretaries replied, that ' they had every possible disposition to remove slavery and every other evil and sin as speedily as possible from the mission churches,' and that one of their number would visit the missions in question, and the whole subject of their slavery relations would come up on his report the following year.

" Mr. Secretary Treat accordingly visited those Indian missions, and the result of his visit, his report, and the correspondence connected with it, are before the public. The material facts shown by his report are, the one con tained in the Brooklyn report of 1845, viz: that the mission churches receive slaveholders to fellowship ; and slaves, to a certain extent, are hired of their owners to work at the Choctaw boarding-schools. While this is the fact, the Indian youth must of course learn contempt of labor along with the rudiments of science, and slavery must become part of their intellectual culture, if not of their religious.

"Of this the Prudential Committee seem to have been convinced, and hence, in Mr. Treat's celebrated letter of June 22d, last year, the Prudential Committee declare, explicitly, that the Board could never have intended that slaveholders should be received to church-membership, 'WITHOUT INQUIRING AS TO THEIR VIEWS AND FEELINGS IN REGARD TO SLAVERY.' And if 'he holds and treats those for whom Christ died with A SELFISH SPIRIT AND FOR SELFISH PURPOSES,' they say, 'for admitting such an one to the privileges of the people of God, especially in the advanced stage to which your mission has arrived, we know no warrant whatever.' And while they hold this strong and explicit language on the subject of receiving slaveholders into the church, they use far stronger and more explicit language on the subject of employing slaves at the schools. They say on this subject to the missionaries, 'If you can discover no method by which a change can be effected, we submit for your consideration whether it be not desirable to request the Choctaw government to relieve us from our engagement in respect to the boarding-schools.'—*Treat's Letter*, June 22, 1848.

"The report of Mr. Treat of his visit to the Choctaw and Cherokee missions, with the correspondence growing out of it, were reported to the Board at their meeting in Boston last year ; and while the anti-slavery portions of the American churches regarded the ground taken by the Prudential Committee, and the Board as silently acquiescing in it, as essentially anti-slavery and satisfactory to reasonable Christians,* loud and bitter complaints were raised by the missionaries among the Choctaws, and generally by the pro-slavery portions of the church. These complaints against the Prudential Committee have been extensively published during the last year in the *New York Observer, Christian Observer*, and other Presbyterian papers further South.

---

* With perfect respect to the Committee that drafted, and the Association that adopted this paper, the author submits that the ground taken by the Prudential Committee, even if it had been maintained by the Board, *ought not* to be satisfactory to "reasonable Christians." By the implication that slaves are sometimes held *otherwise* than " with a selfish spirit and for selfish purposes"—and that *such* slaveholding is consistent with church-membership, the very gist of the whole controversy is relinquished. Such a diluted testimony only invited the resistance it received. If slaveholding is *wrong*, there is no occasion or propriety in asking the candidate's " views and feelings in regard to slavery" while he continues the practice, and is to be indulged in it. But if the practice be *right*, the question becomes manifestly useless.

" In these circumstances, the public looked with intense interest to the late meeting of the Board at Pittsfield, Massachusetts. If the Board ever intends to cease to sustain slaveholding mission-churches, and slave-hiring mission-schools, it would seem that thirteen years is ample time for the Board to make up its mind to declare, at least, that such is its FUTURE intention. But, instead of any such intimation, Mr. Secretary Treat simply reported to the Board an apologetic and deprecatory note issued by the Secretaries during the year, in answer to the complaints against Treat's letter, and the reply to that letter of the Choctaw missionaries. In this note, issued from the mission-house in February last, the Secretaries say : 'The committee have never had any intention of " cutting off " the Choctaw mission from its connection with the Board,' but repeat the expression of their ' undiminished confidence in the integrity of these servants of Christ.'

" The reply of the Choctaw missionaries to Mr. Treat's letter is written in a softer tone than their letter to which Mr. Treat's was a reply, but it abates no whit of their former pretensions, and surrenders no principle laid down in their former letter.

" On the subject of receiving slaveholders to church-membership, a principal point of Mr. Treat's letter of June 22d, THEY DO NOT DEIGN TO SAY ONE WORD ; but simply observe, that five and twenty years ago they thought ' the subject of slavery, as it relates to their mission, was settled upon a scriptural basis.'

" On the subject of hiring slaves of their owners to do the work of the mission-schools, they at great length VINDICATE THEIR RIGHT TO DO SO, placing it upon the same ground with using slave-grown produce in the free States. They, however, feebly intimate their willingness to ' employ none but free help, provided it can be obtained ;' but assert, over and again, their intention to hire slaves, if necessary.

" The above papers were submitted to the Board, with an intimation that no action upon them was desired, on the ground that the correspondence (now of thirteen years' standing) is not yet completed !

Dr. Bacon, of New Haven, moved the reference of the subject to a special committee ; but this motion was overruled by a proposition of Chancellor Walworth, and the subject passed off without action or discussion, with a remark of the Secretary's report, as reported by the *N. Y. Evangelist*, ' That the mission are willing to do all that can properly be required of them to place this subject on the desired basis.'

" In respect to the above, it will be observed :

" 1. That the missionaries intimate no intention ever to cease receiving slaveholders to their churches, but vindicate the practice as scriptural.

" 2. That the Board, by its Brooklyn report, to which it adheres, has constituted them and their churches SOLE JUDGES ON THE SUBJECT.

" 3. It follows, that contributors to the Board's fund must PERPETUALLY, so far as any contrary hope appears, contribute to the propagation of a slave-holding Christianity. And,

" 4. That slaves are to do the work of the mission-schools till, in the missionaries' judgment, it is PRACTICABLE to obtain free help."

If anything further be wanting to define the position of the American Board, it may be furnished by an inspection of the rejected amendments to the celebrated Brooklyn Report of 1845. On that occasion, the late Amos A. Phelps presented and advocated a series of resolutions, characterizing the "practice of slaveholding a great moral evil, entirely opposed to the spirit and principles of the gospel"—declaring that the Board could not appoint or sustain slaveholders as mission-aries—and calling on the missionaries to treat slaveholding as they do other sins.

Dr. Leonard Bacon, of New Haven, Conn., who said he could not consent to the amendment of Mr. Phelps, introduced in room of them the following:

" 1. *Resolved*, That inasmuch as the system of domestic slavery, under every modification, is at war with the principles of Christianity, with natu-ral justice, with industry and thrift, with habits of subjection to law, and with whatever tends to the advancement of civilization and the ascendency of the gospel ; and inasmuch as it brings upon every community which establishes and upholds it, the righteous displeasure of God, and the repro-bation of the civilized and Christian world, the existence of slavery in the Cherokee and Choctaw nations is deeply to be lamented by their friends, and particularly by this Board, as having been, for more than a quarter of a century, engaged in labors tending to their moral, intellectual, and social advancement.

" 2. *Resolved*, That while the strongest language of reprobation is not too strong to be applied to the system of slavery, truth and justice require this Board to say that the mere relation of a master to one whom the constitu-tion of society has made a slave, is not to be regarded as in all cases such a sin as to require the exclusion of the master, without further inquiry, from Christian ordinances.

" 3. *Resolved*, That the missionaries of this Board, everywhere, are expected to admit to Christian ordinances those, and only those, who give satisfactory evidence of having become new creatures in Christ.

" 4. *Resolved*, That the master who buys and sells human beings, as mer-chandise, for gain—who does not recognize in respect to his servants the divine sanctity of their relations as husbands and wives, and as parents and children—who permits them to live and die in ignorance of God, and of God's word, who does not render to his servants that which is just and equal, or who refuses to recognize, heartily and practically, their dignity and worth, as reasonable and accountable beings, for whom Christ has died, does not give satisfactory evidence of being born of God, or having the Spirit of Christ."

Though these resolutions abstain carefully from condemning slave*holding* as sinful—a doctrine which the mover, in his speech, earnestly disclaimed, saying, " *the churches cannot stand such nonsense* " (producing a broad laugh among the members of the Board), yet they too clearly condemned known and existing practices, called *abuses*, to meet the exigencies of the Board.

Dr. De Witt, very sagaciously, said—" These resolutions will introduce a disturbing influence, and occasion *future inconvenience.*"

On motion of Chief Justice Williams, of Connecticut, they were referred, together with Mr. Phelps' resolutions, to a select committee of five, of which he was made chairman. The committee reported, verbally, the next morning, recommending the adoption of the original report of Dr. Woods, without the amendments. Mr. Phelps then promptly renewed the substance of his former resolutions, in a more condensed form, which he moved as an amendment, as follows:

" And finally, in accordance with, and in reply to the memorials submitted to it from Worcester county and elsewhere at its present meeting, the Board deem it right and proper to say, that its funds cannot and will not be expended in maintaining slaveholding missionaries, or building up slaveholding churches; that in carrying out the general principles laid down in the first part of the foregoing report, in their practical application to the question of receiving slaveholders to, and retaining in the missionary churches, the Board will expect its missionaries and churches to treat slaveholding, in the matter of instruction, admonition and discipline, in the same manner as they should and would treat drunkenness, gaming, falsehood, bigamy, idolatry, and the like; and that whenever and wherever it shall appear that the missionaries and the churches, in exercise of their appropriate liberty, do not do so, it will be the duty of this Board, in the exercise of its liberty, to dissolve farther connection with them."

After some ineffectual efforts to dodge a direct vote on this amendment, it was voted upon, and voted down, a few voices only being heard in its favor.

This meeting of the Board was also made famous by the advocacy of the doctrine, involved in the report, that "*organic sins,*" or sins "interwoven in the structure of society," or sanctioned by civil government, are not to be considered and treated, in the administration of church discipline, as *personal* sins—as though personality could be impaired, or individual accountability set aside, by practicing an iniquity framed or allowed by civil rulers, or by following a multitude to do evil!

THE AMERICAN HOME MISSIONARY SOCIETY.

This society, supported by Presbyterians and Congregationalists, builds up, with professions of the most liberal and dignified impartiality, either a pro-slavery or an anti-slavery religion, provided it be manifested in accordance with the approved forms and technicalities of the allied sects, north and south, co operating in the enterprise. In this, it stands, substantially, on the same ground with the American Board.

" There is, to this day, no vote, or rule, or usage of *either* Board, to keep slaveholders, who are unobjectionable in other respects, out of their churches at home or abroad, or even to prevent slaves being hired of their masters to labor at the Mission Schools, where pagan youth are congregated to form, under Christian education, their ideas of Gospel principles and practice.

" The Home Society has, moreover, instead of diminishing, *increased* its slaveholding dependencies during the present era of anti-slavery agitation. Since 1842—that is, in the seven years preceding the last report— the American Home Missionary Society lacks but *five* of having *trebled* the slaveholding churches under her patronage, while it has added but little more than *one-fifth* to its whole Missionary force."—*Letter of Pres. Blanchard and others to the Cincinnati Convention*, April, 1850.

" The American Home Missionary Society has fifty-six churches in slave States, all open to the reception of slaveholders."—" *J. B.,*" in *Chr. Era,* Oct. 2, 1851.

And how is it with the Missionary Societies of other sects? We answer in the words of Pres. Blanchard.

"The American Board of Commissioners for Foreign Missions and the Home Missionary Society certainly contrast favorably with the corresponding agencies in their sister sects. Their records show at least enough hostility to slaveholding mingling with their councils, to keep the subject in agitation from year to year."—*Ib.*

OTHER AGENCIES.

"The missionary piety of a country is its *popular* piety. Bible, Tract, Sunday School, and other subordinate operations, walk in the light of the missionary enterprise, and are merely an expansion and part of it. We have not the statistics at hand, but a table showing the sum annually collected and disbursed in this country for religious and benevolent uses, under circumstances which imply the admission of slaveholding to the communion table, is alone sufficient to keep up the evangelical character of slavery. For every subscriber who pays, and every agent who collects, and every person who receives a shilling of the conscience fund of the United States, which is raised by that religion which allows slavery to its communion table, either consciously or unconsciously utters a silent confession of his faith, that slaveholding is privileged in the Church of God."
—*Ib.*

THE AMERICAN BIBLE SOCIETY, at an early day, aroused the religious community with the proposal to supply *every family* in the United States with Bibles. The auxiliary societies, the agents, and the ministry in general, for a number of years, kept the enterprise prominently before the public; large and general contributions were made for the object; the widow's mite was cast into the treasury, and, at length, the report went forth, re-published by the presses of Christendom, that the magnificent work had been accomplished. On investigation, some time afterwards, it appeared that there had been a slight oversight in the statement. The bulk of the *laboring* population, in *half* the states of the republic had, somehow, been overlooked in the distribution. The only reasons of this neglect were, that they were of a darker complexion than their neighbors, were of African descent, were chiefly held as slaves, and for these causes were not encouraged or permitted to read. The number of the families left destitute (regarding every five persons as a family) was four hundred and sixty thousand, or, a population of two millions three hundred thousand, comprising a little more than *one-sixth* part of the population of the whole country.

This was quite an important destitution. With a view to its supply, the American Anti-Slavery Society, in May, 1834, (through a committee representing several religious denominations,) submitted a written proposal to the American Bible Society, in which they offered to contribute to the funds of the society five thousand dollars, provided the society would appropriate the same amount to the supply of the destitute colored population, and carry the measure into effect in two years from the 4th of July, 1834.

The offer was not accepted by the Bible Society, and no mention was made of it in its Annual Report. Prominent members and supporters of the institution professed to regard the offer as a rude attack, amounting to an insult. The chief apologies for the course of the society were, (1) that the laws of the slave states did not permit the slaves to read, and (2), that the work of distribution belonged to the auxiliaries, and not to the parent society. To these apologies it is sufficient to answer that in its foreign operations the society does not hold itself circumscribed by the legislation that interdicts the scriptures—nor did its structure nor the proper province of its auxiliaries debar the parent society from proposing the supply of *every* family in the United States with Bibles. It would have been as easy for it to have proposed the *completion* of that supply, and undoubtedly this would have been done, if there had been no fear of offending slaveholding church members.—See *Emancipator*, May 27, and June 24, 1834.

An agent of the Bible Society, some time afterwards, was detected in furnishing a Bible to a colored person in New Orleans. He was arrested, but released on the ground of his not being acquainted with the laws, and his promising not to repeat the offence. The Bible Society of New Orleans, auxiliary to the American Bible Society, publicly disclaimed the act, and protested its innocency of any intent to furnish the colored people with Bibles. The "*Parent Society*" is not known to have uttered any reproof or remonstrance to its "*auxiliary*," or any regret at the course it pursued.

At a meeting of the Orleans County (N. Y.) Bible Society, "a Resolution was introduced, that the society request the American Bible Society to make a donation of Bibles for the fugitive slaves in Canada West. *This was opposed, and finally lost.*" No laws against the distribution could be pleaded in this case.*—*Oberlin Evangelist*, July 2, 1845. *Chr. Inv.* March, 1846.

Whatever of progress, or *appearance* of progress, has been made by the American Bible Society, will be shown by the following.

"Public attention, says the Annual Report of the A. and F. Anti-Slavery Society (1849), has been drawn, more than at any previous time, towards the obligation of circulating the Bible among the slave population. The South begins to feel that ' considerations of sound policy, as well as Christian obligation,' require attention to the subject.   Some Christians in that portion of the country realize the duty of supplying slaves with the Bible, and are doing it to a limited extent.   At the North, unwonted interest has been manifested on the subject.   The American Bible Society has been urged to take up the matter.   In their monthly ' Record,' under the head of ' Slaves,' they acknowledge receipts for this purpose ; but in a circular issued some months since, they say, ' Local distributions should be made under the direction of the auxiliaries.   On these organizations at the South devolves the duty, beyond doubt, of supplying the slave population of that region—*so far as this work is to be done ;*' and they request that contributors to the income of the Society would not restrict their contributions to this object, as the funds must remain in part unexpended.   It has also been stated to applicants, at the Bible House, that they have no fund for slaves, that they do not intend to have, and rather than have, they would prefer to return to the donors money sent for that object.   At the same time, it is but just to say, that the managers of the American Bible Society resolve that they will promptly avail themselves of every opportunity to further the distribution of the Bible among the slave population at the South, and that copies will be supplied to any responsible person for that object.   The secretary acknowledges that the applications of the Anti-Slavery Society have done good, and the managers avow, in the circular, that ' so far as

---

* The excuse made was, that the measure would be thought to savor of abolitionism, would hazard the peace and welfare of the society, and therefore it should be left to individuals to make the request.

there are colored freemen, or slaves within the limits of an auxiliary, who can be reached, who are capable of reading the blessed word of God, and are without it, they should unquestionably be furnished with it, as well as any other class of our ruined race."—*Liberty Almanac for* 1849.

THE AMERICAN TRACT SOCIETY prepares, publishes, and circulates tracts against every sin forbidden in the decalogue, except that particular form of sin which involves the violation of the entire code—the sin of subverting the family relation, reducing the image of God to a chattel, and robbing a man of himself.

The charge is not that they decline circulating the writings of "modern fanatics," on this subject. They equally avoid circulating the testimonies of Hopkins, of Edwards, of Wesley, of Grotius, of Hannah More, of John Locke, of John Jay, of Dr. Primatt, of Dr. Price, of the Abbe Raynal, of the Abbe Gregoire, of James Beattie, of Dr. Adam Clarke, of Arch Deacon Paley, of Edmund Burke, of Dr. Johnson, of Bishop Horsley, of Bishop Porteus, of Dr. Robertson, of Bishop Warberton, of Thomas Scott, of Granville Sharp, of Thomas Clarkson, of Fowell Buxton, of Dr. Dick, of John Angell James—of the Christian poets, Cowper, Pollok, and Montgomery. The volumes of general Christian literature since the beginning of the African slave trade, furnish, it would seem, no suitable materials from which the Committee of the American Tract Society, with all their tact and skill in the art of pruning, could cull an eight page tract against human chattelhood, against slaveholding, against the slave system, or even in relation to those topics.

More marvellous, still:—In all the ranks of the learned, the wise, the good, the discreet, of our own age and nation, who cherish the American Tract Society as an instrumentality for teaching human relations and duties, for admonishing an erring world of its sins; among all the writers on whom the Tract Committee depend, and to whom they look for tracts adapted to the times we live in, *not one*, it seems, has been prevailed upon or has succeeded, in furnishing a page of instruction upon a subject in respect to which—it is said—imprudent and rash writers are leading Christians astray ! What a wonderful condition of things is this? What sorcery has paralyzed this arm of the Church—the arm that should wield the Christian press, amid the influences that corrupt and destroy?

But this is not the worst of the case. The Society is not merely guilty of neglect. It commits a positive injury. By its mutilation of books it compels the common christian literature of the English language to bear false witness. By its garbled biographies of the sainted dead, by its suppression of their earnest testimony againt slavery, by its smothering the expression of the purest christian affections of their hearts, it hides the distinctive traits of their christian character, and falsely holds them up as specimens of the kind of piety that expresses no abhorrence of slaveholding. It is a perversion of truth. It is a deceitful representation of the character described :

"A case has recently appeared; the memoir of Mary Lundie Duncan, of Scotland, by her mother. It first had a wide circulation abroad; then was published in this country, in full, by the Carters, in various styles, and some of them as cheap as could be desired; but now has been published, *abridged*, by the American Tract Society. It is, however, abridged very slightly, its size being scarcely at all lessened, but some important omissions are made.

"According to the *Independent* (for January 22), the following is omitted on page 79 :

"'We have been lately much interested in the emancipation of slaves: I never heard eloquence more overpowering than that of George Thompson. I am most thankful that he has been raised up. O that the measure soon to be proposed in Parliament may be effectual !'

"In the following paragraph, the sentences in brackets are expunged in the Tract Society's edition :

"'August 1. Freedom has dawned this morning upon the British colonies. [No more degraded lower than the brutes—no more bowed down with suffering from which there is no redress.] The sons of Africa have obtained the rights of fellow-subjects, the rights of man, the immortal creation of God. [Now they may seek the sanctuary, fearless of the lash; they may call their children their own.] Hope will animate their hearts, and give vigor to their efforts.'

"Such mutilations have their object. We are sorry to see in them an unworthy subserviency to the foul behests of slavery."—*Oberlin Evangelist*, 1852.

Such is a specimen of the methods of those who superintend our religious literature, and who cannot approve "the measures" of abolitionists.

THE AMERICAN SUNDAY SCHOOL UNION is prompt to expurgate from her Sunday School libraries whatever may have incidentally crept into them, in familiar abstracts of Scripture history, which might be construed into a disapproval of American slavery, though the books may not have been written for that end, nor by writers at all identified with present efforts for the abolition of slavery.*

CONCLUDING REMARKS.

We must not pursue, further, the specific action of the American churches, and the organizations that have grown out of them. Apart from what has been presented already, and much more of the same character, which it would be easy to add, there is one general fact, the consideration of which might suffice, of itself, to determine the question of their relation to slavery. The Northern churches commonly foster the spirit of caste by repudiating social equality with the colored man, and by maintaining the negro pew. This fact has been adverted to by legislators in the free states, (once in a Report by a Legislative Committee of the State of New York) as furnishing *the* reason why it is impossible for the State Governments to restore to the colored citizens their acknowledged political and civil rights. So long as this unrighteous prejudice is indulged by the churches, it must bind them to the car of the slave-power as its voluntary victims and tools. It must seal their lips from the utterance of God's words of rebuke. While such diseases prey upon the vitals of the Church, while she "refuses to be healed, and knows not

---

* The late Mr. Gallaudet, who was never identified with active abolitionists, revised an English book for the American Sunday School Union, called "Jacob and his Sons," in three small volumes, which, after being circulated awhile, was dropped by the committee, because, in its biography of Joseph, it contained a passage alluding to slavery, which gave offence to the South.

that her strength has departed," in vain shall her prophets cry " Peace! peace!" or her physicians prescribe panaceas for her wounds.

In the preceding records, we have aimed not only to guard against the injustice of indiscriminate censure, but have endeavored, as far as practicable, to separate the topic of this chapter (the position of the Churches in respect to *slavery*) from their relation to " *modern abolitionists* " and their peculiar and distinctive " *measures.*" That topic we propose to take up in another chapter. We have not obtruded it here. We have not written them down " pro-slavery " because they " followed not with us "—nor because we have been earnestly opposed by them. They claim to be "as much opposed to slavery as the abolitionists themselves." The impartial reader will now judge for himself of that claim. He has seen what they have done and said on the subject, and what they have declined saying and doing; and he has seen this, by itself, disconnected with any controversies concerning " modern abolitionists and their measures." Whatever may be said of *them*, the single point presented in this chapter is the relation of the American Churches, as organized bodies, to the practice of slaveholding. On *that point alone*, let the reader now make up his opinion.

And when he has done this, let him next inquire whether it is probable that the Churches, other ecclesiastical bodies, and leading ministers, of the different sects in this country, could hold such a position in respect to slaveholding, church discipline, religious instruction, and the missionary enterprise, without being brought, of necessity, into a state of hostility to any body of earnest, persevering, and consistent men and christians, who should seek, from high moral, religious and benevolent considerations, the present and entire abolition of slavery.

He will do well to inquire also whether any ordinary or even possible manifestations of wisdom and circumspection, on the part of such a body of men, would be likely to prevent, or could prevent, their collision with religionists holding such a position respecting slavery and slaveholding. And when he comes to examine the facts reserved for another chapter of this history, he will be able, perhaps, to make up his mind, intelligently and conclusively, on the whole subject.

The verdict of an impartial posterity can easily be foreseen. Already that verdict is beginning to be anticipated by men of calm minds, who have stood aloof, as lookers-on, during the whole struggle, or until quite recently, and who are far enough, even now, from adventuring to co-operate with any class of active abolitionists, or severing their ecclesiastical connections.

"Let the time come," says Albert Barnes, "when, in all the mighty denominations of Christians, it can be announced that the evil is ceased with them forever; and let the voice of each denomination be lifted up in kind, but firm and solemn testimony against the system—with no mealy words, with no attempt at apology, with no wish to blink it, with no effort to throw the sacred shield of religion over so great an evil—and the work is done. There is no public sentiment in this land—there could be none created—that would resist the power of such testimony. There is no power *out* of the church that could sustain slavery an hour, if it were not sustained *in* it."

How idle then, is it, for churches and ministers to think of shielding themselves from censure, by dwelling on the real or supposed faults of abolitionists! Why have they not accomplished the work themselves? Why, at the least, are they not now attempting it?

Their real position is revealed clearly by the continual recurrence of a class of significant incidents, too numerous and too scattered for convenient classification and record. We present here a few specimens :

At the Religious Anniversaries in New York in May, at an early period, some time between 1832 and 1835 inclusive, (we have not the precise date) a number of ministers and others from the country, in attending the early morning prayer meetings, before the public exercises, were heard to pray for the poor slaves—some of them, perhaps, for the abolition of slavery. Among these was the venerable Rev. ETHAN SMITH, the writer on the prophecies. The incident, without mention of names, was conspicuously heralded in the New York Observer and kindred prints, in illustration of the meddlesome and mischievous expedients of abolitionists to disturb the harmony of the anniversaries, and mar the peace of the Church.

Similar complaints of anti-slavery prayers have been common all over the country, and have not yet ceased ; and quite recently, Dr. Spring has said,—"If, by one prayer I could liberate every slave in the land, I would not dare to offer it." This might deserve the commendation of honest frankness, if the same class of persons would not claim (especially on visiting England) to desire the abolition of slavery, as much as anybody, and complain that "the imprudence of abolitionists had put back the event half a century."

When news of the British Act of Emancipation reached America, there was a general prediction of bloodshed, and American abolitionists were implicated with those of England, in the responsibility and the guilt. The religious presses were forward in this. After the first panic was over, they spoke of it as "an experiment." The New York Observer, yielding to public sympathy, went so far as to say that if all went on peacefully, the abolition controversy in America would be at an end, as there could be but one sentiment among Christians. And there *could* not be, aside from the influences represented by such papers as the New York Observer. Well; the testimony of the West India authorities and of Queen Victoria to the peacefulness and benefits of emancipation at length reached us. Edward Everett (who, as Governor of Massachusetts, had been forward to intimate that abolitionists should be "indicted at Common Law,") was now ready, in a published letter, to recognize the glorious event. But the co-operation of the leading churches, ministry, and religious presses, has not been secured to the cause of freedom. Their opposition has scarcely been relaxed. With some it is more bitter than ever. The benefits of West India emancipation must be learned through other channels than those directed by them.

The "imprudence" of the immediatists was magnified. Some plan of "gradualism" was preferred. When John Quincy Adams, after great deliberation and labor, prepared and presented in Congress his plan for gradual abolition, he doubtless expected the ready co-operation of the religious portion of the community not committed to the immediatists. But he met with, *literally*, NOTHING of the kind, that reached the public ear. Not a sermon, not a clerical letter, not an ecclesiastical resolution, not a paragraph of a religious editor, not a correspondent of a religious periodical, so far as we could ever learn, commended the measure. Political editors were equally silent. The proposition fell like a weight of lead to the ground. This *one fact* (almost forgotten already) decides the position of the leading churches and ministry of the North on the slave question.

CHAPTER XIX.

ACTION OF THE FEDERAL GOVERNMENT, TO THE CLOSE OF THE FIRST PRESIDENTIAL ADMINISTRATION.

Preliminary observations—Secrecy of the Convention of 1787—Names and dates of the different Presidents—Federal action under the first President—Action in Congress on the Anti-Slavery petitions—Acceptance of Slave territory (now Tennessee), ceded, under restrictions, by North Carolina—Cession of the Federal District—Congressional re-enactment of Slavery—The act unconstitutional—Fugitive Slave Bill of 1793—Examination of it—Unconstitutional provisions—Escape of a female slave of the President—Slavery in the Federal District—Naturalization Law, 1790, for "*white* persons"—Act of 1792 for organizing a "white" militia—Admission of Tennessee as a Slave State, 1796—Kentucky previously.

FROM the Church, we now turn again to the State. Having seen the position of the former, we need not be surprised by any similar manifestations in the latter. When the salt loses its savor, we may expect to meet with putrefaction in the masses around it. The political morality of a nation may sometimes fall below the level of its current religion, but never rises above it. When the leading religious teachers of a country maintain that sins "interwoven by legislation into the structure and frame-work of society," may therefore find a quiet home in the Church, there can be no effectual security against unrighteous enactments. A high premium—so to speak—is thus bid, before hand, for wicked laws.* When such teachers denounce the doctrine that iniquitous enactments are, before God, null and void, and that the laws of God are

---

* The Fugitive Slave Bill was enacted in 1850. The doctrine that "organic" or national sins must not be excluded from the Church, was promulgated at the meeting of the American Board, in Brooklyn, in 1845.

of higher authority than the edicts of man, the defences of liberty as well as the foundations of morality will be likely to give way, and the land be inundated with despotism and crime. So long as moral causes continue to produce their appropriate effects, it must remain true that a people consenting to come under the influence of such teachers, must be exposed to the loss of their liberties. And while a God of equity controls human affairs, a people that voluntarily sustain such enactments must fall under his displeasure.

It must be a short-sighted ambition, whether in ecclesiastics or statesmen, that overlooks, in its estimates, the sure verdict of coming years, and purchases the popularity of an hour at the price of a perpetual future infamy. They should know that no arts of cunning can cover them from the scrutiny of posterity, and no power of patronage protect them from the reproving pages of history. And in this anticipation they should read the presage of the still surer sentence of their Supreme Judge, in the world to come.

Wicked rulers may be canonized by false teachers, and, for a season, be reverenced for saints, as well as lauded for statesmen. But Time, (to say nothing of Eternity) will tear off the mask, and their names will stand for the representatives of falsehood and folly.

In the State, as in the Church, the downward course of declension is often silent, stealthy, and for a time, unperceived, but without repentance and amendment, apostacy and ruin must be the final result.

Sustained by such sentiments, and commending them to the reader, we now approach the inner sanctuary of our political temple, (the temple, perhaps, of our nation's idolatry,) into which it has been thought sacrilege to gaze. The reverence with which we have been accustomed to regard the doings of our half-deified statesmen, may now be sadly disturbed. But the scrutiny must proceed; and though the Hebrew prophets' "chambers of imagery" should be revealed, we must brace wide open the doors. If the sight reduces our reverence of men, it may increase our veneration of God.

SECRECY OF THE FEDERAL CONVENTION OF 1787.

One of the most important facts in our national history, so far as the connection of the Federal Government with slavery is concerned, bears the same date with the sittings of the Convention of Delegates, in 1787, by whom the draft of our Federal Constitution was prepared ; and it stands connected with the circumstances and manner of their procedure. It is the fact that that most important Convention, (a knowledge of whose discussions was of deeper interest to the people, than the knowledge of any other discussions ever held in the country,) *sat constantly with closed doors, and under an injunction of secrecy*, the veil remaining unlifted, till the generation whose responsibilities required a knowledge of those delibera- tions, had not only acted, but had passed off the stage.

It is in no spirit of censoriousness that we allude to this important historical fact. We neither say nor believe that the arrangement was adopted for unworthy ends. Assuredly this was not the purpose of the noble friends of universal liberty who were members of that body. The arrangement may nevertheless be regarded a most important historical fact, and one upon which the entire political history of the country, as connected with slavery, has ever since hinged. It may also be regarded as a most calamitous fact, and one for the existence of which, there seems to have been no adequate cause. The Convention was not a military council, delibe- rating upon measures that might have been reported in the camp of an enemy. It was a political body, sitting in time of peace, and among constituents who were entitled to know *how* and *why* they were acting. It is natural to suppose that the policy of secrecy resulted from habits and maxims imbibed under a kingly dynasty. This apology may excuse the delegates, but it could not do away the effects of their arrange- ment. It was anti-democratic in its character, and could not but produce corresponding results. It is important that the friends of freedom observe this, and derive from it a maxim for future guidance: '*The slightest departure from democracy endangers freedom.*'

Had the Convention sat with open doors, with their deliberations gazetted daily, as in Congress, there is no room to believe that the slave question in America could ever have stood where it now stands. What is now shrouded in mystery would have been held up in the light of the sun. Had the people of that generation found in those proceedings, the "compromises" and "understandings" now claimed for slavery, the draft reported would never have been "the Constitution." No draft, in connection with such "understandings," would ever have been reported. The reader of the preceding history will judge of this, for himself.* But if (as we believe) there were no such "understandings" and "compromises," other than those found in the draft, the gazetted discussions would have disclosed none, and no pretensions of them could have been afterwards set up. In either case, the open Convention would have given us a free country, instead of a conquered territory of the Slave-Power, ruled by a petty oligarchy of slaveholders.

It is easy to see how the arrangement of secrecy gave rise to the pretensions of the Slave Power, in the first place, and has favored it ever since. It could not fail to favor the arts of any in the Convention (if there were such) who might choose to make use of the Constitution for purposes of evil, of which the people, *whose instrument and act it was,* never dreamed. It opened the door for conjecture, for insinuation, for assumption, for the monopoly of occult interpretation, for the claim of unexpressed "understandings, compromises and guaranties." It afforded opportunity to give direction to technical ambiguity and circumlocution, in the document itself. It enabled Cabinets, Legislatures, and Courts of Law, if they pleased, to foist, unperceived, a Constitution of their own devising, in the place of the Constitution submitted to the people. The people, in such a case, can have no secu-

---

* See Chapters VIII. and IX.

rity from the most monstrous perversions of the Constitution, but by insisting upon a rigorous adherence to that righteous rule of legal interpretation, based upon the Common Law, that imperatively forbids any construction to be put upon any instrument which shall make it conflict with equity and justice, so long as the language employed will possibly admit of a construction which would make it equitable. What a revolution would an adherence to that righteous rule produce!

The following Table will be useful for reference, as we proceed:

George Washington was President from 1789 to 1797.
John Adams   "   "   "   1797 to 1801.
Thomas Jefferson   "   "   "   1801 to 1809.
James Madison   "   "   "   1809 to 1817.
James Monroe   "   "   "   1817 to 1825.
John Quincy Adams   "   "   "   1825 to 1829.
Andrew Jackson   "   "   "   1829 to 1837.
Martin Van Buren   "   "   "   1837 to 1841.
William H. Harrison, and }   "   "   1841 to 1845.
John Tyler   }
James K. Polk   "   "   "   1845 to 1849.
Zachary Taylor   "   "   1849 to July 9, 1850.
Millard Fillmore   "   "   (July 9) 1850 to

Slaveholding Presidents, about 49 years—Non-Slaveholding, about 14 years, up to 4th of March, 1852.*

FEDERAL ACTION UNDER THE FIRST PRESIDENT.

The anti-slavery petitions of 1790, before mentioned,† though they evidently found favor with the majority of the members of Congress, nevertheless failed of securing their object. A somewhat favorable Report was made by the

---

* Washington was inaugurated April 30th; his successors (except Tyler and Fillmore), March 4th. Harrison survived his inauguration but one month, Taylor one year and above four months.

† Chapter X.

Committee to whom they were referred, in which the confidence was expressed that the State Legislatures would revise their laws, from time to time, when necessary, and *promote the objects mentioned in the memorials*, and every other measure that may tend to the happiness of *slaves* "—also assuring the memorialists that "in all cases to which the authority of Congress extends, they will exert it for the humane objects of the memorialists, so far as they can be promoted on the principles of justice, humanity, and good policy."—2 *Deb. Cong. Old Ser.* 1465, as quoted by S. P. Chase, U. S. Senate, March 26, 1850.

In deference to the members from South Carolina and Georgia, this Report was frittered away till it embraced only these points, viz: that Congress could not interfere with slavery in the States, nor prohibit the importation of slaves till 1808, but could prohibit American citizens from importing slaves for the supply of foreigners, and provide for the humane treatment, on their passage, of slaves imported here. Thus was taken the first step in the policy of evasion and compromise, in the Congress of the United States, from which has followed its downward course ever since. *Vide Speech of S. P. Chase, as above.*

In the same year (1790) North Carolina tendered to the United States a cession of territory including the present State of Tennessee, on condition that the provisions of the Ordinance of 1787, for the North Western territory, prohibiting slavery, should not be extended over that region. The cession was accepted on these terms. Thus the policy of the country, on that subject, was reversed, and *Congress was led, for the first time, to give its direct sanction to slavery.*—(*Ib.*)

By the Constitution of the United States, Congress was empowered "to exercise exclusive legislation in all cases whatsoever, over such district (not exceeding ten miles square) as may, by cession of particular States, and the acceptance of Congress, become the seat of Government of the United States."—*Art. I., sec.* 3.

On the 22d of December, 1788, Maryland made an act of cession for this purpose. On the 3d of December, 1789, Virginia made a similar act of cession, and the two parcels fixed upon by Congress, in accordance with these acts, comprised the District of Columbia, ten miles square.* And on the 16th of July, 1790, Congress passed an act, accepting these cessions, and providing that the laws of the two States over their respective portions of the District should *remain in force* " UNTIL the time fixed for the removal of the Government thereto, and UNTIL Congress shall otherwise by law provide."

By this wholesale and summary though covert process, the Federal Government re-enacted over the Federal District those slave laws which, had they *not* been thus re-enacted, would have become inoperative at the very moment the cession was accepted, upon the admitted maxim that slavery can exist only by force of positive municipal or local law. Yet Congress had no more power or authority, under the Constitution, to make a slave, than it had to establish an order of nobility, or create a king. The procedure was a flagrant usurpation of power, a violation of the Federal Constitution, and the act, so far as the existence of slavery in the Federal District is concerned, should be set aside by the Courts of the United States, as unconstitutional, null, and void.

This point is of too much importance to be lightly passed over. We will fortify our position by introducing a brief outline of an argument in the Speech of Hon. Horace Mann, of Massachusetts, in the House of Representatives of the United States, February 23, 1849. No answer to the argument is known to have been attempted.

We quote only the propositions of Mr. Mann, without the luminous illustrations and ample authorities by which he elucidated and sustained them. But the propositions shine with sufficient clearness, in their own light.

" 1. Slavery has no legal existence unless by force of positive law."

" 2. A man's legal condition may be changed by a change in the government over him, while he remains in the same place, just as effectually as it

---

* The portion west of the Potomac, ceded by Virginia, has recently been retro ceded back again.

can be changed by his removal to another place, and putting himself under another government."

3. "The jurisdiction under which the inhabitants of what is now the District of Columbia lived, prior to the cession of the District by Maryland to the United States, was utterly and totally changed at the moment of the cession—at the moment when, according to the provisions of the Constitution, they ceased to be citizens of the State of Maryland, and became citizens of the District of Columbia."

4. "Congress, in attempting to re-enact the Maryland laws, to uphold slavery in this District, transcended the limits of its constitutional power. It acted unconstitutionally. It acted in plain contravention of some of the plainest and most obvious principles consecrated by the Constitution. If so, no one will dispute that its act is void. I do not deny, then, that Congress used words of sufficient amplitude to cover slavery; but what I deny is, that it had any power to give legal force to those words."

5. "My next proposition therefore, is this: that as Congress can do nothing except what it is empowered to do by the Constitution, and as the Constitution does not empower it to establish slavery here, it cannot establish slavery here, nor continue it."

The case is plain. There only needs a Granville Sharp to press the question before the Federal Courts. Its Blackstones and Mansfields, though steeped in prejudice, and fettered by precedent, as their English predecessors were, would be forced to yield, and the charm of judicial infallibility would be broken.

KENTUCKY, which had been under the jurisdiction of Virginia, was admitted into the Union in 1792, as an independent State. This commenced the policy of admitting *new slave States*.

We come next to the law of 1793, under cover of which the Federal authorities assist in returning fugitive slaves to their masters.

The Constitution of the United States contains the following provision:

"No person held to service or labor in one State, under the laws thereof, escaping to another, shall, in consequence of any law or regulation therein, be discharged from such service or labor, but shall be delivered up on claim of the party to whom such service or labor may be due."—*Art.* IV., Sect. 2.

From the *mere language* of this section, no one would suspect that it referred to slaves. It makes no mention of such a class, but very accurately describes the case of apprentices and other persons who were under a voluntary contract to perform labor, having received an equivalent in advance, and being in debt for the same. *Strictly* construed, it *could not* apply to slaves.

It speaks of *persons:* but according to the "*laws*" of the slave States, a slave is *not* a "person," but a chattel. It speaks of persons "held to service or labor," but slave law holds no one to "*service or labor*,"* any more than it does to a life of prostitution and idleness. It only holds its victim as *property*—and of reclaiming *property* the section under review *says nothing.* The clause provides that no "law or regulation" of any State shall "discharge" the party owing service. It does not say that either the State into which he has escaped, or that the United States shall enforce the claim, or help carry him back. No "service or labor" can be *due* from a chattel to its proprietor. The slave can owe no *debt*, because he "can form no contract." And were it otherwise, and if the State to which he had escaped, or the United States, were required to act in the case, it must be an act of adjudication between debtor and creditor, in which, after hearing both sides, and balancing the "labor" performed against the debt "due," a decision would have to be made whether any "service or labor" remained "due," or otherwise.

This is all that can be gathered from the *mere language.* Not only does it fail to describe the case of fugitive slaves, but if the provisions of the bill were honestly and rigorously applied to them, it would, in most cases, result in their dis-

---

* Mr. Madison tells us explicitly, that when the framers of the Constitution used the word "*service*," they were careful to make choice of that term, because it did *not* express the condition of *slaves*, but of *free* persons.

"On motion of Mr. Randolph, the word '*servitude*' was struck out, and '*service*' UNANIMOUSLY inserted—the *former* being thought to express the condition of *slaves*, and the latter the obligation of *free persons*."—*Madison Papers*, Vol. III., p. 1569.

How then could they have expected that when they used the word "*service*," the people would understand them to mean "*servitude ?*" But unless the above clause *does* mean "servitude" and not "service," it cannot mean fugitive slaves!

charge, as nothing would be found "due" from them, even admitting that they *could* sustain the relation of debtors.

But, as already noticed, the language does describe the case of persons owing service or labor, by voluntary contract. And there were circumstances that might be supposed to call for some such provision at that time, and in the city of Philadelphia, where the Convention was sitting. It was common for ship-masters there, in accordance with previous contract, to advertise and sell at public auction, whole ship-loads of "German redemptioners," as they were called, or emigrant laborers. That is, their *services* were sold for a term of time, sufficient to pay for their passage. And this shows, by-the-by, that the mere phrases "buying and selling" men, does not prove them to be chattel slaves. These "persons held to service and labor in one State, under the laws thereof," were in the habit, in great numbers, of "escaping to another" State, and thus evading the payment of their just dues. This was the ground of much complaint, and it would be considered proper that they should "be delivered up, on claim of the party to whom such service or labor (might) be due."

And is there the slightest evidence that *the people* of the Northern States, in adopting the Constitution, understood that the clause referred to fugitive slaves?*   While the Quakers

---

* An unexpected answer to this query comes to hand while we are penning it, in a speech of Hon. Daniel Webster, in the Senate of the United States, July 17, 1850. Alluding to a letter of Gov. Berkeley of Virginia, to Gov. Endicott of Massachusetts, in 1644, in which the latter is *requested* to return some fugitive " *servants*," Mr. Webster proceeds to say :

" At that day, I do not suppose there were a great many *slaves* in Massachusetts, but there was an *extensive system of apprenticeship, and hundreds of persons were bound apprentices* in Massachusetts, some of whom would run away. They were as likely to run away to Virginia as anywhere else ; and in such cases, they were returned, upon demand, to their masters. So true is that, that it was found necessary, in the early laws of Massachusetts, to make provision for the seizure and return of *runaway apprentices*. In all the revisions of our laws, *this provision remains ;* and here it is in the revised statutes now before me. It provides that *runaway apprentices* shall be secured upon the application of their masters, or any one on their behalf, and put into jail until they can be sent for by their masters ; and there is no trial by jury in their case, either."

A very important and timely distinction of Mr. Webster, unless he means to insinuate the identity of " *bound apprentices* in Massachusetts" with *slaves !*

of Pennsylvania and Rhode Island, and other friends of freedom, objected so strongly to the twenty years of respite to
the slave trade (Rhode Island withholding her ratification
from that clause), *is it credible* that no complaint would have
been made against a provision understood to require the
return of fugitive slaves?

In "*The Federalist*"—by Madison, Jay, and Hamilton—in
defence of the Federal Constitution,* removing objections,
and persuading the people to adopt it, Mr. Madison himself
devotes ample space to a consideration of the objections
against the apportionment of representation, and the twenty
years respite to the slave trade, the latter of which Mr. Madison regrets. Is it credible that he would have omitted to
notice the clause requiring the return of fugitive slaves, if
the people *had understood* that there was such a provision?
Could he have passed it by, as he does, in silence? Or, what
can we imagine he would have said of it, with those memoranda
in his desk, since published, affirming that the Convention
unanimously defined the term "*service*" as applying only to
"the obligation of *free persons*"—affirming, also, that, as a
member of the Convention, he would not "introduce into
the Constitution the idea that there could be property in
man.†"

In the whole volume, of nearly five hundred pages, we have

Compare this statement with the language of the Constitution, and it is easy to
see how the good people of Massachusetts (in the absence of any of our more modern
expositi(ns and uses of that instrument), would be likely to understand the provision. Whatever he may have *intended* by alluding to these facts, he *entirely* fails
to sustain the claims of the *slaveholders.* He turned their boasted constitutional
requisition in *quite another direction!* He shows us how the people of Massachusetts would have required such a provision if there had been no slaves in the
country!

Another fact, before noticed, becomes particularly interesting in this connection.
The attentive and thoughtful reader of the preceding history will be very likely,
just here, to remember that there is no evidence that there were, *legally,* any
"*slaves*" *in Virginia* in 1644, when Gov. Berkeley requested the return of some
"*servants.*"—See Chapter II.

* These papers were at the time circulated among the people in the public journals, and were afterwards collected into a volume.

† *Madison Papers*, Vol. III., pp. 1429-30.

been unable to detect a single paragraph referring to the subject of fugitive slaves, though much space is devoted to an enumeration of the causes and dangers of disagreement between the States, and the importance of harmony between them.

These facts are introduced, here, *not* as forestalling or even as discussing the constitutional question involved, but for the simple purpose of showing, distinctly and fully, under what circumstances the law of 1793 was enacted.

Six years had now elapsed, since the Constitution had been drafted, and *four years* since it had gone into operation. *During all this time there had been no law for returning fugitive slaves,* as there had been none under the old confederation. There had been no public anticipation of such a law—no general understanding that the duty of such an enactment devolved on the Federal Congress—and, what is still more remarkable—no complaints, much less, no loud and boisterous clamors, from slaveholders, on account of the absence of such a law. Nor is it credible, that at a time when manumissions were so extensive, and the spirit of liberty and opposition to slavery so widely diffused, there were not considerable numbers of successful escapes. A female slave of President Washington himself is understood to have escaped to New Hampshire, during some part of his administration, whether before or after this enactment we cannot now say. The President, it seems, sent a messenger after her, but Gov. Gilman, not having learned his ethics from Moses Stuart nor his constitutional expositions from Daniel Webster, neglected a fair opportunity to arrest her—though apprized of the wishes of the illustrious claimant —and even assisted in putting her out of the reach of her pursuers ; an act for which the present Federal courts would have subjected him to a heavy fine—a process not to be adventured, in those days.*

Very possibly it may have been in consequence of some

---

* The particulars, which went the rounds of the papers a few years since, were taken from the lips of the aged woman herself, who was then living in New Hampshire.

cases of this description that the slaveholders in Congress introduced the law of 1793. They seem to have understood the
tactics of such legislation. The act is couched in language resembling that of the Constitutional provision already cited.
Without any direct mention of slaves, it is so framed that a
court of slaveholders, or those who are appointed by them,
could make it answer their purpose. It is no new thing for
those who would " frame mischief by a law " to cover up their
designs by ambiguities that the people will not, at first, understand, and thus prevent opposition and excitement. The consequence, not unfrequently, is, that the enactment is constructed so loosely, that honest statesmen and jurists, whenever they come upon the stage, will set them aside, as usurpations, or as inadequate for the purposes to which they had
been applied. An example we have, in the acts of Parliament
under which the slave trade was sheltered, but which Mr.
Pitt, (as before noticed) declared to be even *prohibitory* of the
practice.*

The enactment now under review bears marks of a similar
character, and nothing on the face of it would be likely to excite general alarm or suspicion. Yet the courts, in due time,
took care to give it a meaning adverse to freedom; though
eminent jurists are beginning to deny the constitutionality of
some of its provisions, particularly that cardinal feature of it,
sustained by the Federal Courts, hitherto, by which it assumes
for *Congress*, on behalf of the *United States*, the prerogative of
providing for the return of fugitive slaves.†

---

* The enactments under cover of which the courts have carried on religious
persecutions, have very commonly been of the same vague and ambiguous character, and for the same reasons. Even the intended victims of such laws have thus
been quieted and prevented from a timely opposition to them. How important to
guard the people against such arts !

† See Jay's View of the action of the Federal Government in behalf of Slavery,
p. 30. Since penning the above paragraph, the testimony of an aged and prominent
citizen has thrown further light on this subject. An "immense meeting" of
citizens of Boston, for repudiating the Fugitive Slave Law of 1850, was held in
Faneuil Hall, October 14, of the same year. The "call" to this meeting was headed
by the venerable JOSIAH QUINCY, formerly Mayor of Boston, and since President of
Harvard University, Cambridge, "more than four score years of age." In a letter

" By the act of 1793, the slaveholder may, himself, without oath or process of any kind, seize his prey, where he can find him, and at his leisure (for no time is specified), drag him before any justice of the peace, in the place, whom he way prefer." " Before this magistrate, who is not authorized to compel the attendance of witnesses in such a case, the slaveholder brings his victim, and if he can satisfy this judge of his own choice, 'by oral testimony or affidavit,' and, for aught that appears in the law, by his own oath, that his claim is well founded, the wretched prisoner is surrendered to him a slave for life, torn from his wife and children, bereft of all the rights of humanity, and converted into a chattel, an article of merchandize, a beast of burden."—*Jay's View*, pp. 31–2.

" The Federal Constitution declares, ' In all suits at common law, where the value in controversy shall exceed *twenty dollars*, the right of trial by jury shall be preserved ;' but the act of 1793, in suits in which ' the value in controversy' exceeds all estimation, dispenses with trial by jury, and indeed with almost every safeguard of justice and personal liberty."—*Ib.*, p. 32.

To suppose that such a statute is constitutional, is to suppose that the Constitution does not secure our liberties. To suppose that it could be legally binding, would be to reverse the foundation maxims of universal Common Law, and to deny that " Statutes contrary to fundamental morality are void."

---

addressed to J. I. Bowditch, Esq., and read at the meeting, Mr. Quincy states that the law of 1793 excited, from the first, " the surprise and utter disgust" of " every class of citizens in Massachusetts," and that " they regarded that law as *violating the principle of the compact, as they understood it, when they acceded to the Constitution of the United States.*" He states that in the year 1794, he was sent for to defend, as counsellor at law, a slave who had been arrested under this act. In his defence, he " denied the authority of the law of Congress, and of the magistrate under it, to deliver an inhabitant of Massachusetts into the custody of another, unless after trial by jury according to the constitution of this State." While he was speaking, a confusion and loud noise interrupted him, and the alleged slave passed out and escaped ! About two weeks after, Rufus Greene Amory, a lawyer of eminence, received a letter from the master of the slave, directing him to prosecute Josiah Quincy for obstructing his agent ! Mr. Amory, who showed the letter to Mr. Quincy, " felt the folly of the pretense," and Mr. Quincy heard nothing more of the prosecution.

It is said that for many years after the passage of this bill, the owners of fugitive slaves seldom, if ever, made use of it, or attempted it, except in the case at Boston. Instead of this, they resorted to various stratagems to decoy them. Long afterwards, and up to a recent date, the process was a covert one, under pretense of arrests for petty thefts.

We next glance at the *legitimate workings* of that manifestly unconstitutional act of Congress of 16th of July, 1790, by which the Federal Government extended the then expiring slave laws of Maryland and Virginia over the District of Columbia.

A Committee of Congress on the District of Columbia, reported, 16th July, 1827, that, in the County of Washington, ceded by Maryland,

"If a *free* man of color should be apprehended as a runaway, he is subjected to the payment of all *fees* and *rewards* given by law for apprehending runaways ; and upon failure to make such payment, is liable to be sold as a slave ! "*

"That is" (says Judge Jay), "a man *acknowledged to be free*, and unaccused of any offence, is to be sold as a *slave*, to pay the fees and rewards given by law for apprehending *runaways !*"—*Ib.*, p. 37.

The Committee's report further states, "that in the part of the District ceded by Virginia, a FREE NEGRO may be arrested, and put in jail for three months, on *suspicion* of being a fugitive. He is then hired out to pay his *jail fees*, and if he does not prove his freedom within twelve months, is to be sold as a SLAVE ! "—*Ib.*, p. 36.

And yet, on hearing this Report, Congress made no alteration of these laws.

Mr. Jay has further shown how *the law offers to the only* JUDGE, *in this case* (the Marshal of the District) *a high bribe to sell men he knows to be free, and thus become a manufacturer of slaves!* The proceeds of the sale remain in his pocket, after the sale, unless the master of the person arrested appears, and claims the balance.—See *Jay's View*, p. 35–6.

All this appears to be under the Maryland act of 1719, May session, chap. 2, (as cited by Sunderland, in his Anti-Slavery Manual, page 92,) and re-enacted in the manner already noticed, in 1790, by the Congress of the United States !

---

* That this law is not a dead letter, or an empty abstraction, is proved by the statement of Judge Cranch, and more than one thousand citizens of the District, who say, in their petition to Congress in 1828, against the slave trade in the District, that colored persons entitled to freedom are lodged in jail as runaways, and then sold to the traders ! And they narrate a particular instance.—See *Sunderland's Anti-Slavery Manual*, p. 93.

Another item will indicate the incipient apostacy of that period. The Federal Constitution had recognized no distinctions on account of *color*. Any attempt, in that direction, would have been abortive. In the forming of the Articles of Confederation, in 1778, the proposal to introduce the word "white" before "inhabitants" had been significantly rejected. Now, notice the contrast.

"So early as 1790, Congress passed an act describing the mode in which 'any WHITE person' might be naturalized and admitted to the rights of an American citizen."—*Jay's View*, p. 24.

"Two years after (1792), an act was passed for organizing the militia, which was to consist of 'each and every free, able-bodied, WHITE male citizen.'"—*Ib.*

Thus were the free colored population degraded and spurned from the national defense. The bad precedent was followed by succeeding administrations, in other acts of indignity toward that class of citizens; and all at the bidding of slavery.

In 1796, Tennessee, *another* Slave State, was admitted into the Union. Kentucky has been previously admitted.

Up to this point we have only traced the action of the Federal Government, in behalf of slavery, *under the administration of the first President*, with some of the direct effects of that policy. During this period, we have seen the beginning of compromise, servility, and evasion, on the part of the National Congress. We have seen the acceptance of the territory constituting Tennessee, on the condition, imposed by North Carolina, that it should remain sacred to slavery. We have seen the unconstitutional establishment of slavery in the District of Columbia, through the re-enactment, by Congress, of the Slave Laws of Virginia and Maryland, including the authorized sale of free citizens into slavery, for the payment of the expenses of their unwarrantable imprisonment! We have seen the admission into the Union, of two new Slave States. We have seen the Constitution again violated, and the sacred right of trial by jury cloven down, where the question of freedom and slavery is involved, by the law of 1793, for reclaiming fugitive slaves. We have seen the Constitution further violated by the introduction of caste, and the virtual establishment of a privileged order, founded on birth, or blood, in our naturalization and militia laws.

And all this, under the administration and with the sanction of GEORGE WASHINGTON, whom we have been taught to consider the pattern of everything that is republican and christian.

We would gladly cast the veil of oblivion over such facts, but they form a part of the public history of our country. There they stand, on the imperishable record of the past, which we may neither falsify, nor overlook, nor obliterate. We *must know* them, or not understand the history of our country. We must *ponder* them, and *judge righteously* concerning them, if we would solve the problem on which is suspended our nation's freedom. We are permitted to console ourselves with the refreshing remembrance, that Washington, by his last Will and Testament, emancipated all his slaves at his decease, thus writing *his own* condemnation and recantation of all he had ever done in support of slavery. But *his own* condemnation of the wrong, should not silence *ours*. The administration even of Washington exhibits its catalogue of national sins, which must be penitently confessed and put away, if we would enjoy, as a nation, the forgiveness and the blessing of Heaven. Above all, we must learn to repudiate the folly, and abhor the impiety of thrusting the name or the statue of *Washington* between the sin of oppressive legislation and the laws of the most High God. As well might we set up the graven image of any *other* national idol as to set up *his*.*

---

* It might serve to correct our *extravagant* adulation of Washington, Jefferson, and our other national idols, if we would remember their almost violent opposition to each other, as the heads of rival parties, criticising and even criminating each other, quite as eagerly as their successors have ever done. By some of the journalists supporting Mr. Jefferson, the retirement of Washington was hailed as a national deliverance. On the other hand, the zealous partizans of Washington and Adams regarded the elevation of Jefferson as a great public calamity, preached sermons to prevent it, and fasted and lamented when it took place. We have no occasion to renew those contentions, which became personal and bitter between the first

CHAPTER XX.

SUBSEQUENT ACTION OF THE FEDERAL GOVERNMENT—COLORED
PEOPLE—SLAVE TERRITORY—NEW SLAVE STATES—FEDERAL
DISTRICT.

Cession of Georgia and South Carolina—Mississippi Territory—Admission of Kentucky, Tennessee, Alabama, Mississippi—Missouri—Purchase of Louisiana and
Florida—Four more Slave States—Missouri Compromise—Instances of prohibiting
Slavery—Government of the Federal District—A great Slave mart—Testimony of
a Grand Jury of the District (1802)—Of Judge Morrell (1816)—John Randolph
and Alexandria Gaz. (1827)—Petition of Judge Cranch and others (1828)—" Wash.
Spectator" (1830)—Insecurity of Northern Citizens—Crandall, Chaplin, &c.

HAVING traced the beginnings of our national declension,
we must proceed with the remaining part of the history.   The
whole might almost be read, by anticipation, from the germ
already examined.   No subsequent administration, amid all
our fluctuations of national policy, has run counter to the pro-
slavery precedent furnished by the first.

The insult to colored citizens, commenced by the naturalization and militia laws, under the administration of Washington,
was renewed and extended by the law organizing the Post
Office Department, under Mr. Madison, in 1810, providing
that "no other than a free WHITE person shall be employed
in carrying the mail of the United States, either as a post
rider or *driver* of a carriage carrying the mail," under a penalty of fifty dollars.—*Jay's View*, p. 24.

---

two Virginian Presidents. We may admire much in the one and in the other, but
we must be indeed stupid to regard them infallible, or shipwreck our liberties in
order to follow them implicitly, or revise or throw away our Bibles and declarations
of self-evident truths, in order to avoid seeing their inconsistencies, or in deference
to the imaginary and immaculate saintship of either of them.

In 1820, under Mr. Monroe, Congress authorized the WHITE citizens of Washington to elect WHITE city officers! These WHITE officers were authorized "to prescribe the terms on which *free negroes* and *mulattoes* may reside in the city," and they exercised this absurd and wicked authority in the very spirit in which was conferred.—*Ib.* p. 25–26.

SLAVE TERRITORIES AND NEW SLAVE STATES.

Slavery under jurisdiction of Congress, and commencing under the administration of Washington, has been continued ever since. Not only in the District of Columbia has this been done, but in Territories belonging to the United States, has the institution been fostered, preparatory to the admission of them as new Slave States into the Union.

In 1802, Georgia ceded to the United States the country lying between her present western limit and the Mississippi, stipulating that the Ordinance of 1787, in all its provisions, should extend to the ceded territory, "that article only excepted which forbids slavery." This cession was accepted, and the territory placed under a Territorial Government, *restricted from all interference with slavery.*"—*Speech of S. P. Chase,* U. S. Senate, March 26, 1850.

This was under the administration and with the concurrence of Mr. Jefferson, author of the Notes on Virginia, the Declaration of Independence, and the Ordinance of 1787. This added, in due time, the two Slave States of Mississippi and Alabama, to "our glorious Union!" The former was admitted in 1817, and the latter in 1819, both under the administration of Mr. Monroe.

Thus it appears that since the adoption of the Federal Constitution, in 1789, we have admitted into the Union the four Slave States of Kentucky, Tennessee, Alabama, and Mississippi, from territory within our original limits; and, except in the case of Kentucky, the National Government has previously protected slavery in them, while exercising authority over them, as territories, previous to their admission into the Union as independent states.

But this is not all. The national resources have been expended to purchase new territory for the erection and admission of new Slave States.

In 1803, we acquired Louisiana by purchase from the French Republic.* There were at that time about forty thousand slaves held within its limits, under the French law. The treaty contained this stipulation :

" The inhabitants of the ceded territory shall be incorporated in the Union of the United States, and admitted as soon as possible, according to the principles of the Federal Constitution, to the enjoyment of all the rights, advantages, and immunities of citizens of the United States ; and, in the meantime, they shall be maintained in the free enjoyment of their liberty, property, and the religion which they profess."—8 *Stat. at Large*, *U. S.*, 202.

This stipulation, interpreted according to the plain sense of its terms, and carried into practical effect, would have enfranchised every slave in Louisiana ; for no one, I apprehend, will venture to affirm that the slaves were not inhabitants. Independently of this stipulation, it was the duty of the Government—even more imperative than in 1787, for since then the whole country south of the Ohio and east of the Mississippi had been formed into slave States and slave Territories—to establish freedom as the fundamental law of the new acquisition. But this duty was not performed. There was some feeble legislation against the introduction of slaves from foreign countries, and of slaves imported since 1798 from the other States ; but that was all, and that was useless.—*Speech of S. P. Chase*, U. S. Senate, March 26, 1850.

This, too, was under the administration of Mr. Jefferson. The purchase was, with him, a favorite measure, and it is not known to the writer that he proposed the abolition of the slavery existing there. So strong were his impressions, at one time, that the purchase transcended the Constitutional powers of the Federal Government, that he contemplated recommending an amendment to the Constitution for that special object, but he finally persuaded himself that *the people* were so desirous of the purchase that the formality of an amendment might be waived !

Then came the cession of Florida by Spain in 1819. The stipulation in the treaty was substantially the same as in the treaty with France ;† the

---

* This was at a cost to the nation of fifteen millions of dollars.

† 8 U. S. Stat. at Large, 256, as quoted by Mr. Chase.

duty of the Government in respect to the acquisition was the same; and there was the same failure to perform it.

Finally, Texas came in, in 1845, not as a Territory, but as a State.— *S. P. Chase*, as above.

The purchase of Florida, for the sum of five millions of dollars, was under the administration of Mr. Monroe. The annexation of Texas was under that of Mr. Tyler.

The purchase of Louisiana resulted in the admission of three new Slave States, formed out of the purchased territory, viz: Louisiana, admitted under the administration of Mr. Madison, in 1812; Missouri, (after much debate, and a so called "compromise") under Mr. Monroe, in 1821; and Arkansas, under General Jackson, in 1836. Florida was admitted under Mr. Tyler, March 3, 1845.

The dates and the names of the Presidents show the continuity of the policy, during the long lapse of time, and under the successive administrations of the Government.

The contest concerning the admission of Missouri as a slave state, occurred during the Congressional session of 1819–20, and was decided in March, 1820. The proposal for the admission of Missouri, was artfully coupled with a proposal for the admisson of Maine, a free state. It was contended that the one was an equitable balance for the other. But this plea did not satisfy the North. The "compromise" consisted in the introduction of a provision that in the future admission of States from the residue of that territory, the line of division between slavery and freedom should be the parallel of 36° 30′ North latitude, the northern side of that line being appropriated to freedom. This proposal was resisted manfully for a time, but under a threat of dissolving the Union, it was carried by a small majority in the House. But the vote fixing the conditions of the future admission of a State could not bind a future Congress, so that the "compromise," as usual, gave the South all, and the North nothing.

Four new slave states from our original territory, four more from territory acquired by purchase, and one from annexation, make *nine* added in all, to the dominion of slavery, and to the strength of the Slave Power.

It is proper to record here, the instances of Federal legislation of an opposite character.

By the 7th section of the act organizing a Territorial Government for Mississippi, passed in 1798,* the importation of slaves into said Territory from any place without the United States, was prohibited under severe penalties. This was ten years before Congress had the power, under the Constitution, to prohibit the importation of slaves *into* the States.—*Speech of Mr. Bingham, of Michigan*, in Congress, June 4, 1850, *Nat. Era*, July 18.

This was under the administration of John Adams.

On the 7th of May, 1800, an act was passed for the organization of a territorial Government for Indiana, and *slavery expressly prohibited therein.* This act was approved by John Adams.

January 11, 1805, the northern part of Indiana was erected into the territory of Michigan, and *slavery prohibited.* February 3, 1809, the Territory of Illinois was established, with the like prohibition as to slavery. These two latter acts received the approval and signature of Thomas Jefferson.

On the 20th of April, 1836, Wisconsin was organized as a Territory, and *slavery prohibited* within its limits. This act was approved by General Jackson.

The Territory of Iowa was established by act of Congress of the 12th of June, 1838, under the administration of Mr. Van Buren ; and here also was *slavery prohibited.*

On the 14th of August, 1848, the Territory of Oregon was organized, which contained the same provision in the memorable and time-honored words, " there shall be neither *slavery nor involuntary servitude* therein, except for the punishment of crime."—*Ib.*

This was under the administration of Mr. Polk.

These acts concerning Indiana, Michigan, Wisconsin, Iowa and Oregon, were only in pursuance of the Ordinance of 1787, yet they are so many attestations to the Constitution-

---

* This territory, organized in 1798, comprised only a region of country ceded by South Carolina, but was afterwards, in 1804, enlarged, so as to include a part of the country ceded by Georgia in 1802, as stated by Hon. S. P. Chase, in his speech before quoted. This statement will explain an *apparent*, but not real discrepancy in dates, in the two quotations.

ality of that measure, and the consequent *power* of Congress to prohibit slavery in the Territories of the United States.

The same principle was likewise involved, and recognized, in the act, before noticed, for authorizing the admission of Missouri, in 1820, containing, as it did, a clause "*to prohibit slavery in certain territories*," that is, in all the Louisiana purchase North of 36° 30' North latitude.

And there had been a previous recognition of that principle, in its application to a part of the same purchase.

By the act of the 26th of March, 1804, that part of Louisiana south of the Territory of Mississippi was organized into a Territorial Government, by the name of Orleans. By this act, the importation into said Territory of slaves from abroad was prohibited, and also the importation of any slave from within the United States who should have been brought into the country since the 1st of May, 1798, or who should thereafter be brought into the United States. It further provided that no slave should be brought into said Territory, except by a citizen of the United States, who should remove there for actual settlement, and who should at the time be the *bona fide* owner of such slave; thus directly interdicting the domestic as well as the foreign slave trade in this Territory of Orleans. This act was approved by Jefferson.—*Speech of Mr. Bingham.*

When President Monroe was about to give his signature to the Missouri act of 1820, he required each member of his Cabinet, (the Heads of Departments and Attorney General,) to give their opinions in writing, on the questions whether the act was consistent with the Constitution, and whether "Congress has a right, under the powers vested in it, by the Constitution, to make a regulation prohibiting slavery in a Territory?" All the members of the Cabinet, including the late John C. Calhoun and John Quincy Adams, gave written answers in the affirmative. This is proved by the diary of J. Q. Adams.—*See Speech of T. H. Benton*, at Jefferson City, Mo., May 26, 1849, in New York Evening Post, June 14, 1849.

The Federal Government, then, in establishing and fostering slavery in the Territories, has done so *with the full knowledge of its Constitutional power to prohibit it.* The moral and political responsibility, therefore, rests upon it.

Another circumstance connected with the admission of Missouri deserves notice.

The act of Congress authorizing the people of Missouri to form a Constitution, preparatory to admission, was passed in March, 1820. The State Constitution, presented at the next Congress, contained a clause "*to prevent free negroes and mulattoes from coming to and settling in this State, under any pretext whatever*." As this provision was contrary to the Constitution of the United States, which secures "to the citizens of *each* state all the rights and immunities of citizens in the several states," (many of the states having *colored citizens*) Congress passed an act, in March, 1821, authorizing the President to admit Missouri, *on condition* that said clause should not be so construed as to exclude citizens of any other States. Missouri complied with the conditions, and by proclamation of the President, was admitted, August 10, 1821. [See Speech of T. H. Benton, at Jefferson City, May 26, 1849.]

This instance of the supervision by the Federal Government, over the Constitution of a State asking admission, and in a point touching the rights of "*negroes and mulattoes*," involves important principles, and may be of use as a precedent, hereafter.

GOVERNMENT OF THE FEDERAL DISTRICT.

The District of Columbia is under the exclusive jurisdiction of the Federal Government. In another connection we have shown how that Government was administered at the beginning, and so far as the condition of things there could be traced *directly* to the act of Congress of 1790. We then saw *free* colored citizens, on suspicion of being fugitives from slavery, thrown into jail, and then sold into slavery with their posterity forever, for the payment of their jail fees—the expenses of their causeless arrest! We will now look again at the continuance of that enormity, in its connection with the *domestic slave trade*, systematically carried on in the District.

From a number of causes, the Federal District has been, at

some periods, the principal slave mart in America. The policy of Virginia and Maryland has, at times, forbidden the traders to bring in slaves from other States, and expose them for sale, while the Federal District, under the policy of *Congress*, has been under no such restriction. The fact that the District is the resort of citizens from all the states, including Senators and Representatives, who may desire to buy or sell slaves, has given it an advantage over other slave markets, which has been eagerly improved.

As early as 1802, the grand jury of Alexandria complained of this traffic as a grievance demanding legislative interference. In 1816, Judge Morrell, of the U. S. Circuit Court, took notice of the nuisance, in his charge to the grand jury of Washington. The same year, John Randolph, of Virginia, himself a slaveholder, moved, in the House of Representatives, for a committee to inquire into the "inhuman and illegal traffic."* The *Alexandria Gazette*, of June 22, 1827, described, in terms of just abhorrence, the scenes witnessed in connection with the traffic. In 1828, a petition, headed by Judge Cranch, and signed by more than one thousand citizens of the Federal District, was presented to Congress, imploring its interference. In 1830, the *Washington Spectator* described the traffic, and exclaimed, "Where is the O'Connell in this Republic that will plead for the emancipation of the District of Columbia?"

Merchants of large capital engaged in the lucrative business, with their establishments in Alexandria and Washington City, and advertised, "Cash for five hundred negroes," with as much coolness as if they were so many horses! Franklin & Armfield, Alexandria, J. W. Neal & Co., Washington, Wm. H. Williams, George Hephart, William H. Richards, &c., are or have been among the number of these. Some of them have had large prison-houses built for the purpose; and some-

---

* This traffic is doubtless as "*legal*" as any part of the system. Henry Clay, in his famous speech in the U. S. Senate, in 1839, declared the traffic inseparable from the tenure of slave property. But here we find John Randolph declaring the traffic "*illegal!*" Was he in error?

times the *public jails*, built by money appropriated by Congress, have been put to the same infamous use. Large vessels were advertised and employed to transport slaves to New Orleans.

One dealer advertised for " *any* number of young and likely negroes from *eight* to forty years of age." As a *general* fact, little or no regard is paid, either in the purchase or the sale to the sanctities of the family relation, which, in fact, the laws and the usages of the system do not recognize as existing at all! Yet all this, says Judge Jay, is " *in virtue of authority delegated by Congress,*" and he cites his authority.

" The 249th page of the laws of the city of Washington, is polluted by the following enactment, bearing date 28th of July, 1831 :

" For a LICENSE to trade or traffic in slaves, for profit, four hundred dollars."—*Jay's View*, p. 87.

The petitioners of 1828, before mentioned, including Judge Cranch, express themselves in the following language:

" While the laws of the United States denounce the *foreign* slave trade as piracy, and punish with *death* those who are found engaged in its perpetration, there exists in this District, the seat of the Federal Government, a *domestic* slave trade, scarcely less disgraceful in its character, AND EVEN MORE DEMORALIZING IN ITS INFLUENCE. The people are, without their consent, torn away from their homes ; husband and wife are frequently separated, and sold into distant parts ; children are taken from their parents, without regard to the ties of nature, and the most endearing bonds of affection are broken forever. *Nor is this traffic confined* to those who are legally slaves for life. Some who are ENTITLED TO FREEDOM, and MANY who have a limited time to serve, are sold into unconditional slavery, and, owing to the defectiveness of our laws, they are GENERALLY carried out of the District before the necessary steps can be taken for their release."—" The people of the District have, within themselves, *no means of legislative redress*, and we appeal to your honorable body as the ONLY ONE vested by the American Constitution with power to relieve us."

But that "honorable body"—a controlling majority of whom were from the non-slaveholding States—found other business, it would seem, more to their taste, than the granting of the prayer of these petitioners ! Yet this was under the administration of a northern President (John Quincy Adams), whose power of appointment, assuredly, could not have been a rod over the heads of northern aspirants, as is commonly the case. Could there have been a fear, among rival partisans, that an agitation of "the delicate question" might affect the elections?

The liberties of Northern citizens are not secure in the Federal District, "under exclusive jurisdiction of Congress." In 1835, Dr. Reuben Crandall, from the State of New York, was arrested, imprisoned, and tried for his life, in Washington City, for having loaned to a white citizen, at his own request, a pamphlet against slavery. In 1850, Gen. Wm. L. Chaplin, from the same State, was arrested by the authorities of Washington City, on the charge of assisting fugitives. While we are now writing, two citizens of free States, Messrs. Drayton and Sayre, are incarcerated in the jails of the Federal District, for the alleged crime of having assisted* certain citizens of that District to emigrate, in "pursuit of happiness," to another portion of the country, and enjoy "all the rights and immunities of citizens in the" "States" of their intended residence.

---

* More correctly, perhaps, we might say, "On suspicion of having intended to assist;" for the vessel in which these emigrants took passage was found, and the arrest was made, in the *waters of Maryland*, the very State under whose laws they were claimed to be held!

CHAPTER XXI.

FURTHER ACTION OF THE FEDERAL GOVERNMENT—AMERICAN SLAVE TRADE—AFRICAN SLAVE TRADE.

Slave trade between the States, under jurisdiction of Congress—Its nature and extent—Testimony of T. J. Randolph—Niles' Register—Natchez Courier—Virginia Times—Virginia Exports—U. S. Gazette—Prof. Andrews—Prof. Dew—C. F. Mercer—Mr. Gholston—H. Clay—Negro Speculation of 1837—Mississippi Imports —Northern losses by Southern bankruptcy—Funds of the Presb. Church—Shipments from Federal District—*Acts of Congress regulating the traffic*—Brig Comet —Brig Encomium—The Enterprise—Negotiations with Great Britain for payment for Slaves—Case of the Brig Creole—of the Schooner Amistad. *African Slave Trade,* though abolished, connived at—Duplicity in Negotiations with G. Britain —Refusal to take effective measures for suppression—Negotiations with Republic of Colombia—Deceptive Act declaring the trade piracy—A plan of the Virginia Slave-breeders—Connected with the project of Colonization—Notice of various Acts of Congress concerning the Slave trade—1794, 1800, 1803, 1807, 1809, 1818, 1819, 1820—Allowed enslavement by Louisiana, of slaves known to have been illegally imported—The abuse founded on an Act of Congress—No instance of a slave trader being punished with death, according to law. La Coste convicted by Judge Story, but pardoned by President Monroe.

THE slave trade in the District of Columbia is only a part of that detestable traffic carried on under the Federal jurisdiction. The slave trade between the States is under the *same* jurisdiction, for " *Congress shall have power to regulate commerce with foreign nations and among the several States.*"— *U. S. Constitution, Art. I., Sect. 8, Clause 3.**

---

* The legislative acts of some of the slave States, prohibiting, from considerations of local policy, the importation of slaves from other States, have been set aside, if we mistake not, by their own courts, as unconstitutional, on the ground that the regulation of inter-State commerce devolves upon the *Federal* and not the *State* Governments.

Of the nature and extent of that traffic, we will present a few particulars.

In the Legislature of Virginia, in 1832, THOMAS JEFFERSON RANDOLPH declared that " the State had been converted into one grand MENAGERIE, where men are reared for the market, like oxen for the shambles."

Comparing the foreign with the domestic slave trade, he says :

"The *African* trader receives the slave, a stranger in aspect, language, and manners, from the merchant who brought him from the interior. But *here*, sir, individuals whom the master has known from infancy, whom he has seen sporting in the innocent gambols of childhood, who have been accustomed to look up to him for protection, HE TEARS FROM THE MOTHER'S ARMS, and sends into a strange country, among a strange people, subject to cruel task-masters. In my opinion, it is much worse."—*A. S. Lecturer.*

No historian need seek a higher authority for his statements than the " *Register*" of the late Hezekiah Niles, of Baltimore, and, indeed, few books of history are equally authentic and trustworthy. Hear Mr. Niles :

" Dealing in slaves has become a LARGE BUSINESS. Establishments are made, at several places in Maryland and Virginia, at which they are sold like cattle. These places of deposit are strongly built, and well supplied with iron thumb-screws and gags, and ornamented with cow-skins, and other whips, oftentimes bloody."—*Niles' Register*, Vol. XXXV., p. 4.

" According to New Orleans papers, there were imported into that port DURING THE WEEK commencing on the 16th ult., from all ports of the United States, 371 slaves, principally from Virginia."—*Ib.*, Oct. 22, 1831.

" It was stated in the *Natchez Courier* that during the year 1836 no less than two hundred and fifty thousand slaves were carried into Mississippi, Alabama, Louisiana, and Arkansas."—*Sunderland's A. S. Manual*, p. 117 ; also *An. Report Am. A. S. Soc.*, 1837.

At an average price of $600, this would amount to one hundred and fifty millions of dollars. This was a year of unprecedented activity in the domestic slave trade.

The *Virginia Times* proposed that the banking capital of the State be increased, from the money brought into the State from the sale of slaves. The editor said :

" We have heard intelligent men estimate the number of slaves exported from Virginia within the last twelve months at 120,000, each slave averaging at least $600—making an aggregate of $72,000,000. Of the number of slaves exported, not more than one-third have been sold (the others having been carried by their owners who have removed), which would leave in the State the sum of $24,000,000 arising from the sale of slaves."*—*An. Rep. Am. A. S. Soc.*, 1837.

In January, 1840, a correspondent of the *U. S. Gazette,* who signed "*Spectator,*" and whose accuracy the editor vouched for, gave an account of the speculations in negroes in 1835–6 and '37, in which he said:

"In three years the slave population of Mississippi increased from 70,000 to 160,000 slaves, at an average cost of at least $1000 each, making the debt, for slaves alone, in three years, swell to $90,000,000."†—*A. S. Almanac*, 1846.

---

* The winding up of the business, however, left little to increase the capital of the Virginia banks. The slave traders and Southern purchasers swindled the Virginians out of a large part of it. The courts of Mississippi, under their State laws, decided that the importations into that State had been illegal, and so the Mississippi purchaser on credit got his supply of slaves for nothing! Virginia took the insult very quietly, without a single threat of "dissolving the Union," and made ample reprisals, by stretching her now swollen credit, in lavish expenditures, to double the amount, with the dough-face merchants and bankers of Philadelphia and New York, for which she paid them less than ten cents on a dollar, in return for their pro-slavery riots and the burning of Pennsylvania Hall! Such are the gains of the wicked, and such are their friendships! Whether the Virginian bankruptcy, at the time of this reaction, was artificial or inevitable—a question once mooted—the loss to the North was the same. The treasury of the whole conspiracy, indeed, Northern and Southern, was "a bag with holes," as even the Trustees of the Presbyterian Church found, to their cost. [See next note.]

† Hereby hang some other thrilling items of history. This negro speculation, growing out of or connected with a previous cotton speculation, had its *reaction*, involving the negro importing and negro raising States, together with the principal Northern commercial and manufacturing cities that trade with the South, in a general and overwhelming bankruptcy, in which all concerned, *except the slave traders*, shared together. The slave purchasers failed, and the *slavers* secured themselves by "deeds in trust and mortgages upon nearly the whole property of the State of Mississippi." (In other States, similar operations were witnessed.) The planters failed, the Southern banks failed, the Southern merchants failed, their Philadelphia and New York creditors failed. New York City alone lost about one hundred millions of dollars, the little manufacturing town of Newark, N. J., five millions, and so on! Capitalists all over the country lost by the Southern banks, which had offered a bribe of high interest for funds wherewith to facilitate this delectable "commerce among the several States!" Among the rest, and richly deserving it, was "*the General Assembly of the Presbyterian Church*," whose funds, to the amount of $94,692 88 (a part of it piously and conscientiously withdrawn from the

Such are a few specimens of the " *commerce among the several States,*" which, by the Constitution of the United States, " *Congress shall have power to regulate.*" Not a little of it was carried on, under its own eye, in the Federal District, the slaves being brought in there for sale and shipment from the adjoining States.

"Franklin and Armfield, (Alexandria, D. C.) *alone,* shipped to New Orleans, during the year 1835, according to their own statement, not less than a thousand slaves. They owned brigs of about 160 to 200 tons burthen, running regularly, every thirty days, during the trading season, to New Orleans, and carrying about one slave to the ton."—*Sunderland's A. S. Manual,* p. 112.

Professor Andrews, in his work on " the domestic slave trade," repeats a conversation he had with a slave trader on board a steamboat in the Potomac, (1835), in which the trader informed him, " children from one to eighteen months old are now worth about one hundred dollars."—*Page* 147.

Professor Dew, afterward President of William and Mary College, in his review of the debates on slavery in the Virginia Legislature, 1831–'2, speaking of the revenue arising from the domestic trade, says, " a full equivalent being thus left in the place of the slave, this immigration becomes an advantage to the State, and does not check the black population as much as at first we might imagine, *because* it furnishes every inducement to the master to attend to the negroes, to encourage breeding, and to cause the greatest number possible to be raised. * * Virginia is in fact a negro-raising State for other States."

Mr. Charles Fenton Mercer asserted in the Virginia Convention, (1829) : " The tables of the natural growth of the slave population demonstrate, when compared with the increase of its numbers in the Commonwealth for twenty years past, that an annual revenue of not less than a million and a half of

---

Sabbath-breaking Hackensack Bridge Company, N. J.), were invested in the South-Western banks engaged in this "*patriarchal*" operation, which, on the coast of Africa, would have been "*piracy!*" The bottom line of the *loss* of the Presbyterian Church, in May 1842, was estimated at $68,893 88. The documentary statements may be found in the *A. S. Almanac,* New York, 1846. It turns out that this "*successful operation*" "to increase the revenues of the Church" had been gone into just before the celebrated Pittsburg meeting of the General Assembly, in 1836, at which meeting the Trustees reported their doings in this matter, to the great edification of that body, who must have felt a *double* interest in the adoption, at that same meeting, of Dr. Miller's Report, and the circulation of Dr. Hodge's biblical argument, both in favor of the " peculiar institution," in which their Church funds were to be so profitably employed! Thus rapidly, upon the heels of recreancy, trode retribution ! Thus the Church guides the community, and both fall into the ditch, yet both grope on, in darkness, still.

dollars is derived from the exportation of a part of this population."—*Debates*, p. 90.

Mr. Gholson, when in the Virginia Legislature, 18th January, 1831, claimed the right of " the owner of *brood mares* to their product, and of the owner of female slaves to their increase ;" and added, " the legal maxim of ' partus sequitur ventrem' is coeval with the existence of the right of property itself, and is founded in wisdom and justice. It is on the justice and inviolability of this maxim that the master foregoes the service of a female slave—has her nursed and attended during the period of her gestation, and raises the helpless infant offspring. The value of the property justifies the expense ; and I do not hesitate to say that in its increase consists much of our wealth." It is no wonder this same gentleman was anxious for the annexation of Texas, declaring that " he believed the acquisition of Texas would raise the price of slaves fifty per cent. at least."

Hon. Henry Clay, of Kentucky, in 1829, delivered an address before the Kentucky Colonization Society. After showing that when the option existed of employing free or slave labor, the first was the most profitable, he remarked—" It is believed that nowhere in the *farming* portion of the United States would slave labor be generally employed, if the proprietor were not *tempted to raise slaves* by the *high price* of the *Southern market*, which keeps it up in his own."

We might go into the details of the Virginia trade, and show the barbarities and loss of life which attend it, but we forbear, and content ourselves with notices of two dealers in a single town in South Carolina. John Wood, of Hamburgh advertised that " he has on hand a likely parcel of *Virginia* negroes, and receives new supplies *every fifteen* days." John Davis, of the same place, advertised for sale, from *Virginia*, " one hundred and twenty likely young negroes of both sexes," and among them " small girls suitable for nurses, and several SMALL BOYS WITHOUT THEIR MOTHERS."*

If any one is disposed to doubt that this slave trade between the States, as well as that from the Federal District, is under the control, regulation, and supervision of the Federal Government, a few *matters of fact* will not only settle that question, but show *how* this " commerce among the several States" has been hitherto " *regulated*" and protected.

By act of Congress, March 2, 1807, Congress *prohibited* the coastwise slave trade, in vessels of under forty tons burthen. This *exercise* of the power of prohibition shows that it *exists*, and that Congress is *conscious* of its existence. The silence of

---

* Communication signed A. B., in *National Era*, Aug. 22, 1850.

the slaveholders and slave traders under this exercise of that power is a sufficient evidence that *they* understood it to be legitimate and constitutional. And, undoubtedly, the authority to prohibit a traffic, in vessels of *under* forty tons burthen, implies an authority to prohibit it in vessels of *over* forty tons burthen. But this is not all.

By the same act, masters of vessels, of *over* forty tons burthen, intending to transport slaves, are required to make out duplicate manifests of their human cargoes, one of which is to be deposited with the Collector of the port; who is to furnish the master with a "*permit*"—"AUTHORIZING *him to proceed to the port of destination !*"—See *Jay's View*, p. 90–91.

Without this "permit" "*authorizing*" the coastwise slave trade, and issued by an officer of the United States, under directions of a special act of *Congress*, this species of "commerce among the several States" cannot be carried on at all. On the arrival of the slaver to his port of destination, he must moreover, have *another* "permit" from *another* United States' Collector, before he may land a single slave. Thus notoriously is this detestable "commerce among the several States" directly "AUTHORIZED" by the National Congress. And if Congress wishes to discontinue this policy, it has only to *extend* to "vessels of forty tons burthen" and *upward*, the prohibition of the act of 1807.

Instead of this, the National Government not only "permits" and "authorizes" the American slave trade, but prostitutes its foreign diplomacy to the shameless purpose of sheltering and protecting it. The evidences are at hand.

In 1831 the brig Comet, a regular slaver from the Federal District for New Orleans was wrecked off the island of Abaco, and the slaves carried into New Providence. In 1833, the brig Encomium, a slaver from Charleston for New Orleans was also wrecked near the same place, and the slaves carried into the same port. In 1835, the Enterprise, another slaver from the District for Charleston, was driven into Bermuda in distress. In each of these cases, the slaves, instead of being accounted cargoes of brute beasts, were regarded by the inhabitants and the authorities of the British provinces as passengers—human beings—treated with hospitality, and suffered to go where they pleased. *They were free,* and their pretended owners were neither assisted nor permitted to re-capture them. All this was in accordance with the usages of civilized nations, and with that English Common Law upon which our pilgrim fathers had reposed, and which they claimed as their heritage. Prompt measures were, however, taken by the Federal Government to demand of the British Government the *market value* of these *cargoes of " Native Americans !"*

This was under the administration of Andrew Jackson. Instructions on the subject to our Minister at the Court of St. James, were sent from Washington, in 1831. Another dispatch was forwarded in 1832, and a third in 1833. Fresh instructions were sent in 1834, 1835, and 1836. The claim was importunately urged by the Secretary of State, in 1832, as a matter which "must be brought to a conclusion." In 1836, our Minister was reminded that "in the present state of our diplomatic relations with the Government of His Britanic Majesty, *the most immediately pressing* of the matters with which the United States Legation at London is now charged, is the claim of certain American citizens against Great Britain, for a *number of slaves* wrecked in British Islands in the Atlantic." Thus instructed, Mr. Stevenson, our Minister, in a communication to Lord Palmerston, went so far as to hint that a further neglect to satisfy this demand, might " possibly *tend to disturb and weaken the kind and amicable relations now so happily subsisting between the two countries.*"

In plain English, it might involve the two nations in war !

This negotiation was made public by the President, in response to a call from the Senate, in Feb., 1837, for " a copy of the correspondence with the Government of Great Britain in relation to the *outrage* committed on our flag," &c., "by *seizing* the slaves on board the brig 'Encomium' and 'Enterprise,' engaged in the *coasting trade !*" &c. &c.—*See Jay's View,* p. 58–63.

" We, the people of the United States," are thus made to support a Minister in London, at a cost of nine thousand dollars outfit, and nine thousand per annum salary, to negotiate matters, "*the most immediately pressing*" of which is, to protect the American slave trade! To do this by demanding pay of the British Government for slaves liberated by the good Providence of God! To demand this, as if at the point of the bayonet, and with the implied threat of war!

Who, then, is responsible for this infernal traffic, if not the Federal administrations who carry on such negotiations, and the people of the free states who sustain them in it by their votes?

Another illustration presents itself in the

CASE OF THE CREOLE:

" Nov. 7, 1841, the American brig Creole, bound from Richmond, Va., to New Orleans, with a cargo of 102 slaves, was seized by 19 of the slaves, and carried into Nassau, New Providence, one of the British West India islands. One passenger was killed, and the captain and a few others wounded. The whole affair was managed with a remarkable degree of bravery, discretion, and mercy. Every movement indicated an earnest desire to do as little mischief as possible, consistently with securing their own freedom. The ring-leader, a very large and strong mulatto, was named Madison Washington. He had previously run away from bondage, and staid in the family of Hiram Wilson, in Canada. But he grew homesick for his wife, whom he left a slave in Virginia; and he determined to rescue her at all hazards. He went back for this purpose, and was probably caught by his master, and sold to New Orleans as a punishment. At all events, he was next heard of, as the hero of the Creole. It is believed that his beloved wife was with him on board that vessel. The authorities of New Providence declared all the slaves free. Four or five of the women (supposed to be mistresses of the white men), were at first inclined to go back to the United States; but when the case had been truly represented to them by the colored people of the island, they took their freedom.

" Daniel Webster, Secretary of State, officially demanded of Great Britain redress of these grievances, in a style which slaveholders applauded to the echo."—*N.Y. A.S. Almanac*, 1843.

This was under the Presidency of John Tyler.

There was still *another* and a *previous* case, of a character too unique to admit of appropriate classification, but which may as well be related, in this place, as anywhere else. The readiness of the Federal Executive and other officers of Government to subserve the interests of *slavery in general*, is here strongly exhibited, though, for once, the Federal Judiciary was prevailed upon to interpose, and prevent the consummation intended.

THE CAPTIVES OF THE AMISTAD.

"Nearly all these unfortunate Africans came from Mendi, a country in the latitude of the Gallinas River, and probably from three to five hundred miles from the Atlantic coast. Their average age was about twenty. Some were as old as thirty; and some as young as eight or nine. They were seized, and, with many others, hurried down to the coast about the last of April, 1839, and there, with three or four hundred men and boys, and about two hundred women and children, were put on board a slave ship for Havana. After the terrible "middle passage," placed between decks, where the space is less than three feet, they arrived at Havana. Here they were put into one of the large pens, or prison-houses, called Barracoons, and offered for sale. In a few days Joseph Ruiz and Pedro Montes bought them. Ruiz bought forty-nine, and Montes bought the children, three little girls. They put them on board the schooner Amistad, a coaster, for Puerto Principe, Cuba, a few hundred miles from Havana. When they were two or three days out, they were beaten severely, threatened with death, &c. A quarrel took place. The cook and captain were killed, and two sailors fled in a boat. Cinquez, the master-spirit of the whole, assumed the command. He established a strict government over his comrades, and compelled Ruiz and Montes to steer the schooner for the rising sun—their own native Africa. They did so by day, but in the night they deceived the Africans, and ran towards the United States.

"In this way they arrived on the American coast, and came to anchor off Culloden Point, Long Island. Here some of them landed, made purchases (paying for all they took), and shipped water, intending to proceed on their passage, but they were taken possession of by Lieutenant Gedney, of the U.S. brig Washington, and carried into New London, Conn. Judge Judson bound them over to the Circuit Court for trial, on the charge of murder, &c.; but Judge Thompson decided that our courts have no cognizance of offences committed on board Spanish vessels on the high seas. As, however, the vessel, cargo, and Africans had been libelled by Gedney and others for salvage, it was determined that a trial must take place in the District Court. It was held in January, 1840. Judge Judson decided that the prisoners were native Africans; had never been slaves legally. He dismissed the libels with costs, and decreed that the Africans should be delivered to the President of the United States, to be sent back to Africa. *But our government, on the demand of the Spanish minister, appealed to the Circuit Court.* This Court was held in April, 1840. Judge Thompson sustained the appeal, and as one party or the other would appeal to a higher tribunal, whichever way he might decide, the case went up to the Supreme Court of the United States as a matter of form, for decision, in January, 1841. Thus, these FREE MEN were kept in an American jail eighteen months!

"Nine of the Africans died. They were instructed daily by benevolent persons. They made some progress in reading and speaking the English language; and their conduct was very exemplary. James Covey, a native of Mendi, providentially brought to this country, acted as interpreter.

"President Van Buren, at the request of the Spanish minister, sent a U.S. ship to New Haven, to convey the Africans to Cuba, to be given up to the Spaniards, in case Judge Judson had not decided as he did."

At the final trial before the Supreme Court of the United States, the Africans were released, and afterwards returned to Africa, in company with Missionaries, who went to reside among them.

THE AFRICAN SLAVE TRADE.

The Federal Government has neglected to take appropriate measures for suppressing the African slave trade, and has winked at the illegal introduction of slaves into this country. Though the trade has been interdicted on paper, it has been permitted to continue in practice. While the slave *breeding* states have, from motives of interest, desired earnestly the non-importation of slaves from abroad, the slave *consuming* or planting states have, nevertheless, persisted in the illicit traffic, and the Federal Government, with a full knowledge of the fact, has, at times, winked at its continuance; and the national policy, in regard to the subject, has been self-contradictory and unstable. In 1811 and in 1814, under the Presidency of Mr. Madison, in 1817, in 1818, and 1819, under Mr. Monroe, official information of the introduction of foreign slaves was in possession of the Government, or the fact was successively noticed by official functionaries, as Collectors of Customs, the Secretary and officers of the navy, Judges of the Supreme Court, the Attorney General, and Members of

Congress. Yet, in 1819, it was certified by Joseph Nourse, Register of the Treasury, that the Department contained no records of any forfeitures under the Act of 1807 abolishing the slave trade! He had, however, *heard* of two recent forfeitures. It turned out that *one* of these cases was an *accidental* capture of a slaver, that a collusive or sham forfeiture of the bonds had been enacted, and that the owners, master, and supercargo, were *discharged!* In 1820, a slave vessel, the Science, fitted out from New York, and commanded by A. Lacoste of Charleston, was captured on the coast of Africa, brought home, and Lacoste convicted before Judge Story, *but pardoned by President Monroe!*—*Jay's View*, p. 94–108.

The history of negotiations carried on between the Governments of the United States and Great Britain in 1823 and 1824, under Mr. Monroe, in connection with other facts, affords evidence of a persevering and settled duplicity, on the part of the American Government, in regard to the suppression of the African Slave Trade. By the treaty of 1814, the two Governments had mutually promised to use their best endeavors to abolish the "*traffic in slaves.*" Mr. Canning, British Minister at Washington, in January, 1823, addressed a letter to the Secretary of State, J. Q. Adams, reminding him of this treaty, (which, by-the-by, he had assisted to negotiate,) and calling on the American Government to assent to the plan proposed by Great Britain,* or suggest another. The House of Representatives, soon after, requested the President to negotiate with the maritime powers of Europe and America, "for the effectual abolition of the African slave trade, and its *ultimate denunciation as piracy, under the laws of nations by consent of the civilized world.*" The President adopted this as the basis of his proposal to Mr. Canning. Thus far all seemed sufficiently zealous and in earnest. But, mark the existing circumstances and the final result: At this time the British law had not made the slave trade piracy; and, as it could not

---

* The British Government, in 1819, had proposed to our Government a mutual right of search to detect slavers, with slaves actually on board, and a positive refusal to this proposal had been returned.

be done by treaty, the action of Parliament would be needed, and might long be delayed or withheld. The *offer*, therefore, was less hazardous. But the British Minister made no demur, and proceeded to propose a mutual right of search, under limitations and restrictions, to detect slavers. *This was the practical point.* But this the American Government *declined*, though Britain, France, Spain, Portugal, Netherlands, Denmark, Sweden, and Sardinia, have come into the measure.

Yet the American Government renewed its proposition, by authorizing our Minister in England to conclude a treaty, on condition of a *legislative* prohibition of the slave trade as PIRACY. Great Britain took us at our word, and accepted the offer. The treaty was regularly drawn up and signed in London, March 13, 1824, and Parliament passed a corresponding Act, as *our* government had required. The Senate of the United States, however, delayed to ratify the treaty. The British Minister at Washington remonstrated. The President, as in honor bound, urged the ratification, suggesting, naturally enough, that the refusal would expose us to "the charge of *incincerity* respecting the great result of the final suppression of the slave trade." The Senate, after long debates, ratified the treaty, in a mutilated form, adroitly striking out certain words, thus destroying its efficacy, giving full security to slavers while on the coast of "*America*," and also to the traffic carried on in "*chartered*" or *hired* vessels, &c. &c.!

The British Cabinet, of course, refused to agree to a *sham* treaty, but made several attempts to accommodate or compromise the matter, which our Government promptly declined.

Negotiations have since been renewed, but the final answer of the American Government (as we learn from the Edinburgh Review for 1836,) was, "*that under no condition, in no form, and with no restriction, will the United States enter into any convention, or treaty, or combined efforts of any sort or kind, with other nations for the suppression of this trade.*"—*Jay's View*, pp. 109 to 118. Under whose administration this answer was given, is not stated; but it was probably Gen. Jackson's.

A treaty similar to that formed in London, yet exempting the coast of *America* from its operation, had been concluded with the Republic of Colombia, in 1824, but rejected by the United States Senate.—*Ib.* p. 117.

In November, 1825, the Colombian Minister at Washington, while inviting the United States to send delegates to the proposed Congress of Panama, alluded to the suppression of the African slave trade, as an object deserving attention in that Congress. The document was submitted to the Senate, and a committee of that body made a Report, 16th January, 1826, deprecating, in strong terms, any interference with the subject.—-*Ib.* 118–119.

All this enables us to appreciate the pretense of desiring to make the African slave trade piracy! Or, if the Cabinet and House of Representatives were honest in that measure, it betrays a different state of feeling in the Senate.

The zeal shown by the Government for suppressing the African slave trade, and declaring it *piracy*, in 1817, 1819, 1822, &c., has, however, a ready solution. It was urged on by the Virginia *slave breeders*, intent upon monopolizing the market of the planting states to themselves. "*Piracy in Africa, and protection in America,*" would have been the appropriate motto on their escutcheon! A protective tariff, in favor of home products, of which the prohibitory tax was to be the halter! A beautiful harmony among the successors of the "Patriarchs!" The rising sentiment of the civilized world against the slave *trade*, was surreptitiously subsidized to subserve the interests of the slave *breeders* for the southern *market!*

Very naturally did *such* a zeal against the *African* slave trade connect itself with the Virginian project of colonizing their *free* blacks in Africa! Quite conveniently were the measures for suppressing the African slave trade connected with measures, much more efficient, for assisting the Colonization Society, and the former made a cover and pretext for the latter, at the expense of the National Government, and with the semblance of philanthropy. But if the Act making the slave trade piracy, can be readily harmonized with the policy of Virginia, it is not as readily reconciled with the refusal of the Federal Government, the year previous, and ever afterwards, to co-operate with other nations in any efficient efforts for suppressing it.—*See Jay's View*, p. 103–109.

It may be in place, here, to note down a few brief memoranda of the Acts of the Federal Government, against the foreign slave trade.

By act of 1794, March 22, Congress prohibited, under forfeitures and fines, the building or equipping of any vessels in the United States, for carrying on the traffic in slaves TO ANY FOREIGN COUNTRY.—*Ingersoll's Abridgment*, 670.   *Stroud*, 158.

By act of May 10, 1800, it was made unlawful to be concerned or employed in the transportation of slaves *from one foreign country to another*, on pain of forfeitures, fines, and *imprisonment* not exceeding two years.—*Ib.* 672–3.   *Stroud*, 158–9.

By act of February 28, 1803, Congress, in behalf of the Federal Government, co-operated with such of the *States* as had already prohibited the importation of slaves, assisting them in carrying into effect such laws.—*Stroud*, 159.

By act of Congress, March 2, 1807, the importation of slaves from abroad was utterly prohibited after January 1, 1808.*

---

* One provision of this act, prohibiting the transportation of slaves from one port to another, in certain vessels, excited the jealousy of John Randolph, of Roanoke, who, the day after its passage, thought he saw in it something hostile to the *domestic* slave trade, and brought forward a supplementary bill to avert the danger.

"Sir," said he, "we may say what we please about alien and sedition laws, but this law, in my opinion, is the most *frightful*, the most *abominable* that was ever passed! If this law went into operation, unless the owners of slaves were asleep, protests would be sent against it from every State south of the Potomac. As well might they pass a law prohibiting the transportation of slaves in wagons. He doubted whether they would ever see another Southern delegate on that floor. For one, he had no hesitation in saying—if the Constitution is to be violated, if the entering wedge is to be driven, *let us secede and go home.*"

Old Mr. Smylie answered him: "The gentleman from Virginia says he will not trust Congress, and talks of the Southern States seceding from the Union. If they do not like the Union, let them say so. In the name of God, let them go; *we can do without them.*"

This answer somewhat cooled Mr. Randolph. "He complained that he had been

Judge Stroud has elaborately and clearly pointed out the discrepancies of this act, according to which, "the negro, though *illegally* imported, yet, if so directed by the *State Legislatures, he and his offspring should be absolute slaves.*" "The Legislature of Louisiana was not tardy in improving the *privileges* thus preposterously conferred by Congress." By act of March 20, 1809, all slaves imported, in *violation* of the act of Congress of 1808, were directed " to be delivered into the hands of the *treasurer of the territory,* to be afterwards disposed of as the legislature should think proper!"—*Stroud,* pp. 159—162. 1 *Martin's Digest,* 664. "North Carolina and Georgia, respectively, adopted a similar law, the former in 1816.—*Hayward's Manual,* 545 *et. seq :* the latter in 1817—*Prince's Digest,* 463." The act of Georgia, however, authorized the Governor to hand them over to the Colonization Society, on payment of expenses, &c. !—*Stroud,* p. 162.

By the act of April 20, 1818, more severe penalties were imposed upon the prosecution of the slave trade, but "*re-enacting* the odious sixth section of the act of 1807, and *recognizing* the laws of the several state legislatures on the subject, which have just been commented upon."—*Stroud,* p. 163 ; *Ingersoll's Abridgment,* 680.

By act of March 2, 1819, the President was empowered to employ the Navy for the suppression of the traffic, also to provide for keeping and supporting the slaves re-captured, and remove them out of the United States, and finally *repealing* the obnoxious provisions of the *former* acts which authorized their enslavement by the state governments.

By act of May 15, 1820, (a few weeks after the infamous Missouri compromise, and by the same Congress,) the *African* slave trade was made *piratical!* "But laws do not execute

---

misrepresented. He had not threatened a dissolution of the Union. However, he said, if union and manumission of slaves are put in the scales, *let union kick the beam.*"

This account is taken from the *Providence Gazette,* of July, 1820, now before us, in which (during the political contest in Rhode Island, growing out of the Missouri question) it was " copied from a newspaper printed in the year 1807."

themselves, and if any slave trader has suffered death in the United States, as a pirate, we confess our ignorance of the fact."—*Jay's View*, p. 108.

Notwithstanding this repeal, the State of Alabama, Jan. 1, 1823, passed "an act to *carry into effect* the laws of the United States, prohibiting the slave trade," in which—with singular effrontery—"the laws of the United States" on the subject, were grossly violated, by authorizing the Governor *to sell, for the benefit of the state, all persons of color who should be brought into the state contrary to the laws of the United States prohibiting the slave trade ! ! !*—*See Toulman's Digest*, 643 ; *Stroud*, 164.

"The laws of the United States," in accordance with the Constitution, are "the supreme law of the land; and the judges in every state shall be bound thereby, anything in the Constitution or laws of any state to the contrary notwithstanding."—*U. S. Constitution, Art. V.* And yet we know of no action of the Federal authorities, or of the courts of Alabama, for setting aside this open and flagrant insult to a law of Congress by a state legislature.

Thus it is that the Federal Government puts down the *African* slave trade by *calling* it "*piracy.*"

CHAPTER XXII.

FURTHER ACTION OF THE FEDERAL GOVERNMENT.—CONTIN-
UED SUBSERVIENCY OF THE NATIONAL DIPLOMACY TO THE
DEMANDS OF THE SLAVEHOLDERS.

Negotiations with Great Britain and Mexico for the surrendering of fugitive slaves—
Compensation obtained of Great Britain for slaves captured—Negotiations with
Spain and the South American Republics, to prevent emancipation in Cuba—
Threat of preventing it by force of arms.

WE have already seen the corps diplomatic employed at the
national expense (both of money and honor) for the protection of the American domestic slave trade, and in shameful
evasion of the admitted obligation of assisting to suppress
the African slave trade. But this is not the only vile service
to which the diplomacy of the nation has been subjected by
the slave power.

The Federal Government has negotiated with Great Britain
and with Mexico, for the surrendry of fugitive slaves, and
has actually obtained compensation from Great Britain for
slaves captured in war, or taking refuge on board their armed
vessels.

During the last British war, American slaves sometimes
absconded, and took refuge on board the armed vessels of the
enemy. Slaves were also *captured*, at times, and carried off.
In negotiating the treaty of peace, this matter was not forgotten. Our Commissioners at Ghent, (Messrs. Clay, Bayard,
Russell, Gallatin, and John Quincy Adams,) were carefully
instructed by Mr. Monroe, then Secretary of State, under Mr.
Madison, to "insist" upon the return of the slaves taken

from the southern states, or full payment for their value. So adroitly did the Commissioners fulfil their trust that they not only obtained compensation for the slaves *captured*, but also, (as ultimately settled) for those who had *absconded* to the vessels of Britain. The application of the treaty to the case of the *latter*, was contested by the British Cabinet. The decision was referred to the Emperor of Russia, who, in 1818, decided in favor of the American claim, which, at length, in 1836, was liquidated, with interest, amounting to *one million two hundred and four thousand dollars.—Jay's View*, pp. 53–58.

Thus, though the treaty of peace did *not* contain a single stipulation for securing *either one* of the objects for which America had ostensibly declared the war, (" free trade, sailors' rights," &c.,) yet it *did* contain ample and even exorbitant remuneration for *fugitive slaves*. On *this* issue, during the negotiation, was suspended the question of peace or continued war !

Another negotiation with Great Britain, concerning fugitive slaves, took place under the administration of John Quincy Adams, Henry Clay being then Secretary of State, and had special reference to those who had taken refuge in Canada. The House of Representatives, May 10, 1828, requested the President to open a negotiation with the British Government, for the surrendry of these fugitives. At the next session, the House called on the President to inform them of the result. "The President immediately submitted a mass of documents to the House, from which it appeared" (says Mr. Jay,) "that the zeal of the Executive in behalf of 'the peculiar institution' had *anticipated* the wishes of the Legislature. Two years *before* the interference of the House, viz: on the 19th of June, 1826, Mr. Clay, Secretary of State, had instructed Mr. Gallatin, American minister in London, to propose a stipulation for 'a mutual surrendry of all persons held to service or labor, under the laws of either party who escape into the territories of the other.'" Mr. Clay dwelt on the number of fugitive slaves in Canada, and suggested the benefits, to West India planters, from such a stipulation. In

February, 1827, the subject was again urged upon Mr. Gallatin, informing him that a similar treaty had just been negotiated with Mexico. In July, the British minister declined
the proposal. Mr. Barbour, the successor of Mr. Gallatin,
was directed to renew the application. He did so, but was
answered promptly by the British minister, that the "*law of
Parliament gave freedom to every slave who effected his landing
on British ground.*"—*Jay's View*, p. 47—50. The reader will
readily trace this "law of Parliament" to the decision of
Lord Mansfield in the Somerset case, and to the sagacity and
perseverance of Granville Sharp.

As to the treaty negotiated with Mexico, the Mexican
Congress refused to ratify it. The refusal, as will appear in
the sequel, was among the real grounds of our quarrel and
war with Mexico, but it was not prudent to invade the dominions of Great Britain.

The Federal Government, by its diplomacy, has labored
effectually to prevent the abolition of slavery in the neigh-
boring Spanish Island of Cuba, lest such an occurrence should
seriously affect the stability of slavery in our own Southern
States.

The immediate cause of alarm was the war raging between
Spain and her American Colonies, and the prospect that the
latter would throw off the dominion of the parent government, as the North American Colonies of Great Britain had
done. The ordinary vicissitudes of war might emancipate
the slaves of Cuba, but the danger was increased by the fact
that the Spanish Colonies on this Continent had shown a disposition to extend to *all* their inhabitants, irrespective of color
or condition, the liberties for which they were contending.
Some of them had already abolished slavery, and others of
them were taking measures in that direction. If Cuba
should share in the revolution, the Cuban slaves would doubtless become free.

Through the American Minister at Madrid, Mr. Everett,
the Spanish Government was accordingly implored by the
Cabinet at Washington to become reconciled to the colonies.
Could this interference be traced to a love of peace, or an

earnest desire for the independence of Spanish America, it might be regarded with admiration. But the instructions of our government to Mr. Everett, by the Secretary of State, Mr. Clay, forbid us thus to interpret the proceeding. "*It is not for the new Republics,*" (said Mr. Clay to Mr. Everett,) "that the President wishes you to urge upon Spain the expediency of concluding the war." He proceeded to hint at the probable effects upon Porto Rico and Cuba, intimated that the " people of the United States could not be indifferent spectators," and that the possible contingencies of a protracted war *might bring upon the Government of the United States duties and obligations the performance of which, however painful it should be, they might not be at liberty to decline.*"

In other language, it would be the duty of the American Government to prevent those *islands* from becoming the theatre of the war, even if the effort should involve the *United States* in a war to prevent it !

This letter was dated April 27, 1825. Of course it was under the Presidency of Mr. Adams, and among the earliest acts of his administration. The significancy of the transaction is made, if possible, still plainer, by the tone soon after held by the administration towards our incipient sister republics, who, in the enthusiasm of their young love of liberty, had confidingly invited us to sit in council with them, at their proposed Congress of American Republics at Panama; an invitation to which the public pulse in the United States—at least at the North—beat a hearty response. Messrs. Anderson and Sargeant were appointed our Ministers to that Congress. But in his letter of instructions to them, May 8, 1826, our Secretary, Mr. Clay, gives them to understand the real object of their mission to that Congress of Freedom. It was rumored, and doubtless with good reason, that Colombia and Mexico meditated a descent upon Cuba, with a force that should confer upon *its inhabitants* a share in the blessings they were seeking. *Such* an enterprise, however, the Government of the United States would *by no means permit.* THIS message, their Ministers at Panama were required to convey to them. And it was given in language sufficiently explicit and peremptory.

"The United States," (they were to be told,) "*have too much at stake in the fortunes of Cuba to allow them to see a war of invasion prosecuted in a desolating manner, and* ONE RACE *of the inhabitants combating against another.*" "*The duty to defend themselves against the contagion of such a new and dangerous example,* would constrain them, even at the *hazard of losing the friendship of Mexico and Colombia,* to employ all the means necessary to their security."

That is, the United States would sooner go to war with Colombia and Mexico—would sooner join with despotic Spain in reducing them to their former condition—than to stand neutral and see the same liberation extended to Cuba!

Cold comfort this to the new republics in our neighborhood, just throwing off the yoke of European bondage! THIS was the message conveyed them by the administration of Mr. Adams, at a time when the bulk of our northern citizens were exulting, in their simplicity, at the idea of holding a friendly and fraternal conference, at Panama, with our new republican neighbors. They knew, indeed, that certain southern members of Congress had blustered when the subject of the mission was under debate in both Houses, had denounced the new republics as "buccaneers, drunk with their new-born liberty," because they had abolished slavery; even threatening to prevent the liberation of Porto Rico and Cuba, by force of arms. But they *did not* then know that the Federal Executive and Cabinet were in sympathy with them.

The threat had the desired effect upon Colombia and Mexico; the enterprise was abandoned, and *Cuba remains enslaved!*

The fears of our Government were not, however, at once allayed. The war continued, and Cuba might yet become free. Mr. Van Buren, Secretary of State under President Jackson, on the 22d of October, 1829, instructed our Minister at Madrid, Mr. Van Ness, to press on Spain a termination of the war. "Considerations," he remarked, "*connected with a certain class of our population, make it the interest of the southern section of the Union* that no attempt should be made in that island to throw off the yoke of Spanish dependence."—*Jay's View,* p. 120–127.

CHAPTER XXIII.

FURTHER ACTION OF THE FEDERAL GOVERNMENT—HAYTI— FLORIDA—THE SEMINOLE WAR.

Non-intercourse with Hayti—Refusal to acknowledge its independence—Invasion of Florida, while a Spanish province, to break up a fortress of fugitive slaves— Threatened Conquest of Florida by the Georgians—Purchase of Florida—Florida Indians—Seizure of Osceola's wife, as a slave—Seminole War—Indians hunted with blood-hounds.

WE are burthened with the accumulated instances and modes in which our Federal Government has sustained slavery. We cannot proceed with the minute details. We will hastily advert to a few other topics.

TREATMENT OF HAYTI.

The American Government has manifested an inveterate and continual hostility to Hayti, for no reason but because Hayti is an independent nation of emancipated slaves. To the present hour we have neglected to recognize the independence of Hayti, and maintain no diplomatic relations with her, though our commercial intercourse with the island has been more important than with several of the European nations, with whom, at a great expense, we maintain such relations. By this neglect, numbers of our citizens having claims on the Haytien Government have been provided with no means of indemnity. The American Congress, in February, 1806, during the administration of Mr. Jefferson, suspended commercial intercourse with Hayti, in servile obedience to the arrogant and peremptory demand of Napoleon, who was intent on reducing the inhabitants to submission, by starvation. At the Congress of Panama, before mentioned, our Ministers were instructed to decline any recognition of Hayti.—*Jay's View*, pp. 127–144.

INVASION OF FLORIDA AND DESTRUCTION OF FUGITIVE SLAVES WHILE FLORIDA WAS A SPANISH PROVINCE.

This demonstration was made under the administration of Mr. Madison, and in conformity with directions from Mr. Crawford, Secretary of War, addressed to General Jackson, March 15, 1816. General Jackson had, however, anticipated these directions. The object, openly avowed, was to break up a fort of between 250 and 300 blacks, who, it was said, enticed and protected negroes from the frontiers of Georgia. A gun-boat, by order of Commodore Patterson, fired upon the fort; the magazine exploded, and nearly three hundred Indians and negroes, *men, women, and children*, were killed or mortally wounded.—*Ib.* p. 50–52.

PURCHASE OF FLORIDA.

But the trouble did not cease. President Monroe was harassed with numerous letters from slaveholders in Georgia, declaring that their slaves were escaping continually into Florida, and finding an asylum there,* and if the Province was not secured by treaty, the Georgians would take it by force. These facts, according to Timothy Pitkin,† were stated in a secret session of the House of Representatives, on the subject of the treaty, in 1819. The treaty of purchase (*at the national expense, five millions of dollars*) was concluded that same year.

---

* Though slavery existed in Florida, it was of a much milder type than that of the United States. Free colored people enjoyed greater security, and the country afforded facilities for the secretion of fugitives, or their subsistence in retreats of difficult access, and among Indians.

† *Quarterly A. S. Mag.*, Jan., 1836, p. 197.

THE SEMINOLE WAR.

Florida was nevertheless destined to be the theatre of a pro-slavery war, prosecuted by the government of the United States. The Seminole Indians inhabited the marshy portions of that country. Fugitive slaves took refuge with them, and sometimes intermarried among them. Osceola, one of their chiefs, became the hero of a painfully interesting tragedy, illustrative of this condition of things. The following is from an account of him by M. M. Cohen:

"Osceola, or Powell, as he was called by the whites, had a wife to whom he was much attached, whose MOTHER was a mulatto, who ran away, was adopted by the Indians, and married one of their chiefs. Though the FATHER was free, yet the children, by the law of the South, take the condition of the MOTHER. Osceola's WIFE was seized as a slave by a person claiming her under the right of her MOTHER'S FORMER MASTER! The high spirited husband attempted to defend her, but was overpowered, and put in irons by Thompson, who commanded the party." "This transaction has been said to be the origin of the war in Florida."—*Quar. A. S. Mag.*, Vol. II., p. 419.

In this war Osceola was a conspicuous leader. He was perfidiously captured by the American Generals Herandez and Jessup, being surrounded by two hundred horsemen while "holding a talk," or negotiation, with his captors, in October, 1837. This was under the administration of President Jackson.

The cost to the United States of this long protracted slave hunt (for it was nothing else), has been estimated at forty millions of dollars. "What has the North to do with slavery?"

In this war, the American flag was disgraced by the importation of blood-hounds from Cuba, and the employment of them in hunting down the Indians, by advice and under the direction of General Zachary Taylor, whose services in the Seminole and Mexican wars—both for the benefit of

slavery—were rewarded with the Presidency of the United
States. It is quite remarkable that many who were loud in
their condemnation of the administration of Gen. Jackson,
on account of the use of the blood-hounds, were afterwards
the zealous supporters of Gen. Taylor, the idol of the South.
Thus do our parties bind us to slavery.

CHAPTER XXIV.

FURTHER ACTION OF THE FEDERAL GOVERNMENT—ACQUISITION OF TEXAS.

Slavery abolished in Mexico, including Texas—Emigration of American Slaveholders and Slaves to Texas—Attempted seizure of Texas by Americans in 1819—Conspiracy of settlers at Nacogdoches, in 1826—Scheme to purchase Texas, 1827—Mexican refusal to sell—Texan Land Companies in the States—Armed emigration to revolutionize Texas—Meetings of sympathy in the States—No Executive action against it—Standard of revolt raised in Texas—Proclamation of Independence and re-establishment of slavery—Remonstrance of the Mexican Minister—Mendacious reply of Mr. Forsyth—Gen. Gaines stationed near the frontier to countenance the revolters—Battle of San Jacinto—Defeat of Santa Anna—Acknowledgment by the American Government of Texan Independence—Proposed union with the States—Various obstacles and delays—Final admission of Texas, in 1845, and speedy hostilities with Mexico.

TEXAS was a province of Mexico, and Mexico was a colony of Spain. In the general struggle of the Spanish American colonies to throw off the Spanish yoke, Mexico took a part, and asserting her independence, took measures in forming her constitution of government, in 1824, for the prospective but complete abolition of slavery. Having achieved her independence, she proceeded to cut short the tardy process of gradual extinction, by proclaiming the immediate and entire abolition of slavery, and the emancipation of all the slaves, September 15, 1829.*

Texas was of course included, with the rest of Mexico, under these acts. But Texas was in process of settlement by emigrants from our American slave States, who had gone

---

* *Quarterly A. S. Mag.*, Jan., 1836, p. 195; *Jay's Mexican War*, p. 12.

thither with slaves, and with the view of extending their favorite "institution" into that new and fertile country. Lawless adventurers from the United States, under James Long, had attempted the forcible seizure of Texas for this purpose, as early as 1819,* while the country was a portion of Mexico, and under the jurisdiction of the Spanish Government, with which we were at peace; but the enterprise had failed. When it was seen that the young Mexican Republic, by its Constitution of 1824, had provided for the gradual extinction of slavery, a body of American settlers, near Nacogdoches, under a leader of the name of Edwards, raised the standard of insurrection in 1826, declaring Texas independent, but were soon put down by the Mexican forces. "The united Provinces of Coahuila and Texas formed one State, and its Constitution, adopted in 1827, contained an article giving freedom to all who should be hereafter born, and prohibiting the introduction of slaves."†

Such was the position of things in Texas when the Mexican proclamation, of Sept. 15, 1829, emancipated every slave in the Mexican dominions. This produced the greatest dissatisfaction among the American emigrants in Texas, and they determined to resist the execution of the law. For this purpose, one of them was deputed to the United States to procure arms and ammunition. In the distracted and feeble condition of Mexico, the new party then just coming into power felt it politic or necessary to relax the decree, so far as Texas was concerned, permitting a modified apprenticeship of the emancipated slaves, but providing that no indentures or contracts should be valid for more than ten years from their respective dates.‡

This relaxation prevented an immediate rupture, but neither the Texan settlers, nor their friends in the United States, were satisfied, nor had they been before the emancipation decree had gone forth. The settlers wanted the unrestricted

---

* *Jay's Mexican War*, p. 12.   † *Ib.*

‡ *Quarterly A. S. Mag.*, Jan., 1836, p. 195.

restoration and perpetuity of slavery. Our slave *consuming* States wanted an open field for slave emigration and security from a free border for fugitives. Our slave *breeding* States could brook no curtailment of their prospective privilege of a growing market. Texas must be made slave territory at all hazards. But the settlers were too weak to resist successfully the Mexican government. Expeditions fitted out from the United States, *at the expense of the slaveholders*, in 1819 and in 1826, had been found insufficient. What could be done?

The plan was soon decided upon. Texas must be purchased of Mexico, *at the expense of the United States*. The Federal Government must do for the slaveholders, what they could not do for themselves.

The prosecution of this plan was attempted under the administration of Mr. Adams, Mr. Clay being Secretary of State, by whom, in March, 1827, Mr. Poinsett, our Minister in Mexico, was instructed to offer one million of dollars for the purchase. Under President Jackson, in 1829, the bid was raised to *five* millions, and when the offer was declined, Mr. Poinsett offered the Mexican government A LOAN OF TEN MILLIONS, proposing to take Texas *in pawn* until repaid, intending, of course, to get possession, stock it with slaves, and keep it at all events! This offer was justly considered an insult. This same year, Thomas H. Benton, Judge Upshur, Mr. Gholson, and other prominent Southern statesmen as well as editors, openly urged the necessity of acquiring Texas as a means of *extending slavery and improving the slave market.*

The negotiation was relinquished as a failure. The Mexicans refused to dismember their republic by selling Texas. This, too, after having also refused, in 1827, as before noticed, to stipulate for the surrendry of fugitive slaves. *From this time it was resolved to get Texas by force.* If the vineyard of Naboth could not be purchased from him for money, he could be killed, and the field taken for nothing.*

---

* 1 Kings, chap. xxi.

Now came the era of Texan land companies—armaments—invasions—insurrections. Extensive tracts of land, said to have been obtained by grants from the Mexican government, came into our American market, and were speculated upon by capitalists, gamblers, politicians, and demagogues. These purchases secured only a title to the *soil*, under *Mexican juris-diction*. But that which the *purchasers* were after was *slave plantations*, and this end could not be obtained without wresting Texas from the jurisdiction of Mexico. Not a little of this capital was invested by citizens of the non-slaveholding states. Three of the principal Texan land companies were established in the City of New York, the scrip being of little value while Texas remained under the anti-slavery laws of Mexico, but was expected to rise rapidly whenever Texas became independent. Recruits of volunteers from the United States were at length openly enlisted for this enterprise, and proceeded to Texas, under popular military commanders, who publicly announced their intentions, and advertised in the public prints for the number of men they respectively wished to employ. *Armed emigration* was now all the rage. Public meetings of the "Friends of Texas" were advertised and held, at which speeches were made in favor of assisting the Texans, military companies of emigrants were paraded, and the enthusiasm raised to a high pitch. In Mississippi, in Florida, in North Carolina, in various parts of the Slave States, and even in Cincinnati, Ohio, were these scenes witnessed, and arms and ammunition openly purchased to aid in these expeditions. On their starting from their places of rendezvous, the Gazettes and Journals of the day exultingly heralded their departure.

All this was in flagrant and gross violation of our peaceful relations with Mexico, in violation of the laws of nations, and the laws of the land, which forbid any expeditions against nations with whom we are at peace. Aaron Burr had been arrested and tried for the crime of attempting a similar invasion of Mexico, in 1807. Presidents Washington, in 1793, Jefferson in 1806, Madison in 1815, and Van Buren in 1838, had issued proclamations forbidding our citizens to invade the provinces of other nations, or intermeddle with their internal dissensions. But no such proclamation was issued by President Jackson on this occasion, though no emergency more loudly demanding the measure had ever before occurred.

Under these circumstances it was, and by these means, that the standard of revolt was raised in Texas, by the American settlers, against the government of Mexico, which was, at that time, weakened by dissensions at home. The colonists, in 1833, organized themselves into a distinct and separate state, preparatory to independence, because the people of Coahuila, with whom they were associated, were not favorable to the measure. Mexico refused to recognize this new organization. The standard of open rebellion in Texas was then raised, the small body of Mexican troops were driven out, and "on the 2d of March, 1836, the insurgents issued their *declaration of independence,* and fifteen days afterwards adopted a constitution establishing PERPETUAL SLAVERY." "Of the *fifty-seven* signers to this declaration" of independence, *fifty* were emigrants from the slave states, and only three Mexicans by birth, and these, it is said, were largely interested in Texan land speculations.*

"Nothing," says Mr. Van Buren, "is more true or more extensively known than that Texas was wrested from Mexico, and her independence established through the instrumentality of citizens of the United States."† Mr. Clay, while the question of the annexation of Texas was pending, alluded to the same fact as a reason why our government should not be precipitate in that measure, in advance of the recognition by Mexico herself, lest the civilized world should upbraid our rapacity.‡

The Mexican Minister at Washington, in the meantime, had remonstrated against these proceedings. In October, 1835, he informed the Secretary of State that large numbers of vessels were about to sail from New York with military stores for the

---

* *Jay's Mexican War,* p. 22.   † *Ib.*
‡ We state the substance from memory, the speech not being at hand.

insurgents, and that an armed schooner had sailed for Texas from New Orleans, without papers from the Mexican consul. Our Secretary, Mr. Forsyth, then addressed circulars to the several District Attorneys, ...ng them, *in general terms*, to prosecute violations of treaties with foreign nations, but no efficient measures were taken, and no offenders were punished. A District Attorney in Ohio, soon after, made an address at a Texan meeting, in favor of assisting the Texans! To a second remonstrance of the Mexican Minister, Mr. Forsyth very coolly and mendaciously replied that the Government had done all in its power to prevent interference!

A few days before this assurance, General Gaines was directed by the President to take a position near the frontier, ostensibly to prevent the contending parties *from entering our territory*, of which there was no danger. He was *not* directed to prevent regiments raised in the United States from invading Texas! Under pretense of defending our frontiers, he next marched his troops into Texas, against the remonstrances of the Mexican Minister, with the evident object of affording countenance to the insurgents, and, if necessary, assist them against the Mexican forces, under pretense of defending our frontier. Some hundreds of his soldiers deserted and joined the Texans. There they remained and served *while they were wanted*. General Gaines then offered them a *full pardon* on condition of their return.

Thus encouraged and aided, the Texans, or rather the American armed emigrants, fought the decisive battle of San Jacinto, and defeated Santa Anna, in May, 1836. The intelligence was transmitted to our *American President*, Jackson, by the *American General*, Gaines, who indulged the anticipation that, in consequence of the victory, "THIS MAGNIFICENT ACQUISITION TO OUR UNION" would grace his administration.—*Jay's Mexican War*, p. 30.

And all this is said to have been done without violating our relations of peace with Mexico!

On the opening of Congress in December, 1836, President Jackson recommended a prudent delay in acknowledging the independence of Texas, till "*the lapse of time or the course of events*" should have proved her ability to maintain her position. This proved to have been a ruse to allay the fears of the friends of freedom. Not long after, the President urged Congress to put at his disposal a naval force to act against Mexico in case she failed to make prompt arrangements for satisfying our pecuniary claims against her. With such a force he could easily get into a war with Mexico, and then "*the course of events*" would soon lead to the acknowledgment of Texan independence. "This proposition was coldly received." "The session was to close the third of March, 1837." By the most dexterous management of the House of Representatives, and the concurrence of the Senate, near the close of the session, the independence of Texas was acknowledged, and a salary provided a Minister to the new nation! A Minister was immediately nominated by the President, and confirmed by the Senate, the last day of that administration.—*Jay's View*, p. 153.

Nothing was now wanting to complete the drama of Texas, but her admission into the Union. The strong opposition, at the North, against this measure, delayed it for about eight years, and until near the close of Mr. Tyler's administration, in March, 1845.

The Texan Congress took measures, as early as 1836, (before our government had acknowledged their independence,) for proposing a union with the United States, but on the express condition of the "FREE AND UNMOLESTED AUTHORITY OVER *their slave population*." In 1837 the negotiation was opened by the Texan Minister at Washington. Mr. Van Buren prudently declined on the ground that the United States were, at present, at peace with Mexico, and that power had not acknowledged the independence of Texas. As the excitement against annexation increased in the free States, the proposition of Texas was formally withdrawn, and the apprehension of annexation was, by this movement, allayed.

In the mean time, the emigration to Texas from the free States began to alarm the guardians of slavery. In 1842 the ex-President of Texas, General Lamar, addressed a letter to his friends in Georgia, urging the necessity of annexation, lest the anti-slavery party in Texas should change the Constitution, and abolish slavery. He added that though the anti-slavery party were now a minority, yet the majority of the people of Texas were not slaveholders. The clamor of the South for annexation was now revived. A false alarm, without the least shadow of foundation, was got up, that England intended in some way, to interfere in the affairs of Texas, and insist on the abolition of slavery. The British Government disclaimed any such intention.* Yet President Tyler negotiated with Texas a treaty of annexation, in the face of earnest remonstrances from the Mexican Minister at Washington, and the instrument was signed by the Secretary of State, Mr. Calhoun. The Senate of the United States, however, refused its ratification of the treaty. This was in April, 1844, and it was not until March 1st, 1845, just before the close of Mr. Tyler's administration, that the measure was carried by joint resolution of both Houses of Congress, after a severe struggle, and in direct violation of the Federal Constitution, which invests the treaty-making power in the President and Senate. Texas assented July 4th, and was formally received the 22d of December.

Hostilities with Mexico soon followed; but we must, in a way of digression, go back and give some account of an attempt of the slaveholders upon that country, about forty years previous.

---

* Mr. Calhoun, while Secretary of State, in April, 1844, officially declared, in a letter to the American Agent at Mexico, that the annexation of Texas had been "forced on the Government of the United States in self-defense, in consequence of the policy adopted by Great Britain *in reference to the abolition of slavery in Texas.*"

The *accusation* was false—the *confession* was true. *Slavery* was at the bottom of the matter. Eight years before this (May 27, 1836), long before there was any pretense of British interference, Mr. Calhoun had said in the Senate, "There are powerful reasons why Texas should be a part of this Union. The Southern States, owning a *slave population*, were deeply interested in preventing that country from having the power to annoy them." On the 19th of February, 1847, General Houston, under whose directions the treaty between Texas and Mexico had been negotiated, declared, in the Senate, "England never proposed the subject of slavery or of abolition, to Texas."

CHAPTER XXV.

CONSPIRACY FOR THE CONQUEST OF MEXICO AND THE DISRUP-
TURE OF THE FEDERAL UNION IN 1806—CONTROLLING POW-
ER OF THE CONSPIRATORS OVER THE FEDERAL JUDICIARY.

Arrest of Colonel Aaron Burr, 1807—His previous history—Detection of the plot by
Gen. Wm. Eaton—Sketch of his history—Object of the conspiracy—A South-
Western Empire, including slaveholding Mexico and the American slave States—
Extent and power of the conspiracy—Prominent men—Trial of Burr—Sympathy
of the South—Arts successfully employed for his acquittal.

WE shall venture to fix here an earlier date than is commonly given, to the machinations and attempts of prominent
citizens, statesmen, capitalists, and military men, chiefly,
(though not exclusively,) of the South and Southwest, for the
conquest or dismemberment of Mexico, and with a special
view to the security and expansion of the slave system. The
time, we think, has now fully come, when, upon a full review
of the past, connecting nearer and more familiar events with
those more remote and obscure, and reading the more distant
in the light of the more recent, we may better understand the
secret springs of certain movements which caused no little excitement and surprise, in their day, presenting a riddle which
few Northern statesmen then on the stage appeared fully to
comprehend.

The arrest and trial of Col. Aaron Burr, under Mr. Jefferson's administration, in 1807, fills a brief paragraph or two
in our popular histories. But a well-digested manual and
review of the facts that came out on the trial, and that occupied the political journals of that day, could they now be collected and published, would make a thrilling and highly

instructive volume. The details were altogether astounding.

Colonel Burr, as a politician, as a statesman, and as a military man, held rank among the first men of the country. As a competitor with Mr. Jefferson for the Presidency, he received from the people precisely the same number of electoral votes. In the House of Representatives, in 1801, it required thirty-five ballotings to decide between the two, when a change of one vote resulted in the election of Mr. Jefferson ; but, as the Constitution then stood, Colonel Burr was, of course, invested with the Vice-Presidency for four years.*

The sudden arrest of so prominent a statesman for high treason, and in a time of general quiet, was like a clap of thunder out of a clear sky. It produced a sensation the most profound and extensive. Except for his slaughter of Gen. Alexander Hamilton, in a duel, in July, 1804, Col. Burr, though of loose private morals, had stood before the country in general, unsuspected of crime. The occasion of the duel was this: Col. Burr, having been supplanted in the affections of the democratic party by his only rival, Mr. Jefferson, became cool in his party attachments, and was apparently in the attitude of changing sides. At this crisis, a portion of the Federal party in the State of New York proposed him as their candidate for Governor. Gen. Hamilton, as a leading member of that party, strongly opposed the nomination, denouncing Col. Burr as an unprincipled aspirant and "*dangerous to the country.*" Col. Burr sent him a challenge, which Gen. Hamilton accepted, and fell. His strong declaration concerning Col. Burr excited wonder at that time, but it was afterwards conjectured that he entertained secret suspicions, or had received intimations, of his treasonable designs. It appeared at the trial, and afterwards, that Burr had made secret overtures to several prominent men who had

---

* *Willson's American History*, p. 443. The votes were given only for a President, and after electing the President, the candidate having the next greatest number of votes was Vice-President.

declined co-operation with him, but who had considered themselves bound by Masonic obligations or otherwise to observe
silence. He had carried on a very extensive correspondence
in "the Cypher of the Royal Arch Masons," and it was believed, during and after the trial, that his connection with
that fraternity did much to shield and acquit him.

Be this as it may, to Gen. William Eaton, of Massachusetts, was reserved the honor of detecting the dangerous
conspiracy, and lodging information with the Government.
Gen. Eaton had been American Consul at Tunis, during our
war with the piratical Barbary powers, and had concerted
with Hamet, the legitimate but exiled sovereign of Tripoli,
an expedition against the usurper who had dethroned him,
and with whom this country was at war. Communicating
this project to his Government, and obtaining due authority
from it, he had embarked in the perilous expedition with a
few followers of Hamet and some Egyptian troops. He had
marched, with incredible fatigue and suffering, over a desert
of a thousand miles in extent, had taken Derne, a Tripolitan
city, by assault, had fought two battles with the reigning
Bashaw, and had obtained terms of peace which had been
accepted by our agent, Mr. Lear, thus suddenly and successfully closing our long and expensive naval war of five years
in the Mediterranean.* He returned to America, the military
idol of his times. The whole northern country was resound-
ing with his exploits against *the barbarians who had captured
and enslaved so many American citizens!* But Gen. Eaton was
a New Englander and a Federalist. The South could never
permit such an one to wear military laurels. Worse than
all this—Gen. Eaton, while residing at Tunis, had written
letters home to his wife, which had, somehow, appeared in
print, in which he described the horrors of Tunisian slavery, but had declared, that he blushed at the remembrance
of having witnessed worse scenes in his own country !† This

---

* *Willson's American History*, pp. 444–5.
† *Liberty Bell*, p. 33.

sealed the fate of Gen. Eaton. Not only was he coldly received at the seat of Government, but the most mean and frivòlous cavils were raised and charges preferred against him. His accounts of necessary expenditures were disputed and disallowed, reducing him to bankruptcy, and attempts were made to cashier and disgrace him. Triumphantly vindicating himself, at every point, but literally plundered by his Government, he retired, in deep disgust, from its service, carrying with him the sympathies of his New England fellow-citizens, who found in his wrongs, fresh aliment for their hatred of Mr. Jefferson and his administration.

Then it was that Col. Burr conceived the idea of adding Gen. Eaton to the long list of his military adventurers, and approached him accordingly. But he mistook his man. The General listened silently till he had unfolded the whole scheme. *A new Southern and Western Empire was to be established, with New Orleans for its capital, and extending, if possible, over Mexico.* The extreme Southern with the South Western States were confidently calculated upon to oppose no serious obstacle to the measure, and in fact, to come into it, quite greedily. As many of the southern states as possible were to be drawn into it. To the question, what disposition was to be made of the existing Federal Government, the ready answer was, " They can probably be managed easily enough, but if not, we will assassinate the President, and turn Congress, neck and heels, into the Potomac." General Eaton declined the overture, and, nobly forgetting his own personal grievances, lost no time in communicating the particulars to the Government that had wronged him. Col. Burr and several others were arrested. Col. Burr was charged, first, with high treason ; second, with *a high misdemeanor, in attempting an invasion of Mexico*, a province of Spain. The single testimony of Gen. Eaton was thought sufficient to have convicted him, but it was only a tithe of what could be brought forward. So extensive and so powerful was the conspiracy found to be, and so wide-spread appeared to be the sympathy of the South with the prisoners, that it was feared, at one time during the

trial, that, whether the arraigned were condemned or acquit-
ted, the enterprise would in some way be resumed. It was
currently understood that prominent men at the South, who
were as deeply implicated as Col. Burr, and who were, in fact,
the originators of the plot, were not arrested because it was
not deemed prudent to proceed further. Among other rumors,
one was, that Col. Burr was about to turn States' evidence
against some of them, to procure indemnity for himself. But
the matter appears to have been compounded more easily.*
Quite evident it was that the northern states were mainly
depended upon to sustain the Government, at that crisis,
though nearly all the political opposition to the administration
was northern.   Except Col. Burr, few northern citizens, we
believe, were implicated, or even suspected of being in the
conspiracy.   Whoever succeeds in ferreting out the names of
the prominent southern men implicated or falling under strong
suspicion at that period, need not be surprised to meet with

---

* The arts employed to shield the accused from conviction, are quite apparent
even upon a cursory glance at the records of the trial. The indictment was so
drawn up as to charge him *only* with treasonable acts or misdemeanors committed
by him on Blennerhassett's Island, in the river Ohio, the residence of one of his
accomplices, while the great mass of the evidence in the hands of the prosecuting
attorney had respect to acts committed *elsewhere!* By this barefaced fraud, "*almost all the important testimony was excluded by the court from coming before the
Jury.*" The testimony of Blennerhasset was rejected likewise. So well was this
stratagem understood by the Jury, that after retiring, for a short time, they returned
with the following written verdict, read by Col. Carrington, their foreman :

" We, of the Jury, say that Aaron Burr is not proved guilty *under this indictment,*
by any evidence *submitted to us.* We, therefore, find him not guilty."

Exceptions were taken to this verdict, that it was unusual, and that it seemed to
"*censure the Court for suppressing irrelevant testimony.*" The Jurors, however,
"*would not agree to alter it.*" " The Court then decided that the verdict should
remain *as found by the Jury,* and that an entry should be made on the record of
Not guilty." — *Burr's Trial,* reported by David Robertson, Esq., Counsellor-at-
Law. Philadelphia : Hopkins and Earle, 1808. Vol. II., pp. 446–7.

The writer well remembers the prevailing public impression at the North. The
feeble efforts of the prosecution, the evident bias of the Court, and the apparent
apathy of the Executive, suggested the suspicion that the matter was better understood at the South than at the North, and that the Administration had either
favored the project, and did not wish, or did not dare, to press the prosecutions
with vigor. Partisan feelings may have entered into these suspicions, but they were
extensively entertained.

several names that have appeared among the advocates of forcible pro-slavery extension, since. The writer will not trust his youthful reminiscences further than to say, that the name of *Andrew Jackson*, in 1807, was pretty familiarly coupled, in the public prints, with that of *Aaron Burr*, and that the circumstance was again freely alluded to *by the political opponents of Gen. Jackson, who were supporters of William H. Crawford, at the South, during the Presidential canvass of* 1824. It was a Georgia Editor, if we remember correctly, who spoke of it as though it were a fact well understood, that Jackson was an accomplice of Burr.

The acquittal of Col. Burr astonished the people of the North, little less than did his arrest. The secret was not understood. So overwhelming was the *public condemnation* of Burr, notwithstanding his *judicial acquittal*, that, with all his easy and graceful assurance, he could never again lift up his head in American society. He soon left the country, and was, for years, a voluntary exile, in different countries of Europe. He seems to have hoped, at first, that the verdict of his acquittal would have been his passport abroad. But it was not so. The *facts* elicited at the trial had preceded or soon followed him. With a polish and fascination of manners that would have graced any royal court, with talents that would have rendered him an acquisition to any European cabinet, with an energy of action that might have made him the admiration of a Napoleon, he sought employment in vain. He sued for a military post under the French Emperor, but was repulsed. Obscurity, thenceforward, was the doom of Aaron Burr. He returned to the city of New York, and earned his bread, till his death, at an advanced age, by the labors of a counsellor-at-law and a draftsman of legal instruments, without ever again appearing as a barrister in a court of justice. He was a disgraced man. If the Federal Judiciary could save his neck, it could not save his good name. A free people had assumed to act as a jury in the case, and the decision could not be reversed.

That the Federal Courts could not convict a traitor, whose

treason consisted in fealty to the *Genius of slavery extension,* is a phenomenon not very difficult of explanation, *now.* Nor need the secret spring of the Burr conspiracy be a problem of wearisome conjecture. At a time when the expected prohibition of the Foreign Slave trade was approaching, the natural instincts of the southern country, as since exhibited, must have impelled, with almost resistless energy, the appetency for western expansion. The purchase of Louisiana, about the same period, was only another symptom of the same insatiable thirst. Whether the acquisition of Louisiana were cause or effect of the great Southern Conspiracy that exploded in 1807, or which of them, *in reality,* was in progress first, or whether the purchase was not designed to satisfy the conspirators, it might be difficult, at this distance of time, to determine. That there was a close affinity between them, no one can deny. The taste of Louisiana would as naturally whet the appetite for Mexico, *then,* as did the taste of Texas the appetite for California, *more recently.*

Not more truly characteristic was the acquittal of Burr, than the significant silence observed respecting the conspiracy ever since. The *suspected* treason of the Hartford Convention has swollen into volumes. The taint of affinity with it is fatal. The orator's tongue never tires in execrations of it. But the great Southern conspiracy (for such it was, though with a Northern accomplice) is seldom mentioned, and history almost passes it over in silence. High time were it to restore that long suppressed chapter, and let posterity know that but for the fidelity of Gen. WILLIAM EATON, of Massachusetts, "our glorious Union" would probably have been shivered to atoms by the slaveholders, in the year 1807, without even a show of resistance at the South.

CHAPTER XXVI.

FURTHER ACTION OF THE FEDERAL GOVERNMENT—THE WAR WITH MEXICO—ACQUISITION OF CALIFORNIA, NEW MEXICO, AND UTAH.

The project of Mexican Conquest never relinquished since 1807—Suspension of effort till 1819—War of 1846—Its causes—Federal Government bent on a Conquest or Dismemberment of Mexico—Testimony on this point—Review of relations with Mexico since 1836—Unreasonable and fraudulent claims of our Government —Insolent demands—Territory wanted, not money—Naval armament—Com. Jones—His Annexation of California by proclamation, in 1841—Its failure— Attempts to intimidate Mexico, and to provoke a War—Demand that she should acknowledge the Independence of Texas—Negotiations for territory—Their failure —War determined on, and commenced—False claim of boundary of Texas—Gen. Taylor ordered to occupy Mexican territory—Manœuvres to provoke hostilities— Their failure—The first blow struck by Gen. Taylor—False announcement to Congress by the President—Corresponding declaration by Congress, May 11, 1846— Prosecution of the War—Adventure of Col. Fremont—Testimony that it was a War of Conquest—Barbarities and depredations—Subserviency of Congress— President's request for money to purchase Territory—Wilmot Proviso twice passed in the House—Defeated in the Senate—Then lost in the House—Negotiations with Mexico for Territory—Offered on condition of excluding Slavery—Offer rejected— Final adjustment—Cost of acquired Territory.

THE LATE WAR WITH MEXICO.

THE detection and exposure of the great Southern conspiracy against the Federal Union and against Mexico, though it interposed a temporary check on the enterprise, removed neither the cause nor the disposition that had engendered it. There is not the slightest reason to suppose that the purpose of invading and conquering Mexico was ever for one moment relinquished. From the trial and acquittal of Aaron Burr, in 1807, to the actual beginning of military excursions into Texas, then a province of Mexico, in 1819, as already related, there was an interval of *only twelve years*, less time than could have been supposed needful to allay public apprehension, to divert attention to other topics, to draw the veil of oblivion over the past, to transfer the odium of incipient treason from the South to the North, to place the Slave Power on a high ground above Free Labor, to organize the conspiracy anew, and to subsidize the Federal Government itself for the accomplishment of its objects, instead of attempting again its direct overthrow.

How effectively those twelve years were thus occupied, the history of the country will show. A glimpse of it we may take before long; but will first follow out the Mexican drama to its close.

The annexation of Texas, while she was at war with Mexico, was equivalent to a declaration of war against the latter. But Mexico was not in a position to wage war against us; and had the Slave Power, that controls the Federal Government at its pleasure, been satisfied with the acquisition of Texas, our amicable relations with Mexico, if not undisturbed, might have been easily restored. Indeed, there were no actual hostilities between the two republics until the invasion of Mexico, in the summer of 1845, by the American forces, by direction of President Polk, and without authority from Congress.

In his "*Review of the Mexican War*," Mr. Jay has clearly and conclusively shown that the Federal Government, not content to wink at and even encourage and aid the lawless invasion and revolution of Texas, to acknowledge its independence, and to annex it to this country, was resolutely bent upon a still *farther* dismemberment of Mexico, either by purchase or conquest.

So early as April, 1842, Mr. Wise, of Virginia, in a speech in Congress, openly avowed the policy of conquest, and predicted its accomplishment, for the purpose of extending slavery. He boasted that it was the people of our own Western Valley that had *conquered Santa Anna at San Jacinto.* He gloried in the prospect that they would join the Texans and proclaim a crusade against the rich States of the South, "capture towns, rifle churches," and "plant the lone star of the

Texan banner on the Mexican capital." "Let the work once begin" (said Mr. Wise), "and I do not know as this house would hold me very long. Give me five millions of dollars, and I would undertake to do it myself"—"*I would place California* where all the powers of Great Britain would never be able to reach it. SLAVERY SHOULD POUR ITSELF ABROAD, AND FIND NO LIMIT BUT THE SOUTHERN OCEAN." "War is a curse, but it has its blessings too. I would vote for this mission" [of Waddy Thompson to Mexico], "as a means of preserving peace, but if it must lead to war, I would vote for it *more* willingly."

This was under the administration of President Tyler, of whose policy Mr. Wise was the recognized leader in the House of Representatives. The *real object* of Mr. Thompson's mission, as disclosed by his course and the results, fully justified the foreshadowings of this speech. Mr. Tyler showed his affinity with Mr. Wise, by appointing him Minister to France. But the effort to get into a war with Mexico was of a still earlier date than this.

OUR CLAIMS UPON MEXICO.

The only ostensible cause of complaint against Mexico, was the claims of certain American citizens for depredations committed on their property by Mexicans, or by subordinate officials of the Mexican government. Mr. Jay has thoroughly sifted these claims, and shown that they constituted no just ground or necessity of war.

The first claim, in July, 1836, under President Jackson, consisted of fifteen distinct specifications of alleged facts, requiring time for their proper investigation. Of the existence of many of them, the Mexican *Government* may well be supposed to have been wholly ignorant, as they claimed to have been, until the complaint was presented. Yet the American Minister, Mr. Ellis, was directed to obtain a satisfactory answer within *three weeks*, or announce that, unless satisfaction was made without unnecessary delay, his further residence would be useless. If this threat proved unavailing, he was to give notice that, unless he received a satisfactory answer in *two weeks*, he should demand his passports and return home. Mr. Ellis was a Mississippi slaveholder, eager to extend the area of slavery by a dismemberment of Mexico. Another remarkable feature of this demand was, that Mr. Ellis was informed by our government that it was not in possession of "*the proof* of all the circumstances of the wrong done in the above cases !" The reparation was to be demanded *first*, under a threat of war, and the justice of the claim ascertained *afterwards !* Mr. Ellis was to be sole judge whether there was "unnecessary delay," and whether the answers were "satisfactory." The alleged aggressions were mostly of recent date. Similar claims on France and England had been matter of negotiation for ten or twenty years, without a threat of war, but Mexico was required to finish up the whole business in *five weeks !* Before Mr. Secretary Forsyth's dispatches reached Mr. Ellis, *two* out of the *fifteen* wrongs had been settled to the satisfaction of the parties, and many of the remainder were proper subjects of investigation in the Mexican courts, to which, by treaty, our citizens had access, as their citizens had to ours. Of this the Mexican Secretary reminded Mr. Ellis, but promptly proceeded, nevertheless, to an investigation of the claims. Mr. Ellis thought proper to add five more complaints, without waiting for any directions from his Government. These, added to the thirteen remaining original ones, made the number eighteen. In respect to each of these, the Mexican government returned suitable explanations and assurances *within the time specified.* Some of them were shown to be unfounded. Others of them required proof. Others required further time for investigation. Others of them having been investigated, and being found just, the claimants should be compensated. Others of them were under litigation, and the results would soon be ascertained. In one case, an American vessel had been seized by the custom-house officers and condemned for want of the proper papers, but an appeal having been taken to a higher court, before whom the missing papers were produced, the vessel had been discharged. The detention was not the fault of the Mexican officers, but of the master of the vessel, in losing his papers. In every case the answer appeared to be fair and reasonable. Mr. Ellis, nevertheless, as had been determined beforehand, *demanded his passports* and returned home, refusing to give the Mexican Government a reason for so extraordinary a course. And on his return home the country was made to ring with the falsehood that Mexico *had refused* to pay our just demands!

The Mexican Minister, in the meantime, had left Washington, on account of the march of American troops into Texas, as before related. All diplomatic relations between the two republics were thus suspended. American troops were in a province claimed by Mexico, and the wishes of the administration seemed about to be realized. Accordingly in Feb., 1837, President Jackson, in a message to Congress on the claims against Mexico, requested an act passed authorizing reprisals, and the use of a naval force of the United States for that purpose, unless an amicable adjustment could be made, upon another demand, *to be made on board one of our vessels of war on the coast of Mexico!*

The President evidently intended WAR. Indeed his message affirmed, distinctly, that these injuries justified an "IMMEDIATE WAR." But, in a semi-official letter to Governor Cannon of Tennessee, only six months before, which had somehow got into print, he had distinctly said "It does not seem that offenses of this character" (i. e. such as would justify war) "have been committed by Mexico."

But, thanks (under God) to the little band of northern agitators against slavery, the people of the North were not yet prepared for such a measure, and the war proposition of President Jackson received little favor by their representatives in Congress. There needed new machinations and a more favorable opportunity, before the desired result could be reached.

The treaty between the two countries forbade any act of reprisal, by either party, on account of grievances or damages until they had been "verified by competent proof," and until

the demand for satisfaction "refused, or unreasonably delayed." We have seen that the eighteen complaints against
Mexico had *not* been thus verified, nor had the demand for
satisfaction been "refused or unreasonably delayed." Yet
the President, as we have seen, desired authority to make
"reprisals" unless prompt reparation should be made, on a renewal of the demand from on board one of our armed vessels
on the coast of Mexico. And in making this request, he laid
before Congress a list of grievances amounting to FORTY-SIX,
making twenty-eight new cases that had never been presented
to the Mexican Government at all ! Some of these additional
claims—strange to tell—dated back as far as 1816 and 1817,
when Mexico was a province of Spain ! And some of them
were claims for insurrectionary services against the Spanish
Government !

Mr. Ellis was then re-appointed Minister to Mexico, but he
remained at home, and a courier was dispatched with the bud-
get of grievances, with an allowance of ONE WEEK to examine
and determine upon them all. By incredible zeal and industry, the list of grievances was now swelled to FIFTY-SEVEN.
This was in July, 1837, under the administration of Mr. Van
Buren. Many of these demands, as Mr. Jay well observes,
and has clearly shown, "were in the highest degree insolent
and ridiculous."

The messenger to Mexico tarried his "*one week*" and returned. But before the list of these fifty-seven grievances
reached Mexico, the Mexican Government, intent upon an
equitable settlement of all the difficulties it *had heard* anything about, viz.: the *eighteen* specifications made by Mr.
Ellis, had passed an act offering to submit to the award of a
friendly power, the claims of the United States. In the same
peaceful spirit, another Mexican Minister was sent to Washington, and the arbitration proposed, in December, 1837.

The warlike designs of the Federal Administration were
thus again baffled. The offer was too fair to be rejected, in
the face of the nation and the world, yet for four months no
notice was taken of it, but the *new* claims were three times

distinctly urged by our Secretary, Mr. Forsyth. Not until the offer had become public, and Congress plied with northern petitions to accept it, and remonstrances against the annexation of Texas, was the overture heeded, and negotiations commenced. At length an arrangement was made, by which the claims were to be presented to Commissioners to sit at Washington, two to be appointed by each party; the board to sit not more than eighteen months, the decision of cases by it to be final, and the cases on which they could not agree, to be determined by an umpire to be named by the King of Prussia.

Here, then, were allowed *eighteen months* to go through with an investigation which Mexico had been required to complete in *three weeks !*

After many delays, the Commission assembled two years after their appointment, giving ample time for all the claimants to collect their evidences.

After sitting *nine* months, they passed upon all the claims that had sufficient vouchers; but, in order to give further time for collecting evidence, the Commission was kept open the remaining nine months, when it was dissolved. The King of Prussia named as umpire his Minister at Washington, Baron Roenne. Now notice the result.

The total amount of claims presented was	$11,850,578
But of these there came, *in the last nine months*, too late to be examined, and evidently of a speculative and fraudulent character, ...	3,336,837
Thus reducing the amount to . .	$8,513,741
Referred to Umpire, and undecided by him for want of time, ...	928,627
Amount of Claims adjudicated, . .	$7,585,114
Rejected by Commissioners and Umpire, .	5,568,975
Allowed " " " .	*2,016,139

* See *Jay's Mexican War*, p. 70. The bottom line (allowed) is there stated

Just look at it! Our government had been demanding of Mexico nearly *twelve millions of dollars*, had demanded a prompt settlement on pain of "reprisals" and war. And here, after the most laborious investigation, and giving ample time, twice over, for proving the claims, they are dwindled down to a little over *two millions*, not much more than ONE-SIXTH PART of the claim. It is true that only about SEVEN AND A HALF millions were acted upon; but this was the fault of the claimants, if they had any valid evidences to bring forward. Again, of the claims brought forward in season and investigated, viz.: about *seven and a half* millions, *only about one-fourth* was adjudged to be due.

The award of over two millions remained unpaid, in consequence of the pecuniary embarrassments of the Mexican treasury. Adding to this the amount of claims that had not been adjudicated, the Federal Government was furnished with another opportunity of urging its claims upon Mexico. Another arbitration treaty was negotiated; the commissioners, for this time, were to sit in Mexico, and Mexican citizens having claims against the United States were also to have an opportunity of presenting their claims for adjudication. One feature of the treaty was to change the mode of payment by Mexico, from the tender of her depreciated treasury notes to specie payments in instalments—an object of great importance to our government. And yet, the United States Senate virtually rejected the treaty, by changing the place of adjudication from Mexico to Washington, and striking out the clause referring the Mexican claims on the United States to the tribunal of arbitration. Thus mutilated, and divested of its reciprocal character, the treaty was returned to Mexico, where no further notice was taken of it.

So much for our claims against Mexico. Except for delay of payment growing out of its poverty, it does not appear that there was any backwardness on the part of the Mexican Gov-

---

2,026,236, which does not agree with the arithmetical subtraction, owing probably to a misprint.

ernment to do all that could reasonably be asked at its hands. And this is the sum total of all our causes of war against Mexico—a war for the collection of a debt of about two millions, and a pretended debt of about five or six millions more,* the proper adjustment of which had never been refused or needlessly delayed. And this debt was collected, by the war process, at an expense of above one hundred millions of dollars!

It was territory, not money, that the Federal Government wanted of Mexico, and territory for the extension of slavery. Every step in the entire process affords evidence of this.

Under the administration of Mr. Tyler, in December, 1841, Mr. Upshur, Secretary of the Navy, made a report, recommending the employment of a naval force in the Pacific, on the coast of California, to protect "a considerable settlement of Americans" in Upper California, to explore the Gulf of California, &c. A few days after, Commodore Jones, a Virginian, was dispatched with a squadron accordingly, where he arrived in 1842. On receiving a newspaper report that Mexico had ceded California to England—one of the lying rumors of the day, for effect—learning, likewise from the Mexican papers that the government of that country had protested against American interference with Texas, and suspecting that a British naval force then in the Pacific was about to seize upon California, Com. Jones, on consultation with his officers, assumed the responsibility of taking possession of Monterey in California. He had brought with him, either from the United States or from Callao, a supply of *printed proclamations*, in the Spanish language, claiming the people "henceforth and forever" as citizens under the protection of the American flag.

The day after distributing his proclamation, the Commodore discovered his mistake. The report was a fabrication. The fruit was not yet ripe. He apologized to the Mexican authorities of Monterey, and withdrew. The Federal Government was obliged to disavow the act, but "in vain was his punish-

---

* The reader will find evidences of the character of these claims as we proceed.

ment demanded by Mexico." He was too faithful a representative of his government to fall under its censures. He had only mistaken the time to strike.

The refusal of Mexico to acknowledge the independence of Texas was an obstacle, in the minds of the Northern people, to the annexation of the latter, and hence the Senate, as we have seen, had refused the ratification of Messrs. Tyler and Calhoun's treaty for that object. The next step was to intimidate Mexico into a recognition of Texan independence. Accordingly, in October, 1844, our Minister to Mexico, Mr. Shannon, in conformity with his instructions, presented an insolent remonstrance on that subject. In reference to a projected attempt of Mexico to reduce her refractory province, Mr. Shannon represented the importance of Texas to this country, and intimated that his Government could not see it invaded, without taking part in the controversy. The Mexican Minister replied that his government was not capable of yielding to a menace which the President of the United States, "*exceeding the powers given to him by the fundamental law of his nation*, has directed against it."

He added:

"While one power is seeking more ground to stain by the SLAVERY of an unfortunate branch of the human family, the other is endeavoring, by preserving what belongs to it, to diminish the surface which the former wants for this detestable traffic. Let the world now say which of the two has justice and reason on its side."

Mr. Shannon demanded a retraction of this language. The Mexican Government nobly refused to retract, but repeated it. And President Tyler laid the correspondence before Congress, complaining of the language of the Mexican Government as an affront, that "might well justify the United States in a resort to any measure to vindicate the national honor." He contented himself, however, with urging "prompt and immediate action on the subject of annexation."

The successful annexation of Texas in 1845, encouraged the slaveholding party in Congress to broach, openly, the project of entering into negotiations for the cession of Cuba. Their papers began also to dwell on the importance of adding California to the United States, and President Polk was evidently determined to obtain that province, either by negotiation or war. A new bluster was made about our claims upon Mexico, and Mr. Slidell was dispatched on a mission to that Government to make an offer for New Mexico and California. He was to offer *the claims* and *five millions* for New Mexico, and the claims and twenty-five millions for both New Mexico and California.

To facilitate this land speculation, "*the claims*" were conveniently swelled to upwards of eight millions, although Mexico had paid the interest of the award, and above three hundred thousand dollars of the principal, by forced loans, and notwithstanding her financial embarrassments, so anxious was she to retain her relations of peace with this country.

The award under the treaty, as before stated, was above -	$2,000,000
Claims then unsettled were above -	4,000,000
New claims presented, above -	2,000,000
Amount due (after deducting payments) about	$8,000,000

Let it now be remembered that the previous claim of our Government upon Mexico was nearly	$12,000,000
Add to this, the new claims afterwards fabricated as above,	2,000,000
Total claim from Mexico, -	$14,000,000

How much *ought* to have been claimed the reader will judge when he sees, not only (as already exhibited) the amount of above five and a half millions rejected by the Commissioners and Umpire, but when he sees, likewise, how the whole matter was settled when Mexico was afterwards dismembered by our forces, when we had her in our power, and when we had obtained all the slave territory we wanted ! We could afford to be honest then, in respect to these claims. In the final settlement, at the close of the war, the award of the Commissioners was put down at TWO MILLIONS of dollars, and the remainder of the claim, above SIX millions, was put down at only THREE AND A QUARTER millions, the Federal Government stipulating to pay the claimants all "valid claims" *not exceeding* the latter sum, yet releasing the Mexican Government from further responsibility! Thus our Government *itself* repudiated above three millions. But this is not all. As five-sevenths of the claims investigated were found spurious, and as the claims presented later were evidently of a still worse character, it is calculated by Judge Jay, who has presented and studied these statistics, that "one million will be more than sufficient to meet every equitable demand," that is (as we understand it) in addition to the award of two millions; thus reducing the FOURTEEN millions claimed, to THREE millions, and repudiating ELEVEN millions of it as spurious!— *Jay's Mexican War*, p. 118.

Such were "the claims" of which EIGHT MILLIONS were to be used as purchase money to obtain California and New Mexico, through the mission of Mr. Slidell. In his person, the American Government presented itself before Mexico in the character of an importunate creditor demanding more than double his just due, with a bowie knife in one hand and a purse, with his bill, in the other. Now, says he, sell me half of your land at my own price, and take this purse and my bill receipted, for your pay. If not, receive this knife into your bosom. The offer of Mr. Slidell was rejected, as was foreseen, and he returned home. The correspondence, with the attendant circumstances, betray the extreme anxiety of the Federal Administration to provoke Mexico into a war, and raise a clamor against her in this country.

Another occasion or pretext of quarrel with Mexico was sought in a pretended question respecting the western boundary of Texas. Mr. Jay has clearly shown that the acts of this Government had recognized, in several ways, a boundary far to the eastward of that which, on his accession to the Presidency, about the time of the annexation of Texas, was resolutely maintained, and with a military force, by President Polk. Under pretense of defending Texas, which needed no defense, General Taylor was stationed beyond the *real* borders of Texas, with discretion even to cross the Rio Grande, the new boundary now claimed by the President, in case hostilities were commenced by Mexico. The slightest skirmish on the newly claimed territory, would sufficiently answer the purpose of throwing on Mexico the odium of commencing the war. All this was sheer Executive usurpation, without the authority or knowledge of Congress. In the meantime, five states were required to be in readiness to furnish aid to Gen. Taylor, though the documents show that our Cabinet were not under the least apprehension of any invasion from Mexico.

On the very *next day* after the reception at Washington of advices from Mr. Slidell, Jan. 12, 1846, from which it was inferred, that there was no hope of a cession of California, peremptory orders were given to Gen. Taylor to advance to the Rio Grande, and the "points *opposite* Metamoras and Mier, and the vicinity of Laredo, were suggested for his consideration." The evident object was to provoke a collision. After a variety of ineffectual manœuvres to provoke the Mexicans to strike the first blow, it was in fact given by our own army, and Gen. Taylor announced to his government that HOSTILITIES HAD COMMENCED; on the receipt of which President Polk announced to Congress and to the world the untruth that "*Mexico had passed the boundary of the United States, had invaded our territory, and shed American blood on American soil.*" Congress, thereupon, (rejecting a motion to read the documents) and sustaining a call for the "previous question," which precluded discussion, adopted a vote asserting the existence of war by *act of Mexico!* This was on May 11, 1846, the same day the House received the President's war message!

Gen. Taylor immediately took possession of Metamoras; and the war was vigorously pushed westward to its intended destination, the conquest of New Mexico and California.

In anticipation of these military movements, by land, a naval force had been stationed in the Pacific, near the coast of California, with secret orders to Com. Sloat, June 24th, 1845, to possess the port of San Francisco, and blockade or occupy other ports, *as soon as he should hear of an inland war with Mexico.* These orders were now carried into effect, possession taken of Monterey, and a proclamation immediately issued announcing that " *California now belongs to the United States.*" This was on the 7th of July, 1846. Two days after, San Francisco was also in our possession. All this in less than two months after the declaration of war by Congress, plainly showing that the conquest of California had been determined upon and provided for, a year beforehand, and while neither the people of the United States nor Congress were permitted to know the designs of the President. The declaration of war by Congress did not reach the squadron in the Pacific till the 28th of August, fifty-two days after the Commodore, by proclamation, had annexed California to the United States.

Another incident illustrates the same general fact. A party of adventurers, overland, under Col. Fremont, of the United States' army, ostensibly set out on an exploring expedition to Oregon, but in reality destined to aid in the conquest of California, arrived there, among " the American settlers," and commenced his revolutionary movements a little in advance of the invasion by the Commodore. The little settlement proclaimed the independence of California. The new republic existed only *four days*, the insurrection very readily merging itself in the Commodore's proclamation of annexation to the United States. Col. Fremont afterwards presented pecuniary claims upon our Government for services in California, and the investigation drew out the fact that he had acted in accordance with the designs of our Cabinet, through whose misrepresentations of the matter it had however been supposed that he had acted on his own responsibility.

Mr. Jay introduces into his volume some confessions of Mr. Thompson, our Minister in Mexico, clearly showing the designs of the Federal Government, in 1843, under the administration of Mr. Tyler, to get possession of California, and to provoke

Mexico into a war for that purpose.* He cites also Mr. Calhoun, as having said in the Senate of the U. S., Feb. 24, 1847, (in reference to the precipitate action of Congress in declaring, May 11, 1846, that " war existed by act of Mexico")— " *We had not a particle of evidence that the Republic of Mexico had made war against the United States.*"† Mr. C. J. Ingersol, as chairman of the Committee on Foreign Relations, in Feb., 1847, made a report avowing the sentiment that the war was necessary, in order to get possession of territories that " *every American administration has been striving to get by purchase.*"‡ And in the same report, as well as in a previous speech (Jan. 19th) in the House, Mr. Ingersol has the robber-like effrontery to throw the blame of the war and its continuance upon Mexico, because she refused to sell us her provinces, which, says he, " *she has now constrained us to take by force, though even yet we are disposed to pay for them, not by blood merely, but by money too!*"§ Mr. Stanton of Tennessee, Mr. Beddinger of Virginia, Mr. Sevier of Arkansas, and Mr. Giles of Maryland, openly avowed, on the floor of Congress, that the war was a war of conquest. Mr. Polk had, however, in his message, a little time previous, adventured the extraordinary assertion, that " the war has not been waged with a view to conquest." In echo to this declaration, a resolution was introduced in the House (Jan., 1847), disclaiming a view to conquest, *but the House refused to adopt the resolution.* The Southern press abounded in gratulations at the prospect of conquest, and of the extension of slavery. Henry Clay, in a speech in Kentucky, declared that the bill of Congress, of May 11, 1846, " attributing the commencement of the war to the act of Mexico," was " a bill with a PALPABLE FALSEHOOD stamped on its face."‖ A new House of Representatives, "fresh from the people," elected *after* the declaration of May 11, 1846, " Resolved," in the December following, " that *the war was unnecessarily and unconstitutionally begun by the President of the*

---

* *Jay's Mexican War*, pp. 108–9.   † *Ib.*, p. 161.   ‡ *Ib.*, p. 164.
§ *Jay's Mexico*, p. 164. App. to *Cong. Globe*, 1847, p. 125.   ‖ *Ib.*, p. 285.

United States."* That portions of Mexico, including California, were unconstitutionally conquered, and *treated and governed* as conquered territory by the President, before the
treaty of peace, was strongly affirmed and clearly shown in
the U. S. Senate, in March, 1848, by both Mr. Webster and
Mr. Calhoun.†

Of the *manner* in which the war was prosecuted, we have
not room to say much. The reader of Mr. Jay's Review will
find some sickening details of lawlessness, of rapacity, of
plunder, and of outrage, disgraceful to the American name.
Barbarities were committed which should make humanity
weep and blush. General Taylor himself, in a communication to the War Department, said:

" I deeply regret to report that many of the twelve months' volunteers, in
their route hence of the lower Rio Grande, have committed extensive outrages
and depredations upon the peaceable inhabitants. THERE IS SCARCELY ANY
FORM OF CRIME THAT HAS NOT BEEN REPORTED TO ME AS COMMITTED BY
THEM."

General Kearney communicated a similar statement. The
Californians, he says, "*have been shamefully abused by our own
people.*"

When such testimonies come from such witnesses, we may
conjecture the rest.

But depredations on private property were not confined to
the soldiers. Gen. Scott, by proclamation, assessed provinces
and cities at his pleasure, on the following conditions:

" On the failure of any State to pay its assessments, its functionaries, as
above, WILL BE SEIZED AND IMPRISONED, AND THEIR PROPERTY SEIZED,
REGISTERED, AND REPORTED, AND CONVERTED TO THE USE OF THE OCCUPA-
TION, in strict accordance with the general regulations of this army."

No resignation of office was to excuse them, and if the
money was not promptly raised, the commander would
"immediately proceed to collect, from the *wealthier inhabitants*
(other than neutral friends) *within his reach*, the amount of the
assessment due from the State." And this was according to

---

* *Jay's Mexico,* p. 254.   †*Ib.*, pp. 246–7.

instructions from Pres. Polk, without the authority of Congress. *A million of dollars* were extorted from the Mexicans in this way, and three gambling-houses were licensed in the capital, by the American commander-in-chief, in consideration of the annual payment of eighteen thousand dollars! Pillage, desolation, violence, vice, crime, demoralization, and death, kept equal march with the progress of the American arms.

The Congress that had declared the beginning of the war unconstitutional, and the members who had denounced the measure as criminal and wicked, were nevertheless so corrupt and hardened as to vote money for its continuance! A few only had the consistency and honesty to record their votes in the negative.

Though Mr. Polk had declared our title to the whole of Oregon to be "clear and unquestionable," yet he had surrendered much of it to Great Britain, to maintain relations of peace. For Oregon was too far North for the convenient use of the slaveholders, and it might be made into free States. But without the slightest claim to New Mexico and California, he prosecuted a war of conquest to obtain them, because the slaveholders desired them, and they were expected to add to the number of slave States, to help govern the Union. These objects were openly avowed by the Southern press.

All wars of conquest have their limits. It is not certain that the administration sought to conquer and retain all Mexico. The central and southern provinces might be difficult to be managed—might be found too populous and too refractory to admit, at present, the quiet restoration of slavery. The war was expensive. The administration (and partly on account of the war, and its attendant usurpations) was becoming unpopular. Desirous of securing permanently what was in his power, and what was originally contemplated by the war, Mr. Polk turned his thoughts on peace. For this purpose, Aug. 8, 1846, he recommended to Congress an appropriation of two millions of dollars, to be placed at his disposal for that purpose. This request plainly indicated his desire to make an offer of money for a cession of territory, and gave the lie to his former pretense, that war was not waged for conquest. A bill was introduced into the House for this object, and was passed, but with the celebrated proviso offered by Mr. Wilmot, that the territory thus acquired should be free from the polluting touch of slavery. The bill went to the Senate the last day of the session, but was not acted upon, and Congress adjourned.

At the next session, the President's application was renewed, but asking now for three millions. A bill was introduced into the House for that object, and this opened the way for another introduction of the proviso against slavery. A stormy debate ensued. The Southern members were enraged, declaring they would have no territory under such restrictions, and threatening, as usual, a dissolution of the Union. The bill was nevertheless passed, and with the proviso, by a vote of 115 to 106. In the Senate, the proviso was stricken out, 31 to 21. Returning back to the House, the proviso was finally dropped, 102 to 97, no less than 22 members absenting themselves. But though now rejected, the proviso might afterwards be applied, in providing for the government of the territories. This, the friends of liberty contemplated, and this, the slave party feared.

Under this state of things, a great demonstration of sentiment, by public meetings, was got up at the South. Legislatures fulminated their Resolves against the proviso, and the line of the Missouri compromise 36° 30′, began to be proposed by the more moderate.

In August, 1847, negotiations were opened with Mexico through our agent, Mr. Trist. The Mexican Commissioners were instructed, by their government to insist that " the United States shall engage not to permit slavery in that part of the territory which they shall acquire by treaty." Mr. Trist promptly refused to negotiate a treaty under such restrictions, declaring them as obnoxious as "an order to establish the INQUISITION," that "the *bare mention* of such a treaty was an impossibility," and that no American President "would dare to present any such treaty to the Senate."

" I assured them," says Mr. Trist, (in his official dispatch to our Secretary of State,) " that if it were in their power to offer me the whole territory described in our project, increased ten-fold in value, and, in addition to that, *covered a foot thick all over with pure gold*, UPON THE SINGLE CONDITION THAT SLAVERY SHOULD BE EXCLUDED THEREFROM, I could not entertain the offer for a moment, nor even think of communicating it to Washington."

A previous attempt at negotiation for peace had been abortive, because Mexico had declined to cede all New Mexico, and Upper and Lower California.

In the final close of the Mexican war, these territories were obtained at a cost of FIFTEEN MILLIONS of dollars paid to Mexico, in addition to the relinquishment of our long contested " claims." Besides this, the direct expenditures of the war are estimated at over ONE HUNDRED MILLIONS. Adding extra pay, pensions, bounties of land, &c., Mr. Jay puts down the money cost of our new territory at ONE HUNDRED AND THIRTY MILLIONS OF DOLLARS. And all this to extend the area of slavery beyond Texas.

CHAPTER XXVII.

FURTHER ACTION OF THE FEDERAL GOVERNMENT—RESULT OF
THE CONQUEST OF CALIFORNIA—ITS ADMISSION AS A FREE
STATE—" THE COMPROMISE."

Renewed demand for the " Wilmot Proviso"—Southern cry of " non-intervention "
—Attempt, in Dec., 1848, to introduce California as a State—Attempt to clothe
the President with despotic power over the conquered provinces—No government
provided for them—California forms for herself a provisional Government—Scheme
of the South of bringing in California *as a State* without restriction—Mission of
Thomas Butler King from the Cabinet at Washington—Usurpations of General
Riley—His Proclamation to choose delegates to form a Constitution—The Californians comply, *and form a Constitution prohibiting Slavery!*—Sudden change at
the South—Opposition to the admission of California—Controversy in Congress—
New Mexico follows the example of California, and asks admission, without Slavery—Demands of Texas on Territory of New Mexico—Mr. Clay's plan of " Compromise," nominally defeated, but substantially carried—Admission of California
as a free State—Territorial Government provided for New Mexico and Utah, without restriction—Boundary of Texas adjusted—Slave trade abolished in the Federal
District—New Fugitive Slave Bill (1850)—Its infamous provisions.

THERE is an overruling Providence that defeats the plans
of oppressors, and covers the councils of the crafty with confusion. A more remarkable illustration of this consolatory
truth is seldom furnished than in the winding up of the historical drama of the Mexican war. Should kindred arts
seem to succeed in future, we may trust that the same beneficent Providence will, in the end, triumph.

At the very moment when the wishes of the slave power
seemed about to be consummated, a new obstacle presented
itself, as already seen, in the Wilmot proviso, that threatened
to exclude slavery from the conquered and purchased provinces. This proviso, twice adopted in the House of Representatives, in response to the voice of the people, had been

smothered in the more aristocratic Senate, and by extraordinary arts of intimidation, corruption, and management, had, at last, been deserted, for the moment, by a small majority of the Representatives. But the spirit of the people was roused, and throughout the Free States, the indispensable condition of support at the polls, was the profession, on the part of the candidate, of sustaining the proviso. The rival Whig and Democratic parties vied with each other in these professions. The last session of Congress under President Polk's administration, was expected to grapple with this question, and give it a final decision, in the act of providing, in accordance with usage, *for the government of newly acquired territories.*

So wide spread and so unequivocal was the expression of this sentiment, that " no less than fourteen States protested through their legislatures against any enlargement of the area of slavery," and even the "voice of Daniel Webster was raised to warn his countrymen of the impending calamity."*

Alarmed at this aspect of things, and fearing to meet the question again in Congress in that shape, the leaders of the slave party resorted to a new stratagem. They determined to forestal any action by Congress for the government of the *territories,* by urging their immediate admission as *States,* with the right of shaping their domestic institutions as they pleased. The doctrine of "*non-intervention*" was now the watchword, and it was acceptable to those numerous Northern politicians, in Congress, who wished for a pretext to dodge a direct vote on the proviso. If the principle of throwing the responsibility upon the new *States* were admitted, it would relieve *them* from the responsibility, and shelter them, in some degree, from the displeasure of their constituents at home.† The democratic

---

* Address on behalf Am. & For. A. S. Soc., p. 2.

† The real *spirit* of their pledges and professions would indeed oblige them to vote against the admission of a new *State* whose Constitution did not exclude slavery. But the doctrine of "non-intervention," deriving its plausibility from the democratic theory of leaving the people of the States to govern themselves, would relieve their embarrassment. The sophistry lay in forgetting that the *slaves* are a part of "the people," and that the business of majorities wielding civil government, is to protect the equal rights of all.

candidate for the Presidency, General Cass, had occupied this ground. The whig candidate, General Taylor, though not publicly pledged, had been represented, by his friends at the North, as not being disposed to veto the proviso, and being now about to take the Presidential chair, the prospective alternative of being obliged to commit himself on that point, was disagreeable to him, and especially to his party. All this favored the new plot of the slave interest.

In the early part of the session, Dec. 11th, 1848, a bill was introduced into the Senate by Mr. Douglas of Illinois, for the admission of California as a State, which was read twice and ordered to be printed. The boundaries were to include "all that portion of territory which was acquired by the treaty of peace, &c., with Mexico," Congress reserving the right to form new states out of it.* This would include all of Utah and all of New Mexico that was not intended to be absorbed by Texas! It was soon found that this project would not succeed; but Mr. Douglas presented a new bill in another form, leaving New Mexico out of the question. These bills contained, of course, no interdict of slavery.†

Mr. Foote of Mississippi, on the introduction of the first bill, seemed anxious to be considered as its author, and it doubtless had its origin with slaveholders. The Washington Union, the special organ of President Polk, advocated the second bill, and answered the objections of some southern members against it.‡ In the House, Mr. Hilliard proposed a similar bill. The project underwent various modifications, and finally, near the close of the session, a substitute for them all came under debate in the Appropriation Bill, and the amendment of Mr. Walker of Wisconsin, which provided for the despotic government of the territories by the President, at his discretion, and without any restriction in respect to slavery. It contained, likewise, a virtual concession of the claims of slaveholding Texas to all the territory of New

---

* *National Era*, Dec. 14, 1848.　　　　† *Ib.*, Jan. 25 and Feb. 1, 1849.
‡ *Ib.*, Feb. 22, 1849.

Mexico east of the Rio Grande, and it transferred to California certain laws regulating the domestic slave trade on the Atlantic seaboard. All this was passed in the Senate 29 to 27—absent 4,*—but was defeated in the House.

The session was thus occupied in a manner that staved off direct action on the proviso, but neither provided for the government of the acquired provinces as territories, nor admitted them into the Union as states. Being thus left unprovided for, in a condition bordering on anarchy and under military misrule, the Californians established for themselves a Provisional Government, and elected an Assembly, in Feb., 1849. In the United States, the controversy was still undecided, neither the friends nor the opponents of slavery extension having carried any decisive measure.

On the accession of President Taylor, March 4, 1849, the policy of his administration, from which there appears to have been, at that time, no dissent among the friends of slavery extension, was evidently to facilitate and hasten the organization of a State Government in California, without a prohibition of slavery, and bring her forward with her new constitution at the next session, for admission into the Union. "*Non intervention*" was now the doctrine of the entire South, and of its Northern allies. The party supporting President Taylor, even including that large and influential portion of it at

* *National Era*, March 1 and 8. It is proper to add that only seven senators from the free States voted in the affirmative, viz: Messrs. Dickinson of N. York, Dodge of Iowa, Douglas of Illinois, Fitzgerald of Michigan, Hannegan of Indiana, Sturgeon of Pennsylvania, and Walker of Wisconsin.

Mr. Hannegan was immediately appointed by Pres. Polk, Minister to Berlin (one of the last acts of his administration), and (it is said) with the concurrence and advice of leading friends of the President elect (Gen. Taylor), who was known to have used his influence with members of Congress before his inauguration, in favor of Walker's amendment, thus showing the united sympathy of the two slaveholding Presidents with that measure, as a substitute for the defeated project of immediately admitting California, without restriction, as a State. Gen. Taylor's earnest desire for such admission was affirmed by the editor of the *National Intelligencer*, in a labored article in support of that policy, in which it was maintained that as soon as California should present herself with a Constitution, asking admission, *Congress would have no right and no pretense to interfere in the slave question.*—See *N. Y. Evening Post*, Nov. 15, 1849.

the North, that had abounded in anti-slavery professions, and had carried elections on the merit of its zeal for the Wilmot proviso, began now to represent that the measure was not important—that Mexican law remaining in force and not repealed, would be a sufficient guaranty of liberty, or that the climate and other similar causes would prevent slavery—and finally, that if California should present herself with a constitution containing no prohibition of slavery, she would be entitled to admission. In absence of other evidence, the policy of the administration and of the slaveholders would have been sufficiently apparent from these indications. But other facts are at hand.

In the Cabinet, the slave interest was predominant. Mr. Preston of Virginia, Mr. Crawford of Georgia, Mr. Johnson of Maryland, were slaveholders. John M. Clayton, Secretary of State, was accustomed to compromises with slavery, and solicitous to pursue a course that would prevent agitation, while not one of the remaining members, Meredith, Collamore, and Ewing, were counted upon by the advocates of freedom. The course of such a cabinet might well be supposed (in the absence of any opposition) to represent the policy of the South.

By this President and Cabinet, Thomas Butler King of Georgia, member of Congress, an earnest advocate of slavery extension, and a slaveholder, was dispatched on a special mission to California. No sooner was he arrived there than he was found urging the people "to form a State Government, pledging the support of the administration in the movement, and insisting that the measure was necessary to save Congress and the old states from a fearful struggle on the subject of slavery."* And Mr. King stood not alone. Along with him (whether as volunteers or emissaries from the southern country) there were Hon. Wm. M. Gwin of Mississippi, ex-member of Congress, Ex-Governor Boggs, and Peter H. Burnett, of Missouri, &c., exerting a similar influence,—Governor Boggs

---

* *National Era*, Aug. 7, 1849.

writing home to his friends that a few slaves could be used to advantage in the territory.*

A public meeting was held at San Jose, which was addressed by Mr. King and Mr. Gwin.

Mr. King related the history of the Wilmot proviso, and the divisions growing out of it, and said:

> "We cannot settle this question on the other side of the Rocky Mountains. We look to you to settle it by becoming a State. The people of the old States ardently desire it."

He then added,—

> "I speak knowingly, when I say the Administration desire it; and from extensive intercourse with the members of the last Congress, I am convinced they are most anxious for the question to be settled in this way. You will have no difficulty in being admitted as a State. I pledge myself to it, and I pledge the Administration, and I think may speak equally confidently for the next Congress. Form a State Government, send on your senators and representatives, and then admission is certain."

Mr. Gwin followed in a strain still more unreserved. He represented that a "spirit of fanaticism" in Congress had prevented, for two sessions, the provision of any form of government for California, and intimated that "the steadfast friends of California" were those who were opposed to this fanaticism. He was not so sanguine as Mr. King of their ready admission as a state. He feared "we will have to pass through an arduous struggle before we obtain our rights,"—insinuating that the "spirit of fanaticism" at the North would oppose the admission. "I do not refer to these difficulties," said he, "to deter us from acting. *Let all minor questions be merged in the great question before us,*" . . "*dropping all local questions that may excite angry discussions,*" &c. &c.

The drift of this advice was not misunderstood, nor the quarter from whence it came. Col. Hand, one of the speakers at the same meeting, administered a timely rebuke. After denouncing the usurpation of Gen. Riley, he said:

> "Let the manaic politicians of the Atlantic, who have so kindly volun-

---

* *National Era,* Oct. 25, 1849.

teered to teach us semi-barbarians the duty we owe to our would-be leaders, remain at home, and when, after a residence of five days in California, they again attempt to feel the popular pulse in regard to slavery, let your indignation at their uncalled for interference be expressed in such a manner that Gov. Clayton cannot again say, without telling an unblushing falsehood, we are incapable of self-government."*

The friends of liberty at the East had no members or ex-members of Congress at this meeting, to counteract the influences exerted there. The administration, however, had other instruments to do its bidding. *Gen. Riley,* acting under orders of our Federal Executive, was the well-known autocrat of California. The provisional government had not recognized his authority, but were in possession of no organized means of resisting his usurpations. His authority was however destined, for once, to facilitate a better organization. In strict accordance with its settled policy, as already exhibited, the Cabinet at Washington instructed Gen. Riley† to issue a Proclamation directing the choosing of delegates to form a State Constitution, which was accordingly done,—the terms of the Proclamation prescribing the time and mode of elections, and even *assuming the existence of slavery,* by making a distinction between bond and free, in defining who should be electors.‡ This specification was founded, doubtless, on the fact, that slaves were then in the territory and in process of not infrequent introduction there by slaveholding immigrants, a fact very generally understood. The Alabama Journal had declared that the experiment had been tested, that slaves had been carried there and were held in safety, and it urged the "slaveholders to emigrate there with their property in sufficient numbers to control the policy of the country."§ Gen. Riley likewise "apportioned the delegates so as to throw the

---

* *National Era,* Aug. 7, 1849.

† We have met with no contradiction or disclaimer of this alleged action of the administration on the part of Pres. Taylor or his friends, Northern or Southern, though it has been made the subject of free animadversion by opposite classes of citizens, first at the North, and afterwards at the South.

‡ See *N. Y. Weekly Evening Post,* Nov. 15, 1849.

§ *National Era,* Nov. 1, 1849.

weight of political power into the towns where the officers and dependents of the United States Government exercised most influence."*

The Provisional Government, which had been but feebly sustained, considered it the best policy to acquiesce in this movement of Gen. Riley, and the Assembly therefore ceased to exist.† The delegates were accordingly elected and assembled in convention at Monterey, Sept. 1, 1849.

Up to this time, nay, on the receipt of this intelligence at Washington and New York, about the middle of October, and for some time afterwards, the common impression among all classes in the States was, that the new Constitution of California would contain no prohibition of slavery; that a slaveholding population from the southern states would rapidly rush in, that the effort for the admission of the new slave State into the Union would be vigorously pushed, and would most probably succeed. The tone of the journals opposed to the extension of slavery was generally marked by apprehensions of this character,‡ while the southern editors heralded the passing events with an air of assurance and satisfaction. It was known, indeed, that some of the inhabitants of California were opposed to slavery, but the controlling influences were supposed to be on the other side. Mr. Gwin, it was predicted, would be President of the Constitutional Convention. The pro-slavery ticket had triumphed in San Francisco. Thomas Butler King, Mr. Gwin, and Ex-Governor Boggs of Missouri, and Ex-Governor Shannon, a pro-slavery democrat, were the prominent candidates for Senators, from the new State.§ Had John C. Calhoun, and other statesmen of that stamp, entertained any serious apprehensions of a prohibition of slavery by the Constitution of California, it is not to be supposed that

---

* *National Era*, Aug. 7, 1849.

† *Alta California* of July 26, copied into *N. Y. Weekly Evening Post* of Sept. 20, 1849.

‡ Witness the *N. Y. Weekly Evening Post*, of Oct. 18, 1849, and *National Era* of Oct. 25 and Nov. 1.

§ *National Era* of Oct. 25, 1849.

they would have been silent while these measures were in progress. As it was, the country heard nothing of their complaints against the administration, till the result of its policy disappointed them.

Few items of newspaper intelligence ever took the American people more completely by surprise than the following in the new Constitution of California:

" NEITHER SLAVERY NOR INVOLUNTARY SERVITUDE, EXCEPT FOR THE PUNISHMENT OF CRIME, SHALL EVER BE TOLERATED IN THIS STATE."

The public mind was not relieved of suspense, till the acceptance of this Constitution by the people was, some weeks afterward, ascertained.

The result is to be traced to a number of causes, neither foreseen nor understood in the United States, till the result had developed them. The immigration from the South appears to have been less extensive than had been supposed, owing to apprehensions on the part of slaveholders, that the Wilmot proviso would be applied to the territory, or that California would not be admitted, as a slave state. Of the southern settlers, some too, had come there for the very purpose of escaping from the blight of slavery, and others who had come to explore the country, leaving their slaves behind them, were content, on observation and reflection, to try a new order of things. A preponderating population had poured in from the free States, in quest of California gold, some few of whom were opposed to slavery on principle, and most of them, enlightened by the recent discussions at the north, on that subject, understood the irreconcilable antagonism between free and slave labor. As their chief capital was their own industry, they knew better than to welcome the competition of unpaid laborers, and the affinity of free laborers with slaves. Commercial adventurers understood that free labor was the only substantial element of enduring wealth. Politicians and editors, and through them the whole community, knew that the admission of California as a slave state would be opposed by the moral stamina of the North and the North-West.* Add to all this, the Californians had had a taste of the autocratic control of the Slave Power, under the military despotism that had been provided for them; the original inhabitants had no affection for the invaders who had conquered them, and all except the interested few had been disgusted by the air of superiority and dictation that had been displayed by the slaveholders who had just come among them, to prescribe for them, as by authority from Washington, what institutions they should frame.

A review of this result shows us that, in more ways than one, the anti-slavery agitation at the North had contributed largely to shape the public sentiment and the destinies of California. The wisdom of the masses of people in that territory, heterogeneous and undirected as they were, in deciding so correctly and so promptly the great moral, economical, and political problem that still perplexes the precedent-ridden and demagogue-befooled citizens of the old states, presents a splendid exemplification of the safety of the democratic principle, under the Providence of God, and illustrates the great foundation truth of religion and morality, that the *moral sense*, in man, left to itself, and acting freely, without bias, is often found a safe guide, in cases that baffle the skill and confound the calculations of the crafty.†

The doctrine of " non-intervention," so sedulously cultivated, demanded now the prompt admission of California as a *free state!* But the demand was destined to knock at bolted doors. President Taylor indeed, and the northern wing of his party, desirous of his re-election and their own preserved power, were in no condition to repudiate their own doctrine and eat their own words. Their chosen policy of non-committal on the Wilmot proviso, still led them to seek the admission of California as a State. The northern democrats who

---

* See *Alta California* of July 2, copied by the *National Era* of Aug. 16, 1849.

† Since the above paragraph was written there have appeared strong indications of a desperate attempt to extend slavery into California, accompanied with partial success. We will still hope for the best, and that the safety of California will be secured in the liberation of the whole country.

had supported Gen. Cass, under the motto of "non-intervention," could make no show of self-consistency, could hold up
no manly front, at the North, if they deserted California now.
And those who had been elected under pledges to sustain the
Wilmot proviso should be expected to be prompt in rendering
this easier service. What pretext, indeed, could any Senator
or Representative from a *free* state, devise, for not urging, earnestly, the admission of a *free* State? The North, as being a
majority, had the matter in their own hands. Add to all this,
the slaveholding President himself, in his Message on the
opening of the Session, (in December, 1849,) had mentioned
the reception of California with favor, and the less violent and
rabid of slaveholding statesmen, including two prominent
leaders of the rival parties, Messrs. Benton and Clay, were
understood to approve the President's course. An easy victory should have been anticipated for the friends of California.

Instead of this, the struggle was, perhaps, the most violent
and long-protracted ever witnessed in our national councils.
The extreme slave party, led on by Mr. Calhoun, demanded
not only the rejection of California, but other concessions to
the slave power, including an amendment of the Constitution
that should equalize the political power of the free and slave
states, as a condition of the continuance of the Union. The
application of California for admission was repelled on the
ground that she came without leave of Congress and under
executive direction. The administration of President Taylor
was arraigned for its activity in the measure, and intimations
were made by Mr. Calhoun, that the policy might have had
its origin under President Polk. Whether by Mr. Polk, Gen.
Taylor, or Gen. Riley, it was unequivocally denounced.

While this controversy was raging in Congress, New Mexico, from similar causes, and in imitation of the example of
California, adopted a State Constitution, excluding slavery,
and applied also for admission into the Union.

The slaveholding State of Texas, alarmed by this movement, now urged her pretensions of a western boundary that

should include a large portion of New Mexico, by whom this pretension was repelled, and Texas threatened a resort to arms.

In this state of things a plan of so-called compromise was introduced into the Senate by a committee of thirteen, of which Mr. Clay was chairman, embracing the following particulars, viz: 1. The future admission of new slave States, to be formed out of Texas. 2. The admission, forthwith, of California, with her proposed boundaries. 3. The establishment of territorial governments without the Wilmot proviso, for New Mexico and Utah. 4. The combination of the two last mentioned measures in one bill. 5. The establishment of the Western and Northern boundary of Texas excluding from her jurisdiction all of New Mexico, with a grant to Texas of a pecuniary equivalent. 6. More effectual enactments to secure the return of fugitive slaves, (as previously introduced in a bill by Mr. Mason of Virginia.) 7. The abolition of the slave trade, but not slavery, in the District of Columbia.*

Mr. Clay's project of securing all these measures simultaneously, by the adoption of this Report of the Committee, did not succeed. After a tedious and protracted effort, the plan was marred by amendments, till the Report, as a whole, was defeated and abandoned. A similar project was next attempted by separate bills, and with the following results:

1. The admission of California as a free State, with her proper boundaries.

2. Territorial governments for New Mexico and Utah without excluding slavery, and with the provision that the States hereafter formed out of them shall be admitted into the Union either with or without slavery, as the Constitutions of the new States shall decide.

3. The boundary of Texas is so fixed as to surrender to that slave State at least ninety thousand square miles of free soil, and yet the same bill creates a national debt of ten millions

---

* See *National Era* of May 16, 1850.

of dollars to buy off the notoriously fraudulent and unfounded claims of Texas to New Mexico.*

4. The abolition of the slave trade, but not of slavery, in the District of Columbia. This does not prevent citizens of the Federal District from selling their slaves into any of the States. It only prevents traders from bringing slaves into the District for sale and transportation.

5. An act, supplementary to the act of 1793, for facilitating the recapture of fugitive slaves. By this new act all the remaining defenses of personal liberty, in the non-slaveholding States, are effectually broken down, and every man, black or white, (for the law makes no distinction,) holds his exemption from chattelhood, so far as legal protection is concerned, at the mercy of any Southern man who may choose to claim him as his slave, in connection with any one of a horde of government officials, to be appointed for the special purpose, who is authorized to surrender him, without jury trial, with no testimony but that of the claimant or his agent, while the testimony of the person claimed is not to be received. All citizens are commanded to assist in seizing and surrendering fugitives, and all persons are forbidden to harbor them or aid their escape, under penalty of one thousand dollars, with imprisonment not exceeding six months, besides one thousand dollars to be recovered in a civil suit for damages, for each slave so aided or harbored.†

---

* *National Era*, Sept. 12, 1850.

† It will be seen that the substance of Mr. Clay's Compromise bill was reached by these separate enactments. According to Thomas H. Benton, Senator from Missouri, there was still another item in the Compromise, not included in the Report of the Committee of Thirteen, but the subject of a verbal understanding among the members. The cotton manufacturers of New England were to be propitiated by a high tariff. But after the Southern members had got all they could, and especially the Fugitive Slave Bill, they deserted their Eastern friends, and defeated the tariff in the House of Representatives. The following is from the *National Era* of Oct. 3, 1850:

"Mr. Benton is apt to be very pithy in colloquial comment. Conversing with a senatorial friend the other day, about the Compromise or Omnibus, in which he took so tender an interest, he remarked: 'Sir, there were four inside passengers in that Omnibus—there was California, sir; there was New Mexico; there was Texas; there was Utah, sir!—four inside passengers. There was two outside passengers,

CHAPTER XXVIII.

FURTHER ACTION OF THE FEDERAL GOVERNMENT—GENERAL POLICY AND POLITICAL ECONOMY CONTROLLED BY SLAVERY.

Considerations and testimonies in point—Commercial prosperity of the North—The Embargo—Non-intercourse—Second Embargo—Destruction of the Old National Bank—Calhoun's War of 1812 with Great Britain—Treatment of New England—Southern ascendency established—Rise of manufactures—Their wreck on return of Peace—Revival of Northern Commerce—Calhoun's Protective Tariff of 1816—Southern call for a National Bank, and why?—Pecuniary embarrassments of 1819–20—Southern bankruptcy of 1824—Cotton Speculations of 1826 and 1837—Bankruptcy of U. S. Bank, and why?—Its demise—Clamors of Calhoun against his own Tariff system—Nullification—Recapitulation—Note concerning State action.

WITH the facts of the preceding history before us, it is very natural to inquire on what maxims, with what aims, and for what objects, the *general policy* of the Federal Government has been moulded, from the beginning to the present time. Not a single administration of that government have we found free from the controlling influence of slavery. Not only has slavery been steadily fostered as an important interest of the country, but as *the paramount*, the all-absorbing interest, before whose claims every other interest and all other interests combined, have been forced to give way.

We have, thus far, considered only the *direct* action of the

sir: There was the fugacious Slave Bill, and the District Slave-trade Abolition Bill. They could not be admitted inside, but they had outside seats, and the inside and outside passengers could be seen and known, sir. But there was another passenger, under the driver's seat, sir; carefully concealed in the boot, sir; breathing through chinks and holes like Henry Box Brown, sir—the Tariff, sir! But he had a worse fate than Box Brown—he was killed—killed in the House, sir—and I hope we shall have no more Omnibuses and no more passengers in the boot, sir!'"

Federal Government, in manifest support of slavery. But the general policy and the political economy of the country could scarcely fail to have had the most important bearings either for or against the slave interest. Is it credible that this has been overlooked? With the ever watchful eye that we know the slave power has had over its own interests, with all the successive administrations of the Government under its control, and ready, as we have seen, to do its bidding, with slaveholding Presidents and Cabinets of their selection, forty-nine years out of sixty-one, and while the support of slavery has been their constant care, can it be believed that the ever conflicting and totally irreconcilable interests of *free and slave labor* have never been thought of, nor taken into consideration, in shaping our national policy? Or can it be supposed that the always dominant slave power, everywhere else true to its own rapacious instincts, has, just here, where the chess games of political economy are constantly played between the rival interests of the country, been inattentive, or neutral, or that it has held the balances between the slaveholding and non-slaveholding States, with an even and impartial hand? No intelligent citizen can believe this. We might almost be certain, therefore, in advance of all direct scrutiny of the facts of our history, that the general policy of the country has been moulded by the slave power, for the benefit of slavery, and in consequent hostility to the interests of free labor. The law of self-preservation would require this, especially as the interests of slave labor are always destined to grapple with the inherent thriftlessness, imbecility and decline incident to the system, in striking contrast to the ever buoyant and recuperative energies of free labor. It would not be enough for the slave power, acting as a political economist, and mainly intent on retaining its political supremacy, to content itself with devices and expedients to prop up and encourage *slave* labor. It must do more than this. It must adroitly stab and cripple its rival. It must so shape and shift public measures as to disarrange, thwart, perplex, and unsettle the pursuits and the arrangements of free laborers, or else itself fall into inevitable eclipse, sustain certain defeat, and let go the sceptre of power. An illustration and proof of all this we have in the recent demand of the late Mr. Calhoun, that the Constitution should be so amended as to restore to the slave States the same relative power that they had, at the first organization of the government, and which we know they have lost, in despite of their political ascendancy, by the opposite tendencies of freedom and slavery. In making that desperate demand, Mr. Calhoun laid bare his own heart, and the settled policy of the oligarchy of slaveholders. *The free North must be shorn of her own natural strength, when needful, that slavery may preserve her balance of power.* With this simple key, the historian may unlock the otherwise inexplicable labyrinths of American politics, for the last sixty years. Thus instructed, he will be enabled to read into one straightforward and undeviating chapter of national policy the fluctuations of eleven Presidential administrations, amid all the idle clamor of rival aspirants, and the rise and fall of the contending factions that have alternately affected to be *the Government.* In all. these apparent changes, the slave power has governed, and with one steady purpose, and never more steadily and effectively than in the midst of seeming change and caprice.

If any one considers this a severe charge against the South, a southern witness shall be summoned to the stand. The torturing rack of party exigences and of personal rivalry, on one occasion, extorted the confession, on northern soil, from a statesman of the South. At a New York State Whig Convention in Utica, in 1839, Mr. Stanley, "the eloquent member of Congress, from North Carolina," declared that "John C. Calhoun introduced a certain measure (the sub-treasury bill) as a southern measure." " *Mr. Calhoun,*" continued Mr. Stanley, "*knew that it must break down northern manufactures and capital, and destroy the North.* I conversed with Mr. Calhoun; he expressed himself contemptuously of Mr. Van Buren; he spoke of him only as a 'fly on the wheel.' It was not his measure, but *our* measure. *We could retrieve all or destroy.*"

It is in no spirit of sympathy with the whig party, and with no particular hostility to the sub-treasury bill, (on its own merits) that we record this disclosure of Mr. Stanley. What we would bring into notice is the fact that influential southern statesmen, of opposite political parties, are in the habit of commending to each other, in familiar conversation, their respective measures of national policy, as being *adapted to derange northern capital, and perplex the arrangements and operations of free labor.* We shall see how effectually this has been done as we proceed.

The clause of the Constitution directing the apportionment of "representatives and direct taxes," by the same complex and unequal estimate of inhabitants,* affords evidence that direct taxation was contemplated by the framers of that instrument. It is not credible that the northern members would have consented to yield up their due share of representation, but for the prospect that the southern states, as being the gainers in that part of the bargain, would return an equivalent by paying the larger portion of the taxes. It was characteristic of the North to stipulate for a *pecuniary* compensation, as it was of the South to grasp after an undue share of *political power.* How rigorously the South has claimed and exercised her stipulated political power, has been exhibited already in part. In completing the picture, we shall show how, in the use of that political power the North has been defrauded of her stipulated pecuniary equivalent. One word tells this part of the story. No "*direct taxes*" or none of any importance, have ever been levied! And the device by which the fulfilment of this constitutional compromise was evaded, furnishes a clue to the policy which has controlled the fiscal arrangements of the country ever since.

It was among the first cares of the slaveholding oligarchy, after the organization of the Federal Government, and under its first administration, to evade the payment of any "direct taxes" into the treasury. Well knowing, that if a revenue could be derived from duties on merchandize imported, the

---

* *Art.* I., *Sec.* 2, *Clause* 3.

burden would fall mainly on the states that imported and consumed most of foreign merchandize, and that these would be the non-slaveholding states, a tariff sufficient for the purposes of revenue, yet ostensibly designed to favor the gradual growth of domestic manufactures, was thus early introduced; and so far as the *raising of revenue* is concerned, has continued the settled policy of the country ever since. Amid all the fluctuations and controversies respecting the tariff, a sufficient impost *for purposes of revenue* has been conceded by all parties—controlled as all parties have been by slavery—till it almost seems to have been forgotten that a revenue can be raised in any other way, or that the power to levy "direct taxes" was ever vested in the government. This was the first triumph of slavery over the political economy of the country, and is closely connected with all its triumphs since. By thus replenishing the National Treasury by a method of taxation, bearing chiefly on the free states, and from which the slave states are comparatively exempt, the Slave Power that wields the National Government has been supplied with an ample revenue with which to carry on its more direct operations in behalf of slavery—its purchase of new slave territory—its pro-slavery diplomacy—and its pro-slavery wars. With only a revenue raised by "*direct taxes,*" very little in these directions could have been realized.

The present century opened with a remarkable state of things. Our country was at peace with all the world, and, with exception of a contest with the petty states of Barbary, we remained at peace, until the war with Britain, in 1812. Europe was embroiled in war. England, with some of the continental powers, contested the fearful strides of Napoleon. Every European nation was enlisted on one side or the other, and Europe became one vast encampment. Her agriculturists and artizans were under arms. Her commerce was swept from the sea by her own contending navies. Even Britain, "lord of the ocean," was powerful only to destroy, but could not protect her own merchantmen. America, as the only neutral and maratime nation, reaped rich harvests. She was the carrier of all christendom. She not only vended her own products at her own prices, but levied tribute at her pleasure, upon the produce of all nations, upon those of South America, the Caribbean Islands, Eastern India, and China. Not a chest of tea, not a bale of nankins, not a bag of coffee, not a barrel of flour, not a bale of cotton, at treble•their present prices, could purchase the insurer's passport to cross the ocean, unless covered by the stripes and stars of the North American States. Within less than two hundred years after the landing at Plymouth was this wonderful phenomenon witnessed; and by the sons of the pilgrims, chiefly, was this immense contribution gathered. In the counting-houses of New England and New York, were seated the merchant princes, more potent and more comprehensive in their sway than those of ancient Tyre, by whom this vast tribute was levied.

But where was the sunny South at this period. Did *she* thrust in her sickle, and gather golden harvests, when the earth was reaped? Where were *her* gallant ships? Her princely merchants—*where?* The South had no foreign commerce. The cheerful music of the caulker, the rigger, and the sailor, mingle not with the sound of the driver's lash. The spoiled sons of effeminacy, lawlessness and sloth, the heroes of the whip and the bowie-knife, are not merchants. The traffickers in women and babes excel not in lawful commerce. The land of slavery did not prosper. The curse of omnipresent justice, interwoven into the slave system itself, was gnawing at her vitals. She turned her eye of anguish and envy at the free and prospering North, inquiring within herself how she could preserve her balance of power.

The Slave Power, like the power of the pit, never lacks for a stratagem. The Slave Power ruled in the Cabinet, and stood behind the Presidential Chair. I sin not against the democracy of Mr. Jefferson. His *democracy*, however correct in theory, was here, as on his plantation, held in abeyance, and cherished "in the abstract." There was nothing of Mr. Jefferson's democracy in his slaveholding: and there was nothing of it in the embargo. That measure, dictated probably against his wishes by the Slave Power,* was levelled at the commercial prosperity of the free North. Democracy, as expounded by Mr. Jefferson, was jealous of Federal encroachment, and watchful of State rights. The embargo was the utmost stretch of Federal encroachment, in open contempt of the wishes of the commercial States. Democracy was the guardian of "free trade," the boasted champion (before and after the embargo) of "sailors' rights." The embargo annihilated commerce, and thus prohibited the avocation of the sailor! Democracy had claimed, through Mr. Jefferson, "the equal rights of every citizen in his person and *property*, and their *management*." The embargo singled out a most important class of citizens, while in the act of adding, beyond any ancient or modern precedent, to the wealth of their nation, wrested "the management of their property" out of their hands, prohibited their lawful and honorable business, and condemned their property—their shipping, richly laden with their country's produce—to rot at their own wharves.

And what was the pretext for the embargo? The rival edicts and contending fleets of France and England had perpetrated some depredations on our commerce, for which we had obtained no redress or security, to the possible amount of five or ten per cent. of the nett profits of our commerce, after paying a high insurance. Did our merchants, the direct sufferers under these depredations, desire the protection of an embargo? Not they! With all their united influence of petition, remonstrance, and suffrage, they protested against it. They even contested the constitutionality of the embargo in the Federal courts. They pleaded that the power "to regulate commerce" was not a power to annihilate it.† The

---

* It was commonly understood at the time, that the embargo policy did not originate with Mr. Jefferson, but was urged upon him by the extreme South. This was the apology of his partisans in the Northern and Eastern States.

† The petitions to Congress to abolish the interstate slave trade, under this same clause of the Constitution, have been successfully parried by this plea, which did not suffice for the Northern merchants. Our constitutional expounders would have us believe that Congress has power to annihilate *all* commerce *except the traffic in slaves!* Is it not time to distrust such expositors?

defense of the Government was, *not* that commerce was not annihilated (for not a coasting packet might navigate Long Island Sound!) but that the power to regulate commerce *did* involve the power of its annihilation. And the Federal Courts sustained the Federal Administration. Thus Northern commerce was destroyed, to protect it from petty depredations! As a measure of retaliation or coercion against France and England, the embargo could never have been supposed to be of any value.

The theory of political economy then in vogue at the South, adopted by the administration party, and promulgated through all its presses, bears testimony that the protection of Northern commerce from European depredation *was not* (as it *could not* have been) the object of the embargo. The theory was that commerce is corrupting—that the spirit of commerce is the spirit of cupidity and subversive of the spirit of freedom— that "great commercial cities are great sores" upon the body politic—that the concentration of capital is dangerous in a republic—that independency of foreign nations requires us to be agriculturists and manufacturers, not merchants — and that, like the Chinese, we should stay at home, and let foreign nations who want our products come after them. By this teaching, a jealousy against merchants and commerce was fostered, even among the yeomanry and mechanics of the North. Whatever of plausibility or mixture of truth there may have been in this philosophy, its propagation by the slaveholders at this juncture throws light upon their policy, and confirms the conclusion that the embargo and non-intercourse policy was designed to cripple and destroy, instead of protecting and fostering, Northern commerce. Nor can we overlook the coincidence by which this visitation was inflicted upon the North, almost simultaneously with the abolition of the African slave trade, and the explosion and defeat of the great South-Western Conspiracy under Aaron Burr, by the disclosures of a citizen of New England. The embargo was laid in December, 1807, and was continued till March, 1809, when it was exchanged for an act of non-intercourse with

England and France. In this policy the administration was unexpectedly sustained by an influential statesman of the North, the distinguished senator from Massachusetts,* who prefaced his vote with this remarkable argument—" The President has recommended it. I would not deliberate :—I would act." He was soon after named Minister to Russia, and was almost constantly in Executive employ, till, having been made Secretary of State under Mr. Monroe (equivalent then to nomination as his successor), he came into the Presidency in 1825, with the aid of Mr. Clay, whom he appointed Secretary of State, and *with* whom he administered the Government in the manner already shown. From the date of that appointment to Russia it has been evident that Presidential patronage, the gift of the slaveholders, is an over-match for any hold the free States may have upon the most gifted of their sons.

The non-intercourse with France was terminated in 1810. That with Great Britain was continued, including a second embargo of two months, till the declaration of war by Congress against that country, in June, 1812. From the beginning of the first embargo, therefore, in Dec., 1807, until the peace of Dec., 1814 (not available to the ship-owners until the opening of navigation in the spring of 1815), the commerce of the free States was either totally prohibited, or rendered of little pecuniary value. A general conflagration among the warehouses and shipping of the free States—all things considered—would scarcely have inflicted so great a calamity, could the merchants have been then left at liberty to repair their losses by resuming their business.

In 1811, the charter of the old National Bank expired, and

---

* John Quincy Adams. We are not at liberty to suppress so instructive an incident in the history of this great man and of the country. The remarkable independence and signal services of Mr. Adams, in the House of Representatives, after having been ejected from the Presidency to make room for a slaveholder, will always be regarded the brightest portion of his political life. A similar destiny may be claimed, perhaps, to have had a similar effect upon Mr. Van Buren—a lesson to be pondered by those who shall succeed them.

was not permitted by the dominant slave power to be renewed, on the alleged ground that a national bank was unconstitutional, a consideration not discovered when it was chartered. The real reason was that the South had become bankrupt, as it periodically does, as often generally as once in ten or fifteen years, throwing off the greater part of its indebtedness upon its creditors in some other community. No country cultivated by slave labor does otherwise. The British West Indies, under the slave system, was always a burthen to the merchants and bankers of England, in the long run, however profitable their custom might appear to be for a season. The slave system never supports itself for any great length of time in continuation. The periodical collapse must inevitably come. In old colonial times, the creditors of the South were chiefly in England, and the South went into the Revolution of 1776 (in despite of her inherent and prevalent toryism) for the purpose, mainly, of wiping out the old score. But since the revolution, the northern cities of New York, Philadelphia and Boston have shared largely in the honors and emoluments of southern custom. The result came upon them in company with other calamities, in 1811. But along with the embargo and non-intercourse, it greatly assisted the South to regain, in a pecuniary view, her endangered balance of power. Almost the sum total of her indebtedness to the North was now to be dexterously shifted from one scale to the other, with the double effect of relieving the South of the same weight that was to be thrown upon the North. In many ways the demise of the National Bank was exceedingly opportune to them at this juncture. The South had got out of the bank in the shape of loans, all it could, and southern securities were now in bad odor with the directors, while northern paper was discounted freely, and the bank was a financial assistant of the northern merchants. More than this. The Bank was the agent employed by the North to collect her debts at the South. What could the South now want of the bank? A National Bank was unconstitutional of course, and had leave to be interred. In mourning over the loss of their bank, and the depredations of the non-intercourse and embargo, the attention of the northern merchants would be diverted, in a measure, from the direct losses they sustained from the indebtedness of the South. The greater the smoke and the more scattered the fires, the better chance for pillage, and the less fear of detection.

Calamities seldom come singly, and crime is the precursor of crime. The slave power now demanded a war. Unhappily a pretext was at hand. The British "Orders in Council" of Nov., 1807, prohibiting all neutral trade with France and her allies, were still in force, though there was a prospect that they would soon be repealed. Deserters from the British navy, who had found a more lucrative and pleasant employ on board American vessels, both national and mercantile, had been not unfrequently demanded and reclaimed by the British commanders. On one occasion, the demand had been refused, but enforced. The British ship of war Leopard had fired into the American frigate Chesapeake, killed three men, and wounded eighteen, after which the seamen claimed were given up. On investigation, it appeared that three of them were American citizens. This event, which took place in June, 1807, had greatly excited the American people at the time, and the impressment of seamen was still a subject of complaint, though the number of actual impressments was afterwards admitted to have been far less than was believed and represented at first, as very few American seamen were finally found missing from our ports. By far the greater portion of alleged impressments were cases of the recovery of British seamen, who, from similarity of appearance and language, had succeeded in procuring American "protections" or passports. It was notorious that many thousands of British seamen were thus certified to be Americans. This matter was coming to be understood. Aside, therefore, from the British Orders in Council, this country could not have been dragooned into a war with that nation. Nor was it done at all, without the earnest remonstrance of the maratime and commercial classes, and indeed almost all the people of New

England, who were the chief sufferers both from impressment and the "Orders in Council." The South undertook, very kindly, the protection of the North. "Free trade and sailors' rights" was now the southern watchword :—that same "free trade" that had been so long denounced by the South as the bane of the republic, a national curse, and proscribed by non-intercourse and embargo! Those same "sailors' rights" that had been so recently cloven down and annihilated by the same arbitrary measures! The pretense of the southern enemies of commerce, of caring for the "free trade and sailors' rights" of the commercial and hated North, was too flimsy to be plausible. To a great extent the thin disguise was soon thrown off, and southern editors and orators fulminated, in the same paragraphs, their anathemas against New England and Old England, avowing the determination to chastise and humble them both, at the same time, and by the same blow.

The war party was led on by John C. Calhoun, of South Carolina, who claimed the paternity of the measure, and drove it furiously through both houses of Congress.* Mr. Clay was

---

* Mr. Madison, then President, recommended the war in a message to Congress, but his proverbial timidity and caution forbid the idea that he was the author of the measure. Mr. Calhoun, as the leader of the extreme Southern party, was commonly regarded as the real instigator of the war message, and his success in carrying the measure, gave him that decided and controlling influence over the national councils, which he ever afterwards retained, and under all the successive administrations of the government, till the day of his death, a period of thirty-eight years, during which time he seldom failed of effecting the *real*, if not the *ostensible*, objects of his occult evolutions, which were little understood. Though charged with fickleness, he never swerved from his one original and single aim—the aggrandizement of the South by the discomfiture of the North. He was never more successful than in the moment of complaining loudly of defeat, and appearing to submit, reluctantly, to a compromise. Even the great compromiser, Mr. Clay, appeared to be but an implement in his hands. He was charged with ambition for the Presidency, but in reality he preferred to govern through *eight* administrations (and he managed for the most part to do so), rather than rule through the brief period of *one*. He had the faculty of governing, through their hopes or their fears, the political party from which he seemed to stand aloof, as effectually as he did the party to which, for the time being, he seemed to belong. The *Slave* party was the only party to which he ever really adhered. The skill with which he concocted a new party, by an alliance of the Southern "nullifiers," of whom he had been the leader, with the National Republicans of the North, against whom he had threatened a civil war, yet

also in favor of the measure. At one stage of the proceedings, early in June, 1812, a motion was made in the Senate to postpone the declaration of war till the opening of the next session of Congress in December, when the policy of the British Government would be developed.* On this question the Senate was understood to be nearly equally divided, and Mr. Calhoun, whose influence was potential in both Houses, exerted himself to defeat the motion. Then it was that, after an adjournment, a large number of northern members, including prominent supporters of the administration, were said to have surrounded Mr. Calhoun in the lobby, imploring him to relent, and allow the country a respite till December. Mr. Calhoun was inexorable, and by extraordinary appliances, one or two members were gained over to his party, and *the postponement was defeated in the Senate by a majority of one vote.* This decided the question of war, which was declared by a vote of 79 to 49 in the House of Representatives, and of 19 to 13 in the Senate. In a few weeks, news arrived, as was expected, of the repeal of the British Orders in Council, thus removing the chief cause of the war. But the object of the Calhoun party was gained. The nation was plunged into a war, in the midst of the pecuniary embarrassments arising from a general southern bankruptcy, (the North being the creditor) and from the sudden demise of the National Bank. New England, at such a crisis, more than Old England, would be the sufferer by the war, and the North would be burdened with the chief expense of the infliction.

The result of the measure, and especially the manner in

---

stepping *out* of his new party before he was fairly seated *in* it, was mistaken for caprice by those who saw not his object. It enabled him to be either Whig or Democrat, as he pleased, to stand with one foot in each scale, to make either side preponderate as he chose, and become Secretary of State when he wished, by the acclamations of a Senate whose party was, even then, denouncing him! Whoever would understand American politics from 1812 to 1850, must study the political history of John C. Calhoun.

* A motion was also made in the House of Representatives to include France in the measure, but the motion failed. The French had no naval force to spare for the coast of America, and could do little for the threatened chastisement of New England.

which the war was conducted and terminated, were such as to justify, fully, this account of its object and its origin. Two commanders, in sympathy with the administration, Generals Hull and Smythe, the latter a Virginian, were sent, successively, on expeditions of pretended invasion of Canada, but in both instances, the enterprise was abandoned when the Canadas were apparently in their power. General Hull surrendered to the British, to their great astonishment. The whole country accused him of treason, a court-martial sentenced him to death, but he was pardoned by the President.* General Smythe " suddenly retreated, to the great surprise of his troops." These facts, together with the systematic and even skillful withholding of supplies from the forces under other commanders, afterwards,† made it perfectly evident that the administration not only never intended the conquest of Canada, but took special care that no such acquisition of territory should add to the number of non-slaveholding States. Had Canada been adjacent to the slave States, and adapted to slave culture, there can be no reasonable doubt that it could have been conquered as expeditiously as were California and New Mexico.

New England, in the mean time, though compelled to furnish largely to the sinews of a war waged, in reality, against herself—New England, in whose cities was the wealth that tempted the enemy, and in whose ports was the shipping that was endangered—New England, whose militia were subjected to drafts for enacting sham invasions of Canada, or massacres of the Indians, and whose seamen were winning victories on the western and northern lakes, and on the Atlantic—New England was systematically left defenseless, while her seaports

---

* A defense of Gen. Hull was, many years afterwards, published, in which it was claimed that he surrendered for want of supplies, and that his course was in accordance with the secret intentions of the Government that so readily pardoned him.

† As a specimen of these tactics, we notice that Virginian corn was sent in wagons to the forces on the Canada frontier, of which only one bushel to each wagon load was delivered to the army, the balance being consumed by the teams on the journey out and home; while large supplies of northern corn might have been purchased near at hand.

were blockaded, a vast amount of her shipping destroyed, her eastern borders exposed to hostile incursions, and the port of Castine held in possession of the enemy for many months. When, under these circumstances, and after all remonstrances had proved unavailing, New England statesmen were found who demanded that New England resources and New England militia should be retained by the State authorities for home defense, the cry of treason was raised against them, which has been continued to the present day.*

The threat of humbling New England was thus signally fulfilled. New England cowered under the lash of the slave-driver, and has never since adventured to lift up her head in the national councils. Her most gifted Representatives and Senators find ample scope for their powers in bowing to the behests of slavery, or only make a brief bluster of resistance, to quail the lower at last, or be deserted by their cotton lords at home.

When the war had accomplished its grand objects, when the bankrupt Slave States had regained and more than regained their balance of power with the North by despoiling it of half its remaining wealth, after the previous inflictions of non-intercourse and embargo, when Old England had been successfully employed to chastise and humble New England, when insult had been added to injury, and the loss of honor and reputation conjoined with the loss of wealth and political influence, the slave power was ready to restore peace. And this was done without a single lisp of " free trade and sailors' rights." Neither the treaty, nor the negotiations, nor the instructions from the Cabinet under which they were conducted,

---

* The claims of Massachusetts on the Federal Government, for the services of her militia under the State authority, in defending her own coasts, at a time when the Federal Government persisted in leaving them absolutely defenseless, was afterwards contemptuously and insultingly disallowed, and the very *act* of this self-defense is still pointed at as evidence of " constructive treason !" And thus the State contributing most largely (in proportion to population and territory) to the Federal expenses during the war, was compelled to defend itself by additional exertions, at its own cost, and be branded with the taint of treason to boot ! Is it a marvel that the politicians of Massachusetts became servile ?

contained the slightest allusion to the ostensible grounds of the war, or provided or sought the least semblance of any security against similar aggressions in future. Thus ended a war of nearly three years, conducted at an expense of nearly thirty millions per annum, chiefly paid by the free States, the price of their own subjugation and disgrace—a war whose "glory" has given us two Presidents, one of them a slaveholder, the other a native Virginian, and a steady supporter of the slave power—a war that virtually enthroned, from 1812 to 1850, the bitter enemy of northern as well as southern liberty, JOHN C. CALHOUN.*

Free labor, ever buoyant and recuperative, had, however, survived. The hardy yeomanry of the North had earned their own bread with their own hands, had paid all the demands of an oppressive government, and aided by the high war prices of their products, while consuming as little as possible of foreign merchandise, had thriftily maintained their ground. The remnant of surplus capital, in the cities, driven from its own field of enterprise, and encouraged by the scarcity of foreign fabrics, had invested itself in the manufacture of

---

* The writer is aware that his account of the embargo, non-intercourse, and war of 1812, will be as distasteful to some of the partisans and admirers of Jefferson and Madison, as his account of Washington's administration and the Federal party will be to some of their political opponents. But history should be impartial; and a writer who has religiously stood aloof from both parties may claim to have seen passing events with his own eyes, and may be permitted to record them as he has apprehended them. In use of the same liberty, he may further say here, once for all, that since the war of 1812, as before, he has found no essential difference, on the whole, between the two parties. The so called Republican or Democratic party, afraid of an aristocracy of Northern capital, has thrown itself into the arms of the slaveholders. The Federal, National Republican, and Whig parties, while they have seen this, have also had their slaveholding allies, whose aid they could not afford to spare, and hence the slave question has never been made an issue by those parties. When in power they have been as servile as their rival. Neither of them have been anti-slavery parties at any period, nor otherwise (at bottom) than aristocratic parties, being all of them governed by one or the other of the rival aristocracies, Northern or Southern. A truly democratic party has never yet come into power. The people have been cheated by professions and names. Since the rise of the Cotton power at the North, allied to the Cotton power of the South, the rival aristocracies have been merged in one, and the two political parties are kept up as mere shams, to prevent a united rally of the people against the now *united* aristocracy of the country, represented by "compromise" legislation and "Union Committees."

cotton and woollen cloths, of a coarse but substantial texture. But the return of peace brought an influx of foreign goods, and a sudden reduction of prices, ruinous to manufacturers as well as merchants. Years were required to repair these fresh depredations, and the new policy of free commerce, it was thought, precluded the prospect that our infant manufactures could be sustained. No "protective tariff" came to their aid, then. The South, no longer fearing the seductive influences of commerce, had become the champion of "free trade." The North, by this time, understood her position too well to bring forward any measures of her own. Manufactures were, for the most part, abandoned, the manufacturing villages were deserted, and where absolute bankruptcy did not prevent, the little remnant of capital was invested in foreign commerce. The merchant who had been compelled by southern policy to turn manufacturer during the embargo, the non-intercourse, the second embargo, and the war, while his shipping was either rotting at his wharf, or had fallen into the hands of the British, was now compelled by the new southern policy to let his factory and village fall to decay, rebuild again his ships, and commence merchant again. In a short time, the settled channel of northern capital and enterprise was again foreign commerce, and a brisk business in that line was again bringing in an influx of wealth.

No sooner was this witnessed or anticipated, than another change came over the political economists of the South. "Free trade" became a political heresy, and the doctrine of the Jeffersonian period, condemnatory of foreign commerce, and in favor of domestic manufactures, was suddenly revived. The South wanted an increasing northern market for her cotton, and northern capital must be forced to become a customer. The South wanted, likewise, a duty on raw foreign cottons that should exclude those imported from South America. The South wanted, more than all, another opportunity to disarrange and perplex her pecuniary rival, the free laboring North. Not the slightest objection was it, in her eye, that some hundred millions of northern capital, as our northern statesmen demonstrated, would have to be sacrificed by the change. The high tariff of 1816 was forced upon the reluctant North by the same John C. Calhoun who had dictated the war of 1812. Northern capitalists demurred. They desired no capricious change. The merchants had rebuilt their ships, and wished for no interference with their "free trade." Of the few remaining manufacturers, some were also merchants, and nearly all of them, with singular unanimity, repudiated the policy of an artificial hot-bed growth of manufactures, predicting, sagaciously, the over production, the reaction, and the fluctuations afterwards realized by such violations of the law of supply and demand. But the North was overruled. Calhoun again triumphed. The Calcutta trade was annihilated, and our commerce with France and England reduced and shorn of its rich profits, in obedience to the new policy. Factory villages sprung up again like mushrooms. Thousands embarked in the new business. Over competition and over production ruined or crippled a large portion of them in four or five years, and instability and uncertainty became inscribed, legibly, upon their edifices and their fabrics. For the dozens who succeeded and amassed wealth, there were to be reckoned hundreds, if not thousands, who were driven into penury and oblivion.

The same memorable era, 1816, was marked by the establishment of a second National Bank, and by the same Slave Power that had dictated the two embargoes, the non-intercourse, the war, and the tariff. It was dictated by the same policy and to subserve the same end—the preservation of the balance of power between free and slave labor, or rather, the ascendency of the latter over the former. A National Bank was deemed unconstitutional in 1811, but it became constitutional in 1816, for the South, after all her depredations upon the North, now condescended to become a borrower of northern capital! Mr. Madison, in particular, whose constitutional scruples were insuperable, in 1811, overcame them in 1816, and not long afterwards became, it was said, a borrower from the National Bank of a large sum. Other slaveholding statesmen conferred upon the bank the same honor. But it cost the northern banks and the northern capitalists and merchants a severe money pressure of three or four years to spare sufficient specie to get the new National Bank under way. So that the pecuniary embarrassment of 1819–20, arising from a reaction of the high tariff policy, was increased by the process of re-establishing a National Bank, and both burthens fell at the same time upon the free laboring North. The general southern bankruptcy of 1824, renewed and aggravated by the southern cotton speculation of 1826, (an infamous process of gambling) trode rapidly upon the heels of the former inflictions of the Slave Power. An extensive, not to say general, bankruptcy visited Boston in 1824, and New York in 1826, from these joint causes, but chiefly from the accumulation of southern debts to the estimated amount of upwards of one hundred millions of dollars, of which, (as afterwards, in 1837,) scarcely five cents on the dollar were ever realized.

Precisely at what date the second United States Bank was effectually pillaged and reduced to bankruptcy by its slaveholding customers, is not certainly known, but it must have been at a very early period, probably in 1823, soon after its specie capital had been supplied, and chiefly by the over-confiding North. Its condition was for many years concealed, perhaps in the vain hope of retrieving its fortunes. At one time, it is said, the directors, having decided on making no more loans to the bankrupt South, adopted the policy of including the solvent North under the same restriction, lest offense should be taken at the invidious distinction, or the fact of southern delinquency at the bank be disclosed. Be this as it may, it proved to have been a rotten concern for years, while the public supposed it solvent. The Federal Government, as appointing a portion of the directors, comes in for a large share in the blame of this shameful mis-management. The bank was in the hands of demagogues, a tool of political corruption, and chiefly for the pecuniary and political emolument of the South at the expense and for the management and subjugation of the North, purchasing editors if not Senators by its loans. Like its predecessors, it was first robbed and then buried, and all through the action of the Federal Government, at the dictation of the Slave Power. A renewal of its charter was refused in 1832, a fortunate event, as it proved, though its insolvency was not suspected then. It expired by limitation of charter in 1836.

Free labor overcoming all its obstructions, contrived at length to flourish under the tariff system. The manufacturing capitalists became first reconciled and then wedded to the policy. Thriving under it, they sought no essential change. But northern labor had long been held incompetent to self-direction, and had been accustomed to watch the motions of the slave-driver. It adventured, however, a slight modification of the tariff in 1832, yet not departing from the principle and the policy upon which the system was founded, in 1816, by Mr. Calhoun. This temerity was made the pretext for demanding a revolution in the policy of the country. The principle of a protective tariff became unpopular at the South as soon as it was perceived that the free labor of the North was thriving under it, and the growth of this dissatisfaction was well nigh simultaneous with the desire to inter the second National Bank. The policy of protection first fastened upon the country by Mr. Calhoun, was now discovered by Mr. Calhoun and his party to be an infraction of the constitution, oppressive to the South, the climax of political injustice, and demanding a dissolution of the Union, unless speedily laid aside. After stretching the exercise of the powers of the Federal Government to the highest degree, by embargoes, war, tariff, and National Bank, the South now hoisted again the flag of "State Rights." A State Convention of South Carolina, under the influence of Mr. Calhoun, declared the tariff acts unconstitutional, null and void, that duties should not be paid, and that if the General Government attempted to enforce the claim, the state would withdraw from the Union. President Jackson could do no less than repel this demand, but through the intervention of Mr.

Clay, a former champion of the protective policy, a compromise was made, by which the duties were gradually reduced till 1843, when they were to sink to the general level of 20 per cent., which was accounted the revenue standard. In recent debates in the Senate concerning the Mexican war, Mr. Webster of Massachusetts, representing the cotton manufacturers of that state, reminded southern Senators that the expenses of such a war would require an additional tariff. At this there was no demur,—not even from Mr. Calhoun; and it is understood that the prospect of a high tariff reconciled the manufacturing capitalists of New England to that iniquitous war.

Thus Slavery controls all the leading measures of the nation and moulds its political economy,—quite as remarkable for its real and inflexible CONSTANCY as for its apparently capricious CHANGE. A comparison of dates, as before hinted, will show how exactly all these changes have corresponded and chimed in with the more direct and palpable action of the Federal Government in support of slavery. Whenever such *direct* action, by the Government or by combinations, has been suspended, a more active control and a more rapid change of general measures has supplied the deficiency. And when the *general* policy of the country has been for any length of time undisturbed, it has been because more *direct* measures in support of slavery have been in progress. Thus, from 1807, on the explosion of the Southern and Western Conspiracy, till the first armed invasion of Texas, in 1819, the slave interest was sufficiently promoted by embargoes, non-intercourse, war, tariff, the destruction of the first National Bank, and the establishment of the second. So, likewise, from 1836 to 1850, while so much direct action in favor of slavery has been witnessed, the questions of tariffs and banks have been left comparatively undisturbed.

With equal skill and tact has the slave power contrived to keep up two political parties, extending through the North and the South, on the most fallacious and deceptive issues, or upon scarcely any issue at all. By this means she diverts attention from the real to the merely nominal issues before the country, while by controlling both parties, she secures her ends through the ascendency of either, makes the one a check upon the other, and manages them through fear or through hope.

THE STATE GOVERNMENTS.

This chapter on the action of the Federal Government in support of slavery, might be appropriately followed by an account of the action of the State Governments, even at the North, in a similar direction. Our limits forbid us to enter into these details. Suffice it to say that most of the free States are disgraced by constitutional or legislative provisions discriminating, invidiously, between white and colored citizens, and depriving the latter of their equal rights of suffrage and eligibility to office. Colored citizens of the free States, employed on board ships visiting the South, are subject to seizure and imprisonment, in violation of their constitutional rights. An effort was made by Massachusetts to obtain a legal redress of these grievances in the courts of South Carolina and Louisiana. But her Commissioners, Messrs. Hoare and Hubbard, were ejected from Charleston and New Orleans under threats of violence, and Massachusetts submits to the insult. In Ohio there were laws enacted designed to prevent the settlement of colored citizens in that State. In Connecticut a law was passed prohibiting schools for teaching colored pupils. But these laws of Ohio and Connecticut have been repealed. Both the enactment and the repeal of these two laws—it may be proper to say—took place during the present agitation of the slave question by abolitionists.

We have carefully confined ourselves in these chapters (as in the preceding ones concerning "the Position of the Churches") to the course that has been pursued *in respect to slavery*, disconnected from any controversies about the measures of "modern abolitionists," or statements concerning the opposition raised against them. And we deem it no vain repetition to propound again, here, the inquiry—Is it credible that those who hold such a position in respect to slavery could have been otherwise than annoyed and offended by any earnest efforts for its immediate and unconditional abolition?

Some further light on this question may be afforded in our next chapter, exhibiting a movement in which the prominent actors, in political and ecclesiastical life, combined their forces and commingled their labors.

CHAPTER XXIX.

COLONIZATION SOCIETY.

Originated with Slaveholders—Object—Discourages emancipation, yet professes to favor it—Violates its own Constitution, by denying to the people of color their rights of citizenship—Justifies Slavery—Condemns emancipation—Slanders the people of color—Justifies oppression—Declares prejudice against color invincible —Pledged, in advance, to oppose Abolition Societies—The representatives of the leading political and ecclesiastical influences of the country—Its leaders in sympathy with the Fugitive Slave Bill—Meeting at Boston—False pretenses of checking the African slave trade and evangelizing Africa.

THE American Colonization Society, with its auxiliaries, is sustained by the leading influences in the *Church* and in the *State*. The position of these, in respect to American Slavery, has already been shown. It would be strange if the Society should differ widely from the course and policy of those who originated it, and who give shape to its measures. Its two-fold character of ecclesiastical and political gives it a wide range. It takes its place in the list of our religious anniversaries, is advocated in the pulpit on the Sabbath, is claimed to be a missionary institution, asks patronage and accepts the widow's mite as a benevolent enterprise; yet it proposes to build up an empire in Africa; for many years it superintended a colonial government in Liberia;* has received indirect aid from Congress, and large funds from State legislatures. Its friends give a two-fold account of its origin. Sometimes they say it was devised and planned by Rev. Samuel J. Mills, a young minister earnestly intent on evangelizing Africa. Some-

---

* The Colony has at length become independent of the Society, yet the Society continues, in other respects, its operations.

times they commend it as having originated in the political sagacity of popular statesmen, Mr. Jefferson, Mr. Clay, Mr. Mercer, and Mr. Madison, *not* remarkable, *all* of them, for evangelizing enterprise. The authentic account appears to be as follows :

1. ORIGIN.—The entire movement grew out of an alarm caused by an attempted slave insurrection. Hence the effort of the Virginia Legislature to induce Congress to colonize free blacks. This measure failing, a society for the purpose was formed.

In December, 1816, the Legislature of Virginia passed a resolution requesting the Governor to correspond with the President of the United States, for the purpose of obtaining territory in Africa or elsewhere for colonizing free people of color and those who might afterwards become free.

A few days afterwards a meeting was held in Washington City composed of southern gentlemen, at which Judge Washington, a slaveholder and slave-vender, presided, and Henry Clay and Mr. Randolph, slaveholders, made speeches. The result was the organization of the American Colonization Society. Judge Washington was chosen President. Seventeen Vice-Presidents were chosen, twelve of whom were in the slave states, and probably slaveholders. The twelve managers were also slaveholders.

2. OBJECT.—"The object to which its attention is to be *exclusively* directed, is to promote and execute a plan for colonizing, (with their consent) the free people of color residing in our country in Africa, or such other place as *Congress* shall deem most expedient. And the Society shall act to effect this object in co-operation with the *General Government* and such of the *States* as may adopt regulations on the subject."—*Con. of the Society, Art. II.*

The "*exclusive*" object here specified precludes and denies the claim of missionary and anti-slavery objects afterwards set up at the North to obtain patronage. The reference to the General and State Governments shows that the "object" was such as those governments were expected to favor. The

Constitution has no Preamble with statements of reasons or motives for Colonization, and gives no hints whether its operations were expected to facilitate emancipation or strengthen slavery. This ambiguity has enabled its advocates to urge one class of arguments at the North and an opposite class at the South, and obtain funds from both the friends and the enemies of slavery. But the *real* object may be known from its operations, of which we present a specimen. The Maryland Colonization Society, auxiliary to the American, received large funds from the State Legislature with which it transported to Africa, in 1834, "two ship loads of colored people, who were coerced as truly as if it had been done with a cart-whip." So said Rev. R. J. Breckenridge D.D., a member of the American Colonization Society, at its annual meeting, the same year. This policy the gentleman censured at the time, but has since openly defended it, as did likewise Mr. Brodnax, in the Legislature of Virginia, when a bill was under discussion, making appropriations to the same object. "It is idle," said Mr. Brodnax, "to talk about not resorting to force. Everybody must look to the introduction of force of some kind or other. If the free negroes are willing to go, they will go. If not, they must be COMPELLED to go." There was a clause in the bill for compulsory transportation. This was, indeed, stricken out to save appearances, but the end was nevertheless reached, by menaces, and ill treatment.

The desired effects of colonization have been abundantly stated in the publications of the Society, and the speeches and writings of its members.

"The execution of this scheme would augment, instead of diminish, the value of the property left behind."—*African Repository* (the Society's organ), Vol. I., p. 227.

"By removing the most fruitful source of discontent (free blacks) from among our slaves, we should render them more industrious and attentive to our commands."—*Address Putnam Co. Geo. Col. Soc.*

"The tendency of the scheme, and one of its OBJECTS, is to SECURE SLAVEHOLDERS and the whole Southern country against certain evil consequences growing out of the present three-fold mixture of our population."—*Address of a Virginia Col. Soc., Af. Rep.*, IV., 274.

"By removing these people (free blacks) we rid ourselves of a large party who will always be ready to assist our slaves in any mischievous design they might conceive."—*Af. Rep.*, I., 176.

"By thus repressing the increase of blacks, the white population would be enabled to reach, and soon overtake them: the consequence would be SECURITY."—*Af. Rep.*, IV., 344.

It would be easy to fill a long chapter with testimonies to this single point. We are warranted, therefore, in saying that the GRAND OBJECT of the Colonization Society is the increased profitableness and security of slavery.

3. IT DISCOURAGES EMANCIPATION.—The Colonization Society has been patronized at the North, under the idea, held up by its agents, that it encourages and assists slaveholders to emancipate and colonize their slaves. It is true that some emancipations have been made in connection with colonization. But the efforts of the Society have been chiefly directed to the colonization of the free. And it is found that the ratio of emancipations, since the Society was formed, has greatly decreased, on the whole. Neither Judge Washington, Henry Clay, Mr. Madison, nor Mr. Carroll, slaveholding Presidents of the Society, have ever emancipated and colonized a single slave, though Judge Washington sold fifty-four at one time, to be sent to New Orleans! The whole amount of the colonization of manumitted slaves, in eighteen years, ending in 1835, was *eight hundred and nine*, equal to the increase of slave population for FIVE DAYS AND A HALF !* It is not known that the process has been more rapid since.

And yet, *colonization* was constantly held up, then and afterwards, as *the only* safe and proper mode of emancipation, thus quieting the consciences of those who thought they could not spare (or who, in fact, could not command) the additional expenses of transportation to Africa.

"Colonization is the ONLY possible mode of emancipation at once safe and rational."—*Speech of Mr. Custiss, 13th An. Report.*

---

* Up to about this time the funds raised by the Society amounted to $220,449, and it had incurred a debt of $45,645, making an expenditure of $266,094.—*Jay's Inquiry*, p. 78.

"Colonization is the ONLY expedient by which these evils (of slavery) can be mitigated."—*Speech of J. A. Dix, Af. Rep.,* IV., 108.

" To this country it offers the ONLY possible means of gradually ridding ourselves of a mighty evil."—*1st Rep. N. Y. Col. Soc.*

" I would urge this system of Colonization, as the ONLY rational plan that has yet been suggested for relieving our Southern brethren of the curse of slavery."—*Speech of Chancellor Walworth.*

A moderate use of common sense and of the rudiments of arithmetic should have sufficed to dispel the delusion of terminating American Slavery by the colonization of the slaves to Africa. It is astonishing how such a project could have imposed itself upon the credulity of the shrewd and calculating people of the North. Emancipation on the soil had been the policy of the northern and eastern states. No other process of abolishing slavery had ever been known or attempted anywhere. The revolutionary fathers, who had sought and expected the abolition of slavery, had expected it in no other way. Before the forming of the Colonization Society in 1816, no friend of freedom advocated any other method. But in a few brief years the propagandists of colonization had saturated the public mind with their new and whimsical dogma. From the pulpit, from the forum, from the press, from halls of legislation, and by itinerating agents, the proposition was continuously reiterated, with all the solemnity of an oracle, that emancipation and colonization must, of necessity, go hand in hand ! The idea came, at length, to be regarded with the reverence due to a self-evident truth, and to question it was to incur suspicion of insanity.

The influence of this sentiment upon the process of emancipation cannot be doubtful. Emancipations on the soil had been constantly going on, at the South, till the doctrine was proclaimed that the free people of color, as a nuisance, must be removed out of the country, and that future emancipations and transportations must go hand in hand. To emancipate and colonize, even when practicable, was a double burden, and all *other* emancipation was now, by the new formed public sentiment, proscribed.

Equally and necessarily proscriptive was the same doctrine, against all plans and efforts to procure a general abolition of slavery *on the soil*, and no other general abolition would be practicable. It might have been predicted, beforehand, that the influence of the Colonization Society would be arrayed against any earnest efforts for the abolition of slavery. It could not be otherwise, while the Society held the language we have quoted, insisting that colonization was the ONLY method of emancipation. And this has involved the Society in the positions hereafter specified.

4. IN VIOLATION OF ITS OWN CONSTITUTION, IT DENIES TO THE FREE PEOPLE OF COLOR THEIR ESSENTIAL RIGHTS OF RESIDENCE IN THE LAND OF THEIR BIRTH, AND IT DENIES THE RIGHT OF THE SLAVE TO EMANCIPATION ON THE SOIL. This is proved by the course of the Maryland and Virginia auxiliaries, and also by the speeches of Dr. Breckenridge and Mr. Brodnax, already quoted. We add another testimony from the highest authority, and of a recent date:

Hon. Henry Clay, in his recent letter to Richard Pindell, (see *New York Tribune*, March 10th, 1849,) "after full and deliberate consideration of the subject," lays it down " as an indispensable condition (of emancipation) that the emancipated slaves should be removed from the State to some colony." " The colonization of the free blacks, as they successively arrive, from year to year, at the age entitling them to freedom, I consider a condition absolutely indispensable. Without it I would be opposed to any scheme of emancipation." The expense of this expatriation is, says Mr. Clay, to "be defrayed by a fund to be raised from the labor of each freed slave." The Af. Repository, April, 1849, says, let the North " show unto us a more excellent way," IF THEY CAN.

"In no other way could (can) it (slavery) be removed, than by planting colonies of free colored people on the coast of Africa." *Speech of Rev. Dr. Bethune at Col. meeting, Phila., Af. Rep., July,* 1846, p. 222.

" He (the colored man) is an exotic that does not and cannot flourish in American soil." *Address of Judge Bullock, Ky., commended by editor of Af. Rep., Ap.* 1847, p. 103.

"No! There is no place for them in this country. It is not their land, and they never can be made at home here. There are difficulties in the way which no power of man can remove." *Af. Rep. Nov.,* 1846, p. 348.

5. It justifies slavery.

"We hold their slaves, as we hold their *other* property, *sacred*." (*Af. Rep.* I., 283.) "We know your rights, and we respect them." (*Ib.* VII., 100.) "It" (the Society) condemns no man because he is a slave-holder." (*Ib.* VII., 200.) "Acknowledging the necessity by which its (slavery's) present continuance and *rigorous* provisions for its *maintenance*, are JUSTIFIED." (*Ib.* III., 16.) "We believe that there is not the slightest turpitude in holding slaves, under present circumstances." (*Ib.* IX., 4.)

"You cannot abolish slavery, for God is pledged to sustain it."—*Letters to Hon. George P. Marsh, copied into Maryland Colonization Journal, September 6, 1847, p. 44.*

"Slavery in the United States has resulted, and is destined still more to result in the permanent good and advancement of the negro race."—*Letter, &c.*, p. 99.

6. It not only discourages but condemns emancipation.

"Policy, and even the voice of humanity, *forbid* the progress of manumission." (*Af. Rep.*, IV., 268.) "It would be as humane to throw them from the decks in the middle passage, as to set them free in our country."—*Ib.* IV., 226.

7. It slanders the free people of color. Without doing this, and fostering prejudice against them, the scheme of colonizing them would have found little or no favor.

"Free blacks are a greater nuisance than even slaves themselves."—*Af. Rep.* II., 189.

"This class of persons is a curse and a contagion wherever they reside." —*Ib.* III., 203.

"A class the most corrupt, depraved, and abandoned."—*H. Clay, Ib.* 12.

"An anomalous race of beings, the most depraved upon earth."—*Ib.* VII., 230.

"They constitute a class by themselves, out of which no individual can be elevated, and below which none can be depressed."—*Ib.* VI., 118.

"With some honorable exceptions, the free negroes are, as a class, indolent, vicious, and dishonest."—*Memorial to Leg. of Va., Af. Rep. Am. Col. Soc.*, Jan., 1846, p. 45.

Speaking of the 60,000 free colored inhabitants of Virginia, the above memorial says, "Worthless and more than worthless."—P. 48.*

---

* Compare these representations with the following:—Says Mr. Clay, "Each *emigrant* is a *missionary*, carrying with him credentials in the holy cause of religion, civilization, and *free institutions!*" And so Africa is to be evangelized by sending out our *nuisances* as *missionaries!*

8. It justifies their oppression.

" Severe necessity places them (free negroes) in a class of degraded beings." (*Af. Rep.*, V., 238.) " This law," (by which *free* negroes are *enslaved* unless they leave the State,) " odious and unjust as it may, at first view, appear, &c., was doubtless dictated by *sound policy*, and its repeal would be regarded with none by more unfeigned regret than by the friends of African colonization."—*Powhattan Col. Soc.*

9. It discourages their education and elevation.

" If the free people of color were generally taught *to read*, it might be an inducement to them to remain in this country. We would offer them no such inducement."—*Southern Religious Telegraph, Presbyterian.*

" It must appear evident to all, that *every endeavor* to divert the attention of the community, or even a portion of the means which the present crisis so imperatively calls for, from the Colonization Society, to measures calculated to bind the colored population to this country, and seeking to raise them to a level with the whites, *whether by founding colleges or in any other way*, tends directly in proportion that it succeeds, to counteract and thwart the whole plan of colonization."—*New Haven, Conn. Religious Intelligencer, Congregational, July*, 1831.

This frank avowal discloses the cause of the opposition made in Connecticut, by leading colonizationists, soon after, to the establishment of schools for colored children and youth in Canterbury and New Haven. The writer remembers when colored children were freely admitted to the public schools in Connecticut, and when there were no separate pews for negroes in the village and country churches. The growth of prejudice has kept equal pace with the progress, influence, and popularity of the Colonization Society.

10. It declares the prejudice against them innocent and incurable. This ground is assumed in self-vindication. For if the prejudice be criminal, the Society is a transgressor. And if it be cured, the enterprise of colonization becomes an abortion.

" All the prejudices of society—prejudices which neither refinement, nor argument, nor education, *nor religion itself can subdue*—mark the people of color, whether bond or free, as the subjects of a degradation *inevitable and incurable.*"—*Address Conn. Col. Soc.*

" Christianity cannot do for them here, what it will do for them in Africa. This is not the fault of the colored man, nor of the white man, but an ordination of Providence, and no more to be changed than the laws of nature."—*Fifteenth Annual Report*, 47.

11. IT WAS PLEDGED IN ADVANCE TO OPPOSE ABOLITION SOCIETIES.

" The Society having declared that it is in no wise allied to *any* Abolition Society, in America or elsewhere, is ready, *when there is need*, to PASS A CENSURE upon such Societies in America."—*Eleventh Annual Report*.

This was in January, 1828, more than four years before the organization of the Massachusetts Anti-Slavery Society, the earliest of the "modern" Societies. There had been no "abolition Societies" in the country, except those formed by Jay, Franklin, &c., soon after the Revolutionary war, and which were now nearly or quite extinct. The possible resuscitation of *those* Societies, or the organization of *similar* ones, must have been the contingency in view of which this gratuitous pledge of "censure" was given, in advance of any knowledge of their particular measures. No reference to the future and unforeseen "fanaticism" or "imprudence" of "modern abolitionists," who had not then appeared, can furnish an explanation of this measure. Hostility to any efforts for the abolition of slavery is evident upon the very face of the declaration.

Such was the Colonization Society, such its positions, and such its influence, at the commencement of the present agitation of the slave question. And such they remain still. Philanthropists and friends of the enslaved were, for a long time, deceived and misled by it, regarding it as an instrument for the abolition of slavery, and some such possibly are deceived by it still, though hundreds of thousands have deserted and abjured it.

The Colonization Society has been, and still is, the true representative of the leading men in Church and State, on the subject of slavery. It furnishes the central point of their united efforts on that subject, where the political and ecclesiastical elements controlling the Church and the State (in the manner described in the preceding chapters) are conjoined. The same statesmen who have controlled our Cabinets and

Senates, the same theologians, professors, and doctors of divinity, who have controlled our General Assemblies, General Associations, General Conferences, Synods, Bible and Tract Societies, and Missionary Boards, have come together and formed and controlled the Colonization Society. The same imposing array of honorable and reverend names are paraded on the various catalogues, and their doings and their policy are the same. Posterity will award to the one the same praise or blame that they do to the other.

After twenty years' discussion, the course and the character of the Colonization Society are not changed. Whatever may be said of other bodies, the increase of light, and the diffusion of intelligence, have made no impression on the Colonization Society. It represents the class of politicians and ecclesiastics resolutely opposed to liberty and progress. Among its leaders are the advocates and apologists of the new Fugitive Slave Bill—who preach against the paramount claims of "higher law." The infamous slave hunts resulting from the so-called "compromise measures," seem to have infused new life into it, and restored the energy it exhibited during the ascendency of pro-slavery riots, and the attempted legislative suppression of free discussion, from 1834 to 1837, of which some account will appear in the proper place.

The Massachusetts Colonization Society held its Annual Meeting in Boston, May 26, 1852. Rev. Dr. Derby, of Philadelphia, made a speech, in which he insisted that the colored people can never have their political rights in this country. He "was born in the South, had been nursed by a slave woman, had seen the black man under all circumstances, and in all parts of the United States, and yet he had never seen one that was a man."—"He dwelt at some length on the great blessing American slavery is conferring on the slave, in affording him an opportunity to become acquainted with Christianity, and secure the salvation of his soul." And yet, according to the same speaker, he could never rise in this country, and must therefore be colonized to Africa. Among the officers and prominent members of the Society present, "were many supporters of Mr. Webster and the Fugitive Slave law, and signers of the celebrated letter to him, congratulating him upon his 7th of March speech, in support of that bill of abominations." Among these was Rev. Dr. Woods, who pronounced the benediction at the close. "These gentlemen, grayheaded Doctors of Divinity, and cotton politicians of Boston, thumped their canes right heartily at the speech" of Dr. Derby. Robert Morris, Esq., a colored lawyer, of Boston, rose modestly, and wished to ask a few questions, but was refused.—Vide *N. Y. Daily Tribune*, May 28, 1852.

It remains to say that the pretensions of the Colonization Society of doing much to evangelize Africa, and to check and limit the slave trade, have been found to be in keeping with its other pretensions.

As late as 1833 or '34, Rev. Dr. Spring of New York, at a colonization meeting in that city, lamented that the Society had *done nothing* for the religious instruction of the emigrants. The remedy he proposed was the employment of missionaries by the managers, acting as a Civil Government, at the expense of the colony, disregarding the objection urged that it would be (as he admitted it would) a "union of Church and State." But his measure was not adopted. J. B. Pinney, who was sent out as a missionary, became Governor of the colony. On his return, in 1836, he told the writer of this book that *nothing* was doing for the conversion of the *natives*. In 1839, Mr. Wilson, the Missionary of the American Board, which is controlled by Colonizationists, affirmed that the neighborhood of the colony was not a proper station for a missionary, and that remoteness from the settlements was far more desirable. (*See Missionary Herald, Sept.*, 1839.)

Rum, gunpowder, and spear-pointed knives, have been among the regular exports from this country to the colony of Liberia. These are sold to the natives, and especially to the slave traders, being the indispensable articles of their traffic, and the causes of the wars that furnish captives to be sold to them as slaves. The slave trade, instead of being repressed, (as had been pretended) has been stimulated and encouraged.

The colonists have maintained a regular traffic with them, and have visited their stations for that purpose. Shackles have been sold to them at the colonial settlement at Mensurado. The pages even of the African Repository (the Society's official) bore testimony, in 1828, that the trade was increasing.* In 1837 or '38, Dr. Goheen, agent of the Society, residing at Liberia, wrote *in defense* of the slave trade, and his letters were published without rebuke in the colonization papers of this country.

Liberia has now become an independent Government. The political control of the Colonization Society over it has terminated, but it continues to busy itself with the task (according to its own account) of supplying it with " nuisances " whom " Christianity can never elevate in this country" for " missionaries" and "statesmen"—to "evangelize the heathen, and build up an empire in Africa!"

---

* We have not room for the particulars; but if the reader will refer to JAY'S INQUIRY, pp. 55 to 61 (sixth edition), he will find ample evidence, furnished by the Colonization Society itself, that the boast of suppressing the slave trade was unfounded, and that it was even *carried on in the Colony.*

CHAPTER XXX.

ABOLITION OF SLAVERY IN THE BRITISH COLONIES.

Premature triumphs over the supposed abolition of the Slave Trade—Effects of this illusion from 1807 till 1823—Revival of anti-slavery effort in England—Organization of a Society on the basis of gradualism—Writings of Elizabeth Heyrick in favor of *immediatism*—Pamphlet of Clarkson on the *illegality* of Slavery—Change of views and measures—Increased efficiency—Petitions to Parliament—Commencement of Anti-Slavery Reporter, 1825—Parliamentary discussions, 1828-9-30—Anti-Slavery meetings—Eminent Advocates—Methodist Conferences, Rectors and Curates, and Doctors of Divinity, enlisted—Dr. Andrew Thomson of Edinburgh, Bishop of Bath and Wells—Daniel O'Connell, George Thompson and others—Protest of Clarkson and Wilberforce against American Colonization Society—Other political reforms advanced abolition—Ministry of William IV.—Prominent statesmen—Influences in the West Indies—Missionaries among the Slaves—Opposed by the planters—Increased feeling in England—Numerous petitions—Candidates for Parliament questioned—Treatise of Judge Jeremie—Persecutions of the Missionaries—Outrages against the negroes, 1831—Trial of Mr. Knibb—His return to England—Increased agitation—Memorials of Missionary Societies—Government orders the demolished chapels to be rebuilt—Orders insolently disregarded—Committees of Inquiry in Parliament—Pretended preparations for freedom—Witnesses examined before Parliamentary Committees—Feeble defenses of the Slave party—Plans of emancipation—Passage of the Act of Abolition—Apprenticeship—Final Results—Testimonials—Slavery abolished in the British East Indies—Lessons of instruction.

THE slave trade and the slavery of this country, during its colonial state, were substantially the same with the slave trade and the slavery of the other British American Colonies, including the British West India Islands. A common origin, a common character, and a common relation to British law and to the British Government, pertained to them. They grew up together, claiming the shelter of the same royal grants, the same acts of Parliament for regulating the trade to Africa. They claimed the benefit of the same judicial precedents and legal opinions. The friends of liberty in England, for a century past, have sympathized and corresponded with those in this country, on the subject. It seems proper to present a brief account of the recent anti-slavery struggle in Great Britain and Ireland, the abolition of slavery in the British West Indies, and the results of that measure.

The error of supposing that the slave trade could be, in reality, abolished, while slavery itself was permitted to exist has been already noticed,* as also the kindred error of supposing that the abolition of the slave trade, even if it could be accomplished, would virtually abolish slavery.† These delusions prevailed among the friends of liberty, on both sides of the Atlantic, with few and solitary exceptions. The legal abolition of the African slave trade by Great Britain and America, in 1807–8, was hailed as the grand jubilee of the colored race. The warfare was supposed to have been accomplished, and that nothing more remained but to celebrate the achievement, and immortalize the names of the victors. Celebrations were held, orations were delivered, pictures were painted and engraved, and poems were written and dedicated to noble Dukes.‡ Nothing, in fact, in the way of gratulation, triumph, and glorification, was left undone. Demonstrations, to a certain extent, in this direction, might have been very well, had they been so shaped as to furnish incentives to farther and similar efforts, not forgetting that the slaves were still left in their chains, that not one of them had been released by the prohibition of the slave *trade*, and that, in Great Britain at least, the measure had been carried, in certain circles, by arguments conceding the undisturbed continuance of slavery itself. As it was, the gratulation was disproportionate and premature, tending to relax effort, to repress inquiry, and discountenance further aggressive measures. On both sides of the Atlantic has this influence been felt; and in America it is felt still. We content ourselves to garnish the sepulchres of the early British and American abolitionists, while refusing to give effect to their labors.

---

* Chapter VII.   † Chapter X.   ‡ *Copley's History of Slavery*, 311.

It required the whole time from 1807 to 1823, for British abolitionists to recollect that the slaves in the colonies were still in bondage, and to discover that the African slave trade* was undiminished in extent and horrors. Even then the measures adopted were inadequate to the exigency.

In 1823 was formed the "Society for the *mitigation* and *gradual* abolition of slavery throughout the British dominions," of which the "Patron and President was the Duke of Gloucester." Among the Vice Presidents, twenty in number, were the Marquis of Lansdowne, the Earl of Bristol, Earl Nugent, Lord Suffield, Lord Calvert, Henry Brougham, M. P., Thos. Fowell Buxton, M. P., Thomas Clarkson, Stephen Lushington, LL.D., M. P., and William Wilberforce, M. P., &c. Among the Committee were James Cropper, Esq., of Liverpool, Samuel Gurney, Esq., Zachary Macauley, Esq., T. B. Macauley, Esq., Thomas Sturge, Esq., Wm. Wilberforce, Jun., Esq., and Rev. H. Venn.

The ground of immediate and unconditional emancipation was not yet taken by the great body of British abolitionists, as the name of this society gives evidence :

" About this time considerable attention was excited by a small tract, widely circulated, entitled ' Immediate, not gradual, Abolition, or an Inquiry into the shortest, safest, and most effectual means of getting rid of West Indian Slavery.' This tract, though published anonymously, was generally understood to be the production of a talented and benevolent Lady, Miss Hope, of Liverpool."†—*Copley's History*, p. 329.

The more common and prevalent account, however, is, that Elizabeth Heyrick was the first public advocate, in England, of the doctrine of immediate and unconditional abolition, as

---

* It should be mentioned, perhaps, that Messrs. Stephen and Wilberforce, in 1816, introduced and supported in Parliament the Registry Bill, designed to " prevent the illicit introduction of slaves from Africa," which was carried against a strong opposition from the Colonists and their partisans. But the history of the slave trade, since that time, as already shown (Chap. VII.), demonstrates the utter inefficiency of all measures for its suppression, during the continuance of slavery.

† On inquiry, since writing the above, we have been told, on authority of John Scoble, of London, that the pamphlet here attributed to Miss Hope was written by Elizabeth Heyrick (or rather Herrick, which is now said to be the correct spelling.)

before taught by Hopkins and Edwards in America, and that she was the author of a pamphlet in vindication of that doctrine.—Vide *British Reforms and Reformers*, by H. B. Stanton.

Another advance position, of almost equal importance, was, about this time, taken, in a pamphlet by the venerable Thomas Clarkson. The reader will recall the fact, already noticed, that little progress was made in Parliament towards the legislative prohibition of the slave trade, until William Pitt demonstrated, on a certain occasion in the House of Commons, that the slave trade (all its high pretensions of legality notwithstanding) had been, from the beginning, *illegal*. A similar position was now taken by Mr. Clarkson, concerning *slavery itself*, in the British Colonies. In doing this, however, he only revived and re-affirmed the old doctrine of Granville Sharp.*

In this pamphlet Mr. Clarkson showed, to the satisfaction of the British people, that there never had been any *legal* slavery in any of the British Colonies. All had been usurpation and assumption from the beginning.

He affirmed "that the planters can neither prove a moral nor a *legal* right to their slaves." Having examined the moral right of the claim, he proceeded to argue the *illegality* of slavery:

" He brought the slaveholder's claim to the test of original grants, or permissions of Government, act of Parliament, charters, or English laws." He showed " that neither the African slave trade, nor West Indian slavery would have been allowed at first, but for the misrepresentations and falsehoods of those engaged in them "—" that the original Government grants and permissions had their origin in fraud and falsehood ; and if the *premises* fall, all conclusions and concessions grounded on them must fall, too."— " Then, as to *charters*—slavery had indeed been upheld and kept together by the laws which the charters gave those Colonies power to make ; that now SLAVERY, NEVERTHELESS, WAS ILLEGAL, for in all the charters it was expressed that the laws and statutes made under them must not be repugnant, but conformable to the laws of Great Britain. But these did not allow of slavery."—" Indeed, the slaveholders themselves admitted that if debarred whatever was repugnant to the laws of England, they did not see how they could have any title to their slaves, likely to be supported by

---

† See Chap. VI.

the laws of England. In fact, the Colonial system was at constant variance with the whole spirit and letter of the English Constitution."—*Copley's Hist.*, pp. 317–18.

There can be no doubt that the dissemination and reception of these views exerted a most powerful influence in producing a Parliamentary prohibition of slavery in the Colonies of Great Britain. It is difficult to conceive how these views could be controverted without virtually demanding a reversal of the decision of Lord Mansfield in the Somerset case, in 1772; and equally difficult to see why, if that decision was correct, the reasoning and the inferences of Mr. Clarkson do not apply to the Continental as well as to the Island Colonies of Great Britain, continuing, as they did, until July 4, 1776, under the ægis of Great Britain. This being established, it would be natural to inquire whether or how the memorable Declaration of the States, at that date, could have legalized the previously illegal slavery of this country.

But to return. The meliorating and gradual policy terminated, as might have been foreseen. The British Government, in response to anti-slavery petitions, entered readily into measures for mitigating the condition of slavery, as cheap as they were useless, proposing to provide means of religious instruction for the slaves, to extend their privileges, to receive their testimony in courts, to protect their rights of marriage and property, to remove obstructions to manumissions, to prevent the separation of families, to restrain the power of arbitrary punishment, especially the flogging of females, and to establish a Savings' Bank for the use of slaves. All these reforms were committed to the care of the Colonial Legislatures, showing that the British Government and people had much to learn concerning slavery and slaveholding legislators. This was in 1823.

These moderate concessions were rejected and trampled upon by the local authorities as subversive of all the control of the master over the slave, ruinous to the Colonies, and unsafe for the inhabitants.

In 1825, the Anti-Slavery Society commenced publishing

and circulating " *The Monthly Anti-Slavery Reporter*," by
Zachary Macauley, Esq., the father of Thomas B. Macauley,
the Essayist and Historian. The second Annual Report
lamented that so little had been accomplished for the benefit
of the slaves. Very little indeed had been attempted in the
Colonies, and even this had proved a failure. The slaves
understood that the home Government had provided something for them, which had been withheld. This made them
the more discontented, and these discontents were magnified
by the enemies of progress, and turned into arguments against
it. Petitions were now circulated for the abolition of slavery
in the Colonies.

During two sessions of Parliament, little was done except
in respect to particular abuses, as the persecution and expulsion of certain missionaries and free persons of color, &c.,
also in respect to the Mauritius slave trade, the conduct of the
Colonial Assemblies in rejecting or delaying the proposed
reforms, &c. Much important information came to light in
the discussions. In 1828, the discussion of this latter topic
was resumed. The Secretary of State, Mr. Huskisson, represented that some improvements had been made. Mr. Canning, then deceased, was quoted as having said, " Trust not
the masters of slaves in what concerns legislation for slavery."
A great public anti-slavery meeting was held, the Duke of
Gloucester presiding, and Mr. Brougham, Mr. Wilberforce,
Mr. Buxton, Rev. G. Noel, and other distinguished men, took
a part in the proceedings. From this time petitions against
slavery began to load both Houses of Parliament.

In May, 1829, Mr. Brougham introduced in Parliament the
subject of slave evidence, and a reform of Colonial judicature.
Sir George Murray agreed to the propriety of this measure.
Anti-slavery petitions were now multiplied. Discussions became general, and earnest debates among the people were
frequent. Important meetings were held in different portions
of Great Britain and Ireland. The Catholic emancipation
bill brought in a new accession of strength from Ireland to

the cause of the enslaved. The friends of liberty were encouraged also by the abolition of slavery in Mexico.

In May, 1830, a general meeting of the Anti-Slavery Society was held, Mr. Wilberforce presiding; called to the Chair by Mr. Clarkson. The result was an earnest petition to Parliament no longer to postpone the subject, but to fix a day, after which all children born should be free.

This petition was presented to the House of Commons by Mr. Brougham, in July. A motion made by him, pledging the House "to take steps for the immediate mitigation and final abolition of slavery," was lost, fifty-six against twenty-seven.

"Meantime, public meetings were held, and anti-slavery petitions prepared throughout the kingdom. One petition from Edinburgh received twenty-two thousand signatures, and from other places in like proportion."

Men of learning, talent, piety, and influence, espoused the cause in public meetings, and missionaries who had been driven home from their field of labor in the West Indies, appeared in these meetings to bear their testimony against the slave system. The question became a political one, and elections to Parliament turned on the position of the candidates. *The Methodist Conferences and ministers, in a body, exhorted their brethren, for the love of Christ, to vote for no candidates not known as pledged to the cause of abolition.* Rectors and curates of the Established Church, as well as ministers of the dissenting sects, took an active part in anti-slavery meetings, and even lectured from place to place. Doctors of Divinity, instead of searching their Bibles in quest of apologies for slaveholding, made use of them for the purpose of urging upon the people and their rulers the duty of "breaking every yoke, and letting the oppressed go free." Among these, Rev. Andrew Thomson, D.D., of Edinburgh, signalized himself as a most efficient public advocate of immediate emancipation. The influence and the efforts of such men as Rev. John Angell James, of Birmingham, and the Rev. J. G. Pike (the author of "Persuasives to Early Piety"), were enlisted on the same side. In one word, the learning and the piety of Great Britain were earnestly, honestly, and without reserve or equivocation, thrown into the anti-slavery enterprise.

At an anti-slavery meeting in Bath, the Bishop of Bath and Wells presided, and Mr. Wilberforce, after forty years labor to secure gradual and prospective measures, came forward to advocate immediate action. At this meeting an attempt was made to create a disturbance by clamor and hisses. Order being restored, a debate was held on the claims of the slave-holders to compensation.

The excitement in the country ran high. " At Bristol, a most disgraceful uproar was made by the upholders of slavery, who interrupted a meeting, regularly commenced." At a subsequent meeting, there was an earnest debate.

It was during the agitation and debates of this period that George Thompson, who afterwards lectured for a time in this country, became distinguished as an eloquent advocate of the cause, and acquired a reputation which afterwards gave him a seat in Parliament. Charles Stuart, also well known to the friends of liberty in this country, rendered efficient services at that period, both by his pen and his voice. Joseph Sturge, of Birmingham, a wealthy and talented gentleman, of the Society of Friends, was among the efficient laborers in the cause, as was also John Scoble, of London, the laborious and vigilant Secretary of the British and Foreign Anti-Slavery Society.

The doctrines and measures of gradualism and melioration were now abandoned by abolitionists, for those of immediate and unqualified emancipation on the soil, and the claim of any compensation to the master was abjured. In these views, as well as in opposition to the characteristic principles and aims of the Colonization Society, (whose agents had solicited patronage in England,) the venerable Clarkson and Wilberforce heartily concurred. On this latter topic, Mr. Clarkson repeatedly employed his pen. And one of the last acts of Mr. Wilberforce was the signature of a protest against the American scheme of expatriation, a short time before his death, which occurred in July, 1833.

This salutary change in the policy, the measures, and the teachings of British abolitionists produced corresponding fruits. As soon as the public *conscience* was distinctly and pungently addressed, it began to be reached and operated upon to good purpose.

Other causes concurred to favor the revolution in progress. The Catholic Emancipation bill of 1829, brought with it an accession of strength to the cause of slave emancipation, and the celebrated champion of Irish enfranchisement, Daniel O'Connell, was always ready to advocate the claims of the negroes.

The repeal of the odious Corporation and Test Acts, in 1828, placing dissenters on an equal ground of eligibility to office, and the similar concession to Catholic subjects, a few months after, encouraged freedom of discussion on general subjects, and brought into the field of political action large numbers who had learned to sympathize with the oppressed. The celebrated Reform bill of 1832 belongs to the same category, and may be mentioned here, though in advance of its chronological order. By this measure the unjust and disproportionate suffrage of the ancient boroughs, beyond their present proportion of inhabitants, in electing members to Parliament, was done away, and the masses of the industrious people were, in some measure, restored to their political rights. It is pleasing to notice how all these democratic reformations favored the introduction of redress for the enslaved. And the reader will have observed the general fact, both in the British and American legislatures, that measures in behalf of justice and freedom are commonly carried in the popular branch first. The department nearest to the mass of the people and most directly responsible to them, is soonest reached by the voice of humanity and conscience.*

---

* An argument designed to prove the worthlessness of democratic institutions has been drawn from the alleged fact that the enjoyment of universal suffrage in

Add to this the new ministry, formed soon after the accession of William IV., in 1830, were favorable, beyond all former precedent, to the cause of abolition and general freedom. Grey, Lansdowne, Holland, Brougham, Durham, Althorpe, Howick, Melbourne, Palmerston, Goderich, Russell, Auckland, Stanley, Graham, Denman.

To these influences in England, we may add others in the West Indies. Christian missionaries were at work there. Religion, and a knowledge of letters had begun to reach and open the minds of the enslaved, for West Indian slavery had not as effectually bolted the doors of its prison-house against the light of heaven, as has the slavery of our North American States. British Protestantism had not learned nor taught that " oral instruction " was sufficient for slaves. Bibles, to some extent, had been furnished them, and they had been allowed to build chapels for worship.

But the determined advocates of slavery were beginning to discover their mistake. They saw that intelligence and purity were incompatible with the condition of slavery. The missionaries, too, with all their abundant prudence, (forbearing to instruct the slaves in their heaven-conferred rights,) had not learned to teach a religion that justified oppression, or that could be embraced without aspirations after freedom. The missionaries began to foresee a little of the struggle that was before them, if the West Indies were ever to be christianized. They patiently labored on, waiting the event, while the planters regarded them with suspicion, and watched for opportunities and pretexts for ejecting them. The overruling providence of God was visibly at work preparing the way for the change that was to take place.

It was under this state of things that the anti-slavery agitation progressed in Great Britain. " Early in 1831, the num-

---

America has never secured the abolition of slavery. The sophism lies in the notorious fact that the premises are untrue. Universal suffrage is not enjoyed in America; all the slaves, and most of the free people of color, being excluded from the polls. To establish the universal suffrage in America, would be to abolish American slavery.

ber of petitions presented in one session amounted to upward of five thousand." On motion of Mr. Buxton, April 15, the House of Commons resolved to consider, speedily, the best means of effecting the abolition of slavery throughout the British dominions, but a few days after the Parliament was adjourned.

A public meeting of the Anti-Slavery Society was held, Lord Suffield presiding. "The speakers were Mr. Buxton, Sir James Mackintosh, Dr. Lushington, Rev. D. Wilson, (since Bishop of Calcutta,) Mr. O'Connell, Mr. Sheil, Mr. Pownall, Rev. J. Burnett, Rev. Mr. Watson, Mr. Evans, Mr. Stephen, Rev. J. Cunningham. They insisted upon the utter extinction of slavery by act of Parliament, *and, to this end, the importance of "a judicious use, on the part of the people, of their right of choosing their representatives." " The formation of a new Parliament was, in no small degree, influenced by these considerations."* *

At the "hustings," where, after the English custom, the candidates presented themselves to be questioned, while the people were voting, they were constantly and publicly interrogated by the individual voters, as they came up, one after another, " *Will you vote for the abolition of slavery ?"* and as the answer was *yea* or *nay,* (or dubious,) the vote was given or withheld. On these election days was fought the decisive battles of West Indian freedom. Under these influences was elected the first Reform Parliament which assembled at the close of the year 1832,† to signalize itself by one of the most glorious achievements of modern legislation.

At the close of 1831 there appeared an important work on Colonial Slavery, by Judge Jeremie, late of St. Lucia. Its disclosures made a powerful impression upon the mind of the British nation. No longer were apologies needed for the "extravagant statements of over excited abolitionists." The workings of the slave system, the condition of the enslaved, and the demoralization of the masters, were shown to be alto-

---

gether and immeasurably worse than any of the abolitionists
had ever supposed, or could have imagined. Documentary
facts demonstrated that "truth is stranger than fiction," and
"the poetry of philanthropy" became stale by the side of the
records of jurisprudence. Judge Jeremie had been strongly
prepossessed in favor of the slaveholders, had gone out there
with the determination to administer, impartially, the laws
of the country, had found the task utterly impracticable, and
had returned. There could be no such thing as the reign of
impartial law, in a community of slaveholders. One specification, illustrated by a variety of incidents, was this; that, in
no case before a court of justice, where the claims of slavery,
or the interests of master and slave were involved, was the
least reliance to be placed upon the testimony, under oath, of
any slaveholder, however exalted his station, or however sanctimonious his professions.

About the same time that these disclosures were made in
England, the West India Islands were becoming the theatre
of new outrages, the knowledge of which, in England, soon
after, could not fail to swell the tide of public indignation
against slavery.

"It had long been a trick of West Indian policy, when any measure
favorable to negro emancipation, or at all bearing upon it, was in progress,
to excite among the slaves some trifling brawl with their managers, which
was then dignified with the formidable name of an insurrection, the military
forces were called out to suppress it, at a wanton expense of negro blood,
and then intelligence was sent home, by way of proving the unfitness of the
negroes for emancipation."—*Copley's Hist.*, 371.

"In 1815, when Mr. Wilberforce gave notice of a bill for the registration
of all Colonial slaves, a universal clamor was excited in the West Indies;"
and sham insurrections were enacted for producing an effect in England.
In 1823, the movements in England occasioned similar demonstrations.
"Rumors of plots and insurrections were constantly assailing the public
ear."—*Ib.*, p. 371–4.

The close of the year 1831, and the beginning of 1832,
were signalized by a more general and violent outbreak of
slaveholding fury, which proved to be the death struggle of
West India slavery. The moderate measures of melioration

proposed by the British Government, produced the greatest excitement among the planters of Jamaica. They held public meetings, threatening to resist the mother country, and renounce allegiance to the King. This was directly calculated to rouse the slaves, yet they remained quiet, and measures were next resorted to, designed evidently to produce an appearance of disturbance among them. The term of their usual Christmas holidays was unlawfully abridged, and when they were ordered to their work, before the close of their accustomed recreations, a portion of them refused. This refusal was magnified into an insurrection, and proclamations in the name of the King were solemnly issued, announcing the pretended fact, and spreading consternation and alarm in every direction. The militia were ordered out, attacks were made upon the defenseless negroes, they were shot down in great numbers, and their cane-sheds and houses destroyed. "It does not appear that the negroes attempted the life of any person, but their determined insubordination was very evident." By the testimony of the more moderate among the planters themselves, as well as of the missionaries, afterwards, there was no necessity, for any purposes of self-defense, for this wanton attack upon the negroes.

But the malice of the slaveholders did not exhaust itself thus. The missionaries, Baptists, Wesleyans, and Moravians, shared a large portion of their fury. In their religious instructions, they had abstained, even to a fault, from teaching the slaves the wickedness of slaveholding and the extent and sacredness of their own rights. It does not appear that they had directly admonished the slaveholders of their great sin. But they had undoubtedly done something for the moral and intellectual improvement of the slaves,—they had treated their converts as brethren in Christ—and this was an unpardonable sin against the slave system ! From the beginning of the disturbances already mentioned, they had done all in their power to keep the slaves quiet, and to dissuade them from acts of insubordination and aggression. They had taken pains to disabuse some of them of the mistaken impression

that the King had made them free. They had even entreated
them to resume their labors. But all this did not suffice to
conciliate or pacify the slaveholders. The missionaries were
arrested, insulted, threatened with hanging, imprisoned, tried
for their lives, and no arts of bribery or intimidation left un-
tried to extort testimony against them that should seem to
warrant their conviction and execution. The newspaper
presses, in the meantime, teemed with the most inflammatory
and shameless falsehoods against them, declaring that "it
would be a grateful exhibition to the island to see a dozen of
them gibbeted." One editor called on the public to "raze
their chapels to the ground, and then take away their lives."
When no charges could be substantiated against them, they
were nevertheless incarcerated in filthy prisons, and by this
means, perhaps, chiefly, they escaped, for a season, the rage
of the mob. When, at length, they were bailed out, the
magistrates who had extended to them this favor, were denounced and villified in their turn. Even the more moderate
and enlightened portion of the inhabitants were led to conclude that the missionaries must have been very imprudent.
Their friends strongly urged them to leave the island, assuring them that their usefulness was at end. On every side
they encountered countenances distorted by expressions of
malice and revenge.

At this critical juncture, the arrival of some new missionaries, along with Mr. Burchell, a missionary who had been to
England for his health, was made the occasion for a new outbreak. Mr. Burchell was immediately arrested, and absurdly
charged with having participated in the rebellion. He was
liberated on bail. Mr. Knibb and his companions were again
summoned to answer to charges of having preached in an un-
licensed house to a large congregation of negroes and others.
After examination they were discharged. But the fury of
the slaveholders could no longer be restrained. They assembled in mobs, demolished the chapels of the missionaries, and
threatened their lives. "Both magistrates and militia were
actively engaged in this work." Finding it unsafe to remain

on shore, the missionaries sought shelter on board some British vessels in the harbor, but the captains were afraid to receive them, lest the inhabitants should refuse to load their vessels. At length, Captain Trefusis consented to receive them, till the excitement subsided.

The missionaries memorialized the Governor, protesting their innocence, and asking redress for the loss of their chapels. The Governor issued a proclamation denouncing these acts of violence, and enjoining on the magistrates to quell all disorderly meetings, to protect property, and bring the offenders to justice. But the proclamation was torn down from the walls. The very persons called upon to bring offenders to justice, were themselves the offenders.

"The most base and malignant efforts were still made to implicate the missionaries." Negroes were threatened, and even cruelly tortured to make them testify that the missionaries—especially that Mr. Burchell—had excited them to rebel. But they steadily affirmed the contrary, and the persecutors were defeated in this part of their scheme. Public meetings were, however, held by them, at which "*gentlemen*" regretted that they were not present at the destruction of the chapels; others made speeches, declaring that they must "get rid of the Baptists;" that if the House of Assembly would not expel them, other measures must be taken ; that "neither ought the Wesleyans to be allowed to remain ;" that Mr. Murray (a Wesleyan missionary) should be informed that "it would be at the risk of his life that he attempted to preach," &c. Resolutions to the same effect were adopted at meetings in different parts of the island, declaring that they must "get rid of all sectaries," or dissenting ministers. Clergymen, however, of the Church Establishment, who favored the religious instruction of the negroes, found little less favor at their hands.

Mr. Knibb was released the 14th of February, after a period of imprisonment, but was soon after informed of a design against his life, and his house was the same evening assaulted. Similar attacks were made upon others.

" On the evening of Mr. Burchell's release, a white mob

collected around his lodgings, vowing they would tar and feather him." By the exertions of the colored people, and the presence of the chief justice, they were deterred from their purpose, on the condition that Mr. B. should leave the island, to which he consented, and a detachment guarded him through the streets to embark. Messrs. Gardner and Knibb were subjected to trial the following week, and the next thing we hear is "that this very same William Knibb, who had been treated as an incendiary, a promoter of rebellion, was employed to examine certain negroes, and find out, if possible, the causes of the rebellion." The result proved that the violent meetings of the slaveholders, already mentioned, at which they threatened to resist the British Government and throw off their allegiance to the King, was the first thing that made the slaves suspect that the British Government and the King had ordered their liberation.

Mr. Knibb was, nevertheless, urgently requested by some of the magistrates to leave the island, and finding it impossible to be longer useful in that field of labor, he consented, in April, 1832, to do so, and was appointed by the other missionaries to represent their case to the people of England. This act sealed the overthrow of slavery in the British West Indies. The revelations of Mr. Knibb, on his return home, convinced the British nation that Slavery and Christianity could not co-exist in the Islands, and the doom of slavery became certain. Some attempts were, in the meantime, made by the missionaries remaining in Jamaica to resume their labors, but in vain. The further preaching of the Gospel among the slaves awaited the abolition of slavery.

The Missionary Societies in England, through their committees, represented to the Colonial Secretary of State, Lord Goderich, the outrages that had been committed in Jamaica. " Instructions were accordingly forwarded to Lord Mulgrave, the newly appointed Governor of Jamaica, and by him recommended to the House of Assembly, to provide means for rebuilding the thirteen Baptist and four Wesleyan chapels, so wantonly and illegally destroyed." "These recommendations were disregarded, or rather, insolently rejected," thus revealing to the British Government the temper of the slave party. But it was found necessary, for the security of all houses of worship, to enact a law for the future, that if any such building should be injured or destroyed by a mob, the damage should be repaired by the county. Committees of inquiry were instituted in Parliament respecting these outrages, and respecting the pretended rebellion on the part of the negroes, and the whole truth of the case, at last, came to light. The pretense of preparing the slaves for freedom, while opposing by violence their instruction, was thoroughly exposed. The meetings of Missionary Societies became anti-slavery meetings. The Anti-Slavery Society took the ground of immediate and unconditional emancipation, and from every part of the United Kingdom there came up one united demand for the utter abolition of slavery.

"On the 9th of June, 1832, Lord Goderich addressed a circular to the Governors of the Colonies, announcing to them the formation of a Committee in the House of Commons, in consequence of the numerous petitions for the abolition of slavery, to consider and report what measures it might be expedient to adopt with that view."—*Copley's Hist.*, 430.

A similar committee was appointed in the House of Lords. A large number of witnesses were examined before both of these committees, and voluminous statistical facts were introduced, particularly by Mr. Buxton, touching the main questions concerning slavery, and the workings of emancipation wherever it had been tried. The slave party did their best to sustain themselves during these investigations, but their efforts only served to establish the positions of the abolitionists. Their "reluctant admissions and awkward apologies or evasions of adverse witnesses," says Copley, "only served to confirm and establish the views of all thinking and impartial persons on the other side."

The objections that emancipation would not be safe, that the liberated slaves would rise against their masters, that the Islands would be reduced to a state of anarchy and overrun with idlers and vagabonds—objections once so powerful as to stagger the faith of philanthropists themselves, were now completely overthrown, and all the terrors they had created were dispelled, in the light of well attested historical facts. The "horrors of St. Domingo" were shown to be the horrors of *slavery*, and not of *freedom*. The history of emancipation was found to be the history of the most beneficial results.

The ancient Romans had tested the policy of emancipation, to obtain soldiers in their wars against Hannibal. The testimony of Tiberius Gracchus, confirmed by Cicero, and approved by Montesquieu, assures us of the salutary effects. Christianity had abolished slavery throughout the Roman Empire without disaster. The feudal system had been displaced in modern Europe, and nobody deplored the change. English slaves liberated, a few centuries ago by their Irish masters, did not cut the throats of their benefactors. In Chili, every child born after the 10th of October, 1811, was declared free: in Buenos Ayres, after January, 1813. In Colombia, all slaves bearing arms were emancipated July 19, 1821, and provisions made for emancipating the remainder, amounting to two hundred and eighty thousand. In Mexico, Sept. 15th, 1829, instantaneous and unconditional emancipation was extended to every slave. In Guadaloupe, eighty-five thousand slaves were set free in 1794, when there was a population of only thirteen thousand whites. At the Cape of Good Hope, thirty thousand Hottentots were emancipated in 1823. In all these instances, the change had taken place without producing any unhappy results.

Facts, of which these are a specimen, when spread out before the British Government and the British public, prepared the way for a still more signal and illustrious exemplification of *the safety of doing right!*

Matters in Jamaica, in the meantime, were ripening for the final result. Lord Mulgrave, the new Governor sent from England, in his speech to the Colonial Assembly, had recommended the religious instruction of the slaves. So far from responding to the sentiment, the Assembly recorded its threats of revolt from the British Government, whereupon the Governor dissolved the Assembly. A new election, under the Reform bill, which extended, it seems, to the Colonies, secured an Assembly of more moderate and liberal views.

The first reformed British Parliament assembled about the close of the year 1832. Mr. Buxton soon gave notice of a motion for the abolition of slavery, unless the Government should take the matter into its own hands. Lord Althorpe stated, in reply, that it was the intention of the Government to do so, and that he would shortly bring a bill before the House, which he trusted would be both safe and satisfactory. The nation now waited for this measure in almost breathless suspense.

The 23d of April, 1833, was the day appointed for bringing it forward, and the Anti-Slavery Society improved the interim by holding a public meeting in Exeter Hall, at which speeches were made by Lord Suffield, Mr. Buxton, Joseph John Gurney, Earl Fitzwilliam, Rev. J. W. Cunningham, G. Strickland, M.P., Rev. J. Burnet, H. Pownall, Esq., Mr. Geo. Stephen, Lord Milton, Dr. Lushington, and others.

" A still more important meeting was held in the same hall a few days afterwards," consisting of three hundred and sixty-nine delegates from various parts of the United Kingdom. "More than three hundred of the delegates attended at the house of Earl Grey, to present a memorial, which was read by Mr. Gurney." The deputation had an audience with Lord Althorpe, and with Mr. Stanley, the Colonial Secretary of State. They represented the necessity of *immediate and total emancipation*, in the full confidence that *such* an emancipation would be *peaceable*. These views were embodied in a memorial to Lord Grey, and exerted, no doubt, a strong influence upon the Government.

The plan first proposed, however, was unsatisfactory. It contemplated a compensation of £15,000,000 to the planters, which was to be paid out of the earnings of the negroes. It proposed a twelve years' apprenticeship, during which time the compensation money was to be earned.

Abolitionists justly contended that compensation was due,

if at all, to the slave, and not to the master. They contended that emancipation should be entire and immediate. The planters, on the other hand, petitioned for compensation. While these questions were pending, the friends of emancipation held another meeting, July 20, and protested against the objectionable features of the bill.

The details of the act of emancipation were finally adjusted on this basis, viz:

1. The entire extinction of slavery, to take place on the 1st of August, 1834.

2. Field laborers, above six years old, to serve as apprentices for six years, ending 1st of August, 1840.

3. Domestic or house servants to serve as apprentices four years, ending first of August, 1838.

4. Children under six years, to be free, without apprenticeship. Children hereafter born to be free.

5. The slaves to pay no part of their redemption money, but a compensation of £20,000,000 out of the public treasury to be paid to the planters, *at the close of the apprenticeship.*

Other regulations were specified, for securing the rights of the apprentices and their masters.

The bill passed the House of Commons August 7, the House of Lords, August 20, and received the royal assent August 28th, 1833.

It remains to record the results of this measure.

The first of August, 1834, came and passed peacefully, without the slightest disturbance, in any of the islands. And there has been none since.

In Antigua and Bermuda, the Colonial Legislatures preferred to dispense with the apprenticeship system, believing immediate and complete emancipation to be safest, and desiring likewise the earlier reception of the compensation money, to which this measure would entitle them. They reaped the double reward of their sagacity, experiencing none of the perplexity occasioned by the apprenticeship system elsewhere.

In Jamaica, Barbadoes, and the other islands, the apprenticeship went into operation, and worked as well as could have been anticipated. But its inconveniences and vexations led to its voluntary abandonment, and the entire freedom of the field laborers, on the first of August, 1838, two years before the time limited in the statute.

In Barbadoes, with a population of 140,000, only 20,000 were whites. In Jamaica, with a population of 450,000, only 37,000 were whites.

In *all* the British emancipated colonies, with a population of about 1,125,000, only about 131,000 were whites, being a little more than one-ninth part. Yet the tranquillity of the inhabitants was not in the slightest degree disturbed. The testimony on this point has never been questioned. The Governor of Jamaica, Sir Lionel Smith, in his speech to the Assembly, October 30, 1838, said:

" The conduct of the laboring population, who were the objects of your liberal and enlightened policy, entitles them to the highest praise, and proves how well they deserved the boon of freedom." " I trust there is every prospect of agricultural prosperity."

To this speech the Assembly of Jamaica responded thus:

" The House join with your Excellency in bearing testimony to the peaceful manner in which the laboring population have conducted themselves in a state of freedom."

Queen Victoria, in her speech to the British Parliament, February 5, 1839, said:

" It is with great satisfaction that I am enabled to inform you, that throughout *the whole* of my West India possessions, the period fixed by law for the complete and final emancipation of the negroes, has been anticipated by acts of the colonial legislatures, and that the transition from the temporary system of apprenticeship to entire freedom, has taken place WITHOUT ANY DISTURBANCE OF PUBLIC ORDER AND TRANQUILLITY."

The islands, since emancipation took place, have been repeatedly visited by philanthropists well known in both hemispheres, for the purpose of collecting information concerning the workings of freedom. James A. Thome, of Kentucky, (afterwards Professor at Oberlin,) in company with Joseph H. Kimball of New Hampshire, went thither in November, 1836, and returned in June, 1837. Joseph Sturge and Thomas

Harvey of England took an elaborate survey in 1837. Joseph John Gurney followed in 1839–40. The results of these several investigations are before the public in three interesting volumes.* The trustworthiness of these highly respectable and competent witnesses has never been questioned. They all agree, substantially, in the particulars which follow, and which are extracted from the work of Thome and Kimball. Similar facts and testimonials have since been officially reported to the British Government, and published in the British Anti-Slavery Reporter. The information on which the following propositions were founded, was obtained from large numbers of the principal planters, magistrates, and professional gentlemen on the island of Antigua, whose names are preserved in the volume, with their testimony in their own words. We give only the substance of the principal statements.

1. " The transition from slavery to freedom was a great revolution, by which a prodigious change was effected in the condition of the negroes."

2. " Emancipation (in distinction from apprenticeship,) was the result of political and pecuniary considerations, merely."

3. " The event of emancipation passed peaceably. The gloomiest anticipations had been previously entertained."

4. " There has been, since emancipation, not only no rebellion in fact, but no fear of it."

5. "There has been no fear of house-breaking, highway robberies, and like misdemeanors, since emancipation."

6. " Emancipation is regarded, by all classes, as a great blessing to the island."

7. " Free labor is decidedly less expensive than slave labor."

8. " The negroes work more cheerfully, and do their work better."

9. " The negroes are more easily managed as freemen, than they were when slaves."

10. " The negroes are more trustworthy, and take a deeper interest in their employer's affairs, since emancipation."

11. " The experiment of Antigua proves that emancipated slaves can appreciate law."

---

* (1.) Journal of J. A. Thome and J. H. Kimball.
(2.) The West Indies, in 1837, by Joseph Sturge and Thomas Harvey.
(3.) Letters to Henry Clay, &c., by Joseph John Gurney.

12. " The emancipated negroes have shown no disposition to roam from place to place."

13. " The gift of unrestricted freedom, though so suddenly bestowed, has not made the negroes more insolent than they were while slaves, but has rendered them less so."

14. " Emancipation has demonstrated that gratitude is a prominent trait of negro character."

15. " The freed negroes have proved that they are able to take care of themselves."

16. " Emancipation has operated at once to elevate and improve the negroes."

17. " Emancipation promises a vast improvement in the condition of woman."

18. " Real estate has risen in value since emancipation, mercantile and mechanical operations have received a fresh impulse, and the general condition of the country is decidedly more flourishing than at any former period."

19. " Emancipation has been followed by the introduction of labor-saving machinery."

20. " Emancipation has produced the most decided change in the views of the planters."

21. " The progress of anti-slavery discussions in England did not cause the masters to treat their slaves worse, but, on the contrary, restrained them from outrage."

For other similar statements we have not room. Distorted rumors have sometimes reached us from the islands, set afloat by interested managers and speculators, who, in the absence of the owners (many of whom reside in England) desire to depreciate the price of property, that they might become purchasers. The droughts have, once or twice, occasioned short crops. The embarrassments of estates arising under the old system have not disappeared instantly, and sometimes have resulted in bankruptcy as formerly.

It is painful to add, that in Jamaica and Barbadoes, and some other islands, the Colonial Governments have, in various ways, oppressed and harassed the laborers, to diminish their wages, and prevent them from becoming proprietors of land. The fact that the negroes, to some extent, were becoming self-employers, has been made a pretext for introducing coolies from the East Indies, and treating them as though they were slaves, insomuch that the British Government has been obliged to interfere.

The abolition of slavery in the British West Indies liberated 800,000 slaves. This was followed, in 1843, by the abolition of slavery throughout the British dominions, which liberated more than TWELVE MILLIONS in the East Indies.

The history of British anti-slavery effort and its results, is instructive in more aspects than one. It shows, in the strong light of practical experiment, the worthlessness of all partial, temporizing efforts, all schemes of preparation, amelioration, and gradualism, in striking contrast with the efficiency, power, safety, and success of efforts for a thorough, uncompromising, and radical removal of the evil. It shows the utter incompatibility of slavery with a Christianity that earnestly attempts anything for the religious instruction and education of the slaves. It shows the resistless power of the religious sentiment of a country to mould at its pleasure, to preserve or to overthrow the legislation of a country. It assures us that whenever the prevailing and recognized religion of America decrees the downfall of American slavery, it will fall. It reveals to us the power of an enlightened public sentiment over a government less popular than our own. It exhibits to us the fiction of the *legality of slavery* holding a great nation in fetters until exploded by the kindling lights of religion and freedom. It shows us the power of a right-minded and persevering minority, through the good Providence of God, to overcome mountains* of opposition, and dispel a chaos of error. It demonstrates that the increasing rage and madness of oppressors is the sure presage of hastening deliverance to the oppressed.

---

* It is a mistake to suppose, as some do, that because the West Indies were remote from Great Britain, the slave power exerted but little influence on the home Government. There was a time when it virtually bribed the courts, controlled Parliament, and stood behind the throne. Statesmen and nobles, not to say monarchs and members of the royal family, were suspected of being secret partners in the African slave trade, or openly held investments in West India plantations. A large portion of the West India proprietors resided in England, and wielded a commanding influence. A large share of the £20,000,000 compensation voted by Parliament,

CHAPTER XXXI.

DISTINCTIVE FEATURES OF AMERICAN SLAVERY.

Its essential principle—Human Chattelhood—Integral parts of the system—Its consistency and unity—Agreement of the theory with the practice—Slavery cannot co-exist with liberty.

FROM the scenes and achievements of British philanthropy, and of West India Emancipation, we come back again to our own land of boasted liberty and cherished human chattelhood,—the land in which about 113,000 slaveholders control TWENTY MILLIONS of human beings,—and where the question still hangs in suspense, whether the yoke can be broken. Before entering upon the history of the present struggle, it may be well to look directly into the face of the monster to be grappled with, and see wherein its strength lies.

WHAT IS SLAVERY?

" The slave is one who is in the power of a master to whom HE BELONGS." —*Louisiana Civil Code*, Art. 35. " Slaves shall be deemed, sold, taken, reputed, and adjudged in law to be CHATTELS PERSONAL, in the hands of their owners and possessors, and their executors, administrators, and assigns, to all intents, constructions, and purposes, whatsoever."—*Law of South Carolina*, 2 *Brev. Dig.* 229, *Prince's Dig.* 446, &c.

" The cardinal principle of slavery, that the slave is not to be ranked

---

never went to the West Indies to improve the plantations there ; but remained in England, some of it in the hands of dissolute nabobs, some in the hands of merchants and mortgagees, in consequence of the West India estates being deeply involved in debt by the system of slavery. This, with the continued absence of owners from their plantations, partly accounts for the reports which we still hear, of the pecuniary embarrassments and thriftlessness of many West India plantations.

among sentient beings, but among THINGS, as an article of property, a chattel personal, obtains as undoubted law, in all these [slave] States."—*Stroud's Sketch*, p. 23.

This, then, is slavery, as it exists in America. God created man in His own image. He made him a little lower than the angels, crowned him with glory and honor, and gave him dominion over the beasts of the field. But slavery reduces him to a thing, a commodity, an article of merchandise!

This is no flourish of rhetoric—no idle abstraction. So far as the power of man can accomplish such a result, it is accomplished by slavery. If it cannot take away the immortal soul of man, it deems, reputes, and adjudges him to have none! It ranks him, not a little lower than the angels, but on a level with the beasts that perish!

The question of slavery or emancipation is not a question of cruel treatment or of kind treatment—of starvation or of full feeding. It is a question whether a man is to be recognized *as* a man, or as a brute—a person or a thing—a spiritual, moral being, or a mere lump of matter—a being gifted with volition and clothed with responsibility, or a mere piece of machinery—a being with, or without, RIGHTS, which the laws should PROTECT.

INTEGRAL PARTS OF THE SLAVE SYSTEM.

These are such as are involved, of necessity, in the cardinal principle of slavery, viz.: *human chattelhood*. We enumerate the following:

1. The unlimited authority of the slave-master or owner.

2. The abrogation of marriage, and the family relation, among slaves.

3. The power to enforce labor without wages.

4. The incapacity of the slave to acquire or hold property.

5. His incapacity to make contracts or bargains.

6. His incapacity to enjoy civil, domestic or political rights.

7. The liability of the slave to be sold, like other chattels, and separated from relatives. The authorized prosecution of the SLAVE TRADE!

8. The absence of any adequate legal protection for the slave.

9. The power of the master to forbid education and social religious worship, at his own discretion.

10. The power of the legislatures of slave states to prohibit education, even by the masters, and to prohibit or restrict free social worship.

11. The power of the legislatures of slave states to abolish freedom of speech and of the press, in general.

CONSISTENCY AND UNITY OF THE SLAVE SYSTEM.

The *theory* of American slavery agrees with its *practice*. The whole system of slave legislation grows legitimately out of the chattel principle upon which slavery is founded. And the most revolting usages and practices to be detected among the incidents and workings of the system are found to be in perfect keeping and harmony, both with the principle of human chattelhood and with the slave code.

1. The very idea of human chattelhood involves the idea of the unlimited control of the master, and the absolute defenselessness of the slave. Habits of tyranny and of servility must follow, of course, with all the insecurity and outrage that grow out of them.

2. The absence of legal marriage, and of the protected family relation, is manifestly essential to the idea of human chattelhood. Chattels are not married, and cannot constitute families. Chattels may be transferred, bought, sold, and *used*. The promiscuous intercourse of the sexes, especially at the bidding of the master, follows, of course, and is not to be censured by those who consent to the system, or to the practice of slaveholding.

3. Chattels never receive wages, or acquire or hold property. The deep poverty of the slave, and all the effects of that poverty, with the absence of a motive to labor, follow, of course.

4. Chattels can make no contracts, not even the contract of marriage. And this is the law of the slave.

5. Chattels can have no rights, and hence the slave can have none.

6. Chattels may be bought and sold. Hence the existence of slavery involves, of necessity, the slave trade, as Henry Clay testifies.—*Speech in the U. S. Senate*, 1839.

7. Chattels can claim no legal protection, and therefore the slave can have none. And all the cruelties of slavery must be tolerated.

8. Chattels are not to be educated, or instructed in religion! The idea is an absurdity. If the slaveholders are right in holding slaves as chattels, they cannot be blamed for withholding education and religious privileges from them. If the government may sanction or permit slaveholding, it must, to be consistent with itself, prohibit literary and religious instruction.

9. The same may be said of the laws forbidding freedom of speech and of the press. Such freedom is manifestly impracticable and unsafe in the presence of chattel slavery. The entire South attests this; and thus far the testimony is truthful. If slavery is to be maintained, or even tolerated, then liberty, of course, is to be relinquished. This is self-evident.

The statutes of the slave states abundantly confirm the preceding statements, as will appear by consulting Judge Stroud's "Sketch of the Slave Laws," published at Philadelphia in the year 1827. The "Black Code of the District of Columbia," by W. G. Snethen, Esq., will show that *some* of the worst features of the system are sanctioned on the national hearthstone, and under "exclusive jurisdiction of Congress." And "Wheeler's Law of Slavery," (a large volume of "Reports") attests that slave enactments are not a dead letter.

It has sometimes been represented that the severe laws of the South, especially those forbidding education and free religious meetings to slaves and free people of color, are wholly or chiefly owing to the impertinent agitations of abolitionists, whose mischievous efforts, it is said, have made such regulations necessary, or have furnished occasions or pretexts for them. The ready answer to this, is that the enactments in question are found in "Stroud's Sketch," published in 1827, *five* years before the organization of the "modern" anti-slavery societies commenced, *four* years before the "Liberator" was issued by Mr. Garrison; and that, according to Judge Stroud, the principal acts of that character, cited by him, bear date from 1740 to 1770, long before the organization of the old Anti-slavery Societies, by Jay and Franklin. So well known is this fact that occasion has sometimes been taken from it, to represent these severe laws as being antiquated, obsolete, and a dead letter! For the refutation of this falsehood, we have only to cite the testimony of the Presbyterian Synods of Kentucky and of South Carolina and Georgia, and the Virginia Revised Code of 1819. A mass of authenticated facts, chiefly sustained by Southern testimony, and showing that the practical workings of the system correspond, at all points, with the statutes defining it, may be found in a volume entitled "American Slavery as it is, by the testimony of a thousand witnesses,"—also in several unimpeachable narratives, and the Southern newspapers of every month in the year. "No people," says the philosophical and learned Dr. Priestley, "have ever been found to be better than their laws, though many have been known to be worse."

Such is the system that controls and wields the Government of the United States, as shown in preceding chapters.

Such is the system, sheltered and sanctioned, as we have already seen, in the prominent religious sects in this country, —the system which the Christianity of the country must overthrow,—or to which it must succumb and conform.

Such is the system with which *human liberty*, in America, is summoned to contend, or to which it must yield.

Who are enlisted in the struggle? What are they doing? What are the prospects before them? These are amongst the questions before us, in the succeeding chapters.

CHAPTER XXXII.

THE PRESENT ANTI-SLAVERY AGITATION IN AMERICA—ITS CAUSES, ORIGIN, AND CHARACTER.

Discussions caused by the Missouri Compromise—Rebuke of the dough-faces at the ballot-box, 1820—Benjamin Lundy, 1821 and afterwards—Missionary enterprise advocated as the harbinger of universal liberty—Revived doctrine (among active Christians) of immediate and unconditional repentance—This doctrine antagonistic to conservatists in the Church, and their Colonization Society—Spirit of ethical inquiry—Social Reforms—Temperance—Peace—An age of newspapers, lecturers, lyceums, popular discussions, and voluntary Associations—William Lloyd Garrison, a printer, a Temperance Editor—Associates with Benjamin Lundy at Baltimore, 1829—Imprisonment, trial, and release, 1830—Established his "Liberator" at Boston, 1831—Panic caused by insurrection in Virginia—New England Anti-Slavery Society formed, 1832—Other Journals—Anti-Slavery tracts issued by Messrs. Tappan and others, New York—N. Y. Emancipator commenced, 1833—Miss Crandall's School, Connecticut—N. Y. City A. S. Soc. organized, Oct., 1833—American A. S. Soc. at Philadelphia, Dec., 1833—Principles and measures of Abolitionists.

IF the reader of the preceding chapters shall have sufficiently pondered the character of American slavery, and the position of the churches and of the Federal Government in respect to it, he will now perhaps be able to form some intelligent opinion concerning the condition and prospects of liberty in America, at the time when the present agitation of the slave question commenced. He will be able to judge whether such an agitation then was unnecessary, impertinent, ill-judged, unfortunate, or ill-timed. And when he learns, in the perusal of this chapter, the principles, the aims, and the measures of the abolitionists, he may be ready to judge whether, or how far, they offended against the rules of decorum and prudence; and whether the opposition they encountered was anything more than might have been expected from the leading men, and the controlling influences, in Church and State, that have already been described, however wise and prudent may have been the persons earnestly and resolutely engaged in the effort against slavery.

It is not easy, perhaps not possible, to trace all the latent causes which, like little rivulets running together, produced the present agitation of the slave question, as other popular agitations are produced. We shall mention such as are within our knowledge, without pretending to enumerate them all.

The year 1820, after a long period of quiet, was distinguished by a pretty general and earnest discussion of slavery, growing out of the debates in Congress concerning the admission of Missouri, and the adjustment of that controversy by the Missouri Compromise. Mr. Clay, the author of that measure, and those who co-operated with him, congratulated themselves with the success of the policy. As lately as 1850, Mr. Clay alluded to it in the Senate, while his "omnibus" compromise was pending, reminding senators of its success, and boastfully assuring them that his second compromise would be equally efficacious in allaying the popular ferment, and restoring peace.

It is undoubtedly true that the Missouri Compromise, like all other compromises between right and wrong, did induce a moral paralysis in those who assented to it, and this is what Mr. Clay denominates *peace*. But the people did not all hold themselves parties to that compromise, nor participate in its benumbing effects. The spark of liberty was a fire pent up in their bones. Though temporarily baffled, they were not conquered. If the national "Vesuvius was capped" for a few years, it was only that it might burst forth again with fresh vigor. If Henry Clay could but have known how many were made uncompromising abolitionists by their disgust with that unholy compromise, he would have found less occasion to congratulate himself with the results. The present antislavery excitement may be distinctly traced, in part, to the earnest debates among the people elicited by that same Missouri Compromise. The "settlement" of the question by Congress was only the signal for its agitation among their constituents.

The Congressional elections of 1820 were extensively affected by the previous votes of the Representatives on the admission of Missouri. The recreants to liberty were regarded as marked men, especially those who had falsified their own previous professions, and richly merited the expressive epithet, "dough-faces,"* then coined and bestowed upon them by the eccentric John Randolph, of Roanoke. In some instances they took the hint of their friends, and quietly withdrew from public life. In other cases, their old associates declined to nominate them. Some were nominated, only to be defeated. Others, who had previously defied all competitors, were subjected to the mortification of being re-elected by a diminished vote, barely escaping defeat, after the most strenuous exertions of their supporters, admonishing them never to hazard the chances again.

This latter was the fate of the very distinguished and highly-gifted Representative from Rhode Island.† The controversy was carried on during the whole summer by newspaper discussions, and public meetings, and debates. Party tactics and party discipline were resorted to, with little effect; party lines, for the time being, were well nigh erased, and the terms "anti-slavery" and "pro-slavery" took the place of Federalist and Republican. The files of newspapers, particularly the *Providence Gazette*,‡ bear testimony that the discus-

---

* This term, as now commonly used and understood, expressively characterizes the politician, whose face, as flexible as " dough," and belonging to a head equally soft, may be moulded by others into any shape that best suits them. But it is thought by some that the epithet intended by Mr. Randolph was " doe-faces," in allusion to the timidity of the female deer, who attempts to drink, but starts back at the reflection of its own face in the water. " They saw," said he, " their own doe-faces, and were frightened."

† The late Hon. Samuel Eddy, of Providence. Mr. Hazard, his associate, a less popular candidate, was dropped from the ticket, on election day, by his own partisans.

‡ The *Providence Gazette* was a Federal paper. Mr. Eddy was supported by the

sion became as "radical" then, as it is now, and that nearly the same arguments, *pro* and *con.*, were then in use. Some who commenced writing against slavery and "compromise," then, have not ceased writing against them still. The author may be permitted to record himself among these. Mr. Eddy was elected by a majority of less than one hundred votes.

The anti-slavery agitation of 1820 was not confined to Rhode Island, or even to New England. It extended throughout the non-slaveholding States. By many of the "Friends" and other opponents of slavery, the "Missouri Compromise" was unsparingly condemned; but the deed was done, and there seemed no political remedy at hand, but the political repudiation of the authors, which, very extensively, took effect. To this day, we find, in various parts of the country, a remnant of the anti-slavery agitators of that period, and recognize some of the old familiar names in the proceedings of the Anti-slavery and Free Soil conventions of the present times. The late BENJAMIN LUNDY was probably moved by the Missouri contest and compromise, to engage in his arduous anti-slavery labors. He seems to have entered the field that same year, and commenced the publication of his monthly periodical, the "Genius of Universal Emancipation," the year following, 1821. In an appeal to the public in April, 1830, he says:

"I have, within the period above mentioned, (ten years,) sacrificed several thousand dollars of my own hard earnings, have travelled upwards of five thousand miles on foot, and more than twenty thousand in other ways ; have visited nineteen States of this Union, and held more than two hundred public meetings—have performed two voyages to the West Indies, by which means the liberation of a considerable number of slaves has been effected, and, I hope, the way paved for the enlargement of many more."

At Philadelphia, at Baltimore, at Washington City, he successively published his paper. In 1828, while located at Bal-

---

Democratic papers, as being the nominee of that party. Until his obnoxious vote in Congress, he was so acceptable to both parties, that no opposing nomination was made against him. But now he was deserted by the "rank and file" of both parties, to a great extent.

timore, he visited various parts of New England, to extend the circulation of his paper, and stir up the friends of the enslaved. He visited Texas twice, and penetrated into Mexico, in search of some better asylum for fugitive and emancipated slaves. Though failing to accomplish this object, he possessed himself of much invaluable information, which afterwards became of the highest importance to the cause in which he was engaged, and to the country at large. It was chiefly to communications from Benjamin Lundy that John Quincy Adams was indebted for those astounding disclosures concerning the Texas plot with which he so suddenly electrified Congress and the nation, in 1836. A more full account of the particulars was afterwards published by Mr. Lundy himself in a paper issued at Philadelphia for that purpose. This timely information put the friends of liberty upon the track by which, though failing to exclude Texas from the Union, they have succeeded, thus far, in arresting the quiet march of the slave power to the Pacific, thus sending a thrill of alarm and rage through the whole South. Thus does Divine Providence raise up and direct the voluntary instruments of its high designs. Benjamin Lundy was a member of the Society of Friends; he was small in stature, of feeble health, afflicted with deafness, less definite than some abolitionists in his anti-slavery ethics and measures, but of indomitable purpose, perseverance, faith, courage, patience, self-denial, endurance, and by dint of these, became a pioneer in the cause. At one time he traversed the free States, lecturing, collecting, obtaining subscribers, writing for his paper, getting it printed, monthly, wherever he could conveniently have it printed, for once, stopping himself to read the "proof," and direct and mail his papers, then travelling on again another month, and carrying in his trunk his "direction book," "column rules," and type "heading," (with the date of "Baltimore,") to facilitate the process. Such are the labors of men who commence moral revolutions, to be completed by others after they have gone off the stage.

Among the early pioneers of the cause, should be mentioned

the name of Rev. John Rankin, a Presbyterian minister of Kentucky, now of Ripley, Ohio. In 1824 or 1825, he published his Letters on Slavery, maintaining its inherent sinfulness, and enforcing the duty of its present abandonment. Through his influence an anti-slavery society, on the same principle, was formed in Kentucky, at that early period. It was afterwards, however, "laid asleep" (to use the words of Mr. Rankin,) by the illusive pretensions and seductive influences of the Colonization Society.

There were moral, religious, and social influences at work, preparatory to an unprecedented agitation of the slave question. The missionary enterprise, in its youthful vigor, was an effort for "evangelizing the world." It was deliberately proposed as a *work to be done*. It was based on a belief that the promises and predictions of the Scriptures afforded a divine guaranty for its accomplishment. Bible, Tract, and Education Societies were commended and patronized as auxiliaries to this magnificent undertaking. The anniversaries of these were enlivened with glowing descriptions of the approaching millennium, when all should know the Lord, from the least to the greatest, and sit under *their own* vines and fig-trees, secure in their rights. The eloquence of a Beecher, a Rice, a Cornelius, a Summerfield, and a Spring, on such occasions, had sent a thrill through the churches, and the promised day was believed to have already dawned. The time was set for furnishing every family on the earth with Bibles. The chronology of the prophetic periods was computed, and the close of the present century, it was believed, was to witness the completed work of the "conversion of the world." To be "up and doing" was the watchword, and our American love of liberty, equality, and "free institutions," was gratified with the assurance that all the despotisms of the earth were to crumble at the Prince Emanuel's approach !

Was all this to be accomplished without Bibles, and education, and marriage, and family sanctities, and liberation for American slaves? Who could believe it? Whatever our missionary and evangelizing orators intended, whatever *they* were thinking of, they were God's instruments for putting into the minds of others "thoughts that burned," for the emancipation of the enslaved. The writer and many others well remember that the tone of our May anniversaries of religious societies, from 1825 to 1832, was such as has been described. And the suddenness with which this tone was changed, when bibles, education, and family sanctities were demanded for slaves, did not escape notice. But the fires kindled could not be extinguished.

The same period was distinguished by "revivals of religion," in which prominence was given to the old doctrine of Hopkins and Edwards, demanding "immediate and unconditional repentance" of all sin, as the only condition of forgiveness and salvation. This was urged in direct opposition to the vague idea of a gradual amendment, admitting "a more convenient season"—a prospective, dilatory, indefinite breaking off from transgression—an idea that had been settling upon the churches for thirty or forty years previous,—an incubus upon every righteous cause, and every holy endeavor. It is easy to see the bearing of such religious awakenings upon the mode of treating the practice of slaveholding, unless it were believed to be righteous. A more perfect antagonism to the ethics and operations of the Colonization Society could not well be imagined. A collision was inevitable, whenever the subject should be introduced, and the Society itself could scarcely avoid introducing it.

Simultaneously with all this, and more or less connected with it, there came over the religious community an increasing spirit of inquiry in respect to Christian ethics, and the bearing of the religious principle upon the social relations and political duties of man. Peace Societies had been formed. Temperance Societies were in progress. The Institution of Free Masonry had been arraigned. The influence of theatres, of lotteries, and the morality of lottery grants by legislatures, were brought under rigorous review. The treatment of the aborigines of our country, especially of the Cherokees, by Georgia and the Federal Government, and the imprisonment of the missionaries among the Cherokees, became subjects of earnest attention. Christians began to be reminded that they were citizens, and that Christianity had its claims upon them in their civil relations. The Sabbath Mail question—whether wisely or unwisely managed—became an exciting topic of animadversion from the pulpit and religious press. The application of the principle may have been a mistaken one, or it may have been unhappily argued and urged; but the principle was, in some fashion, brought into view, that though our institutions secure religious freedom, yet religion and politics are in some way connected, after all, and civil Governments have no right to disobey God. In short, it was a period of unwonted if not unprecedented moral and political inquiry. Was it possible that the slave question should escape the scrutiny of such an age? Assuredly it *did* not, and for the obvious reason that there was in progress a new and strong development of the human mind in the direction of such investigations. How short-sighted are those who think that the agitation originated only with a few "fanatics," and that all would be quiet if they could be silenced or crushed!

Along with the new spirit of moral enterprise and inquiry, there came likewise the new and appropriate methods of their manifestation and culture among the masses of the people. Newspapers were no longer confined to party politics and commerce, nor the reading of them to the select few. Religious newspapers were among the novelties of the times. These were followed by papers designed to promote the reforms and discuss the moral questions of the day. Voluntary lecturers and agents of societies were abroad. Promiscuous conventions as well as protracted religious meetings were held, and laymen found they had tongues. To write for the public was no longer the monopoly of professional authors and quarterly and monthly reviewers. Whoever pleased might become an editor of a newspaper, and whoever chose to subscribe for it, at a trifling expense, was introduced into the "republic of letters." Not only did the great masses become readers of public journals, but to a great and growing extent, contributors, likewise. The custom of writing anonymously, encouraged the timid : the most dependent could stand here on a level with the most powerful, and sometimes smile to see their productions arrest the public attention. Farmers and mechanics, journeymen and apprentices, merchants and clerks—females as well as males—participated in the privilege. From the counting-house, from the anvil, from the loom, from the farm-yard, from the parlor, perhaps from the kitchen, there came paragraphs for the perusal (perhaps for the reproval and instruction) of Senators and Doctors of the Law. History, that often busies itself with petty details pertaining to those who have been falsely called great, need not count it undignified to notice revolutions in human condition like these—revolutions more sublime than those that transfer from one dynasty to another, princely crowns. No one can comprehend, in their causes and distinctive characteristics, the existing agitations in America, who does not take into account the new power and the changed direction of the public press, constituting a new era in human history.

Was it strange, at such a period, when *laborers* of almost all classes were giving free utterance to their thoughts, that the morality of unpaid and forced labor began to be questioned—that the chivalry of whipping women, and the civilization of selling babes at auction by the pound—began to be scrutinized? The rail-car, in 1838, the electric telegraph ten years afterwards, were scarcely greater innovations or greater curiosities than were voluntary lecturers, free public conventions, and moral and religious weekly journals, with their free correspondence, from 1825 to 1830. Was nothing, then, to have been expected—is nothing now to be attributed to this new moral and educating power?

WILLIAM LLOYD GARRISON was a printer's apprentice—then a journeyman printer, at Newburyport, Massachusetts. He wrote paragraphs, perhaps stanzas, for the newspaper, on the printing of which he was employed. His pieces were copied. He became known. He was invited, in 1827 or '28, to edit, for a few months (perhaps to assist also in printing), a weekly paper in Boston, the only one then devoted *exclusively* to the Temperance cause, the first of the kind ever attempted, and then in its second or third year.* He afterwards edited, by invitation, for a short period, the "*Journal of the Times,*" in Vermont, and took strong ground against slavery.

In the autumn of 1829 he became associated with Benjamin Lundy, in the publishing and editing the "*Genius of Universal Emancipation,*" at Baltimore. Not long afterwards, the ship Francis, belonging to Francis Todd, of Newburyport, Mass., being at Baltimore for freight, was employed in taking from thence a cargo of slaves for New Orleans. Mr. Garrison noticed the fact in his paper, and spoke of it in terms of such severity that Mr. Todd directed a suit to be brought against him for a libel. He was tried by a Maryland Court, in Feb., 1830, convicted, and thrown into jail for non-payment of the fine (one hundred dollars) and costs. This circumstance roused an excitement at the North that has never since slept.† From that time the anti-slavery cause took its place among the moral enterprises of the age; small indeed in the beginning, and for sometime after, but constantly widening and deepening its channels.

---

* The *National Philanthropist*, commenced in 1826, by the late Rev. William Collier (a Baptist), by whom Mr. Garrison was employed. The *Investigator*, by William Goodell, commenced in 1827, and published at Providence, R. I., was devoted to moral and political discussion, and reformation in general, including temperance and anti-slavery. In Jan., 1829, it was merged by him in the *National Philanthropist*, at Boston, Mr. Collier retiring. In July, 1830, it was removed to New York, and published as "*The Genius of Temperance,*" by W. Goodell and P. Crandall—afterwards by W. Goodell, till the close of 1833, when it was discontinued, and W. Goodell took charge of the *Emancipator*, which had been issued by him from the same office, though in the name and by the aid of Rev. C. W. Denison, from the spring preceding. In conducting both these papers he received assistance, for a season, from the late Stephen P. Hines, one of the earliest advocates of the anti-slavery cause.

† By the popular orators and paid agents of the Colonization Society, Mr. Garrison was afterwards stigmatized in public meetings of that Society, in the city of New York and elsewhere, as "*a convicted felon,*" on account of this trial and imprisonment!

After lying in jail about fifty days, Mr. Garrison was released by the payment of his fine and costs, amounting to upwards of one hundred and fifty dollars, contributed chiefly by Mr. Arthur Tappan, merchant, of New York, well known as the munificent patron of Foreign Missions and other kindred efforts. His name thenceforward, with that of his brother, Lewis Tappan, was identified with the anti-slavery cause. Mr. Garrison, dissolving partnership with Mr. Lundy, issued the prospectus of his "*Liberator*," to be published at Washington City, but his arrangements were afterwards changed. Mr. Lundy removed with his paper to Washington, and Mr. Garrison commenced his "*Liberator*" in Boston, in Jan., 1831.

Mr. Tappan, Rev. Simeon S. Jocelyn, and others, projected the establishment of a seminary of learning at New Haven, for the benefit of colored students, the same year, but a strong opposition manifested itself, a public meeting at New Haven denounced the project, and it was necessarily abandoned.

The insurrection of Nat. Turner at Southampton, in Virginia, the same year, alarmed the South, and quickened the discussion of the slave question throughout the country. The insurgents, about sixty in number, were put down by United States' forces. The Legislature of Virginia discussed the measure of gradual emancipation, but indefinitely postponed the whole subject.

On January 30, 1832, the New England Anti-Slavery Society was organized in Boston, and went into operation, but with limited means.

The "*New York Evangelist*," conducted for a time by Rev. Samuel Griswold, and afterwards by Rev. Joshua Leavitt, entered into the discussion, and espoused the enterprise. The "*Genius of Temperance*," as before mentioned, was already committed to the cause. The circulation of both these papers was, at that time, extensive, through all the non-slaveholding and many of the slaveholding States.

By pecuniary aid from the Messrs. Tappan, the "*Emancipator*" was commenced, in the spring of 1833, as before stated, by the publishers of the "*Genius of Temperance*."

By co-operation between the Messrs. Tappan and a few others, very large issues of anti-slavery tracts were circulated monthly, during the greater part of this year, and sent by mail to clergymen of all denominations, and other prominent men throughout the country. A great amount of important information was thus diffused.

This year was also distinguished by the visit of Mr. Garrison to England, where he obtained important information, and was cheered with the hearty sympathy of Wilberforce, Clarkson, Buxton, Macauley, and other friends of the cause. At home, the excitement was increased by the disgraceful and ever memorable prosecution and imprisonment of Miss Prudence Crandall, for teaching a colored school at Canterbury, Conn., under a law enacted for the special purpose, through the influence of leading friends of the Colonization Society.

By this time the doctrine of immediate and unconditional emancipation of the soil, as held by " modern abolitionists," was pretty thoroughly proclaimed throughout the country. To the mass of the people it was a new and strange doctrine, though taught by Hopkins and Edwards the previous century. It roused the people from their slumbers. The majority were alarmed; some hesitated, many inquired, and not a few, including individuals of high moral worth and established reputation, were attracted to the new and definite standard, and rallied round it. Among these were many whose earnest opposition to slavery was no new and hasty impulse. Evan Lewis, of Pennsylvania, of the Society of Friends, for many years an active friend of the enslaved, was of the number of these. Hon. William Jay, the worthy son of Gov. John Jay of New York, was another. Moses Brown, a very aged member of the Society of Friends, of Providence, R. I., more extensively known by his exalted virtues and rare wisdom than by his great wealth, was another.* Nathaniel Emmons, D.D., of Massachusetts, the dis-

---

* Moses Brown died in 1836, aged 98. A few days before his death he penned an important communication on the subject of slavery, for publication in an anti-slavery

tinguished theologian, of the school of Edwards and Hopkins, and formerly their associate, being then eighty-eight years of age, but retaining his full mental vigor, was another.* Rev. Thomas Andros, of Berkeley, Mass., upwards of seventy years of age, yet active, a "self-made man"—of strong powers and extensive literary acquirements, a theological writer, though a mariner in his younger years, and once a prisoner in the Revolutionary war on board the far-famed Jersey prison-ship, (from which he escaped by almost superhuman exertions and miraculous providences, while prostrate with yellow fever,) was another. Chief Justice Hutchinson, of Vermont, was another. To this list might be added others less extensively known, but of a similar character, men minutely acquainted with the history of slavery and emancipation, veterans, some of them, for more than half a century in the cause of human freedom, and well qualified to judge what expedients were to be regarded as inadequate, and what the exigencies of the times required. The wisdom and experience of such men should have sheltered the anti-slavery agitation from the flippant charge of a "hair-brained fanaticism"—the charges emanating, in most instances, from younger and less considerate men, many of whom had never devoted a month's candid attention to the most profound and momentous problem of the age. If younger men, under the manifest Providence of God, originated the movement, they were not destitute of the sympathy, council, and co-operation of the

---

paper. He was consequently 94 years of age in 1832, when the New England Anti-Slavery Society was formed.

* Dr. Emmons had incautiously taken for granted that the Colonization Society was doing some good, though he never seems to have relied upon it to remove slavery. When Mr. Garrison came out against the Society, in 1832, Dr. Emmons, who was "never too old to learn," sat down to an examination of the Society's periodical magazine, the "*African Repository*," which was lying on a shelf in his own study. A few hours' reading opened his eyes. "There is no disinterested benevolence about it," said he, as he laid up the numbers. "It is all a scheme of selfishness, from beginning to end. It is all wrong." At the Anniversary of the American Anti-Slavery Society in New York City, in May, 1835, he was present, and presided at the opening of the meeting for business. He died Sept. 23, 1840, in the 96th year of his age.

patriarchs of liberty in both hemispheres. And practical business men, from forty to sixty years of age, were not wanting among them. New recruits, of all ages and professions, came forward. , President Storrs, and Professors B. Green* and E. Wright, Jr., of the Western Reserve College, Hudson, Ohio, were hailed among the accessions of this period. [James G. Birney, James A. Thome, Rev. Dr. Nelson, Rev. Dr. Brisbane and others, from the slave States, espoused the cause afterwards.]

The time had now come for a more general organization of the friends of the cause. A New York City Anti-Slavery Society was organized, October 2, 1833, but not without demonstrations of tumult and violence. The meeting had been advertised to be held at Clinton Hall. A counter notice, signed by " Many Southrons," invited a meeting at the same time and place. The abolitionists, therefore, as many as on the sudden emergency could be notified, assembled at Chatham Street Chapel. Their opposers, finding Clinton Hall closed, adjourned to Tammany Hall, and made speeches and adopted resolutions against them. Before separating, they learned where the abolitionists were assembled, and adjourned, by acclamation, and shouts of " Let us route them," to Chatham Street 'Chapel, which they entered tumultuously and riotously, just as the meeting there had adjourned, but before the persons in attendance had left the house. Loud threats were uttered—" Ten thousand dollars for Arthur Tappan!" Several abolitionists were called for by name, but they all escaped personal violence. The Tammany meeting was organized by prominent citizens, addressed by popular public speakers, and their proceedings published in the city papers, along with gratulations for the " security of the Union!"

By the same class of citizens, a Colonization meeting was promptly called, which was held at the Masonic Hall, precisely one week after the Tammany Hall and Chatham Street Chapel meetings. The Mayor of the city presided. The orators

---

* Afterwards President Green, of Oneida Institute, N. Y.

dwelt on the reckless agitations of the abolitionists. Not a word of disapprobation of the late outrage against them was uttered. Theodore Frelinghuysen, United States Senator from New Jersey, charged them with "seeking to dissolve the Union." Chancellor Walworth was in attendance, from Albany, to declare their efforts "unconstitutional," and to denounce them as "reckless incendiaries." David B. Ogden, Esq., declared " the doctrine of immediate emancipation to be a direct and palpable nullification of the Constitution." Mr. Frelinghuysen further declared that " nine-tenths of the horrors of slavery are imaginary," and the "crusade of abolition" he regarded as " the poetry of philanthropy."

In pursuance of a previous public notice, a National Anti-Slavery Convention was held in the City of Philadelphia, December 4th, 5th, and 6th, 1833, consisting of upwards of sixty members, from ten States, viz.: Maine, New Hampshire, Vermont, Massachusetts, Rhode Island, Connecticut, New York, New Jersey, Pennsylvania, and Ohio. Beriah Green, President of Oneida Institute, was chosen President of the Convention, and Lewis Tappan and John G. Whittier Secretaries. The members united in signing a declaration of their sentiments, objects, and measures, prepared in committee, from a draft by Mr. Garrison. This Convention organized the American Anti-Slavery Society, of which Arthur Tappan was chosen President, Elizur Wright, Jun., Secretary of Domestic Correspondence, and William Lloyd Garrison Secretary of Foreign Correspondence, A. L. Cox, Recording Secretary, William Green, Jr., Treasurer. The Executive Committee was located in New York City, the seat of the Society's operations; which were now prosecuted with vigor. The "Emancipator," under editorial charge of William Goodell,* one of the Executive Committee, became the organ of the Society. Tracts, pamphlets, and books were published and circulated,

---

* This arrangement continued till July, 1835, when Mr. Goodell left the city for another field of labor in the same cause, and the *Emancipator* was conducted, successively, by E. Wright, Jr., Amos A. Phelps, and Joshua Leavitt, and was finally removed to Boston.

a large number of lecturing agents were employed, conventions were held, and State, County, and local Anti-Slavery Societies were organized throughout the free States, auxiliary to the American, and contributing to its funds. The New England Anti-Slavery Society became the Massachusetts State Society. Mr. Garrison continued to issue the Liberator at Boston, some time as organ of the State Society, and afterwards again in his own name.

These particulars may serve to give some idea of the origin of the Anti-Slavery movement, sufficient to show that it was of no mushroom growth, or capricious origin, but came up, naturally, not to say necessarily, under the moral government of God, and in the onward and upward march of human improvement and progress. In the light of the preceding history, this remark can scarcely fail to be appreciated, as well as understood. To what destiny, without such a healthful, timely, and necessary agitation, could the country have been tending? What would have become of the interests of humanity, of morality, of religion, of civilization, and of liberty, affected as these are by the position and the activities of the Church and of the State? Was it not high time that *something* were attempted to be done? What should that something be, if not the measures that were then put in operation? If there were wiser men, who could have propounded better measures, why did they not come forward? If it be said that the Colonization Society was, (as was claimed by its friends,) ·that better measure, let the unprejudiced reader judge.

We cannot further pursue, in minute detail, the history of the anti-slavery agitation. A well-digested and condensed account of it would require a large volume. We will hastily group together a few classes of facts that may afford light upon the present position and aspect of the slave question in America, and the duties and prospects before us.

PRINCIPLES OF ABOLITIONISTS.

These may be briefly and comprehensively stated as follows:

"All men are created equal, and are endowed by their Creator with certain inalienable rights, among which are life, liberty, and the pursuit of happiness."

Slavery, or more properly, the practice of slaveholding, is a crime against human nature, and a sin against God.

Like all other sins, it should be immediately and unconditionally repented of, and abandoned. It is always safe to leave off doing wrong, and never safe to continue in wrongdoing.

It is the duty of all men to bear testimony against wrongdoing, and consequently, to bear testimony against slaveholding.

Immediate and unconditional emancipation is pre-eminently prudent, safe, and beneficial, to all the parties concerned.*

No compensation is due to the slaveholder for emancipating his slaves; and emancipation creates no necessity for such compensation, because it is, of itself, a pecuniary benefit, not only to the slave, but to the master.

There should be no compromise of moral principle, in legislation, jurisprudence, or the executive action of the Government, any more than in the activities and responsibilities of private life.

No wicked enactments can be morally binding. "There are, at the present time, the highest obligations resting on the people of the free states to remove slavery, by moral and political action, as prescribed in the Constitution of the United States."—*Anti-Slavery Declaration of* 1833.

THE MEASURES OF ABOLITIONISTS were such as grew out

---

* The precise date of the adoption of this sentiment by "modern abolitionists" generally in America, we do not find. Mr. Garrison had not adopted it at the time of his 4th of July discourse at Boston, in 1829, but it was embodied in the Declaration of the Convention at Philadelphia, in 1833.

of their *principles*, and consisted in their promulgation and practice.

Among the publications circulated by them, at an early day, were the Dialogue of Dr. Hopkins, and the Sermon of Dr. Jonathan Edwards, before mentioned, together with Wesley's Thoughts on Slavery. The first two, as we have seen, had been circulated long before, by the Anti-Slavery Societies, patronized by Stiles, Jay, and Franklin. The latter had been circulated by Methodist preachers, by direction of the Conferences, as late as the year 1804. But in 1834, the circulation of these writings was proscribed as treasonable, and condemned as insurrectionary. No writings of "modern abolitionists" were more severe against slaveholders than these, as an examination of them will show.

CHAPTER XXXIII.

OPPOSITION TO ABOLITIONISTS.—ITS CAUSES—ITS ELEMENTS—
ITS NATURE AND METHODS.

Why abolitionists were opposed—False reasons assigned for it—Elements of the
opposition—Conservatism in the Church—Commercial cupidity—Political rivalry
—Scheme of Colonization—Servility of Literary Institutions—Nature and modes
of opposition—The religious and political press—Mob violence—Early and remarkable instances—New York, Philadelphia, Worcester (Mass.), Canaan (N. H.),
Boston, Utica (N. Y.), New Haven (Conn.), Alton (Ill.)—Murder of Lovejoy—
Burning of Pennsylvania Hall—Three Riots in Cincinnati—Three in Philadelphia—Similar scenes elsewhere—Fomented by "the higher classes of Society"—
"Gentlemen of property and standing"—the Conservative Clergy, and leading
influences in the Colonization Society.

WHY were abolitionists opposed? And for what? It was
for the agitation of the slave question. It was for the attempted propagation and practice of their principles, *and for
nothing else,** that abolitionists were violently assailed and villified.

It was *not* because they were "fanatics" or "incendiaries,"
nor because they insisted upon or recommended "amalgamation," or sought to incite the slaves to insurrection and bloodshed. These charges were only the unfounded aspersions of
their enemies.

It was *not* because they had any of them, at that time, assailed either the Churches, the Sabbath, the Bible, the Ministry, the Constitution, the Union, or the political parties. They

---

* It is admitted that many worthy men, including sincere friends of the enslaved,
dissented from the distinctive views of abolitionists, and argued against them. Dr.
Channing, to some extent, did this, as did many others. But this was no part of
the kind of opposition of which we are speaking.

had simply assailed *slavery*, invoking all the powers of the Church and of the State, with their institutions—all religious sects and all political parties in the country—to join *with* them, in opposition to slavery. They were mostly themselves supporters of the different religious sects and political parties: and so far from anticipating any separation from them, or controversy with them, they fondly expected to secure their co-operation and assistance. To ministers of the gospel, especially, were their appeals confidingly and respectfully addressed.*

It was *not* because, in the first instance, they opposed, or thought of opposing, the Colonization Society. Mr. Garrison himself addressed, on invitation, a meeting of the Colonization Society, held in the Park-street Congregational Church in Boston, on the 4th of July, 1829.† The Colonization Society was not opposed by abolitionists until it was found to be the opposer of abolition, and the persecutor of the free people of color.

It was the "*agitation of the subject*" that was opposed, and not any particular measure or mode of treating it.

ELEMENTS OF THE OPPOSITION.

As the anti-slavery agitation was, primarily, the natural

---

* The writer accompanied Mr. Garrison, in 1829, in calling upon a number of prominent ministers in Boston, to secure their co-operation in the cause. Our expectations of important assistance from them were, at that time, very sanguine.

† This elaborate and able discourse was published in the *National Philanthropist*, under the title of "NATIONAL DANGERS," among which the speaker enumerated "infidelity"—"the tyranny of government which compels its servants to desecrate the holy Sabbath"—the "desolations of liquid fire"—the abuse of the elective franchise—the general exclusion of religious men from office—"the profligacy of the press," which attacks every holy enterprise, (*e. g.* the missionary cause, &c., which was then villified), and finally, the great abomination of slavery. On this latter topic the speaker dilated at length, and said—"*I call on the ambassadors of Christ* everywhere, to make known this proclamation, 'Thus saith the Lord God of the Africans, Let this people go, that they may serve me.' I ask them to 'proclaim liberty to the captive, and the opening of the prison to them that are bound.'" "*I call on the churches of the living God* TO LEAD *in this great* ENTERPRISE!"

Had the churches and ministry responded, as they should have done, to this appeal, they would have been spared the trouble of opposing "infidel abolitionism," and the pretext of being repulsed from the anti-slavery enterprise by it.

working of a religious sentiment in the religious community, so the *opposition* to it was, primarily, the natural working of a *counter* sentiment in the *same* religious community. There was not a religious sect that did not experience the shock of the two antagonistic principles contending against each other in the same ecclesiastical communion.

From the times of the Edwardses, there had been a progressive and a conservative party in the Churches; the former aspiring after an enlarged liberty, and the latter seeking to repress it; the former insisting upon the doctrine of immediate and unconditional repentance (as did Hopkins); the latter pleading for indulgences, postponement, gradualism, and temporizing expedients; the former responded promptly to the call for the immediate and unconditional abolition of slavery; the latter had previously intrenched and fortified itself in the fortress of the Colonization Society, and was determined to permit no disturbance of its supremacy and its quietude.

The first collision, therefore, was manifested in the bosom of the principal religious sects at the North, including especially the Congregationalists of New England, and the Presbyterians of the Middle States, and speedily followed in the Methodist, Baptist, and other communions. The religious presses of these, particularly of the Congregational sect, in the hands of the conservative party, were the first to traduce, to misrepresent, to villify, and to oppose the abolitionists, representing them as anarchists, Jacobins, villifiers of great and good men who had been slaveholders, (but who had not been directly mentioned by abolitionists*) incendiaries, plot-

---

* The *Vermont Chronicle*, edited by Rev. Joseph Tracy, early in 1833, represented that the *Liberator* had called Washington a man-stealer and a robber, now in hell! But this was only the *inference* of Mr. Tracy from a communication in the *Liberator*, written by a Presbyterian clergyman of New York (Rev. Geo. Bourne), formerly a resident of Virginia, in which the *doctrine* of Edwards—and in nearly the same *language*—was affirmed (without any allusion to Washington), that slaveholding was man-stealing, and an act of robbery. Yet the charge went the rounds of the religious papers, was copied at the South, then by the New York City editors, and repeated by the mob who sacked the house, and burnt the furniture of Lewis Tappan

ters of insurrection and disunion, and enemies of the public peace. By these artful and injurious appeals, other than religious elements of opposition were soon roused.

Commercial cupidity in the cities trading with the South, was one of these elements, very early brought into action.

Political corruption and rivalry came next in order. Abolitionists were found in both political parties. The leading whig presses first,* and the democratic afterwards, exerted themselves to throw off the imputed contamination, and assure the South that their party was "sound to the core, on the subject of slavery."

All these elements of opposition found their centre, their home and their manifestation, from the beginning, in the Colonization Society, the pet of the conservatists both in the Church and the State. The meetings, the publications, the agents, and the advocates of this Society, were almost uniformly and invariably at the head of every movement and of every disturbance in which the abolitionists were assailed.

Literary Institutions at the North desiring or enjoying Southern patronage, Northern watering-places the resort of Southern visitors, manufacturing establishments and villages of artizans and mechanics vending their fabrics and wares at the South—these were points from which an influence was almost certain to emanate, opposed to all earnest agitation of the subject of slavery.

Over all these elements and posts of opposition, presided *the slave interest itself*, the power that controlled so extensively both the Church and the State ; the mammoth oligarchy of the nation, assimilating and wielding for its own ends, all the minor interests and elements of aristocracy in the land.

---

in the streets, in July, 1834. Mr. Tracy would not retract the charge. He was afterwards editor of the *Boston Recorder*, and then of the *New York Observer*, the two oldest religious papers in the country, and advocates of the Colonization Society.

* This priority of action was perhaps owing to the fact that a greater number of *prominent* abolitionists were then found in the Whig party than in the Democratic, which latter was in the ascendant, and therefore identified with the pro-slavery action of the Government, and averse to agitation.

NATURE AND METHODS OF OPPOSITION.

To " put down the discussion "—to " silence the agitation." was the evident object—and to a great extent, this design was openly avowed. The " public indignation," in some form, was to overawe the agitators, and overwhelm them with defeat.* In perfect consistency with this, was the policy of closing against them the ordinary avenues of access to the public mind—the pulpit, the forum, the public journals, (political, commercial, literary, and religious,)—the arena of public debate. Or, if a discussion was attempted, inflammatory appeals and injurious aspersions were substituted for manly argument and dignified debate. A colonization meeting or anniversary was the precursor of a mob against the abolitionists; or, on the other hand, the riotous dispersion of an anti-slavery meeting prepared the minds of a sympathizing populace, with their gifted orators, for a public demonstration in favor of the colonization enterprise, connected with bitter denunciations of abolitionists, and apologies or defenses of slaveholding.

EXTENSIVE MANIFESTATIONS OF MOB VIOLENCE.

An attempt to hold an anti-slavery meeting in the city of New York, on the 4th of July, 1834, was made the occasion of a frightful and protracted riot. The meeting was broken up; and for several successive days and evenings, the city was in possession of the rioters, who assaulted private dwellings and places of public worship, attempting and threatening personal violence upon abolitionists. Similar scenes were enacted in Philadelphia a few weeks afterwards. Extensive damages were done to the private dwellings and public building of the unoffending colored people who had been cruelly

---

* It is important that the reader notices distinctly this statement, and watches the evidences of its truthfulness, as the narrative proceeds. Great efforts have been made to produce the impression that only some peculiar and offensive " *measures*" of abolitionists were opposed. The " measure" *most* obnoxious was the agitation and discussion of the subject.

maligned, and wantonly held up to public odium at a coloni-zation meeting a short time previous. During these riots, which were of several days' recurrence, many of the colored people were wounded, and some of them lost their lives.

These early examples of lawlessness, notoriously counte-nanced as they were by men of wealth and influence, excited by eloquent orators, and palliated afterwards by the public press, furnished precedents for similar outrages throughout the non-slaveholding states for a series of years.

At Worcester, Mass., Aug. 10, 1835, while Rev. Orange Scott was lecturing, a son of an Ex-Governor of the State, assisted by an Irishman, tore up his notes and offered him personal violence.

On the same day, a mob at Canaan, (N. H.) demolished and dragged away an academy, because colored youth were ad-mitted to study there.

At Boston, Oct. 21st., 1835, a mob of 5000 "gentlemen of property and standing," as the city editors called them, mobbed the Boston Female Anti-Slavery Society, dispersed them while the President was at prayer, and dragged Mr. Garrison through the streets with a rope about his body. He was roughly handled, threatened with tar and feathers, but finally con-ducted to the Mayor, who lodged him in jail till the next day, to save him from further violence. After an examina-tion, he was released from prison, but at the earnest entreaties of the city authorities, left Boston for a time.

The same day, at Utica, N. Y., a committee of twenty-five prominent citizens, appointed at a public meeting, and headed by a member of Congress, broke up a meeting convened to form a New York State Anti-Slavery Society, and threw down the press of a democratic journal that had espoused the anti-slavery cause. By invitation of Gerrit Smith, who, on that occasion, identified himself with them, the abolitionists re-paired to his residence at Peterboro', twenty-five miles dis-tant, where the next day they finished the transaction of their business, after a portion of them had been pelted with stones, mud, and missiles, at Vernon, on their way from Utica to Peterboro'.

In Dec. 1836, an anti-slavery meeting at New Haven, Conn., was broken up by some southern students of Yale College.

At Alton, Illinois, Nov. 7, 1837, the press of the Alton Observer was destroyed by a mob, and the editor, Rev. Elijah P. Lovejoy, shot dead, receiving four balls in his breast. The murderers were not brought to justice.

Pennsylvania Hall, in Philadelphia, was opened May 14, 1838, for the free discussion of all subjects interesting to American citizens. On the 17th of the same month it was burned by a mob, because abolitionists had been allowed to hold a meeting there.

At Cincinnati, Ohio, Sept. 5, 1841, a ferocious mob destroyed, for the *third* time, the printing-press of the Philanthropist, a paper devoted to anti-slavery. The first of these outrages was in 1836. JAMES G. BIRNEY, a repentant slaveholder, from Kentucky, was then editor and proprietor of the paper.

At Philadelphia, on the 1st of August, 1842, occurred the worst of several mobs against the colored people of that city. A church and hall, built by their hard earnings, were burnt down, their houses demolished, and their persons beaten and mangled in the most ferocious and cowardly manner. The city authorities afforded no efficient protection till the mischief was done, in a riot of two days. The only provocation, on their part, was a peaceful temperance celebration of the anniversary of British West India emancipation, and walking in public procession on that occasion.

These instances present but a specimen of the riots enacted against abolitionists in almost all parts of the country. Not only in cities and large towns, but in rural villages, and country parishes, and townships, the attempt to hold a meeting for the discussion of slavery was, very frequently, the signal for a disturbance and breach of the peace.*

---

* It would be easy to fill a respectable volume with accounts of these mobs, and

One uniform feature of these lawless proceedings has been that they have been either countenanced, instigated, or palliated by that description of citizens who complacently consider themselves and are commonly denominated "*the higher class of society*,"—the men of wealth, of office, of literature, of elegant leisure, including politicians,—and that portion of the clergy who naturally associate with the class just described, or are dependent upon them. The aristocracy of a city or village, and its mobocracy, if not exactly identical, or even if exhibiting the strong contrasts of splendor and squalor, were found to be the inseparable ingredients, the *sine qua non* of a riot against the claims of emancipation and the exercise of free speech. We speak of the general fact, not forgetting the noble exceptions.

Another remark in place here, is the uniformity and efficiency with which the influences sustaining the scheme of Colonization, (with the rare exceptions just now conceded,) have been arrayed against the free discussion of the slave question, and bent, at all hazards, upon its suppression. We might specify the riots in New York, in Philadelphia, at Utica, and at Alton, as having been obviously excited beforehand, or palliated and excused afterwards, by the editors and public speakers devoted to the Colonization cause. The pledge of the Society, beforehand, to visit with its censures, when needful, the existence of Abolition Societies in America, has been amply and even more than literally redeemed.

---

the means by which they have been roused. The writer has often been solicited to prepare such a volume, and had intended to afford more space in the present work for the details.

CHAPTER XXXIV.

ATTEMPTS TO SILENCE THE DISCUSSION BY AUTHORITY—STATE
LEGISLATURES—FEDERAL EXECUTIVE—U. S. MAILS—GAG
RULES IN CONGRESS—RIGHT OF PETITION.

Presentment of a Grand Jury—Literary and Theological Review—Pamphlet of Hon.
Mr. Sullivan—Rewards offered by Southern Governors for the abduction of North-
ern Abolitionists—Violent language of pro-slavery clergy and ecclesiastical bodies
—Southern demands on Northern State Legislatures—Responses of Northern
Governors—Bill reported in Legislature of Rhode Island—Violation of U. S. Mails
—Pillage of Post-office at Charleston—Postmaster General—President's Message
—Accusation against abolitionists—Recommends a prohibition of the circulation
of their papers by mail—Answer of the Anti-Slavery Ex. Com.—Legislature of
Massachusetts—Joint Committee—Interview with Anti-Slavery Committee—Their
defense silenced—Reaction—Prohibitory Legislation defeated—Action in Congress
—Calhoun's Mail Report—Recommendation of the President defeated—Act to
prevent a violation of the mails—Anti-Slavery Petitions—Various "gags" from
1836 to 1845—John Quincy Adams.

BUT measures of mere riotous, irregular, unauthorized violence against abolitionists, were soon found inadequate to the
objects of those who had set them on foot. It was not every
day that a popular tumult could be roused. By a reaction
which might have been foreseen, the better part of community,
touched by sympathy, and excited to reflection and inquiry,
were led to protest against these disorderly proceedings.
Some of them became abolitionists themselves, and others who
did not, became justly alarmed at the progress of anarchy, and
the absence of protecting law. There was danger that the
tables might be turned, and mobs against abolitionists be followed by mobs against their opposers. It became important,
therefore, to put down abolitionists by the strong arm of civil
power.

Intimations in this direction began to manifest themselves

at an early day, and in close connection with the riotous demonstrations already noticed. About a month before the
great mob at Utica, a Grand Jury of that county, (Oneida)
comprising a portion of the incipient rioters, or persons in
sympathy with them, made a presentment in which they say
that those who form abolition societies are guilty of *sedition*,
and of right ought to be punished, and that it is the duty of
all citizens friendly to the Constitution of the United States,
to destroy all their publications wherever found.

The "Literary and Theological Review," published in the
city of New York, conducted by Leonard Woods, Jr., a son
of Professor Woods of Andover, Mass., (himself afterwards
Professor of a College in Maine) elaborately defended the
position that the "radicals" (meaning the abolitionists) were
"*justly liable to the highest civil penalties and ecclesiastical censures.*"*

The Review was patronized by prominent clergymen in
New York and New England, was approvingly quoted by
leading religious journals, without eliciting a word of public
dissent, (except from the proscribed abolitionists) either by
the school of theologians represented by and in special sympathy with the "Review," or—what is still more remarkable
—by the Reviews and Journals of the rival theological party,
in the habit of controverting disputed points, against them.

Another specimen of the literature of those times may be
found in a widely circulated pamphlet from the press of a
popular publishing house in Boston, the same year, from the
pen of a titled LL.D.,† the previous author of a "Political
Class Book" for schools, that had gone through several
editions. The drift of the pamphlet, of 1835, will appear
from the following:

"It is to be hoped and expected that Massachusetts will enact laws declaring the printing, publishing, and circulating papers and pamphlets on
slavery, and also the holding of meetings to discuss slavery and abolition,

---

* *Literary and Theological Review* for Dec., 1835.

† Hon. WILLIAM SULLIVAN.

to be public indictable offenses, and provide for the punishment thereof in such manner as will more effectually prevent such offenses."

If it be thought wonderful that such sentiments could emanate from the high places of New York and New England, is it not still more so that no earnest remonstrance, either from press, pulpit, or forum, was raised against it, excepting only from the threatened victims?

The prevalence and the publication of such views at the North could not fail to encourage and embolden the enemies of liberty and free discussion at the South. Accustomed to legislative enactments against the agitation of the slave question among themselves, it was natural that they should expect something of the kind from the legislatures of the non-slave-holding States, especially when there appeared to be so much evidence that leading men at the North were already ripe for the measure. A disposition to silence the northern abolitionists by public authority, as well as by other forms of violence, had been manifest at the South from the beginning, and there now seemed to be a prospect of securing the co-operation of the legislatures of the nominally free States.

As early as Dec. 26, 1831, Gov. Lumpkin, of Georgia, gave his approval to an act of the Legislature of that State, offering five thousand dollars to any one who would arrest and bring to trial, *under the laws of that State*, the editor or publisher of the *Boston Liberator*. By the laws of Georgia he would have been sentenced to death. Mr. Garrison was a citizen of Massachusetts, owing no allegiance to Georgia, but here was an attempt, by the Government of Georgia, to secure his felonious abduction. Yet the Government of Massachusetts took no notice of the insult, nor in any way provided for the security of its citizens.

Other public bodies and popular meetings at the South followed this example, and offered rewards for the abduction of Northern abolitionists. Twenty thousand dollars were offered at New Orleans for the seizure of Arthur Tappan, and ten thousand dollars at some other place for arresting Rev. Amos

A. Phelps. Another advertisement specified the names of *several* of the Executive Committee of the American Anti-Slavery Society at New York, offering a reward for each or either of them.

Even ministers of religion shared largely in the feelings that prompted to these advertisements and did much to countenance and inflame them.

Rev. Robert N. Anderson, of Virginia, writing to the Sessions of the Presbyterian Churches of Hanover Presbytery, in 1835, said:

" At the approaching stated meeting of the Presbytery, I design to offer a preamble and string of resolutions on the subject of the treasonable and abominably wicked interference of the Northern and Eastern fanatics with our political and civil rights, our property, and our domestic concerns."— " If there be any stray goat of a minister among you, tainted with the blood-hound principles of abolitionism, let him be ferreted out, silenced, excommunicated, AND LEFT TO THE PUBLIC TO DISPOSE OF IN OTHER RESPECTS.

" Yours in the Lord, ROBERT N. ANDERSON."

Rev. Thomas S. Witherspoon, of Alabama, writing to the editor of the *Emancipator*, said:

" Let your emissaries dare to cross the Potomac, and I cannot promise you that your fate will be less than Haman's. Then beware how you goad an insulted but magnanimous people to deeds of desperation."

Rev. William S. Plummer, D.D., of Richmond, Va., in July, 1835, wrote to the Chairman of a Committee of Correspondence for calling a public meeting of the clergy of Richmond, on the subject of abolition, in which he said:

" Let them (the abolitionists) understand THAT THEY WILL BE CAUGHT IF THEY COME AMONG US, and they will take good care to keep out of our way." " If abolitionists will set the country in a blaze, it is but fair that they should receive the first warming of the fire."

A few days after the famous forcing of the Post-office, the violation of the U. S. Mail, and the destruction of anti-slavery publications, at Charleston, S. C. (July 29, 1835), a public meeting was held for completing that measure, and ferreting out and lynching abolitionists. At this assembly, the *Charleston Courier* informs us,

"The clergy of all denominations attended in a body, lending their sanction to the proceedings, and adding by their presence to the impressive character of the scene."

The thanks of the meeting to the clergy for this service, was expressed in a resolution for that purpose.

Rev. J. C. Postell (Methodist), of South Carolina, some time afterwards, addressed a letter to Rev. La Roy Sunderland (Methodist), editor of *Zion's Watchman*, New York, in which he said:

"If you wish to educate the slaves, I will tell you how to raise the money, without editing *Zion's Watchman*. You and old Arthur Tappan come out to the South this winter, and they will raise one hundred thousand dollars for you. New Orleans itself will be pledged for it. Desiring no further acquaintance with you," &c. &c.!

It was in the same year (1835) that the ministers and messengers of the Goslein Baptist Association, assembled at Free Union, Virginia, having adopted resolutions affirming the right to slave property, proceeded to denounce the abolitionists as incendiaries and assassins, and intimating that they dared not show themselves at the South.

At the Anniversary of the American Colonization Society at Washington City (so late as 1839), Hon. Henry A. Wise, M. C., of Virginia, a slaveholder and duellist, said:

"THE BEST WAY TO MEET ABOLITIONISTS WAS WITH DUPONT'S BEST (*i. e.* gunpowder) AND WITH COLD STEEL." The *N. Y. Sun* reported that, after Mr. W. had made his speech, Rev. Dr. Gardner Spring, of New York CITY, SPOKE WITH SYMPATHY OF THE SENTIMENTS OF THE SOUTH, AS EVINCED IN THE SPEECH OF MR. WISE!"

We can bear testimony that the language here attributed to Mr. Wise is but little more violent or reprehensible than was frequently used at Colonization meetings that were attended by Dr. Spring (one of them in his own "session room") in the city of New York, both preceding and after the riots against abolitionists, in 1833 and '34. To "silence" and to "put down the incendiaries," were expressions very frequently employed.

The reader will now be prepared to understand the records

that follow, and appreciate the situation of the friends of liberty at that period.

Gov. McDuffie, of South Carolina, in his message to the Legislature, in Dec., 1835, declared slavery to be "the corner-stone of our republican edifice." The laboring population of any community, "bleached or unbleached," he pronounced to be a "dangerous element in the body politic." He predicted that the body of the laboring people of the North would be virtually reduced to slavery within twenty-five years.[*] Of the measures of abolitionists, he said: "The laws of every community should punish this species of interference with death without benefit of clergy,"[†] &c. &c.

In pursuance of his recommendation (and, as if desirous of fulfilling his prophecy), both branches of the Legislature of that State (Dec. 16) adopted the following:

" *Resolved*, That the Legislature of South Carolina, having every confidence in the justice and friendship of the non-slaveholding States, *announces her confident expectation*, and she earnestly requests, that the Government of these States will promptly and EFFECTUALLY SUPPRESS all those associations within their respective limits, purporting to be abolition societies," &c., &c.

December 19, 1835, the General Assembly of North Carolina adopted the following:

" *Resolved*, That our sister States are respectfully requested to enact PENAL LAWS, prohibiting the printing, within their respective limits, *all* such publications as *may have a tendency* to make our slaves discontented."

January 7, 1836, the Alabama Legislature adopted the following: ˙

" *Resolved*, That we call upon our sister States, and respectfully request them to enact such PENAL LAWS as will finally put an end to the malignant deeds of the abolitionists."

Gov. Gayle, of Alabama, had previously demanded of Gov. Marcy, of New York, that R. G. Williams, publishing agent

---

[*] The Fugitive Slave law of 1850 seems well calculated to fulfil the prediction !

[†] The reader will notice the striking coincidence between this language of Gov. McDuffie and that of the " *Literary and Theological Review*," viz : "justly liable to the highest civil penalties and ecclesiastical censures."

of the American Anti-Slavery Society, should be delivered up to be tried by the laws of Alabama, (a State into which he had never set his foot,) on an indictment against him by the Grand Jury of Tuscaloosa County, Ala., for publishing in the Emancipator, at New York, the following sentences:

" God commands, and all nature cries out, that man should not be held as property. The system of making men property has plunged 2,250,000 of our fellow-countrymen into the deepest physical and moral degradation, and they are every moment sinking deeper."

In making this demand, Gov. Gale says:

" It is admitted that the offender was not in this State when his crime was committed, and that he has not FLED therefrom, according to the strict literal import of that term."

Gov. Marcy, as may well be supposed, declined acceding to the demand. But it was expected that that class of offenses might be punished under laws to be enacted in New York.

Feb. 16, 1836, both houses of the Legislature of Virginia agreed to the following:

" *Resolved*, That the non-slaveholding States of the Union are respectfully but *earnestly* requested promptly to adopt PENAL ENACTMENTS, or such other measures, as will EFFECTUALLY SUPPRESS ALL associations within their respective limits purporting to be, or having the character of abolition societies."

Resolutions adopted " unanimously," about the same time, by the Legislature of Georgia, included the following:

" *Resolved*, That it is deeply incumbent on the people of the North to CRUSH the traitorous designs of the abolitionists."

These demands were officially communicated to the Governors of the non-slaveholding States, and by them were laid before the respective Legislatures, as matters deserving grave consideration and decision. It is not known to the writer that in doing this, a single northern Governor availed himself of the opportunity to express an opinion adverse to these demands, much less to speak of them in terms of merited indignation and rebuke. On the other hand, we have to record such specimens of servility and treachery as the following:

Edward Everett, (whig) Governor of Massachusetts, in his message communicating the southern documents, held the following language:

"Whatever by direct and necessary operation is *calculated* to excite an insurrection among the slaves, has been held, by highly respectable legal authority, an offense against the peace of this Commonwealth, which may be prosecuted as a MISDEMEANOR AT COMMON LAW."

William L. Marcy, (democratic) Governor of the State of New-York, in his message on the same subject, spoke as follows:

"Without the power to PASS SUCH LAWS the States would not possess all the necessary means for preserving their external relations of peace among themselves."

This was in January, 1836. In the Legislature of Rhode Island, Feb. 2d, Mr. Hazard, of Newport, Chairman of a Committee appointed on the subject, at a previous session, in October, 1835,* reported a bill in conformity with the southern demands.

While this question was pending in the legislatures of the northern states, the influence of the Federal Executive was brought to bear on the side of the Slave Power, and against the freedom of the press. The occasion for exerting this influence was presented by the excitement growing out of the transmission of anti-slavery publications, through the United States' Mails. Some of these publications were gratuitously sent, NOT to any portion of the colored people, either the free or the enslaved, but to prominent citizens, statesmen, clergymen, merchants, planters, and professional gentlemen at the south, whose names and residences were known at the north. There could be no reasonable pretense that this measure could excite an insurrection of the slaves. Gen. Duff Green, Editor of the Washington Telegraph, one of the most violent oppo-

---

* This, it will be noticed, was about two months *previous* to the earliest action in the Legislatures of the *Southern* States—so that, in reality, the measure of legislative suppression was first broached in the Legislature of a *Northern State!* The subject was introduced into the Legislature of Rhode Island by Mr. Hazard, who had presented resolutions of a public meeting in Newport, recommending the measure.

sers of abolitionists, admitted that there was little or no danger of this; and that the real ground of apprehension was that the publications would "operate upon the consciences and fears of slaveholders themselves, from the insinuation of their dangerous heresies into our schools, our *pulpits* and our domestic circles."—"It is only," (said he,) "by alarming the consciences of the weak and feeble, and by diffusing among our own people a morbid sensibility on the subject of slavery, that abolitionists can accomplish their object. Preparatory to this, they are now saturating the non-slaveholding States with the belief that slavery is a sin against God," &c.

The riotous outrage upon the Post-office and the U. S. Mail at Charleston, (S. C.) July 29, 1835, has already been alluded to. From an editorial of the Charleston Courier, it appears that "arrangements had previously been made at the Post-office in the city, to arrest the circulation of incendiary matter, until instructions could be received from the Post-office Department at Washington." The Editor therefore thought "it might have been better, perhaps, to have awaited the application for instructions before proceeding to extremities." In reply to this application, Aug. 5, the Postmaster General, Amos Kendall, (a northern man) said:

"I am satisfied that the Postmaster General has no legal authority to exclude newspapers from the mail, nor to prohibit their carriage or delivery on account of their character or tendency, real or supposed." " But I am not prepared to direct you to forward or deliver the papers of which you speak." " By no act or direction of mine, official or private, could I be induced to aid, knowingly, in giving circulation to papers of this description, directly or indirectly. We owe an obligation to the *laws*, but a *higher* one to the communities in which we live, and if the *former* be permitted to destroy the *latter*, it is patriotism to disregard them. Entertaining these views, I *cannot sanction*, and will *not condemn*, the step you have taken. Your justification must be looked for in the character of the papers detained, and the circumstances by which you are surrounded."

Other Postmasters followed the example of the Postmaster at Charleston. The measure of suppression was not confined to the South. The Postmaster at New-York, Samuel L. Gouverneur, Esq., proposed to the Anti-Slavery

Society, "*voluntarily* to desist from attempting to send their publications into the southern states, by public mails." The proposition was declined. In answer to a letter from Mr. Gouverneur to the Postmaster General, Mr. Kendall wrote an elaborate reply, Aug. 22, in which he said:

" I am deterred from giving an order to exclude the whole series of abolition publications from the Southern mails only by a want of legal power, and if I were situated as you are, I would do as you have done."

President Jackson introduced the subject into his annual message, Dec., 1835, accusing abolitionists of "unconstitutional and wicked attempts," and recommending as follows:

" I would therefore call the special attention of Congress to the subject, and respectfully suggest the propriety of passing such a law as will prohibit, under severe penalties, the circulation, in the Southern States, through the mail, of incendiary publications, intended to instigate the slaves to insurrection."

The winter of 1835–6 was a dark day for the prospects of northern freedom. Except by the intended victims of this proscription, few, feeble, and hated as they were, no voice of remonstrance was uttered, no symptoms of alarm were exhibited. The adoption of the measures proposed to Congress and to the Legislatures of Massachusetts, New-York, Rhode Island, and other free states, was anticipated, as a matter of course. The majority of intelligent citizens expected no other result. Abolitionists redoubled their efforts, knowing that all was at stake.

A searching Review of his Message, in the form of a solemn protest, was addressed to President Jackson, by the Executive Committee of the American Anti-Slavery Society at New York. In the bold and dignified language of conscious innocence, they denied the charges he had brought against them, of insurrectionary designs. They invited investigation by a Committee of Congress, and offered to submit to their inspection all their publications, all their correspondence, and all their accounts, and promising to attest them, and to answer every question under oath. No notice was ever taken by the President of this Protest, but it must have had its effect. His charges were never repeated by President Jackson, or by any of his successors.

An Anti-Slavery Convention at Providence (R. I.) for forming a Rhode Island State Anti-Slavery Society, Feb. 2, 1836, had been invited by a call of respectable citizens in all parts of the State. It was numerously attended, well sustained, and did much to revive the spirit of Roger Williams in that part of New England.

A joint Committee of both Houses of the Legislature of Massachusetts, Senator Lunt, Chairman, was appointed to consider and report, upon the southern demands. Abolitionists requested the customary privilege of a hearing before this Committee, but no notice, for a long time, was taken of the request. It was believed that no hearing would be given. The Anti-Slavery Committee at Boston, were at length unexpectedly notified that an audience would be given them, the very next day, March 4th, 1836. They hastily rallied, selected their advocates, and prepared for their defense. The interview was held in the Representatives' Hall, neither of the houses being in session, but most of the members of both houses, and many prominent citizens being present. After remarks by Rev. Samuel J. May, and Ellis Gray Loring, Esq., they were followed by Prof. Charles Follen, who, in the course of his remarks, alluded to the recent outrages against abolitionists, observing that any legislative enactments or censures against the already persecuted party, would tend to encourage their assailants, and increase their persecutions. Taking offense at this remark, the Chairman, Mr. Lunt, silenced Prof. Follen, and abruptly terminated the interview; whereupon the abolitionists took prompt measures for issuing their suppressed defense in a pamphlet form, which, comprising above 40 pages, was prepared for the press in the two following days. A Boston Editor, Benjamin F. Hallet, Esq., gave some account of the proceedings, and said the abolitionists were entitled to a fair hearing. The Legislature directed their Committee to allow a completion of the defense, which was accordingly notified for Monday, P. M., the 8th inst.

The adjacent country was by this time roused, and the hall of the Representatives was crowded. Prof. Follen concluded his speech, and was followed by Samuel E. Sewall, Esq., William Lloyd Garrison, and William Goodell, the latter of whom, instead of making any farther defense of abolitionists, or proving that their publications were not insurrectionary, proceeded to charge upon the southern states who had made these demands, a conspiracy against the liberties of the free North. This opened an entire new field. Great uneasiness was manifested by the Committee, but the speaker, though repeatedly interrupted by the Chairman, succeeded in quoting the language of Gov. McDuffie's message, and in characterizing the southern documents, to which he pointed, lying on the table of the Committee before him, as being fetters for northern freemen. He had commenced making the inquiry—"Mr. Chairman! Are you prepared to attempt putting them on?"—but the sentence was only about half finished, when the stentorian voice of the Chairman interrupted him:—"*Sit down, sir!*"—He sat down. The Legislative Committee presently began to move from their seats, but the audience sat petrified with suppressed feeling. The late Dr. William E. Channing was seated among the abolitionists, though not in form nor in sentiment fully identified with them. On such an occasion he could not be absent, and his presence was felt. His countenance seemed to express what words could not have uttered; more eloquent in silence than even *he* could have been in speech. The Legislative Committee themselves lingered, as in vague expectation. Then rose a respectable merchant of Boston, Mr. Bond, unaccustomed, as he said, to public speaking, and begged the Committee to wait a few minutes. It was growing dark, and the hall unlighted, but they sat down. Mr. Bond briefly reminded them that freedom of speech and of the press could never be surrendered by the sons of the pilgrims. He was followed by another volunteer, a Dr. Bradley, from old Plymouth rock. The Committee then rose again, and, with the audience, slowly and quietly retired. A low murmur of voices, though *too* low to be distinctly articulate, was heard through the dim hall of the People's Representatives, but the very tones of which, like the distant roar of the sea, told of power. The printed plea of the abolitionists was, three days afterwards, on the desk of each member of the Legislature, in the hands of the Governor, and in process of circulation through the Commonwealth. Mr. Lunt and his Committee delayed their Report, till near the close of the session, several weeks afterwards. It was a stale repetition of trite declamation on the subject, but recommending no distinct action by the legislature. What disposition was made of it we do not remember, and the political prospects of Mr. Senator Lunt shared its oblivion.

" As goes Massachusetts, so goes New England." The bill of Mr. Hazard, in the Legislature of Rhode Island, was defeated by the energy and spirit of two members from Providence, George Curtiss and Thomas W. Dorr.

By the Legislature of the State of New-York, a Report was adopted in May, 1836, responding to the sentiments of Gov. Marcy's Message, and pledging the faith of the State to enact such laws whenever they shall be requisite. This Report appears to have been sent to the Governors of the Southern States, but never appeared in the organ of the New-York State Administration, (the Albany Argus) in which the acts of the State Government are " by authority " published. The citizens of the State of New-York, in general, (including abolitionists who were watching for the document) were unapprized of its contents until they saw it quoted, the winter following, in the message of the acting Governor of Virginia. There were indications, in the year 1837, in the State of New York, that the project of legislative suppression was not relinquished.

The proposition of President Jackson to Congress, for an act prohibiting, under severe penalties, the circulation of insurrectionary publications through the mails, was referred to a Select Committee, of which John C. Calhoun was Chairman, by whom a Report was submitted, Feb. 4th, 1836, of a very remarkable character. It conclusively proved and maintained that the measure recommended by the President would be a violation of the Constitution and an infringement of the liberties secured under it. It would, moreover, be unsafe for the interests of slavery.

" Nothing is more clear," says the Report, " than that the admission of the right to Congress to determine what papers are incendiary, and, as such, to prohibit their circulation through the mail, necessarily involves the RIGHT to determine what are NOT incendiary, and ENFORCE their circulation." . . . " If Congress may this year decide what incendiary publications ARE, they may, next year, decide what they are NOT, and thus laden their mails with real though covert abolitionism." . . . " It belongs to the STATES, and not to Congress, to determine what is or is not calculated to disturb their security."

The Report, therefore, proceeded to maintain that when the several *states* had determined, severally, what publications were incendiary, the Federal Government and all the *other* States, were bound to conform to those determinations, and act accordingly. Congress must enact a law prohibiting the transmission of *such* publications through the mails, and every other State in the Union is bound to pass laws in concurrence, that is, prohibiting publication and discussion! Thus Congress and *all* the States were to be controlled by the legislation of *one* State! And powers unsafe to be conferred by the people upon their Representatives in Congress, (as the Report had shown) were nevertheless to be exercised by the legislature of a single slave State, over the whole country! The Report was accompanied by a Bill in accordance with its recommendations. It contained the following:

" *Be it enacted*, &c., That it shall not be lawful for any deputy postmaster, in any State, Territory, or District, of the United States, knowingly, to deliver to any person whatsoever, any pamphlet, newspaper, handbill, or other printed paper or pictorial representation, touching the subject of slavery, where, by the laws of the said State, Territory, or District, their circulation is prohibited, and any deputy postmaster who shall be guilty thereof, shall be forthwith removed from office."

On the question of a third reading in the Senate, the votes were eighteen to eighteen. The Vice President, Mr. Van

Buren, came forward and voted for the reading. It was however defeated on the final vote.

The project of restrictive legislation over the mails, was abandoned. Not only so: the credit of the Post-office Department was found to have received such a shock by the disorders that had given rise to these projects, that, instead of an act *requiring* such a discrimination as the President had recommended, the nation was astonished with an enactment, approved by the Presidential signature, (after having been passed without debate) *prohibiting* such a discrimination under severe and degrading penalties. The right of abolitionists to the use of the United States' mails was thus established! And before the close of the same session, Mr. Calhoun conceded, in the Senate, that the purposes and operations of the abolitionists were only moral and suasive, and *not* violent and insurrectionary.

ASSAULTS ON THE RIGHT OF PETITION.

Since neither riots nor legislation were likely to crush the abolitionists, the next expedient was to break down the right of petition, and to stifle the discussion in Congress. Abolitionists had deluged the Senate and House of Representatives with petitions for the abolition of slavery in the Federal District and Territories, and for the prohibition of the interstate slave trade. Now came the era of the "*gags*."

We give a list of them with the names of the movers, the dates, and the votes in the House, by which they were carried.

    1. Pinckney's, May 26th, 1836.—Yeas 117—Nays 68.

    2. Hawes',   Jan. 18th, 1837.—Yeas 115—Nays 47.

    3. Patton's,   Dec. 21st, 1837.—Yeas 122—Nays 74.

    4. Atherton's, Jan. 12th, 1838.—Yeas 126—Nays 78.

    5. Johnson's, incorporated into the standing rules of the House, and thenceforward known as the 21st rule. Jan. 28, 1840.—Yeas 114—Nays 108.

On the 7th of June, 1841, during an extra session, the vote by which this rule was "discarded" was—Yeas 112—Nays

104.   This was done by a vote adopting all the standing rules, *excepting the* 21*st,* but a *special* rule was immediately afterwards adopted, applicable only to the extra session, by which it was established that on the presentation of petitions on subjects not included in the President's Message, (except a bankrupt law) " objection to the reception shall be considered as made, and the question of reception shall be laid on the table." This was, in effect, a new gag of a *general* character, operating upon anti-slavery petitions, but not confined to them. *All* petitions as well as *abolition* petitions, were excluded, and people began to open their eyes to the fact that the entire nation, as well as the troublesome agitators, were gagged !

The original gag of Mr. Pinckney was as follows :

" *Resolved,* That all petitions, memorials, resolutions, and propositions, relating, IN ANY WAY, or TO ANY EXTENT, WHATEVER, to the subject of slavery, shall, without being either printed or referred, be laid on the table, and no further action whatever shall be had thereon."

The succeeding ones were substantially the same.

In the session of 1841-2, a Report was prepared re-enacting the gag ; but fearing to trust a vote upon it in the House, its authors adroitly laid it on the table, under the previous question, where it could not be taken up without a two-thirds vote. The effect of this (the extra session having passed) was to restore the 21st Rule. This was continued until December, 1845, when it was finally rescinded.

JOHN QUINCY ADAMS.

The long protracted efforts of John Quincy Adams, who was not an immediate abolitionist, to restore the right of petition, are too well understood to require a minute record in this place. They constituted the crowning act of his laborious public life, and rendered him the benefactor of his country. Mr. Adams also opposed the annexation of Texas, and the Mexican war. He declared that the General Government, in time of war, had a discretionary power to emancipate the slaves. He proposed in Congress a plan for the prospective abolition of slavery, through an amendment of the Constitution, a proposition which, by-the-by, received no favor either at the North or the South, thus testing the sincerity of those who professed to be opposed to slavery, and in favor of its gradual removal, while they only deprecated the imprudent measures of the *immediatists*. Mr. Adams was threatened with assassination, with an indictment by a Grand Jury of the District, and with expulsion from the House. A formal effort was made to pass a censure upon him, but it did not succeed.

CHAPTER XXXV.

OPPOSITION FROM LEADING CLERGY AND ECCLESIASTICAL BODIES.

Recapitulation of Preceding Statements—Theological Seminaries—Ecclesiastical Bodies—Law of Lane Seminary against discussion (1834)—Conference of Meth. Epis. Ch., Cincinnati (1836)—Ohio Annual Conference (previous)—New York Annual Conference, (June, 1836, 1838)—Sentiments of Methodist Ministers—Official course of Presiding Elders and Bishops—Presbyterian Synod of Philadelphia—Associations of Congregational Ministers in Connecticut and Massachusetts in 1836—"Pastoral Letters" of 1836, and 1837—Extraordinary claims of Congregational Pastors—Origin of disaffection towards the Clergy on the part of a class of Abolitionists.

WHILE these efforts were making to put down abolitionists by mob violence, by State legislation, by denunciations from the Federal Executive, by violations of the U. S. Mails, by closing the Post-offices against their publications, by gagging discussion in Congress, and overthrowing the people's right of petition, there was still *another* power, more potent than all the others, standing behind and sustaining them all, with which abolitionists were called to contend. We mean the prevailing and predominant *religious* influences of the country, represented by and controlling theological seminaries, religious associations, churches, and *ecclesiastical bodies*. It is the religion of a country that shapes its political and social manifestations, under all forms of government, more especially under those of a popular character.

The position of the principal religious sects, respecting slavery, was exhibited in former chapters.* It appeared also in their support of the Colonization Society.† The opposition

---

* Chap. XII. to XVIII.   † Chap. XXIX.

of Theological Reviews, of religious journals, and of prominent clergymen, has been adverted to in the present connection.* It was to be expected that corresponding manifestations should be witnessed in Theological Seminaries and the
action of ecclesiastical bodies. A few specimens must suffice,
in this record.

Among the earliest and boldest attempts to suppress the
discussion of the slave question in America, we have to record
the gag law of Lane Seminary, Ohio, October 6, 1834, by
which the students were ordered to disband both their Anti-
Slavery and Colonization Societies, (for it was important to
appear impartial,) and, in a standing rule, forbidden to lecture,
deliver addresses, or hold meetings among themselves, except
of a devotional character. This was during the reign of mob
violence against abolitionists, and more than a year before
the demands of Gov. McDuffie and his Southern associates
upon the free States of the North. The well known occasion
was the formation of a flourishing Anti-Slavery Society.
Though most of the students left the Seminary in consequence,
and the laws were soon after repealed, yet the same spirit pervaded theological and literary institutions in general, and influences were generally exerted in them which prevented free
discussion and inquiry.

In showing the position of the Methodist Episcopal Church
on the slave question, we have already noticed the declaration
of its General Conference at Cincinnati, in 1836, in which
they "disclaim any right, wish, or intention, to interfere in the
civil and political relation between master and slave, as it exists in the slaveholding States of this Union." At this same
Conference a preamble and resolutions were adopted deprecating "the great excitement on the subject of modern abolitionism," and the course of some of its members, as "calculated
to bring upon this body the suspicion and distrust of the community." They declared themselves "decidedly opposed to
modern abolitionism." It was also

---

* See last two chapters.

" *Resolved*, by the Delegates of the Annual Conferences, in General Conference assembled, that they disapprove, in the most unqualified sense, the conduct of the two members of the General Conference, who are reported to have lectured in this city recently, upon, and in favor of, modern abolitionism."

This resolution was adopted by a vote of 122 to 11. The mover, Rev. S. G. Roszell, was reported to have said, in the debate, that he wished the Rev. Orange Scott (one of the censured members) was in heaven—(that is, he wished he was dead:)—in perfect keeping with the murderous sentiments so freely expressed by pro-slavery clergymen at that period, some specimens of which the reader has already seen.

This same Conference received a friendly address from the Methodist Wesleyan Conference in England, on the subject of slavery, but refused to publish it. They adopted, moreover, a pastoral address to the communicants of the M. E. Church, in which, after stating that the "Constitutional Compact" between the *States* precluded *Church* action against slavery, they added,

" These facts, which are only mentioned here as a reason for the friendly admonition which we wish to give you, constrain us, as your pastors, who are called to watch over your souls, as they must give an account, to exhort you to abstain from all abolition movements and associations, and to refrain from patronizing any of their publications," &c. &c.   *   *   *

" From every view of the subject which we have been able to take, and from the most calm and dispassionate survey of the whole ground, we have come to the conclusion that the only safe, scriptural, and prudent way for us, both as ministers and people, to take, is, WHOLLY TO REFRAIN FROM THIS AGITATING SUBJECT," &c.—*Signed by order and in behalf of the General Conference of the M. E. Church, by the Bishops.*

The General Conference represented both the northern and the southern portions of the M. E. Church, acting together. But northern Annual Conferences took the same ground.

The Ohio Annual Conference had, a short time *before*, Resolved,

1. " That we deeply regret the proceedings of the abolitionists and anti-slavery societies in the free States, and the consequent excitement produced thereby in the slave States, that we, as a Conference, disclaim all connection and co-operation with, or belief in the same, and that we hereby recommend

to our junior preachers, local brethren, and private members within our bounds, to abstain from any connection with them, or participation of their acts, in the premises, whatever.

2. " That those brethren and citizens of the North who RESIST THE ABO-LITION MOVEMENTS with firmness and moderation, are the true friends to the Church, to the slaves of the South, and to the Constitution of our common country," &c.

The New-York Annual Conference, in June, 1836, approved the doings of the General Conference, and disapproved the patronizing of Zion's Watchman, an anti-slavery Methodist paper, edited by Rev. La Roy Sunderland. It also Resolved that—

* * * " We are, decidedly of the opinion that none ought to be elected to the office of a deacon or elder in our church, UNLESS HE GIVE A PLEDGE TO THE CONFERENCE THAT HE WILL REFRAIN FROM AGITATING THE CHURCH ON THIS SUBJECT," &c. &c.

In 1838, the same Conference resolved that any of its members or probationers who should patronize Zion's Watchman, recommend it, circulate it, obtain subscribers, or collect or remit moneys for it, "shall be deemed guilty of indiscretion, and dealt with accordingly."

" The Rev. George W. Langhorne, of North Carolina, in writing to the editor of *Zion's Watchman,* June 25, 1836, said :

" If you have not yet resigned your credentials as a minister of the Methodist Episcopal Church, I really think that, as an *honest* man, you should now do it." " You are bound to submit to their authority [the General Conference], or LEAVE THE CHURCH."

This sentiment, that abolitionists ought to quit the churches or cease disturbing their peace by anti-slavery agitation, was very current in the churches of most sects, even at the North, at this period, though much has been since said against the sin of schism, when abolitionists secede.

Presiding Elders refused to put anti-slavery resolutions in Quarterly Conferences, but readily put pro-slavery ones.

Bishops Hedding and Emory addressed a Pastoral Letter to the New England and New Hampshire Conferences, in which the anti-slavery excitement in that part of the country was discountenanced. They "advised the preachers, the trustees, and official and other members, to manifest their disapprobation, and to refuse the use of their pulpits and houses for such purposes."

" Bishop Waugh refused to put a motion to raise a committee on slavery at the N. E. Conference of 1837, and declared 'that there should be no appeal from his decision to the Conference. Bishop Hedding, at the N. E. Conference, in 1837, refused a motion to raise a committee on slavery, only on certain conditions.' "

" Bishop Soule, presiding at the New England Conference of the M. E. Church in 1840, refused permission asked by Rev. O. Scott to read a memorial from private members of the church, requesting the Annual Conference to express an opinion against the 'Colored testimony Resolution' of the General Conference."—*True Wesleyan*, Dec. 27, 1851.

The Presbyterian Synod of Philadelphia, about the same time, re-echoed the stale and truthless slanders of the newspapers against the abolitionists.

It is to be borne in mind that these ecclesiastical efforts to suppress the discussion of the slave question, in May and June, 1836, came as closely as possible on the heel of the legislative attempts to the same effect, in the national and state legislatures, the previous winter, being the first opportunity that had presented itself by the accustomed annual meetings of these bodies, since the famous demands of the Governors and Legislatures of the Slave States. They are to be interpreted in the light of the silence and apparent acquiescence of the leading clergy and religious journalists, during that dark period, except when, as already stated, their influence was on the side of "the highest *civil* penalties and *ecclesiastical* censures." The *former* had been attempted, and (though, in some states, they were still pending,) there was a prospect of their failure. Now came the time to try the power of the *latter*. The authorities of the Methodist Episcopal Church were speaking. It would not do for the guardians of New England Congregationalism to be behind them.

The Associations of Congregational Ministers, first of Connecticut, and, immediately afterwards, of Massachusetts, moving evidently in concert, and with the aid of prominent *Presbyterian* clergymen from New-York and Ohio, in attendance for that object, united in adopting a series of Resolutions, among which was the following:

" *Resolved*, That the operations of itinerant agents and lecturers attempting to enlighten the churches in respect to particular points of Christian doctrine and of Christian morals, and to control the religious sentiment of the community on topics which fall most appropriately within the sphere of pastoral instruction, and pastoral discretion, as to time and manner, *without the advice and consent of the* PASTORS and REGULAR ECCLESIASTICAL BODIES, are an unauthorized interference with the RIGHTS, duties, and discretion of the STATED MINISTRY, dangerous to the influence of the PASTORAL OFFICE, and fatal to the PEACE and good order of the churches."

The evident design of this was to close the Congregational meeting-houses and pulpits against anti-slavery lecturers and anti-slavery meetings, which were at that time beginning to be greatly multiplied, and which were exerting a powerful influence. It became necessary, for the sake of consistency, and also to maintain the high powers thus claimed for Congregational *pastors*, to apply the same rule to "itinerating *evangelists*," which was accordingly done in another Resolution. The series was closed by a pledge of the clergy, " that we consider ourselves *bound to sustain each other*, and the churches, in standing against all these invasions of our ecclesiastical order."

Under this pledge, even abolitionists belonging to the pastoral body, felt themselves bound to exclude anti-slavery lecturers and preachers from their pulpits, in deference to the wishes of the clerical body to which they belonged. This *Congregational* precedent was followed, (as designed by the movers,) in Presbyteries and Synods of the *Presbyterian* church, all over the free states. It was a flagrant violation of the " ecclesiastical order" of Congregationalism, sustained only by the bad usages under the old "Saybrook Platform," by which Whitefield, Tennant, and Finley had been shut out of the pulpits, and even made liable to imprisonment and banishment, through joint ecclesiastical and legislative action, a century previous.

It was objected to these Resolutions, while under discussion in the Connecticut General Association, that they would tend to encourage the mobs against anti-slavery lecturers, which were then rife in that region. The taunting retort was, that abolitionists, according to their own motto, ought not to shrink from the consequences! Among the abolition lecturers then at work in Connecticut, was a Congregational minister of that state. He persevered in the work, till, finding his way hedged up by his clerical brethren, he retired from the field;—*not* because a portion of the *people* in the parishes were not desirous to hear him, but because the *pastors* would not suffer him to be heard!

A Pastoral Letter to the churches accompanied the Resolutions of 1836, and breathing the same spirit. A still more famous Pastoral Letter was sent forth by the General Association of Massachusetts, a year afterwards, June, 1837. The evils of anti-slavery agitation had not ceased. A new class of anti-slavery lecturers had appeared, creating still greater alarm. Two talented Quaker ladies, the Misses Grimke, daughters of the late distinguished Judge Grimke, of South Carolina, once slaveholders, but now earnest abolitionists, were lecturing in the old Commonwealth. They had commenced by addressing female audiences, but had been prevailed upon to admit listeners of the other sex, who could seldom hear without going away convinced. Another clerical manifesto was deemed necessary to avert the calamity impending over the commonwealth and the churches.

" We would call your attention" (say they) " to the importance of maintaining that respect and DEFERENCE TO THE PASTORAL OFFICE which is enjoined in Scripture, and which is essential to the best influence of the ministry on you and your children. One way in which this respect has been, in some cases, violated, is in encouraging *lecturers* and *preachers* on certain topics of reform, to present their subjects within the parochial limits of settled pastors *without their consent.* YOUR MINISTER is ordained of God to be your teacher, and is commanded to feed that flock over which the Holy Ghost hath made him overseer. If there are certain topics on which he does not preach with the frequency or in the manner that would please you, it is a VIOLATION of SACRED and IMPORTANT RIGHTS to encourage a STRANGER to present them."

The Pastoral Letter then dilates upon the appropriate sphere of woman, and the danger of her stepping into the wrong place. Quaker women had long been accustomed to preach in New England, and occasionally in Congregational meeting-houses, without alarming ecclesiastical bodies, but they were now preaching successfully in favor of immediate emancipation, and against the prejudice that fed the Colonization Society ;—and the clergy became alarmed.

When it is remembered that " the parochial limits of settled pastors" are intended to cover (if they do sometimes lack a little of it) the entire area of the Commonwealth—every foot of the soil in it—the modesty of the demand becomes as apparent as the condition of a people who should be led to recognize such "sacred and important rights." Whatever the pastor might preach, or omit preaching, his "rights are violated" if any one else is encouraged to lecture or preach ! The religious " rights" of the *community*, if proportionately circumscribed to meet this demand, may be represented by a cypher —they utterly vanish away.

Whether it was *too late* in the day, or *too early*, to set up pretensions like these, it was certainly attempted at a very unfortunate moment. A small portion of the " prudence" so much commended, would have withheld the conservative clergy from broaching so exciting a topic. The great are not always wise.

If a portion of abolitionists have come to regard the institutions of Church and Clergy with unreasonable aversion, the reader may now see, as posterity will certainly see, the school in which they have been trained. If Christian institutions, if the Bible, if anything pertaining to true religion falls into temporary disrepute, a fearful weight of responsibility rests on the clerical bodies who have so recklessly and needlessly furnished the occasion. It would be difficult to fasten upon any class of abolitionists the charge of having been disrespectful towards the church and the clergy, until manifestations like these had appeared. Had the pastors manfully discharged their duty in reproving the giant sin of the country, instead of waiting for the stones to cry out, they might have magnified their high calling, promoted the cause of religion, delivered their country from thraldom, and their own memories from merited disgrace.

CHAPTER XXXVI.

PERSECUTIONS OF ABOLITIONISTS.

Ecclesiastical persecutions—La Roy Sunderland—Lewis Tappan—E. W. Goodwin—
Presbyteries and Church Sessions—"Friends"—Charles Marriot and Isaac T.
Hopper—Other modes of persecution—Principal victims—Benjamin Lundy—
William Lloyd Garrison—Miss Prudence Crandall—Dr. Reuben Crandall—George
Storrs—Jonathan Walker—Elijah P. Lovejoy—John B. Mahan—Alanson Work
—James E. Burr—George Thompson—Charles T. Torrey—William L. Chaplin—
Messrs. Drayton and Sayres.

NEITHER northern legislative enactments, nor riots, nor
personal assaults, could prove of much permanent service in
the work of suppressing free discussion and punishing deeds
of mercy to the poor, without other and more permanent
instrumentalities. These were furnished by the ecclesiastical
machinery of the sects at the North, and the sanguinary slave
code of the South. Whenever active abolitionists fell into
the hands of either of these, they expected no mercy, or expected only to discover their mistake.

No persecutions of abolitionists have been perhaps so vex-
atious, so annoying, so exhausting, or, on the whole, so
effective, as those suffered by some of the more active among
them, in their church or ecclesiastical relations. Not that
their anti-slavery principles and measures were, in very many
cases, charged directly against them as heresies or crimes. It
was not commonly the policy of their persecutors to pursue
precisely that course. It was always easy to harass them
with unfounded charges of disorderly or disorganizing conduct, and thus cripple, and harass, and disgrace, and discourage them. The trials of La Roy Sunderland, of Lewis Tappan,

and of E. W. Goodwin, were but specimens of the persecutions of scores and hundreds, if not thousands, of less prominent, but equally faithful and abused men. The records of Presbyterian Church Sessions and Presbyteries, would alone furnish ample materials for a humiliating but instructive volume of such details, even in a very condensed form. Similar persecutions have been encountered all over the country in the walks of social and domestic life. The "gospel of deliverance to the captives" has "not brought peace upon the earth, but a sword"—"a man's foes have been those of his own household;" and if the "prophets" of emancipation are looking for "honor," it seems not likely to come from those of their "own country and kindred." Even those who are now preparing to "enter into their labors" have already learned the art and policy of disparaging them.

The vast powers wielded by clerical bodies, missionary boards, conventions, and managers and committees of benevolent societies, have been exerted to cripple and crush abolitionists who would persist in agitating the slave question.

These ecclesiastical annoyances and persecutions have not been confined to the sects whose general associated action has been found recorded on the side of slavery, or whose recognized leaders have labored to press the Bible into its support. Sects claiming the reputation of being decidedly anti-slavery —sects that do not allow slaveholding among their members, nor maintain any ecclesiastical connection with slaveholders, have opposed the agitation of the subject by anti-slavery societies, and have censured and even excommunicated their members for their activity in them. The Hicksite Friends, for example, in the City and State of New York, disowned two of their most estimable members, Charles Marriot of Athens, and Isaac T. Hopper of New York city, solely for that cause. The only excuse was the sanctimonious plea that "Friends" must not mingle with "the world," nor co-operate with other sects. The *real* fact was, that "Friends" in general had so "mingled with the world" in its commercial cupidity and its political servility, as to sympathize with

"other sects" in their hatred of active abolitionists. Their
members can co-operate with their fellow-citizens of other
sects, to elect slaveholding and slave-hunting Presidents of the
United States, without fear of church censure. The "Friends"
in New England are extensively and largely interested in the
cotton manufacture, and like most of that class, are averse to
an agitation which is offensive to the planters. And hence
an earnest and active Quaker abolitionist loses caste with his
sect.

It would be strange if there were not many apostacies
under such trials. Yet unremitting persecution has proved
less effective than a brief season of it, alternated with patronage, and flattery, and favor. It has been by these adroit appliances that the ranks of reformers, especially among clergymen and leading laymen, have been corrupted and thinned.
There are many who withstood manfully the tempest of
popular fury, and even the prospect of imprisonment, who
have since fainted under the sunshine of political or ecclesiastical favor, or been laid asleep by the fireside of domestic
quiet. But others have taken their places. "The last have
been first, and the first last, for many are called, but few are
chosen."

We will now notice some other forms of persecution, and
in doing this, will briefly recapitulate some of the prominent
cases, with the names of the victims.

BENJAMIN LUNDY was repeatedly assaulted in the streets
of Baltimore, and once brutally beaten by Austin Woolfolk,
a slave-trader, before any of the modern Anti-slavery Societies were organized. Mr. Lundy was a feeble man, a quiet,
unresisting Quaker, but the "peculiar institutions" of Southern Chivalry provided no protection for him.

WILLIAM LLOYD GARRISON'S imprisonment in Baltimore,
and the violent assault upon his person, and his imprisonment
in Boston, have been narrated already.—(*See Chap.* XXXII.)

MISS PRUDENCE CRANDALL, a pious and benevolent young
lady, established and taught a school for colored pupils, at
Canterbury, Conn. Through the influence of leading mem-

bers of the Colonization Society, an Act of the State Legislature against such schools was procured, and was enforced by the imprisonment of Miss Crandall, in 1833. The school having been resumed, was finally broken up by lawless violence in September, 1834.

DR. REUBEN CRANDALL of Westchester county, (N. Y.) a brother of Miss Prudence Crandall, having located himself in Washington City to teach botany, was arrested and thrown into prison, Aug. 11, 1835, on charge of circulating incendiary publications, with intent to excite the slaves to insurrection. After lying in jail above eight months, till April 15, 1836, he was brought to trial before Judge Cranch. The evidence against him only proved that he had in his trunk some anti-slavery pamphlets and papers, that the latter were used by him in wrapping up his botanical specimens, and that, on request, he had lent to a white citizen, one of the pamphlets. The "incendiary" matter read in court from these papers, were articles against slavery, and in favor of the right of the free colored people to reside in this country. The effort to prove Dr. Crandall a member of an Anti-slavery Society failed. Yet the District Attorney, Francis S. Key, Esq., a leading advocate and an officer of the Colonization Society, by whose vigilance Dr. Crandall had been indicted and arrested, (avowing, from the first, his determination to subject him to capital punishment,) persisted, vehemently, and in the use of the most inflammatory and approbrious language, to urge upon the jury a verdict of guilty. The counsel for the accused urged that the "incendiary" matter read in court did not exceed in severity the language used by Mr. Jefferson, Patrick Henry, and other Southern gentlemen, including even Mr. Key himself, when declaiming against slavery.* He attributed this excitement and prosecution to the rivalry between the Colonization and Abolition Societies.

---

* It was a constant ruse with the orators of Colonizationism, to declaim against *slavery*, in order to enlist and use up the energies and means of philanthropists, while, in almost the same breath, they would justify *slaveholders*, and denounce the "*incendiary abolitionists.*"

The jury, after a short deliberation, returned a verdict of *not guilty*.* But the murderous work of the prosecutors was effected. His damp dungeon and close confinement, while awaiting the trial, had fixed upon him a lingering consumption, of which he died at Kingston, Jamaica, about the first of February, 1838. He was a gentleman of high literary and scientific acquirements, captivating manners, and dignified deportment, a scholar, a devoted Christian, and one of the purest, most disinterested, and most amiable of men. Thus was a worthy citizen of a free state incarcerated and, in effect, murdered, though adjudged innocent, in the Federal District, on the national hearth-stone, under "exclusive jurisdiction of Congress," for no fault but having come under suspicion of having disseminated publications hostile to slavery and the Colonization Society!

AMOS DRESSER of Ohio, a young student in theology, travelling in Tennessee to distribute Bibles, was flogged twenty lashes on his bare back in the public square in Nashville, July 25, 1835. His crime was being a member of an Anti-slavery Society, and having some anti-slavery publications in his trunk. Some church members assisted in the outrage.

GEO. STORRS, a Methodist preacher, and agent of the Anti-slavery Society, having accepted an invitation to address an Anti-slavery Society in Northfield, (N. H.) assembled with them for that purpose, December 14, 1835, but was dragged from his knees, while at prayer, by the deputy sheriff, David Tilton, in virtue of a warrant issued by Nathan Wells, Esq., Justice, on complaint of Benjamin Rogers, charging Mr. Storrs with being an "idle and disorderly person"—"a common railer and brawler"—"going about the town and county and disturbing the public peace." On trial before Judge Atkinson, he was discharged. But on the 31st of March, 1836, after having lectured at Pittsfield, N. H., Mr. Storrs was

---

* Vide " *Trial of Reuben Crandall, M.D.,* &c., published in Washington City, 1836—a pamphlet of 48 pages.

arrested again in the pulpit, while on his knees, while another minister, Mr. Curtiss, was offering the concluding prayer. This was by authority of a writ issued by Moses Norris, Jr., Esq. He was tried the same day, and sentenced to three months' *hard* labor in the House of Correction. He appealed from the sentence, and we find no further account of the proceedings.

These specimens of riotous demonstrations, connected with mockeries of legal proceedings, illustrate the nature, design, and moral affinities of the legislative and ecclesiastical attempts at gag-law, for which that precise period was distinguished. They show us what was intended, what was well nigh accomplished, and what would have been the condition of liberty in America if the conspirators had succeeded.

CAPT. JONATHAN WALKER, a citizen of Massachusetts, for assisting the escape of a slave, was branded with a hot iron in the hand, the letters SS, *by an officer of the United States!*

ELIJAH P. LOVEJOY was a native of Maine, a graduate of Waterville College, in 1828. He practiced law at St. Louis, Missouri, but, being desirous of entering the ministry, spent some time in preparatory study at Princeton, N. J. He was employed as an agent for the Sunday School Union, and was afterwards selected to conduct a religious paper at St. Louis. In this station he advocated the right of free discussion in opposition to the persecutors of Dr. Nelson. When a free colored man was burnt to death near St. Louis, he rebuked the savage outrage. For this he was obliged to leave the State, and located himself at Alton, Illinois, where, in July, 1837, he avowed his sentiments as an abolitionist, and published a full declaration of his views in his "Alton Observer." This raised against him a storm of violence. Three several times were his press and office destroyed, before the fatal catastrophe, and three times were they replaced by the friends of liberty and law. At a public meeting, early in November, ostensibly got up for the purpose of allaying the excitement, but really with the design to intimidate him and crush the liberty of the press, Mr. Lovejoy appeared, and, in a noble speech, defended his cause and his rights, "like Paul before Festus, or Luther at the Diet of Worms."

On the arrival of his new press, it was lodged in a stone warehouse, and here Mr. Lovejoy and some of his friends stationed themselves, armed, apprehending an attack, which took place the same night. After several volleys of firing, an attempt was made to set fire to the building. Mr. Lovejoy went out to prevent their purpose, and soon fell, pierced with three buckshot. His companions effected their escape. This was on the 7th of November, 1837.

Mr. Lovejoy left a widow and children. His wife had stood by him, like a heroine, when he was brutally assaulted, some time previous, at St. Charles. When the mother of Lovejoy heard of his death, she said, "It is well. I had rather he should fall a martyr to his cause than prove recreant to his principles."

JOHN B. MAHAN, on requisition of Gov. Clark, of Kentucky, was delivered up by Gov. Vance, of Ohio, as a fugitive from justice, "going at large in the State of Ohio," to be tried on an indictment for assisting the escape of certain slaves.

John B. Mahan was a citizen of Ohio, a local minister of the Methodist Episcopal Church, residing in Sardinia, Brown Co., Ohio, and had not been in Kentucky for nineteen years! Yet he was given up by the Governor of Ohio, was arrested, at his residence, Sept. 17, 1838, torn from his family, hurried to Kentucky, and shut up in jail, without allowing him time to procure a writ of habeas corpus, or summon evidence in his defense. He was tried at the Circuit Court of Kentucky, in Marion County, the 13th of November. It was admitted by the Attorney for the Commonwealth that the prisoner was a citizen of Ohio, and not in Kentucky at the time of the alleged offense ; yet he made an effort to procure his conviction. The jury returned a verdict of not guilty. A civil suit against him, for damages, was still left pending, to be tried the May following. The result of this suit we do not ascertain.

ALANSON WORK, JAMES E. BURR, and GEORGE THOMPSON,

in July, 1841, were seized and imprisoned in Missouri, for attempting to assist the escape of some slaves.

Alanson Work, a native of Connecticut, about 40 years old, having a wife and four children, was residing at the Mission Institute at Quincy, Illinois, for the sake of educating his children, and training them up for usefulness. James E. Burr and George Thompson were young students at that institute, preparing for the ministry.

Quincy is separated by the river Mississippi from the slave state of Missouri. Having crossed the river on an errand of mercy, these three men were seized and imprisoned. In September they were tried, convicted, and sentenced to the Penitentiary at Jefferson City for twelve years. Here, their conduct was such as to win for them many friends, and to commend their principles to the people of the surrounding country. Their persecutors found it a matter of policy to get rid of their presence. Mr. Work was pardoned and released, Jan. 20, 1845, Mr. Burr, Jan. 30, 1846, and Mr. Thompson, June 14, 1846. Mr. Thompson was afterwards employed on a mission to Africa, by the American Missionary Association.

CHARLES TURNER TORREY was born at Scituate, Mass., Nov. 21, 1813. He was educated at Yale College, and entered the Theological Seminary at Andover in October, 1834, where he studied one year, and left the institution on account of ill-health. Completing his studies afterwards, under private tuition, he was licensed to preach by the Mendon (Mass.) Association of Congregational Ministers, in October, 1836. In March, 1837, he was ordained pastor of a Congregational Church in Providence, R. I., and was married soon afterwards to a daughter of his theological instructor, Dr. Ide, of Medway. Miss Ide was a grand-daughter of the distinguished theologian, Dr. Emmons. Leaving Providence, Mr. Torrey preached a while at Salem, Mass., in 1838, but in 1839 we find him in the less sedentary avocation of an anti-slavery lecturer. He had been an earnest abolitionist from the beginning of his ministry, and in this active and laborious enterprise he was preeminently at home. He wrote much for the anti-slavery papers, during his travels. The winter of 1841-2 he spent chiefly at Washington City as a reporter for several papers, and with a primary and special view to the interests of the anti-slavery cause. His writings were vigorous, rapid, bold, free, and discriminating. While at Washington, a Slaveholder's Convention was held at Annapolis, Maryland, January, 1842, and Mr. Torrey adventured to attend it, for the purpose of reporting the proceedings. But slavery shrinks, instinctively, from the penetrating eye of a freeman. He was excluded from a seat among the reporters, afterwards forbidden to take notes in the gallery, and finally arrested and thrown into prison. A few days afterwards, on a judicial examination, he was released on giving bail in $500 to "keep the peace" till April, and returned to his post at Washington.

In the autumn of 1842, Mr. Torrey became editor of the "Tocsin of Liberty," afterwards the "Albany Patriot." While engaged in this work he was entreated by a fugitive from slavery, to go to Virginia, and assist him bring his wife out of bondage. He could not refuse. This undertaking was a failure and they narrowly escaped arrest. It led Mr. Torrey, however, into other and more successful enterprises of the same character, but which, ultimately, cost him his liberty and his life.

His arrest took place June 24, 1844. He was thrown into jail at Baltimore. Finding it certain that he could not have a fair trial, he made an unsuccessful attempt to escape from confinement. His trial came on November 29, 1844. He was convicted, as he affirmed, on evidence of perjured witnesses, who testified that they saw what they did not see.* He learned, what Judge Jeremie had certified before, and what has been verified since, that in all trials of this kind, any requisite amount of false testimony is always at hand! He was

---

* Of course, it is not denied that Mr. Torrey was instrumental in releasing many slaves. But this does not alter the fact, that the witnesses in the present case perjured themselves. As a specimen, one of them testified that he had seen the prisoner at the residence of his (Torrey's) mother, in Hereford County, Maryland! The mother of Mr. Torrey died in Massachusetts when he was a child!

convicted, and sentenced to hard labor in the penitentiary for six years. To this place he was removed the 30th of December, 1844. Great efforts were made to procure his pardon. His father-in-law, Dr. Ide, made a visit to the Governor of Maryland, for the purpose. It was all in vain. He died in the penitentiary, May 9, 1846, of a lingering consumption, the effect of his confinement. Such are the tender mercies of slaveholders. The God of the oppressed, the avenger of the widow and the fatherless, will remember them. The murderers of Torrey and of Lovejoy are alike guilty in his sight.

The most fiend-like expression of hatred against Torrey and against the holy cause in which he was enlisted, remains to be told. On the arrival of his remains at Boston, the residence of his brother-in-law, Mr. Ide, and where the widow and children of Torrey, with her parents had come to attend the funeral solemnities, arrangements had been made, on leave duly obtained, to hold the services in the meeting-house of the Park Street Congregational Church, in which Mr. Ide was a stated worshiper. A Congregational minister, Mr. Lovejoy (brother of the martyr) was selected to preach on the occasion. Mr. Torrey had lived and died an orthodox Congregational minister in good and regular standing, and no heresy or misconduct had been imputed to him except his excessive sympathy for the poor slave. Dr. Ide, like his father-in-law, EMMONS, who had died about six years previous, was among the most honored Congregational ministers in the commonwealth. Who could have believed that arrangements so appropriate would have been broken up, by *a refusal to allow the house to be used on such an occasion?* But so it was! The corpse of the martyred Torrey was denied, what would *not* have been denied to the worst of malefactors—the decencies of a temporary resting-place in the house of prayer during the accustomed religious exercises of such an occasion. This single incident will suffice, centuries hence, to certify the position held by the leading religious influences of the orthodox Congregational sect in Boston, in the great struggle for christian liberty, in the nineteenth century in America.* The Tremont Temple (Baptist) was opened for the occasion, and the services appropriately performed. This was followed by a public meeting in Faneuil Hall, and commemoration meetings and funeral discourses, all over the free states. From across the water, the voice of British Christianity, as represented by the Anti-Slavery Committee in London, and attest ed by the world-honored signature of the aged CLARKSON, brought expressions of sympathy for the "widŏw and orphan children" of Torrey, and admonition to "every section of the professedly Christian Church in the United States to separate itself from all participation in, or sanction of the system of slavery."†

He died in the 33d year of his age. Though few men have made a deeper impression upon society in so brief a life, his various powers both of thought and of accomplishment were little known and little developed, in comparison with what they would have been had his life been prolonged. He was a man of genius as well as of rare courage. His little book " *Home*, or the Pilgrim's Faith Revived"—however some may dislike its old fashioned Puritan theology—is among the few sketches of the kind that will live. " It will be matter of astonishment to all who read this book of two hundred and fifty-five pages, that it should have been written by a prisoner in twelve days." This was in the interim between the verdict against him and the sentence of the Court.

This place may be a proper one for the remark that while the commonly recognized leaders and great men among the

---

* We could wish that the same spirit had not been witnessed in other places than Boston. The meeting-house of the Richmond-Street Congregational Church, in Providence, R. I., of which Mr. Torrey had been pastor, was not permitted to be opened for a sermon commemorating his death ! Very few, in the comparison with the whole, was the number of Congregational churches in the cities whose houses could be occupied for such services. Is it strange that some abolitionists connected with such churches should secede from them ?

† *Memoir of the Martyr Torrey*, by J. C. Lovejoy. Boston : J. P. Jewett & Co. 1847.

American clergy have disgraced themselves, the ministry, the churches, and the religion they profess, by the course they have taken on the slave question, and while the great majority of inferior men in the ministry have servilely followed in their wake, adding much to the multiplied mischiefs of their unfaithfulness, there has nevertheless been a noble band of true christian ministers, (though few in comparison with the great body) who have been among the most self-sacrificing and efficient laborers in the cause of freedom. Not only should the more distinguished be honorably mentioned, but a much greater number of equally laborious though more obscure ministers of Christ, who, in their retired places, have done what they could, though known only in their own narrow circles, or where they have sojourned or traveled. They have been driven, for support, from parish to parish, sometimes have itinerated as lecturers, and sometimes have been driven *out* of the ministry, as a stated avocation, altogether, resorting to other means of subsistence, and patiently suffering out their pilgrimage, as they best could. The rectified vision of a future age may recognize in these "the salt of the earth," who have preserved the true Church.

GENERAL WILLIAM L. CHAPLIN, a lawyer by profession, a native of Groton, Massachusetts, a citizen of the State of New York, since 1837, and frequently spending the winters in Washington City, is too well known to the friends and the enemies of American liberty to require a biographical sketch in this volume. As a lecturer, as an editor, as a reporter of proceedings in Congress, as a leader, and as a candidate for office, in the Liberty party, he has an established reputation among the public men of his times.

Gen. Chaplin was arrested, sometime in August, 1850, by the police of Washington City, though out of their appropriate jurisdiction, and within the borders of Maryland. It was in the night season; his carriage wheels were blocked, he was knocked from his seat, conveyed back into the city, and thrown into prison, on the charge of carrying away slaves. The Governor of Maryland also made a requisition on the

Federal Executive, for the delivery of Chaplin, to be tried for an assault committed in that State. Having been bailed in the District, in the sum of six thousand dollars, he was immediately conveyed to Maryland, and imprisoned at Rockville, where he remained until the latter part of December, when he was released on the extravagant bail of nineteen thousand dollars, which was raised by his friends in the free states. After all this, there have been intimations that he would be demanded by the Governor of Maryland!

Messrs. DRAYTON and SAYRES, citizens "of the free North," are now, (June, 1852) incarcerated in Washington City, for the alleged crime of assisting 74 or 76 slaves to escape from Maryland in the schooner Pearl, which was seized in the waters of Maryland, in April, 1848. They were convicted on 75 indictments. The prosecution was conducted by Francis S. Key, Esq., who, "in disregard of usage," procured their indictment for "stealing *slaves*," after having failed to obtain a verdict against them for *larceny.*—*National Era, May* 31, 1849.

CHAPTER XXXVII.

OF THE ELEMENTS AND OCCASIONS OF DIVISION AMONG
ABOLITIONISTS.

Unity in measures the result of unity in principles—Complex problem before American Abolitionists—Their points of agreement and of disagreement—Natural variety of measures and of organization—Change of views incident to reformatory experiment—Actual changes in most abolitionists and of opposite schools—These changes described—Division naturally followed.

IN common with the Protestant Reformers, and many other earnest men of progress, the abolitionists of America suffer the reproach of being divided among themselves. There may be a great fault in this; but the fault may lie in another direction than is commonly supposed, and in things that seldom fall under censure. It is easy to say that reformers should be united and present an unbroken front to the common enemy. So they should. They should be "perfectly joined together in the same mind and judgment." They should "all speak the same thing," and do the same work.

In other words, they should harmonize in their principles and their measures. Unless they do harmonize in their principles, they *cannot* harmonize in their measures—that is, if they are what all reformers should be, earnest, honest, consistent, conscience-controlled, God-fearing men. The harmony that grows out of compromises of principles, is worse than useless, in any moral reform.

Or, if expedients instead of principles be proposed as a basis of co-operation, the result will commonly be a still greater diversity of judgment. Men's sense of right and wrong are less various than their calculations of advantage and disadvantage. Anything but unity comes of running after mere expedients.

It has been asked why American abolitionists should be distracted by divisions any more than British abolitionists were. Many answers might be given,* but we choose, first, to demand what progress was made by all that unity of British abolitionists that preceded their unity in correct principles and in measures growing out of them? What trophies are to be shown of the unity in which the principles of Granville Sharp were held in virtual abeyance by a co-operation with the wrong principles then acted upon by Wilberforce and Clarkson?

Reformers should all and always be agreed. That is to say, the profound problems of human nature, of moral philosophy, of theology, and of ethics, should be correctly solved and acted upon by them. It ought to have been done, doubtless, long ago. And the reforms still before us should have been consummated accordingly. The world waits, and must wait, for reformers to unite in acting according to correct principles, before the world can be reformed. Right measures grow out of right ethics. And all systems of ethics have their theological foundations.

It is easy to deride abstractionists, and to extol practical business men. But who *are* practical business men, except those who honor the laws of nature and of God, in the activities they put forth? The steam-ship, the rail-car, the magnetic telegraph—could any array of numbers, could any expenditure of funds have reached the results of these, if a compromise requiring a departure from the laws of nature (the laws of God) had been deemed requisite, or had been consented to, in order to obtain the men, or the means, or to purchase patronage?

---

* In England, the Slave Power had not taken *entire* possession of the high places of the Church and of the State. The wide Atlantic separated the mass of the slaveholders from the British Legislature, the British Cabinet, the British throne, the British Church, whether " established" or " dissenting." The plans and modes of operation first agreed upon among abolitionists, were therefore found adequate to overcome opposition.

You see a delicate and complicated machine, a chronometer, out of order. You see half a dozen "*reformers*" debating the *principle* upon which the machine is constructed, and the consequent measures of repair. Will you exhort them to unity of *action* in repairing, without waiting for any agreement in the *principle* upon which the action must proceed?

Society, the Church, the State, legislation, jurisprudence— here are machines quite as delicate, and requiring as much study as a chronometer. The principle, in both cases, may be very simple. But it needs to be understood, and applied.

When abolitionists first commenced their labors, they did not know how completely the Slave Power had controlled, and how much it had marred, deranged, and subverted, our whole social machinery—the Church, the State, the Constitution, the laws, the judiciary—everything which they hoped and expected to *wield* for the overthrow of the slave system. The implements of their warfare were out of order—the machinery did not work. Or rather, it worked only in the wrong direction. What was to be done?

The Church, the Ministry, the State, the Constitution, legislation, jurisprudence, religion, law—what *are* all these? What is to be *done* with them?

We sought from them assistance, guidance, light, order, protection, *defense*. But behold, opposition, confusion, darkness, injury, invasion! Are they perverted? or are they only doing their appropriate work? Are they to be rescued and wielded? or are they to be abandoned, repudiated, and overthrown?

Different answers would be likely to be given to these questions, especially as abolitionists were men of diverse theologies and conflicting politics; and some of them, perhaps, had given to neither theology nor politics any very consecutive attention, but had become abolitionists from instinctive sympathy and impulse.

Other problems besides the slave question might have a bearing on the decision. If the principles of peace or non-resistance were so held and embraced by one class of abolitionists as to preclude an approving recognition of any civil government operating by physical compulsion, or the sanctions of penal law, a foundation would be laid for a course in respect to political action, widely different from any that could consistently or conscientiously be pursued by those holding to the opposite theory.

Just so of the Church. If the idea of individuality were carried so far by some, as to suggest the inutility and mischiefs of all regularly established church organizations, there would, of necessity, arise corresponding views of reformatory measures in relation to the Church, which men of other theories could not reasonably be expected to patronize.

If the question of slave emancipation be considered (as it commonly is in America) one phase of the broader question of human equality and inalienable rights, it might come to suggest the question of woman's entire equality and identity of position with man, and thus another problem, perhaps an intricate one, might present itself, in respect to which the friends of slave emancipation might differ.

That questions of this nature had more or less to do with divisions among abolitionists, it would be in vain to deny. Equally plain is it that these questions had a strong inherent tendency to produce division, whatever may be said of the possibility of avoiding a rupture.

So far as abolitionists were agreed in their *principles*, so far, but no farther, could they consistently agree in their *measures*. It is in vain to anathematize non-conformity, and to call it bigotry, illiberality, and prejudice. No bigotry is more narrow and intolerant than that which would enforce a unity of *measures* without a unity in the *principles* upon which they must be founded. The body of men who demand that I shall adopt their *creed*, are not more arrogant, and are much less unreasonable, than another body that condescendingly permits me to retain my *creed*, but denounces me as a bigot or a disorganizer because I hesitate to patronize the *measures* which nothing but the adoption *of their own* creed could warrant or justify.

Abolitionists *were* and still *are* agreed in respect to the inherent criminality of slaveholding, the duty and safety of immediate and unconditional emancipation, the right of the slave to liberation on the soil, and of the free people of color to remain in the land of their birth or of their choice, in the full possession and exercise of their equal rights as men, and as American citizens. In the promulgation of these sentiments, and in the answering of objections against them, all abolitionists could agree; and for a time they found themselves sufficiently occupied with this labor.

But as assuredly as they made much progress, the time would soon come—and it *did* come—when the majority of abolitionists felt other work pressing on their hands. When a large body of the people *were* convinced of the truths abolitionists had taught them, the question arose, How shall they best be led to put their principles in practice? Some of them felt themselves to be, by the act, the ordinance, and the Providence of God, a part and parcel of the State and Nation in which they resided, holding political power themselves, and sharers in the responsibilities thus resting upon them. These had work to do in which those who held opposite views of civil Government could not be expected to co-operate—a work from which others had no right to deter them. Just so, those who were members of organized churches, and who believed church organizations to be proper and Heaven-appointed institutions for religious activity and culture, found a work before them in which those of *other and opposite* views could not participate, and could not be supposed to be the best advisers.

It was not enough to say that abolitionists, as *individuals*, were left at liberty to pursue their own course of political and ecclesiastical action, yet retaining their connection with an anti-slavery society composed of men of all political and religious views, and even administered and directed by those holding to *no* measures of political or ecclesiastical operation. All this might be plausible, and even possible, in the exercise of great mutual forbearance and candor. But it would still remain true that no mere isolated individual action without co-operation in some way, could suffice for those who intended to pursue ecclesiastical and especially political action against slavery. Organization among themselves, in some form, might be quite as important there as in the Anti-Slavery Society. Those who thought so, had, at least, the right to act in accordance with their convictions. Be it so, that their connection with the Anti-Slavery Society might have been retained. The progress of the cause would inevitably require, in their view, the greater part of their efforts and means to be expended in some form of *definite* action which the Anti-Slavery Society, if confined to mere "*moral suasion*," (as understood by many,) could not be expected to endorse. The *diminished* operations of such societies, even without a rupture, would have been the inevitable result. But, for this state of things, the leading men in the societies might not be prepared—and might regard it as an evil, to be counteracted and opposed; perhaps vehemently denounced.

Aside from such differences of principles, among abolitionists, it is easy to see that unexpected occurrences, a change of position, and habits of observation and inquiry, might introduce widely different views of the policy proper to be pursued. And these different views might lay a foundation for a diversity of organizations. The jealousy of centralized power, so common among friends of liberty, would tend to a similar result.

The preceding suggestions, it is believed, will furnish a clue to the divisions among American abolitionists. When they formed the American Anti-Slavery Society, and adopted a Constitution and a Declaration of Sentiment, at Philadelphia, in 1833, there appeared to be an agreement in their principles, and in their understanding of the prominent facts of the case. This laid a foundation for an agreement in their measures, and, consequently, for an unity of organization.

They were agreed in their views of civil government and of its legitimate powers. They were agreed in the following declaration of their duty as citizens :

" There are at the present time the highest obligations resting upon the people of the free states, to remove slavery, by moral and political action, as prescribed in the Constitution of the United States."

They appear to have been substantially agreed in their construction of the Federal Constitution. While they repudiated the ultra Southern construction, they nevertheless admitted " the compromises" as commonly understood and conceded, at that time, in the non-slaveholding States. They disclaimed the idea of a direct interference of the Federal Government to abolish slavery in the States, though they insisted that it should, in no way, support slavery or extend it anywhere, but abolish it in the Federal District and Territories, and interdict the inter-state slave trade. This, they then thought, would secure the general abolition of slavery, by State action, and with this they were content. Into any close scrutiny of the Constitution they had not gone.

Anticipating, as they did, the speedy co-operation of the principal religious sects in the free States, and of a majority of one or both the great political parties, they contemplated no measures of separation from either of them—no political or ecclesiastical organizations of their own. Their disclaimers of any such intention were honest, and were continued for a long time. Connected with this, to a great extent, was the vague notion, so generally entertained, that a religious and moral question was too sacred to be mingled with politics. And yet, as has been seen, they contemplated, in some way, " political" as well as " moral action."

They seem also to have been agreed in their views of the proper action of females. Though many earnest and gifted ladies were present at the sittings of the Convention at Philadelphia, when the Society was formed, and some of them (on invitation) suggested amendments of the " Declaration," yet no one of them became members or officers of the Convention or of the Society. By common consent, the separate organization of Female Anti-slavery Societies was recommended, then, and for some time afterwards.

These statements are made here for no other object than to

record the simple facts of the case, and to show the position of the Society at the beginning. Whether deviations from this course have been wise or unwise, is not the point now in hand. But the fact of deviation, by somebody, connects itself with the fact of division. Without a change, no division would have occurred.

The truth is, a very small portion of abolitionists, if any, at the present time, occupy precisely the original ground as above described. If any organization *does* now occupy that ground, in every particular mentioned, it probably represents but a very small minority of American abolitionists.

Deviations have taken place; and the history of them is the history of division. The mere fact of change criminates no one, and the record of it should give no offense.

Some changed their views in respect to the proper methods of female co-operation, and wished to change their usages accordingly.

Some changed their views in respect to the practicability of obtaining legislative action against slavery, through the instrumentality of the old political parties, and therefore desired the organization of a new one.

Some, on investigation, changed their views of the Federal Constitution, and, believing it to contain no "guaranties" of slavery, but a distinct guaranty of free institutions, they could no longer continue to concede those pro-slavery guaranties, but, on the other hand, demanded that the "guaranty" of Republican State Governments should be redeemed, and rendered available.

Some changed their views of the Constitution in the opposite direction—perhaps changed twice;—repudiating, in the first place, "the compromises," and holding the Constitution (as did N. P. Rogers) to be thoroughly anti-slavery—and then (assenting to the pro-slavery construction) denouncing it, very consistently, as a "covenant with death, and an agreement with hell."

Some changed their views of the prospect of divorcing their churches and other ecclesiastical bodies from slavery, and therefore wished to withdraw from them, and form other ecclesiastical organizations better conformed to their own ideas of the Christian religion.

Some changed their views in respect to the propriety of any compulsory civil government, making use of physical compulsion. On this ground they could not, themselves, conscientiously vote or hold office, and they could not but desire, as earnest men, to draw other philanthropists into their own views and methods.

Some changed their views in respect to the value of all organized Church institutions, (whether pro-slavery or anti-slavery) and the desirableness of their being sustained by the friends of humanity. It would be a libel on such to insinuate that their activities and their influence would not correspond with their convictions.

It may be said that this influence concerning civil government and Church organizations, was not exerted by them "as abolitionists," nor "on the anti-slavery platform." This statement might be either conceded or questioned, (as some do question it) but the main fact, as before stated, would remain. We reproach no one. We only record the facts.

And, finally, a long time afterwards, some changed their views in respect to the moral obligation of directing their political activities, and wielding their right of suffrage, in such a manner as to sustain no statesmen except those pledged to the *abolition of slavery.* They therefore consented, as will be seen, to a political platform less rigid, and permitting the support of those who only promised to oppose the *extension* of slavery.

In respect to this last item—perhaps some of the others— *some* who admit that they occupy the ground described, may say also (and say truly) that *they* have not changed. But, the majority, doubtless, under each specification, *have* changed.

In recording these general facts, with the particulars that may follow, the writer understands that he treads on delicate ground. Each party mentioned would, perhaps, wish him to modify some part of the record—to add something—or erase something from the statement. It is, perhaps, difficult, for one who has been an earnest actor in such scenes, to write the history of them without some bias. We claim no exemption from such influences, and can only promise our best efforts at impartiality and fairness, consoling ourselves with the thought that no one *but* an earnest actor would be likely to see clearly all that is to be seen. We must write as we see, and must see with our own eyes,—leaving it with others to judge, and to write, too, if they shall think fit.

CHAPTER XXXVIII.

DIVISIONS IN 1839–40.

Division in the Massachusetts Anti-Slavery Society, in 1839, at Boston—Circumstances connected with or preceding it—Division in the Parent Society in 1840, at New York—Its attendant circumstances and results—General neutrality of abolitionists in the interior—Distinct origin (and from other causes) of the Liberty Party.

A DIVISION in the Massachusetts Anti-slavery Society took place at Boston, in May, 1839. The Liberty Party was regularly organized by a Convention at Albany, N. Y., April 1, 1840. A division in the American Anti-slavery Society, occurred in New York, in May, 1840.

The division at New York appears to have been connected, more or less, with the division at Boston.

By Mr. Garrison and his associates, the organization of the Liberty Party has been regarded as only one form of the opposition made to *their* State and National Societies, by those who separated from them.

The writer thinks them mistaken in the general fact, (admitting, perhaps, local exceptions) and that the Liberty Party was projected in the interior of the State of New York, by those who had not entered at all into the dissentions in Boston and New York. We must briefly notice the prominent facts.

THE DIVISION IN MASSACHUSETTS.

It was in Boston that the Liberator of William Lloyd Garrison was published—for a season as the organ of the Massachusetts Anti-slavery Society—and afterwards (when complaints were made of his introduction of other topics, and of the expression of sentiments obnoxious to some abolitionists) its publication was resumed in his own name, and on his own account. Officially, or in form, the difficulty was obviated, but the prominence of Mr. Garrison, as an abolitionist, throughout the country, and his official connection with the Massachusetts Anti-slavery Society, appeared, in the minds of some, to identify his peculiar views with the anti-slavery cause, to its injury. Such persons were still annoyed with the continued appearance, in the Liberator, of the views they deemed so objectionable. They conceived that the Society was coming under their influence, and that its activities were in process of becoming mis-directed and injurious.

It was in Boston, therefore, that the first division took place.

Among the new views objected against, were the principles of "Non-Resistants," so called, who had organized a "Non-Resistance Society," and established a paper promulgating their views, in addition to the advocacy they received in the Liberator. The definition of "non-resistance," as gathered from the writings of its advocates, included, not merely the absence of war, of military armaments, and of "the death penalty," but, likewise, if we have rightly understood it, of all physical coercion in a way of punishment by civil government; the absence, consequently, of all that is commonly understood by the term, *penal law.* This view connected itself, then, and afterwards, with the peculiar theological tenets of those who had, for a long time previous, promulgated similar views of the Divine administration here or hereafter.

Political action, by voting, even for the abolition of slavery, under a civil government based on physical force, could not but be regarded as sinful by those who held, consistently, these new views. Such was indeed the fact. The inference was not merely admitted, but avowed and insisted on. For a long time, and on this ground alone, did this peculiar class of abolitionists decline and discountenance voting, before they raised any objection to voting on the ground of the pro-slavery character of the Constitution of the United States—before, indeed, some of them seem to have *discovered* those traits of that document which have since become so palpable and manifest to them.

Here, then, was a division among the abolitionists of Massachusetts, *in fact*, in respect to their *measures*, before there was any division, *in organization*. What some of them regarded a most solemn *Christian duty*, others of them regarded a *malum in se*—a sin!

Another question resulting in division, appears to have been that concerning the proper position of females. The "Pastoral Letter," before mentioned, sent forth by the Association of Congregational Ministers in Massachusetts, in 1837, had strongly censured the public lectures of females. This created a re-action, and drew forth strong and startling assertions of "woman's rights." A "clerical appeal," signed by five Congregational pastors, in the ranks of the abolitionists, but on the side of the "Pastoral Letter" of 1837, increased greatly the excitement. In this "clerical appeal" there was manifested a strong sympathy for the pro-slavery portion of the clergy—a disposition to shelter them from the censures of abolitionists—and an effort to sustain them in their claims of high clerical authority. A very able reply to the "clerical appeal" was promptly issued by Rev. Amos A. Phelps, of the same religious denomination, who, afterwards, in the division, did not go with Mr. Garrison, and never embraced his peculiar views. The signers of the "clerical appeal," and those who agreed with them, would, of course, separate themselves from Mr. Garrison in the division that followed. But the case of Mr. Phelps shows that a division from Mr. Garrison and his associates afforded no certain evidence of sympathy for the appellants, or approbation of their "appeal."

The editorial tone of the Liberator, in the mean time, was spirited and stirring. The assaults of the "Pastoral Letter" and of the "Clerical Appeal" were not merely parried, in a way of self-defense. In such a warfare, not even "Non-Re-sistants" were to be restrained from aggressive and even retali-atory movements. The body of the "orthodox clergy" with a few exceptions, were regarded by them as the aggressors, and that, too, in a bad cause. The most provoking as well as the most alarming feature of the assault was, that it had been successful in bringing to its aid a portion of the clergy that held rank among abolitionists. " What is this clerical institu-tion ? Where is its charter ? What are its claims ? And what is the theology that lends it its sanction ?" Questions like these must have arisen. Mr. Garrison was earnest and ardent. The distinctions between an institution and its per-version—between an office and its incumbent—between " or-thodoxy" and the supposed conservators and expounders of orthodoxy, were very intelligible distinctions. Mr. Garrison may have lacked neither the discriminative powers nor the magnanimity to understand and admit them. Yet he may not have been in the best mood or position, at the moment, to perceive, to appreciate, or to inquire after them. The first impulse, if followed, would naturally be—" Is *this* the institu-tion of the ministry ? Then, away with it ! Is this ortho-doxy ? Let it fall." The Liberator, about this time, abounded in sneers against the " clergy"—against " orthodoxy" and the " orthodox." It questioned or denied the obligation of ob-serving the first day of the week, as the Sabbath. It broached speculations concerning the "law" and the " decalogue," as contrasted with " the gospel"—which, to many ears, conveyed an impression of speculative antinomianism. In all this, though connected (*contrasted* as some thought) with his terribly " orthodox" denunciations of the Divine wrath against op-pressors and their apologists, there was much to alarm, per-plex, and alienate a class of New England minds that had, until then, been warmly and affectionately drawn to him. He could not have intended to repel the " orthodox" aboli-tionists around him—nor to do them or their theology injus-tice. But his editorials seem to have had that effect. No protestations that his " anti-slavery platform was broad enough for men of all creeds," served to satisfy them. They felt that there was a want of sympathy and confidence towards those of their creed—that to be "orthodox" was to lie under suspicion of latent pro-slaveryism.* In the mean time, those of other theological views clustered naturally around Mr. Garrison; attracted, in some cases, it may be, by his warfare with "the orthodox," as well as by his warfare with slavery. From about this time, we date the change that came over the theological sentiments of Mr. Garrison, who, in 1830, is known to have been rigidly "orthodox" himself, having been educated in the sentiments of orthodox Baptists and being a warm admirer of the Puritans.†

Differences in theology, having a bearing on ethics, on politics, and on reformatory measures, and, especially, theological *jealousies*, mutually entertained, may therefore be reckoned, to a certain extent and degree, an element of division among the abolitionists of Massachusetts. We will not say that, in this, either party has been wholly free from blame. Yet it is evident that a theology that places the ballot-box and the yoke of slavery in the same category, could hardly be expected to shape antislavery measures for those who believed in the divine institution of civil government and the political responsibilities of the citizens.

In April, 1839, a new paper called the Massachusetts Abolitionist, and conducted by Elizur Wright, Jr., (formerly Corresponding Secretary of the American Anti-Slavery Society, and Editor of the Anti-Slavery Quarterly Magazine,) was commenced in Boston.

A new State Society, called the Massachusetts Abolition Society, was organized in Boston, the 27th of May, in the same year.

The new paper and the new society based the movement on their views of the importance of political action—views not

---

* We find Benjamin Lundy, a Quaker, expressing in his paper, his regret,that the course of Mr. Garrison tended to introduce sectarian divisions among abolitionists.

† Mr. Garrison is not, and never has been a Quaker, as many, at a distance, have supposed.

held by the Editor of the Liberator, and by other leading members of the Massachusetts Anti-Slavery Society. Yet it does not appear that, at that time, the leaders of the new movement contemplated the organization of a separate political party.

The Old (Massachusetts Anti-Slavery) Society affirmed, in a manifesto sent out on the occasion, that so lately as the 10th of August previous, the Board of Managers had urged political action, that fourteen out of eighteen members of the Board believed in "*the duty* of upholding civil government at the polls," and that they doubted whether one-hundredth part of the members of the Society held the peculiar views of Mr. Garrison.*

To this, it was responded that such facts furnished a strong argument against the tone of the only anti-slavery paper in the state, seeking and receiving anti-slavery support—that, at least, so large a majority of Massachusetts abolitionists were justified, in establishing a paper that advocated instead of opposing the political measures they approved: and that they were called upon to organize an anti-slavery society in which, without contention, they could *advocate* " the duty of upholding civil government" and likewise of abolishing slavery " at the polls."

DIVISION IN THE PARENT SOCIETY.

A few days before the consummation of this rupture in Boston, a kindred dispute had been introduced, May 7, 1839, into the business meeting of the American Anti-slavery Society in the city of New York. Two points of disagreement were presented; the one related to the co-operation of females; the other to the duty of political action.

A question arose whether the roll of the meeting should, as on former occasions, be composed only of the names of *men*,

---

* This statement, in making the same argument, was repeated long afterward. In 1841 or 2, it was alleged that there were not, probably, to exceed one or two hundred " Non-Resistants" in all New-England.

or whether it should include also those of *women*.* The yeas and nays were taken, from which it appears that the delegates from Massachusetts gave 72 ayes and 25 nays; state of New York, 45 ayes, 76 nays; Connecticut, 14 ayes, 11 nays; Pennsylvania, 21 ayes, 7 nays; Rhode Island, 10 ayes, 1 nay; other States, 18 ayes, 20 nays—Total, 180 ayes, 140 nays. Majority, in favor of enrolling names of women, 40.

On the list of ayes we notice several prominent names afterwards conspicuous in the Liberty party, and not in sympathy with the distinctive views of Mr. Garrison, viz: Alvan Stewart, Rev. Joshua Leavitt, Gerrit Smith, Wm. L. Chaplin, Rev. Cyrus P. Grosvenor, A. F. Williams, S. M. Booth, Rev. Otis Thompson, Rev. Francis Hawley, Rev. Samuel Wells, &c. &c. Several of them "orthodox" ministers of the gospel.†

A resolution was reported, containing the former testimonies of the society, on "the duty of political action," nearly in the language of the Declaration of 1833, as then drawn up by Mr. Garrison. Mr. C. C. Burleigh moved an amendment, to the effect that those who use the elective franchise and neglect to use it for the cause of emancipation, are false to their principles, and fail to do their duty. The result was 84 votes for the original resolution, and 77 against it.

The annual meeting of the society at New York, in May, 1840, resulted in a division :—the election of new officers for the Old Society, and the organization of the "American and Foreign Anti-Slavery Society;" the former in accordance with the views of Mr. Garrison; the latter, with the co-operation of Messrs. Arthur and Lewis Tappan.‡

The majority of those in attendance at the "business meet-

---

* On the one hand, it was claimed that the Constitution of the Society made no discrimination between males and females. On the other, it was urged that the uniform usage indicated the original intentions of the society.

† Alvan Stewart moved the appointment of a Committee to reply to the protest filed against the vote, but the motion was laid on the table.

‡ Mr. Arthur Tappan, in anticipation of the controversy, absented himself from the "business meeting." He was re-elected President of the Old Society, and declined serving, but accepted the Presidency of the newly formed American and Foreign Anti-Slavery Society.

ing," appeared to have been from New England, mostly from Massachusetts; many were females from particular localities where the peculiar views of Mr. Garrison were known to be prevalent. Arrangements had been made for the cheap conveyance of the company by steamboat. The Liberator said:

" On making an enumeration, it appeared that there were about four hundred and fifty anti-slavery men and women *in our company*, of whom about four hundred were from Massachusetts. Probably one hundred went by *other routes*."

This would make 550 in all. The proceedings afterwards showed only 1008 recorded votes, from all in attendance, from all the States. Of these, Mr. Garrison's rally of 550 would, if unanimous, secure a majority of 92 without any votes from any of the other States. Yet the business to be transacted was that of a Society scattered in all the free States, and numbering, perhaps, one or two hundred thousand, the majority of whom anticipated nothing of what was going forward; and, if they had known, could have had no opportunity of attending.

On the motion to insert the name of Abby Kelly on a committee, 557 votes were given in favor, and 451 against the appointment, a majority of 106. The women who came in company with Mr. Garrison, and voted with him, were more than enough to secure a majority.

Resolutions were adopted disapproving the Liberty Party Nominating Convention at Albany, the April previous, disapproving of anti-slavery nominations in general, and deprecating, in the same sentence, and without distinction, the support of Harrison, Van Buren, and *Birney;*—the latter being an abolitionist who had emancipated his slaves, and the two former opposers of the anti-slavery movement. The consistency of this must be found, perhaps, in the principle that all voting, under a compulsory civil government, is alike sinful. The pro-slavery character of the Constitution—not yet discovered—was not alluded to, in the proceedings.*

---

* The division gave rise to new contentions. Mr. Garrison and his friends complained that the "*Emancipator*" newspaper (originally established at great expense

The historical evidence seems not quite clear that the abolitionists who did not hold themselves bound by these proceedings were therefore untrue to the cause of the slave.

While these divisions produced a strong sensation in New England, and in the sea-board cities, the sound of them going across the Atlantic, and awakening kindred responses, pro and con, from among the abolitionists of Great Britain, the blast died away, like a Massachusetts North-Easter, as it traveled westward, spending its strength by the time it had reached the valley of the Mohawk, and was scarcely felt beyond the waters of Lake Erie.

There were reasons for this. The contention about women's acting in the Societies was, at the West, considered a frivolous one. There were differences of opinion, but the question would not have been pressed, on the one hand, nor have been made a ground of withdrawal, on the other. The voice of women, in conference and prayer-meetings, in those days and previously, in the wide west, had been too familiar to the ears of the most fastidious, to admit of their being greatly alarmed.

As to the new policy of not voting, and the theories upon which it was based, the march of political anti-slavery was

---

and labor by Mr. Tappan and others, and afterwards transferred by them without compensation to the Society) was gratuitously transferred again by the Society to the N. Y. City Anti-Slavery Society, a short time before the division, and thus prevented from passing into the hands of the newly elected committee. The answer to this complaint was, that as the paper did not support itself, as the treasury was empty, and individual members of the committee had already assumed heavy liabilities, there was no means of paying the printer, and the publication must have been suspended but for the acceptance of the offer. To this it *might* have been added (if it was not), that if the paper had passed into the hands of the new committee, it would have been used to oppose the sentiments and measures of those who had originally established it, who had mainly supported it, and whose subscriptions, after the division, could not, to any great extent, have been retained by the publishers.

Another complaint was, that a member of the old committee had taken possession of the Anti-Slavery depository of books, pamphlets, &c., and refused to deliver them over to the newly elected committee. The justification was that members of the old committee had become individually responsible for the payment of debts contracted for the Society, which liabilities the new committee and its members had refused to assume ; and the proceeds of the depository would repay only a part of the amount due them from the Society. Their final loss was above $3,400.

too steadily and too resistlessly on the advance, in the interior of the country and at the far west, to be arrested by the rumor of what had been said and done in the cities of New-York and Boston.

Apart from all this, the abolitionists of the interior, including those of the far west, were too busily at work in their own localities and in their own way, to think it necessary that they should affiliate with either of the rival National Societies, or be under the supervision of either of them. The bonds of national organization had, indeed, set lightly upon them from the beginning. And with the progress of the cause and the consequent increase of local activity and effort, those bonds had grown looser and looser. There was a mistake in supposing that any one great central Committee could transact any great proportion of the anti-slavery business *to be* transacted in the country. A central committee in London, with a few others in some of the chief cities, might suffice for Great Britain. The wider territory of the American States, with our more democratic methods of procedure and agitation, could not be thus managed. Not only state, but county, village, and township organizations were needed. The Committee of the New-York State Society, at the central point of Utica, could not effectively reach the more western parts of the State. A Western Committee had to be organized. Not only so, County Societies were encouraged by the two State Committees to do up their own work in their own way. In other States, the same manifestations were witnessed. In short, the previous tendencies to centralization were subsiding. Abolitionists, having felt the evils of too much centralized power in the other National Societies, were beginning to guard against similar evils, among themselves. Aside from any unpleasant rupture in the National Society, and before it was foreseen, it was becoming evident that the functions of such a Society must decrease, instead of expanding, with the progress and expansion of the enterprise itself, which was, everywhere, cutting its own local channels.

Thus, while in Boston, New-York, and their vicinities, the

great pending question seemed to be, which of the two National Societies should superintend the activities and absorb the contributions of American abolitionists, the great majority of them, in the interior, found themselves in a convenient position to withdraw from the control and from the support of either. Within a year from the division in New-York, most of the State Anti-Slavery Societies out of New England, declined sustaining the position of auxiliaries to either of the National Societies, a measure which, it was believed, would greatly tend to discountenance divisions. In the States of New-York and Ohio, however, (perhaps in other States,) the friends of Mr. Garrison succeeded in forming State Societies, sometime afterwards.

The neutrality we have described may have been wise or it may have been unwise. It was assumed at a time when the controversy was little understood in the interior, and when the changes in progress had been but imperfectly developed.

The fact of so extensive a neutrality respecting the "New" and the "Old organizations" belongs to the record, and throws light on the *true origin of the Liberty Party;* which could have had no important or general connection with this controversy, as has been represented and supposed, on both sides of the Atlantic.* It is claimed that the large class of abolitionists who wished to escape that contention, have not been, as a class, behind others, in their uncompromising fidelity to the enslaved.

---

* We mean to say that the Liberty party, which originated in Western New York, did not arise from a wish to oppose the "old organization" or Mr. Garrison—nor from a wish to support the "new organization." Some individuals in Massachusetts, who had encountered Mr. Garrison's theory of non-voting, may have been the more ready to fall in with an organized party. A letter of E. Wright, Jr., published in the *Liberator,* shows this. It is equally possible that Mr. Garrison's antipathy to voting, and his desire to have other abolitionists come into his views of voting, might have made him adverse to the organization of such a party, though he may not have been distinctly conscious of such a motive himself. We have never doubted that if Mr. Garrison had not become a "Non-Resistant," he would have been an early and zealous leader of the Liberty party.

CHAPTER XXXIX.

ORGANIZED POLITICAL ACTION—LIBERTY PARTY—LIBERTY
LEAGUE—FREE SOIL PARTY.

Necessity of distinct organization—Early anticipations of this—Garrison, Follen,
Stewart—Convention at Albany, July, 1839—Nominations in Monroe Co., N. Y.—
Myron Holley—Rochester "Freeman"—Convention at Arcade—Liberty Party
organized at Albany, April 1, 1840, and James G. Birney nominated for President
—Second Nomination, in 1844—Number of votes—Course of other voting abolitionists—What was accomplished ?—Occasions of instability—Tendencies to re-absorption—Different views of its true policy—Nomination of Gerrit Smith by " the
Liberty League," and why ?—Position taken by the " League"—Unconstitutionality of Slavery—Other features—Nomination (by the Liberty Party) of John P.
Hale—Rise of the Free Soil Party—Nomination of Mr. Van Buren—Buffalo Platform—Position of Mr. Van Buren—Various views of that movement and of its
results—Hints for the future—Remnant of the Liberty Party.

THE Liberty party arose from the fact, that, after a protracted experiment, the candidates of the old parties could
not, to any extent, if at all,—however " questioned " and
"pledged "—be depended upon, to do the work which abolitionists demanded of them. When they really intended to
do it, their party associates would not suffer them. It would
be easy to prove this, if we had room for the details.

Another fact, lying behind this, must not, as we value the
impartiality of history, be withheld. Abolitionists themselves,
connected with the political parties, and who " questioned
the candidates," could not generally be weaned from an undue
bias in favor of their political leaders. They too readily
persuaded themselves that the candidate of their own party,
though but slightly or ambiguously pledged, or even if not
pledged at all, would probably do more for the slave, if elected, than the candidate of the opposite party, whatever his

anti-slavery reputation or his pledges might be. This delusion and its effects began, at length, to afford candidates an excuse for not answering the questions of abolitionists. They said, "It will be of no use, for abolitionists will generally vote for the candidates of their respective parties." The statement was exaggerated. But on many occasions and in many localities, there was enough of truth in it, to render the "questioning of the candidates" a farce.

It was hoped that by the organization of a distinct political party, this delusion might be dispelled, and abolitionists be led to honor their principles at the polls. Though a minority, they could exhibit a correct example, and thus preserve their integrity, and increase their moral power.

Mr. Garrison had advocated, sometime previous, the forming of a distinct political party, though he was not now in favor of it. His recommendation is, indeed, the earliest that we find on record. In his Liberator, in 1834, he advocated "a Christian party in politics"—with particular reference to the slave question.

Prof. Charles Follen, sometime after, suggested the utility of a new political party of democratic progress, of which one prominent object should be the abolition of slavery. This, if we rightly remember, was as early as 1836.

Alvan Stewart strongly urged upon the Executive Committee of the New York State Anti-Slavery Society, in February, 1839, the organization of a distinct party. The Committee were not then prepared for the measure, but some of them saw, clearly, and had long seen, the necessity of strenuous efforts to counteract the partisan tendencies of abolitionists, by inculcating the highest principles of political morality.

At the annual meeting of the Society, at Utica, Sept. 19–21, 1838, a series of Resolutions, twenty-two in number, had been presented, discussed, and adopted, setting forth the principles of political action, and solemnly pledging those who adopted them to vote for no candidates who were not fully pledged to anti-slavery measures.* Though not designed,

---

* These resolutions, which had been prepared by Wm. Goodell, were reported by

at that time, to favor distinct anti-slavery nominations, nor expected to introduce them, these resolutions recognized a *moral principle*, in voting, which, it was afterwards found, could not be acted upon, in the existing state of the country, without a new political party. Both parties, then and afterwards, were completely under the control of their slaveholding members.

A National Anti-Slavery Convention was held at Albany, commencing July 31, 1839. It was called by a Committee appointed for the purpose at the annual meeting of the American Anti-Slavery Society, the May previous. Its object, as specified in the call, was " to discuss the principles of the anti-slavery enterprise " and "the measures suited to its accomplishment in the United States, especially those which relate to the proper exercise of the right of suffrage by citizens of the free states." The mode of political action against slavery, including the question of a distinct party, was fully discussed, but without coming to any definite decision by vote, farther than to refer the question of independent nominations to the judgment of abolitionists in their different localities.

This suggestion was improved to sanction some local nominations in the State of New-York, which, with the discussions of the Convention, prepared the way for further progress.

The Monroe County Convention for Nominations at Rochester, N. Y., September 28, 1839, adopted a series of Resolutions and an Address prepared by the late Myron Holly, which have been regarded as laying the corner stone of the Liberty Party. In his "*Rochester Freeman*," commenced in June previous, Mr. Holley successfully advocated the policy of independent political action, and came to be recognized as —more than any other one person—the founder of the Liberty Party.

A New-York State Anti-Slavery Convention was held at

a business committee of which the late Myron Holley was Chairman. They were eloquently advocated in the Convention by Gerrit Smith, and extensively circulated in anti-slavery papers.

Arcade, (then) Genesee County, January 28th and 29th, 1840, attended by Myron Holley and Gerrit Smith; Reuben Sleeper, of Livingston County, presiding. This Convention issued a Call for a National Convention to be held at Albany, April 1, 1840, "to discuss the question of an independent nomination of abolition candidates for the two highest offices in our National Government, and, if thought expedient, to make such nomination, for the friends of freedom to support, at the next election."

The National Convention at Albany was accordingly held, at the time appointed, Alvan Stewart presiding. After a full discussion, the Liberty party was organized, and James G. Birney and Thomas Earle were nominated for President and Vice-President of the United States. The traveling, at that season of the year, was exceedingly bad, but delegates were in attendance from six States.

The entire vote of the Liberty party at the Presidential Election, in the autumn of 1840, amounted to a little less than 7000. In 1844, the Liberty candidates, James G. Birney and Thomas Morris, received upwards of 60,000 votes. These were but a small part of the professed abolitionists of the United States. A few hundreds, perhaps, abstained from voting, from conscientious scruples, and other considerations. But the great majority of those who did not vote for the Liberty candidates, unquestionably voted for the nominees of the old parties, Harrison, Van Buren, Polk, and Clay, the two latter being slaveholders, and the two former openly opposed to the measures and objects of abolitionists.

Politicians accustomed to identify "success" with the election of their candidates may ask: What was effected by the organization of the Liberty party? Let the question be answered by asking another: What would have been the condition of the anti-slavery cause now, if *all* the voting abolitionists of the country had continued to vote (as all except "Liberty" men did) for the candidates of the old political parties? If any intelligent and candid politician will say, on reflection, that it would have stood on as high a ground as it does now, we have nothing further to say to him on that subject.

A more pertinent inquiry would be: What would, probably, have been the effect, if the sixty thousand Liberty men who voted for Birney in 1844, had held firmly *that position?*

But there is a question lying back of this:—Why did they not continue to maintain that position?

A number of particulars might be adverted to, in reply to that question.

The old party attachments of many who joined the Liberty party, were not broken off. They were not steady in their adhesion to the Liberty party. Some voted, occasionally, with the old parties to accomplish particular objects. Some voted for Mr. Clay, as they said, "to keep out Texas." Some voted with the old party to procure amendments in State Constitutions. Some, if they would confess the truth, to secure a "protective tariff." Thus, the Liberty party was weakened, and confidence in its stability, and even its integrity, was undermined. There are thousands of whigs and democrats who will affirm that the reason why they never joined the Liberty party was because the vacillating course of its members led them to anticipate what they say has since taken place—its general absorption in a party with a lower basis—and, finally, in one or the other of the old parties. Why should they quit their party, when those who had done so, were evidently on tip-toe for an opportunity to get back into it?

The ecclesiastical connections of many Liberty party men, must have exerted a similar influence upon them; for their religious teachers, to a great extent, exerted a political influence in harmony with the old political parties, and directly in favor of their candidates. On the eve of Presidential elections, their efforts were seldom wanting. When a celebrated Doctor of Divinity, on one occasion of the kind, inculcated the Christian duty of "voting for the least of two devils" that might be in nomination, if one or the other of them must succeed—is it credible that Liberty men, confiding in such

teachers, would be likely to retain their position ?* It is difficult for any class of men to maintain a higher tone of morality in their political relations than they do in their Churches,
thus exalting their politics above their religion. The history
of the Liberty party has shown this. The little remnant of
that party exists, because its leading members commonly hold
a corresponding ecclesiastical position.

Another cause of instability, connected with causes already
mentioned, was the idea in many minds that the Liberty party
was to be available only on one subject, and was pledged to
neutrality on all other questions, so that whenever any other
important political duties were to be performed, the Liberty
party must be temporarily deserted of course.

Closely allied to this was the idea that the Liberty party
was only to be a "balance of power" party, to be re-absorbed
by either of the parties who should give promise of doing
most for the cause of freedom. This would naturally encourage an attitude of unreasonable expectancy on the part
of Liberty men, and give undue importance to any real or
apparent concessions that might be held out to allure them.
In short, the policy of "choosing the least of two evils," as
commended by Dr. Taylor and others, would be embraced,
and the stern political morality that had originated the Liberty party would be abandoned.

---

* Edmund Tuttle, of Meridan, Conn., in a Letter to Rev. Dr. Taylor, of New
Haven, propounded this inquiry :

"Can a Christian, consistently with the word of God, cast his vote, either for a
duellist, or for an oppressor of the poor, for Chief Magistrate of this nation ?"

In an elaborate answer, sustaining the affirmative of the above question, Dr.
Taylor said :

"To put a stronger case. Suppose that there is no reasonable doubt that one of
two devils, one of which is less a devil than the other, will be actually elected, let
the Christian vote as he may ; and that his vote will therefore be utterly lost if he
does not vote for one of them ; I think that an enlightened Christian would vote
for the least devil of the two.   "NATHANIEL W. TAYLOR."
"*Yale College, October* 5, 1844."

The date and circumstances of the letter oblige us to infer that the highly com-
plimentary comparison which it contains was intended for the political benefit of
Henry Clay, as being, in the writer's view, a lesser devil than James K. Polk.

Such at least were the apprehensions of some active Liberty men, who began, as early as 1845, to propose safe-guards against the re-absorption they so much dreaded and feared.

They contended that the Liberty party was originally designed to be a permanent and progressive exponent of human rights, and not a mere temporary expedient—that its foundations were accordingly laid in the first principles of civil government—that its platform was as broad as those of republican institutions and of protecting law—that whatever the State and National Governments ought to *do*, the Liberty party ought to seek and *propose*—that while the abolition of chattel slavery was to be the prominent, the paramount measure of the party, it was not to be the *only* one. They quoted the writings and speeches of Myron Holly and the early resolutions and addresses of the Liberty party, to prove that such were the views with which the Liberty party was formed.

The most that could be said in reply to this representation was, that the sentiments quoted were expressed, for the most part, in general terms.

To supply, then, this alleged deficiency in a party of progress, it was proposed to specify some of the particular measures which the principles and professions of Liberty men required them to espouse, such as free trade, gratuitous distribution of public lands, limitation of land ownership, the inalienable homestead, retrenchment of expenses, free suffrage, and the abolition of all legalized monopolies and castes.

In further support of this policy, it was urged that slavery was only to be overthrown through the destruction of the minor monopolies and aristocracies subsidized by and sustaining it; and that the forces needed at the ballot box to overthrow slavery must consist, to a great extent, of the masses of men who feel that they have wrongs of their own to be redressed, and who could have no confidence in a Liberty party not committed to universal equality and impartial justice to all. They predicted that unless this advice was heeded, the Liberty party would, ere long, be scattered to the winds. They contended that, as civil government is an ordinance of God for the protection of *all* the rights of *all men*, we have no right to administer it, or to seek to administer it, for any lower or partial ends, and that if an *Anti-Slavery Society* may confine *its* attention to one form of oppression and robbery, it does not follow that the functions of CIVIL GOVERNMENT may be thus circumscribed.

LIBERTY LEAGUE.

A State Convention was held at Port Byron, (N. Y.) June 25th and 26th, 1845, at which an address was presented, embracing the preceding views. It was not adopted by the Convention, but was printed and circulated, and gained adherents. By a number of Liberty men embracing its sentiments, a nominating Convention was called, which was held at Macedon Locke, Wayne Co., N. Y., June 8th, 9th, and 10th, 1847; at which Gerrit Smith and Elihu Burritt were nominated for President and Vice-President of the United States. Mr. Burritt having declined, the name of Charles C. Foote was afterwards placed on the ticket, by another Convention, at Rochester. The Macedon Convention sent forth an address which was widely circulated, and elicited much debate. The Convention separated itself from the Liberty party, and took the name of the Liberty League.

These measures were adopted in the confident anticipation of the speedy absorption of the Liberty party in some other organization holding a receding instead of an advanced position, in respect to slavery itself, to say nothing of kindred reforms. Unequivocal indications of this, were believed to have appeared.*

UNCONSTITUTIONALITY OF SLAVERY.

It should be mentioned in this place that the doctrine of the unconstitutionality of American Slavery had, before this time,

---

* Among these was the proposal to defer making a Presidential nomination in 1847, leaving it till the next year, to see what course would be taken *by prominent men in the other parties*. It was commonly understood that the nomination of Gerrit Smith by the Macedon Convention, induced a majority of the National Committee to call the Buffalo Convention. A minority still dissented from that course. Four years previous, there had been some similar tendencies.

gained a strong foothold in the Liberty Party, and was coming to be embraced by many in the old political parties. Rev. Samuel J. May, an abolitionist of the Garrison school, had written an argument to prove that the Federal Constitution is not pro-slavery, which appeared in the Quarterly Anti-Slavery Magazine for October, 1836 and May, 1837. The late Nathaniel P. Rogers, Esq., a lawyer of New Hampshire, an abolitionist of the same school, writing in the same magazine, for January, 1837, took the same ground. He even challenged the proof that slavery had ever been legalized in Carolina. He affirmed that a rising of the slaves would be no "insurrection;" and intimated that the "guaranty to every State in this Union of a republican form of government," was a guaranty against slavery. An anonymous writer over the signature of "Seventy Six," in the Emancipator of January 4, 1838, threw out hints which put many of the friends of liberty on the track of further investigation. Alvan Stewart prepared an argument, based on the "due process of law," [Amendments, art. v.] which was presented to the annual meeting of the N. Y. State A. S. Society in September, 1837, and of the American A. S. Society in May, 1838. In 1844 appeared a pamphlet on the subject, entitled "Views of American Constitutional Law, in its bearing upon American Slavery," by William Goodell.* This was followed, soon after, by another, "The Unconstitutionality of Slavery," by Lysander Spooner, Esq., a gentleman never connected with the Liberty Party. The subject now elicited general inquiry. Discussions and public debates were held. Prominent lawyers, of the old parties, declined the solicitations of their political associates, to combat, in public debate, the new doctrine, declaring that the printed arguments in its favor were impregnable. Others, having entered the lists, admitted, afterwards, that they had been baffled. Promiscuous audiences, not distinctively abolitionists, having heard the question debated, voted, by strong majorities, the unconstitutionality of slavery. The doctrine was espoused by Liberty Party editors,

---

* Upwards of 13,000 copies of this (in two editions) were soon circulated.

was affirmed by a State Convention of the Massachusetts Liberty Party, by other State Conventions, and at large Liberty Conventions all over the State of New York, and at the West. The Liberty Party of the country, if remaining in the field, and active, was expected to have affirmed the doctrine, ere long, in its National Conventions. But most of its leaders were apparently marking out for it a course which would require that such a doctrine should be abandoned, or held in abeyance. It was however made prominent, and strongly insisted upon by the Liberty League.

OBJECTIONS AGAINST THE LIBERTY LEAGUE.

Among objections against the Liberty League, one was, that it would divert attention from the Slave Question by the introduction of other topics. The call of the Macedon Convention had stated the views of the signers in nineteen distinct propositions, nearly one half of them affirming abstract propositions which no republican denies, and some of the rest expressing sentiments frequently embodied in the resolutions of anti-slavery Conventions. Occasion was nevertheless taken from this, to satirize the League, as having put forth a creed of nineteen articles, and as having set up nineteen new measures as tests.* The *truth* was, the number of its proposed *measures* of government did not exceed those often *professed* before by the old political parties, and by the " Free Soil" party since. Yet a party with so wide a platform was, in this case, pronounced impracticable, and abolitionists were warned to adhere strictly to their "one idea," as the only antidote against apostacy from primitive abolitionism.

THE " FREE SOIL" PARTY.

In the midst of these exhortations, the National Convention of the Liberty party assembled at Buffalo, October 20th, 1847. Gerrit Smith, still a member of the Liberty party, was propo-

---

* Some of the measures objected against, have since been claimed by other political parties, including the Free Soil party, and have been rapidly gaining public favor.

sed as a candidate for the Presidency. His nomination would
have secured the co-operation of the Liberty League, in his
support. But the course marked out by the leading men in
that Convention, beforehand, required the nomination of a
different man from Gerrit Smith. The Liberty party, for the
first time, adopted the policy of going out of its own ranks for
a presidential candidate. After debating, awhile, the question
of nominating at all, till next year, they nominated the Hon.
John P. Hale, United States' Senator from New Hampshire, an
"Independent Democrat," who had certainly done himself
honor in refusing to do homage to the slave power, and who
had drawn off a portion of the "democracy" of New Hampshire to his support. But he was not prepared to advocate
all the measures of Liberty party abolitionists. So far from
believing in the unconstitutionality of slavery, he did not perceive (what Daniel Webster* had long before affirmed) the
constitutional power of Congress to abolish the inter-state slave
trade. The candidate for the Vice-Presidency was Hon.
Liecester King, of Ohio.

But the nomination of Mr. Hale was only a temporary one,
and answered its temporary purpose.† Gentlemen active in
making it, united with others, of other parties, in calling
another Convention, which was held at Buffalo, Aug. 9, 1848,
composed of *the opponents of slavery extension*, irrespective of
parties, and including, of course, as was designed, large numbers who did not intend to be committed to "the one idea" of
abolishing slavery. On that occasion was organized "the
Free Soil party," in which the Liberty party was designed to
be wholly absorbed. Martin Van Buren, of New York, and
Charles F. Adams, of Massachusetts, neither of them recog-

---

* See Quarterly A. S. Mag., April, 1837, p. 232.

† "The Buffalo Convention *had to be* summoned, because the Macedon Convention
had been held, and had done precisely what it did. The Buffalo Convention, when
assembled, *had* to nominate, because a secession had been made from the Liberty
party, a Liberty League organized, and its presidential nominations made and announced."—[*Charter Oak*, W. H. Burleigh, editor, a supporter of Mr. Hale and Mr.
Van Buren.]

nized as being distinctively "abolitionists" or Liberty party men, were nominated as candidates for the Presidency and Vice-Presidency of the United States. Messrs. Hale and King, as was expected, withdrew their names, in consequence or in anticipation of this new nomination.

"THE BUFFALO PLATFORM."

The following resolutions, with the response of their Presidential Candidate, define the "platform" of the Free Soil party:

"*Resolved*, That we, the people here assembled, remembering the example of our fathers in the days of the first Declaration of Independence, putting our trust in God for the triumph of our cause, and invoking his guidance in our endeavors to advance it, do now plant ourselves upon the National Platform of Freedom, in opposition to the Sectional Platform of Slavery.

"*Resolved*, That slavery in the several States of this Union which recognize its existence, depends upon State laws alone, which cannot be repealed or modified by the Federal Government, and for which laws that Government is not responsible. We therefore propose no interference by Congress with slavery within the limits of any State.

"*Resolved*, That the proviso of Jefferson to prohibit the existence of slavery after 1800 in all the Territories of the United States, Southern and Northern; the votes of six States and sixteen delegates, in the Congress of 1784, for the proviso, to three States and seven delegates against it; the actual exclusion of slavery from the North-Western Territory, by the Ordinance of 1787, unanimously adopted ·by the States in Congress; and the entire history of that period clearly show that it was the settled policy of the nation not to extend, nationalize, or encourage, but to limit, localize, and discourage slavery; and to this policy, which should never have been departed from, the Government ought to return.

"*Resolved*, That our fathers ordained the Constitution of the United States, in order, among other great national objects, to establish justice, promote the general welfare, and secure the blessings of liberty, but expressly denied to the Federal Government, which they created, all constitutional power to deprive any person of life, liberty, or property, without due legal process.

"*Resolved*, That, in the judgment of this Convention, Congress has no more power to make a slave than to make a king; no more power to institute or establish slavery, than to institute or establish a monarchy—no such power can be found among those specifically conferred by the Constitution, or derived by just implication from them.

" *Resolved*, That it is the duty of the Federal Government to relieve itself from all responsibility for the existence or continuance of slavery, wherever that Government possesses constitutional authority to legislate on that subject, and is thus responsible for its existence.

" *Resolved*, That the true, and, in the judgment of this Convention, the only safe means of preventing the extension of slavery into territory now free, is to prohibit its existence in all such territory by an act of Congress.

" *Resolved*, That we accept the issue which the slave power has forced upon us, and to their demand for more slave States, and more slave Territories, our calm but final answer is, No more slave States, and no more slave Territory. Let the soil of our extensive domains be ever kept free, for the hardy pioneers of our own land, and the oppressed and banished of other lands, seeking homes of comfort and fields of enterprise in the new world."

These were followed by resolutions in favor of cheap postage, retrenchment, abolition of unnecessary offices, elections by the people, river and harbor improvements, free grant of public lands, payment of public debts, and revenue tariff. Here were seven distinct objects enumerated, besides the nonextension of slavery.

It may be asked, how much was intended to be included in the sixth of these resolutions. It will not probably be claimed that *this* Convention intended to set up a *higher* standard than that of the Liberty Party Convention that nominated Mr. Hale, who was not prepared for the abolition, by Congress, of the inter-state slave trade. The following extracts from the Letter of Mr. Van Buren, accepting the nomination, will show *his* understanding of the position of the Convention and the new party :

" I have examined and considered the platform adopted by the Buffalo Convention, as defining the political creed of the ' Free Democracy,' with the attention due to the grave subjects under which it is presented. It breathes the right spirit, and presents a political chart which, with the explanations I am about to make, I can, in good faith, adopt and sustain.

" In regard to the chief topics of the resolutions, it is not to be doubted, that the present movement of the public mind in the non-slaveholding States, upon the subject of slavery, is caused mainly by an earnest desire to uphold and enforce the policy in regard to it, established by the founders of the Republic. That policy, in addition to the prospective prohibition of the foreign slave trade, was—

" 1st. Adequate, efficient, and certain security against the extension of slavery into territories where it did not practically exist.

" 2d. That, in the language of your own condensed and excellent resolution, ' Slavery, in the several States of the Union which recognize its existence, should depend upon State laws, which cannot be repealed or modified by the Federal Government ;' and—

" 3d. A SPIRIT OF CONSIDERATE FORBEARANCE TOWARDS THE INSTITUTION, IN LOCALITIES WHERE IT WAS PLACED UNDER THE CONTROL OF CONGRESS." * * * * * * * *

" The sixth resolution embraces the subject of slavery in the District of Columbia ; and I observe in it a generality of expression, in respect to the time when, and the circumstances under which, it was the opinion of the Convention that it should be abolished, which has not been usual on the part of the friends of immediate action. Most reflecting and philanthropic minds live in the hope, that they will one day see slavery abolished, not only in that District, but in the States also, in the latter through the agency of the State Governments, to whom the Constitution wisely leaves exclusive power in the matter, and in the former by Congress. I may be mistaken, but I think I see in the guarded language of the resolution, evidence of an apprehension, on the part of the Convention, that a difference in opinion, to some extent at least, existed among its members, upon the point referred to, and of an enlightened and truly patriotic resolve, not to suffer that circumstance, if it existed, to weaken the moral power of their unanimity on the great question which had brought them together."

It is not known that the leading members of the Convention that nominated Mr. Van Buren, ever complained that he had misunderstood their position. They certainly did not withdraw from him their support.

Here, then, was a platform containing as many collateral measures as had been proposed by the Liberty League, but omitting " *the one idea*" of a direct abolition of slavery. Yet it was eagerly embraced by many who had scarcely ceased from protesting against the introduction of other topics by the Liberty League, in connection with the highest standard of anti-slavery action.

The position of Mr. Van Buren, and of the party that selected him as their chief representative, may be further seen from the reference he made to his course during his Presidency in respect to the slave question, in his widely circulated letter of June 20th, 1848, a few weeks previous to his nomination at Buffalo :

" But deeply penetrated by the conviction that slavery was the only sub-ject which could endanger our blessed Union, I was determined that no effort on my part, within the pale of the Constitution, should be wanting TO SUSTAIN ITS COMPROMISES AS THEY WERE THEN UNDERSTOOD, AND IT IS NOW A SOURCE OF CONSOLATION TO ME THAT I PURSUED THE COURSE I THEN ADOPTED."

The manner in which Mr. Van Buren sustained the "com-promises of the Constitution" when he was President, the reader has already seen.

The enemies of the Liberty party, whigs, democrats, "non-resistants," and "Garrison abolitionists," rejoiced greatly at its supposed "death and burial."

REMNANT OF THE LIBERTY PARTY.

But a little remnant remained. Besides those who had organized the Liberty League, there were a few who were inclined to favor their views, and there were others who pro-ferred to support Gerrit Smith rather than John P. Hale, or any candidate that would be likely to be substituted for him. *These*, rallied as "the Liberty Party," and in Convention at Buffalo, June 15th, 1848, concurred with the Liberty League in nominating their candidates. At a subsequent Convention at Canastota, Sept. 28th, they adopted the documents defining the platform of the Liberty League, which has not, since that time, maintained a separate organization.

RESULTS AND POSITION OF THE "FREE SOIL PARTY."

After an experiment of three years and a half, from the time of its organization at Buffalo, not a few members of the Free Soil party found themselves in the position described in the following extract, which appeared in the National Era of March 4, 1852 :

" I confess myself disappointed in the results of the Buffalo Convention. To one at the time it did seem that the people had become thoroughly awake, both to their rights and their duties, and that party attachments are no longer to prevent a manly, fearless assertion of the rights of the free North to take the control of the Government, and to wield it in favor of liberty.

" While I believe that that demonstration did exert a salutary influence on the then pending election, I am constrained to admit that the high hopes then formed have faded away, and left the sad conviction that the people of the free States are yet to learn lessons of deep humiliation, before they will rise to the true position and dignity of freemen."—*Extract of a Letter from A. A. Guthrie to the Free Soil Convention of Ohio.*

Others were found who freely expressed their regrets that the platform of direct abolition should have been virtually exchanged for that of non-extension.

The editor of the National Era, in commenting upon the letter of Mr. Guthrie, thus sums up the result, as he understands it, of the Free Soil organization :

" We did not succeed in obtaining a positive act from Congress prohibiting slavery in the Territories, but the power of the movement we represented was such as to constrain the new administration to countenance measures favorable to our views, such as to weaken the confidence of the slaveholders in their own doctrines respecting the title to their slaves in free territory, such as to impregnate the tide of emigration to California with the anti-slavery spirit, thereby inducing the formation of a non-slaveholding State on the Pacific, by which our entire Western seaboard was consecrated to Freedom.

" Among the other results attributable to this movement, directly or indirectly, are the repeal of the Black Laws of Ohio ; the election of from ten to fifteen members of the House for two successive Congresses, acting independently of organizations when controlled by slavery ; the election of Messrs. Chase and Sumner to the Senate of the United States; the control of Wisconsin, Ohio, New York, and Massachusetts, by coalitions, not to be coerced into submission to the dictates of the Slave Power ; distraction in the old political organizations always subservient to slavery, which thus far no efforts have succeeded in allaying ; a more general discussion of questions of slavery, in Congress and out, than had ever taken place before ; and such a state of the public mind as to have checked, if not extinguished, the project of Cuban annexation. Nor must we forget that it was under the pressure of this Buffalo Convention that the Oregon Bill, with its clause prohibiting slavery, was carried through Congress."

This, then, it may be presumed, is the most favorable account that can be given of the results of the Buffalo Convention of August 9, 1848, and of the nomination of Mr. Van Buren.

On the other hand, there are many who think all the favorable results above-mentioned, and many more now unrealized, would have been secured by taking higher instead of lower ground on the slave question. Aside from the *principle* involved, they maintain that since all congressional contests on the subject result uniformly in compromise, it was *bad policy* to set the claims of liberty on the lowest possible ground, that of the non-extension of slavery. They judge that a vigorous and bold push for the *abolition* of slavery (at least where it is confessedly under jurisdiction of Congress) would have cut out other work for the pro-slavery party than opposition to the admission of California as a free State! They have no doubt that its prompt admission, together with the adoption of the Wilmot proviso, would have been eagerly proposed as a "compromise" to stave off the abolition of slavery in the Federal District, and the prohibition of the inter-state slave trade—to say nothing of the still higher ground of the abolition of slavery in the States. Instead of acting merely on the defensive, and on their own territory, they would push the war into the citadel of the enemy. If "compromises" must needs be submitted to, they think a position should be chosen that should not inevitably result in placing all the concessions on the wrong side. More than all this, they believe in *the moral obligation of a practical conformity to all ascertained truth*, believing that the God of truth can control "consequences" and bring to pass results which no human sagacity could calculate or foresee beforehand. Though they were glad to see whigs and democrats leave their old parties, to take the advanced ground of the Free Soil party, they deeply deplored that Liberty party men, especially those who believed in the unconstitutionality of slavery, should have abandoned the ground indicated by their own convictions, for the sake of co-operation with those who held lower views.

It is questioned by many others, whether the organization of the Free Soil party produced all the results attributed to it in the above extract from the National Era. The questions that, of necessity, came before Congress, produced great excitement and drew forth earnest debate. The position of the ultra Southern members rendered it inevitable. And many members of Congress, not belonging to the Free Soil party, were quite as efficient in their advocacy of Northern interests as some who did. Among these are to be reckoned such men as William H. Seward, whig Senator from New York, and several others, though their party connections naturally tended to cripple them.

It should be noticed that some statesmen in Congress and the State Legislatures, who were elected as Free Soil men, or by help of the votes of that party, have found their way *out* of the Free Soil party into one or the other of the old parties. Among these are some who were formerly in the Liberty party, and who exerted themselves most strenuously, first, in favor of the "one idea" policy in opposition to the Liberty League; and, soon afterwards, to merge the Liberty party in the Free Soil party.

In the State of New-York, where the "Buffalo platform" was erected, it seems to have fallen down entirely. The Free Soil party is extinct in that State, having been absorbed by the old Democratic party, and that too, upon a basis which unites the "Old Hunkers" and the "Barnburners,"—the pro-slavery and the anti-slavery sections of the party. It is not seen that that party, since the re-absorption, is at all in advance of the Whig party, on the slave question. The friends of Mr. Seward, in the Whig party, appear to be rather in advance of them.

In Massachusetts and in Ohio, where there are yet some signs of life among "Free Soilers," their activity chiefly consists in temporary and local coalitions with one or the other of the old parties, or with portions of them, as circumstances may seem to require. It has, in fact, become a question, whether, as a national party, the "Free Soil party," as organized at Buffalo, in 1848, may be said to exist.

Party ties, even in the old parties, are, to an increasing extent, held loosely. At one time, there were indications of a division in both of them, by the organization of a new " Union" or Slavery party, to maintain the fugitive slave bill.

On one point, the Free Soil party, if it exists, is now in unity with the remnant of the Liberty party, and the platform of the late Liberty League. It repudiates the " one idea" policy, insisted upon, in 1847-8.* This bone of contention is now removed. If the members of the Free Soil party perceive that the time (if there ever was one) for a rally on the low ground of the " Buffalo platform" has now passed away—if they feel that the name " Free Soil "—indicating non-extension, is too narrow to describe their present position, as friends of liberty, they would do well to study the constitutional question, and the measures of political economy that harmonize with the principle of equal rights. Such a course, on their part, might result in a re-union of all the friends of political action against slavery.

---

* See editorial in *National Era*, March 4, 1852.

CHAPTER XL.

ANTI-SLAVERY CHURCH AGITATION—NEW ANTI-SLAVERY CHURCHES AND MISSIONARY BODIES.

Consideration, among abolitionists, of their Church relations—Consultations at Albany, in July, 1839—Previous " Anti-Slavery Conference and Prayer-Meetings" —"Christian Anti-Slavery Conventions," 1840 and onward—Paper devoted to the subject—Organization of Independent Anti-Slavery Churches—" Wesleyan Church," a secession from the Meth. E. Church—"Free Presbyterian Church" —"Free Missions"—Several early Missionary organizations—"Union Missionary Soc."—" W. India Committee"—" Amistad Committee"—" Western Miss. Asso." —Merged (1846) in "Am. Miss. Association"—Church agitation at the West— Large Conventions at Cincinnati and Chicago—Papers devoted to these movements —Church agitation among Baptists—Correspondence with English Baptists— Mission of Cox and Hoby—Organization of a "Baptist Anti-Slavery Convention" (as a permanent body), in 1840—Panic among Southern Baptists—Renewed opposition by Northern Baptists—Records of pro-slavery action among them—" Compromise Article"—Expulsion of Elon Galusha and others from the Missionary Board, in obedience to Southern demands—Baptist " Free Miss. Soc." organized 1843, by abolitionists—Old Boards, Slaveholding Missionaries—"Triennial Convention" dissolved—A new " Baptist Miss. Union" succeeds it—Its character— Its anti-slavery professions examined ; also other Baptist organizations—Missions of the " Am. Bap. Free Mission Soc."—N. Y. Central College.

IT would be interesting to trace the history of anti-slavery CHURCH agitation, for the last sixteen years. The items lie so scattered among different sects, and in various localities, that it would be a great task to collect, to classify, and to present them. There are materials sufficient for volumes, but we have room for only a few pages.

It was seen by many, at an early day, that the same principle that required *political* secession, required, in like cases, *ecclesiastical* secession; and the more especially as the Church is naturally expected to be purer than the State, and to constitute the guide and teacher, by which, on great moral questions, the legislation of a country must be moulded.

This was seen and felt by many who attended the National Anti-Slavery Convention for political discussion at Albany, commencing July 31, 1839. A large portion of those in that Convention who were church members, and who were then looking forward, though vaguely, to some new modes of political action, assembled each morning before breakfast, during that Convention, for mutual prayer, and for a free consideration of their ecclesiastical relations.* The result was a general determination among those present to push the slave question in the churches, to "abolitionize" them if possible, and if not, secede from them. A resolution was adopted and afterwards published, recommending "Christian Anti-slavery Conventions" for this end. Even before this date, something of the kind had been done on a limited scale in the region of central New York, where "Anti-slavery Conferences and prayer meetings" had been frequently held, attended by abolitionists from a few adjoining towns.

The same connection was perceived by some at the Albany Convention just mentioned, who were opposed to *political* secession, and who urged, as an objection against an anti-slavery party in politics, that it would lead to similar schisms and difficulties in the Church. The right course, we were told, was to "abolitionize" all the sects and all the parties in religion and politics, and then the work would be done. The question, nevertheless, recurred, "What shall we do when we find it impossible to reform them? Shall we continue to sustain them, to be corrupted, perhaps, by them, and to become a partaker of their sins?"

"CHRISTIAN ANTI-SLAVERY CONVENTIONS" were accordingly notified and held at various points in the State of New York,—at Auburn, Penn Yan, Clinton, Syracuse, and a large number of other places,—beginning soon after the rise of the Liberty party. They were attended by many of those who

---

* The prominent exceptions to this statement, should we specify them, would be found to be those who are not now (1852) in the ranks of the Liberty party, nor active in political efforts against slavery.

have been active in the Liberty party,—Smith, Birney, Stewart, Green, Chaplin, Torrey, Goodell, and others,—and were, some of them, among the largest and most interesting anti-slavery conventions ever held in the State.* A little paper, conducted by Wm. Goodell, devoted mainly to this object, was commenced in 1841, and was published occasionally till the beginning of 1843, then monthly till the summer of 1848. It was circulated in all the free and some of the slave States, and was supported mainly by members of the Liberty party.

INDEPENDENT CHURCHES.

As a result of all this, a large number of *local independent Churches* have been gathered by secession from the old Churches of several different sects, and holding no ecclesiastical connection with them. This movement is chiefly in the State of New York and farther west.

WESLEYAN METHODIST CHURCH.

From an early period of the present anti-slavery discussion, there has been an efficient body of Methodist abolitionists, the denomination has been extensively agitated, and the result has been a secession from the M. E. Church and the organization of a new ecclesiastical connection, known as the " Wesleyan Methodist Church."

In the latter part of the year 1834, a number of ministers and members of the New England and New Hampshire Conferences, addressed an appeal to their brethren on behalf of the anti-slavery cause. This drew forth a "counter-appeal," signed by the late Pres. Fisk and others. Earnest discussions and debates followed. The cause of anti-slavery made progress, and an anti-slavery delegation from the above conferences to the General Conference (with exception of one dele-

---

* A pamphlet, entitled " *The American Churches the Bulwarks of American Slavery*" (the first publication of the kind that we know of), was published by James G. Birney, the Presidential candidate of the Liberty party, while in England, where he attended the " World's Anti-Slavery Convention." Its republication and circulation in America did much to forward the church agitation of the slave question.

gate) was secured. The opposition was however so strong, even at the North, and the course of the General Conference was such, that a secession was deemed unavoidable. Local secessions commenced in Michigan in 1839. Three ministers —Jotham Horton, Orange Scott, and La Roy Sunderland,— signed an act of withdrawal from the M. E. Church, dated at Providence, R. I., Nov. 8, 1842. At a Convention held for the purpose, at Utica, N. Y., May 31, 1843, the Wesleyan Methodist Church was regularly organized. Its polity is not Episcopal, but provides for an itinerancy under a modified supervision of conferences, recognizing the rights of congregations, and the participancy of laymen. At the South and West, E. Smith has been an effective pioneer in the enterprise. The Wesleyans have made an inroad into North Carolina, and gained a promising foothold, though some of their ministers have been ejected. The connection now (1852) embraces "twelve annual conferences." The "General Conference, which is the rule-making body, meets once in four years, and is composed of an equal number of ministers and laymen." Churches may elect their own pastors.—Vide " *Grounds of Secession*"—*Matlack's History—and MSS. by Luther Lee.*

FREE PRESBYTERIAN CHURCH.

This church was organized, a few years ago, during the sittings of the General Assembly at Cincinnati. It embraces Presbyterians of both the Old and New School in Theology, who agree in respect to the necessity of separation from slaveholders. Among the pioneers of this movement is the Rev. John Rankin, of Ripley, Ohio, formerly of Kentucky, who wrote and published in favor of immediate emancipation, in 1824 or '25, before the commencement of Mr. Garrison's labors. In the connection there are about fifty Churches, and three Presbyteries, extending through portions of Pennsylvania, Ohio, Indiana, and Illinois, the whole composing the "Free Synod of Cincinnati."

FRIENDS.

A division among the Society of Friends in Indiana, has grown out of the slave question, and the manner in which active abolitionists in the Society had been treated in their yearly and annual meetings.

Except the Wesleyan secession, there has been but little Church secession and re-organization in New England, but abolitionists of the Congregational sect in that quarter, extend a pretty liberal support to the new "American Missionary Association," in preference to the "American Board."

FREE MISSIONS.

An Anti-slavery Missionary Committee was organized at Boston at an early day, in principal reference, we believe, to operations in the British West Indies. The "Amistad Committee," having in charge the captives taken in that vessel, provided missionaries to accompany them home, and established a mission among them. A "Union Missionary Society" was formed by a number of white and colored ministers and others, in New York and Connecticut. The Western Missionary Association, at Oberlin, Ohio, was also of an anti-slavery character. All these were afterwards merged in the "*American Missionary Association*," which was formed by a Convention of delegates at Albany in the autumn of 1846, on a new and broader basis, encouraging the local efforts of Churches and auxiliaries to sustain and superintend their own missionaries. The Executive Committee, instead of being a "close corporation," like the American Board, is chosen annually by the contributing constituency; they exercise limited functions, and their proceedings are subject to examination and revision at the annual meetings of their constituents, the members of the association. The association has missions in Africa, in Siam, in the West Indies, among the Ojibue Indians, at the Sandwich Islands, and in Canada. It also occupies, to a considerable extent, the field of Home Missions, which are included in its plan.   It has a missionary in Kentucky, where two new Churches have been organized that exclude slaveholders.   An important auxiliary to this association has recently been organized in Ohio, carrying on its own operations in that region, in a manner provided for in the Constitution of the American Missionary Association.

CHURCH AGITATION AT THE WEST.

The subject of Anti-slavery Church Reform has recently received a fresh impulse in the Western States.   In April, 1850, a large and influential Christian Anti-slavery Convention was held at Cincinnati, Ohio, invited by a committee representing several religious denominations.   Members were in attendance from most of the Middle and Western States. A similar convention was held at Chicago, Ill., in July, 1852. At these conventions, after long and earnest discussions, resolutions were adopted in favor of withdrawing from churches, ecclesiastical bodies, and missionary organizations, connected with slaveholding.   Among the active members of one or both of these conventions were Rev. B. P. Aydellotte, D. D., late President of Woodward College, Rev. C. G. Finney, President of Oberlin College, Rev. Asa Mahan, President of Cleveland University, Rev. Jona. Blanchard, President of Knox College, Illinois, Rev. John Rankin, Rev. Dr. Wilson, of Pittsburg, Rev. E. Smith, Rev. J. B. Walker, Rev. E. H. Nevin, Rev. Samuel Lewis, Rev. Dr. Brisbane, Rev. C. B. Boynton, Rev. E. Goodman, Rev. John G. Fee of Kentucky, &c. &c., and some from the more easterly States.

"The "Christian Era," Chicago—the "Christian Press," Cincinnati—and the "Free Presbyterian," are journals devoted to Free Missions and Anti-slavery Church Reformation. The "Free Wesleyan," New York, is the organ of the Wesleyan connection.   Baptist abolitionists have had their "Christian Reflector," "Christian Contributor," "American Baptist," &c. &c.

BAPTISTS.

The history of anti-slavery agitation among Baptists connects itself so closely with the history of pro-slavery movements in the same sect, that we must present them together.

The position of the Baptist denomination, Northern and Southern, concerning slavery, was shown in a former chapter,* so far as it could be done without distinctly anticipating the account of the struggle between abolitionists and their opposers in that sect. Some further particulars are in place here, connected with the anti-slavery Church agitation among them.

The leading influences in this sect, as in the others, were brought to bear, at an early day, against all agitation of the subject. The violent denunciations against abolitionists, by a Baptist Association in Virginia, in 1835, has been noticed already.† A spirit of servility, as in the other sects and in the political parties, was already manifest among Baptists at the North. The Baptist Magazine, as early as 1834, like the leading periodicals of the other principal sects, was closed against the discussion.

The "Board of Baptist Ministers, in and near London," Dec. 31, 1833, addressed a fraternal letter, signed by Eld. W. H. Murch, their Chairman, to "the Pastors and Ministers of the Baptist denomination throughout the United States of America." In this letter they gave an account of their own struggle in England against slavery in the British West Indies, and made some very modest suggestions respecting slavery in the United States. It was directed to "Rev. Spencer H. Cone, President, the Board of Managers, and the Delegates of the Baptist Triennial Convention," supposing this to be the most ready method of access to Baptist churches in America. Eld. Howard Malcom, afterwards a slaveholder in Kentucky, though then a Northern man, was clerk of the convention. The letter was kept at Boston several months,

---

* Chapter XV.   † Chapter XXXV.

then sent to Elders Cone and Somers, New York, and by them returned to the Board at Boston.

By Sept. 1, 1834, an answer was prepared by a Committee of the Board, accompanied with a series of resolutions. The tone of these was apologetic of slaveholding, yet disclaiming responsibility for its existence, declining to interfere with the subject, and adducing the "consideration" that "there is now a pleasing degree of *union* among the multiplying thousands of Baptists throughout the land." To this was added a warm eulogium of "our Southern brethren" who "are generally, both ministers and people, slaveholders," yet "liberal and enterprising in the promotion of every holy enterprise for the extension of the gospel." This reply, as well as the letter from England, were kept secret. And it was not until the publication of both documents in England, and their re-publication by the editor of the (Presbyterian) New York Observer, (who was gratified with the American answer) that the editor of the Baptist "Christian Watchman" in Boston, after request by Eld. Grosvenor, gave them to his Baptist readers, *thirteen months* after the date of the English letter.

Another answer, and of an opposite tone, " with more than one hundred and eighty signatures," was however sent to the "Baptist Board in and near London," by a Baptist Convention held in Boston, May 26 and 27, 1835.—*Facts for Baptist Churches,* p. 15–29.

" Soon after (this) correspondence, Elds. Cox and Hoby, delegates from the Baptist Union, (England) visited this country. The influence of the Triennial Convention was employed to keep them as silent as possible in regard to the enormous sin of American slavery."—*Ib.* p. 29.

The delegates were sent to America, charged by the English Baptist Union with the following mission:

" We send our deputation to promote most zealously, and to the utmost of their ability, in the spirit of love, of discretion and fidelity, BUT STILL MOST ZEALOUSLY to promote the sacred cause of negro emancipation."

The delegation attended the Triennial Convention at Richmond, Virginia, but said not a word in public concerning slavery. One of them, Elder Cox, declined an invitation to take part in the proceedings of the American Anti-Slavery Society in New York. He also declined a similar invitation at Boston. But soon afterwards, at the Free-Will Baptist Yearly Meeting in New Hampshire, he adventured to speak against slavery.—*Ib.*, pp. 296-302.

This was in 1835. On the return of the delegation to England, and their report to the English Baptist Union, in June, 1836, resolutions against slavery were adopted, and it was voted that the committee take an early opportunity to address a letter to the American Baptist Triennial Convention on the subject. This was accordingly done, under date of London, Sept. 13, 1836.

From this letter it appears that the English delegation, while in this country, "although they did not mention the subject of slavery in the *public* proceedings of the Convention; yet, at a private meeting assembled for the purpose," they made known the import of their errand. The letter argued against slavery at some length.

It was answered, Jan. 7, 1837, *not* by the Board, to whom it was addressed, but by *one* of the members, Elder Baron Stowe, of Boston, informing that "the Board, under existing circumstances, will not, in any way, intermeddle with the subject of slavery."

A number of English Baptist Associations adopted resolutions on the subject of American slavery, and expressive of their deep mortification and regret at the position of Baptists in America.

The English Baptist Union, May, 1837, adopted a resolution of sympathy with American abolitionists, and addressed a letter "to the Ministers and members of Baptist churches in the United States," entreating them to "listen to the cries of the oppressed, at whatever cost." Fraternal correspondence, between American Baptist abolitionists and Baptist bodies in England, was continued, afterwards.—*Ib.*, pp. 30-44.

Thus encouraged, Baptist abolitionists in America, a few weeks after the organization of the Liberty party, and simultaneously with similar movements, in some form, among abolitionists of other sects, assembled in a general or National Convention. It was held in Macdougal-Street Baptist Church, New York, April 28, 1840, "for the purpose of considering the connection of the denomination with slavery, and inquiring, 'What could be done?'"

An organized "National Baptist Anti-Slavery Convention" was the result. An address was issued to the Baptist churches of the North, and another to "Baptist slaveholders in the Southern States."

This was the signal for renewed opposition. The slaveholders threatened. And influential ministers at the North sent forth their "Counsels and Cautions."—"*Facts*," &c., pp. 44–45.

"In 1841, the Triennial Convention was to hold its appointed meeting in Baltimore. All parties, North and South, looked forward with deep interest to this session."—*Ib.*, p. 49.

The Savannah River Baptist Association

1. "*Resolved*, That we deem the conduct of northern abolitionists highly censurable and meddlesome, and request our State Convention to instruct their delegates to the Triennial Convention to DEMAND of our northern brethren WHETHER THEY CAN ACKNOWLEDGE THOSE FANATICS AS THEIR CO-WORKERS IN THE GREAT WORK OF EVANGELIZING THE WORLD, and to state fully to them the impossibility of our further co-operation, UNLESS THEY DISMISS SUCH FROM THEIR BODY."

2. "*Resolved*, That the State Convention be requested to retain the funds sent by this Association until the Triennial Convention shall publish their repudiation of the whole spirit and conduct of Baptist abolitionists."—*Ib.*, p. 49.

The Camden (S. C.) Baptist Church unanimously

"*Resolved*, That we recommend to our Association to use their influence to have Elon Galusha EXPELLED from his office of Vice-President of the Board of Foreign Missions; that they have a right to REQUIRE it, and should make his EXPULSION the condition of their future connection with the Board."

"*Resolved*, That we extend to Northern Baptists opposed to the abolitionists our warmest affection and fraternal regard. They will ever have an interest in our prayers."—*Ib.*, p. 50.

The editor of the (Baptist) *Religious Herald*, Richmond, Va., after describing the Baptist Anti-Slavery Convention and its doings, in connection with the foregoing action of the Camden Church, says : " In North Carolina, South Carolina, Georgia and Alabama, Conventions, Associations and Churches, have noticed this Address to Southern Baptists."—*Ib.*

About this time a correspondent of the (Baptist) *Recorder & Watchman* (N. C.) stated that the President and seven of the fifteen Vice-Presidents of the Board of Foreign Missions live in slaveholding States and District of Columbia, &c., adding, "It is also well known that the Acting Board in Boston *are decidedly in opposition to abolition measures.*"—*Ib.*, p. 51.

" *The Circular of the Boston Board,*" (Daniel Sharp, President, Baron Stowe, Secretary,) as published in the *Christian Reflector*, Dec. 2, 1840, manifests great solicitude to exclude " *irrelevant subjects.*" It describes the one exclusive object of the Association, the promotion of Foreign Missions, and deprecates the withdrawal of support by contributors. The Board must not be held " accountable for things done and not done, *in relation to all which, alike, the Board has done nothing, because it had nothing to do.*"

This was an elaborate effort to retain the support of both abolitionists and slaveholders, and it satisfied neither party. The Georgia Baptist State Convention expressed their dissatisfaction ; the Board replied, and sent out their Treasurer, Mr. Heman Lincoln, to explain, verbally. But all in vain. The Chairman of the Georgia Executive Committee said :

" If the object of the Board in sending their delegate to us, is to try to steer between us and the abolitionists, they might have spared themselves THE EXPENSE AND TROUBLE."—*Ib.*, p. 57.

The American and Foreign Bible Society, Feb. 3, 1841, sent out an address to its members and supporters of a similar character, signed by S. H. Cone, President, C. G. Somers, Cor. Secretary.

A kindred " Circular of the Executive Committee of the *American Baptist Home Missionary Society,*" S. H. Cone, Chairman, Benj. M. Hill, Cor. Sec., was issued a few days after, Feb. 16th. This was addressed " *to the Churches.*" It has less the appearance of neutrality than the preceding documents. It alludes to " the action of Anti-Slavery Societies formed at the North." " Our brethren at the South, with great unanimity," says the Circular, " deprecate the discussion as unwarranted, the measures pursued as fatal to their safety, and complain of the language occasionally employed as cruel and slanderous." But the Society could not act on the subject. " *We need union*," say they, " *as a denomination: And as patriots, we must cherish religious union, as one among the strongest, although not the most prominent, of the bands that hold together the Union of these States.*" Thus " the churches" were exhorted to shape their *religious* union, for the promotion of *political ends*, though, in the same Circular, the same churches were warned not to " furnish an armory for the *secular* conflicts of the times," but to say with Nehemiah, " I am doing a great work, and I cannot come down!"—*Ib.*, pp. 67–71.

Such were the teachers under which northern Baptists were trained for the Triennial Convention, which assembled at Baltimore, in April, 1841. In a secret caucus, a so-called " Compromise Article," drawn up by Eld. S. H. Cone, was adopted and signed by 74 persons, including prominent northern men. Like all other " compromises" on the slave question, it gave all to slavery. It discouraged " innovation" and " new tests." This would be understood as a censure of abolitionists who contemplated a separation from slavery, or who refused to commune with slaveholders. If any should think of its possible application to the southern " demand" of excluding abolitionists from office in the Missionary Board, the illusion would soon be dissipated by the action of the Convention.

In the election of officers, those " demands" were substantially complied with, to the full satisfaction of the South, as was afterwards expressed. All known abolitionists were *left off the Board of Foreign Missions.* Eld. Baron Stowe was not an exception. He had been obnoxious to the South, but in a letter to the Foreign Secretary, read at the meeting of the Southern Delegates, he expressed his unwillingness " to deny any courtesy to a Christian brother because he is a slave-holder."

Elder Elon Galusha, whose expulsion was demanded by name, was accordingly ostracized. Eld. Richard Fuller, of S. Carolina, a slaveholder, and a Biblical defender of slavery, was elected in his room.—*Ib.* p. 82–3.

The delegation from the South held a meeting before leaving Baltimore, and addressed a letter to their constituents, in which they say—"The election of the Board of Managers resulted agreeably to our wishes." Signed by F. Stocks, Chairmon, J. B. Jeter, Sec. pro. tem.—*Ib.* p. 85–6.

But the Baptist abolitionists were not discouraged. The anniversary of the American Baptist Anti-Slavery Convention was, soon after, held in New York City, and another Convention was held in Boston.

The extreme solicitude of the northern Conservatists to preserve "union" only precipitated the inevitable rupture. And the "Compromise article" of 1841, like the later "Compromise measures" in Congress, instead of settling "the vexed" question, only opened the controversy afresh. The excinding of the abolitionists, like the Fugitive Slave bill, only served to show the North its degraded position. The continued employment of slaveholding missionaries was too glaring an outrage to be tolerated in the free States. The proposed change in that policy would be equivalent to open war on their "brethren of the South." The two Missionary Boards, (the Home and the Foreign) were placed in no enviable position. The slaveholders on the one side, and the abolitionists on the other, like the upper and nether mill-stone, were likely to grind them to powder.

The Baptist Anti-Slavery Convention and its labors resulted in the permanent organization of "The American Baptist Free Missionary Society," in Boston, May 4, 1843. It was a timely and decisive step, forming an era in the history of American Baptist Missions.—*Ib.* p. 384.

The old Boards met again, at Philadelphia, in April, 1844. "The chief theatre of discussion was the Home Mission Society; yet as the same individuals constituted both societies, the influence told with equal power on the Triennial Convention." The point in debate was the employment of slaveholding missionaries. In neither society was any definite action reached, further than the adoption of resolutions evading the question, disclaiming any action for or against slavery, and leaving each member free to be a slaveholder or an abolitionist, as he pleased. In the Home Society, this passed by a vote 121 to 61. In the Foreign (from which abolitionists were, perhaps, either displaced or had withdrawn,) it was said to have been adopted unanimously. But neither abolitionists nor slaveholders could be conciliated or satisfied, for both were in earnest, and wished for some decision of the matter. A motion, in the Home Society, for a Committee to report on " *an amicable division,*" was also adopted unanimously!—*Ib.* p. 87–94.

Similar action was had by the Foreign Board, at a meeting at Providence, in 1845.

The division was, in fact, rendered inevitable, by the position in which the Acting Board, at Boston, found themselves placed. Determined to maintain a neutral position, they were reluctantly driven from it, by the action of the Alabama Baptist State Convention. By this body a letter was addressed to the Board, Nov. 25, 1844, transmitting resolutions, in which they " demand the distinct and explicit avowal that *slaveholders* are eligible and entitled to all the privileges and immunities of their several unions, and especially to receive any agency, *mission,* or other appointment which may fall within the scope of their operations and duties." This was a test which could no longer be evaded. Abolitionists as well as slaveholders were watching them. In their reply, dated Boston, Dec. 17, 1844, the Acting Board said—

" Allow us to express our profound regret that they" (the Resolutions) " were addressed to us. They were not necessary. We have never, as a Board, done, or omitted to do, anything which requires the explanations and avowals that your resolutions 'demanded.' They also place us in the new and trying position of being compelled to answer hypothetical questions,"

&c. They further said that they had "never called in question your (the slaveholder's) social equality, as to all the privileges and benefits of the Foreign Missionary Union." "Nor," say the Board, "have we ever employed our official influence in impeaching you."

After much ingenious circumlocution, they, however, proceeded to say:

"If, however, any one should offer himself as a missionary, having slaves, and should insist on retaining them as his property, we could not appoint him." * * * "We disfellowship no one." * * * "If our brethren in Alabama, with this exposition of our principles and feelings, can co-operate with us, we shall be happy to receive their aid. If they cannot, painful to us as will be their withdrawal, yet we shall submit to it, as being neither caused nor sought by us."

Of the consistency of this we say nothing. The reader will judge of it, and whether a principle of disfellowship with slavery, or only a reluctant compliance with a northern sentiment avowed by abolitionists, occasioned the refusal to appoint slaveholding missionaries.

The decision produced of course a great sensation at the South. Conventions and Associations recommended a general Southern Convention to form a new Missionary Board. The Tennessee Baptist Foreign Missionary Society, however, at a meeting in Nashville, April 2, 1845, expressed their regret that the Acting Board at Boston should have been suspected and interrogated; yet they said, the Acting Board, by its answer, had "rendered themselves justly *obnoxious to the censures of the whole church,*" and they "*Resolved, that, in our opinion, the Convention will not sustain the position of the present Acting Board in regard to slavery.*"

These proceedings were transmitted "to the Board of the Triennial Convention soon to convene in annual session at Providence, R. I.," and the closing prediction was then verified. The neutral position there assumed (as already seen) was a virtual reproof of the Acting Board. Resolutions approving their course were offered by Eld. B. T. Welch, but being warmly resisted, were withdrawn.—*Ib.*, pp. 104–13, also 145–6, &c.

But nothing could now save either the " Acting Board" of Foreign Missions, or the " Triennial Convention." Their dissolution was manifestly inevitable.

" *The Home Mission* Board was subjected to a similar test. The Georgia Baptist Convention sent to this Board the name of Mr. James E. Reeve, STATING THAT HE WAS A SLAVEHOLDER, and requesting the Board to appoint him as a missionary."

It was also stated explicitly that this application was made to test the position of the Board. The Board declined making the appointment, *not* because the candidate was a slaveholder, as they were careful to explain, but because the Board, having taken neutral ground, would not permit that neutrality to be disturbed by the mode of requesting appointments. In this respect they placed abolitionists and slaveholders upon precisely an equal footing. They said:

" When an application is made for the appointment of a slaveholder or an abolitionist, or an anti-slavery man, *as such*, or for appropriations to fields where the design of the applicant is apparently to test the action of the Board in respect to the subjects of slavery or anti-slavery, their official obligation either to act on the appointment, or to entertain the application, ceases. Therefore,

" *Resolved*, That in view of the preceding considerations, it is not expedient to introduce the subjects of slavery or anti-slavery into our deliberations, nor to entertain applications in which they are introduced.

" *Resolved*, That, taking into consideration all the circumstances of the case, we deem ourselves not at liberty to entertain the application for the apppointment of Rev. James E. Reeve."—*Ib.*, pp. 124–26.

The action at Providence was adapted to soothe and appease the slaveholders, but they had already committed themselves extensively to a Southern Convention. " The South anticipated the co-operation of the North in entering into their organization." The North, too, (equally opposed, as the leading men were, to abolition,) would also be compelled to re-organize. On both sides it was an amicable as well as a reluctant separation.

THE SOUTHERN BAPTIST CONVENTION assembled at Augusta, (Geo.,) May 8, 1845, and formed a new missionary organization, of the same name. A sympathizing letter from

President Wayland was read, in which he said: "Your rights have been infringed." "We" (of the North) "have shown how Christians *ought not* to act. It remains for you to show us how they *ought* to act." Mr. Burroughs, of Pennsylvania, was present, and said: "The Middle States were opposed to the action of the Boston Board, and were at a loss what course to pursue." The address put forth by the Convention, said:

"Let not the extent of this disunion be exaggerated. At the present time it involves the Foreign and Domestic Missions of the denomination. Northern and Southern Baptists are still brethren."

A correspondence with the Boston Board was immediately opened for negotiating a convenient "*transfer* of a portion of the missions under their charge to the patronage of the Southern Baptist Convention." The project was fraternally entertained, and the object was ultimately effected. Columbian College, also, was given to the South.—*Ib.*, pp. 163–169, &c., also 214.

"THE AMERICAN BAPTIST MISSIONARY UNION" is the name of the new organization at the North, which takes the place of the old. The time and circumstances of its formation are as follow:

A special meeting of the Baptist General Convention was held in New York City, Nov. 19, 1845. Eld. Francis Wayland, President, Eld. R. H. Neale, Assistant Secretary. Eld. Spencer H. Cone presented and explained the Constitution of "The American Baptist Missionary Union," which, after discussion, was adopted; and a committee appointed "to inform the Trustees of Columbian College that the *Triennial Convention is now dissolved*, in order that they may take such measures as in consequence may be necessary."

"The Baptist General Convention" was a delegated body, responsible to those who appointed them; and were neither authorized to "dissolve," nor to form a new organization. But they did both, and in doing it they constituted themselves life members of the new "Union," free of cost, providing that "*other* persons" might become life members by paying one hundred dollars. "This Union shall be *composed* of life members." The representative principle was thus set aside. The "Union" of "life members" is neither responsible to the contributors, nor to the churches.

Eld. Cone, in explaining the Constitution, said :

"They did not want a Missionary Convention to be divided eithei by Mason and Dixon's line, or any other line ; and under the proposed Constitution, no extraneous question of slavery or ANTI-SLAVERY, or TEMPERANCE, or anything else, apart from the one great question for which they were organized. Any member may pursue his private predilections as he lists, BUT HE CANNOT BRING THEM FORWARD IN THE 'AMERICAN BAPTIST UNION FOR FOREIGN MISSIONS.' "

It was objected that the terms of Union would admit either Universalists or slaveholders, but the article was not changed.

Eld. M. D. Miller, of Vermont, moved to add to the "Qualifications of Officers," the words, "*and not slaveholders*"— thus excluding such from office. The amendment was lost.

" Eld. J. W. Sawyer, of Maine, presented a communication on the subject of slavery, from the American Baptist Free Mission Society, which was unanimously laid on the table."

Eld. B. T. Welch offered a resolution in commendation of the " Acting Board" at Boston. It was opposed by Elders J. M. Peck, Turnbull, Cone, Stowe and Neale, and finally withdrawn. [The " Acting Board" had refused to employ slaveholding missionaries.]

A communication presented by Eld. Sawyer proposed the following:

" *Resolved*, That in the secession of Southern Baptists from the Baptist Triennial Convention, we recognize a division between free and slaveholding missions, which we wish, on the grounds of Christian principle, to remain perpetual, as to the American Baptist Missionary Union."

The Resolution was not adopted.

" Many have blamed the *Free* Mission Society, because it did not disband at the formation of this Union." But *why* should it disband? Should it do so, a re-union of the North with the South, in support of slaveholding missionaries, would not, probably, be long delayed.

" Ever desirous of union with their brethren of the North, the Free Missionists sent an address to the ' Union,' at its second Annual Meeting at Troy, May, 1848. It was with difficulty that an opportunity was gained, of presenting it to the Body. When it had been presented and read, immediately a motion was made to lay it on the table. The motion prevailed, one or two voting in the negative."—*Ib.* p. 171-180.

" The Union," by a vote, constituted the members of the Triennial Convention life members of the Union : and this includes some slaveholders.—*Ib.* p. 201.

" At the first anniversary of ' the Union' at Cincinnati, five members are set down from Kentucky. The Banner and Pioneer (a Southern Baptist paper,) calls them ' our representatives.' "—*Ib.* p. 207.

Eld. J. G. Binney, formerly pastor of the Savannah Church, Georgia, and highly eulogized in the address of the Southern Convention, is sustained by the A. B. M. Union as Superintendent of the institution for training native Missionaries.—*Ib.* p. 168.

" Finally, the ' Union' has maintained slaveholding in its Indian Missions, up to the present time (1850)."—*Ib.* p. 216.

The fact that the Baptist Cherokee and Choctaw Churches were slaveholding, was alluded to, in the proceedings of " the American Board," at Worcester, in 1844, and again at Brooklyn, in 1845. Thus countenanced by Baptist example, they felt sustained in their own position.—*Ib.* p. 249-253.

These churches came under care of the " Union."

At the anniversary of the A. B. M. Union in Philadelphia, May, 1849, "Eld. Colver rose and declared in the presence of the whole Board, that the Cherokee churches were sanctioning slaveholding."—*Ib.* p. 252.

After much effort, a Report of the Committee was obtained, touching lightly on the subject, speaking of it as a *rumor*, and saying that they were " taking measures to ascertain the facts of the case." But the facts appear to have been sufficiently ascertained !—*Ib.* p. 253-268.

The Baptist Home Mission Society survived the Triennial Convention and the Foreign Board, notwithstanding
the secession of slaveholders. But its character, like that of
the newly organized " Union," seems to run in the old channel. Like the " Union," it is controlled, mainly, if not wholly,
by the northern leaders of the Baptist sect, who are in close
fellowship with slaveholders, but have no sympathy with
abolitionists—except with those who co-operate with them, in
preference to the " Free Mission Society."

" In New York, 1846, a new Constitution was presented
and adopted. The chief change was the casting off of the
auxiliaries," the northern as well as the southern. In a circular to the Baptist churches and associations, composing the
Baptist Missionary Convention of the State of New York,
written by Eld. Wheelock, agent of the society, *the reason* assigned for this change was, that attempts had been made " in
some quarters to control the parent society, about matters of
local policy, concerning which there were different opinions.
That which brought the evil to a crisis was the Slave Controversy." By cutting off auxiliaries and delegations, the Board
became independent of the people, and their voice was hushed.
In other respects, the new Constitution took no new ground
on the slave question.—*Ib.* p. 307-318, 19.

" Elder N. Colver gave notice, that at the next annual meeting he should
move, so to alter the Constitution as to instruct the Missionaries of the Society not to administer baptism to adhering slaveholders, nor the ordinances
to a slaveholding church."

In 1847 the matter was called up, and laid over again, till
1848, when, it was *indefinitely postponed.*

And yet, it is asserted that " the society has cut loose from
slavery !"—*Ib.* 308.

The Society and its Reports maintain studied silence on the
subject of slavery. It has a large number of slaveholding life
members or life directors, whose names are given in the " Facts
for Baptist Churches." " The number of members in the
Slave States is two hundred and eighty-five."—*Ib.* p. 316-18.

Mr. J. Finch, a slaveholder, was a missionary of the Society,

in 1846, and the term of his appointment did not expire till
1st Feb., 1847. From the Report of 1848, it is evident that
the Society was in the receipt of slaveholders' funds.—*Ib.* p.
311–13.

THE AMERICAN AND FOREIGN BIBLE SOCIETY also continues
its former position. It receives slaveholders to membership,
and says nothing against the laws or the usages which withhold bibles from slaves.

The " Baptist Banner and Pioneer," of Kentucky, one of the most bitter and vindictive of all the southern religious papers, in 1846, said—

" The Am. and Foreign Bible Society may now be regarded as the only
ligament that binds the North and the South in union, and we trust that this
bond will not be infracted."

It was *not* the " *only*" ligament, but it was a prominent one.
In 1848 the annual report showed the receipt of $6,753 53
from the slave states.—*Ib.* p. 333, 4.

In 1849, while the choice of officers was pending, a motion
that the Nominating Committee should report no names of
slaveholders, was negatived, and slaveholders were accordingly elected.—*Ib.* p. 337, 8.

THE AMERICAN BAPTIST FREE MISSION SOCIETY, organized
in 1843, admits no slaveholding members, nor any who do
not possess "an acknowledged Christian character." It is
"amenable to the Churches, and earnestly invites them to
control its affairs by its annual delegations." It recognizes no
distinction founded on color. Its plan embraces both Foreign
and Domestic Missions—also Bible and Tract operations. It
has a Mission in Haiti, another in Canada, others at the West,
and contemplates missions in several portions of the South.—
President of the Society, Harvey Hawes, Maine ; Corresponding Secretary, Eld. C. P. Grosvenor, McGrawsville, Cortland
Co., N. Y.; Treasurer, George Curtiss, Utica, N. Y.

THE NEW-YORK CENTRAL COLLEGE, at McGrawsville, (N.
Y.) incorporated in 1848, is an institution "pledged to the
morality of anti-slavery," knows no distinction of color,* and

---

* In another connection, similar mention might have been made of the COLLEGE

welcomes accomplished colored Professors, as well as students. It originated with the founders of the Free Mission Society, as a part of their movement.

Whether Baptist abolitionists will be able to maintain these free movements without separating from pro-slavery influences in local churches and in associations, remains to be seen. But they deserve much credit for their efficient labors, hitherto, in the cause of Free Missions. If the other Baptist Missions should ever be divorced from slavery, it will be in consequence of their efforts, and especially of their persevering support of the Free Mission Society.

AT OBERLIN, but the Institution is of too long standing to need a particular notice. ONEIDA INSTITUTE, at Whitesboro, N. Y., while it existed, and under the Presidency of Beriah Green, was thoroughly anti-slavery in its character.

CHAPTER XLI.

THE ANTI-SLAVERY SOCIETIES—THEIR RELATION TO POLITICAL AND CHURCH ACTION.

Limited, yet appropriate labor of the National Anti-Slavery Societies—Reasons why their operations became more circumscribed—AMERICAN AND FOREIGN A. S. Society—Its course and policy—AMERICAN ANTI-SLAVERY SOCIETY since the division in 1840—Its exclusive claims and proscription of other organizations—Early indications of its policy, political and ecclesiastical—Albany Convention of 1839—Tone of the Liberator in Jan., 1840—Of the National Anti-Slavery Standard, after the division—Solution of an enigma.

WHILE these political and ecclesiastical agitations were in progress, it will readily be seen—as might have been anticipated beforehand—that the two Anti-Slavery Societies and their auxiliaries could occupy, in respect to those agitations, only a subordinate position. Each political and each ecclesiastical movement would be carried on by those more immediately interested in it, while the Societies, as such, were not prepared to recommend, nor adapted to carry forward, any particular measures of political or church action.

And yet, they were not left altogether without a field of appropriate and beneficial action. Though moral considerations were by no means out of place, in a political movement, (as politics should be founded on ethics) and though the moral bearings of slavery would, of course, come directly under review in a discussion of the Church question, yet an appeal having no direct reference either to the religious sects or to the political parties, would be of great service, and be well adapted to exert an influence on many minds unduly sensitive when the course of their sects or parties is called in question. The Anti-slavery Societies, therefore, in the measure of their limited means, and in proportion to the wisdom and efficiency of their management, continued to urge forward the general cause. Yet, owing to their dissensions, and other causes, their usefulness has been, in a degree, circumscribed, and the State and local auxiliaries of the two rival national societies have either become extinct, or have fallen into a state of comparative decline.

THE AMERICAN AND FOREIGN ANTI-SLAVERY SOCIETY—ITS COURSE AND POLICY.

Since its organization, in 1840, this Society has pursued an equable and steady course. If it has not been a pioneer of new aggressive movements, ecclesiastical or political, it has not chosen the policy of interposing obstacles to them. It has been conducted by those who honestly consider themselves in occupancy of the original ground, and in the practice of the early usages of the American Anti-Slavery Society, at its organization, in 1833. Though this will be controverted by the leaders of the rival Society, an examination and comparison of documents would perhaps exhibit as near an approximation to that ground as could be exhibited elsewhere. If the strict letter of the old Society's Constitution does not describe their course on the position of females, the early usages of the Society may be pleaded as their precedent. Its leading members would not, perhaps, claim, that they hold precisely the same views that they once held, concerning distinct political action. As a Society, or, as a Committee, they have had little or nothing to say, pro or con, in respect to distinct political or ecclesiastical organizations of abolitionists. Yet their annual reports, from time to time, have embodied important political and ecclesiastical records, with interesting and valuable statistical information connected with slavery, and with the progress of the anti-slavery cause. However violently they may have been denounced by another class of abolitionists, whatever they may have failed to undertake or to accomplish, whatever differences of opinion may be entertained in respect to the division in 1840, or in respect to their course afterwards, impartial history will give them an honorable place among the sincere and laborious friends of the enslaved. The writings of William Jay will ever retain a high place in the anti-slavery literature of his age and nation, and the ceaseless vigilance and untiring activity of Lewis Tappan will leave their marks upon every year and month of anti-slavery progress. No power of party prejudice, no narrow bigotry, not even connected with the most signal services and brilliant exploits in the cause of freedom, will ever be able successfully to write down such names, along with those of their associates, Rev. Simeon S. Jocelyn, Rev. Theodore S. Wright, Dr. J. W. Pennington, &c. &c., as recreants to the anti-slavery cause. As there are limits to the dissensions of earnest reformers, so there must also be limits to their power of crippling and injuring one another, by unjust accusations.

AMERICAN ANTI-SLAVERY SOCIETY—ITS COURSE AFTER THE DIVISION OF 1840.

This Society, after the division of 1840, retaining the same Constitution and the same name as before, claimed to occupy its original position, as at its organization in 1833, and not only regarded the new Society as "schismatic" but stigmatized it as untrue to the cause. More than this. The Liberty party, distinct in its origin and in its peculiarities, as has been shown, from the American and Foreign Anti-Slavery Society, has been perseveringly identified with it, in these representations, and both together have been characterized as "a hateful form of pro-slavery," originating in a desire to shelter the pro-slavery churches, to cripple "the only efficient abolitionists," and to crowd off woman from the sphere of anti-slavery activity.

Had these things been said only by a few individuals, on their own responsibility, or on the spur of an exciting moment, the circumstance might need little or no notice in our records. But it is not so. The repetition of these charges has been incessant, on both sides of the Atlantic. It has been the theme of lecturers and agents, has been embodied in resolutions, addresses, and annual reports, and has occupied columns upon columns of periodicals devoted to the interests of the Society. So prominent a part of the Society's operations, has it been, to propagate and repeat these representations, that the historical view of the Society that should fail to give this feature of it a corresponding prominence, would fail to record truthfully its history.

And since this leading feature of the Society must needs be noticed, including the corresponding claim that the American Anti-Slavery Society and its auxiliaries represent "the only genuine abolitionists in the country," it becomes needful, as a matter of historical integrity, to record more minutely than would otherwise be requisite, the course of a Society setting up such exclusive claims.* While we give due credit for the important anti-slavery labors of Mr. Garrison and his associates, before and since the division, we shall be compelled to record some particulars—both in respect to their political and ecclesiastical position—which may throw light on the validity of their exclusive claims.

Their course *since* the division of the Society, and the organization of the Liberty party, in 1840, should be studied in connection with the position held by them *at* that time and for some time previous.

It has already been seen that Mr. Garrison and his friends had taken their stand against voting, not on account of the pro-slavery character of the Federal Constitution, but on account of their principles as "Non-Resistants" in respect to compulsory civil government and penal law.

---

* The very last " Annual Report of the Massachusetts Anti-Slavery Society," dated January, 1852 (page 48), designates its partisans as "the only efficient anti-slavery men" in America—and represents the " New organization" (meaning the American and Foreign Anti-Slavery Society) as having "sprung into existence for the protection of pro-slavery churches." It speaks of "the Apostacy of 1840." It uses still more offensive language, which we will not repeat, and applies opprobrious epithets to distinguished abolitionists on both sides of the Atlantic, by name. Since the Report reached us, we have heard a lecturer of the American A. S. Society use similar language, expressly including in his remarks " the Liberty party," and boasting that he and his associates had " broken it down"—threatening also that they would break down an Anti-Slavery Society then in process of organizing, unless it would become auxiliary to the American A. S. Society.

It was about the same time, if we correctly remember, that, in connection with his new views of the Sabbath, Mr. Garrison threw out hints in disparagement of the commonly received ideas of the Ministry and the Church. The pro-slavery position and the authoritative tone of leading ministers in Massachusetts and elsewhere, must doubtless be charged with no small share of the responsibility of giving rise to these views and occasions for the manifestation of them. To some extent, they may have grown out of corresponding estimates of civil government. Be this as it may, the distaste appears to have been entertained against the institutions themselves, and not merely against pro-slavery influences and action *in* them.

At an Anti-slavery Convention in 1839 or '40, Stephen S. Foster, a Garrison abolitionist, introduced into an Anti-slavery Convention a resolution denominating the American Churches a "brotherhood of thieves." To "come out" from pro-slavery churches was soon insisted upon by Mr. Foster and others as the duty of the abolitionists connected with them. We do not remember that Mr. Garrison expressed any dissent, and the general tone of his paper was in harmony with it.

Yet, at the Albany Convention, in July, 1839, as before noticed, the partisans of Mr. Garrison, in his presence, and without his dissent, objected to a distinct political party, that it would lead to similar divisions in the churches, and to new ecclesiastical organizations by abolitionists.

Again, January 31, 1840, (before the organization of the Liberty party or the division of the American Anti-slavery Society) Mr. Garrison, in his Liberator, in reply to "Gerrit Smith on political action," held the following language:

"If we must have a new political party to abolish slavery, must we not also have a new religious sect for the same purpose? Is the necessity greater in the one case than in the other? YET, WHO, AMONG ABOLITIONISTS IS PREPARED FOR SUCH A MEASURE?* As to the RIGHT of abolitionists

---

* The "measure" had already been a subject of earnest consultation in Albany, the July previous, in the morning prayer-meetings, as before noticed.

to withdraw from the existing sects and start a rival one to them all, it is as indisputable as it is to organize themselves into a separate political party. But such a course, we are persuaded, WHETHER PURSUED POLITICALLY OR RELIGIOUSLY, WOULD BE PRODUCTIVE OF SERIOUS MISCHIEF TO THE ANTI-SLAVERY CAUSE. Nor is it demanded by anything in the history of that cause. The progress of abolitionism is strong and sure ; and, by its own inherent power MUST AND WILL OVERCOME, ERE LONG, BOTH CHURCH AND STATE, AS NOW ORGANIZED."

Comparing together these apparently conflicting positions of Mr. Garrison and his friends, we can reconcile them only by supposing that they wished abolitionists to "come out" from the pro-slavery churches, but were not pleased with the prospect of their organizing anti-slavery ones. The non-voting policy, and the absence of a distinct anti-slavery party in politics, would harmonize with this. "The progress of abolitionism" would then "overcome the Church and State as *now* organized," but without producing any *new* organizations of them. We are bound in all charity to believe, on their own testimony, that such earnest reformers would seek to guide and shape reformations in accordance with their own views.

The "National Anti-slavery Standard"—the organ of the American Anti-slavery Society, soon after the division in 1840—held a language equally revolutionary—equally conservative. The very foundations of society were to be overturned. Yet the political parties must not be disturbed !

" See if the cause of the division be not closely connected with the nature of the reform itself. Anti-slavery is a word of mighty power. Oh ! IT STRIKES AT THE VERY CORNER-STONES AND KEYSTONES OF SOCIETY. It aims a death-blow at long cherished habits and opinions. It robs life of all factitious honors ; but above, and more than all, IT WOULD PUT AN END FOR-EVER TO THE UNRIGHTEOUS DOMINATION OF ' THE CHURCH.' IT WOULD UN-SEAT POPULAR THEOLOGY FROM ITS THRONE, break down the barriers of sect, and, in short, RESOLVE SOCIETY INTO ITS NATURAL ELEMENTS, saving all the real progress that has been made in the scale of improvement. Here is the true issue on which division in our ranks is made up."

But in the same paper there appeared also the following :

" The GREATEST danger, in our opinion, is the organizing of a third political party, STRIVING TO BREAK DOWN political organizations."

At this same time, and afterwards, the Standard condemned anti-slavery church secession and re-organization, as being a part of the same policy that organized the Liberty party. It repeated this in particular reference to the forming of an independent anti-slavery church in Utica, of which Alvan Stewart, a pioneer of the Liberty party, was a member.

Now, how are we to decipher and harmonize all this? Anti-slavery, after the model of the "Standard," is to "strike at the keystones of society," but it dreads, as the "greatest danger," the breaking down of the old pro-slavery political parties! It is to "unseat popular theology," and "put an end forever to the unrighteous domination of the church"— but there must be no secessions with a view to organize anti-slavery and reformatory churches!

We see only one solution of the enigma. If it were determined to "put an end forever" to ALL civil and ecclesiastical institutions, and if their unhappy and unholy connection in this country with slavery was to be improved as the excuse and occasion for doing this, then the course of the official "Standard" becomes at once intelligible and consistent. For nothing could so effectually defeat the desired operation as the united and successful efforts of abolitionists to redeem those institutions from disgrace and subversion by divorcing them from slavery, and wielding them for its overthrow, which could only be done by organizing new churches and political parties, if the existing ones could not be reclaimed.

A resolution of Mr. Garrison, adopted by the Middlesex County Anti-Slavery Society, about this time, demanded that "the alliance that now subsists between the *religious sects* and *political parties* of the North and South, be INSTANTLY BROKEN UP."

The *principle* here laid down would require abolitionists to secede "*instantly*" from the existing parties and sects. And if organized political and church action were to be, for any purposes, continued, it would require them to re-organize. But Mr. Garrison was strongly opposed to the efforts making in that direction. It seems to follow, that he required of all

abolitionists that they should act in accordance with *his* principles concerning politics and religion, by *virtually withdrawing from the Church and the State.*

"Here," according to the 'Standard,' "is the true issue on
which division in our ranks is made up," or its language has,
to us, no intelligible meaning.

CHAPTER XLII.

THE AMERICAN ANTI-SLAVERY SOCIETY—ITS FURTHER COURSE ON POLITICAL ACTION.

Political element in the division of the Societies—Facts in illustration—Position of
" Non-Resistants"—Position of abolitionists in the old parties remaining with the
Society—Course of Mr. Garrison—" Moral suasion" abolitionists—Resolutions at
Worcester and Springfield—Presidential election of 1840—Subsequent develop-
ments—Opposition to the Liberty Party—State Election in New York—Political
ethics.

Two resolutions of the Quarterly Meeting of the Old Massachusetts Anti-Slavery Society, some time beforehand, were
understood to portend a revolution of some sort in the American Anti-Slavery Society, in May, 1840. The previous
annual meeting had decided in favor of women's voting, yet
the officers had not resigned, and the business of the Society
was going on as usual. What elements then, or what indications of a revolution, were foreseen?

At the World's Anti-Slavery Convention in London, soon
after the division in America, the question of admitting 'women
to participate in the proceedings, was introduced by some of
the American delegation. The proposition, being accounted
an innovation on the customs of British abolitionists, including
" Friends,"* did not succeed, whereupon Mr. Garrison and
some others declined taking seats.

During the discussion of the question, Wendell Phillips,

---

* It will be remembered that " Friends," both in America and England, transact
their ecclesiastical business in separate meetings of males and females—not by organizing them together. This usage probably gave rise to the separate organization of
male and female Anti-Slavery Societies in both hemispheres.

Esq., of Boston, a delegate associated with Mr. Garrison, "denied that the WOMAN question had occasioned the late division in New York. He said that it was POLITICS that occasioned it."

Without denying, with Mr. Phillips, that the "woman question" was one occasion of division, we may agree with him that "*politics*" had a large share in the transaction—the politics of those who wished in some way to wield civil government against slavery—the politics of those who foresaw in this the disturbance of their political parties—and the politics (perhaps we should say the anti-politics) of those who desired no compulsory civil government at all.

The combination, for the time being, between the two latter against the first, appears to have presented the political element of division, and their union in the American Anti-Slavery Society, after the division, furnishes the key to the political manifestations that followed, including the bitter hostility towards the Liberty party for which that Society was distinguished. With a "rank and file" of whig and democratic abolitionists, wedded to their old parties, the Society was "officered," to some extent, with Non-Resistants, who would have preferred to witness in their ranks no voting at all, but who were unfortunately led to regard with more forbearance the pro-slavery voting of the whig and democratic members of their own Society, than the rigid anti-slavery voting of the members of the Liberty party.

The division in the Society at New York, and the organization of the Liberty party, took place, it will be borne in mind, in the spring of 1840, on the eve of the Presidential election of that year, and in the midst of stirring preparations for the contest. The resolution adopted by the Garrisonian majority, placing the support of the pro-slavery and the anti-slavery candidates on equal grounds of disapprobation, has already been mentioned. This was the *beginning* of a political course for a long time pursued by that Society. It was the beginning, but not the consummation; for before election day arrived, it was openly taught that the securing of votes for Harrison and Tyler was less to be deplored than the securing of votes for Birney and Earle. This was the language of N. P. Rogers, one of their leading editors, and of the agents and lecturers of the Society.

The annual meeting of the Massachusetts Anti-Slavery Society, in January or February, 1840, had said nothing against the support of Harrison and Tyler, though there was known to be a strong tendency of the majority of abolitionists in that State to support them. After the nomination of Birney and Earle, by the Liberty party, in April, the American Anti-Slavery Society, as we have seen, could impartially dissuade from pro-slavery and from anti-slavery voting, in the same breath. But now, a decided preference, as a choice of evils, was given to the political support of a slaveholder over an abolitionist who had emancipated his slaves.

The action of the great majority of the society and its supporters was in accordance with these teachings. Non-Resistants, who, on the ground of their peculiar views of civil government, abstained from the polls, were admitted to be (as we have seen) but a small minority of the society and of its leading men—"less than an hundredth part of the society" in Massachusetts, at the time of the division, there, in 1839—"not exceeding," in 1841, or '42, "one or two hundred in all New England," and still more sparse in the other States. And nothing, at *that* time, was heard of abstaining from the polls, on the ground of the pro-slavery character of the Federal Constitution or the Federal Government. The vast majority of the society claiming to embody "the only true abolitionists of the country" voted either for Van Buren or for Harrison and Tyler, opponents of abolitionism, while the Liberty party, designated by them as "apostates," voted for Birney, the emancipating abolitionist.

Some of their active and official members were earnestly engaged in electioneering for a slaveholder. A member of the "business committee" of the meeting of the Massachusetts Anti-Slavery Society just now mentioned, having assisted to shape its proceedings, was found, not long afterwards, a prominent speaker at political meetings, in support of Harrison and Tyler.

The Executive Board of the same Massachusetts A. S. Society, during the pendency of the same presidential election, addressed a letter to the abolitionists of the United States, against independent anti-slavery nominations, but said nothing against the support of the pro-slavery candidates. Like the "Standard," they seem to have felt that " the greatest danger was the organization of a third party, striving to break down political organizations."

Soon after the nomination of Birney, in April, 1840, the same Massachusetts State A. S. Society, held a quarterly meeting, and adopted six labored resolutions, deprecating the support of Birney and Earle, but uttering not a word against the support of the pro-slavery candidates. Nothing was said, (as formerly) of " scattering votes" at State or National elections, nor in favor of staying away from the polls. Of this meeting, the same prominent supporter of Harrison and Tyler* was chairman. The proceedings of the meeting were published in the Liberator without dissent, accompanied with sarcastic mention of the nomination of Birney, which was spoken of as "the Albany farce."—See *Liberator*, of April 17, 1840.

Some time before this, (March 13) Mr. Garrison labored, in his Liberator, to show that " it is most unphilosophical for abolitionists to expend much time, expense, or thought, upon the approaching presidential election,"—that " *it matters very little who is President*," because there is no probability that within four years there will be a Congress who will vote for the abolition of slavery in the District of Columbia. Yet he would have abolitionists bear their testimony against elevating either of the candidates.

---

* Mr. Tyler was a slaveholder. He was elected Vice-President, at this election, and, in consequence, became President by the demise of President Harrison. His course, as President, we have seen. Gen. Harrison, by his public speeches at Vincennes and Cheviot, had been one of the earliest and most violent opposers of abolitionists. By this means, and by his letters to southern politicians, he had gained southern favor, and thus he became the Presidential candidate of his party.

In all this, we heard nothing of the wickedness of voting under the pro-slavery constitution. We saw nothing of the motto of "no union with slaveholders." A close union with the *supporters* of slaveholders was quite evident, nevertheless.

The previous policy of "questioning the candidates" of the old parties, was now, by general consent, laid aside. Liberty party men had candidates of their own. Non-Resistants desired none. And other abolitionists, (whether of the "Old" or the "New" organized anti-slavery societies,) appeared to be tolerably well content with the candidates furnished them by their old political parties. Except the seven thousand votes polled for Birney and Earle by the Liberty party, and perhaps two or three hundred non-voting Non-Resistants,* excepting, also, the sect called "Covenanters," who never vote, there were not, probably, any considerable number of abolitionists who did not, at that election, cast pro-slavery votes.

Now was the noon-tide glory of "moral suasion" abolitionism, as it was called. "We must abolitionize the people," said the advocates of this doctrine, and all will come right. And again, "Do not bring down our holy cause," said they, "into the dirty waters of politics." These had a holy horror of the Liberty party. They preferred the "Old organization," and hastened to vote for the pro-slavery candidates of their old parties.

Let it not be inferred that Mr. Garrison and those of his associates who were thorough abolitionists, could silently witness all this, to the close of the contest, without a word of rebuke. It was not so. The Old Massachusetts Anti-Slavery Society, though late in the season, at Worcester, October 6th, and at Springfield, October 8th, adopted the following, from the pen of Mr. Garrison :

"*Resolved*, That no man can vote for William H. Harrison, or Martin

---

* Some who called themselves Non-Resistants were scarcely restrained from the polls, when election day came. It is confidently said that some of them did vote. Be this as it may, the political preferences and influence of some of them was no secret.

Van Buren, without voting directly to sustain slavery, and he who votes for slavery, HAS NO TITLE TO THE NAME OF AN ABOLITIONIST."

Mr. Garrison was himself again. He here repeated the old anti-slavery doctrine, held before the division—the doctrine of 1838—the doctrine that compelled voting abolitionists to form the Liberty party. Its severe but just censure lighted upon not one single adhering member of that party, accused as that party was, of apostacy from genuine abolitionism. But it fell, like a thunder-bolt, upon seven-eighths, if not nine-tenths of the members of the American Anti-Slavery Society and its auxiliaries, to which Mr. Garrison himself belonged, and which claimed then, and still claims, to embody or repre-sent all the genuine abolitionism in America.

If it fell equally upon a portion of the rival Society, (the " New Organization ") it fell only upon that portion of it that failed to come into the Liberty party, thus revealing the dis-tinction between them, and also the affinity of political ethics between portions of the New Organization and the Old.

The language of the Resolution justifies the estimate we have already made of the advice previously given, in the op-posite direction.

Such a Resolution, at the meetings of the Society in the winter and spring, consistently carried out, and not neutral-ized by contrary teachings, would have had a salutary effect, though it would have swelled the vote of the Liberty party. As it was, it came too late to prevent the mortifying result already described. It had scarcely reached central and west-ern New-York, ere those who needed it had either deposited their votes or had committed themselves too deeply to retract.

Nor did the infatuation die with the Presidential contest. It was publicly stated and never denied, that two lecturing agents of the American Anti-Slavery Society, professing to be non resistants, boasted, afterwards, that they had saved thousands of votes for the whig party; in other words, for Harrison and Tyler. It is known that, in their travels they sought out whig committees, and made such representations to them as induced them to subscribe for packages of the " National Anti-Slavery Standard." "No union with slaveholders" was not, then, the motto of that paper, nor of the Society of which it was the official organ.

A great convention of "old organization" abolitionists was held at Le Roy, N. Y., January 6th and 7th, 1841, under the auspices of the Corresponding Secretary and General Agent of the Old American Anti-Slavery Society. The proceedings were published in more than nine columns of the National Anti-Slavery Standard.

" The largest and most spirited anti-slavery Convention" (say the editors) "ever held in the State of New York." "Several hundred delegates were in attendance, and acted without distinction of sex. The third party movement was voted down by a very large majority, as it had been in four State Conventions previously in that State." "We publish the proceedings entire." " Send it to the four winds, that it may do the work of PRIMITIVE ABOLITIONISM !"

In this Convention, as appears in the proceedings, a Resolution was introduced, discussed, amended, and put into various shapes, upon the subject of voting for slaveholders, but, finally, the Resolution was lost. In rejecting it *the Convention* REFUSED *to say, in any form, that it was inconsistent to vote for a* SLAVEHOLDER! In all the proceedings, there was no expression of regret in view of the course of voting abolitionists, except those who voted for the abolition candidate, Mr. Birney. Among the letters to the Convention, read and published as from "distinguished abolitionists," deprecating the Liberty party, were several from zealous supporters of Harrison and Tyler.

The proceedings of this Convention were hailed in the Liberator as a signal triumph of the American Anti-Slavery Society over the Liberty party and " new organization."

By the Liberator and the National Anti-Slavery Standard it was apparently assumed as a settled axiom, that politics, of necessity, must be impure—that they must be conducted on principles of mere expediency, and that moral principle, for the time being, must be laid aside. They derided the efforts of the Liberty party, its lecturers and its editors, to raise the tone of political morality, to teach the duty of honest, conscientious, political action, to be performed religiously, in the fear of God, and looking to him for assistance and direction.* Moral action and political action were spoken of, as antagonisms, that cannot exist together, or be reconciled.

It was not strange that those who thought thus of political action, and then undertook to direct it, should realize, in the results, the appropriate effects of their own theory. He is not to be regarded an unsuccessful operator whose work comes up to his ideal—his model.

In the Autumn of 1842, an important State election took place in the State of New York, and the agents of the American Anti-Slavery Society, with the " National Anti-Slavery Standard," were again in the field, in opposition to the Liberty party, its editors, its lecturers, and its candidates.

The " Standard" of July 7, took the ground that abolitionists should not insist on the " genuine" abolition of those for whom they were called upon to cast their votes. They were not to insist on " filling the State House with *true* anti-slavery men." Instead of this, they were advised to make calculations whether or no " fifty men who have a strong motive for obliging abolitionists," would not do us more service than a *few* abolitionists who are anti-slavery to the back-bone ?"

The comparison here instituted describes and concedes the distinction between the candidates of the Liberty party, and the candidates of the old parties, whom other voting abolitionists would have to support. The choice was between the two, and the suggestion was in favor of the latter.

In the same paper, of Sept. 29th, an effort was made to persuade abolitionists to vote for a gubernatorial candidate who was a partisan of Henry Clay.

" Politics is a game of expediency, its science consists in a nice calculation of present availability. Those skilled in such calculations can decide

---

* " ' Under certain circumstances,' Mr. Goodell thinks, ' that the days of approaching the ballot-box, and of preparing for its solemn duties, might be set apart as days of fasting and prayer to Almighty God, by those who are accustomed to observe such appointments.' Pardon us, if we smile at this."—*Liberator*, March 20, 1840.

for themselves, whether Luther Bradish, as Governor, would be likely to do more to support Henry Clay, than Luther Bradish, as a private citizen."

It might have been added, that those abolitionists who had openly supported Harrison and Tyler, could have no conscientious scruples against supporting Henry Clay.

In the same paper, of the same date, was inserted, without comment or dissent, a long letter from a Whig statesman, William Slade, of Vermont, in which he justifies the policy of making the tariff question the paramount one, for the time being, instead of the slave question; and then adds as follows:

"May not abolitionists better subserve the cause of abolition by thus aiding to secure the election of men who are willing to take MODERATE ground against slavery, than to lose their influence, as to present PRACTICAL PURPOSES, by shutting themselves up within the straightened enclosure of a third political party?"

Such was the political morality inculcated and exemplified by the official organ of the American Anti-Slavery Society, up to the autumn of 1842, on the eve of an important State election, and looking forward to the Presidential campaign of 1844. Posterity will compare such political ethics with those of the Liberty party, and decide upon the claims of the former to represent the only true abolitionism of America, and whether the latter gave evidence of apostacy from the anti-slavery cause, in not acting with them.

CHAPTER XLIII.

SECOND REVOLUTION IN THE POSITION AND POLICY OF THE AMERICAN ANTI-SLAVERY SOCIETY, IN 1844.

"No Union with Slaveholders"—The Federal Constitution "a covenant with death and an agreement with hell"—Import of the "No Union" motto—Some advantages of this new position—Its origin and history.

PASSING over an intervening space of about one year and a half, we find the American Anti-Slavery Society, at its annual meeting in May, 1844, raising the flag of "No Union with Slaveholders,"* demanding a dissolution of the Union,

---

* It has not always been easy for other abolitionists to understand precisely what, and how much, is included by Mr. Garrison and his associates, under the phrase, "No union with slaveholders." If they mean only a separation of the non-slaveholding States from the slave States, the meaning would be sufficiently clear, and the proposal deserves attention. But such a separation would not be a separation between the pro-slavery and the anti-slavery portions of the nation. It would leave the slaves, free colored people of the South, and many of their white friends on the South side of the line; while many of the most despotic statesmen and servile voters would remain on the North side. It would leave the "black law" legislation of the free States in full force. Neither morally nor politically would the geographical line of division describe the true separation. Appeals sometimes made in favor of "no union with slaveholders," seem to overlook this. It seems to have been assumed that the relation of a common citizenship between a slaveholder and a friend of liberty is, *per se*, a sinful relation—that it is wicked to sit in the same Congress where a slaveholder sits, or to go to the same ballot-box with him. This idea would accord with the theory of no civil government. Its adoption would render civil government impossible, so long as there remained a wicked lawless man in the nation; in other words, so long as a civil government, to repress crime, is needed. This idea also assumes that civil government is merely a voluntary association, into which the citizen may enter, or not, as he pleases. This too accords with the non-government theory, and its advocates doubtless understand themselves as holding no political connections *either with slaveholders, or with any body else*. The separation, on their part, involves no self-denial, and consists in no new or discriminative act. To those of other views, who hold themselves *in fact*, whether

denouncing the Federal Constitution as pro-slavery, "a covenant with death, and an agreement with hell," under which no abolitionist can consistently hold office, or vote for another to hold office. This was a memorable revolution in the Society and its policy.

In many respects there was an advantage gained by the Society in taking this new ground. The favorite policy of *not voting* could now be placed on an anti-slavery basis, and openly urged "on the anti-slavery platform," with the aid of anti-slavery funds, instead of depending upon the still moderate number of "Non-Resistants," who were consistent enough to abandon the polls. The experiment of keeping other abolitionists away from the polls had proved, thus far, a manifest failure.* The anti-slavery reputation of the Society, as well as the interests of the cause, had suffered severely, and the lost ground must be regained. The startling doctrines and measures thus propounded would arrest attention and excite discussion. Instead of lagging behind the Liberty party, and hanging on to the skirts of the old pro-slavery parties and their slaveholding candidates, they could now claim to outstrip them in the march of separation from slaveholders, and retort upon them the charge of inconsistency in their political associations.† How far, or whether at all, these considerations had weight, we pretend not to say. They naturally suggest themselves on a review of the history. The reader will judge.

---

they will or no, a part of the nation they reside in, *some* of their appeals have therefore no force. But when they urge the duty of dissolving the Union between the free and slave States, on the ground that the Union upholds slavery, they propound a serious and intelligible question, and one that comes home to the conscience and interests of every northern citizen.

* So well known and almost universal was the desire to vote, that Stephen S. Foster and some others, it is understood, proposed among their associates some mode of anti-slavery voting, distinct from the obnoxious Liberty party. But either the proposal was overruled, or no other platform of anti-slavery voting could be devised.

† In October, 1842, a Liberty Party Convention at Syracuse, N. Y., had issued a circular describing the political influence of the American Anti-Slavery Society, which was not to be conveniently answered till the course of the Society was changed.

So radical a change could not have been effected in a moment. A strong under-current must have been at work during the enactment of the scenes before described. The particulars are not fully before us, and we have little space for them. We are told that Wendell Phillips, Esq., first affirmed the pro-slavery character of the Federal Constitution and the inconsistency of voting under it, at a Convention in Dover, N. H., in October, 1841.* Mr. Garrison is said to have expressed in conversation, at that time, his dissent. It is believed that he once held the anti-slavery character of the Constitution, along with N. P. Rogers and S. J. May.

But at the next anniversary of the Society in New York, May, 1842, the proposition was brought forward by Mr. Garrison himself. His annunciation of it beforehand, caused some excitement, and the Executive Committee in New York were alarmed. A note of disavowal was sent by them to the pro-slavery editor of the N. Y. Courier and Enquirer, stating that the committee did not approve the annunciation—that Mr. Garrison was not the Society, &c., or words of that import.

Two years afterwards, May, 1844, after an earnest debate, a majority of those present at the annual meeting adopted the new policy, and many withdrew from the Society.† The change in the course of the Society thenceforward was strongly marked, and the tone of the "National Anti-Slavery Standard," under the charge of other editors, also changed.

The political history of the Society, however, does not end here. But we must digress a little at this point to notice another schism in the Society.

---

* We are not quite certain of the accuracy of some of these dates, but think them sufficiently early.

† Whether it was on this occasion, or before, or afterwards, we cannot say, but at one period two or more lecturers of the Society found it difficult to pronounce the new shibboleth of a "pro-slavery Constitution" having been so long accustomed to promulgate the contrary doctrine, as learned from N. P. Rogers and Samuel J. May, in 1836. The Federal Courts were cited on the other side, but theirs was interested testimony, and ought not to have been received.

CHAPTER XLIV.

FURTHER DIFFICULTIES IN THE AMERICAN ANTI-SLAVERY SOCIETY.

Natural working of the new theories concerning Church and State—N. P. Rogers—
His inflexible adherence to his theory—The Collision.

THE particulars that follow may illustrate the effects of excessive exclusiveness among reformers. They may also throw light on that phase of attempted reformation that seems to look in the direction of displacing all organized control in human society.

Some of the leading minds in the American Anti-Slavery Society, after the division of 1840, were understood to repudiate the ideas commonly expressed by the term " *Church*," and the term " *State*," as regularly constituted organizations. It seemed to many, however, that their cherished organizations, the Non-Resistant Society and the Anti-Slavery Society, together or separate, constituted, to them, both a Church and a State,—the union of Church and State being of the most intimate kind, amounting to identity; the discipline and polity being of the most rigorous and stringent character—the anathema tremendous—the infliction precipitate and unsparing. The absence of any other Church or any other State, would naturally tend to concentrate and vitalize, at this central point, whatever of the governing propensity in human nature (if there be any) that remained in them. This was believed to be the case.

If it were so, the fact would be likely to develop itself among the subjects of this government. Attracted within its jurisdiction by perhaps an excessive dread of subordination, they would be likely to feel it the more keenly, if it should ever happen to be exercised upon themselves. The contingency was not long lingering.

Nathaniel P. Rogers, Esq., of New Hampshire, was a man of genius—of strong mental powers—an original and rapid thinker—a racy and vigorous writer—a non-resistant—and an abolitionist of the Garrison school. For a time he edited the National Anti-Slavery Standard, New York, then again the Herald of Freedom at Concord, N. H. In energy of purpose and weight of talent, he was second to no man among his associates, except Mr. Garrison—perhaps not second to him. He held himself subordinate to no man. There may have been a latent and unconscious rivalry between the two. Together, and with the concurrence perhaps of one other, a lady, the Society was easily managed. Pitted against each other, Greek against Greek, there must be schism.

With N. P. Rogers, his phase of abolition and his theory of non-government were no empty abstractions. At least he could not consent to be governed. He had not abjured the Church, to recognize a Bishop, nor the State, to bow before a Throne, or to any power, male or female, behind it. He spurned, as instinctively, and as indignantly, the rules of order observed in Anti-slavery Conventions and annual meetings, as he would those of Senates or Synods. When he spoke, as he often did with great power, he would not confine himself to reported resolutions. In Executive Committees he saw Sanhedrims, in Presidents of Societies, Popes, in recorded minutes, precedents, in Constitutions of voluntary associations, forms of government. These, as a consistent Non-Resistant and lover of liberty, he abjured. He became "a disorganizer" in the view of some who had been stigmatized as disorganizers themselves. In meetings of the Society, these points became matters of earnest debate. On one occasion of the kind, at Concord, in 1841, we were incidentally a witness, while Stephen S. Foster maintained against Rogers the claims of order, organization, and official prerogative.

The same sentiment forbade that Mr. Rogers should recognize the supervision of his "Herald of Freedom" by the
Executive Committee of the New Hampshire Anti-Slavery
Society, that claimed it as their organ. "I have to edit the
Herald," said he, "and what I have to do, nobody else is to
do or direct for me." A dispute arose concerning the control and the proprietorship of the paper. The merits of the
case we do not know; but both sides had their warm partisans. The controversy was carried to Boston. Mr. Garrison
was among those who took sides against Mr. Rogers. The
paper went out of his hands, but he started another of the
same name, and maintained a controversy while he lived, for
his health declined and he died, but not until the breach had
extended beyond the boundaries of New England. Where-
ever there were supporters of the American Anti-Slavery Society in central and western New York, there were found
some who sympathized with Rogers. The denunciations of
his opponents against him were quite as severe as anything
that had ever been fulminated against the "new organization"
and the Liberty party. How the breach in the Society was
healed—if it be healed—we cannot exactly say, but the penalty of insubordination and "schism," under the administration of the American Anti-Slavery Society, is now well understood. Its governors have evinced their capacity to bear
rule.

CHAPTER XLV.

POLITICAL COURSE OF THE AMERICAN ANTI-SLAVERY SOCIETY SINCE ITS REVOLUTION OF 1844.

The Society not wholly composed of "Non-Resistants"—Position of its politicians— Welcomed as members of the Society—Commonly connected with the old political parties—Consequent standard of their political action, as compared with the Liberty party, or with the motto of "No Union with Slaveholders"—On a level with the mere "Wilmot Proviso" politicians, or the platform of the Free Soil party— Their reception of the nomination of Mr. Van Buren, in 1848—Charges of apostacy against those Liberty Party men who came into the same measure—Relation of "Non-Resistants" in the Society to this political standard of their associates— Their policy read in the light of their theory—Facts in confirmation—Embarrassments of political abolitionists in consequence of this opposition.

It may, perhaps, be inferred, from the features of the revolution of 1844, that the American Anti-Slavery Society was afterwards or is now composed wholly of abolitionists who decline political voting—some on the principles of the Non-Resistance Society, and some or all on the ground of "no union with slaveholders," and the "pro-slavery Constitution of the United States."

Such a conclusion would be wide of the mark. The society that, on the ground of these features, (so recently acquired,) claims to be and to *have been, since* 1840, the only true Anti-Slavery organization in America, contains political voting members still. How numerous they are, or what proportion of the entire body, we say not, now:—but it contains them. It welcomes them. It chooses to retain them. By its agents it invites the co-operation of such, assuring them that the "anti-slavery platform is as broad as ever—broad enough to receive those who vote under the Federal Constitution as well as those who decline doing so."*

And this is not all. It has no rules and it desires none, for excluding those who vote for slavery, and even for slaveholders. We have the authority of Mr. Garrison in his Liberator, for saying this, although he declared, in his Springfield and Worcester Resolutions, in 1840—before cited—that such a voter "*has no title to the name of an abolitionist.*"

When reminded by a Liberty League correspondent that the American Anti-Slavery Society, as well as other anti-slavery societies, contained pro-slavery voters and members of pro-slavery churches, he denied not the fact, and pleaded that the original Constitution of the Society, which remained unchanged, did not exclude them, but only excluded slaveholders. He went further, and vindicated the policy, even at that late day, maintaining, in substance, that assent to the anti-slavery *principles* of the Society was the proper test of membership, and that each member must be left free to judge whether or no he honored his principles in his *practice*, so long as he did not become a slaveholder. He might vote for slaveholders, and hold religious fellowship with them, and remain in the Society.

In the light of this avowal, the exclusive claims of the American Anti-Slavery Society to purity of membership may be tested. The relation of the Society to politics, since 1844, may also be understood.

The Society is not a Society of self-disfranchised non-voters, after all, as the " Covenanters " are. While some of its members hold that position, others of them do not. In the matter of membership, it is not a test. To the merits of that position, whatever they may be, the Society, as such, has no valid claim.

Still further, the test of membership in that Society—as in

---

* This language was lately held, in our hearing, at Rochester, by Mr. S. S. Foster, agent of the Society, who was laboring to persuade an Anti-Slavery Society then organizing, and composed chiefly of political voters, to become auxiliary to the American A. S. Society.

others—opens the door to those voters who, in Mr. Garrison's view, "*have no title to the name of abolitionists.*" How then does he ascertain the claims of the Society to the name of abolitionist, in contrast with the claims of other societies? He need not institute a comparison with the Liberty party, which contains no such voters.

The Society is composed, to an unknown extent, of political voters*—perhaps of pro-slavery voters. In the *Society* they have an equal right with Mr. Garrison and faithful abolitionists. How then does the motto of "no union with slaveholders" expurgate the Society? Is there no union with slaveholders in a voluntary and fraternal union with those who vote for them?

Being composed, to a certain extent, of political voters, the Society must have a standard of political ethics and action.

It has one. How does it compare with the standard of other anti-slavery societies, and with the standard of the Liberty party?

No anti-slavery society that we know of has a lower standard, in this respect, than the American Society. The Liberty party has a much higher one.

Political voters connected with the American Anti-Slavery Society, since 1844, it may be presumed, with possible exceptions, have not voted with the Liberty party. The dread of being branded "apostates," if nothing else, will have restrained them from that.

For whom, then, have they been casting their votes? And what tone of political ethics has been indicated by their voting?

The candidates of the Liberty party, before its incipient absorption into the embroyo Free Soil party, in the autumn of

---

* It is not known that the number of non-voting Non-Resistants has increased since they were estimated at "one or two hundred in all New England." Some prominent advocates of the doctrine have resumed voting. We know of few who abstain from the polls on account of the "pro-slavery Constitution," but there are some. If political voters do not compose a majority of the supporters of the Society, it must be feebler than we have supposed it to be.

1847, were always pledged to the abolition of slavery in the District of Columbia, and Territories, the prohibition of the inter-State Slave trade, and the non-extension of Slavery. This was the old demand of abolitionists. The Liberty League, and the remnant of the Liberty party since the absorption, have gone farther, demanding the abolition of Slavery in the States—the highest standard of political abolitionism.

Have the candidates receiving the votes of members of the American Anti-Slavery Society, since 1844, been pledged to the measures of even the old Liberty party?

To ask such a question is to answer it. Though the tone of anti-slavery feeling in portions of the Whig and Democratic parties has been rising, their candidates have not been pledged to these measures.

The measures of the Free Soil party, and the pledges of its candidates, have already been described. The Annual Report of the Old Massachusetts Anti-Slavery Society, for 1852, affords a similar description. It designates the standard of that party as falling short of the demands of consistent abolitionism. It is so, precisely at those points wherein it falls short of the position of the Liberty party, as just now recorded.

But the very highest standard indicated by the votes of members of the American Anti-Slavery Society, even since 1844, is that of the Free Soil party, or that of certain members of the Whig and Democratic parties. *To no higher standard of voting could Mr. Garrison himself point them, without advising them to vote for the candidates of the Liberty party.*

But this he has not done. It follows that the highest standard of political action countenanced by the American Anti-Slavery Society, even since its revolution in 1844, has been lower than that of the old Liberty party.

Since 1844, as truly as in 1842, the influence of that Society upon its political voters has been to lead them not to "insist" on the "genuine" abolition of those for whom they cast their votes, but to prefer voting for those who "have a strong motive for obliging abolitionists."

The *lower* standard of political abolitionism has uniformly been preferred by the Society and its leading members to the *higher*. And the voting members of the Society, when voting with any reference at all to the slave question, have voted accordingly. Let facts testify.

When certain "progressive" whigs and democrats espoused "the Wilmot proviso," they constituted the only political element then in the country adverse in any degree to the ascendency of slavery, except the Liberty party. For this these statesmen deserved due honor, but they did not come up to the higher political ethics and demands of the Liberty party. The leading influences and the voting members of the American Anti-Slavery Society supported the *former* (though standing in their pro-slavery parties, and sometimes voting for slaveholders) in preference to the *latter*.

Did this course honor their new flag of "No union with slaveholders?"

Measure the distance between the platform of mere "Wilmot proviso" and that of the Liberty party, pledged to the abolition of slavery, and you have the distance at that period, between the political ethics of a voting Garrison abolitionist, and a voter in the Liberty party. The former voted only against the *extension* of slavery—the latter against its extension and in favor of its *abolition*.

The lower standard was again preferred to the higher, when indications appeared of the organizing of a "Free Soil party." That measure encountered none of the virulent opposition that had been manifested against the formation of the Liberty party.

And yet again, when the question presented itself, of the absorption of the Liberty party in the Free Soil party, the same preference was again witnessed—though amid some confusion of tongues, as different aspects of the transaction presented themselves. The leaders of the American Anti-Slavery Society could not fail to see that in such a movement the

members of the Liberty party would lower down their standard of political abolitionism, and the first impulse was to reproach them for their defection. "Leading Liberty party
men" said they "are preparing to desert the slave. Have we
not always said they would prove untrue?" A second glance
revealed to them the fact that in such a movement the members of the Liberty party would be coming into close political
affinity with the "Wilmot proviso" voters in the old American Anti-Slavery Society. Above all, the troublesome Liberty
party would be crippled, perhaps disbanded. "Liberty party
men" said they "are coming to their senses." "We have
strong hopes of this new movement."

We may fail to recall the precise words, but the import of
both these conflicting comments came close on the heels of
each other in the Liberator and Standard.

At the Free Soil nomination of Martin Van Buren at Buffalo in 1848, Rev. Samuel J. May, a "non-resistant" abolitionist, a leader from the beginning of the "old organization,"
gave his approbation of the movement in a speech, and invoked upon it the blessing of Heaven in prayer. At no
Liberty party nomination that we know of, was his approving
voice ever heard or his prayers offered. *Thus* deep into "the
dirty waters of politics," he could not have descended. Yet
Samuel J. May is one of the most liberal minded men, one
of the most earnest abolitionists, in the Society to which he
belongs.

And after all this, at a convention of all descriptions of
abolitionists at Syracuse, (the residence of Samuel J. May)
an abolitionist of the Garrison school vehemently insisted
upon the rottenness of the Liberty party, and adduced, in a
way of evidence and illustration, the fact that so large a portion of it had lowered down the high and holy standard of
abolitionism, by becoming absorbed in the Free Soil party!
He seemed to forget that in this transition—however it was
to be described—they had come upon the highest platform
of political action ever sanctioned by the "old organization"
—that the high and holy standard of abolitionism apostatized

from, was that of the old "one idea" Liberty party—though even this was not deemed as utopian and ultra as that of the Liberty league.

The question forces itself upon our attention: How can such radical abolitionists as Mr. Garrison and his associates undoubtedly are, prefer that those who *do* make use of the ballot box, should espouse a lower instead of a higher standard of political abolitionism?

It seems hardly compatable with their known sagacity and characteristic dread of compromise to suppose that they fall in with the shallow policy of attempting to achieve great ends by temporizing expedients.

Their views of the Federal Constitution and of the limited powers of the Federal Government, cannot account for it. Though they decline voting themselves, they willingly and without conscientious scruple, make political suggestions for the guidance of those who do vote. They have not questioned the constitutional powers of Congress over the slavery of the Federal District, the Territories, and the inter-state slave trade—as well as the non-extension of slavery. Yet we have seen them steadily prefer that voting abolitionists should rally on the latter issue alone, rather than that they should include likewise the former and the more important. Politically, they are non-extensionists, rather than abolitionists.

If it be said that they had hopes of accomplishing the one and not the other, we repeat that such compromises and expedients do not come within the scope of their accustomed activities and methods.

It must be remembered that they are non-resistants as well as abolitionists. They believe that slavery is wicked; but they believe, too, that the compulsory abolition of slavery by the strong arm of civil government, would also be wicked. How then can they consistently or conscientiously advise efficient political action for the compulsory abolition of slavery? An incident or two will show the pertinency of the question.

When the platform of the proposed Liberty league was published, it encountered, of course, the searching scrutiny of Mr. Garrison. He evidently saw that it was free from some of the objections that had been made against the Liberty party, and that it was adapted to find favor with the most radical class of such reformers as make use of the ballot box. It was equally plain that he did not wish them to fall·in with it. He found no fault with its proposed objects—abolition, free trade, &c. It became necessary to state his objections. In doing this, the key-note of all his political advice was clearly revealed. He objected distinctly to the compulsory action of civil government, even for the abolition of slavery. And, with some seeming warmth he affirmed, that if the penman of the document, his old friend, were placed in the position of Chief Magistrate, he could not carry out the measure without a practical rejection of Christianity in using physical force.

The same sentiment was again uttered distinctly, by Mr. Garrison and Henry C. Wright, at the anniversary of the American Anti-Slavery Society, May, 1851, at Syracuse. A discussion with Liberty party men concerning political action against slavery, drove them, at last, to that position.

If this had been understood on both sides, and kept in mind, from the beginning, much angry and misdirected altercation might have been spared. If it can be remembered hereafter, it may prevent similar wranglings, in time to come.

Non-Resistants do not seek to suppress crime—not even the crime of slaveholding, by the strong arm of civil government. Their appeal is rather to the slaveholder. They would have the slave-laws repealed : but they understand that, under a compulsory civil government, such a repeal would be followed, if needful, by the forcible suppression of slaveholding. For this they are not prepared, and cannot be, while they remain Non-Resistants. They are shut up (if consistent) to mere moral suasion. This is their field. Let them occupy it without being reproached. They have a right to their own principles and to corresponding measures.

Abolitionists believing (as most abolitionists do) in a compulsory civil government, have an equal right to their own principles and measures. If they understand themselves, they will not follow the political advice of those who do not seek the compulsory suppression of slaveholding. For refusing such advisers, they do not deserve to be denounced as untrue to the slave; nor denied the honorable name of abolitionists because they do really seek the *abolition of slavery*,* and not merely the *emancipation of the slaves.*

Among the obstacles which political abolitionists in America have been called to encounter, one of the most formidable and perplexing (because, by many, unperceived) has been the influence of political advisers, earnest emancipationists, who have believed it *wicked to suppress slaveholding by a government wielding physical force.* Had they always and steadily exhibited the ethical foundations of their political advice, that advice would have been understood, and there would have been no occasion for complaint.

If the boast, already begun by lecturing agents of the American Anti-Slavery Society, Non-Resistants, that they have broken down the Liberty party, should prove well-founded or prophetic, the reader will see how, on what principles, by what methods, and with what auxiliaries, the work was, or will have been, accomplished. And posterity will judge how much the exploit facilitated the abolition of American slavery, or vindicated the claims of the victors to the title of " the only true abolitionists in the country."

Those who would understand the history of political abolitionism in America—its origin—its nature—its objects—its obstacles—its future prospects—will find no occasion to complain that we have detained them too long on this topic. Its study will furnish them with a key to many intricacies otherwise inexplicable.

---

* The phrase " *abolition of slavery*," in strictness of speech, as well as in popular usage, expresses the act of repealing the slave code, *and* suppressing the practice of slaveholding. This was the " abolition of slavery" in the British West Indies. If all the slaveholders in America should emancipate all their slaves to-day, that would not be the abolition of American slavery. Slaves might be held again to-morrow. Non-Resistants opposed to slavery, are properly *emancipationists.* We will call them *abolitionists*, if they prefer it, but in doing so we must use the word in a new and accommodated signification.

CHAPTER XLVI.

COURSE OF MR. GARRISON, AND THE AMERICAN ANTI-SLAVERY SOCIETY AND ITS MEMBERS, SINCE THE DIVISION IN 1840, IN RESPECT TO ANTI-SLAVERY CHURCH ACTION.

Sympathizers with the " Clerical Appeal"—an inconsiderable and local minority of the Liberty party—Unhappy ecclesiastical connections (nevertheless), of a majority of its members—Same inconsistency found in the American A. S. Society—Anti-Slavery Church agitations, extensive, but overlooked by the Journalists of the Society—Anti-Slavery Church and Missionary re-organization little noticed by them— Position of the Amer. Society—Of its members who desire no Church relations— Causes which repulsed many Church members from that Society—Ecclesiastical position of those members of the Society who *do* sustain Church relations. Connection with pro-slavery bodies—Few Anti-Slavery re-organizations, or agitations to that end—Other side of the picture—Anti-Slavery Universalists—Testimony of Mr. Garrison.

WE have seen that Mr. Garrison and his associates in the American Anti-Slavery Society, at an early day, discountenanced withdrawal from pro-slavery parties *and churches*, with a view to the organizing of new ones ;—that they nevertheless, at the same time, favored and raised the cry, to " come out," of pro-slavery churches—that then, and since, to the present time, they have perseveringly charged upon the American and Foreign Anti-Slavery Society (with which they connect the Liberty party), "that it sprung into existence for the protection of pro-slavery churches"—claiming for themselves and their Society the exclusive credit of fidelity to the slave, in this particular.

Here are claims to be scrutinized, charges to be examined, apparent discrepancies to be reconciled, or accounted for.

The facts of the case must be impartially presented. In no other way can these problems be solved, or posterity put in possession of any trustworthy history of the anti-slavery movement in America. This we shall endeavor to do, so far as our limits will permit.

We have already said that those abolitionists in New England, who sympathized with the "Clerical Appeal," in its tenderness towards pro-slavery ministers, took ground against Mr. Garrison and were drawn into the "New Organization"—perhaps some of them into the Liberty party. Hence the claims and representations to which we have referred. But *these* were only a small part of the New Organization—a very small part, certainly, of the Liberty party.

We have also said that a large portion of the Liberty party, including, of course, a considerable number of those who preferred (on the whole) the "New" to the "Old" Society after the division, continued in their old Churches, (many if not most of them pro-slavery,) and that this, in our view, was among the causes why the majority of the Liberty party could not perseveringly maintain the high standard of political ethics which gave rise to that party.

With this full and free statement concerning the party with which we have acted, we must be permitted to connect another concerning those who stood aloof from that party, who opposed it, and who belonged to "the Old Organization" with Mr. Garrison.

According to the best information we have ever been able to collect, the portion of the American Anti-Slavery Society *who wish to sustain any Church relations at all*, are quite as commonly and as extensively (in proportion to numbers) connected with pro-slavery churches as abolitionists connected with the "New" (the American and Foreign) Anti-Slavery Society, or the Liberty party.*

---

* It may be said (as it has been,) that those who withdraw from pro-slavery political parties, and yet cling to pro-slavery Churches, are less consistent than those that cling to both. And it may be retorted, that those who withdraw from pro-slavery political parties, exhibit, at least, *one* more phase of progress than those who cling to *both*. It may further be said, that in sects maintaining some degree of local Church independency, yet remotely related to large ecclesiastical bodies, the character of the body, the nature of the relation, and the prospect of a salutary change, are not as readily ascertained as in the two great political parties.

Our own strong impression is, that, in respect to the Liberty party, (especially as it now stands) the difference is greatly on the other side. A large portion of its members are members of anti-slavery churches.

The agitation in the churches has been a very important part of the anti-slavery movement, especially where Christian abolitionists, to so wide an extent, and for so long a time, have associated themselves for the purpose of holding Christian Anti-Slavery Conventions, sustaining lecturers, circulating books, papers, and tracts, with a direct view to bring the churches into an anti-slavery position, or, in case of failure (as has been the general fact), to secede and gather new churches. The extent to which this has been done (as briefly recorded already), has been sufficient, one would think, to deserve some approving record in the official organs and other leading journals of "*the only*" trustworthy Anti-Slavery Society in America, the Society that claims to be distinguished from all other organizations for fidelity on the church question; and that charges its rival with having "sprung into existence for the protection of pro-slavery churches." Common justice would seem to have required at the hands of such a Society and such journalists, that so dark a picture should be relieved by a presentation of any important facts of a more encouraging character. The readers, in Europe, of their Liberator, their National Anti-Slavery Standard, and their Annual Reports, might have been interested to know that among the proscribed and anathematized class of abolitionists, some such manifestations had been witnessed. But so far as we have been able to learn, this class of important facts have been almost wholly ignored or overlooked by them.

When General Associations, General Assemblies, General Conferences, smaller ecclesiastical bodies, Missionary Boards, &c., &c., embracing a majority opposed to abolitionists, have met, and debated, and taken action, or refused to take any, the facts have not escaped due notice from them. But when abolitionists connected with those bodies have banded themselves together for efficient anti-slavery agitation and action

among the constituencies of such bodies; when new missionary boards, new churches, and extended ecclesiastical bodies,
have been organized on anti-slavery principles, very little, if
any, recognition or notice has been taken of such facts by the
leaders and organs of the American Anti-Slavery Society.*
The historian must look elsewhere than to the columns of
their journals and the pages of their annual reports, for information concerning this movement. He must seek it in the
papers of the Liberty party, and in the religious papers conducted by those engaged in these enterprises. If it be said
that the records of these extensive movements were too
voluminous for the Liberator and Standard, and similar journals, it may be asked, whether there could not have been
found room for occasional notices and recommendations of
them, even if some of the discussions in the Liberator concerning the Sabbath and the Bible, and proceedings of conventions on those topics, had been somewhat curtailed or
abridged. If it be so that even a condensed record of these
movements (which were before them in their "exchange
papers") would inconveniently encumber their columns, it
would seem to follow that the sweeping charge against other
anti-slavery bodies, of "having sprung into existence for the
protection of pro-slavery churches," requires essential modification. For, with very inconsiderable exceptions, if any,
these movements have been carried on by active members of
the organizations thus censured. And no anti-slavery movements have been more bitterly assailed by the leaders and
organs of the pro-slavery churches and missionary bodies.

We now inquire, more particularly and directly, concerning
the relation of the American Anti-Slavery Society to pro-
slavery churches, and the efforts of its members in respect to
anti-slavery church reformation.

It *may be true* that a smaller proportion of the members of

---

* The only exception we remember to have met with, was a favorable notice, in
the National Anti-Slavery Standard, of the organization of a single local anti-slavery
church, as though it were a new thing, some years after hundreds, probably, of
similar churches had been organized, and after a change of editors of that paper.

the American Anti-Slavery Society are connected with pro-slavery churches, than are to be found in the "new" organization (or were in the Liberty party prior to 1848), because *it may be true* that a much smaller proportion of them (especially leading members, editors, and lecturers) are, or desire to be, members of any organized churches whatever.

If this be so, it may be remarked, that while abolitionists who rejected all church organization had an equal right to their own views and usages, it must be remembered that their separation from pro-slavery churches may have had other grounds than their abolition principles; and that it was comparatively easy for those who, on such other grounds, had "come out" or remained out of the churches, to raise an outcry against those who remained in them. This zeal *may* possibly have sprung, in some measure, from another source besides their superior fidelity to the slave. It is not to be assumed that they were free from the common infirmities of human beings. Nor is it quite clear that they gave evidence of greater self-denial in the anti-slavery cause than did the many thousands (unrecognized as true abolitionists by them) who, with strong attachments to long cherished church institutions and loved associates, severed these strong ties, and with great sacrifices of social feeling and of pecuniary expenditure, established new church relations, in accordance with anti-slavery principles, amid opposition and scorn.

If large numbers of anti-slavery church members, particularly those called "orthodox" or "evangelical," separated from Mr. Garrison, and consequently from the American Anti-Slavery Society, on the division, some facts already stated may suggest reasons for their course, aside from the derelictions that have been imputed to them. Men seldom, if ever, retain organized religious or moral co-operation and affinity with leaders who deride their religious principles and the institutions to which they have attached themselves. This may be accounted *consistency and sagacity*, or it may be accounted *bigotry and weakness*. The general fact, nevertheless, remains. The cause existed, and was sufficient to produce the effect; and there is no occasion, in the absence of evidence (with the exception of those favoring the "Clerical Appeal") to impute additional ones. It would be the extreme of bigotry, in such a case, to assume that their withdrawal from a particular anti-slavery society, and joining another one of the same anti-slavery creed, where their religious predilections would not be outraged, gave evidence of unfaithfulness to the anti-slavery cause.

Similar causes, after the division, continued to produce and perpetuate similar effects. Conventions were held to discuss the Sabbath question. In March, 1842, if we correctly remember, a Convention was held to discuss the divine inspiration and authority of the Bible. These Conventions were invited and attended by leading abolitionists in the American Anti-Slavery Society, and ground was taken by them, and language used, in those Conventions and in the columns of the Liberator, adverse to the principles of "orthodox" or "evangelical" Christians, and highly offensive to them. We say nothing here of the merits of these discussions. We say nothing against their right of free expression. We only record the facts along with the effect which they naturally and evidently produced—the alienation of many abolitionists from that Society, on other grounds than differences of anti-slavery principles, or even of anti-slavery measures—unless to "unseat popular theology from its throne" (in the language before quoted from the National Anti-Slavery Standard), and the overthrow of commonly accredited religious institutions, are to be recognized as anti-slavery measures.

It was said that the Liberator, at that time, was not the official organ of the Society. But its editor was the recognized leader of the Society. It was said that these conventions were not Anti-Slavery Conventions, and that the sentiments objected against were not promulgated "on the Anti-Slavery platform," nor by "the Society as such."* But some feared

---

* A certain Colonization Society, "as such," may not have forcibly expelled the colored people, nor enacted the Fugitive Slave bill, nor advocated either of those

that the society would not be guided right, if its leaders refused to be guided by the Bible.

Sometime after this, similar conventions were held in different parts of the country, and as far west as Ohio, in this manner. Anti-slavery lecturers, agents of the Society, sustained by its funds, and holding the new views of civil government, of penal law, of church institutions, of the ministry, of the Sabbath, and of the Bible, had their appointments for anti-slavery conventions published in their papers, beforehand, under the head of "One hundred Anti-Slavery Conventions." How many of them were held we do not know, but in several places where these appointments were fulfilled, the same speakers, by previous arrangement, would remain in the same place long enough to hold another convention on one or more of the other topics. Thus the funds of the Anti-Slavery Society appeared to have sustained the lecturers on the other topics, and the notices of anti-slavery conventions drew together hearers for them. If this was not the promulgation of their other sentiments, "on the anti-slavery platform" and by "the society as such," it so nearly resembled it that many simple-minded people were so dull as to fail of perceiving the wide distinction.

It will be seen from all this, that causes remote from pro-slavery and anti-slavery, withdrew many anti-slavery Church members from the Anti-Slavery Society conducted by Mr. Garrison and his associates—whether wisely or unwisely, on either side, is not the point to be here examined. We are recording the facts.

And the facts being so, it might be inferred that this withdrawal of so many Church members from the American Anti-Slavery Society, (or this withholding them from joining it,) might possibly leave it in a position in which only a small

---

measures "on the Colonization platform." But when those who hated those measures found the leaders of the Colonization Society supporting them, they were led to identify them with the Colonization Society. We intimate no farther parallel in the cases than the natural workings of cause and effect on a community, when leaders in a great society give offense by their position.

proportion of its members, in comparison with those in the other society, would *have* any Church relations *to be* attended to, especially when it is remembered that some of the leading members neither held nor desired any such relations.

It is evident that in any equitable comparison of the two societies, in respect to their course on the Church question, the comparison must be instituted between the ministers and Church members and their supporters, in the two societies.

For some time after the division it was however claimed by the friends of Mr. Garrison that a considerable number of respectable orthodox ministers and Church members remained in their Society, whence they inferred that all *genuine* abolitionists among the "orthodox" would do so. We remember some prominent names of ministers and others who did remain. And they also remained, so far as we know, in their old ecclesiastical connections, without being spurned by Mr. Garrison as "apostates." We never heard of their making any attempts at new Anti-Slavery Church organizations. If any of them did afterwards break off their connection from "pro-slavery Churches," it must have been, we think, by discarding all Church organizations. As for the rest, they stood in the same pro-slavery ecclesiastical relations with the members of the "New" organization, who were and still are denounced as untrue, for standing in precisely the same ecclesiastical relations. The historical evidence seems not quite clear that the one deserved a welcome place in "the only" true Anti-Slavery Society, while the other came justly under the condemnation of seeking "the protection of pro-slavery Churches."

But, in addition to the "orthodox," there was probably a much greater number of ministers and Church members connected with the Old Society, who belonged to what are called "the liberal" denominations, as Universalists and Unitarians, to which we may add Swedenborgians, not to mention one branch of "the Friends." If to these we add numbers who, though not technically Church members, assisted in sustaining Churches, and ministers, and religious sects of some sort, we shall find, if we mistake not, a large body of men connected with the American Anti-Slavery Society, who were, and still are, supporters of the different religious sects. We should not be surprised to be assured that they still constitute a considerable majority of the members of the Society.

Except in the case of the "Friends," it will not probably be claimed that the sects just mentioned are more free from the imputation of being pro-slavery than the sects denominated "evangelical" or "orthodox." As being more recent in their origin, they may have extended less into the slave States than *some* others. They may be, from the same cause, less easily controlled by their leaders. There is the less excuse for their being pro-slavery, but, *as sects*, they nevertheless are so. Of few of their local congregations, perhaps, could it be said otherwise. As sects, (most commonly as local churches,) they have deprecated Anti-slavery agitation, denounced abolitionists, fostered prejudice against color, and by the votes of the majority of their members, maintained slavery at the ballot-box. This last item alone, according to Mr. Garrison, decides that they "do not deserve the name of abolitionists." Under this count, if not some of the others, we must reckon most of the "Friends." In the "Hicksite" connection, Charles Mariott and Isaac T. Hopper were "disowned" for their activity in Anti-slavery Societies. Yet abolitionists in the American Anti-Slavery Society continue in that religious connection.

Now then, if the American and Foreign Anti-Slavery Society deserves censure, for its support, through its membership, of pro-slavery Churches, the American Anti-Slavery Society, under the guidance and with the consent of Mr. Garrison, deserves the same censure, and for the same reason.

If a majority of its members sustain the old existing sects and Churches—then a majority of them sustain *pro-slavery* Churches, and the position of the Society is thus defined.

If, on the contrary, a majority of its members, including most of its leaders, support no *churches at all*, either pro-slavery or anti-slavery, most of them not desiring to support any, then their complaint against those who sustain pro-slavery Churches can have comparatively little weight, with those who understand their position in respect to *all* churches.

Still farther, if a controlling majority of the Society (in either case) regard it regular and proper to receive and retain members who support pro-slavery Churches, then it is evident that no Anti-Slavery Society in the country has a lower standard of membership, so far as the Church question is concerned, than the American Anti-Slavery Society.

And this is the fact of the case, as before shown. The Society has no rule for excluding such members, and Mr. Garrison says it ought to have none. Thus much for its exclusive claims.

But the comparison invited by those claims may not end here. Among those charged with having separated from Mr. Garrison, and re-organized "for the protection of pro-slavery churches," we have witnessed a long protracted and widely extended anti-slavery church agitation, resulting in a series of secessions, and ecclesiastical and missionary re-organizations, on an anti-slavery basis. It is natural and proper to inquire after similar manifestations among the members of "the only genuine anti-slavery society" that sets up such a high standard for its neighbors.

And where shall we look for any such manifestations? It has been seen that there has been, and still is, sufficient room and occasion for them. For the Society (on any estimate that can be made) contains not a few, ministers and others, connected with and sustaining pro-slavery church organizations.

On some occasions we see names of ministers enrolled among the active friends and members of the Society. Some of them we know as earnest and long-tried laborers in the cause, and under that banner. We thank and honor them for their anti-slavery labors. But what are the ecclesiastical connections that they sustain? To what churches are they ministering? Is there one of them, or are there many of them, that can claim connection with an anti-slavery church? With a church that, at best, can be more favorably described than a church tolerating an anti-slavery minister and a few anti-slavery members, who, on their part, agree to hold fellowship with pro-slavery members? Are the "liberal" churches often in advance of this position? Is "the negro pew" an abomination with them?

We ask these questions without being able, with confidence, to answer them, or being able to specify an exception to the position indicated by them. There may be exceptions. We think there cannot be many.

We have known of scores, and have heard of hundreds of ministers, who have conscientiously left their pro-slavery ecclesiastical connections to join or establish anti-slavery ones, or whose earnest anti-slavery preaching has driven them from their churches, or subjected them to persecutions from ecclesiastical bodies. Among all these we can recall to mind only two or three that we think may have been connected with the American Anti-Slavery Society since the division. It is to be presumed that there are others, but they are not probably very numerous in the comparison with those not belonging to the Society.*

There has been a division, in some form, among "Friends" in Indiana, on account of the slave question. A small secession from Hicksite Friends, perhaps partly on anti-slavery ground and partly for the enjoyment of local church independency, has taken place in Western New York. In both these movements there must have been members of the American Anti-Slavery Society. These are the only instances we know of, with exception, perhaps, of a few individuals, belonging to that Society, who may have come into the general church secession movement, the Wesleyan, the Independent, or the Presbyterian, originated by and almost wholly composed of

---

* Since writing the above paragraph, we have seen a statement of Rev. Theodore Parker, of Boston, that "*several* Unitarian clergyman have been driven from their parishes in consequence of opposing" "the Fugitive Slave bill." We think it very probable that some or all these may have been members of the American Anti-Slavery Society. There may be many others, of whom we have no knowledge.

Liberty party men, and of those who held what are called "evangelical" views in theology.

We have yet to hear of the first Convention among ministers and church members belonging to the "old" Society, to consider their pro-slavery church connections, and with a view to withdraw and re-organize, if a reformation could not be effected, or to form an Anti-Slavery Missionary Society.

In attending more than a hundred such conventions, we have met very few known to us as members of the old Society, or called Garrisonians. We can remember still fewer of them, if any, who seemed disposed to assist in gathering anti-slavery churches, or to favor anti-slavery missionary societies.

These are negative statements. They are presented for want of information of a positive character. We can tell less of what *has* been done, than of what (to our best knowledge) *has not*. The Liberator, the National Anti-Slavery Standard, and other journals of that class, and of the "liberal" sects, have not afforded us the information, as they should have done, if it were accounted important.

It is in the same category that we must place the inquiry, How many, in the old Society, have "come out" from their old church organizations, *without* organizing new ones? We have no means of forming an estimate. But we suppose they can by no means equal the numbers of those in the other Society and in the Liberty party who have left pro-slavery churches and organized anti-slavery ones. If the class of abolitionists who repudiate all church organizations are not far more numerous than those who repudiate compulsory civil governments, their number cannot be great. And it is known that a very considerable number of those among this class of abolitionists, who reject such civil governments, are church members and pastors of churches.

It is but proper and just to add, that if Garrisonian abolitionists who are church members, and who desire to sustain church relations, have not, to any extent, adopted the measure of separation and re-organization, as such large numbers of other abolitionists have done, they have nevertheless their own way of agitating the subject, and no one questions their right to mark out their own course of operations. We have noticed the preceding facts merely to correct the erroneous statement that Garrisonian abolitionists are exclusively or peculiarly free from the inconsistency of supporting pro-slavery churches. Though we should be glad to see Garrisonian Universalists and Unitarians adopting the more stringent and radical measure of separation and re-organization, of which other abolitionists have set them an example; yet we love to see them at work by voluntary associations of a denominational character, calculated to have a beneficial influence upon their ecclesiastical associates. We record the following specimen with much pleasure:

"Boston, May 27, 1852.

"At the session of the Universalist Moral Reform Society, to-day, composed in part of leading Universalist ministers, the following resolution was offered, and after discussion adopted without opposition:

"Resolved, That we view with deep concern the present attitude of our country on the subject of slavery, believing, as we do, that earnest efforts must be made for the overthrow of slavery, or the just judgment of God will descend on our land; and seeing, with great pain, a disposition on the part of those called statesmen to patch up Compromises, which merely hide, but cannot cure the evil, we feel called on, as Christians, to testify against the unrighteousness of slavery, and to request our fellow-Christians, of every sect, to unite with us in striving to break down that loathsome institution."—N. Y. Daily Tribune, May 28, 1852.

SWEDENBORGIANS, or members of the "New Jerusalem Church," who are abolitionists, have done effective service in the cause, though we have not heard of any movements among them for severing religious connection from those of the same faith at the South, who are slaveholders. And numbers of abolitionists of this sect, as among others before mentioned, belong to the American Anti-Slavery Society.

From the preceding statements it must not be inferred that Mr. Garrison has regarded it consistent for the members of the American Anti-Slavery Society to continue their support of pro-slavery churches. They would learn otherwise from his general writings on the subject, as well as by his rebukes of the " new organization." What was " apostacy" and " hypocrisy" in the one case, could not be less than " inconsistency" in the other, and as such it has been mildly censured.

The "Society as such"—whatever may have been the position of *some* of its officers and leading members—bore a similar testimony. Its resolutions and the speeches of its lecturers, were in conformity with the language of Mr. Garrison. The question remains whether either the Society or Mr. Garrison were consistent or just in making so wide a distinction between the supporters of pro-slavery churches in their own Society and those in other organizations—whether there has ever been, or now is, any proper foundation for their exclusive and extraordinary claims of being the only true and efficient Anti-Slavery Society, the only Society true on the Church question, while the other Society is to be spurned as "apostate" for its "protection of pro-slavery churches." With the preceding statements of facts before him, the reader will judge.

CHAPTER XLVII.

GENERAL ESTIMATE OF THE AMERICAN ANTI-SLAVERY SO-
CIETY AND ITS LABORS, SINCE 1840.

The Society an earnest and active organization against Slavery—Energy, talents, and
perseverance of its leading members—On some points censured unjustly—No
heresy in placing Justice and Liberty above human "compacts" and the "Union"
—Their orthodoxy to be distinguished from their heresy—Orthodox truth not to
be abjured because promulgated by them—Pro-slavery Churches and Ministers
responsible for their aberrations—An unfaithful church and ministry must reap the
fruits of their unfaithfulness.

DISMISSING the history of "*the only*" true Anti-Slavery Society in America, we will proceed to consider the American
Anti-Slavery Society as *an* earnest and active organization
against slavery. As such, the Society (apart from its connection
with other topics, its exclusive claims, and its injustice to the
Liberty party, and to the American and Foreign Anti-Slavery
Society,) deserves honorable mention. Except in the instances
and the particulars already recorded, and in which its exclusiveness betrayed it into unworthy associations, or its false
theories withheld it from efficient political action, it has been
doing good service to the cause of freedom. It has been *one*
among several organized instrumentalities which Divine Providence has been wielding against slavery. Its leading members have been persevering and untiring. They have exhibited a fixedness of purpose, and an energy of resolution
that challenge admiration. With talents of a high order, and
a hearty hatred of slavery, they have struck heavy blows
which have taken effect, in despite of all their mistakes. Of
William Lloyd Garrison it is needless to say much. As a
writer, he will take a high rank among the strong men of the

age. As a speaker, (though less celebrated in that department) he has a simple, sober, solemn, straightforward earnestness that, with many minds, outweighs all charms of elocution
and arts of rhetoric. Wendell Phillips is among the most
accomplished orators of New England. Charles C. Burleigh
is little behind him. In power and tact he may sometimes go
beyond him. Edmund Quincy has a sharp pen and a ready
tongue. When he is fortunate enough to direct his artillery
against the enemies instead of the friends of the cause he
loves, he is sure to do good execution. It would be pleasant
to mention others, and to draw parallels between them and
such men as Gerrit Smith, Beriah Green, Alvan Stewart,
Myron Holly, Samuel R. Ward, William L. Chaplin, and
others, of whose powers we might have spoken in our account of the Liberty party—and Frederick Douglass and
others who have made a trial of both platforms. But we
must desist. Prominent abolitionists have been too much
villified and too much praised. They have too much lauded
and too much censured each other. Mutual flattery (so seem-
ingly necessary in the ranks of the persecuted) erects hierar-
chies, and these occasion schisms, and beget confusion of
tongues. Divine Providence, in the meantime, vindicates its
own claims to superintendency, and to the glory of every reformatory achievement.

On some points, respecting which Mr. Garrison has been
much censured, even among earnest friends of freedom, we
cannot, ourselves, join in the censure.

Though he may have erred in swerving from our own "orthodox" estimate of the divine inspiration of the Hebrew
prophets, we cannot see that he has sinned against orthodoxy
or the Bible, in repeating and in emulating the terrible denunciations of the Hebrew prophets and of Christ himself,
against a priesthood that strikes hands with oppressors.

Though (misled by the Federal Courts, the Federal Administration, and the prevailing public sentiment,) he may have
misinterpreted the Federal Constitution, as we think he has,
we cannot say that he has erred in declaring such a constitu-

tion, *as thus construed,* in the strong language of scripture, "a covenant with death and an agreement with hell." We should feel that we were putting the Constitution above the Bible, and above humanity, and above conscience, and above God, should we say otherwise.

He may have erred in demanding, in unqualified terms, the immediate dissolution of the Union, as a means of abolishing slavery. It may be that the Union furnishes the best occasions of agitation, the best means of abolition, with a constitution rightly construed. It may be that our relations to the slave forbid our virtual desertion of him, by a dissolution of the Union. Here are things to be considered—perhaps to be determined by coming events.

So far as Mr. Garrison and his associates, and their Society, have contributed to bring this great problem before the people, so far as they have rebuked the servility that dares not "calculate the value of the Union" at a time when the Federal Administration declares the price to be the surrendry of freedom ; so far as they have helped to expose the atheism that, in the name of religion, and from the pulpit, and by perversions of the Bible, has attempted to deify "the Union" in rivalry and in defiance of Jehovah, bidding us disobey Him by obeying the Fugitive Slave Bill, (by which it is said the Union is to be preserved) so far they have deserved well of their country, have done service to the cause of freedom, and have vindicated the first principles of true religion.

It is said that some of these men have become infidels. If it be so, under what influences have they become such ? If it be so, what is the proper cure of such infidelity ? If it be so, shall we repudiate the truths they utter because they have uttered them ? Should a Witherspoon withhold or blot his signature from the Declaration of "self-evident truths" because penned by a Jefferson, or vindicated by a Paine ? *That* must be a sickly, purblind, faint-hearted, half-doubting "orthodoxy," that fails to recognize or fears to honor the essentials of its own creed, on the lips of a heretic. Heresy lives upon its retained orthodox truths. It drives its most brisk and most lucrative business upon its capital of such truths, cast aside, forgotten, or unwisely relinquished to them, by the conservators of orthodoxy. The orthodox should learn to discriminate between the truths and the heresies of Mr. Garrison and his associates. There is no cause for alarm. Their orthodoxy will stand. Their heresy will fall. The Bible is in no danger. The Sabbath, the Church, the Ministry, the ordinances of the gospel, and civil government, are in no danger. They will come brighter out of the ordeal. They will be better understood and more highly valued, though those who have perverted them may be less esteemed, and held mainly responsible for their temporary disrepute.

When the Church and the Ministry—Heaven's own appointed organizations for promoting human progress—lag behind the necessities of a progressive age: when they do worse than this, and throw themselves as blocks under the chariot wheels of the Messiah, they must, of necessity, reap the fruits of their unfaithfulness. The work of human redemption, if "orthodoxy" be true, must go on, in despite of them, and, though it crushes them. The sublime truths of their creed, in their practical form and extended social applications, must find utterance. And "if these hold their peace, the stones of the street" shall find tongues for the task, and "shall cry out." We hold it altogether and distinctively "orthodox" to say this, and to add that "the eternal purpose of redeeming mercy" requires the chastisement, and, if not thus reclaimed, the removal of a church and ministry that cannot "open their mouths for the dumb." The true Church and the true ministry, not yet extinct, (and already striking deep their roots) will survive.

The same principle applies to abolitionists themselves. If untrue to their task, they must be displaced by a better instructed and more stable generation, who will come after them.

CHAPTER XLVIII.

REVIEW OF THESE DIVISIONS AND THEIR RESULTS.

No body of abolitionists free from mistakes—Natural tendencies to division in an age of progress—Overruling Providence of God—Good resulting from evil—Tendency of the division to reach, with anti-slavery truth, opposite classes—An antidote to the fear of centralized power—Democratic phase of development—No escape from abolitionism of *some* phase—Objection against anti-slavery "*measures*" becoming obsolete—A sufficient *variety* of measures to accommodate all earnest men—The main question, now, a question of measures—This question rapidly narrowing down—A great work to complete the enterprise, but an impossibility to undo what has been done—An indefinite amount of half-developed abolitionism needing guidance.

IN a review of the divisions among abolitionists, we may see much to rebuke human pride, and much to exalt the superintending Providence of God—much to admonish, and much to inspire hope.

No class or organization of abolitionists can claim exemption from mistakes. None of them have been free from blemishes, inconsistencies and defects. To pretend it, would be to give evidence of partiality. If one of the societies has crippled itself by erratic progression—if the other has failed to make all the progress that the crisis demanded—if the Liberty party, except a handful, lost its hold upon its "one idea" by refusing to apply it in every direction, in the Church and in the State—if Liberty League men attempted a political organization without the previous preparation and selection of materials—if the Free Soil party sought strength and comprehensiveness in numbers, rather than in a high tone of political ethics—there was nothing, in all this, out of the ordinary range of diversity, in times of revolution and progress. Whenever a mighty truth, vitalized and glowing, is thrown into a community, like a mass of melted metal into running water, the commotion tends to separate the disturbing force into shapeless fragments. But the principle of unity is not thus destroyed. The parts may afterwards come together and adhere. The unity of truth, will, in the end, be revealed.

Under the good Providence of God, the dissensions among abolitionists, however humiliating to them, and however mischievous in some respects, have been over-ruled, in other respects, for good. Abolitionism, before the division, was a powerful elixir, in the phial of one anti-slavery organization, corked up tight, and carried about for exhibition. By the division, the phial was broken and the contents spilled over the whole surface of society, where it has been working as a leaven, ever since, till the mass is beginning to upheave.

Had abolitionists remained in one compact and well defined body, with a uniform mode of action, the whole mass of the community might not have been as soon reached, and as thoroughly permeated by them. A powerful and growing National Anti-Slavery Society, before the division, with its affiliated auxiliaries, and its central committee, was already exciting jealousy against the cause. It was matter of fear among its friends. Dr. Channing was not alone nor singular in this feeling. It was more operative in the mass of the community than most abolitionists supposed. Had the Society remained united, and had its means and operations increased, this element of resistance would have soon made itself felt. By the division of the great National Society, and the consequent dwarfing of the two rival divisions, this central point of dreaded influence was rendered almost invisible. Divided further and cut up by state, county, city, town, and village Committees, the work was going on, everywhere, without presenting an alarming concentration of power anywhere. The democratic principle in abolitionism underwent a democratic phase of development, and propagated itself as Christianity did, when the disciples, that were scattered abroad, went everywhere, preaching the word. Yet the element of power, whatever it might be, in the principle of episcopal supervision, had its medium left, for those who chose to employ it, and they could look for this, to the centre of spiritual unity most congenial to them. The division between Rome and Byzantium did not destroy Christianity or the Church.

With the rise of the distinct political party, there were manifested other phases of development. There was moral suasion abolitionism and political abolitionism. Then came also Church Reform abolitionism—Missionary abolitionism—Methodist, Baptist, Congregational, Independent, and Presbyterian abolitionism. Politicians were careful to supply a Whig and a Democratic abolitionism. No man knew where to go to escape the infection. He could not elude it in the religious sect, nor in the political party. If he cried out against abolitionism as " bigotry, priestcraft, and Puritanism," behold! there was the most rampant abolitionism, at his elbow, railing lustily against "bigotry, priestcraft, Puritanism, and pro-slaveryism"—placing them all in a row. If one sought, in view of this, to disparage abolitionism as heretical and infidel, behold! the gathering of an anti-slavery conference and prayer meeting met his vision, and on his ears came quotations from Isaiah, and Hopkins, and Wesley, and Edwards. The simpleton who had but just learned from his political editor to curse the abolitionists, was puzzled to find the same editor, or perhaps his Congressional candidate, professing to be as good an abolitionist as anybody.

And when earnest and even acrimonious debates among abolitionists themselves, arrested the attention of the community, displacing the controversy between abolitionists and their opposers, a remarkable effect was produced. Thousands now heard or read them for the first time. The issue before the public mind was soon changed. The question was *not* whether slavery *ought* to be abolished, nor *when* it should be—but, by what methods and motives should the people be brought up to the work. The previous question was taken for granted, as not needing debate. A community could not long listen to able debates on such a question without unconsciously sliding into the idea that, in *some* way, the work was

to be done. The " duty and safety of immediate and unconditional emancipation" had been settled, among intelligent men,
by "the West India experiment."

With all the varied modes of proposed and attempted anti-
slavery agitation and action, arising out of these divisions and
discussions, another objection against abolitionists has become
obsolete—"We do not approve of your measures!"—" *Which*
of them?" might be the inquiry in return. It might be difficult to conceive of any measure, which some class of professed abolitionists have not proposed. And no small progress
has been made towards a disposal of the rival claims thus
presented.

It may be a great work to carry the enterprise forward to
its consummation. But it would be a more difficult, nay, an
impossible task, to carry it back to where it stood twenty
years ago. There is an indefinite amount of latent, half-
developed, incipient abolitionism, in the country, needing
guidance, that is not now embraced under any existing organization. It seems waiting for the solution of a few
remaining problems, of which we shall treat in the next
chapter.

CHAPTER XLIX.

DIFFERENT VIEWS OF THE CONSTITUTION, AND OF THE LEGALITY OF SLAVERY.

Vital importance of the questions—Alternatives presented by them—Almost the only questions remaining to be settled—All public business involving the Slave question must be transacted on *some* theory of the Constitution, and of the legality of slavery—All anti-slavery action must assume some theory—Three General Views of the Constitution—1. The ultra Southern or Calhoun theory—2. The prevalent theory of the "Compromises"—3. The construction in favor of Liberty—Previous question of the *legality* of slavery—References to the preceding history—Principles of interpretation—Features of the Constitution—Comparison of the three theories—Results.

THE relation of the Federal Constitution to slavery must have an important bearing on the Slavery Question in America.

Whether an oath to support the Constitution be an oath to support slavery, is only one of the many important questions involved in it.

If the Constitution requires us to support slavery, then the Constitution requires us to overthrow our own liberties, to declare war against universal humanity, to rebel against God, and incur his displeasure.

If the Constitution does this, it is to be either amended, or overthrown. Otherwise, we must submit to be slaves to one portion of our fellow-men, while assisting to make slaves of another portion of them—we must throw off our allegiance to God, for the sake of maintaining allegiance to the deadly enemy of ourselves, our country, and our race.

But if the Constitution be in favor of liberty and against slavery, then it is our duty and interest to wield it for the overthrow of slavery and the redemption of our country from the heel of the slave power.

In the one case, our line of march out of Egyptian bondage lies through the bloody sea of Revolution—in the other, through the legitimate action of our government, as already organized.

In the progress of the slave question we have now arrived at that point at which the legality and the constitutionality of slavery are among the very few questions that remain to be settled.

The inherent criminality of slavery and of slaveholding, their utter repugnance to natural justice, to Christianity, to the law of nature, to the law of God, to the principles of democracy, to the liberties of the country—no longer present questions for serious discussion among the great body of intelligent citizens in the non-slaveholding States. Here and there a superannuated ecclesiastic (who has, perhaps, a son at the South, or in a college seeking southern patronage) may thumb over his Polyglot, and pretend to find a justification of slavery. But nobody believes him. His disclaimers and self-contradictions prove that he does not—even in his dotage —believe it himself! His friends shield him from the impending avalanche of public scorn, by saying—" Do let him alone—he can do no mischief—he is not worth minding !"

The settlement of this question has disposed of nearly all the one hundred and one objections that, fifteen years ago, were confidently urged against the doctrines and measures of abolitionists. In most circles, it would be difficult to broach them without being voted *a bore*.

Almost the only remaining exceptions are those that cluster around the supposed " guaranties" or " compromises of the Constitution "—the " legal rights "—the " vested immunities " of the slaveholder. Take away these, and what is there left?

The Church question, as well as the political question, as it lies in many minds, hinges just here. The Church must not speak against Cæsar—must be in subjection to " the powers *that be*"—and that, too, without stopping to inquire *whether* they *be*, or *be not!* It may be said that the Church—with her

Bible in her hand—should be able to shape her course, without asking leave of the Federal Constitution. So she should. And in so doing, she should throw out principles before the world that would help us to definitions of "law" and "legal rights"—and enable us to expound Constitutions correctly, in the light of UNIVERSAL LAW.

It is difficult to dispose of any public business in Congress, without involving the slave question, and this involves at once the question whether the Constitution sustains slavery—whether the slaveholder has a legal right to the slave.

If there is to be any political action against Slavery, under the Federal Constitution, we must know what the Constitution authorizes us to do in the premises. If it "guaranties" Slavery, then it forbids us to do any thing. If it has "compromises," they limit our action, and we must know their extent. The questions between Liberty Party (as it was) Free Soil Party, Liberty League or present Liberty Party, turn, very much, on the Constitutional question.

If the Federal Judiciary is to be used, either as a weapon of assault upon the Slave Power, or as a shield of defense against its attacks, the relation of the Federal Constitution to Slavery and the legality of Slavery become the main points at issue before the Courts.

In every view of the task before us, the assumed legality and constitutionality of Slavery thrust themselves directly across our path, and come under our eye. It is one cheering sign that we have traveled nearly the whole distance from our starting-place to the citadel, when so many familiar objects and once formidable obstacles are distanced, and only two or three remain to be grappled with.—Overcome these, and the work is accomplished.

The various views of the Constitution may perhaps be classified under three general heads:

First, the idea that slavery, as a lawful and legitimate interest, in common with other rightful and legitimate interests, is entitled to the protection of the Federal Government, and that it was established for that end.

Second, the idea that, although slavery is not a rightful and legitimate interest, its existence is nevertheless tolerated, and the Government restricted from abolishing it.

Third, the idea that slavery is an usurpation, an abuse *from the beginning*, that it has *never* been legalized, that the *Constitution* has not legalized it, that consequently it *remains* illegal, and that it is the duty of the Federal Government (as well as of the State Governments), in all its branches (legislative, judicial, and executive) to *treat* it as illegal, and repress it, as any other crime or treason against the essential rights of the people is to be repressed.

The limits of the present work will not allow of extended statements of the arguments upon which these conflicting theories are based. The most we can attempt is to give such a view of them as may enable the reader to *see what they are*, that he may examine them at his leisure.

I. The theory first mentioned is the generally prevalent one at the South. With the more ultra (the Calhoun or Carolinian school) it would seem that slavery is considered not only a legitimate interest, but the leading, the paramount one, to which all other interests are to give way. The mildest, the most modified form in which this theory is held (or which is now represented by the Southern delegation in Congress), is that of the border States, and is expounded by Henry Clay. It may indeed *talk* of "compromises," but by Mr. Clay's own showing, they give everything to slavery, and nothing to freedom. The Fugitive Slave bill, defended by Mr. Clay, consists with the mildest type of this theory.

This theory must repose, for its basis, either upon the idea of Calhoun, McDuffie, Dew, &c., that slavery is originally and abstractly right, and that it presents the best state of society; or else upon the idea of Mr. Clay, that "what the law makes property *is* property"—and that "two hundred years of negro slavery have sanctioned and sanctified" the principle of property in man. To complete the argument, it must be shown either that the Constitution affirms the original right of slavery, or the principle that involves it; or that it sanctions and ratifies the process of its previous legality, as described by Mr. Clay.

II. The second theory of the Constitution, that of a "compromise" between slavery and freedom, is so vague and unsettled, and is exhibited in such a variety of shades, that it is difficult to exhibit it with much accuracy or order. The field is wide enough to accommodate Daniel Webster and Moses Stuart, on the one hand, shaking hands with Henry Clay over the Fugitive Slave bill; and the leaders of the Free Soil party, on the other, intent on "divorcing the Federal Government from the support of slavery." However wide the chasm between these opposing parties may be, they occupy the common platform of the supposed "compromises of the Constitution," which have never been satisfactorily agreed upon among those who recognize them.

Whether the alleged "*guaranties*" of slavery should be assigned a place under this theory or the preceding one, may seem, at first view, uncertain. Perhaps they belong to both. The "compromises," as Mr. Webster understands them, involve a pretty strong "guaranty." And the compromises of those who would only "divorce the Federal Government from the support of slavery," would seem to involve a guaranty that—within a certain enclosure, however bounded— slavery should not be disturbed. It is not known to the writer that any of the friends of liberty who admit the doctrine of the "compromises," and who yet adhere to the Constitution, would do otherwise than "guaranty" to the slaveholder the right of seizing his fugitive slave in the *free States*, provided that, by jury trial and other safeguards, due security be given that none *except* fugitives from slavery be given up. This is a "guaranty" that introduces slavery, in one of its most odious features, into the free States themselves. Being done by the conceded structure of the Federal Government, and assented to by the free States, it seems not to consist with the idea of divorcing either the State or Federal Government from slavery. The magnitude of this "guaranty" is seen in the contrast between the position of the Canadas, where the fugitive is safe, and that of a non-slaveholding State of this Union, permitting, under any modifications, the re-capture of a fugitive from slavery.

Southern statesmen, of the school of Mr. Clay, understand "the compromises of the Constitution" to involve ample "guaranties." Those of the ultra Southern school, have sometimes, we believe, disclaimed the proper idea of "guaranties," because they conceived that it might involve the principle that the right of slaveholding was held under the Federal Constitution, instead of the original and absolute State sovereignty claimed by them. They hold the Federal Government to be the servant and instrument of the slave power, rather than its conservator and patron.

The most that any of the friends of freedom, admitting "the compromises" and yet adhering to the Constitution, could claim under their theory, would perhaps be included in the following:

1. The rightful power of Congress to abolish slavery in the Federal District and Territories, including the idea that it is unconstitutional in the Federal District.

2. The right to prevent the extension of slavery into new territories, and to refuse the admission of new slave States.

3. The right to abolish the slave trade between the States, coastwise and inland.

4. The right of the free States to insist on the jury trial and other securities, to prevent *others* than fugitives from slavery from being seized and carried back as slaves.

5. The restriction of the right to reclaim fugitives to the citizens of the original thirteen States now permitting slavery, to the exclusion of the right of citizens of the Federal District, Territories, and States, admitted since the adoption of the present Constitution.

6. The right to refuse recognizing the legality of slavery in Louisiana and Florida where, by the terms of the Treaty of Cession, the "*inhabitants*" were to be received as "*citizens of the United States.*"

7. The right of the Federal Government to decline the use

of its diplomacy, and other powers, in sustaining directly or indirectly the institution of slavery, except in the case of suppressing a servile insurrection—another "guaranty" included in the theory of "compromise"—if we rightly understand that theory.

We are not aware that any abolitionists conceding the "compromises of the Constitution"—yet adhering to their allegiance to it—have claimed anything more under it than this.

This leaves to the several slave states the right of maintaining slavery as long as they please, and yet remaining in the Union, with the right, under modifications, of making the free states their hunting-ground for fugitives.

It concedes the duty of the Federal Government and the free states under the Constitution, to assist in putting down insurrections of slaves.

"The Almighty has no attributes," says Mr. Jefferson, "that could take sides with us in such a contest." Those who construe the Constitution as including such "compromises" and "guaranties," and who nevertheless cling to the Constitution and cry out against anti-slavery disunionists, would do well to "count the cost" of such a contest, which seems to be hastening, and ask themselves whether their forces are sufficient for the emergency, and whether it be quite *safe and prudent* to occupy their present position. Is it consistent for abolitionists—is it right or wise for the non-slaveholding states to adhere to the "Union" and to the "Constitution" as thus construed?

III. We come to consider the construction of the Constitution that acknowledges none of these compromises and guaranties.

This construction is connected with another idea lying back of it, of the illegality of slavery before the Constitution was formed.

It is not commonly supposed that the Constitution *originated* legal slavery, or gave to it a validity that it did not possess before. The two theories already described, do not include such an idea. The most ultra of the Southern expositors of the Constitution would most indignantly spurn it. And the theory of "compromises" supposes *something* already existing to be the subject of the compromise.

If there was no legal slavery *to be* compromised or guarantied, then the Constitution, however constructed or designed, must have failed to effect any such purpose. Had the document recognized a certain river as a Western boundary, which was afterwards found to be only an imaginary one, so much of the instrument must have become obsolete and inoperative of course. Just so of any supposed State laws or institutions which should afterwards be found to have had no valid existence.*

The very first question, then, (as some contend) is, whether there was any *legal* slavery in the States when the Constitution was formed. The *fact* of existing slavery is not to be confounded with its *legality*. The fact may have been only an usurpation, an abuse, a crime. The *fact* of slavery existed a long time in England, and the courts held it to be legal. But it was afterwards ascertained and decided that it *never had* been.†

It has lately come to light that leading lawyers and statesmen at the South are apprehensive that *their* slavery is *not legal*—that they are unwilling to have its legality tested in the courts—that this is the ground of their objection to a jury trial for fugitives—and that the Senate of the United States, participating in the same apprehensions, has shaped its legislation accordingly.‡

---

* This *principle* is thus recognized by the Supreme Court of the United States. "A legislative act, founded upon a mistaken opinion of what was law, does not change the actual state of the law, as to pre-existing cases."—1 *Cranch* 1, *Peters' Digest*, 578.

† See Chapter VI.

‡ In the recent debate in the U. S. Senate, on the Fugitive Slave bill, Mr. Mason, of Virginia, objected to the amendment of Mr. Dayton, providing for a jury trial, because, said he:

"*A trial by jury necessarily carries with it a trial of the whole right, and* A TRIAL

If slavery was legal at the time when the Federal Constitution was adopted, when did it become so? When, how, where, and by whom, was it legalized?

It will not be said, except by the ultra slave party, that the right to hold slaves is a natural right, the same as the right to own oxen. If it were a natural right, then it would be inherent in all men, black and white, slaves and slaveholders. The confusion consequent on this assumption, sets it aside.

The best writers on common law affirm that slavery is so evidently contrary to the paramount law of nature, to justice, to fundamental morality, and the law of God, that it never

---

OF THE RIGHT TO SERVICE *will be gone into,* according to all the forms of the Court, in determining upon *any other* fact."

And where would be the hardship of this? Why *should not* the investigation take place? Mr. Mason had told the Senate why.

"Then, again, it is proposed, as a part of the proof to be adduced at the hearing, after the fugitive has been re-captured, that *evidence shall be brought by the claimant to show that slavery is established in the State from which the fugitive has absconded.* Now this very thing, in a recent case in the city of New York, was required by one of the judges of that State, which case attracted the attention of the authorities of Maryland, and against which they protested," &c. "In that case the State judge went so far as to say that the only mode of proving it was by reference to the Statute book. Such proof is required in the senator's amendment; and if he means by this *that proof shall be brought that slavery is established by existing laws, it is impossible to comply with the requisition,* FOR NO SUCH LAW CAN BE PRODUCED, I apprehend, IN ANY OF THE SLAVE STATES. I am not aware that there is A SINGLE STATE in which the institution is established by *positive law.* On a former occasion, and on a different topic, it was my duty to attempt to show to the Senate that no such law was necessary for its establishment; CERTAINLY NONE COULD BE FOUND, and none was required in any of the States of the Union."—*Liberator,* Sept. 6, 1850, copied from the *Washington Union.*

The pretense set up by Mr. Mason, that slavery can exist under common law, without positive law, is contradicted by numerous legal authorities and decisions. Once, at least, in Louisiana, it was decided that a slave carried to Europe by his master, and returned, was free, because he had been carried out of the jurisdiction of the local laws of Louisiana.

Mr. Mason enlarged on the topic, and said distinctly that he was not willing to trust the question with the Courts in the free States. *The Senate evidently partook of his apprehensions.* They struck out Mr. Dayton's amendment, *lest it should be decided by the Courts that there was no legal slavery in the Southern States.* Hence, also, the peculiar structure of the infamous Fugitive Slave bill, allowing no litigation, no counter evidence, no *habeas corpus,* no "due process of law." If slavery were believed by the slaveholders to be legal, would they fear to have the question litigated in the Courts?

was, and never can be, legalized; and that no legislature nor monarch possesses the power to make it legal.

But, not to insist on this, and coming down to the lowest possible standard of legality that can be made intelligible, that of positive enactment, we inquire—When was American slavery made legal, and by whom?

Was it legalized by the permit of Queen Elizabeth to John Hawkins to import negroes with their own free consent? By the laws regulating the trade to Africa, but forbidding the forcible or fraudulent exportation of the natives?

Was it legalized by the British Constitution? By the common law of England? By the Colonial Charters which restricted colonial legislation to a conformity with English common law? The very reverse of all this was the fact.

Was it legalized by the acts of the colonial legislatures in direct opposition to the Colonial Charters? Or, *are* there any such enactments (whether authorized by the Colonial Charters or otherwise) creating the relation of slavery? If neither Mr. Mason nor Mr. Bayly could find any,—and if the whole course of southern argument concerning slavery in Mexico, unites in the testimony that there are none—may we not pretty confidently conclude that none exist?*

Does not the decision of Lord Mansfield, in the Somerset case, (in 1772,) as clearly prove that there was, *then*, no legal slavery in these Colonies as that there was none in England?

---

* During the long debates of 1850, in Congress, it was abundantly insisted by Mr. Bayly, Mr. Mason and others, that slaves might now be *held legally* in the territory conquered from Mexico, though there were no positive enactments there creating the relation. And in proof they urged the fact that slavery existed in our own slave States without any such enactments. The lame link of the logic was the monstrous assumption that slavery can LEGALLY exist *without positive law*, that is, on the foundation of natural right! After his return home to Virginia, Mr. Bayly addressed a circular to his constituents repeating the argument, in which he said:

" *We all know that slavery* was introduced into *the British Colonies of America* IN ABSENCE OF A STATUTE, and solely under the protection of the *Common law!*"

How the " Common law" protects slavery may be seen in the decision of Lord Mansfield in the case of Somerset. But these Southern testimonies to the fact that slavery in America was introduced in the absence of any statute creating it, may be considered conclusive on that point, and so of the whole question.

If, as he decided, slavery could not legally exist in England, without positive enactment, how could it exist in these Colonies, under the same jurisdiction, and the same common law, without positive enactment?

Was Slavery legalized by the Declaration of American Independence, proclaiming that "all men are created equal?" On the contrary, if there *had* been any legal slavery then existing in the Colonies, would not that unanimous Declaration of the Colonies have abolished it?

Was Slavery legalized by the *State Constitutions* that were framed soon after the Declaration of Independence, and repeating the same "self-evident truths"—in Maryland and other Southern States—the same as in Massachusetts, where the Courts decided that the Declaration had ABOLISHED Slavery? "*Not one of them* RECOGNIZED *Slavery*," nor was there, in one of them, any authority conferred on the legislature to enslave any body.

Was Slavery legalized by the Articles of Confederation, that made no manner of allusion to it?

If Slavery was not legalized, at that time, how has it become legal, since?

And if not *legal*, how can it have become *Constitutional?* Can it be Constitutional while it is illegal?

The Constitution must either receive a strict literal construction, or else it must be construed by the living spirit that pervades the instrument—its main design, its grand leading object.

If construed strictly and literally, what becomes of its "compromises" and "guaranties?" What does it say of "slavery"—of "slaves"—or of "property in man?" What could be made, even of the clause concerning "persons held to service and labor," from whom service is "due?" Is there any proper description of a slave in this clause? Can any thing be "due" from one who cannot even make a contract? The laws of the Slave States do not admit that a slave is "a person." How then can a "person held to service and labor" be a slave?

"Where rights are infringed, where fundamental principles are over-thrown, where the general system of laws is departed from, the legislative intention must be expressed with IRRESISTIBLE CLEARNESS to induce a Court of Justice to suppose a design to effect such objects."—*Rule of Supreme Court of U. S.*, case United States *vs.* Fisher and others. 2 *Cranch*, 390.

The "intentions of the framers" (on this principle of strict construction) is to be gathered only by their words, strictly construed. Besides, "the framers," as they are called, did not *make* the Constitution. They only *proposed* it. They sat with closed doors, and the people knew their *intentions* only by their *words*. It was the *people*, and not the *Convention*, that formed the Constitution, when they ratified it.*

If, departing from this "strict construction," we take the spirit, grand design, scope, aim, and object, of the Constitution, then we are driven to the Preamble, to the Declaration of Independence, and to the literature of the times, the writings of Jefferson, the doings of Franklin, the Ordinance of 1787, &c., for a rule of interpretation. How much the claims of legal and Constitutional Slavery would gain by this process, the reader of the preceding history can inquire at his leisure.

The Declaration of Independence, by-the-by, has never been repealed. It was, for years, the *only* Constitutional law of the United States, and it is *no less* Constitutional law *now*, *than formerly*. Can there be either legal or Constitutional Slavery under such an organic law? Were the Courts in Massachusetts mistaken, when they decided otherwise?

"The first act of our nation (the Declaration of Independence) being a solemn recognition of the liberty and equality of ALL MEN, and that the rights of liberty and happiness are inalienable—was the corner-stone of our Confederacy, and is ABOVE ALL CONSTITUTIONS and all laws."—*John C. Spencer.*

"The United States shall guaranty to every State in the Union a republican form of government."—*Constitution*, Art. IV., Sect. 4.

This is the only "*guaranty*" in the Constitution.

---

* The language of the Constitution shows this—"We, the people of the United States," "do ordain," &c.

and judgment rendered in open court.* What slave has ever been " deprived of liberty " in this manner ?

Admitting that the *original* Constitution contained all the "compromises and guaranties " ever attributed to it, does not this amendment sweep them all away by prohibiting Slavery?

Slaves are either citizens of the United States or they are aliens. If citizens, they are entitled to the rights and privileges of citizens, and these are incompatible with slavery. But if they are aliens, then Congress, under the Constitution, has the power, by naturalization, to *make* them citizens of the United States.

" Congress shall have power to establish a uniform system of naturalization."—*Constitution, Art. I. Sec. 3, Clause 4.*

If the States may reduce to slavery the citizens of the Uni-

---

* JUDGE STORY, in his Commentaries upon the Constitution of the United States, speaking of this provision of the instrument, says :

" The other part of the clause is but an enlargement of the language of Magna Charta, ' *nec super eum ibimus, nec super eum mittimus, nisi per legale judicium parium suorum vel per legem terræ*'—*neither will we pass upon him or condemn him, but by the lawful judgment of his peers, or by the law of the land.* LORD COKE says that the latter words, '*per legem terræ,*' (by the law of the land,) mean ' by due process of law,' that is, *due presentment or indictment,* and being brought in, to answer thereto by ' due process of law.' So that this clause, in effect, affirms THE RIGHT OF TRIAL, according to process and proceedings of Common law."

It has, however, been alleged that " Due process of law is process *sanctioned* by law ; as when a juror is fined by the Court for non-attendance, a spectator imprisoned for contempt, land and money taken by tax-gatherers and assessors, *and a soldier shot by order of a court martial.*"

It may be answered that customs and usages do not define or create law, but should be controlled by it. Convenience, in small matters, or where gross injustice is seldom perpetrated, may tolerate customs not strictly legal. More than this : Gross outrages, in open defiance of Magna Charta and Common law, have been continued through entire generations. Thus, in England, the practice of home impressment of merchant seamen for the Royal Navy—is an admitted violation of English law. Martial law supersedes Civil law, and hence the latter cannot be defined by the former. The Turkish Sultan's order to behead any subject in his dominions may be " sanctioned by law," and the same Congress and President that enacted the Fugitive Slave bill might have conferred upon the President the prerogatives of the Turkish Sultan, with as much reason, or equal legality. The people insisted upon this provision in " Amendment V." for the purpose of securing themselves against such aggressions. But the precaution would avail them nothing, if the *inhibition* is to be construed in conformity with *usages,* instead of bringing usages to the test of inhibitions. If this Amendment cannot protect us from slavery, what can it protect us from ? Or, of what use is it ?

And what is a republican form of government?

" The true foundation of republican government is the equal ⫫
EVERY CITIZEN in his person and property, and in their managei
Jefferson.

Mr. Jefferson repeatedly speaks of the slaves as " ci
— *Vide Notes on Virginia.*

" No State shall pass any bill of ATTAINDER," or "laws impai
obligation of CONTRACTS," or " grant any title of NOBILITY." The
of each State shall be entitled to all the privileges and immunities
zens *in* the several States."

How can Slavery in the States consist with all these
bitions, describing its essential arrangements?

Does Congress possess the powers requisite to enfoi
such salutary restrictions upon the States?

" Congress shall have power to make all laws which shall be nec
and proper for carrying into execution the foregoing powers, and al
powers vested by this Constitution in the government of the United ⫫
or in any department or officer thereof."—*Art.* 1, *Sec.* 8, *Clause* 17.

" This Constitution, and the laws of the United States which sh
made in pursuance thereof, and all treaties made, or which shall be
under authority of the United States, shall be the SUPREME LAW of
LAND, and the judges in every State shall be bound thereby, ANYTHI
THE CONSTITUTION OR LAWS OF ANY STATE TO THE CONTRARY NOT⫫
STANDING."—*Art.* VI., 2.

If this be not sufficient to make the Constitution, *as o
nally framed and adopted*, an Anti-slavery document, ther
an amendment, afterwards added, which seems sufficie
decisive. Let it be borne in mind that an amendment
Constitution, like a codicil to a will, overrules, controls, ⫫
annuls whatever in the original instrument is inconsist
with it.

" No person shall be deprived of life, LIBERTY, or property, without
process of law."—*Amendments* V.

" Due process of law " includes an indictment, trial by jui

ted States, then they may abolish the Federal Government, by depriving it of citizens. If a State may reduce *one* man, under its jurisdiction, to slavery, it may reduce *all* men, under its jurisdiction, to slavery, and thus nullify the Federal Government, so far as the State is concerned.

The organization of the Militia, of the Postoffice, and Mail, and Custom-house establishments, pertain, under the Constitution, to the Federal Government, in its various departments. In these, as in all other Federal appointments, no restriction is imposed, as to *the persons to be* organized, appointed, or employed. If the States, by their legislation, (or if the *citizens* of the States, sustained by State authority,) may *designate the persons* whom the Federal Government may *not* organize as militia, nor employ in the Custom-house, Postoffice, and Mail establishments, or appoint to other offices, then the States, (or *citizens* of the States) may cripple if not abrogate the power and action of the National Government, in all these departments! If they may withdraw one-*fourth* or one-*half* of the people from their allegiance and subjection to the Federal Government, and from their liability or capacity for military or other services under it, then they can withdraw three-fourths, nine-tenths, or ninety-nine one-hundredths, in the same manner, and thus overthrow the national government* in those States.

Such is an outline of the theory that denies the "compromises and guaranties of the Constitution" in favor of slavery.

Those who hold this view, believe that every slave in the United States is entitled to the privileges of the writ of *habeas corpus*, and to the benefits of a judicial decision in favor of his freedom. And they believe that Congress and the Federal

---

* In many of the slave States the militia is of no value to the Federal Government from this cause, and is scarcely sufficient to keep *the slaves* in subjection in time of peace! Has the Federal Government no remedy for this? John Quincy Adams declared a truth in Congress when he said that "the war power of Congress" was adequate to the abolition of slavery. But is this the *whole* of the truth? If Congress *has* any "war power," may it not put the country in a state of preparation for defense?

Executive are bound to provide a judiciary that will discharge its duty, and to protect, (if need be) the Courts, in the efficient exercise of their functions.

COMPARISON OF THESE THREE THEORIES.

The first of these three theories of the Constitution seems to present the friends of freedom with no alternatives but subjection or revolution.

It is too late in the day to dream of liberty for a portion of a people, while another portion of them are enslaved.

Whatever may be said of "moral suasion," it cannot be expected that slavery will soon cease in this country, by voluntary emancipation, on the part of all the slaveholders, or by the great body of them, while they are upheld by the action of legislative and judicial authorities.

Nor can it be thought probable that the authorities of the Slave States will voluntarily change their position, in advance of their constituents, or while the Federal Government maintains (as at present) a position very nearly in accordance with the constitutional exposition now under review.

It is equally evident that the friends of liberty, so far as they shall receive this exposition of the Constitution as the correct one, can have no hope of any political remedy short of disunion or revolution.

Nor does it seem clear that a dissolution of the Union between the free and slave states, without such a general *revolution* as should render *disunion* unnecessary, would do anything, directly, for the cause of freedom, further than to relieve the people of the North, and detach them from the support of the foul system. In such a case there would indeed be a still more appalling prospect than there now is, of that terrible remedy, at which humanity herself shudders, unless, by timely repentance, the South should avert the catastrophe. Yet the principle of self-preservation, not less than the duty of clearing their own skirts from the guilt of oppression, should impel all who fear God and love liberty, to choose, in sadness, the only alternative presented to them. To remain voluntarily in the Union under a Constitution that must be thus construed, would be suicidal to ourselves, as well as treason against mankind, and rebellion against God. Common prudence, to say nothing of principle or of piety, should suffice to direct, in so clear a case, a people not judicially blinded. The "patriotism" and the "chivalry" the "honor" and the "magnanimity," the "sagacity" and the "prudence," that could deliberately plant themselves against every "attribute of the Almighty" and every instinct of human nature, in opposition to every principle of law, and every element of social order—and all this under the hallucination or the pretext of being "*orderly and law abiding*"—invite epithets which we are unwilling to use.

The Second Theory—that of "the Compromises," may appear less appalling, at the first view, but it deserves serious inquiry, whether this be anything more than mere appearance.

An attempted "compromise" between moral right and moral wrong, results always in the ascendency of the wrong, and the overthrow of the right. In matters of civil government, in politics, in legislation, in jurisprudence, this is as certain as everywhere else. The history of the Slavery Question in America furnishes lamentable illustrations in point.

The friends of liberty, adhering to the Constitution, yet admitting its "compromises" and promising to fulfil them, admit themselves to be compromising with moral wrong! What, then, becomes of their moral power? If anything deserving the name of success, is to come from the pursuit of this policy, the historical verification of it is yet future. The annals of the world, thus far, have not supplied it. The good Providence of God, in spite of their moral obliquities and compromises, may have delivered an oppressed people. But their compromises have never deserved the credit of it, any more than the idolatries of the Hebrews deserved the credit (as they stupidly fancied,) of having supplied them with bread.*

---

* Jeremiah 44 : 17.

If the "Compromises of the Constitution" include—as they are commonly understood to do—the "guaranty" of the right (under any restrictions) to reclaim fugitives, and the "guaranty" of northern assistance in suppressing a servile insurrection, then the construction that concedes these compromises, concedes the most atrocious as well as the most effective supports of slavery included in that ultra southern construction which the masses at the North so indignantly repudiate! Conceding these, very little more would be lost, in a moral view, by conceding the whole.

And the extent of the moral concession is the measure of the political. An effort in Congress, or at the ballot box, against slavery, conceding the sacredness of the "compromises" with the "guaranties" involved in them, is an effort for victory after having relinquished the main controversy in debate. Such efforts must be abortive of course. By the operation of well known laws of human nature, they generally fail of reaching the low point at which they are aimed. And if reached, only an unsightly limb is displaced, leaving the root untouched and the trunk less offensive and, perhaps, the more thrifty and vigorous for the pruning.

That local and partial victories may sometimes be gained by this policy is not denied. But a wise general knows that a local victory may be purchased too dearly. A political victory is always purchased too dearly, when it is done by a moral compromise, or when the victor, by his compromises, concessions, and pledges, ties up his own hands, and forecloses himself from doing his main work.

If it be true that the Constitution *does* contain the "compromises and the guaranties" commonly attributed to it, even at the North, then the main battle between slavery and freedom cannot be fought under it, nor otherwise than by a repudiation of it, or the proposal of such amendments as would be regarded as revolutionary to insist upon. And however wise it might be for the friends of liberty to avail themselves of any advantages thrown in their way, to weaken or cripple the slave power, (taking care to avoid giving sanction to any constitutional compromises) it would be evidently impolitic for them to expend their main strength and wear out their energies and dishearten their successors in labors which, if never so successful, would leave their main work unaccomplished and even unattempted, after all. The longer the friends of liberty busy themselves in this manner, the more firmly will they establish the precedents which, sooner or later, must be rebelled against and spurned.

If the Constitution be a "compromise" between slavery and freedom, then those who adhere to it, giving their assent to the compromise, yet expecting to "secure the blessings of liberty" under it for "themselves and their posterity," are only acting over again the folly of their fathers, but with less excuse, after having witnessed the experiment of the last sixty years. The fruits borne by the tree of "compromise" thus far, should warn us to expect nothing better of it in future.

Of the third theory of the Constitution, that which repudiates all its supposed "compromises" and "guaranties," it is sufficient to say that, *if it be correct*, it is all that could be desired as a basis of political action. In the words of another,

"Those who believe that slavery is unconstitutional, are the only persons who propose to abolish it. They are the only ones who claim to have the power to abolish it. Were the whole North to become abolitionists, they would still be unable to touch the chain of a single slave so long as they should concede that slavery is constitutional.

"The mass of men will insist on seeing that a thing CAN be done, before they will leave the care of other interests to assist in doing it. Hence the slow progress of all political movements based on the admission that slavery is constitutional."—SPOONER.

These considerations should not tempt us to put an unwarrantable construction upon our great national document. But they should induce a candid and thorough investigation of the matter, with a determination to take the position demanded by a discovery of the truth of the case. If the organic structure of our National Government does indeed cast us at the feet of the Slave Power, bound hand and foot, let us know the worst of the case, and in view of it, determine whether we have strength and resolution to cut the cords, or whether we will submit to be slaves, with our posterity, forever. But if we have in our hands the Charter of Freedom, let us understand its use, and the responsibilities with which it invests us.

CHAPTER L.

THE SLAVERY QUESTION IN AMERICA AND THE CRISIS.—WHAT SHALL BE DONE?

Effects of Compromise thus far—Shall it be repeated or continued?—The Slavery question, as it now stands, stated—Must be settled by the Church and in the State—A question for *the people*—Can the Church and the State be reformed, and wielded against Slavery?—Questions behind these—What is the organic structure of the Church and the State?—Fallacy of the idea that the Federal Government can occupy a neutral position, divorced from the support of Slavery, yet not wielded effectively against it—Fallacy of the idea that the *peculiar structure* of our Government relieves us from responsibility in respect to Slavery— Suggestions concerning what might be done. *The Church*—Can the politics of a people, or of reformers, rise above the level of their religion?—Responsibility of the Church and its constituent members.

THE reader of the preceding pages will, by this time, comprehend something of the magnitude of the pending slave question in America. Though, primarily a question concerning the liberation of the enslaved, there is involved in it the question of the civil and political liberties of the nominally free. And the crisis seems to have arrived, predicted by one of our prominent statesmen, at the time our present Federal Government was organized.

" I have no hope that the stream of general liberty will forever flow unpolluted through the mire of partial bondage, or that they who have been habituated to lord it over others, will not, in time, become base enough to let others lord it over them. If they resist, it will be the struggle of pride and selfishness, not of principle."—*Wm. Pinckney's Speech in the House of Delegates of Maryland*, 1789.

The North has submitted to compromise on this subject till one of her own Senators taunts her with infidelity to her constitutional engagements, if she insists upon any *legal securities* for the personal liberties of her own citizens, the Senator him-self not excepted;* and he exhorts her to conquer her "pre-judices" in favor of LIBERTY, for the sake of preserving "*the Union!*"

The Slavery Question in America is the question whether liberty shall be relinquished, for the security of slavery, or whether slavery shall be overthrown by the spirit of liberty. It is the question whether civil government shall secure and protect human rights, or whether a ruthless despotism, dis-placing civil government, (properly so called,) shall be wielded by the Slave Power for the subjugation of freemen. It is the question whether the Federal Government shall be thus wielded by a petty oligarchy of one or two hundred thousand slaveholders, over twenty millions of people, (one person con-trolling one hundred,) or whether it shall be a republican government, amenable to all, and administered for the pro-tection of all.

It is, moreover, the question whether Christianity in Ame-rica shall overthrow heathenism in America, or be corrupted or exterminated by it. It is the question whether the Bible, the Church, and the ministry, shall suffer the disgrace of being accounted the handmaids of oppression, or whether they shall be hailed as the deliverers of the captives, proclaiming the Jubilee of the Lord.

This great question is to be decided, mainly, by the concur-rent action of the two great social institutions of the country, the Church, and the State, the ecclesiastical and the civil power.

It is for THE PEOPLE of the non-slaveholding States to say whether these two social institutions shall be redeemed from the foul embraces of slavery, and wielded for their hea-ven-appointed ends, or whether they shall remain, as at pre-sent, in the hands of their enemies.

And the question whether THE PEOPLE will ever effect

---

* If Daniel Webster were seized as a slave, he could have no *legal* redress under the Fugitive Slave bill, to which he urges our submission.

the requisite reformation in the Church and the State will depend, very much, on the ideas they attach to the *organic structure* of the Church and the State, and of their own participancy in the administration of their powers.

If the Christians of the Free States conceive of the Church as a mysterious something in the hands of the priesthood, above the control of the brotherhood, to which they are religiously bound to adhere, right or wrong, and go wherever it carries them, it is evident that there will be no reformation in the Church.

If the *voting* citizens of the Free States conceive of "the Government" as something distinct from themselves, and to which their allegiance is unchangeably due,—if they conceive of the "Constitution" as pledged to "compromises and guaranties" in favor of slavery, and yet hold themselves bound to fulfil those unrighteous compromises and guaranties, thus elevating the Constitution (though conceded to be criminal) 'above all that is called God or is worshiped'—it is evident that there will be no reformation in the State.

And if there is to be no reformation in the Church or the State, it is evident that the sun of American liberty must go down in darkness, or be subjected to a baptism in blood.

The questions arise—"What shall be done?" And "How shall it be done?"

The field may be narrowed, by first inquiring, in the light of the past, and on the stand-point of the present, what ought *not* to be done?

May we not clearly detect some of the main fallacies by which the friends of liberty have been misled, and by which they have been foiled?

Expedients—compromises—gradualisms—postponements—ameliorations—have not the friends of liberty been baffled sufficiently by confiding implicitly in these?

Attempts to overthrow slavery merely by localizing it—preventing its expansion—prohibiting the slave trade, or the transportation of slaves—excluding slavery from new territories—Is it not time to understand that the work of *abolishing* slavery is not to be accomplished by directing attention and effort chiefly to enterprises of this character?

Every opportunity should, doubtless, be improved, to do, in the use of proper measures, whatever presents itself to be done in these directions. But is it wise, as a matter of policy —can it be right, as a question of morals, to postpone or compromise the *main* question of *abolishing slavery*, in order to concentrate strength or enlist numbers, on points of secondary importance? May we consent to one crime for the sake of repressing another? Especially where the greater is indulged that the smaller may be abolished? May we—or may civil government—consent to regulate and thus authorize crime, for the purpose of curtailing its mischiefs?

Is there not a fallacy in the idea that the Federal Government can be divorced from the *support* of slavery without being enlisted *against* it, and *so* enlisted as to treat it as illegal and criminal?

How shall the Federal Government be thus divorced without so exerting itself as to overthrow slavery?

In organizing the militia, in providing for the collection of the revenue, (whether through the Custom-house or by direct taxation,) in providing for the transportation of the mails, in appointing Post-masters and all other officers of Government, in making enlistments for the army and navy, in naturalizing or in refusing to naturalize all classes of aliens—in making or refusing to make compensation to slaveholders for losses of slaves in the public service—must not the Federal Government take sides, one way or the other, on the question of the legality of slavery, and of the right of the slaves to their freedom? And is not the practical decision of the Federal Government, in either case, entirely conclusive of the whole matter? Could the condition of slavery be continued, if the practice of the Federal Government did not acknowledge its legality? And while acknowledging its legality, can it be said to be divorced from the support of slavery? *Can* it be neutral on that question, taking neither the one side or the other?   Or, (however constituted,) has it any moral right to be neutral, were it possible to be so?

Can the United States "guaranty to every State in this Union a republican form of Government" without abolishing Slavery?   Or can they neglect doing this without sustaining and being responsible for Slavery?

Is there not a fallacy in the common assumption (admitted by some of the friends of liberty) that the peculiar structure of our Federal Government, with its delegated powers, its limitations, and the reserved rights of the States, relieves the Government and the people of the free States from their responsibilities in respect to slavery *in the slave States*, provided the Federal Government prohibits it elsewhere?

Can man by his skill, or by his want of skill, in the con struction of a Constitution of Government, relieve that Government of the essential duties devolving upon *all* civil Governments, in the nature of things, in the nature of civil Government itself, and by the express appointment of God?

Can there be a civil Government not invested with the prerogative, and charged with the duty, of protecting human rights, and "executing justice between a man and his neighbor?"   If the Bible or the Declaration of Independence be resorted to for an answer, will they not unitedly respond, *No?* Is there any intelligible theory of civil Government that will not require at its hands thus much?   Does the Constitution of the United States, in its Preamble, *profess less?*   Can it claim the allegiance, or deserve the confidence of the people, if it *performs* less?   Have the Sovereign People, who are responsible for the organic structure as well as for the administration of their Government, any moral right to construct and continue an arrangement which *contemplates* less?   Or can their liberties be secure under such an arrangement?

The Federal Constitution either describes a civil Government or it does not.*   If it does, then that Government is

---

* The great problem of 1787, was the formation of a National *Government* that should supersede the " *Confederation*," and yet leave the *State* Governments in

charged with the *essential duties* of a civil Government. If it does *not* describe a civil Government, then we are *without* any National Government. We are reduced to a mere confederacy of the States. And if we have only a confederacy of States, may it not be dissolved at the option of either of the parties? And are not the free States doubly inexcusable for remaining perpetually in a confederacy that binds them to restore fugitives and assist in suppressing an insurrection of slaves?*

The questions again recur—What shall be done? And how shall it be done?

Without presuming to dogmatize, may we adventure a few farther suggestions?

The powers of the Federal Government—the legality or the illegality of slavery—its agreement or disagreement with the Constitution—present, evidently, questions of the first magnitude, and of vital importance in disposing of the problem—"What shall be done?"

Would it not be the part of wisdom, in the friends of liberty, in the first place, to examine thoroughly, and settle definitely, those questions? Can there be efficient and united political action against slavery till these questions are settled?

If it be found that slavery is illegal, that it is unconstitutional, that the Federal Government has full power over it, the course of action becomes plain. The Federal Courts, sus-

---

existence. After great labor, the paradox was supposed to have been solved. It remains to be seen whether the exultation was not premature. The common theory, according to one of its ablest advocates, concedes that "the Federal Government is not *a complete* civil Government"—but nevertheless adds: "It does not follow, and it is not true, that we have *no* National Government."

The concession then is, that we have only, *in part*, a National Government;—an *incomplete* Government. And the precise point in respect to which its incompleteness is conceded, is the point in which it fails "to secure the blessings of liberty" for "the people of the United States"—and some other little things of that character. A somewhat significant incompleteness—like the performance of "the Drama of Hamlet, with the part of Hamlet left out, by particular request."

* United States' forces were used to suppress the Southampton insurrection of negroes in 1831. And, more recently, they were employed to capture a company of Maryland slaves who were marching off in pursuit of freedom. And every execution of the Fugitive Slave bill is of the same character.

tained by Congress and the Executive, are adequate to administer the remedy. And the power is in the hands of the non-slaveholding States.

The investigation itself might be carried on, to a great extent, by bringing questions, involving the rights of slaves and others, for decision before the Federal Courts, after the example, and with the untiring perseverance of Granville Sharp.

If it comes to be conceded, after a fair investigation, that the Constitution is in favor of slavery, and that it provides no remedy against it, the question returns again—"What shall be done?"

An amendment of the Constitution might be proposed, but it requires the concurrence of two-thirds of the States to carry it into effect. There seems little prospect of a remedy in that direction.

Revolution or disunion appear to be the only direct political remedies that remain. We may conceive of a revolution that should carry with it, or bring after it, the abolition of slavery. The ground of disunion would then be removed. But the mind shudders at the thought of a revolution by violence.

Might there not be effected a peaceful separation between the slaveholding and non-slaveholding States? If a majority of the citizens at the North and at the South should concur, why could it not be done? If the Constitution makes no provision for such an emergency, does it follow that an Administration is bound to enforce union by the sword? Or why might not a vote of two-thirds of the States (Northern and Southern) unite in an amendment of the Constitution for that end?

The Union has its value, but is it anything more than that of a means to an end? And what is that end worth, if it does not include justice, security, freedom, and the right to obey God?

What other alternative remains but the *loss* of the main objects for which the independence of the country was achieved, and the Constitution and the Union established?

Is anything to be gained by clinging to that which was designed to be the *means*, if, in doing it, we must *sacrifice the
end?*

The general and public discussion of these questions would
arrest the attention of all classes of citizens, Northern and
Southern. If any other alternatives exist, they would be
discovered and presented. If the South loved slavery more
than the Union, she would say so. If the North loved the
Union more than liberty, she would say so. The issue would
be presented to every citizen, and it would have to be met at
the ballot-box and decided. If the friends of liberty at the
North were left in the minority, and the country ruined under
the avenging hand of divine justice, they would then be clear
of the blame. But would the impartial award of posterity
acquit them, if, adhering to a Constitution of "compromises
and guaranties" in favor of slavery, they bartered their principles, their consciences, and the liberties of their country, for
an idolized "union" with oppressors? Would it acquit the
entire generation of northern citizens who, in full view of the
crisis, should consign themselves and their posterity to the
degradation of vassalage? Would not their own Declaration
of self-evident truths, and of the rights and responsibilities
of freemen, upbraid them?

"We hold these truths to be self-evident, that ALL MEN are created equal;
that they are endowed by their Creator with certain inalienable rights, among
which are life, liberty, and the pursuit of happiness. That, TO SECURE
THESE RIGHTS, GOVERNMENTS ARE INSTITUTED AMONG MEN, deriving their
just powers from the consent of the governed; THAT WHENEVER ANY FORM
OF GOVERNMENT BECOMES DESTRUCTIVE OF THESE ENDS, IT IS THE RIGHT
OF THE PEOPLE TO ALTER OR ABOLISH IT, and to institute a new Government, laying its foundation on such principles, and organizing its powers
in such form, as to them shall seem most likely to effect their safety and
happiness."

Whatever sentiments may mould the answers that shall be
returned to these questions, *the issue to be met and disposed of*
will remain, if we mistake not, very much as has been stated
already. That is to say: If the Constitution contains the
"compromises and guaranties" commonly attributed to it;

if there is no prospect of its being amended, or of the speedy abolition of slavery by the States; then the free States have no remedy but revolution or disunion. Rejecting this, they must continue to participate in the guilt of slavery, and to suffer its evils, including their own subjugation by the petty oligarchy of slaveholders. But if the Constitution contains no such "compromises and guaranties," then they hold the power in their own hands, and may readily redeem themselves and their country if they will, by the proper administration of the Government.

This view presents what we understand to be *the Slavery Question in America*, so far as the prospect of its abolition by the action of civil government and the political action of the North are concerned.

The Church question is still more comprehensive, more vital, and more solemn. If the religion of a country controls, of necessity, the legislation of a country, then the Church, to the full extent to which it moulds or represents the religion of a country, or is able to mould and represent it, is responsible for its political morality. Is it not so?

Can the political morality of a people rise higher than the religion of a people? Can the political morality of reformers rise higher than the religion of reformers? Can their religion rise, permanently, above the religion of the Churches to which they adhere, and of the ministry in whom they confide for religious instruction? Will they be likely to demand of their political parties, or to secure in the management and direction of them a higher tone of morality than they require of their Churches, or than actually prevails in them? Does the history of past experiments warrant the belief that it can be so? Or would it be honorable to religion and religious institutions, to believe that such could be the fact, and that the world should be the teacher and exemplar of the Church?

The friends of liberty and pure religion, to a considerable extent, have been impressed with the importance of so directing their missionary efforts, as to send none but a pure and liberty loving religion to the heathen. They are contributing their missionary benefactions accordingly. But, are they, in all cases, sustaining and confiding in no other religion at home? Are they supporting by their contributions and by their approving attendance, no teachers of religion whom they would not entrust with the work of carrying the gospel to the heathen? Is it probable that they will consistently and perseveringly insist on exporting a better religion for the acceptance of the heathen abroad, than that which they cherish and confide in for their own edification and the benefit of their families at home? Or, will it be practicable, to any extent, or for any great length of time, to find missionaries of liberty to send abroad, who have been nurtured in the bosom of pro-slavery churches at home,—churches that remain in fellowship with oppressors, that cherish the arrangements of caste, that set up in the sanctuary of prayer the negro pew, and that welcome to their communion, without remonstrance, the politicians whose votes rivet the fetters of the slave?

Or is it to be believed that the peaceful abolition of slavery is to be effected by the labors of those who thus contribute to its support? Can the consciences of the slaveholders be thus reached? Can Christian missionaries be sustained in the slave States to build up churches there, having no fellowship with slavery (for this is one department of our "Free Missions") by Christians at the North who remain in churches holding fellowship with slavery, and who support its apologists as religious teachers? Are the Choctaw and Cherokee Churches to be disowned and abandoned for retaining slaveholders in their communion, by Christians at the North remaining in ecclesiastical connection with the slaveholders of the South, or holding fraternal ecclesiastical correspondence with them? Or, retaining religious fellowship with the corrupt and servile northern demagogues who are more guilty than the slaveholders themselves? Can the friends of liberty and pure religion continue long to remonstrate with churches in fellowship with slavery, while their *own* position is such as has been described? If the churches have any responsibility in respect to slavery, is there no inconsistency in the position of such? What *is* the responsibility of churches aside from the responsibilities of the *members* of which the Church is composed? And how can the individual member urge upon the body a position which he is not ready to take himself?

"There is no power *out* of the Church," says Albert Barnes, "that could sustain slavery an hour, if it were not sustained *in* it." To this we may add the inquiry—How long would slavery be sustained in the churches, if churches sustaining slavery were not sustained by those who complain of their position? If a solemn responsibility rests on the churches, is it not shared by those *in* the churches whose support contributes to sustain them?

There is still another view of the subject. Suppose it were *not true* that the position of the Church could decide the fate of American slavery? Suppose it were certain that, notwithstanding all that could be done by the Church and ministry to overthrow slavery, it would still live and thrive? Would the responsibility of the Church and ministry then cease? Would it not still be their duty to bear their testimony in the midst of a perverse people? How else can they shine as lights in the world? How else can they honor their God and their Savior? How else can they teach and exemplify pure religion? How else can they call sinners to repentance? How else can they preserve a pure seed to survive the terrible overthrow of the nation, or its dark night of disgrace and servility, to take root and germinate and bear fruit in a more genial age?

And if it be true, as we have seen, that the Federal Government cannot hold a neutral position—that it cannot be divorced from the *support* of slavery without being wielded *against* it—if its peculiar structure—fashioned by man—cannot absolve it nor its constituent members from the responsibilities involved in the very nature of the institution itself—how much more clearly and more forcibly do these considerations apply to *the Church*, established by Christ himself, to be "the salt of the earth," and "the light of the world!"

GENERAL INDEX.

[N. B. (1.) The leading topics of this Book, arranged in Chapters, will be found in the Contents, at the beginning. (2.) *Minor* topics, in their order, are inserted under the several head titles, at the beginning of each Chapter. (3.) This General Index, though containing many names, does not include, however, (except in a few special cases,) the names of the numerous authorities that will be found cited in the body of the work.]

Aberdeen, Lord, 66.
Abolition of Slave Trade, by Great Britain, 63.
Abolition of Slave Trade, by U. S., 63
  of Slavery in England, 42.
  British Colonies, 353, 372.
  British E. Indies, 376.
  Massachusetts, 109–11.
  New Hampshire, 109–13.
  Vermont, 110.
  Pennsylvania, 112.
  Rhode Island, 113.
  New York, 114–17.
  Connecticut, 114.
  New Jersey, 115.
  Mexico, 272, 370.
  Roman Empire, Europe, Chili, Buenos Ayres, Guadaloupe, Cape of Good Hope, 370.
Abolition Societies, (last century) 95.
Abolition movement, U. S., present, 382.
Abolitionists, their principles and measures, 398.
Abolitionists, opposition against, 399.
  slanders against, 402.
  mobs against, 404.
  attempted legal suppression of, 408.
  elements of division among, 447.
  agreement in 1833, 452.
  changes afterwards, 454.
  divisions in 1840, 457.

" Abstractionists," 448.
Adams, John, Pres., 73, 241.
Adams, Samuel, 73.
Adams, John Q., 78, 219, 245, 257, 263, 274, 327, 386, 423, 577.
Adams, Chas. F., 478.
Addison, Joseph, 29.
Alabama—African Slave Trade, 262.
  demand on Gov. of N. Y., 413.
Albany Convention, (1839,) 470, 513.
  (1840,) 471.
Alliance of Aristocracies, Northern and Southern, 334.
Althorpe, Lord, 371.
Alton Observer, 459 : mob and murder, *ib.*
American Slavery, features of, 377.
American Revolution, period of, 69.
  Board, (Missions) 202, 220.
  Home Mission Society, 209.
  Bible Society, 210.
  Tract Society, 213.
  Sunday School Union, 215.
  Missionary Association, 491.
  Anti-Slavery So. (See below.)
  and For. A. S. So. (See below.)
Amistad, captives, 255.
Anderson, Robt. N., Rev., 411.
Andover Theo. Sem., 171.
Andros, Thos. Rev., 393.
Andrews, Mr. Rev., (Ct.) 176,
Andrews, Prof., 250.
Antigua and Bermuda, 372.

Anti-Slavery efforts, last century, 91.
Anti-Slavery Society, American, organized, 396. Protest. to Pres., U. S., 417.—Division, (in 1840,) 457, 462. —New measures, 464. General Policy, 511.— Political course, 517.—Second Revolution, (in 1844,) 526.—Difficulties, N. P. Rogers, 529. Politics, (since 1844) 532.—Course on Church action, 541.—General Estimate, 555.
Anti-Slavery So. American and Foreign : Origin, 463.—Course, 510.
Anti-Slavery So., Massachusetts, 457–62, 512, 517, 519, 521, 535.
Arcade, N. Y. Convention, (1840) 471.
Aristocracy, U. S., 126.—N. and S., 334.
Articles of Confederation, 78, 573.
Aves, Thos., (slave case) 111.
Aydellotte, B. P., Dr., 492.

Bacon, Leonard, Dr., 177, 206, 207.
Bank, U. S., 327, 336.
Bankruptcy, (of 1837) 249, (of 1811) 328.
Baltimore Conference, Meth., 148.
Baptists in England, 60, 61, 190, 493, 494.
Baptists in America, (in 1778) 108.
Position, 183, 493.—Missions Cherokees, 187.
Am. and For. Bible So., 189, 507.
Publication So., 190.
Anti-Slavery agitation, 493. Baptist Magazine, 493.
Va. Asso., 495.
Triennial Con., 187, 493–8, 501–2.
Board For. Missions, 187.—Acting Board, 187, 500.
Home Mission So., 188, 499, 502, 506.
Missionary Union, 503–5.
Southern Convention, 501–2.
Tennessee Missionary So. 501.
Alabama Conv. and letter, 500.
Anti-Slavery Conv., 496.— Free Mission Society, 499, 507.
Barnes, Albert, Rev., 217.
Barrow, David, Eld., 108.
Barbour, Gov., 80.
Barbadoes, 372.
Baxter, Richard, 27.
Baxter, G. A., Dr., 155.
Bayard, James A., 97.
Bayly, Mr., of Va., 572.
Beattie, James, 30.
Beecher, Geo., Rev., 157.
Beman, N. S. S., Dr., 154.
Benezet, Anthony, 36, 41.
Benton, T. H., Hon., 274, 316, 318.

Berkeley, Wm., Sir, 20, 229.
Bermuda, (abolition) 372.
Bethune, Dr., 346.
Bible Society, American, 210.
American and Foreign, 189, 507.
Convention concerning, 546–7.
Bibles for Slaves, 210–12.
Binney, J. G., Eld., 505.
Birney, James G., 395, 406, 471.
Blackstone, Judge, 28, 48, 49, 52.
Blanchard, Jona., Pres., 202, 492.
Blennerhasset, 284.
Bloodhounds, 270.
Boggs, Ex-Gov. Miss., 310, 313.
Bolles, Lucius, Dr., 186.
Bond, Dr., 147.
Bond, Mr., (Boston) 419.
Book Concern, Methodist, 149.
Boston Recorder, 182.
Boothe, Abraham, 30, 60, 61.
Boyd, A. H. H., Rev., 164.
Boynton, C. B., Rev., 492.
Bradley, Dr. (Plymouth), 419.
Breckenridge, R. J. Dr., 343.
Brisbane, Dr., 395, 432.
Brissot, 31.
British Colonial Slavery, 6, 7.
Constitution, 51.
Orders in Council, 329.
Brodnax, Mr. (Va.) 343.
Brooklyn Report, Am. Board, 204–6.
Brougham, Henry, M.P., 355, 358–9, 362.
Brown, Abel, Eld., 189.
Brown, Moses, 398.
Buffon, 31.
Buffalo Conv. nom. J. P. Hale, 478.
M. Van Buren, 478.
Burchell, Mr., Missionary W. I., 366.
Burke, Edmund, 28.
Burleigh, C. C., 463, 556.
Burling, Wm., 40.
Burnett, P. H., of Mo., 310.
Burr, Aaron, Col., 280, 284.
Burr, James E., 440.
Bushyhead, Mr., Missionary, 187.
"Business men," 448.
Butler, Bishop, 28.
Buxton, Thomas Fowell, 67, 365, 358, 363, 369, 371.

Calhoun, John C., 279, 301–2, 316, 321, 330, 334, 336, 339, 420–1.
California, acquisition of, 287 ; possession, 300 ; results, 306 ; effort to exclude slavery, 307 ; counter efforts, 308 ; Southern plan, 310 ; Provisional Government, 312 ; Constitution vs. Slavery, 313.

Camden (S. C.) Bap. Church, 496.
Campbellites, 198.
Campbell, Alexander, 198.
Canning, Mr., 257, 358.
Canterbury Colored School, 393, 436.
Capres, W. Dr., 148.
Caribs or Charibs, 4.
Cartwright (slave case), 50.
Cass, Gen., 308, 316.
Cemeteries, col'd people excluded, 200.
Census of Slaves, 114–16.
"Centralization," 466.
Channing, W. E. Dr., 419, 560.
Chaplin, Wm. L., 246, 445, 463, 556.
Charles V., 5, 16.
Charleston (S. C.) Asso. Bap., 184.
    rifling the mails, 411.
Chase, Samuel, Judge, 96.
Chase, S. P., Hon., 225.
Chatham-St. Chapel, mob, 395.
Cheivres, 5, 16.
Cherokees, Bap. Miss., 187.
    Am. Board, 203.
Cherokees and Georgia, 389.
Choctaw, Missions, 203.
Chronicle, Vermont, 182.
Christian Mirror, 182.
    Spectator, 181.
    Observer, 205.
    Anti-Slavery Conv., 488, 492.
Churchman, The, 192.
Churches, American, decline, 135.
    position, 143–219.
Church—Why scrutinized, 449.
Church and Ministry, responsibilities, 558.
Church Anti-Slavery agitation, 487.
    re-organization, 489 ; Independ-
        ent, 489 ; Wesleyan, 489 ;
        Free Presb., 490 ; Friends,
        491.
Cinquez (African), 255.
Clarence, Duke of, 59.
Clarkson, Thomas, 56–9, 66, 355–60, 393,
    444.
Clarke, Adam, Dr., 29.
Clarkson, Matthew, Gen., 95.
Clay, Henry, 140, 244, 251, 264–6, 274–6,
    301, 316–17, 342–7, 380–3, 566.
Clayton, J. M., 310.
Clergy, opposition of, 402, 411–12, 425.
"Clerical Appeal," 459, 542.
Clinton Hall, meeting, mob, 395.
Coke, Lord, 145.
Colonies, Am., dates settlement, 19 ; As-
    sociation of, 1774, 72.
Colonies, Brit., abolition, 353, 372, 376.
Colonial Charters, 18 ; Slavery, 10.
    Legislation, 18.

Colonization Society, 139, 200, 341, 393,
    401, 407, 412, 425–6.
    Meeting, 155.
Colombian Republic, 259, 266.
Columbian College, 503.
Colver, Nathl. Eld., 505–6.
Common Law, English, 18, 63.
Commerce, Northern, 323.
Compromise, Missouri, 240–3, 383.
    of 1850, 317.
Comet, Brig, 252.
Connecticut, Colonial Slavery, 11–13.
    action (in 1774), 75.
    Abol. Soc. (1790), 96.
    Gen. Asso. (Cong.), 173, 429–30.
    "black laws," 340.
Cone, Spencer H. Eld., 187–9, 190, 493,
    497–9, 503–4.
Continental Congress, 78–9.
Congress, U. S., 100, 224–6, 234–5, 240,
    251, 268, 278, 299, 301, 331.
Congress of Panama, 259.
Congregationalists, position, 163 ; pub-
    lications, 181.
    Associations, 173, 429–30.
Constitution U. S. (see Federal Const.)
Convention Cong. Min., Mass., 180.
Convention (of 1789), 83.
Conventions, Chr. A. S., 488–92.
    (See names of places.)
Conspiracy, Burr's, 280.
Corporation and Test Acts, 361.
Cotton Gin, Whitney's, 132.
Cotton manufacture, effects, 134, 334.
    speculation, 249.
Court of King's Bench, 18.
"Covenanters," 198, 533.
Cox, S. H. Dr., 157.
Cox and Hoby, 494.
Crandall, Prudence, 393, 436.
Crandall, Reuben, Dr., 246, 437.
Cranch, Wm. Judge, 234, 244–5.
Creole, Brig, 254.
Crummel, Alex., 193.
Cuba, Slavery and U. S. Gov't, 265.
Cumberland Presbyterians, 198.
Curtiss, H. Rev., 160.
Curtis, Geo., of R. I., 419.

Dana, Rev. Dr., 172.
Davenport, Mr. (Missionary), 187.
Dayton, Mr. (U. S. Senate), 570.
Decline of Liberty, 118.
Declaration of Independence, original
    draft, 16.
    Constitutional law, 574.
Delaware (in 1785), 109–10.
Democratic party, 128, 131.

De Witt, Rev. Dr., 208.
Dew, Prof., 250.
Derby, Rev. Dr., 350.
D'Wolf, James, 11.
Dickey and Beman, Messrs., Presb. Gen.
    Assembly, 154.
Diplomacy, U. S., 252, 263.
Direct Taxes, 322.
" Disciples," 198.
District of Columbia, (see Federal Dist.)
Doane, Bishop, 193.
Dominicans, 27.
Dorr, T. W., 420.
" Dough-faces," origin of, 384.
Douglass, Frederick, 556.
Douglas, Mr. (Ill.), 308.
Dove, James, Eld., 61.
Drayton and Sayres, 246, 446.
Dresser, Amos, 105, 438.
Drummond, Rev. Mr., 145.
" Due process of law," 575–6.
Duffield, Rev. Dr., 157.
Dunbar, Duncan, Eld., 188.
Dundas, Mr. (M. P.), 64.
Dutton, S. W. S. Rev., 176.
Dutch Ref. Church, 195.

Earle, Thomas, 471.
Eaton, Wm. Gen., 282.
Eddy, Samuel, Hon. (R. I.), 384.
Edmundson, Wm., 33.
Edwards, Jona. Dr., 28, 92, 111, 127, 130.
Edwards, —— (Texas), 273.
Elizabeth, Queen, 6, 7, 8, 16, 50.
Ellis, Mr., min. Mexico, 289.
Ely, Mr. Rev., 176.
" Emancipator," 392, 464.
Emancipation, W. I., effects, 373.
Embargo, 324.
Emerson, Ralph, Prof., 172.
Emmons. Nathl. Dr., 393–4.
Emory, Bishop, 428.
Emory, Robert, Rev., 145.
Encomium, Brig. 252.
Endicott, Gov., 229.
England, Slavery and Abolition, 44.
English Statutes, 18.
" Enterprise, The," 152.
Episcopal Church, 191.
Everett, Edward, Gov., 218, 415.
Eyre, James, Sir, 46.

Faulkner, Mr., 80.
Federal Constitution, era of, 81.
    Convention, framing, 83–4, 222.
    Ratifications, 84–5.
    Amendments, 89.
    Views of, 563.

Federal Government, action, 220.
Federal District, cession, 225.
    Slavery by act of Congress, 226.
    Government of, 234, 243.
" Federalist, The," 86–7, 230.
Federal party, 128, 132.
Fee, John G., 492.
Ferdinand V., Spain, 7.
Fillmore, Pres., 162.
Finney, C. G. Rev., 492.
Finch, J., Missionary, 506.
First Congress (1774), 71.
First Presidency, 224.
Fisk, Wilbur, Pres. 167.
Florida, Invasion of, 269.
    Purchase, 239, 269.
    Admission, 240.
    Treaty — " Inhabitants citizens,"
        239–40, 568.
    Seminole War, 270.
Follen, Charles, Prof., 418, 469.
Foote, C. C., 475.
Foote, Mr., of Miss., 308.
Forsyth, Mr., 277, 293.
Foster, S. S., 527–30–33.
Fox, C. J., 28, 62.
Fox, George, 30, 32.
Franklin, B. Dr., 30, 40, 54, 96, 100.
Franklin and Armfield, 244.
Freeman, Mr. Rev., 191.
Free-Will Baptists, 196.
Free Soil party, 478, 482.
" Free trade and sailor's rights," 330.
Free Missions, 491.
Free Presb. Church, 491.
Fremont, Col., 300.
French National Assembly, 57–9.
French Revolution, (1793) 130.
    Infidelity, 130.
Frelinghuysen, Theodore, Hon., 395.
" Friends " in England, 32, 60, 196.
    In America, 35, 435–6.
    Seceders, 491.
Fugitive Slave Bill, (of 1793) 227.
    (of 1850,) 172, 220, 318, 413.
Fuller, R., Eld., (S. C.) 188, 499.
Furman, Rev. Dr., 186–7.

Gallatin, Albert, 264.
Galusha, Elon, Eld., 496, 499.
Gaines, Gen., 277.
Garrison, Wm. L., 396–7, 401, 405, 410,
    419, 436, 458–9, 460, 469, 512, 541,
    455–6.
Gates, Horatio, Gen., 79.
Gayle, Gov., (Ala.) 413.
Gedney, Lieut., 255.
General Conf., Cong., (Me.) 180.

General Asso., Cong., (Ct.) 173, 429.
General Asso. Cong., (Mass.) 178, 429–30.
" Genius of Temperance," 392.
" Genius Universal Emancipation," 391.
George II, act of, 8, 65.
Georgia, Colonial laws, 20–1.
  action, (1774) 74.
  demands, 414.
African Slave Trade, 261.
  annual Conference, (Meth.) 148.
Gholson, Mr, (Va.,) 251, 274.
Gilman, Gov., (N. H.) 231.
Godwin, 27.
Goderich, Lord, 369.
Goodman, E., 492.
Goodwin, E. W., 435.
Gonzalez, Anthony, 4, 16.
Gouverneur, S. L, 416.
Goslein, (Va.) Bap. Asso., 412.
" Gradual abolition," tested, W. I., 357, 372–3.
Graham, Rev. Dr., 158, 166, 170.
Grand Jury, Oneida Co., 409.
  District Columbia, 244.
  Tuscaloosa, (Ala.) 414.
Green, Beriah, Pres., 395–6, 556.
Green, Mr, Sec. Am. Board, 203.
Green, Duff, Gen., 415.
Gregoire, Abbe, 5, 29.
Grey, Earl, 371.
Grosvenor, C. P., 463, 494, 507.
Grotius, 28.
Gurney, J. J., 371.
Gwin, W. M., 310, 313.

Hale, John P., 478.
Hall, E., Rev., 176.
Hallet, B. F., 418.
Hamilton, Alex., Gen., 86, 95, 97, 281.
Hannegan, Mr., 309.
Hand, Col., 311.
Hancock. John, 78.
Harrison, W. H., Gen., 520.
Hawkins, John, Sir, (Capt.) 6, 16.
Hayti, 130, 268, 370.
Hazard, Mr., (R. I.) 415.
Hedding. E., Bishop, 147–8, 428.
Henry, King, (Spain) 4.
Henry, Patrick, 70, 85.
Heyrick, Elizabeth, 355–6.
Hicksite Friends, 435, 551.
Hierra, 5.
Hilliard, Mr., 308.
Hill, B. M, Eld., 188, 497.
Hispaniola, 4.
Hoare, Mr., Hon., 340.
Hodge, Prof., 154.
Holly, Myron, 470, 474, 556.

Holt, Chief Justice, Lord, 48.
Home Missionary Society, Baptist, 188.
Home Missionary Soc, American, 209.
Hopkins, Samuel, Dr., 28, 41, 76, 92, 109, 114, 120–2, 127.
Hope, Miss, 355.
Hopper, Isaac T., 435, 549.
Horseley, Bishop, 28, 62.
Horton, Jotham, Rev., 490.
House of Commons, 62, 66, 372.
House of Lords, 62.
Houston, Samuel, General, 279.
Hubbard, Mr., Hon., 340.
Hull, General, 332.
Hutchinson, Judge, 394.

Ide, Jacob, Dr., 443.
Illinois Central Asso., 202.
  Gen. Cong. Asso., 204.
Impressment Seamen, 329, 576.
Indiana Ter., 241.
Ingersoll, C. J., 301.
Insurrection in Texas, 273.
Invasion of Texas, 273.
Iowa Ter., 244.
Iredell, Judge, 85.
Ives, L. S., Bishop, 191.

" Jacobinism," 130.
Jackson, Andrew, Pres., 267, 269, 274, 276–7, 286, 291, 338, 417.
Jamaica, 370.
James, John Angell, Rev., 360.
Jay, John, Gov., 30, 86, 92, 95, 97.
Jay, John, Esq., 191.
Jay, Wm. Judge, 393, 511.
Jefferson, Thomas, 16, 30, 70, 71–2, 79, 83, 86, 131, 142, 236, 268, 281, 324, 569, 575.
Jeremie, Judge, 363.
Jocelyn, S. S., 392, 511.
Johnson, Samuel, Dr., 28.
Johnson, Wm. B. (S. C.), 187.
Jones, William, Sir, 31.
Jones, C. C. Rev., 199.
Jones, Com., 295.
Judson, A. T., Judge, 255.

Kearney, Gen., 302.
Kentucky (in 1780), 110.
  Admission of, 227.
  Presb. Synod, 152.
Kendall, Amos, (P. M. Gen.) 416–17.
Kerr, John, 47.
Key, Francis S., 105, 437, 446.
King Henry of Spain, 4.
King's Bench, Court, 50.
King, Thos. B., 310, 313.

King, Leicester, Hon., 478.
Knibb, Wm., Missionary (W. I.), 366.

Lacoste (slave Capt.), 257.
Lamar, Gen., 279.
Lane Seminary, 426.
Langhorne, G. W. Rev. (N. C.) 428.
Laird, Capt., 47.
Las Casas, 4.
Lay, Benjamin, 40.
Lear, Tobias, 282.
Leavitt, Joshua, 463.
Leo X., Pope, 27.
Leigh, B. W. (Va.), 80.
Le Roy Convention, 523.
Lewis, Thomas (slave), 48.
Lewis, Evan, 393.
Lewis, Samuel, 492.
Liberty Party, 457, 467–8, 482.
Liberty League, 475, 477, 481.
Liberia, 351–2.
Liberator, 392, 397.
Lincoln, Heman, 497.
Lisle, David, 46.
" Literary and Theol. Review," 409, 413.
Literary Institutions, 403.
Liverpool, mob, 59.
Locke, John, 30.
Long, James, Texas, 273.
Loring. E. G., 418.
Louis XIII. of France, 7.
Louisiana, purchase, 239.
   Af. Slave Trade, 261.
   " Inhabitants citizens," 239, 568.
Lovejoy, E. P. Rev., 406, 439.
Lumpkin, Gov. (Geo.), 410.
Lundy, Benjamin, 385, 391–2, 436.
Lunt, Geo., Hon., 418.
Lushington, Dr., 363, 371.

Macauley, Zachary, 358.
Macedon Lock Convention, 475.
Macknight, (Commentator) 29.
McDuffie, Geo., Gov. S. C., 141, 413.
Madison, James, Pres., 70, 79, 84, 86–7, 102, 228, 230, 336.
Mahan, J. B., Rev., 440.
Mahan, Asa, Pres., 492.
Mails, U. S., laws, 233.
   Report, U. S. Senate, 421.
Malcom, Howard, Rev., 493.
Mansfield. Chief Justice, Lord, 18, 46, 48, 50–1–2, 55.
Mann, Horace, Hon., 226.
Manufactures, N. England, 134, 334, 336.
Marriage, white women with slaves, 23.
Maryland, Colon. Slavery, 22 : laws, 140.

Maryland, action, (1774) 74.—Abolition Society, (1789) 96.
   no legal slavery, 573.
   Colonization Society, 343.
Martin Luther, (Md.) 82.
Marcy, W. L., Gov., 413–14.
Mariott, Charles, 435, 549.
Massachusetts, Colonial Slavery, 12, 13.
   (in 1812,) claims on U. S., 332–3.
   relations with S. C., and La., 340.
   Legislature, (of 1836) 417–18.
   Abolition Society, 401.
   Colonization Society, 350.
Mason, Mr., of Va., U. S. Senate, 570–1.
Masonic Hall, Colonization meeting, 395.
May anniversaries, (1825 to '30) 387.
May, Samuel J., Rev., 418, 476, 537.
Mercer, Charles F., 250.
Metamoras taken, 299.
Methodist E. Church, 106–7, 138, 143–5, 426.
   Division of, 150.
Methodist E Church, North, 150.
Mexico—abolition of slavery, 272–3.
   war against, 287, 299, 302.
   claims U. S. on, 289, 293, 297.
   peace with, 303.
Miller, Samuel, D.D., 152–3.
Milnor, Rev. Dr., 193.
Militia laws, U. S., 233.
Mills, Samuel J., Rev., 341.
Miller, M.D., Eld., 504.
" Ministry," the, 449.
Mississippi Territory, 241.
Missouri, admiss. and comp., 240–3, 388.
Missionary Societies, England, 368.
Missionary enterprise,—effects, 386.
Mobs against abolitionists, 395, 406.
Monroe, James, Pres. 240–2, 256–7, 269.
Monroe Co., N. Y., Convention, 470.
Montez and Ruiz, 255.
Montgomery, James, 4, 5.
Montesquieu, Baron, 28.
Monterey taken, 300.
More, Hannah, 28.
Morrell, Judge, 244.
Morris, Thomas, 471.
Mulgrave, Lord, 370.
Murch, W. H., Eld., 493.

Nacogdoches, settlement, Am., 273.
Napoleon vs. Hayti, 268.
National Bank, 327, 336.
" National Philanthropist," 391.
   " A. S. Standard," 514, 528, 544.
   " Era," 483.
   Anti-Slavery Conv. (1833), 393.
Naturalization laws, 235.

Naturalization laws, power of Congress, through, 576, 586.
Nat. Turner's Insurrection, 392, 588.
Nelson, Dr. Rev., 395, 439.
Nevin, E. H., Rev., 492.
New England, Colonial Slavery, 12–14.
In War of 1812, 332.
Meth. E. Conf, 148.
Anti-Slavery Soc., 392.
New Orleans Bible Soc., 211.
Newport (R. I.) Cong. Ch., 42.
New School Gen. Assembly, 157.
New York—Yearly Meet. Friends, 38.
Abolition Soc. (1785), 95.
City A. S. Soc., 395.
Annual Conf. Meth., 428.
Central College, 507.
"New York Observer," 176, 182, 205, 218.
"Evangelist," 392.
"Non-Resistants," 458, 512, 518–19, 527, 534, 539.
North Carolina, Colonial Slavery, 22.
Convention (in 1774), 72 ; Cession to U. S., 225 ; Af. Slave Trade, 261 ; Demands, 413 ; Bap. Asso., 186.
N. W. Territory, 83.
"Notes on Virginia," 87.
"No Union with Slaveholders," 526.
Nourse, Jos., Reg., 257.
Nullification (S. C.), 338.

"Observations" (1774), 75.
(1779), 78.
O'Connell, Daniel, M. P., 361.
Oglethorpe, Gen., 20, 21, 31.
Ogden, D. B., 193, 396.
Ohio, "black laws," 340.
Annual Conf. Meth., 427.
Olin, S., Pres., 147.
Onesimus and Philemon, 167–9.
Onderdonk, Bishop, 193.
Ordinance of 1787, N. W. Ter., 83.
"Organic Sins," 209.
Oregon Ter., 244.
Orleans Co. Bible Soc., 212.
"Orders in Council," Brit., 329.
Osceola, 270.

Page, Mr. (Va.), 110.
Paley, Dr., 28.
Paine, Robert Treat, 73.
Paine, Thomas, 131.
Panama, Congress, 259.
Parker, Mr. (Va.), 100.
Parker, Theodore, Rev., 551.
"Pastoral Letter," Meth. E. Bishops, 428.

Pastoral Letter, Con. and Mass. Asso., Cong., 431–2, 459.
Pearl, Schr., 446.
Peck, J. M., Eld., 504.
Penn, Wm., 35.
Pennsylvania, Abol. Soc., 95.
Hall, burned, 406.
Pennington, J. W. Dr., 511.
Perkins, G. W., Rev., 174.
Petitions to Congress, 91, 97, 224.
Persecutions, 434.
Phelps, A. A. Rev., 207–8, 410–11, 459.
Phila. "Yearly Meeting" Friends, 36.
Phillips, Wendell, 517–18, 528, 556.
Pigott, Arthur, Sir, 62.
Pike, J. G., Rev., 360.
Pinckney, Wm., 82, 583.
Pinney, J. B., 351.
Pitt, Wm., 28, 57, 62, 64–5, 232.
Plummer, W. S., Dr., 411.
Political Power of Slaveholders, 134.
Economy, controlled by, 319.
Polk, J. K., Pres., 297, 301–3, 309.
Pope Leo X., 27.
Port Byron Convention, 475.
Porteus, Bishop, 27.
Portland, Duke of, 36.
Postell, J. C., Rev., 412.
Post-office, Charleston, S. C., 416.
Postmaster-General, 416.
Prejudice vs. color, 139, 200.
Presbyterian Ch., 107–8, 138, 151, 249.
General Assembly, 152, 155–6.
Old School, 155–6.
New School, 157–9, 161–2.
Synod, Kentucky, 152, 381.
S. Carolina and Georgia, 381.
Press, periodical, 389.
Presidents U. S., list of, dates, 224.
Price, Dr., 29.
Primatt, Dr., 29.
Princeton Repertory, 154.
Theological Seminary, 14.
Protestant Episcopal Church, 191.
Society, &c., S. C., 192.
"The Churchman," 192.
Theological Seminary, 193.
Convention, Penn., 194.
Protestant Meth. Church, 195.
Prohibitions Slavery by Congress, 241–2.
Puritans of England, 12.

Queen Victoria, 218, 273.
Quincy, Josiah, 232.
Quincy, Edmund, 556.

Randolph, Peyton, 73.
Randolph, Mr., (Fed. Conv.) 84, 85, 228.

Randolph, Thos. J., 248.
Randolph, Jno. of Roanoke, 244, 260, 384.
Rankin, John, Rev., 387, 490.
Raynal, Abbe, 29.
Reeve, Judge, 11.
Reform Bill, England, 361.
Reformers, divided, 448.
Religious bodies *vs.* slavery, 32.
    Anniversaries, (1825–1830), 387.
    Revivals, (1825 to 1830) 388.
Restorationists, 196.
Review of divisions, 559.
Rhode Island, colonial laws, 12, 13.—
    Yearly meeting, 37.
    Ratification Fed. Const., 89. Abol.
    Soc., (1786) 96.
    Election, (1820) 384.—Legisla-
    ture, (1835) 416.
Right of Petition, 422.
Riley, Gen., 311–12.
Rio Grande, 299.
Robertson, History, 5.
Robertson, Wm., Dr., 29.
Rochester, Bishop of, 28, 62.
Rogers, W. W., Rev., 172.
Rogers, N. P., 454, 476, 519, 530.
Romans, abolition, 368.
Roman Catholics, 195, 201.
Roszell, S. G., Rev., 427.
Rousseau, J. J., 31.
Royal Navy and Slave Trade, 66.
Rutledge, John, 74.
Rutledge, Edward, 75.
Russell, John, Lord, 66.
Rush, Benj., Dr., 29, 96.

Sabbath, Anti, 460, 546.
St. Domingo, "horrors of," 139, 370.
St. Thomas' Church, 194.
Sandiford, Ralph, 40.
San Jacinto, battle, 277.
Santa Anna, defeat, 277.
San Francisco taken, 300.
    pro-slavery vote, 313.
San Jose, meeting, 311.
Sawyer, J. W., Eld., 504.
Savannah River Bap. Asso., 185, 496.
Scoble, John, (London) 360.
Scott, Mr., of Pennsylvania, 101.
Scott, Winfield, Gen., in Mexico, 301–2.
Scott, Orange, Rev., 427, 590.
"Science, the," (slaver) 257.
Sectarian rivalry, 138.
Secession Church, Kentucky, (1805) 108.
Semple, Robert B., 187.
Seminole War, 270.
Sewell, S. E., 419.
Seward, Wm. H., 485.

Sharp, Granville, 21, 44–60, 77, 104.
Sharp, Daniel, D.D., 497.
Shannon, Mr., Min. to Mexico, 296, 313.
Shaw, Judge, (Mass.) 111.
Sims, E. D., Prof., 147.
Slade, William, Hon., 525.
Slave States, admitted, 237.
Slave trade, African, origin of, 4.
    by the Colonists, 11.
    efforts to abolish, 53.
    unsuccessful, 66.
    denounced by First Congress, 73.
    resumed by individuals, 122.
    Federal Gov., action, 256–260.
    American or Domestic, 247–9.
    in Federal District, 244.
Slavery in American Colonies, 10.
    in England, 44.
    distinctive features in U. S., 377.
    unconstitutional, 475, 573–8, 587.
Slavery question in America, 583.
Slaveholding and traffic illegal :
    Testimony of G. Sharp, 50.—
    Blackstone, 28.—Wm. Pitt, 64–5.
    —Lord Mansfield, 51, 63.—Dr.
    Hopkins, 76.— James Madison,
    84.—Mr. Scott, (M. C.) of Pa.,
    101.—Methodist Confer., (1780)
    106.—John Randolph, 244.—T.
    Clarkson, 356.—Mr. Mason and
    Mr. Bayly of Va., 570–2.
Slaveholding and traffic called "Man-
    stealing," "robbery," or "theft,"
    by Bishop Porteus and Richard
    Baxter, 27—John Wesley, 27–8
    —Grotius, Dr. Jonathan Edwards,
    and Charles James Fox, 28—
    Macknight and Scott, (Commen-
    tators) 29—Abraham Booth, 30
    —Presb. Ch., U. S., (from 1794 till
    1816) 107–8—Philadelphia year-
    ly meeting of Friends, 35–6.
Slaveholding Missionaries—*Am. Board*,
    J. Wilson, Africa, 203—*Baptists*,
    Mr. Bushyhead, Cherokees, 187—
    Mr. Davenport, Siam, 187—Mr.
    Tryon, Texas, 188 —*Twenty-six*
    employed by Am. Baptist Home
    Miss. Soc., 188—J. Finch, 206.
Slidell, Mr., Minister to Mexico, 297.
Sloat, Commodore, 300.
Smith, P. F., (Presb. Gen. Assemb.) 160.
Smith, Ethan, Rev., 217.
Smith, Gerrit, 405, 463, 513, 556.
Smith, E., Rev., (Wesleyan) 492.
Smith, Lionel, Sir, 373.
Smylie, James, Rev., 199.
Smylie, Mr., (M. C.) 260.

Smythe, Alexander, Gen., 332.
Societies, voluntary, 202.
Somerset, James, (slave case) 49.
Somers, C. G., Rev., 494.
Soule, Bishop, 147.
Southampton Insurrection, 392, 588.
South Carolina, Colonial slavery, 22.
    decrease of slaves, (1790) 106.
    African Slave trade, 122.
    Nullification, 338.
    demands, 413.
    Ann. Conf. Meth., 148.
    Synod, Presb., 381.
" S. W. Chr. Adv." 199.
Sparks, Jared, Pres., 172.
Spencer, John C., 574.
Spooner, Lysander, 22, 25, 476.
Spring, Gardner, D.D., 155, 218, 351, 412.
Stanley, Mr., of N. C., 321.
Stanley, Mr., Colonial Sec. (Eng.), 371.
Stapylton, Mr., 48.
State Governments, on Slavery, 339.
State Constitutions (1776) vs. Slav., 573.
Stewart, Mr. (Ill.), 153.
Stewart, Alvan, 463, 469, 471, 476, 556.
Stiles, Ezra, Pres, 96.
Storrs, George, 438.
Storrs, C. B, Pres., 395.
Story, Judge, 576.
Stowe, Baron, Rev., 497–8, 504.
Strong, Jonathan (slave), 46.
Stroud, Judge, 11, 12, 22, 23, 25.
Sturge, Joseph (Eng.), 360.
Stuart, Charles, 360.
Stuart, Moses, Prof., 166, 172.
Suffield, Lord, 371.
Suffrage, Universal, vs. Slavery, 461–2.
Sullivan, Wm., Hon., 409.
Sunderland, La Roy, Rev., 412, 42,8 434,
    490.
Supreme Court U. S., 19, 256, 574.
Swedenborgians, 548, 553.
Synod, Presb. Kentucky, 152, 199.
    Cincinnati, 166.
    Philadelphia, 429.
    S. Carolina and Georgia, 381.

Tammany Hall Meeting, riotous, 395.
Tappan, Arthur, 392, 395–6, 410, 463.
Tappan, Lewis, 392, 396, 434, 463, 511.
Tariff, 322, 336–8.
Taylor, Zachary, Gen., 270, 299, 302,
    308–9, 317.
Taylor, Nathl. W., D.D., 473.
Tennessee, admission of, 235.
    Bap. Miss. Asso., 501.
Territories U. S., 238.
Texas, acquisition of, 272–79.

Thome, James A., Rev., 395.
Thompson, Judge, 255.
Thompson, Waddy, Hon., 289, 300–1.
Thompson, George (Missionary), 440.
Thompson, George (M.P.), 360.
Thomson, Andrew, Dr., 359.
Thornton, Pres., 147.
Todd, Francis, 391.
Torrey, Charles T., Rev., 442.
Tracy, Uriah, Hon., 97.
Tracy, Joseph, Rev., 182, 402.
Trefusis, Capt., 367.
Treat, S. B., Sec. Am. Board, 204.
Triennial Conv. Bap. (see Baptists.)
Tripoli, war, 282.
Trist, Mr., 304–5.
Turner, Nat., insurrection, 392.
Tyler, Bennett, D.D., 176.
Tyler, John, Pres., 275, 289, 295–6, 520.

Unconstitutionality of Slavery, 475,
    573–8, 587.
Union of the Colonies (1774), 72.
Unitarians, 196, 548, 551.
Universalists, 196, 548, 553.
U. S. Mail, rifled, 411.
U. S. forces vs. slave insurrection, 558.
U. S. Bank, 327, 336.
U. S. Supreme Court, 19, 256, 574.
Upshur, Judge, 274, 295.
Utah, 317.

Van Buren, Martin, Pres., 276, 278, 292,
    321, 422, 478, 479–80.
" Vesuvius capped," 157.
" Vermont Chronicle," 182, 402.
Victoria, Queen, 218, 373.
Virginia, early character, 19–20.
    Colonial Slavery, 19.
    Conv. (1774), 71 ; action, 75, 110.
    Abolition Society, 96.
    Revised Code, 381.
    demands on North, 414.
    Colonization Scheme, 342.
    Bap. Asso. 493.
    Friends' Yearly Meeting, 38.
Voluntary Societies, The, 202.

Walker, Mr. (Wis.), 308.
Walker, Jona., Capt., 439.
Walker, J. B. Rev., 492.
Walworth, R. H., Chancellor, 203, 345,
    396.
Warburton, Bishop, 27.
War, Revolution, effects, 123.
    of 1812, Brit., 331.
    Mexican, 287.
Ward, Samuel R., 556.

Washington, George, Gen., 70, 72, 74, 81. 231, 236.
Washington, Madison (col'd), 254.
" Washington Union, The," 303.
Washington, Judge, 342, 344.
Watson's Theol. Inst., 149.
Waugh, Bishop, 429.
Wayland, Francis, Pres., 187, 505.
Webster, Dan'l, Hon., 229, 254, 301, 307, 339, 478, 584.
Welch, B. T., D.D., 504.
Wesley, John, 14, 27, 60.
Wesleyan Meth. Church, 150.
    Meth. Conf. (Eng.), 427.
West Indies, Abolition, 353.
    Colonial Leg., 357.
    English Missionaries, 362.
    Slaveholders, violence, 362–4.
    Wesleyan Chap. destroyed, 366.
White, Bishop, 194.
Whitefield, George, Rev., 14–15.
Whitney's Cotton Gin, 132.
Whittier, John G., 396.
Wilberforce, William, 57–62, 355–361, 393.
William III., statute of, 8.
William IV., 59, 361.
William and Mary, Univer. (Va.), 104.
Williams, R. G., 105, 413–14.

Williams, Judge (Ct.), 203, 208.
Wilson, Dr., Rev., 492.
Wilson, James (Pa.), 84.
Wilson, Mr., Missionary, 203, 351.
" Wilmot Proviso," 304.
Wisconsin Ter., 244.
Wise, Henry A. (Va.), 288, 412.
Witherspoon, Thos. S., D.D., 44, 155.
Wives, bought in Va., 19.
Woolman, John, 41.
Woodbridge (N. J.) Anti-Slavery Meeting, (1783), 94.
Woods, Leonard, D.D., 172, 203, 208, 351.
Woods, Leonard, Jr., 409.
" Woman Question, The," 454, 462, 518.
Work, Alanson, 440.
World's A. S. Conv., 517.
Wright, Theo. S., 511.
Wright, Elizur, Jr., 395, 461.
Wright, Henry C., 539.

Ximines, Cardinal, 5.

Yates, Mr., of N. Y. (Congress), 83.
York and Talbot (Eng.), 45–6, 52.

" Zion's Watchman," 428
Zong, Ship, (slaver), 55.